Jodi has done what Jesus directed His disciples and all of us to do: "Go and make disciples of all nations" (Matthew 28:19 NIV). She has gone into the inner city of Akron, Ohio, and ministers alongside the local community and immigrant children, the latter from numerous countries. Her book is amply illustrated with vivid personal stories of people whom she encounters in the city with the Gospel that transforms her and them. Reading A Call to the Edge is like reading a modern version of Acts.

Dr. Ronald Sauer
Professor of Bible at Moody Bible Institute

A Call to the Edge is the faith-building, true story of the ministry of Urban Vision in Akron, Ohio. Jodi Matthews candidly shares the challenges she and her family faced as they followed God's call to live among and serve the children of North Akron. Her faith is contagious as she shares her experiences of growth in trusting God while doing ministry and raising a family in a low-income neighborhood. We have been privileged to witness God's faithfulness to the Matthews family as Christian community developers for the last twenty-five years. Now, you can be inspired as well, by reading Jodi's biblically thoughtful reflections on how an ordinary woman's call to follow Jesus into the city leads to an extraordinary life.

Duane and Lisa Crabbs
Co-founders of South Street Ministries

A CALL TO THE EDGE

One Ordinary Person of Faith
Embracing an Extraordinary Vision of God

JODI M. MATTHEWS

WESTBOW
PRESS®
A DIVISION OF THOMAS NELSON
& ZONDERVAN

WestBow Press books may be ordered through booksellers or by contacting:

WestBow Press
A Division of Thomas Nelson & Zondervan
1663 Liberty Drive
Bloomington, IN 47403
www.westbowpress.com
1 (866) 928-1240

ISBN: 978-1-5127-9902-6 (sc)
ISBN: 978-1-5127-9904-0 (hc)
ISBN: 978-1-5127-9903-3 (e)

Library of Congress Control Number: 2017912624

Print information available on the last page.

WestBow Press rev. date: 08/17/2017

DEDICATION

To my husband and love of my life, Rodney
To my three sons Micah, Joseph, and Nathanael
To my Mom and Dad, Diane and George White
To my Urban Vision family
But most of all, to my precious Jesus!

CONTENTS

FOREWORD

Urban Vision lives its name and sees the city for sure. But more—they do something about the needs. Their story is told here by the one who saw it begin in her prayers and dreams, and in the hopes of many people who just plain cared, and wanted to come alongside others with a message of hope found in Christ our Lord! Akron, you see, is not just about LeBron, or good hospitals, or rubber and chemical companies, or the strong university downtown, or the many good churches. Maybe God notices even more the actions of love done on the North Hill and more by Jodi and Rodney and their teammates. I think so. Read this and you will see how things do not just happen. Caring people see needs and work together with our Lord to do something about them. Check your own vision for your own city as you give thanks for theirs!

Knute Larson
Pastoral teacher and coach
Pastor Emeritus, The Chapel, Akron

As followers of Jesus and people of the Word we read of God's calling on special people whom He set apart for the work of the ministry. In Jeremiah 1, God says, "Before I formed you in the womb, I knew you, before you were born I set you apart; I appointed you as a prophet to the nations" (Jeremiah 1:5 NIV).

I met Jodi Matthews at a CCDA conference, and as soon as we spent time together, I knew she was one of God's chosen. This young woman had a fire in her heart for Jesus and a burden for the poor, the downcast, and the displaced in Akron, Ohio. As the

Founder of Voice of Hope Ministries, an inner city urban ministry in Dallas, I knew all too well the challenges she was facing and the obstacles that lay ahead of her. Multi-racial, cross cultural, inner city community development work is difficult enough for the experienced practitioner, and here she was: young, white, and a female coming from a conservative evangelical church background. What I saw in Jodi though was the fire that the Holy Spirit had birthed deep in her soul, and I sensed then that this young woman was destined by Jesus to do great things in His name.

She visited Voice of Hope and I spent time listening to her vision as she observed the Voice of Hope model. I believed in Jodi then, and almost thirty years later I still believe in her, and the incredible story of Urban Vision is a testament to her leadership, perseverance, and faithfulness.

A question that the body of Christ must answer is this: How many women throughout the ages were clearly called and gifted by God to ministry and either did not go or did not remain because of discouragement, opposition, or lack of support from the churches, solely because they were women? In these difficult and trying days, the gospel of Jesus Christ is being ridiculed and scorned throughout the Western world by society. The body of Christ needs to embrace a theology of equality that truly empowers both women and men to answer the call of our Lord without battling the church and old traditions, so that more Jodi Matthews are encouraged to step out and be faithful to their calling.

Jodi's work is not done, and I say to her and Rodney, who has stood with her as a partner in love and ministry: Well done.

Kathy Dudley, DMin
President, Imani Bridges

ACKNOWLEDGMENTS

Where do I begin to thank the many people who prayed with me, inspired me, and labored with me to see this book become a reality? How grateful I am for every single person God has placed in my life!

I want to acknowledge my family who loved me and sacrificed for me and supported me through it all....Thank you, Rodney, for always loving me. Thanks to my three sons Micah, Joseph, and Nathanael, for being young men who follow Jesus!

Thanks, Mom and Dad, for always being there to cheer me on! Thanks, Mom, for your love and willingness to rejoice with me in my victories and weep with me in my sorrows. Thanks, Dad, for believing in me.

Thanks Mary and Jerry (Rodney's parents) for your care and support over the years.

Thanks to my prayer sisters who really seek the heart of God and prayed me through. Thanks Susie for inspiring me. Thanks Clorinda, Bethany, and Linda for praying with me. Thanks Miss Chris for your encouragement!

Thanks to the original five who had great faith and love for Jesus (Patricia Holley, Lee Ann Dawson Smith, Chris Dennison, Russ Morgan, Rodney Matthews), along with others who soon followed and were committed early on to pray and work alongside me to see the vision become reality!

Thanks to my Urban Vision family...all the children and families of North Hill community—I love you much! Thanks to the Urban Vision staff, both past and present, mentioned or unmentioned in this book—you serve and have served with a heart like Jesus!

Thank you dear sister in the Lord Bena Paisley for the many hours you put into helping me get this book ready for the editor. Thank you to Patti Lee for helping with this book out of love and obedience to our Lord!

Thanks to Pastor Knute Larson, Kathy Dudley, and Duane and Lisa Crabbs who did not hesitate to stand with me in ministry throughout the years and in this book project.

Thanks to Dr. Ron Sauer, professor at Moody Bible Institute, and his wife, sweet Sue, who have loved and mentored me, and been a shining example of what it means to follow Jesus!

Thanks most of all to Jesus, who continues to call me to the edge of His will! Oh how I love You with all my heart!

INTRODUCTION

A long time ago there was born a little girl into whom God put many hopes and dreams. At the young age of three her mind raced with questions about everything, but the topic she loved to discuss the most was heaven. She had questions like, *What does God look like? Is there really a street of gold?* And, of course the most asked question a child could deliberate over, *Will my dog get to go to heaven too?*

She loved having these conversations with anyone patient enough to listen, but her dad was her favorite audience. She would talk in the car, outside, and yes, even in the bathroom. Her parents wished that she would put the same kind of focus on her potty training skills as she did on spiritual conversations, but all things come in time.

It was not too long after one of these deep conversations that the little girl decided that if Jesus lived in a place called heaven, then she wanted to live there too. So, with a simple childlike faith, this little girl went to the corner of her room and asked Jesus into her heart. Now this little girl could not quote the four spiritual laws, or the Roman road, or even recite John 3:16. However, she did know that Jesus loved her, died for the bad things she had done, and that He came back to life. She knew that if she believed in Jesus, then He would save her and take her to heaven one day.

That little girl was me...Jodi.

CHAPTER 1

CAN I GET A WITNESS?

*"You are my witnesses," declares the LORD, "and my
servant whom I have chosen, that you may know and
believe me and understand that I am he"*
(Isaiah 43:10).

I believe I sensed the strong calling to seek God at an early age because of what was modeled for me at home. I saw love in action as my parents faithfully took us (me, along with my older brother Brett and younger brother Trent) to church in a unique way...on a big brown bus. My dad was the church bus driver and my mom was a Sunday school teacher. Every Sunday morning, Sunday night, and Wednesday evening my whole family would be bouncing around in a very hot and stuffy bus picking up children and families.

Some of the places we picked up children were in very needy parts of town. My dad would pull up the bus and honk the horn and my mom would warmly greet each child with a smile and a hug. Torn dresses and snotty noses aside, each child was treated with love and dignity. I still remember going up to the cold bus garage on Saturday nights in the middle of winter and holding the flashlight for my dad as he tinkered with the engine to make sure the bus would start the next morning.

Nothing kept my parents from picking up the children; not the intense heat of the summer nor snowstorms in the winter. Their faithfulness to what God asked them to do in the midst of their realities impacted me and shaped the vision of what would come in my future. I can look back now and see that there were many lessons learned on that big brown bus.

Dad and his bus riders (mentioned in book:
my dad, Lee Ann Smith, Jodi, brother Brett)

When I was seven I felt God's tug on my heart, calling me to be a missionary. I remember watching a movie at church that was about John Huss, a 14th century preacher whose desire was to preach the Word of God to people in their own heart language so that they could understand. This was considered heresy within the larger church. He was labeled a heretic and asked to recant but he would not. He was tied to a stake and as the flames engulfed him he sang loudly a hymn of praise. One of the last statements he made as the flames consumed his body was, "I will not recant. What I have spoken with my lips, I now seal with my blood."

I learned that day that loving God could potentially mean that I would have to be willing to die. Not many of us are called to a martyr's death, but we are all called to die daily to ourselves as the Scriptures say in Galatians 2:20: *I have been crucified with Christ and I no longer live, but Christ lives in me. The life I now live in the body, I live by faith in the Son of God who loved me and gave himself for me* (NIV).

My home was not perfect and we struggled like most families do. My dad worked a couple of jobs and he was in sales which required him to be gone for weeks at a time, leaving my mom home alone to raise three kids. I wore thick glasses because of severe eye trouble and many kids at school were none too kind to a four-eyed little girl.

But because I knew God loved me and I had the support of my family, I was able to find my joy and security in Him. God uses everything to shape us and conform us to His will. My faith deepened in my high school years with the opportunity to attend Cuyahoga Valley Christian Academy, thanks to great sacrifice from my parents. The teachers loved Jesus and poured into me so I could be rooted in and built up in the Lord. I later went on to Moody Bible Institute where God challenged me to go even deeper still. I began to see how God had a heart for the city and the many different people who lived there. These experiences, along with training in the Word of God, put in me a vision, an Urban Vision, to live Christ out in the midst of the city and to reach families with the gospel of Jesus Christ.

God has blessed me with my husband, Rodney, and we have the honor of serving together in ministry. God has also given us three sons: Micah, Joseph, and Nathanael.

Friends, we all have different backgrounds that have led us to this moment in our journeys. But I don't believe you picked up this book by accident. I believe that if you are reading this now, then God has a word for you. My prayer is that it would be a timely word to encourage you to be obedient to follow God, to see Him fully for who He is, and to become like Christ in the midst of your realities.

Some of our realities are harsher than others but God wants to meet with you in the midst of your praise, in the midst of your thanksgiving, in the midst of your grief, in the midst of your tiredness, and even in the midst of your pain. All of our journeys begin from the moment He called us to be His children. With a simple childlike faith, we believe that Jesus died for sin, the just for the unjust, to bring us to God. *For it is by grace you have been saved through faith, and this is not from yourselves, it is the gift of God, not by works, so that no one can boast* (Ephesians 2:8–9 NIV).

For those who stand on this truth, it then becomes all about the process of becoming like the One who loves, shapes, and forms us to the image of Himself in order to glorify His name and to serve and build His kingdom. *For we are God's handiwork, created in Christ Jesus to do good works, which God prepared in advance for us to do* (Ephesians 2:10 NIV).

Our becoming like Christ doesn't happen in a perfect environment, it happens in the middle of our realities in the daily tensions of life. Trials and temptations come to each of us in many ways and forms. By God's mercy and grace we learn to surrender our responses to Him in order to allow the Potter to form the clay for the use He has intended. This surrender leads to a thirst to know Him more, an intense longing to dwell in His presence. *I want to know Christ and the power of his resurrection and participation in his sufferings, becoming like him in his death and so, somehow, attaining to the resurrection from the dead* (Philippians 3:10–11 NIV).

You may be wondering what is needed for this journey toward becoming more like Him? I am not going to ask you to bring a water bottle, but I am going to ask you to be a vessel and draw from the Living Water of Life. I am not going to ask you to wear your hiking boots, but I am going to remind you to put on the whole armor of God from the helmet of salvation all the way down to the shoes of the gospel. No need for a walking stick, just be sure you have your sword of the Spirit and the shield of faith. Of course, no flashlight is required because His Word is a lamp unto our feet and a light unto our path. No map or directions because God's GPS, "God's Perfect Spirit," will lead and guide us into all truth. Oh, and by the way, I would not encourage Hanes® Her Way or His Way (not to be too personal) under all that armor, but just slip into the garment of praise and you will be sure to get there much sooner. So, with a readiness of Spirit and a prayer for courage, let's take that first step of faith.

It is time for a trip to the edge!

CHAPTER 2

LIFE ON THE EDGE

*What no eye has seen, what no ear has heard, and
what no mind has conceived—the things God has
prepared for those who love Him*
(1 Corinthians 2:9 NIV).

I will never forget the day I went out back to talk with my dad about a vision God had called me to. He was tinkering around in the shed of our suburban middle class home when his only daughter gave him the news that I was called to be a missionary in the inner city. All that he had taught me about God and faith now became a new reality for him to grapple with. *Did I really train her up in the Lord for this?*

Parents never stop being parents no matter how old we get. To my dad I was the little girl that God had given him to provide for and protect, so the news sank deep into his soul when I said, "God has called, I must go." He didn't rant or rave, and he didn't stop tinkering either, not until he finally paused long enough to ask me a question I have since asked myself many times: "Jodi, why is it that you always feel you have to live life on the edge?"

At that moment I was stumped and didn't have an answer. I just knew I had heard the invitation to come, and so I must go.

It wasn't bravery or courage, I can assure you, but a compelling from the Spirit of the Lord. I knew that to turn back now I would miss something that would affect the rest of my life. Little did I realize what scene lay ahead when I, in the midst of my reality, stepped right up to the edge and saw as I had never seen before.

Just Jodi

At that time—in the early 90s—I was a young, single, white female called to a vision way beyond what I could imagine it would become. Definitely out of my comfort zone, I ventured toward the edge that led me to see the needs of the urban poor who were living out many painful realities of hopelessness and despair. My eyes and my heart were captivated with a compassion that I know came from the Lord Himself. I could no longer stay the same.

The irony is that I don't actually like edges of any kind. There is something about coming close to the edge of a cliff that sends my head into a spin and causes my stomach to do flip flops. (I know there are some real edge/rollercoaster thrill seekers out there but that is not me!) Edges prompt me to give a warning to our three boys as they walk a canyon's ridge, reminding them to stay on the path and pay attention to the caution signs along the way. This warning goes out especially to my youngest who takes no precautions as he barges ahead fearlessly thinking himself to be sure-footed and invincible. Not so with me...keep me as far away from the edge as possible.

Edges bring a certain amount of discomfort for fear of plummeting to the depths of the valley below. (I know that is a little dramatic, but my mom always said I was her drama queen.) Walking near an edge keeps my eyes fixed down on where I am stepping, usually missing the sights along the way. Fear of the unknown has a way of limiting our vision.

Even though I have struggled with this fear many times in my past, there has always been something beyond the edge that drew me to get a little closer. It was a persistent nudging of the Spirit that kept me moving forward in my journey of faith to know God better and in my desire to live in His presence, even if the edge was the destination.

There's nothing special about me; no special talents or big degrees. In fact, I have labeled myself *Just Jodi* on several occasions. Yet God through His Spirit compelled me to come. A Scripture that God has put on my heart since I was a young girl is found in Luke 12:48 and says, **Everyone to whom much was given, of him much will be required.** Salvation is a free gift but I have a responsibility to come and see and be all that God has for me.

No fear of an edge could release me from my responsibility to NOT settle for a distant and average view of His presence. It was time for me to get closer, surrender my fear, step up to the edge, and see the vision to which I believe God calls us all. Each of us may receive different visions or callings but one goal will be the common chord: seeing the Lord in the majesty of His presence. Just like Moses in Exodus 33:18, I want to ask God to, **Show me Your glory...!**

So with much trembling (and my dad's blessing) I walked up to my edge, having no qualifications other than an invitation to come and being open to really seeing who God is and what He wanted me to do. And now I can tell you after all this time, that God has not only allowed me to walk up to the edge, He has even compelled me to set up camp and live there until this very day.

Some of you reading this feel that same burning. You have that same compulsion not to settle for mediocrity; you are being drawn to the edge. Let me encourage you to prayerfully take the next step toward that edge, trusting the prompting of the Holy Spirit within you.

Now please stop here and sing with me to Jesus. (Yes, please really sing; it is part of the process!)

Turn Your Eyes upon Jesus
Lyrics by Helen H. Lemmel

Turn your eyes upon Jesus
Look full in His wonderful face

And the things of this earth will grow strangely dim
In the light of His glory and grace.

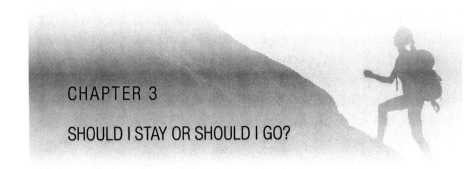

CHAPTER 3

SHOULD I STAY OR SHOULD I GO?

Wrestling with the Will of God

Teach me to do your will, for you are my God!
Let your good Spirit lead me on level ground!
(Psalm 143:10).

Be a missionary every day
Show the world that Jesus is the way
It could be in the country or city avenue
Africa or Asia, the course is up to you

I sang this song a lot growing up in a Baptist, Bible-believing church where we talked much about supporting our missionaries all over the world. From a young age I wanted to be a missionary too. It captivated my heart when one missionary didn't just talk about his story, but actually brought his story with him. I was eight, and I sat up and listened eagerly to the testimony of a new believer this man brought from the village where he loved and labored.

How then can they call on the one they have not believed in? And how can they believe in the one of whom they have not heard? And how can they hear without someone preaching to them? And how can they preach unless they are sent? As it is written, "How beautiful are the feet of those who bring good news!" (Romans 10:14–15).

Later as a teen at church camp I encountered a missionary whose message has stayed with me all these years; he spoke about being a doer of God's Word not just a hearer only (from James 1). This fun-loving, God-fearing, missionary man made an impact on me with that message. But, I kid you not, while I was out on a paddle boat with him, he told me I had ugly feet. Oh, I don't think he meant any harm, but that has stayed with me all these years too. Although my earthly feet might not be at the top of the Who's Who list of the feet world, I know God looks at things quite differently. My feet become beautiful when they take action; moving into His will for my life and toward seeing His Word being taken to those who need to be set free. So, although I might have thick ankles (I never could wear those cutesy ankle bracelets) and hairy toes, God still has a plan for my feet as He also has for yours.

I have already shared how my parents influenced me as lay leaders within the church. They loved God and loved others, bringing hundreds of children to church with them on a big brown bus. We did ministry together as a family. My two brothers and I were part of their bus ministry, reaching out right along with them. If the bus broke down, we were there. If fifty kids were singing *Hallelujah, Praise Ye the Lord* at the top of their lungs, we were there. As my parents walked down long dirt roads on dark nights just to make sure the children got to their houses safely, we were there. I would go with my dad on visitation day and watch him go to the homes of the people to invite them to church; he always left them with a word of encouragement and a prayer for deliverance. A verse that God used in my heart is from Luke 19:10, **The Son of man came to seek and to save that which was lost.**

A desire that God branded on my heart was to seek Christ and to seek out people who are lost and need to be found. I learned the timeless truth of going to the people where they are, not allowing a building or a structure to define where I was to do ministry. I learned this because I saw it lived out in a simple yet impactful way. Moms and dads out there, don't just invest money and focus on fun activities or programs for your kids, it is worth it to take time to serve God in ministry together as a family. You have no idea what God will use to get you or even your children to the edge, in order to accomplish His will and His purposes—for such a time as this.

Another big influence on me was my grandmother. I grew up hearing her tell stories of how she would share Bible stories with kids and teens under a bridge in Akron. (Believe it or not my family still lives under that same bridge...you can't make this stuff up!) There was a group over the years who faithfully worked together, both African-American and Caucasian believers, and made it possible to hear the Word in the Shelter House that stood in the middle of the projects of the Elizabeth Park community in the mid to late 60s. For safety reasons, during the time of all the uprising in urban America after the assassination of Dr. Martin Luther King Jr., my grandmother, under the direction of others in her group, needed to stop going to the little Shelter House where they had church for the neighborhood children. My grandmother grieved over that decision and prayed that God would continue His work in the lives of the children she left behind. Little did she know that God would answer her prayer by giving me that same heart and same vision generations down the line.

Grandpa and Grandma White with
Jodi—A legacy passed along

So, with all these great influences in my life, I dreamed of someday being a missionary, and I always thought I would go to a land far, far away. I loved the Spanish culture and thought maybe I could study the language and expand my vocabulary beyond what I learned on Sesame Street.

I did not take the idea of being a missionary lightly for a moment. I knew I needed to count the cost. That's biblical from the account of a parable Jesus tells us and asks the question: if a builder is going to build a tower, will he not need to count the cost in order to complete the project? (Luke 14:28). Verse 33 of Luke 14 says, ***In the same way those of you who do not give up everything you have cannot be my disciple*** (NIV). Salvation is a free gift but discipleship costs. It's true! To follow Christ, to surrender your will to His, to step up to the edge requires something from each of us: a surrendered, yielded heart.

I did finally get a chance to experience missionary life up close and personal when I decided to take a trip to Mexico. I lived with missionary friends with whom I had become acquainted while attending Bible College. It was a missionary kids' school for all those serving in the region of Pueblo, Mexico. I loved kids and wanted to do God's will, but I couldn't stop wondering whether or not this was the plan God had for me. There were some other issues complicating things that I will share in the chapters to come, but thinking deeply, I wondered whether I would somehow miss God's will for me? Would I somehow go left when I was supposed to go right? Okay, maybe I was over thinking things just a bit, but I really wanted to know and I didn't want to miss a thing!

On a flat roof in the middle of Mexico, really seeking to understand God's will, I have to admit I was a little stressed. I mean I was willing to do whatever, but what if whatever wasn't so clear. I really needed then the advice I got later from my ninety-year-old neighbor. She says she talks to God all the time, especially about her son. She said, "One day I fussed at God all day long until finally I heard Him say, 'Clara, sit down and be quiet. It's my turn to talk!'"

Good advice. Maybe I just needed to stop talking and start listening for a change. Psalm 46:10 says, *Be still and know that I am God* (NIV). And John 10:27: *My sheep hear my voice and I know them and they follow me.* Once I was quiet enough on that flat roof, God did speak into my heart. God made it very clear that I should not get so hung up on the *where* I'm supposed to be concerning God's will, but I should focus more on the *who* I'm supposed to be in His will. It was God's job to get me where I needed to be. If I am seeking Him in the Word, if I am obeying with all my heart, then God will move me in the direction I am supposed to go.

I came home from my Flat Roof Mexico Experience ready and willing to focus my attention on God Himself. I had a passion for children and for the Word of God, and God removed the burden of me trying to figure it all out. He allowed me to rest in what I already knew He had called me to: love God, love children, and preach the gospel of Jesus Christ.

It was then that I went on staff with Child Evangelism Fellowship as an Inner-City field worker within the city of Akron.

Because of my previous introduction to living and working in the urban communities in Chicago (more about this later) with a Hispanic pastor and his wife, my eyes were opened to all the needs of the cities right here in America. Of course, God knew what He was doing. I had to wait and trust that He would lead me along the edge, and it was my job to follow. I began teaching in urban communities on all sides of Akron doing Good News Clubs for many children.

So, should I stay in Akron or should I go to people and lands far away? I still didn't know, but I did start praying specifically for housing in the inner city. *God, I need a place to have children over, maybe some yard space (yeah right, yard space in the city). God, I need to be able to afford it, and I need you to confirm that this is your plan.*

He answered every one of my prayers. I did not have to go searching either! Instead, I got a phone call one night when I was the only staff person at the CEF office. The lady politely told me what she was looking for. Her name was Patricia Holley and she lived in the inner city of Akron and had a passion to reach the children on the streets all around her. She said, "I would love if someone could help me teach the children and maybe even live in the refurbished apartment upstairs from me. Oh, by the way, there is plenty of space in the yard. I happen to have a corner lot for the children to come and find refuge here."

Is God good or what? He answered my prayer and then some. As we spoke further, I discovered there was an even deeper connection between Mrs. Holley and me; one I never could make up in a thousand years. She had served with my grandmother in Elizabeth Park! This woman, whom I had never met before, called with an answer to my prayer AND she was connected to a legacy my grandmother had passed on to me. I love that verse in Isaiah 58:12 that says, **And your ancient ruins shall be rebuilt; you shall raise up the foundations of many generations; you shall be called the repairer of the breach, the restorer of streets to dwell in.**

Getting our feet to move to the edge is difficult, it feels almost impossible, but once we are surrendered, there is no doubt God will move on our behalf! Even as I type these words a group of teens from Urban Vision is in Dayton, Ohio, where Mrs. Holley now lives among the urban poor. They are assisting her in reaching out to her community there. My two oldest sons are there along with a diverse group of teens committed to taking their feet to the street and sharing God's message of love! The legacy lives on and things on the edge start to look a whole lot clearer! I love how the Lord works in such amazing ways!

Well, it seemed very clear now that going was not an option for me as a missionary, but that I was called to stay. I can't rewrite the verse that says "go and preach the gospel" to "stay and preach the gospel," but I think the communication was clear.

So, guess who showed up at my very first club in my new apartment in the city? Three Hispanic children! Yes, Mexico seemed far away, but God had three Hispanic children come and hear the gospel that day. It was as if God said with a megaphone, "Jodi, can you hear me now? I want you to stay." So stay I did!

God's will is not always easy to discern, but we just need to focus our eyes on Him. Rest in Him. Do what you already know to be God's will, and do it with a passion. Be ready to move when God does, and God's plan will unfold for you too. Remember this is a faith journey. So get your Word out and Your ears tuned in and keep moving closer to the edge.

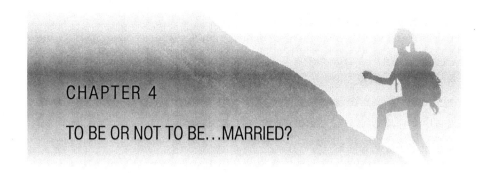

CHAPTER 4

TO BE OR NOT TO BE…MARRIED?

Finding My Identity in Christ Alone

I belong to my beloved and His desire is for Me
(Song of Solomon 7:10 NIV).

Most every little girl dreams that someday her prince will come and sweep her off her (potentially ugly!) feet. I was no different; I wanted to be married, loved, cherished, and the queen of my castle. Isn't that how the fairy tale is supposed to end?

But as we all have come to realize, life isn't as easy as wishing upon a star or hoping that our fairy godmother will someday show up and just wave her wand over life's messy realities. After stepping up to the edge and seeing the vision God had given me, I knew that no ordinary prince charming would do. I knew I was a strong-willed kind of a gal (okay, you could probably label me an *aggressive, control freak, visionary leader…*). Now what kind of a guy would want to take on such a challenge day in and day out?

I dated some in high school and a little in college but my call was secure. How many guys wanted to live in poverty and raise a family there too? It sounds a little adventurous until the first stray bullet comes through the house, through the hall closet, through your husband's dress pants (thankfully he wasn't wearing them at the time) to the center of your bedroom where it lands in a basket of towels near your bathtub. True story! In fact, the hole in our wall is still there; we kept it covered up for the longest time, hoping none of our parents would find out. Don't worry, they all know now. My husband was only a few feet from the direct path and I was nursing my son directly in the room below. We thank God for His hand of protection! We can all pretty much agree that this is not what most people would call "living happily ever after."

Commitment was modeled to me by my parents, who just celebrated fifty years of marriage. Way to go Mom and Dad; congrats to you! There are a lot of ups and downs in life, but I knew that for me to marry someone, he would have to be equally called to the edge and share the same vision. It seemed like an impossible dream. I would date someone only a short time and realize this was going nowhere fast. I wish I could tell you that I always made good decisions and that I never lowered my expectations of what I was looking for in a marriage partner, but that wouldn't be true. However, God in His grace and mercy, kept me for the plan He had for me.

I will never forget the comment an inner-city pastor mentor said to me, "Jodi, if you are going to be a light, you're going to attract some bugs along the way." I had to laugh but it was quite true. No mercy dating for me; been there done that, and it was not helpful at all.

I was never very good with relationships on a deep level. I always felt that no one really understood me or my call to walk up to the edge. Or, if that wasn't enough to dampen relationships, then all my insecurities would. To be perfectly vulnerable and honest, I have often struggled with insecurities and fears, especially in relationships. Yes, I had become—as some of you can relate to—great at masking my insecurities. But just because we fix the outside doesn't mean that something on the inside isn't very broken.

My heart longed to do God's will and His work, but we are all broken vessels needing the glue of the Holy Spirit to fill in our cracks. Most who know me personally might say, "Oh come on, Jodi, you don't seem like you're insecure. I mean, you have walked some streets where angels have feared to tread." Although that may be true, it doesn't mean I don't get afraid. Our confidence with ourselves really comes from understanding that Jesus loves us no matter what; that He is the rock on which we can stand firm. *He set my feet on a rock and gave me a firm place to stand* (Psalm 40:2 NIV).

As a child, I was diagnosed with lazy eye, along with nearsightedness and an astigmatism. I wore a black patch on my thick, brown glasses (styles were very limited back then) and I was not considered a princess but rather, a pirate. I was all right emotionally early on although my mom said she had a real challenge keeping glasses with the patch on the eyes of her busy three-year-old girl. Because I did have loving parents and I knew Jesus loved me, I was secure enough.

Jodi as a little girl with her "pirate patch"

It wasn't until I got a little older and around others my age that I realized my eye was not right. It wandered like crazy and I began to think I was a freak of nature. Now, after having had surgery, when I'm wearing glasses or contacts it is barely noticeable. But while surgery solved my outward problem, every night in the secrecy of my room, I still struggle. Even knowing my husband's acceptance of me doesn't always change how I feel. I am still faced with that same reality that doesn't go away.

All this left an impression on my soul; fears and insecurities that the enemy shackled me with for a very long time. But in recent years I have finally gotten some victory over it. I want to assure you that for me to even speak of this to you is huge, I mean HUGE, for me.

I was saved and I loved Jesus, I had a loving family and really, to be honest, I had no excuse to feel and think the way I did. But the enemy, the father of lies, is pretty convincing. My head was filled with thoughts like, *You're ugly, you're no good, you're a mistake. Dream all you want little girl but no one will ever love you once they know what you really look like. Forget those dreams of prince charming coming to sweep you away; you will be disregarded like a piece of trash.* Pretty harsh thoughts. No one directly told me those words as a child but somehow they were implanted there, maybe by Satan who possibly thought that if he could destroy this little girl and her thought process, she would never grow to make an impact in this world for Christ?

I understood that the lies came from the pit of hell. I knew the truth, I knew who I was. But the enemy would cast doubt that always lingered in my mind, *Lord even if someone had the same call, would they really love me if they knew what I really looked like?*

I am not trying to elicit a "poor me" reaction, by any means. For I know God uses all our weaknesses and that when we yield our imperfections to Him, He makes beautiful things out of us all. Our confidence is in Christ alone. We all, at times, feel like we don't measure up or that we aren't quite good enough;

sometimes because of visible physical imperfections, sometimes due to something emotional and hidden. Don't be discouraged; God takes great delight in all His children. He sees our weaknesses as His greatest opportunities to display His great power in us. My dear mentor friend, Miss Clorinda Tucker, always tells me that man's extremity is God's opportunity. I am starting to get an understanding of what that means.

I have recently written a poem about my hidden thorn in the flesh. Just like the apostle Paul, I asked for Him to remove mine as well. Don't you ever get tired of hiding? I have, many times.

Hear my heart…

Masquerade
—Jodi M. Matthews

Behind the Masquerade hidden so well
From the eyes of all others no difference can tell.

Hidden I thought would be a moment's relief;
What seemed for a moment became my belief.

Beyond the cruelty and judgement I hide
Never the same to my own self have lied.

Always wondering do they love me for me;
Thinking you would never love if you could see what I see.

A hideous truth a freak on display;
God please heal this deformity I pray.

Asked once, asked twice, a million times more,
My plea for a change has seemed ignored.

Of course, the wrestle, the wondering why;
It would seem that my Savior has left me to die.

To drown in self-pity or resentment of one
Who could change my condition with no help from none.

What's the point with this making of me?
When blurred is my vision, can't really see.

Really it's no to my request once again;
Grace is sufficient with my strength you can win.

Die once, die twice, three times and more
Is what is needed to do all the more.

Just give me your gaze and you will see as I do;
You die but you're raised in my power through you.

It's amazing how I long for people to see
With my mask on display, "O what beautiful me."

But hidden beneath the admiring stares and some glares,
A soul of self-pity, shame, and despair.

Ignorant I'm not; I have figured my plight.
As long as I parade with mask I'm alright.

Accepted by others even admired by them,
But chained to my mask, imprisoned within.

Sometimes I catch myself staring at those
Who too look different from this mask I've proposed.

For the world is no kinder who appear different or odd
With no masks to wear, no pretty facades.

Lord let me surrender for these are my eyes
Both outside and in from deception and lies.

I now accept these eyes that can't really see
For they have made me see others instead of just me.

I surrender my being, wholeheartedly I give.
My mask is now yours; please let me live.

Not subject to fear to the prince of this earth
But free as a dark soul that has found rebirth.

Loved by a King, the Master of all.
No masks required to come to His ball.

I am loved, admired, He even takes great delight;
Enthralled with my beauty what a glorious sight.

I now can see with no masks and no chains
Much clearer now, a peace I have gained.

One day my weak eyes will no longer be,
But for now I am thankful they've helped me to see.

A love so deep that goes deep down inside,
Past my mask, beyond all my pride.

I am now free, no more chained to my sin.
Praise the Lord, Hallelujah, I can see once again!

> *But he said to me, "My grace is sufficient for you, for my power is made perfect in weakness." Therefore I will boast all the more gladly of my weaknesses, so that the power of Christ may rest upon me. For the sake of Christ, then, I am content with weaknesses, insults, hardships, persecutions, and calamities. For when I am weak, then I am strong* (2 Corinthians 12:9–10).

I thought I was going to leave my Moody Bridal/Bible College experience in Chicago (as many always joked) without a hitch. But then I met someone the last few months of my senior year who seemed to be headed for missions and loved the Hispanic culture. He was even going to teach at the same missionary kids' school that I already had plans to visit after graduation. We were engaged before my Mexico missions experience.

But on that flat roof in Mexico, God reminded me once again that no person in this world could take His place. Christ alone. I had to know it and I had to live it. I left Mexico a changed person, realizing I was in no way ready to make the marriage commitment. I felt deeply that God had another plan in mind. I left feeling very brokenhearted. I thought I was leaving behind my dreams of marriage and of being a missionary too. I exchanged my plan for His as I continued to get closer to the edge.

I wish I could tell you that one broken engagement was enough, but not so...a couple of years later I found myself engaged again to someone who loved God and worked in the city. Yet the thought of working, living, and doing the kind of ministry I knew God had called me to would not work for both of us. Another broken heart, another point of surrender.

Left very vulnerable, I knew I had to stop putting myself through this. *Maybe marriage is not for me, maybe it was just wishful thinking*, I thought. Surrender again. If you could just indulge me one moment, as I slip back into the pages of my past, you will find a very brokenhearted young woman who just had to let go of her will in the area of relationships, and exchange it for God's. Let me assure you that the point of pain was real. If anyone has gone through a broken relationship or is facing it now, you know it is huge. Yet God is bigger, and I had to rest in the sovereignty of God, for He who knew the plan held my heart as well.

Now I had two broken relationships as baggage in my past. Two times I was engaged, thinking to be happily married, but God had better plans for me. Of course, hindsight is always much clearer than at the moment, but it's the heart of a relationship with God that won out over a dream I thought I could never have anyway (remember those insecurities I have shared with you).

Here is a journal entry of mine in the form of a poem I jotted down and haven't read again until just recently when I was preparing for this book. Now it may seem a bit silly to share what seems to be a woeful heart wondering if there was anyone for her in this world, but God is good. He loved on me back then and once again by His presence, assured me that my ship or my man had not passed me by, but just hadn't come into port yet. I love God's grace for all!

I was on a little trip with my parents who were trying to minister to my broken heart, watching all these huge ships go in and out of the harbor. So here it is:

My Captain's Choice
—Jodi M. Matthews

Ships come and go throughout this life, I wonder which is for me.
Yet I will not fear nor be sad, for my anchor is in Thee.
You're the One who allows these ships to pass by my shore
To remind me of your saving grace, to strengthen me all the more.
It is very painful to watch the ship return to sea
But my Captain who is in charge has the best in mind for me.
One day He will bring a ship for me to anchor and to rest
And then and only then I'll know my Captain chose the best.
Until this time I must let go of ships that leave again
And trust my Captain with all my heart and learn to wait on Him.

Now, almost twenty-five years later, most definitely married to my soul mate and with three sons whom I love dearly, I know without a shadow of a doubt that my Captain did choose what is best for me. (I will share more on how I met Rodney in a chapter to come.) Oh, how I thank Him for keeping me for what is His best. Oh, how I thank God for helping me to surrender to His plan! Hebrews 6:19 says, *We have this hope as an anchor for the soul, firm and secure. It enters the inner sanctuary behind the curtain where Jesus who went before us has entered on our behalf* (NIV).

My soul mate, friend, and partner in ministry:
Rodney and Jodi Matthews, married May 7, 1994

It really is all about knowing that Christ alone is the true lover of our souls; that He is kind and good. Even though light can attract bugs, it can also stand out and pierce the darkness. *Let your light so shine before men that they may see your good works and glorify your Father which is in heaven* (Matthew 5:16 NIV). That light that shines in you can also lead others to you, even—within God's will—your soul mate.

I know some of you are still waiting and wondering whether or not God has a marriage partner in mind for you. Wait on His best and while waiting, be all you can be in Him. God knows your heart, knows what you need, so trust Him on the edge. You will never slip, with your eyes on Him. Be assured that no matter what, your Prince of Peace will come and give you all you need for life and godliness. Whether we are single or married, young or old, male or female, there is always a call to come. He is our guide. He has the plans. Let's trust that He who began a good work in all of us is faithful to complete it (Philippians 1:6). AMEN!

CHAPTER 5

A WALK IN SOMEONE ELSE'S SHOES

So if there is any encouragement in Christ: any comfort from love, any participation in the Spirit, any affection and sympathy, complete my joy by being of the same mind, having the same love, being in full accord and of one mind. Do nothing from rivalry or conceit, but in humility count others more significant than yourselves. Let each of you look not only to his own interests, but also to the interests of others (Philippians 2:1–4).

After my struggles in coming to rest in what God would do with me, married or unmarried, I put my whole heart into loving God and serving Him with a passion. I had more on my plate than I could ever manage to accomplish; more and more needs in the lives of the people I encountered.

Starting one Good News Bible Club where I lived began a multiplication of clubs all over the city of Akron. Any place where children had a lot of time on their hands proved to be a perfect place to proclaim the gospel of Jesus Christ. I found myself in many different government housing areas; struggling communities of need. Single moms trying to make ends meet, young men congregating in throngs, many children free to do whatever they wanted, like getting cooled off by fire hydrants opened to provide some relief to the summer's heat. I would walk around the whole neighborhood inviting children to come meet me in the park or at a nearby yard to come hear a Bible story and play some kickball or soccer. I never lacked for takers; whether a small or large group of children, they were always ready to have fun and always wanting to feel special. We all long to feel special; it is a basic human need to be and feel wanted.

Earliest Kids Club in yard by the building on
Turner Street in Elizabeth Park, 1993

Friends who had the same vision came with me and as the children came, we loved on them the best we knew how. My mom and dad joined me on the edge occasionally, but Mom said it always made her hair a little grayer watching her daughter go walking through projects inviting children to come. But then she told me that God gave her peace of mind through a glimpse of angels surrounding me as I walked. I have always loved the verse in Isaiah 58:8 that says, ***The glory of the LORD will be your rear guard*** (NIV). I knew I wasn't invincible to danger, but I learned, wrestled, and came to terms with the fact that I was safer in the center of

God's will for my life in the roughest part of town than I would be out of God's will in the nicest part of town. No one should recklessly do anything unless they get their directions from above. Yet even so, we must leave the results with God. Thankfully, in all my years of service within the city, I have been unharmed physically, praise be to His name. That doesn't mean I haven't had my share of trials or difficulties, but I trust my beloved, the true lover of my soul, and no matter what comes my way, I am in His hands. He is my Keeper. He has bid me to come. I know and believe that faithful is He who has called me, and He will bring it to pass.

When I was a little girl I loved trying on my mom's clothes from her teenage years, like her party dresses from the late 50s along with her shoes and accessories. I loved slipping on her gloves, but most of all her beautiful wedding dress that, yes, I wore on my wedding day. And my grandmother had worn it as well! Three generations of weddings with one dress is pretty amazing! Dresses are a lot easier to alter in order to fit than shoes. If they are not your size, it just seems awkward to wear them. They just aren't comfortable; in fact, the experience can be downright painful.

However, I so longed to walk in the shoes of my brothers and sisters of color to understand more about what had shaped their culture up to this current day, even if it was uncomfortable at times. I have made my share of mistakes and have had to work through prejudices that have been a part of a majority culture for centuries. At the time I had started many of the clubs in Akron I was spending more and more time in the community with people who very different from me, and I loved it! Yet as much as I tried to fit in, I could never walk in the shoes of so many of my new friends. I have never felt the racism they have as some of my dear friends have very candidly shared with me over the years. I never had to fit in to places where people didn't look like me, talk like me, or dress like me. Yet, as I was maturing in my walk with God, I began praying about this area of how I could truly be reconciled with others cross culturally. God brought something very distinct to my mind and heart from a time gone by. Like a dagger to my soul, I was confronted with the ugliness of sin and it was called indifference. I never thought I needed to walk in someone else's shoes until God said, *You need to try these on, even if you think they won't fit, so you can get to the edge I have called you to.*

I was taking some summer classes at a college, where we lived in dorms for six weeks, which would be short yet intense weeks of study. I was first to arrive at my designated room and got settled, wondering if my roommate would actually come. Secretly I had hopes of even having the room to myself. She did finally arrive late on Sunday, a petite African-American young lady who appeared quite shy with her one suitcase that she never unpacked. We introduced ourselves to each other briefly, but before I knew it I was busily preparing for classes that were to come and was too preoccupied to notice anything particular about my roommate. I didn't think she would mind. After all, we were just going to be there a short time and I was sure she had things to do too, I rationalized. After classes had started I rarely saw her in our room. She always came in late after I was in bed and seemed to be gone early in the morning and she always went home on the weekends. I really didn't think much of it. I was focused on my agenda of classes, pretty at ease in my comfort zone around people who looked like me and felt fairly accepted in a college that reflected the majority culture.

Yet, when I prayed and asked God to show me what reconciliation should look like for me, He did not show me what it should be but showed me what it was *not*. God took me back to this time when I was in a place where I could have shown great love and acceptance to someone who was not a part of the majority culture and who I am sure struggled to fit into shoes she had no choice to walk in. My roommate chose not to stay throughout the whole session; she left early and I never understood why. Let's get something straight, I know it was not because she wasn't smart enough or gifted enough to handle the challenge in front of her, but I never thought twice about how difficult it must be to walk into a place where people see you as different and find your acceptance and identity and stability if no one takes the time to see beyond your differences. Would someone take the time to see into her heart? I blew it totally!

Before the prayer was over I was in tears as God showed me how wrong I was not to go out of my way to love and accept this dear, sweet, young lady. I didn't go out of my way to do her any harm—that would be very "unchristian"—but I didn't go out of my way to extend friendship, or reconciliation either. This most definitely was very "unchristian"!!! God confronted me so directly that He called me to see that it wasn't so much what I did do but what I didn't do to walk alongside another person who was different than me. Indifference towards others is sinful. As a follower of Jesus, I must learn to listen to someone's whole story that gives context to what is being lived out for others to see, and at times can be misinterpreted wrongly. I never put myself in her shoes; I didn't even try. So, therefore, I did not enter her pain, or her story, and the sad thing is since she left school early, I couldn't even tell you her name. At the time, secretly I was just happy to have the room to myself. Is that pathetic or what? I was utterly wrong and sinful and I am ashamed to even share such a story with all of you. Someday I hope and pray I can make my wrong right. I want to tell her how sorry I am for not understanding her and getting out of my world and entering hers. I pray she would forgive me for speaking love from my lips and not living it out in my heart with her. Oh wretched woman that I am, who will save me from my sin? I regret that I allowed indifference to rule in my heart instead of God's love in that instance. May God cleanse me from my sin. I am so thankful for God's amazing grace! Aren't you? **Thanks be to God, who delivers me through Jesus Christ our Lord** (Romans 7:25 NIV)! Praise God He helps us to see!

Back in the early days, there were instances when people may have thought that I did not belong in the communities I became a part of. I would even have to let people in authority know of my intentions of doing Bible Clubs in the many communities of Akron, along with those who volunteered with me. The thought was that if you don't live there, you don't go there unless you're dealing or up to no good. Even my mom and dad were questioned several years later, as they drove through the neighborhood in my mom's red convertible with my toddler in the car seat in the back, listening to Barney the purple dinosaur. One may have thought that they were the wrong color in the wrong community with the wrong car and definitely with the wrong music. These are misperceptions all of us need to process and learn to respond to in a humble, teachable way. As believers we need to constantly go to Jesus and ask Him to help us to see how He sees. We need to ask Him to wash away the inconsistencies in our hearts that need to be confessed as sin so our hearts are tenderer towards the experiences of others.

We could shrug off incidents that seem to be harmless especially when our ending turned out okay. Yet how many lives have been hurt or potentially even lost because of wrong information that leads us to look through distorted lenses. How tragic it is when someone is misjudged no matter who they are or what job they have. God was showing me how wrong stereotyping, indifference, and prejudice can be from any of us no matter what. Something needed to change; some things most definitely still do!

These would be the first of many needed lessons I would humbly learn about how often people can be judged so unfairly by the color of their skin. I highly recommend reading Benjamin Watson's book *Under Our Skin*, (Carol Stream, IL: Tyndale Momentum, an Imprint of Tyndale House Publishers, 2015), which gives great insights into how we as believers can begin to navigate and process issues of race and culture. True reconciliation requires us to see into the hearts of those whom we desire to reconcile with.

A dear sister of color used to ask me, "Jodi, have you ever walked in my shoes?" No, I have not is all I could say to her at that time. Yet from my lessons learned and sins that have been confessed I purposed in my heart to truly genuinely live amongst people who now see me as different. I still have a lot to learn but in a very small, teeny way I began to understand what it meant to be perceived as different. Maybe—just maybe—God used how I felt so different growing up with my eye problems and insecurities to prepare me to better understand the differences of others. In no way have I walked in the shoes of those who have suffered so much. Yet I thank God for the many who have been so patient to help me start to understand what embracing differences means. There is a saying that says, if the shoe fits wear it, but I say, from what I have learned, even if it doesn't feel like it fits, wear it, and just maybe the indifference of our world will seem one size smaller. So much to learn, so much to take in, so much to sink into my soul and bring into focus that which I needed to see.

So Much
—Jodi M. Matthews

Lord, so much my cry to You;
I feel so overwhelmed, out of control, out of view.
Lord, so much I find where I see
And how it must all center on me.
Lord, so much I need to repent
Of all the wasted moments I spent.
Lord, so much of Your greater grace in my life
And so much I have caused You strife.
Lord, so much is Your patience I know;

How You have loved me and caused me to grow.
Lord, so much You help me believe
Beyond my eye with joy I receive.
Lord, so much You have had to give
Despite the rejection You had to live.
Lord, so much is Your love I can't comprehend;
Lord, so much my God and my Friend...
Lord, I know and have learned that
Nothing is too much for You...absolutely nothing!

We all think we know, but in reality we are very limited in perceiving things with our human eyes. That's the reason that getting to the edge is all the more imperative for us as believers. We may not be able to walk in someone else's shoes, but we look to the One we all love and adore. We know no one has ever walked in shoes like His; and He walked in them on our behalf... red and yellow, black and white, we are all precious in His sight.

CHAPTER 6

LEARNING WHILE LOVING

*The Sovereign LORD has given me a well-instructed
tongue, to know the word that sustains the weary. He
wakens me morning by morning, wakens my ear to
listen like one being instructed*
(Isaiah 50:4 NIV).

There is no doubt that I had much to learn about life, culture, and about the people of the city—who would end up being my greatest teachers of all. I can't begin to tell you the many older brothers and sisters of color who came alongside me to encourage, befriend, and teach me things I needed to know about loving God and loving others from another culture.

Reverend Corn and his wife ran a ministry called Operation Jochabed, and they loved and accepted me. Many times, after the Bible Club on Copley Road in Akron, I would stop by and visit with them in their home. I never felt like they were inconvenienced that this young white girl came by to hang out while she cooked and he ironed his clothes. Yes, from the world's perspective I may have seemed out of place, but I was right where I needed to be; learning from an older African-American couple who could teach me how to go in and out amongst people. I would set up my blanket on their sidewalk since there was no room in the yard, and we would teach the Bible right on the streets of West Akron. We jumped rope, we sang, we proclaimed the Truth.

Other African-American dear friends who opened their doors and their hearts on the west side of Akron were Mr. Ernest Calhoun, Sr., and Pastor Gus and Elaine Brown. I loved spending time with each one of these dear servants of the Lord…they loved and accepted me, and the Holy Spirit knit our hearts together.

I met Mr. Calhoun many times at the urban elementary school where he worked as a counselor. Seeing the impact he had on the children there so impressed my soul. A genuine love came from God and was dispersed through the hands and feet and kind words of this elderly African-American man whom the children fondly called *Grandpa*. He introduced me to the concept of reconciliation and to a man named Dr. John Perkins, who was proclaiming this message of reconciliation all over the United States, bringing people from different cultures together to radically love each other in order to point people to Jesus. Little did I know at the time how God was using all these people's lives to shape and mold my own.

We were a team. Mr. Calhoun would bring all the kids, one carload at a time, as the Browns opened their church, and I was given the privilege of sharing the message of hope to so many who needed to hear. Frances of Assisi wrote that it is in giving that we receive; I had no idea of the power of those words until friendships with the children and people in the city grew to become close and precious as I began to know and love them. It was there that I met people who would change my life forever.

One night more than twenty-five years ago I stood with one of the pastors I highly respected from the city in the back of the room where we held the club, looking out over 100 elementary and junior high-aged, inner-city youth. This man really loved those children and wanted to help me understand the sobering reality of what lay before me as I had the weighty responsibility of sharing the Truth and helping them apply it in their sometimes hard lives on the streets. I will never forget what he said to me. He told me to take a good look at all these children and then said, "Jodi, two-thirds of these children will either be dead or in prison by the age of eighteen." I was staggered by the raw fact that these children faced severe challenges on their none-too-kind journeys in life. They looked so happy to be there, so eager to hear the Truth.

It wasn't too long afterwards that his statistics started playing out before my very eyes, and I found myself standing at the grave of my twelve-year-old friend, Jessie. He had attended that very same Bible Club, and his life had been snuffed out all too soon, due to the ills of society; such as, drugs, poverty, and neglect, that he faced in his young life. From the world's perspective Jessie was chalked up to be just another tragic statistic. Yet there is another world to be accounted for. It is one only seen from God's records not man's, from God's perspective not ours.

You see, Jessie was a leader with lots of enthusiasm and energy. Yes, I would have to say he was quite ornery, but even so Jessie wanted to be there and proved it by bringing more and more children with him to Bible Club to hear the good news of the gospel. Mr. Calhoun mentored him along with many other children. Jessie went to Christian overnight camp and never missed Bible Club. A couple of months before his death Jessie was chosen to go on Christian radio to give his testimony of how Jesus changed his life. As short as Jessie's life was, he had found his voice and had clear vision of who he was and where he was going.

Jessie and Jodi at Kids Club/Jessie
giving his money for missions

From time to time, I still visit the humble little grave of this young man who barely has a 10 x 12" flat, metal marker as a memorial to his brief life. Yet this young man's name is written in the Lamb's Book of Life and he has made a mark on my heart forever. God has given me a vision to see beyond the harsh reality of life and death. *Where O death is your victory? Where O death is your sting?....But thanks be to God! He gives us the victory through our Lord Jesus Christ!* (1 Corinthians 15:55, 57 NIV).

The vision means not yielding to the statistics, but clearing our sight and doing something in God's plan about the problem at hand; for Christ and His kingdom. It means stepping all the closer to the edge even if we do begin to see the valley of the shadow of death. Lessons of life and love and even pain and death have taught me so much about His kingdom and His plan, which goes beyond even what the eye can see. God has used these lessons to grow me into a woman who has a deep love for children and a love for the city and all who dwell in it.

I wrote this little memorial poem and dedicated it to Jessie. As I stood before a very mournful group of people on the day of his funeral, I saw many who were full of despair; they didn't know the Truth that Jessie had found at a young age.

The Traveler
—Jodi M. Matthews

A traveler on the road of life starts out so very small, with hands that help in every way to catch him when he falls.

But soon the traveler begins to walk along this road so long, to find this road of life is hard, how can he be so strong?

This road of life much traveled on should not be walked alone, for many are the paths we take but only one may lead us home.

Jessie our young traveler boy chose a path one day, when He heard God's Word so true that Jesus is the way.

Wanting what was right and pure, loved Jesus with all his heart; he said, "I choose to take for me this path!" His journey he did start.

As he began to walk this path so young as others saw him do, he realized that he was not alone for Jesus walked there too.

So young, they cried, for him to walk the path that Jesus took; but God has called both young and old, for it is written in His book.

Jessie learned and grew with others who chose that path as well; he knew that heaven was his end, and others he would tell.

On this journey Jessie walked with his Savior near, while one day Jesus stopped to say, "Jessie you are here."

"There so soon," others cried, "it isn't fair at all. He has so much more he could do to answer to His call!"

But Jesus with His loving eyes turned and shared His heart, "My precious child, he has done his part."

"He brought many to hear my truth that can set them free, but it's his time to come on home and to live with me."

Weep not for him, for he is well in his heavenly home. But weep for those who know not me, whose paths are still unknown.

Jessie is a testimony for all the world to know, so choose the path that Jessie took; your life it too will grow.

For Jessie knew that to live a life abundant, full, and free, started with accepting Christ when He said, "Just believe on me."

> ***Believe on the Lord Jesus Christ and you will be saved*** (Acts 16:31 NIV).

Let me also tell you about Dorothy Morton, an elderly African-American woman who loved Jesus and children. She had a friend named Pastor Batch who was an elderly Caucasian widower. He had a little old church on Arlington Street and Mrs. Morton introduced me to him. Before long we were a threesome, reaching out to children on the east side of Akron for the gospel of Jesus Christ. God used these Bible Clubs all over Akron to show me a need that was profound and extensive.

It's true that the teams God put together were most unusual, but God is creative in how He works and we are all the better for it. I met so many pastors in the city who influenced me by their tireless efforts to reach the hurting all around them. Pastor Duma, Pastor Harris, Pastor Jackson, and Pastor Glen were people who had given much for the gospel. I wondered if I had what it took to walk in places they had walked for many years.

Often I would think, *Really, God?* All the children and all the needs...how could I ever make an impact on something that seemed enormous to take on? I was a far cry from what anyone would think of when someone said urban missionary, but God's qualifications are not the same as man's. Perhaps I was a little like Peter when Jesus called him out to walk on water with Him. In his eagerness to obey, Peter did it, but then loss of focus got him sinking quickly. I needed to keep my focus on Jesus.

John 15:5 says, *I am the vine; you are the branches...apart from me you can do nothing* (NIV). Yet another lesson; a lesson of dependence. In no way could I take on all this need by myself. I had to learn that my source is Christ alone. I wish I could tell you all the stories about the times when children in the projects would come and sit under the awning of the church driveway to hear Bible stories, and about the times when teens and mothers and once in a while—a dad—would come also. God was preparing the vision that I would see once I got to the edge. A vision that would run deep and wide and that involved a message of hope to children and their families. An Urban Vision was soon to be born...

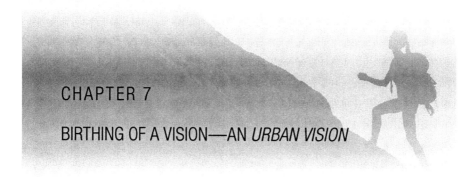

CHAPTER 7

BIRTHING OF A VISION—AN *URBAN VISION*

Where there is no vision the people perish
(Proverbs 29:18 KJV).

At that time in my life God kept nudging me more and more to the edge. Now was no time to turn back. Thankfully, there were some volunteers that came alongside to help with all the inner-city Bible Clubs that sprang up all over Akron on every side of town. It was an exciting time of living out the call that God had on my life in my early to mid-20s. God even brought a childhood friend back into my life (one who had ridden on the big brown bus with me) to serve with me after God drew her back into relationship with Him. We became roommates, living in the city, and ministering to children everywhere.

Prayer is key to any plan that God unfolds in any of our lives. This was modeled to me early in ministry by dear Mrs. Holley. She and I would spend many hours walking and praying through the city, asking God to move on behalf of those who needed Him most. My roommate, Lee Ann, Mrs. Holley, and I spent many times in prayer for those around us, which indeed opened up many opportunities to share the gospel. I remember the security guard that stood watch over the corner bar with whom we often had conversations. The kids in the neighborhood knew that Mrs.

Holley's house was a place of refuge. She called her home and ministry *The Morning Glory House* because of all the morning glories that climbed the fence all along her property. Her prayer that God would use her and all she had in order to reach those around the neighborhood definitely brought glory to His name. What a bright spot her home was within our urban community. I remember coming home late one night and finding some children sleeping in a little play area she had set up under the steps. They had run away and come to a place where they knew they would receive love and help. I could never get used to those unexpected situations and never knew what to do when they arose. I learned what it meant to make 911 prayer calls to our Heavenly Father asking what to do. No textbook or Bible class could prepare us for the task at hand, but God is greater than all; *Greater is He that is in me, than He that is in the world* (1 John 4:4 KJV).

We invited others to pray as we began to seek what God's heart for this city set on a hill (see definition below) meant for all of us. A small group of young people, mostly in their twenties, came to Mrs. Holley's house at 5:00 in the morning to pray. These were people seriously wanting God to move in their lives and in the lives of those around them. It was a mixed group of men and women who had started to volunteer in the various Bible Clubs that we had started throughout the city. I found a list of all the schools in the Akron area that included the names of teachers and principals, along with a list of churches and their pastors, and we began to pray through the lists as often as we could. We prayed that God would move in and through us to see His kingdom come, His will be done, on earth as it is in heaven. It doesn't take God long to respond to hearts set out to seek Him. We continued doing what we knew God placed before us and as we were faithful, God brought other godly people into our group; people who began to give more shape to the vision that had begun to burn deep within my soul. Yes, it was through that early time of meeting with God that an Urban Vision was born.

I was still on staff with Child Evangelism Fellowship living out my dream of being a missionary. I loved the Bible Clubs, the children, teaching God's Word, and doing it all with kindred spirits who wanted to assist in the cause of sharing the gospel. I was even allowed to fulfill a role as the inner-city field worker and my job was to begin Good News Clubs all over the inner city of Akron. It was during this time, through all the mentors God brought into my life that the Urban Vision in my heart began to take on more and more definition.

In Greek, Akron means *high place.* Geographically, Akron is a city set on a hill overlooking the valley below, so how appropriate for me that God talked in Matthew 5 about the city on a hill that could not be hidden. ***Let your light so shine before men that they would see your good deeds and glorify God in heaven*** (Matthew 5:16 NIV). I wanted to be a part of that light that would shine all around Akron.

Clubs sprang up on the west side, on Copley Road with Reverend Corn, on Diagonal Road at Akron Alliance Church with Pastor Gus and Elaine Brown, and near the Edgewood AMHA (Akron Metropolitan Housing Authority). My roommate Lee Ann helped me start and run clubs on the east side of Akron; on Arlington Street with Pastor Batch and also at Macedonia Baptist with Pastor Lorenzo Glenn who graciously opened his heart and church to the vision of reaching children. On Akron's south side the AMHA Wilbeth Arlington Homes, which were remnants of old war houses, provided much opportunity to reach children who lived in the houses and ran the streets. We met with those kids in a small church called Hillwood Chapel, opened for us by Pastor Rufus Hofelt. Also on the south side I connected with Akron Bible Church and Pastor Duma who allowed us to use the Denton Center that was named after Bill Denton and the Furnace Street Ministry from years gone by. One little boy who came to play kickball there grew up to be an Olympic wrestler. We still know his dad, a man who continues to labor for the Lord at Akron Bible Church after giving his life to the service of his King. Sometimes we do not know if what we do makes a difference and to be honest, I am not even sure that the little boy who grew up to be the Olympic wrestler remembers us, but for that time and in that place, we met a need by loving kids, sharing the Word, and keeping them off the streets. Only time can tell how one's obedience affects the lives of others, but I believe that someday eternity will tell the story.

It proved to be more difficult to connect with an already existing church on the north side of Akron in order to reach out to the children of the community. We finally were able to do a CEF five-day club in a small church under the bridge, which stirred my heart even more because my grandma had reached children for Jesus under that same bridge so many years ago.

With every day that passed, God burdened my heart even more. My eyes saw, but my heart did too. I had never known poverty like what I was encountering on a daily basis. I didn't even know how God could use an unqualified young white woman to love and live amongst all of it. Many people said I would never make it. However, just as the Word tells us that love covers a multitude of sins, I know God's love for us also covers a multitude of insufficiencies. If God called me to live and love in a culture and a background so different from my own, then I must move all the closer to the edge in order to see more of Him and less of me.

Over the years I have learned and lived the truth of John 15:5, where Jesus says, *…apart from me you can do nothing* (NIV). But I have also learned that with Him, *I can do all things through Him who gives me strength* (Philippians 4:13 NIV). It is humbling to walk a journey alongside others when we know we are not qualified for the task. That is the point; who we are and what we do is wrapped in Who He is and what He desires for our lives. Again in John 15:5, He says, *I am the vine; you are the branches.* I know where my strength comes from, and I have learned to cling with great tenacity to the One who holds tenaciously to me.

God wants us to be faithful in the small things, and if we have been found faithful, He can entrust us with the larger things of life. I have learned that faithfulness is huge for God; His Word says that without faith it is impossible to please God. I just heard a young African-American teacher who grew up in poverty himself and now pours his life into third grade boys say, "God is not looking for heroes; He is looking for people to be faithful." I must take Him at His word when He says He is the rewarder of those who diligently seek Him. Yes, I was and still am a pleaser by nature, but this desire, this vision that grew in my heart, pressed me on to heights and edges I never thought I would go.

I remember preparing for my first speaking engagement at a CEF fundraiser. I wanted so much to communicate the need I saw in all these clubs and how sharing the good news of the gospel made an impact on the lives we came in contact with. Never had I thought that I would speak to adults about my heart for the children in all these clubs all over Akron, but preparing for the talk began to stir in me a desire to bridge a gap between the people within the Church and the hurting people outside the walls of the Church. Unfortunately, stereotypes and prejudices are still prevalent even within God's people. Asking God to give us His eyes and His ears and His hands is an uncomfortable process, yet it is needed in order to embrace those who need to know that there is hope left in the world.

I shared passionately that night, even sharing a poem I had written about the importance of reaching these children for the kingdom. The streets are a harsh reality for many children and they needed to know that someone loved them and had a plan for them, as it says in Jeremiah 29:11: ***"For I know the plans I have for you," declares the LORD,…"plans to give you hope and a future"*** (NIV). Yet just as God has a plan, so does the enemy who wants to come and steal, kill, and destroy. Oh, how Jesus longed for the children of these clubs and children everywhere to know that there is a Savior who loves them. Here is the poem I shared at that first banquet.

Let the Children Come...
—Jodi M. Matthews

Satan says I will love the children, you bring them unto me;
For I will fill their minds with junk and I will use their bodies.
Satan says I will love the children, the ones who are alone;
To keep them in the darkest night, just hear their painful groans.
Satan says I will love the children, the ones who I can train
To sell the drugs, to make a buck, my evil it will reign.
Then on the scene the Living Word stood and spoke so clear;
He placed a child within the midst and he wiped all their tears.
Then Jesus said, I will love these children, you bring them unto me;
For I loved them through my life and death when I died there on
that tree.
Jesus then asks, do you love these children just as much as me?
For such is the kingdom of heaven for all eternity!

After speaking that night, I shared a slideshow of the children I worked with, using this old song by Steve Green called People Need the Lord as background music. Verse one really captured what I was experiencing coming alongside the many children I had begun to encounter.

People Need the Lord
—Steve Green

Every day they pass me by,
I can see it in their eye.
Empty people filled with care,
Headed who knows where?

On they go through private pain,
Living fear to fear.
Laughter hides their silent cries,
Only Jesus hears.

After this challenge from my heart to anyone who was willing to listen, two men, one Caucasian and one African-American, came up to meet me. Little did I realize what our conversation would lead to. These two men, Ralph Gatti and Bob Sturkey, wanted me to meet a woman named Kathy Dudley, and before I knew it, I was on a plane headed to Texas to visit an urban ministry called Voice of Hope. God was moving and I wanted to move with Him. I had no idea who I was meeting or what it would all mean for my future. Go I must, even when I was not sure of where I was headed, but He provided everything I needed. I arrived at Dallas airport feeling a little apprehensive about this whole experience. I got off the plane and was welcomed by a man holding a sign that said *Jodi White* (my maiden name). I wasn't quite like all the other business people who had drivers waiting for them to arrive, but I was on an adventure, so with a deep breath I introduced myself and off we went to visit a ministry that loved Jesus and loved others well.

I took in so much during that long weekend. Kathy really encouraged me that God does use women to lead in certain situations. I have struggled with this concept because I never set out to prove a point about women in leadership; I just wanted to do what the Lord asked of me. I have carried a lot of insecurity with me over the years, but I have learned to shed it little by little through the grace given to me by the Lord.

I experienced the ministry of Voice of Hope in full swing as they ministered to the poor all around them. I saw a brokenness in the community that needed the loving hand of God's people who were willing to live and love amongst those they served. Voice of Hope had an after school program, dance classes, the teen house, a thrift store, a dental clinic, and so much more. I was caught up in a whirlwind of productive activity that seemed to breathe life into those who participated. I spent time with Kathy and her niece, Selina, and gleaned so much information. I knew God was helping me to form a foundation for the vision He had given me. It was helpful to see something that was years ahead; something that was already what I hoped someday to see in the community of Akron.

At one point I was left alone, bagging mounds and mound of potatoes that had been donated to Voice of Hope. As I worked, I noticed that a staff person who was tending the lawn went inside the building, leaving his lawn equipment unattended. It was all such a blur, but as I watched, a van pulled up out of nowhere and a couple people jumped out, ran over, picked up all the lawn equipment, and jumped back into the van. It was something you would see in a movie. I could not believe it. I witnessed a theft in broad daylight! I walked in, leaving the potatoes to fend for themselves, and said, "I believe someone just stole all your lawn equipment," to which the Voice of Hope staff replied with an exasperated, "Not again!"

We spent time visiting the families in their homes, asking them how we could pray for them, just being Jesus' love in action. It was a truly amazing experience to take in. On the flight back to Akron I found myself processing all that I had seen and what it meant to me. Very clearly as I looked over the city before landing, God spoke to my heart. *Jodi, what you saw in Dallas, bring here to Akron...* As unqualified as I felt, God made it clear that just like the word in Habakkuk 2:2, I was to **write the vision down and make it plain...that he may run who reads it** (KJV).

Faith is walking, sometimes even running, up to the edge even though you are not sure what is in store. What became clear in my heart and mind was that this Urban Vision was God's plan and for some reason I cannot explain He chose to include me in His plan. I am grateful that He allowed this young woman to be a part of His plan to bring the good news of the gospel and to reach the community for Christ, one child and family at a time.

CHAPTER 8

FOLLOW ME AND SEE MY NEIGHBOR

"Come follow me," Jesus said,
"and I will make you fishers of men"
(Mark 1:17 NIV).

Vision became reality as I found myself leading and coordinating with other Bible Clubs that sprang up in the inner city of Akron. As much as I loved having this opportunity for so many children, I began to wonder what more could be done to come alongside those who so eagerly came to hear the Word. So many needs, so many hurting people. The children and teens came, but when moms started to show up and ask to go deeper, it became clear we needed to be ministering to the whole family. As much as I loved all the clubs, I began to think of the importance of going deep with a few instead of wide with many and what that might mean or look like. About that time, I read in Luke when Jesus stood up in the synagogue and recited the part of Isaiah that clearly outlined that He was the fulfillment of this very word.

> *The Spirit of the Lord is upon me because he has*
> *anointed me to preach good news to the poor. He*
> *has sent me to proclaim freedom for the prisoners*

> *and recovery of sight for the blind, to release the oppressed, to proclaim the year of the Lord's favor* (Luke 4:18–19 NIV).

It is amazing to me that He spoke with such confidence. Then in verse 22 it says how amazed the people were, but by verse 29 the people were so furious they were ready to throw him off a cliff. A little mind boggling, yes, but truly, when left to our own deceitful hearts, we turn too quickly on what we know to be truth.

However, it is the verses in between that really got my attention as I was pondering over the issue of going deep with a few. He began talking about Elijah and how there were many widows in the land with the same problem of famine, but in verse 26 we learn that Elijah was not sent to any of them but only to one widow in Zarephath in the region of Sidon. He also talks about the many lepers in Israel at the time of Elisha but only one leper (Naaman) was cleansed. There could be many reasons that God chose these particular people to make known His glory and purpose on earth.

But it was the story of the woman at Zarephath that drove home a point that would mold the philosophy of Urban Vision and continue even to this day. I was drawn to the story in the Old Testament where Elijah specifically asked a widow who had nothing to prepare him food to eat. We know the miraculous story where she obeyed and God caused an overflow of oil in her home even in the famine. Yes, this widow and her son were saved in the midst of many others who also struggled. Surely she was not the only mother in the whole community who had a problem.

It is after this encounter that the Word tells us that Elijah decided to stay on with this widow and her son for an extended visit. In the middle of her issues a lesson on God's character needed to sink in a little deeper in order for real change to happen. Soon after, the widow's son fell ill and died. At this tense point of the story Elijah whisks the dead son upstairs, prays over him three times and the Word says that the Lord heard Elijah's cry and the boy's life returned. Yes, it's an amazing story, but what the woman said next stuck to my soul with power. 1 Kings 17:24 says, **Then the woman said to Elijah, "Now I know that you are a man of God and that the Word of the LORD from your mouth is the truth"** (NIV).

Most people would think that with the first encounter with this man of God the widow would get it and know that God is in control and He has all power and authority in all situations. Yet interestingly enough, it took another miracle before the woman finally confessed her genuine belief and finally understood what Elijah was all about! The widow's decision to allow Elijah to stay with her and her son, witnessing God's power, and her willingness to go deep instead of wide, all made a lasting change and resulted in her confession that said, "I finally get it."

Wow. These very words burned into my heart the fact that in order for an impact to be made, for lasting change in a community, I must go the long haul and live and love amongst the people who I wanted to see reached with the powerful, radical truth of the gospel. There are no quick fixes to problems of poverty in our urban communities. God clearly burdened my heart that to make an impact for His kingdom, I needed to resolve to live up close and personal in a specific community. I needed to dwell with the people, experiencing life like everyone around me, and then humbly share the truth of the gospel that lived in me. Staying with others, like Elijah did, makes it possible for people to see the Truth.

I know God gives people different ways or methods to reach urban communities for Christ, but as I walked to my edge, God unfolded the principles of John Perkins for me. A great teacher and advocate for the poor, John Perkins clearly defined principles of Christian Community Development that could impact struggling communities. I wanted to live out his model of the three Rs: relocation, reconciliation, and redistribution.

- Relocation: go to the people...live among them.
- Reconciliation: be reconciled to God but also to one another across racial and economic divides.
- Redistribution: thinking creatively about using God's resources, through God's people, to meet needs with dignity.

I knew it was time to focus on one community of need and turn all my attention there and go deep for the long haul.

The thought of letting go of all the other clubs really rocked my world, but I was confident that this was how God was leading. So, once again, I found myself getting closer and closer to the edge; beyond my comfort zone. I knew what I wanted to do: reach people in the urban community, one child and family at a time. And I knew I wanted to do this by living, loving, and listening to the people in the community. Now the question remained: where should we put our focus?

It seemed only natural with the connections to Mrs. Holley and the legacy of my grandmother that the North Akron community would be the place I should begin. As I began to follow Jesus to the edge, He began to reveal things I never would have seen unless I had taken the first step to follow Him. The excitement of looking around in the community for a home to fix up and move into just made my blood pump. God began to unfold the vision and all the details that came along with it. I had no idea what lay ahead but I knew that whatever it was, I was headed in the right direction. A lot of prayer, a lot of tears, and most of all, a lot of soul searching surfaced on my journey with Him. Full steam ahead, I was a woman on a mission, but some needed detours were looming around the corner that I needed to take for my good and for His glory.

Miss Sandy, Mrs. Holley, Grandma White,
and me with some children from the community

CHAPTER 9

IT IS ALL IN WHO YOU KNOW

*All of you clothe yourselves with humility toward one
another because "God opposes the proud but gives grace
to the humble." Humble yourselves therefore under God's
mighty hand, that he may lift you up in due time*
(1 Peter 5:5–6 NIV).

Those were some pretty exciting days as I began to look around for houses in the Elizabeth Park community. I had good counsel from my friends the Gattis and we began to look at properties, many of which were in great need of attention and many that were in bad shape. I walked through a couple homes in the community, trying to envision myself living in these places that looked far from habitable. My spirits continued to stay up because I knew it would just be a matter of time before the right place would emerge.

During that time that I was praying for a door to open in the Elizabeth Park community, I began frequenting the community as often as I could, searching for a place where I could set up a Kids Club for the neighborhood children. With no place of my own, I reached out to a man who owned a couple of small stores in the community. He also owned quite a bit of property in the neighborhood, and was well-known by all the neighborhood residents. He had a building on Turner Street that he used on occasion to have certain gatherings for people to come and hang out. It would make a perfect place to set up a Kids Club for the time being so I tried to go and speak to this elderly African-American man. I'll never forget the many times I stopped to see if I could speak to him, and let me assure you I always looked very much out of place. I think he thought that if he ignored me I might just go away, but persistence is something that has always been engrained in my DNA so I was not easily deterred. The man at the front counter of the store I visited would politely tell me how busy the owner was and that he could not speak to me at that time. One time I came in and asked again to speak to the owner and I literally saw him peek through his office blinds. He finally came out to speak to me, probably out of curiosity about this persistent white girl.

I shared my heart for the children and asked him if we could have a Kids Club in his building around the corner. He did concede to my request and my first Kids Club in North Akron began. I passed out flyers, got my kickball ready, and sure enough, the kids started to come.

David, one of the little boys, brought me a wooden cross he had made from two old planks of wood held together with one little nail. He wrote roughly with marker on it: *For Me.*

More than twenty-five years later, I still have that cross sitting in my office, reminding me of how God touches the hearts of children with the truth of the gospel. David's life was not an easy one as far as I could see, but he came in that moment in time and heard a message of love.

I always made sure I got there early enough to get the building aired out and to throw away all the bottles and cans from the previous night. Yes, it took some time to get things together, but the place was central in the community, and I was thankful for a place to be and grateful to the man who let us use his building. God always makes a way!

With the Kids Club started, I knew I needed to connect not just with the children but also with the people who made up the community of Elizabeth Park. It was a small community consisting of four to six streets that connected in a square that sat adjacent to the Akron Metropolitan Housing Authority units where multiple single-parent families lived. Back in the day it was known as Brick City because all the project units were made of brick; it was one of the first of its kind when built in the mid-40s. Elizabeth Park was in the middle of Brick City, where the Shelter House (where my grandmother had taught) stood. There was an area with swing sets, tennis courts, and a neighborhood baseball field adjacent to the Little Cuyahoga, which flowed next to the park. We would often see many of the men washing their cars right out of the river. The area sounds nice but the swings were always thrown over the bar with half of them unusable, the courts' nets drooped, and the old metal spin wheel creaked with motion. But it still offered a place for children to come to escape being cooped up in their apartments.

I did meet one young African-American mom named Miss Beverly who lived in the apartments and became a great friend and would eventually come on staff with Urban Vision for a season. Miss Bev loved the Lord and she wanted to reach her community where she was raising her two sons to see change happen from the inside out. Her joyous spirit with her beautiful smile was a warm welcome to an outsider like me. God knit our hearts together from the very beginning. How I thank God for those who saw the vision and were willing to walk with me across the cultural divide. Miss Bev opened doors for me to meet other moms and children but it wasn't always that easy and I had many more lessons to learn.

Miss Beverly and two sons with other
moms and kids from community

Starting the Kids Club was not too difficult, but gaining acceptance in the community was going to take time. I read a book by Robert Linthicum, called *Empowering the Poor*, (Monrovia, CA: MARC Publishing, 1996), that talked about the different roles people hold in a community of need. One role is that of *gatekeeper* and if you want to gain the acceptance of the people as a whole, you must connect with the *gatekeeper* of the community. The one elderly man, who owned the building where we held the Kids Club, and lots of other land, had a lot of visibility in the community and had what little wealth there was to be exchanged there. However, I believed the title of *gatekeeper* went to an elderly African-American woman whose name was Mrs. Coleman. She loved to advocate for the community and many political officials knew and respected Mrs. Coleman's opinion when it came to the neighborhood. She had raised her family there and kept up her house in such a way that it stood out from the many dilapidated homes that paled in comparison to hers. She took great pride and looked for ways to beautify the neighborhood and inspire others around her to do the same.

I knew that in order to continue to be in her community, I must find a way to connect with her, at least to introduce myself somehow. So I began to visit her home, knocking on the door to meet and talk. What I thought would not be difficult proved to reveal how much of an outsider I really was. Every time I stopped to talk with her, no one ever answered the door. I would try different times of the day, hoping that one time I would catch her there. In the meantime, I had met an elderly woman around the corner who seemed very friendly and willing to talk about her heart for the community. She told me of the block club that Mrs. Coleman had and how she was a part of it. She did not seem to mind talking with a young white girl who just wanted to listen to her story.

I still hoped one day I would get to meet Mrs. Coleman and somehow gain her acceptance. So, one more time I found myself knocking on her door, not really expecting she would answer. As I turned to walk away, the door opened and another woman came out to speak to me. I asked if I could speak to Mrs. Coleman. She clearly made a point in a polite yet direct way of telling me that Mrs. Coleman could not speak to me any time soon. I could not understand and felt really rejected in that moment, but had to accept that that day would not be the day we would meet. Feeling a little sad, I drove around the corner to go speak to my new friend. I knocked and she came to the door and said, "I am sorry, honey, I cannot talk with you today." Seriously, was I stirring up too much trouble for people just to give me a chance? Or maybe they had been hurt one too many times by outsiders like me.

Hurting from my first conversation, I stood crushed to my soul, thinking, *Why won't anyone talk with me...what did I do to offend these ladies...?* I had no idea that this would be a defining moment for me. I drove back to my little apartment on the corner of Hazel and Adams, went upstairs, fell on my bed, and cried. My tears flowed not just because of rejection but because I felt misunderstood and confused. Did God not lead me to do this? Did

He not ask me to focus on this particular neighborhood? On that bed, God let me feel my helplessness and reminded me that I was not chosen to come save the day in a community of need amongst people that looked different from me. Pride camouflages itself at times in a self-righteous, do-good way of thinking. That thinking that says, "I have the answer to save the world around me." This attitude, although hidden from my thoughts, prevailed deep within and revealed itself through a detour I had not anticipated: rejection.

On that bed that night I had to settle a certain issue in my mind and attitude: that God was in control, not me. I also began to realize that this process of seeing a community change from the inside actually started with my heart; a heart that needed to be humbled. I will always be grateful that those women taught me a lesson I needed to learn; that just because I had a grand vision to see something change did not mean that there had not been people all along doing all they could to make a difference where they were, with the resources they had, without me and my grand vision. I had to learn to respect that and see from their eyes and perspectives that they never asked me to come to their community and save the day. They did not need a young white woman or anyone else to come fix anything. I needed to learn the importance of dignity, worth, and value in connecting with community. I knew God asked me to be obedient, and I had to do it His way, not mine. I had to build up trust so they would see that I was willing to stay and invest in the community, side by side as equals, not bulldozing my way in with a vision that did not approach others with genuine humility.

Over the years I finally got my opportunity to sit in the home of Mrs. Coleman. I had the opportunity to serve with her and learn from her when she hosted events like Keep Akron Beautiful, and I made sure I got involved with her agenda, not just my own. Over time I believe we became friends. She loved to share her gardening tips, and her house still continued to stand out among all of ours in the neighborhood. In time she started to come to Urban Vision events like our Thanksgiving Dinner; we have sweet memories of the elderly neighbors in our community coming to enjoy a great meal and fellowship together.

Every year we would also host an Urban Vision fundraiser and I will never forget the time Mrs. Coleman came. I never thought that she would come, but she came with a beautiful smile that said, *Yes, we are now partners in our love for this community.* Her community, which she had loved all her life and would now share with me and my family. How humbled I was to be connected with people like Mrs. Coleman, who had a deep love and care for her community for the long haul. The gate now open has taught me that the key to acceptance was time, trust, persistence, and hope, but most of all: humility.

Shortly after my surrender to God and confessing my own pride, God would show me His path for gaining the acceptance I needed in order to be a part of the community. **He leads me in paths of righteousness for His name's sake** (Psalm 23:3 KJV). None of us likes detours, but the lessons learned have been necessary to get closer to my edge. I still had not found a home and felt alone at times, but God was with me. He humbles us so He can lift us up. Directing my steps, He knew the lesson of humility that needed to be engrained into my soul in order to live and love among the people in the Elizabeth Park community, whom I knew little about then, but who have grown dearer to my heart with every passing moment.

CHAPTER 10

NO ONE QUITE LIKE YOU

As an apple tree among the trees of the forest, so is my
beloved among the young men
(Song of Solomon 2:3).

Life in many ways seemed to be moving on pace. The Lord gave me some good friends, people who prayed with me and for me and this Urban Vision. By now I had gone through yet another great disappointment in another broken engagement (my second). Despite my broken heart God put people in my path who balanced me out and helped define the vision so that it could have a solid foundation from the start. Our early morning prayer group grew and continued to be a source of solid friendships; brothers and sisters committed to the call of reaching a community one child and family at a time. We had intense talks and debates over the mission statement and our statement of faith. Talks that caused us to think biblically about how we could reach out to others in a way that allowed change to happen from the inside out.

I loved to dream and think big about reaching people for Christ. Coming up with budgets and sticking to them was not my cup of tea, but it was for a young man in our prayer group named Rodney. As the formal 501c3 for Urban Vision came together, our little prayer group all agreed that we should form a Board of Directors to help govern the ministry and that the board would include me, as the founder, and Rodney, as a young business-minded person. Ralph Gatti and Bob Sturkey, the two men who originally encouraged me to pursue this desire in my heart to live and love in the community, became our first Board members. Mr. Edgar Lee, who worked with my grandmother in the Shelter House all those years ago, joined as well. Also, Ms. Christy Grant, Randy Fairfax, Sandy Van Kirk and my dad, Mr. George White. It was a good team of people willing to govern and give advice to the direction of Urban Vision.

Rodney and I sometimes had issues because any time I wanted to do something that seemed as if it would push the budget, Rodney would be there telling me that it might not be the best solution. Let me just put it this way: our discussions at times got a little heated until yes, I must confess, I would pick up the closest thing to me (usually a pen) and send it flying through the air toward Rodney's head. Let me assure you, I no longer throw objects in his direction. Not that I am not tempted to at times, but God is merciful and He knows exactly what we need and even *who* we need to refine us to be His usable vessel. God decided to use Rodney to be my sharpening tool back then and to this day. This tall young man who sleepily came upstairs to pray with us at 5:00 am with his Akron University baseball cap on backwards (which I thought was kind of cute) knew how to pack a punch when it came to numbers and facts. Rodney was an accounting student at the University of Akron and also shot on the rifle team. He grew up in Michigan, literally between apple orchards, moved to Columbus in high school, and had been invited to come to Akron to shoot on their team and was offered an opportunity to try out for the Olympics.

It was after one of our *interesting* Board meetings (at which I was not very happy with Rodney's input) that the Board president told us we needed to do something about our relationship or this would never work. Reluctantly, we went out after the meeting to discuss our issues and yes, less than a year later, we were married. I never thought that God would pick someone so different from me, but He brought Rodney into my life as my best friend, partner in ministry, and the love of my life. Yes, this tall prince charming swept me off my feet, budgets and all, to start something beautiful together as one. Rodney's faithful heart and His genuine love for God won my heart with one comment when he said, "Jodi, any man would be blessed to have someone like you by his side." Yep, that did it for me! He saw and expressed to me how valuable he thought I was. How humbling, how crazy, to think someone could love me so much. Yes, once again, God so exceeded my heart's desire.

Rodney and I were engaged on December 24, 1993. New ministry, new relationship, new everything seemed to be the order of the day. With both of us committed to finding a home in Elizabeth Park, we continued to ask the Lord what the next step should be.

Rodney and I were married on May 7, 1994, at 5:15 pm in the Memorial Chapel at The Chapel in Akron. What a celebration it was. Naturally, I had a lot of bridesmaids because I wanted everyone to be involved, and two receptions so I would not leave out the children and teens I had grown to love and care for so much. My only regret is that I wish I had started the party a little earlier than 5:15 pm. (Yes, I know it was a weird time to start but that's what I thought I wanted; you live and learn.)

God's plan continued to unfold as He continued to lead me closer to the edge. He blessed us with our three boys, and so the journey continues. Loving God, loving others, and now raising a family on the edge. I knew I would need all of Jesus to stay focused on Him!

CHAPTER 11

UNLESS THE LORD BUILDS THE HOUSE

*Unless the L*ᴏʀᴅ *builds the house,*
those who build it labor in vain
(Psalm 127:1).

There is something about reading God's Word that makes us think, but there is also something about experiencing God's Word that takes it to a whole other level for me. You see, I have always learned by doing, by living, and yes, I must admit, oftentimes I choose the hard path or, let's just be real, my path. God has called us to be doers of His Word, not hearers only, and I think I am starting to understand why.

It's when I am immersed in a situation that requires me to act that I finally get the message of what God says, instead of just letting it be a passing thought in my brain. I especially need this reminder because I have a little problem, okay—it has been a big problem—remembering who really is in control: God or me. As mentioned earlier, I was so thankful that my husband decided to take up the challenge of choosing me, his lovely control-freak bride. However, under my exterior as a God-fearing woman there was a huge power struggle about who was going to be in charge. No, I am not talking about Rodney or me; that is another discussion for another time, but rather, God or me. I wish I could tell you that this power struggle is over, but it is something I have had to learn to surrender on a daily basis, sometimes even moment by moment.

Prior to getting engaged to Rodney, I had been on the search for the right house to live in. I knew I was called to live out my faith in community amongst people who lived in the neighborhood. I had good reason to believe, based on my past, that God had led me to be a part of the Elizabeth Park community. I looked for a while, but in the end it was not what I found but what actually found me that made the difference. Man plans, but God directs his steps (Proverbs 16:9). It is so true!

I got a phone call from Chris Grant, a dear African-American mentor, who said that she had some interesting news for me. Looking back, I could not have done this without her. She was the kind of woman who just showed up when I needed her most. It was so interesting that she had this radar from the Holy Spirit that went off, saying, *White sister needs some kind of assistance before she gives up. Go see Jodi now!*

Jodi and Miss Chris Grant,
mentor and friend for over 25 years

I met Miss Chris at a Bible study at her work where I had gone to share about Urban Vision as the group met over their lunch break. After the study she came up to me and said, "So you're trying to move into my neighborhood. Okay, I am going to swing by your apartment tonight and take you around." Now keep in mind I had never met Miss Chris before, but God was about building His house His way instead of me running around looking to do it my way. Things would be a lot easier if I would just cooperate a lot sooner. Learning to trust God with my life has been more of a challenge than one would think. I am so thankful God does not give up on us...Amen!

Anyway, sure enough Miss Chris came by my place, picked me up, and drove me through Elizabeth Park. She showed me the apartments where she raised her only son and then pulled around the corner down a dead-end street. She pulled up to a house and said, "We're here."

"Where?" I asked.

She replied, "This is my mom's house; I grew up here. Come inside and meet Mrs. Jettie."

All this time and all the tears shed from trying to find ways to connect to the little urban neighborhood beyond the children, and then it just started in the living room of Mrs. Jettie Neal. Not only did I meet her, but Miss Chris also took me around the corner to meet some other elderly neighbors like Mrs. Verna Lomax who had lived and raised their families for years in this community. Jodi, the young white girl on the outside, now had an invitation from a dear sister of color to be embraced on the inside.

After meeting her mom and others in the community on that first ride with Miss Chris, I turned and said, "Chris you are an angel sent from heaven."

She said, "Nope. I was sent from North Street."

I responded, "To me it is all the same!"

I never thought I could be accepted and embraced the way these ladies did. Little did I know at that moment what kind of impact this introduction would have in shaping the heartbeat of Urban Vision. I would soon be a part of a group called the North Akron Prayer Band, a group of elderly African-American ladies mostly from the community, whose mission was to pray, read God's Word, and sing hymns to those shut in or in nursing homes. They took me to places I never would have gone, with a Bible in one hand and a hymnal in the other. What an impact it made on the lives they touched, and mine was one of them.

North Akron Prayer Band Ladies
enjoying a program at 130 Belmont Street
Mrs. Myricks, Mrs. Hammonds, Mrs. Neal, Mrs. Lomax

So humble, so accepting, so full of wisdom—I soaked it all in like a dry, thirsty sponge. I wanted so badly to understand and love across cultures and these women showed me the way. This lesson of learning from those who have gone before was and is huge in my life. So often we can discount the older generation thinking they are tired, lacking vigor or creativity—not these ladies. Although in their 80s they were still ready to do God's work! I love Psalm 92:13–15, which says, ***They are planted in the*** *house of the LORD; They flourish in the courts of our God. They still bear fruit in old age; They are ever full of sap and green, to declare that the Lord is upright; He is my rock, and there is no unrighteousness in Him.*

I will never forget those introductions to people who then became my lifelong friends. Most of them are now in the presence of the Lord, but my friend Miss Chris still shows up at my house honking her horn and saying, "Hey girl, what's going on with you these days?" What a blessing she was and is in my life. You see, if I had stayed in my comfort zone I would have missed so much that God wanted me to see of Himself in the lives of those whom I met. I am so thankful that God is teaching me to lean hard into Him and to stop trying to do things myself. I can do nothing apart from God. It is Christ in me, the hope of glory.

Miss Chris called weeks later and told me that her uncle was selling his home across from Mrs. Neal and asked if we would like to take a look. I sure wanted to see what God had in mind. Rodney and I went to look at the house to see what kind of shape it was in. Rodney got there before me and Chris' uncle did not know him and told him a little higher price, but when I showed up he lowered the price for me. It was just after Rodney had proposed to me so not only was God supplying a house, He also gave me a roommate!

Well, needless to say, with the help of generous friends we were able to purchase the home for $8500 and let me tell you, it was a real fixer upper! We were a young couple without much income; I was the only staff at Urban Vision at the time, and Rodney was working as a sales person at Kenmore Tailors. Once again, God would have to be the one to help us build this house— literally and spiritually. This was a real test for us; there were so many things to address in the house. Where in the world do we begin with holes in the floors, foundation issues, etc, etc…? Even so, we were happy that God led us to our little house on Belmont Street and we still live there to this day. The view is starting to look a little sweeter but the perseverance needed to do the work seems a lot harder. But oh the joy we have had seeing the hand of God move along the journey.

Picture of 130 Belmont Street before renovations

The inside view of our new home…it needed some love!

Both Rodney and I jumped in with all we had, trying our best to make things work. We even started our daily tutoring program in the middle of all the work being done. The kids sat on carpet rolls and used dry wall as tables. It was quite the adventure. However, we were starting to become weary because one problem led to another, which led to another, and we ran out of time in the house we were living in just up the hill on Dayton Street. It was actually starting to get quite discouraging with limited resources and all we wanted was to live in the community. Points of desperations are good stops to make, I have found over the years. It is at those times I finally come to the end of myself and my trying and I begin to cry out to God in my trusting. It was definitely one of those times. It seemed as if we ran out of everything except Jesus! Good thing He is all that we need, and we would soon see how He would move and literally be the one to build our house.

John Perkins, a strong, African-American activist and preacher of the Word of God, whom I've spoken of in previous chapters, was invited to come to Akron in the fall of 1994. A group of Christians who had a heart for the city began to rally around him, and the CCDA (Christian Community Development Association) movement was happening all over the United States and the world. (Check out their website: www.ccda.org) Having already been introduced to Dr. Perkins' philosophy and his 3 Rs of Reconciliation, Relocation, and Redistribution, both Rodney and I were very excited about the invitation we received to come on a Saturday morning to the John S. Knight Center in downtown Akron.

To be in a room filled with kingdom people who really had a heart to do something about poverty and the social injustice of the lives of people they embraced every day, was a humbling experience. That day Dr. Perkins called for people to take up this idea of living and being a part of the communities of need. He called for an incarnational type of ministry in which people would dwell amongst the people of need and be the hands and feet of Jesus. My soul was in tune with everything he said, but my heart was crying out to God, *This is what we are trying to do, but it doesn't seem like we're making as much progress as we'd like to on our house, and we're running out of resources. What are we to do?*

At the close of the session Dr. Perkins was going to dismiss us all into groups to pray. At that moment my heart beat so fast with the thought that I needed to ask everyone in this room to pray for us. Now let's just clarify a couple things: I was one of the youngest in the room (well, Rodney is two years younger), and I was definitely one of the few women in the room. But I knew it was now or never.

I stood up with a shaky boldness and said to Dr. Perkins, "We are a young couple who wants to do this but we are at the end of what we can do." A friend and mentor in urban ministry who knew us stood up and validated who we were and what we were trying to do. God always speaks up for those who speak for Him. Was I ever thankful for Mr. Duane Crabbs in that moment because with every eye on me, looking at me and wondering where in the world we came from, a positive testimony was indeed appreciated.

Dr. Perkins said, "You heard the young lady, let's pray for them."

I did not know how God would answer but He began to set things in motion that are still being played out even to this day. In our small group, Knute Larson, who was at that time the Pastor of The Chapel in Akron, joined us and after prayer he turned to Rodney and me and asked what he and his church could do to get behind our move into the Elizabeth Park community. All of a sudden it was as if a light switch had turned on. Pastor Larson himself came to visit our little needy house on Belmont Street.

Before long, there were backhoes and trucks and lots and lots of volunteers on Belmont Street. I just could not believe my eyes! God was building our house. Under the direction of a man named Rick Runge and so many others we now had the resources to see such a big job handled through such an amazing God whom we serve! All He was waiting for was for us to get out of the way! As we began the many needed renovations, the skilled workers informed us that our foundation was bad, so bad that there was one moment when they thought the whole thing would cave in. Thankfully it did not, but what a real lesson of building our foundation on the solid rock; building on something firm that can withstand much over the years. You see, Rodney and I would never have been able to fix up the house the way it needed to be fixed and we would never have known of the foundation problems. But God knew, and He led us on His path of righteousness for His name's sake right up close to the edge so we could know that He did this amazing renovation—not only on our house but in my heart.

These lessons burned in my heart and still do, which keeps me longing to go to the edges God has called me to. God has this in mind for all His children no matter what He has asked us to do. The lesson that it is not me but God who is doing this work, is so important. You see, at the end of my journey I don't just want some fruit, but I desire to bear much fruit in my life.

How about you? Are you ready to turn over the hammer to God and let Him build your house? He is the master architect; He will give all of Himself to those willing to turn the control over to Him. So, what are you waiting for? Take a step to the edge. You won't regret it!

CHAPTER 12

THE RHYTHM OF LIFE

For everything there is a season,
and a time for every matter under heaven
(Ecclesiastes 3:1).

There is something about rhythm that I really love and long for in my life. I like to have routine and some sort of discipline to keep me balanced. Well, at least it helps me feel that way. Things that feel familiar, people I know and love to be near and close to so I can know all is well in my little corner of the world. I have to admit that walking to the edge has repeatedly disturbed my rhythm, and each time it does I have to find a way to embrace a new comfort zone—one that's closer to the edge than ever before.

Rodney and I moved into 130 Belmont Street in March of 1995—a little earlier than anticipated. Renovations were taking place and literally took apart the house all the way to the lath. (I didn't even know what lath was—you could literally see through the whole house from one end to the other.) I will never forget some of the neighborhood children coming by and saying, "Wow, Miss Jodi, who blew up your house?" Fair question!

Because we didn't want to stick out from the other homes in the community, we did all we could to maintain the structure of the house. The simple fact that we were the only white couple in the community made us stick out anyway, but God was going to teach us beautiful lessons about Himself and those with whom we longed to reconcile.

We ended up moving in before everything was finished. It turned out that leaving a house vacant with copper pipes and all that was being fixed in the middle of the city was not a good plan. We came to work on the house as usual one day only to find that our little house had been broken into. Fortunately, I think it must have been just curious kids or teens who broke in because nothing was taken and just an old concrete wall in the basement had been smashed. This was a signal that we needed to move in now. But there was a small problem—we had no toilets and the carpeting had not been completed either. So, with a camper toilet I borrowed from my grandma and an air mattress, we moved in, and Belmont Street has been home sweet home ever since. (No worries, we have plumbing now!)

It didn't take too long to get everything mostly together and we then began to seek out what life would be like for us now. I was so thankful for our neighbors and the ladies I already knew from the prayer band. Many times I would go visit Mrs. Neal or Mrs. Lomax and just hear all the stories from the past about family life and the community. Interestingly, one of the families in the neighborhood knew my grandmother quite well from the Shelter House all those years ago. There were two sisters who had attended Sunday school at the Shelter House with my grandmother, and over time on Belmont Street, I would get to know these two sisters fairly well along with their children and even a grandson who still attends Urban Vision on occasion.

I held Bible Clubs and started tutoring children, and we did our Summer Family Night Camp. We decided to host our camp at night because so many of the children were involved in all-day camps throughout the city so evening was the best time to reach the community. We would have over 100 children in our backyard under a big, rented circus tent. (In fact, we rented it so much for so many years that the company decided to give it to us!)

Night Camp 94 at 130 Belmont Street

We had arts and crafts, sit-down dinners, and of course lots of fun games. The kids participated in worship and the lessons all revolved around themes like One Way Camp, Journey with Jesus, and Jesus is the Light. And when our plumbing could not handle so many at our house, we had to rent porta potties! The whole week ended in a special reward trip for those who came most of the week. We went to the zoo, Geauga Lake Amusement Park, rollerskating, or Sea World. Some of these kids had never had an opportunity to do these special things or to go to places like this before.

Let me tell you it was an act of God that we were able to take over 100 children to an amusement park, get them there, watch them, feed them, and make sure they got home safely. Anyone who works with children knows this was nothing short of a miracle, and I thank God for His grace to us over the years at Urban Vision. Even years later I have encountered former UV participants who have told me how much being a part of Urban Vision impacted their lives back then. One young man said, "Mrs.

Jodi, now that I am grown I look back and wonder how in the world you got all of us kids to the zoo or to the amusement park and back safe and sound." It was testimony time and I could say it was all Jesus! Amen and amen!

Our little house on Belmont Street with all its activities caused quite the stir in our little community. Thankfully we had patient neighbors who loved us and often got involved and would help us out at times. Doing something out of the norm causes people to look and see and maybe even challenges them to think about their own lives and purpose. I once went for a week to a Christian camp called Camp Carl, serving as a counselor so I could be there for some of the children from the Bible Clubs. While I was gone, Rodney got a knock on the door and on the step stood a cute and feisty little African-American girl who started the conversation by first asking if his girlfriend was home. After Rodney took a quick moment to clarify that I was not his girlfriend but his wife, the conversation became more and more interesting as it progressed. She chatted away on the step for a while until she made the pronouncement that she did not like white people. She didn't pause after this announcement, but kept on talking as if she had not a care in the world. Now, she didn't seem to mind talking to Rodney who is very tall and white. So Rodney stopped her monologue and said, "Now, wait a minute...you do know we are white, right?"

"Yeah," she said, "I know, but you guys don't count."

We have reflected on this for many reasons, and both Rodney and I took it as an encouragement that at least we knew for sure we were welcomed in the neighborhood by this little girl!

This was our new normal. Bible Clubs, tutoring, having children over to bake cookies, play kickball, or help me plant flowers at our house. I was living my dream and I thought I was living close enough to the edge. However, even in ministry, what might seem abnormal to others can become normal and comfortable in day-to-day life. This is where I have really had to ask God to keep me coming closer to His edge and not just be content to stay where I am. I have learned that we must never stop moving closer to Jesus, closer to His will, and must always watch out for complacency. I am not trying to say that God wants us to always be in a state of discomfort but then again, when I am uncomfortable my dependence on Him does tend to deepen.

There were days in the ebb and flow of life that were good and happy and carefree and I thank Him for those times, but there are times when our edges lead us down through the valley of the shadow of death and yet we must still praise Him. Why? Because in the rhythm of my life I want Jesus to write His new song in my heart. He is the musician; I am His instrument to bring Him the most glory in all my days. Boring days, happy and joy-filled days, confusing days, even grieving days, all belong to Him. I know when I surrender to Jesus, the sweetest tune comes from my heart and before you know it I am singing along even outside my comfort zone, up closer to the edge!

> *O sing to the LORD a new song, For He has done marvelous things; His right hand and His holy arm have gotten Him the victory* (Psalm 98:1 KJV).

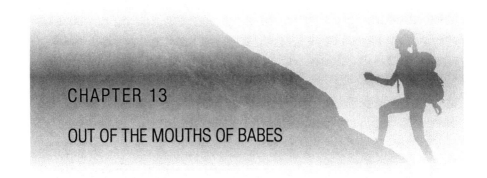

CHAPTER 13

OUT OF THE MOUTHS OF BABES

Out of the mouth of babies and infants,
you have established strength because of your foes,
to still the enemy and the avenger
(Psalm 8:2).

Kids just say the most profound things sometimes. If we really listen, God will use little children to get a point across loud and clear. I will never forget what happened after some long, weary weeks of ministry, wondering at times if what we did really mattered. Yes, I know it mattered but there were days when we needed to be reminded. I went into a classroom of first graders whom I helped tutor in our local urban elementary school and one of the little girls in the class who attended our UV Kids Club greeted me with a big smile. When she had a moment to speak to me alone, she said, "Mrs. Jodi, you really work your behind off at Kids Club, don't you?" God used this little girl to say that it mattered to her, and she knew how much care I had for all the kids. After regaining my composure, I straight up told her, "You're absolutely right. I do work my behind off, but I love you kids and you're worth it!"

I think that was the whole point Jesus was trying to make by putting a small child amongst the disciples. If anyone is going to enter the kingdom of heaven, we must have the faith of a child, see as a child sees. No holding back, simply just trust. Since I have had the awesome privilege of coming alongside lots of little ones I have started to tune into what a child has to say and I have been all the more blessed because of it.

Early days of Duck, Duck, Goose at 130 Belmont Street

Rodney and I were super blessed to start our family and we now have three sons, Micah, Joseph, and Nathanael. This 24/7 caring for children was a whole new deal for us in the middle of the ministry, but I had always hoped to be a mom one day. Because I had the blessing of having a great mom and dad, I hoped I could parent well. I would pray over our boys that they would grow to be Kingdom Shakers who carried out God's plan for each of their lives. Prayer has been so important in my life and even more so since God entrusted these children into our care. I remember the first night home from the hospital when it took both Rodney and me to change a diaper. Clipping Micah's little nails was even worse. Poor Rodney clipped one a little close and it bled just a little and we were both a wreck. We hoped we had not traumatized our son for life, but boy what a change it brought to us. This tiny little baby placed in our arms sank deep into our hearts forever. Walking on the edge seemed a little more complicated now, having this kind of responsibility in our care. However, I knew if God called me to the edge, then He had called my family too. You might wonder how I knew that. Well, if God called us to go and then entrusted us with children, then I believed it was His family plan. If we go, we go together.

Rodney and Jodi with Micah, Joseph, and Nathanael

The boys have been a part of Urban Vision from day one. I don't regret that our kids have been raised in the city or in ministry because I know God has used it all to shape who they are and how they perceive the world around them. My boys know diversity in ways I never did growing up. They know how to go in and out of the people with a comfort level that is real and helps them to connect to the hearts of people of different cultures and different economic backgrounds. My kids are all the richer for it, so I am thankful for the family of God—so large, so beautiful, and so different.

Kids having fun at the zoo

Just because I was thankful didn't mean I wasn't concerned about what at times played out before them. Poverty was evident. Boarded up homes, with many needing a great deal of care. We woke in the middle of the night to find our neighbor's house in flames due to an old electric wiring problem. At times, I had to wait in my mini-van with the kids for the cars in front me to do their drug deals. I had to be more watchful when a child whom I knew had encountered all kinds of abuse wanted to play with my children. I can even remember many times when the police were on our little dead end street dealing with various issues, yet I'm so grateful that somehow God put a shield around the boys.

Most people who lived close to any of us might have wanted to borrow a cup of sugar or some coffee, but instead of being asked for such routine items, we literally have been asked to hold someone's kitchen knives so they would not be tempted to hurt someone in their house. We did, but seriously who gets those kinds of requests? Yet these are things we have had to process and work through and trust God for even when our fears seemed to ever increase. Wanting to go to the edge yourself is one thing but it's different to walk so close to the edge with your children. I didn't want to be naïve, and my faith walk didn't mean that our family was invincible either. I had to settle my fears once and for all and say, *if God is for me who can be against me?* I know that doesn't mean we don't encounter hardship or pain; it means I believe in a Sovereign God who loves me and loves my sons even more. That lesson of release is one I am still learning and my sons are almost grown. Parenting is rough no matter where you are, where you live, married or single—it is just rough. Yet God is bigger than all of it, and I choose His plan. I cry, I struggle, and I even argue with God at times, but in the end when I surrender, a peace comes—it just does.

I have to admit raising my kids in the midst of ministry got a little crazy at times. Yet God was helping me to understand that there will be seasons in life when sometimes you can do a little more and sometimes you have to do a little less. I will touch on this a little later but choices on what we do and how we spend our lives with children was going to be very impactful on our tender children's souls.

There are so many stories I could share because what mom doesn't want to sit and talk about her kids all day? Hopefully what I share doesn't bore you. My prayer is that it will encourage you that God uses all things to work His plan out in our lives and that of our families. Kids Club was just a part of my sons' lives. They came right along with all the kids in the neighborhood and sat with them and participated in everything everyone else did. Rodney and I worked hard to treat our children just like everyone else during the program. We didn't favor them over the others, but my motto was *love them all,* so they felt that love too.

I will never forget one particular Kids Club. There were about forty kids in the room, sitting on metal chairs listening to me teach the Bible lesson for the day. I have always believed in incorporating the gospel in every lesson and giving kids an opportunity to respond to it when they are ready. Honestly, I don't remember the lesson that day but what I do remember is my six-year-old son frantically waving his hand in the back of the room. I tried to ignore him, thinking he would get tired, but the waving continued. I signaled to Rodney with my eyes to go and see what was so urgent for our son. Keeping the attention of forty inner city kids was not always easy so I hoped Rodney would be able to solve Micah's problem. Rodney talked to Micah, but then Micah's hand went right on waving and Rodney just stared at me and shrugged his shoulders. Since Dad hadn't settled Micah's urgency, I called on Micah and asked him what he needed. He said, "Mom, I need to talk to you now. It is very important!"

Micah was determined to talk with me, so I reluctantly stopped and said to the class, "All right, kids, Micah needs to tell me something real quick."

So I paused to hear Micah whisper in my ear, "I have to tell these kids about Jesus! I need to invite them to come!"

Okay, what do I do now? Here my sweet little six-year-old son wanted to share Jesus with all of the kids. I had no idea how they would respond to this little white kid giving them an invitation to Jesus. For all I knew they would laugh and maybe kill his spirit. Yet Micah was so insistent that it was one of those times I needed to let him go and speak. With no fear, little Micah shared the gospel message of Jesus on the cross, urging the children—some twice his age—to give their lives to Him. You could have heard a pin drop in the room. No one laughed and all eyes were tuned into Micah's heart. The Spirit of God used Micah that day and continues to do so even now. Many hands went up in the room responding to the simple truth that Jesus loves me, He died, and rose again, and He can save me. And a little child led them is so true. What treasures children are! So ready to soak in the truth of God's Word. Speak the truth to your kids. Tell them about Jesus. Let them respond to what they know, because believe me, they can get it and begin to give it away in ways you can't even begin to imagine!

Interestingly enough, no matter how close to the edge I am, God still calls me to surrender completely to Him. You would think I have learned the lesson well, but for me and probably for most people, surrender needs to take place daily. On one particular morning God was calling me to surrender my future plans to Him once again. Even though I wanted to, the inner battle raged on. I had the blessing of talking that day to a pastor and he brought the Word out again: surrender all to Him. Later that same day, I met with my sweet little friend, one of the children in our Set On Success after school program at UV. We were playing Connect Four and I was encouraging her in an area where she needed to grow. I was deep in thought and she was focused on wanting to win the game. Finally, she burst out, "Mrs. Jodi, you just need to surrender!" I know she was talking about the game, but God used this little girl to make a point in my heart once again. So all adults out there, listen up! God might be using someone small in your life to get a big point across. Out of the mouths of babes!

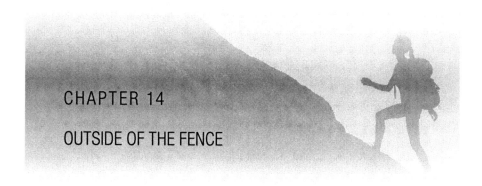

CHAPTER 14

OUTSIDE OF THE FENCE

Search me, O God, and know my heart! Try me and know my thoughts! And see if there be any grievous way in me, and lead me in the way everlasting!
(Psalm 139:23–24).

When Rodney and I moved to Belmont Street we had quite a bit of yard space for a city lot. Our property sits on a dead-end street that goes right up against the woods right below the All-America or what local people call the Y Bridge. Unfortunately, that bridge got to be known as Jumper's Bridge because many would go there to end their lives and plummet to the valley below. I remember early one morning when I was at home trying to have some quiet time before the hustle and bustle of the day began. I believe it was a Sunday and I heard someone yelling off the bridge, "Does anyone hear me? Does anyone care?"

I was in my house but there is an echo off the bridge that you can hear pretty distinctly if someone is yelling loud enough. It was quite disturbing so I got Rodney up and asked him to go check it out. A little reluctant, Rodney went out. He found the man before he was able to do something drastic—like jump and end his life.

The man was intoxicated from the night before and said, "Wow, I didn't think anyone would hear me and come."

I don't think he was going to do anything life threatening but Rodney gave him a ride home, and it probably made his day that he actually got someone's attention. Who knows when that man will yell off the bridge again? (Okay, probably when he needs a ride from us!) Seriously though, hopelessness brings on thoughts that at times make one feel as if there is no way out, no escape from the bondage of life. It is very true when God says, **Where there is no vision the people perish** (Proverbs 29:18 KJV). We need hope, we need purpose, we need to follow God's plan to the edges of our lives.

Thankfully, our yard was partly fenced when we got it, and we were able to finish fencing it in. Mostly it served to keep all the stray dogs out (back then they literally ran in packs through our neighborhood) and our children in. Fences can be good to give some sense of safety but fences can also divide. We felt okay about our fence and thought it would be a good boundary for all the Matthews boys to know and obey. I tried to engrain into their minds that they could play anywhere inside the yard but there was no going outside the fence. Period.

There was one day when I was traveling home from kindergarten with my middle son who was five at the time. As we drove through the city, my son spoke up from his car seat directly behind me and very adamantly said, "Mommy, I see someone who is poor." Wanting to understand my five-year-old's definition of poor, I began a conversation with him that was going to change my life.

I asked him a series of questions like, "Why do you think the man is poor?" "Is it because of where we are?" "Or maybe the clothes he is wearing?"

Every time, Joseph responded by saying, "No, that isn't why."

After I had exhausted the reasons for which I thought a five-year-old would label someone as poor, and really probably any adult would also, I finally just asked, "So, Joseph, why do you think this person is poor?"

I watched in the rearview mirror as he looked up and said very clearly and compassionately, "Mommy, because his eyes were sad."

Yes, my five-year-old little Joseph really was taking me to school that day. His insight into the soul of a person, even while he was so young, is a true gift God has given to him and he continues to be an insightful and compassionate young man to this day.

If that was not enough to get my brain around, I thought this would be a good time to interject some foundational truths of loving God and loving others. I told him that God wanted us to love all people and to reach out to people who are sad and need to know Jesus and His love and the life He can bring. I could really see that he was taking in all that I was sharing with him, so on I continued, telling him that we need to share the good news with everyone; we need to share the hope we have. Joseph reflected on all my comments and then began to have a very thoughtful, concerned look on his face, finally saying to me, "Mommy, I would do this with people…if you would just let me out of the fence."

I about wrecked the car when little Joseph said those words to me! In his little mind, all he needed was permission to get out of the fence so he could share this wonderful news with everyone around us!

I can't tell you how many countless times I have not only reflected on, but also shared this story with people everywhere. There is a powerful truth in the recognition that in order to get to the places God is calling us, we need to be willing to step outside of the fences we have built. We need to ask the Holy Spirit to show us the fences, or maybe I could even say "offenses," that keep us from the very will of God. In my life, I have discovered that I have put up fences of fear, fences of insecurity, fences of control and manipulation, fences of prejudice, and fences of pride. My fences don't look so good written out like that but I need to speak them out, confess them, and ask the Holy Spirit to do His construction work in my life. Sometimes, in order to build, we must be willing to tear down. My fences needed to go. I wish I could say that all is well and I am done with fences, but wouldn't life on the edge be a lot easier with a fence? Not so, in God's plan.

Stop right now and ask God to search your heart for the fences you have put there. Sometimes our fences come up because someone has hurt us, disappointed us, or maybe even betrayed us. Fences are barriers that need to be dealt with. God is a gracious and merciful God, and, **Because of the LORD's great love we are not consumed** (Lamentations 3:22 NIV). God, in His infinite love, can tear down and then build up again—in all of us.

This same son, my middle son Joseph, has endured a lot, growing up in ministry and with a mom who at times was a little overboard. Joseph has always been my sensitive soul. Because of all this, he feels so much more deeply than most would. It's a blessing and also the cross he has had to bear. He has given me permission to share his story, and you will also read his testimony entitled, "Facing Our Fences" at the end of this chapter. Although he has often suffered silently with anxiety and depression, I know God is shaping him to be a mighty man who will be used for His glory!

Years later we were driving in the car together heading toward a time of group counseling for Joseph along with other teens in a program designed to deal with issues that so many young people face today. This was not a Christian program so there were people with all kinds of faith backgrounds and those who had no faith at all. As we drove there, Joseph told me what he had done at a previous appointment, "I hope you don't mind but I took a Bible off the shelf and gave it to a guy who is really struggling with his faith." Joseph told me that this young man had tried everything, even Jesus. Joseph, even in the midst of his own struggles, was able to share with this young man that it is not about trying but trusting. It was not our plan to have to deal with these issues and walk down some dark paths, not knowing what lay ahead. Yet Joseph, even in the darkness, turned his flashlight on and was able to minister to someone he never would have met unless he walked that path as well.

God had used him in this place of darkness to be a great light that this young man could see fleshed out before his very eyes. He could see a real example of faith is not a perfect one but a trusting one. It is not about trying Jesus, but trusting Jesus on our good days and even on our bad days when He just holds on to us. Life is like that, our faith is like that, not just in a nice neat package where the story always ends up with a happy ending. Our faith is living and breathing in the ebb and flow of life's victories as well as in the struggles, the doubts, and fears. In that moment in the car I turned to my son and said, "Joseph, surely you are outside of your fence and I am so proud of you. I know this has been a long road to walk, but I do believe God has something amazing in mind as you step to the edge of His will."

So, let's ask God to start renovating our lives and let's start with our fences.

Facing Our Fences
By Joseph Matthews

I, for one, can tell you of how hard it is to not only tear down the fences that trap us in our comfort zone, but also of the difficulties you will face once you do so. My name is Joseph Matthews, and most of you know me by the many stories about me my mother so often speaks of. It is true that I have faced overwhelming obstacles, or fences (if you will), throughout my life's journey of walking with Christ outside my fences, and of the times I have chosen to walk without Him. And, perhaps, I will write my own book someday to encourage those who struggle with fences that may be like my own, in even more detail than what little of this excerpt of mine will even make the author's cut (love you mom).

I struggle with my everyday anxieties, the lingering effects that my Panic Disorder has on my life, the overwhelming depression from the pains in life I have suffered, the insecurities that follow, and the physical health problems that are linked to my conditions, daily. These obstacles have not only presented as mere fences in my life, but more like giant walls of hopelessness. I can tell you from experience these walls are insurmountable when we are facing them alone. We cannot fully overcome our walls until we have first entrusted them to Jesus. There is a reason He has earned the name "Savior," yet so often we forget that Jesus defeated the greatest walls of all. His life's purpose was to overcome these walls we face on the cross, so that we may all have life and so that we can have the strength to face all our hardships. Knowing that I have a personal relationship with a God who knows what suffering is, on a very personal level, is what helps me know that God understands me and my suffering.

When you give your life to Christ, this doesn't mean you won't face hardships or suffering. In fact, God makes no such promise at all. He tells us in His Word (see John 16:33) that we will endure hardships in this world, because we live in a disease-ridden, sinful world where troubles in this life are a guarantee. Yet, it is God's command to be joyful amid our sufferings (Romans 5:3-5). I know some of you are probably asking, "But, how can God expect us to be happy while we are experiencing so much pain?" That, too, is a question I have often asked myself. This is a question that may not have an answer we like, but I think we still need to hear. God can use your hardships and sufferings in your life to help others who are enduring similar experiences. This, however, cannot be done until you have reached a point where you trust in God and His promises to work for our good in all things, fully. We must be willing to give to God control over our lives. Once you are able to give God back the steering wheel, He can do great and amazing things in your life.

I want to remind you that giving God your complete trust and control over your life is no easy feat, but be encouraged because it isn't something that has to happen overnight (Philippians 4:13). In fact, it's a lifelong process and journey to master this. Even as I am writing this, I have been so low sometimes I feel like giving up completely. But I pray that you and I can continue to trust in God, even in the hard times. Please remember me in your prayers; they are greatly appreciated. I probably wouldn't be where I am today, even as I'm writing this now, without them. God bless and be with you always!

Joseph Matthews

CHAPTER 15

THE PITFALL OF PRIDE

You make known to me the path of life;
in your presence there is fullness of joy; at your right
hand there are pleasures forevermore
(Psalm 16:11).

I love routine. I love the feeling of knowing what I am doing and where I am going. But so often the path that leads me to the edge leaves me feeling out of control and very uncomfortable. Yes, I am learning to lean on Jesus as I have journeyed these many years through unknown paths of life and ministry. I have learned to enjoy the company of my Savior, realizing my joy is only found in Him…but this has not always been the case.

The lesson of stepping beyond my fences has always been a challenge, but one of the most dangerous pitfalls on the pathway before me has been when I have taken my focus off Jesus and placed it more on my circumstances. Somehow I thought it was more important to be focused on what I was doing instead of just being with my Savior. If I can just be straight up blunt: it just comes down to PRIDE; thinking my way is better, more important, and—dare I say—even *necessary* to get where I am going.

It reminds me of the dear disciple Peter with all his zealousness. Sometimes in the Bible I am not sure if this was a gift or a curse. Don't get me wrong, I admire Peter's faith in stepping out of the boat to meet Jesus in the storm. Yet when his eyes wandered, he began to sink, to fall, to drown. I have found myself in similar situations; having faith to move mountains until I realize the mountain is about to move me...yikes! Thankfully, we serve a God who **does not deal with us according to our sins** but who, **is merciful and gracious, slow to anger and abounding in steadfast love** (Psalm 103:8–10).

God was patient with Peter. He is patient with me, and He will be patient with all who struggle with speaking out and falling flat in the follow through. Yet let me be clear: pride has got to go!

After encountering many joyless days, weeks, and evens months, I began to ask God what needed to be addressed in my life on my journey to the edge. God, through the convicting work of the Holy Spirit, began to reveal to me a sin that I did not think I had. That was the sin of pride. You see, I thought I was pretty humble. I mean, I loved God and loved putting others before myself. To the best of my ability, I tried to meet others' needs and so the pitfall sin of pride was definitely not on my radar screen. However, it wasn't long into ministry before I began to think thoughts like, *If I don't get this done, who else will? Or, I will do this myself because it really takes much less time and they won't do it how I like it anyway. Or, I just need to do this because I need to prove to others that I am not weak, but I'm tough and can handle this job.*

Before I knew it, I accepted these lies as they entered through the back door of my life. I would never have verbalized these thoughts to anyone because I was a humble person (come on now!), but a thought that is not taken captive under the scrutiny of the Holy Spirit, especially one of pride, will definitely lead to a downfall, as the Scriptures so clearly say in Proverbs 16:18: **Pride goes before destruction, and a haughty spirit before a fall.** And Romans 8:6-8, **The mind of the sinful man is death, but the mind** *controlled by the Spirit is life and peace; the sinful mind is hostile to God,* (check out that word "HOSTILE"). *It does not submit to God's law, nor can it do so. Those controlled by the sinful nature cannot please God* (NIV).

Whoa, wait a minute here! What happened? I thought I was all about pleasing God on my path to the edge, and where in the world did this pitfall of sin come from? I may have even gone so far as to blame someone else for my sin and for failing to maintain the path a little better. Maybe even have blamed Jesus Himself, saying, "This path made me stumble." How foolish I have been at times.

I was in the middle of doing the ministry and life thing. God was moving, and I loved what He had given us the opportunity to do as a couple and family within Urban Vision. So, as I began to entertain in my heart some of those prideful thoughts, something began to happen that at first I couldn't quite put my finger on. I was still doing all that I had done before: teaching Bible Clubs, helping others, mentoring, and reaching out to the community. But the effectiveness of what I was doing was not there. The impact wasn't there, and I began to realize my joy wasn't there anymore either. No one noticed these things, but because I knew God and His love for me, I knew something was not right. I thought the only thing I could do was what any good woman would do—take control and fix the situation myself!

Once again, unbeknownst to me, pride was rearing its ugly head. I tried putting more hours in at Urban Vision and tried being more creative with my teaching, but it wasn't long before I realized that this wasn't working either. Depression started to set in, I felt trapped without joy, and I struggled just to make one more day of ministry happen. Like in Pilgrims Progress, the good old Giant of Despair had me in his dungeon, because I had let the enemy deceive me with his lies.

If Satan would show up at our front doors in his little red suit, horns, and pitchfork, would we just ask him in for tea and cookies? I most definitely would not do such an ungodly, unholy thing. Don't forget that Satan's plan is to come and steal, kill, and destroy. He will get in any way he can. He just finds the weak areas of our lives and then presses in all the more.

Late one night as I was getting myself into bed, before my head even hit the pillow, God impressed upon my heart to get up and go and read Revelation 2:1–5. I could have pushed that thought out of my head, but I was compelled to get back up to look up these verses. I began reading and it was an address given in the last days to the church of Ephesus, and this is what I read: *These are the words of him who holds the seven stars in his right hand and walks among the seven golden lamp stands: "I know your deeds, your hard work and your perseverance."*

Wait a minute here—God was speaking to me! He knows me, He knows my struggles. He knows about my difficult circumstances. He knows that even through the tough times I have been faithful and have not given up.

The Scripture continued, *"I know that you cannot tolerate wicked men, that you have tested those who claim to be apostles, but are not, and have found them false."*

God knew how I longed to stand for truth and how it was our desire through the ministry of Urban Vision to proclaim Jesus who is the way, the truth, and the life (John 14:6).

The Word continued, *"[Jodi], you have persevered and have endured hardships for my name and have not grown weary..."*

That all sounded good! But then came the next phrase: *"Yet I hold this against you."*

All right, God, I'm definitely awake, and you definitely have my attention!

I don't know how you would feel if God, the creator of all the heavens and earth, who holds the seven stars in His hand was saying to you, "I have this against you..." but I can tell you how I felt: I was shaking in my shoes—literally struck with fear of this God who knows and sees me completely!

"[Listen up, Jodi]," the Word continued, **"Yet I hold this against you: You have forsaken your first love. Remember the height from which you have fallen** (pride). **Repent and do the things you did at first. If you do not repent, I will come to you, [Jodi], and remove your lampstand from its place"** (NIV).

What is a lampstand? A place that holds a light. And God clearly said: *Jodi, you need to repent of your pride and return to the true lover of your soul, your true joy giver.* From Isaiah 29:13 (NIV), God said: *Jodi, you're just like those people who came near to me with their mouths and honored me with their lips, but your heart, like theirs, is far from me.*

I had a choice to make right then. You see, all that God had given me—the opportunities within Urban Vision and within my family—were at a crossroads. It all came down to what I would choose to do with my pitfall of pride. It was my warning, and I felt like my final one. Was I going to continue in my sin and have the impact in my family diminished, and the opportunity to reach many people with the gospel just snuffed out and removed completely?

All I could do was fall on my knees and cry out to our merciful God who is slow to anger and full of compassion. Exodus 34:6–7 says, **The LORD, the LORD, the compassionate and gracious God, slow to anger, abounding in love and faithfulness, maintaining love to thousands and forgiving wickedness, rebellion, and sin. Yet he does not leave the guilty unpunished; he punishes the children and their children for the sin of the fathers** (most likely the mothers too) **to the third and fourth generation** (NIV).

Psalm 38:17–18 says, **For I am about to fall and my pain is ever with me; I confess my iniquity, I am troubled by my sin** (NIV).

The Lord heard the cry of my heart and my longing to truly and humbly repent and turn from my sin and make a 180-degree change in my heart and attitude. I have often revisited this moment as I continue in His plan for me, but now I hopefully and prayerfully walk with my eyes more attentive not only to what appears on the outside but also to what is going on in the inside and at the back doors of my life. I am more diligent on my journey to the edge to watch for the pitfall of pride that could come at any part of the path I am on. We must never be too smug with ourselves, thinking we have got this down. Oh, let us lean hard into our Savior knowing that *the joy of the Lord is my strength* (Nehemiah 8:10 NIV).

There is so much to take in as I journey with my Jesus, but with love and patience He continues to make my path straight.

> *Trust in the LORD with all your heart and lean not on your own understanding; in all your ways acknowledge Him, and He will make your paths straight* (Proverbs 3:5–6 NIV).

CHAPTER 16

TABERNACLED

The Word became flesh and made his dwelling among
us. We have seen his glory, the glory of the one and
only Son, who came from the Father,
full of grace and truth
(John 1:14 NIV).

I love this truth about God and how He sent His only Son to dwell, or in the Greek, to tabernacle in a tent, amongst His people. Think of the Creator of the spectacular world we live in coming to set up His tent among the people He created, loved, and would eventually die for. God came near. God is near.

I love the verse in Psalm 73:28 that says, **But as for me, it is good to be near God; I have made the Sovereign LORD my refuge; I will tell of all Your deeds** (NIV).

This verse tells me that there is a purpose to God drawing near. Several purposes, actually: salvation, refuge, and for all of us to tell of His mighty works. I love sharing God's Word with anyone who will listen. My love for children, for people, and for His Word has given me an unquenchable desire to keep on sharing. I love teaching at our Kids Club program that has grown from forty to over 200 children weekly. I remember my little African-American friend from Kids Club telling me, "Mrs. Jodi, you can really preach the Word."

Some of you may be wondering if it's right for me to preach the Word. All I know is that this is how God made me, so I can't keep silent. I have to preach the Word in power! Something amazing happens as the Spirit of God shows up and each child feels loved and senses God is at work. In the early days of Urban Vision we were predominantly all African-American, except for the Matthews family, but the Lord has truly turned UV into a very diverse group of people representing cultures from around the world. I just love the diversity. I love the richness of culture. It has been beautiful.

As I mentioned before, when I was little I dreamed of going to faraway lands and now I get the joy of meeting new friends here who come from lands far away. Combining the refugee community with the city children of America has made an interesting and unique blend, creating a new culture here at Urban Vision. Walls had to come down. Relationships had to be intentional, but what a picture it is looking over the sea of children that come through our doors. Praise His name!

Let's step back in time once again, to when Rodney was still working full time at a mid-sized manufacturing company which was family owned by our first Board president, Ralph Gatti. Ralph and his wife Bonnie came alongside Rodney and me in the early days of UV and have remained lifelong friends and prayer supporters. We felt it best that Rodney work a full-time job outside of the ministry as an example of loving God, his family, and hard work. Rodney was very much involved with all that happened at UV too, including being our finance guy, which balanced me out well. I have learned to appreciate those with other giftings who have contributed much to this ministry over the years!

With Rodney working and me running the ministry and caring for our small children (with help from my mom and dad), life was never dull. Truth be told, I like a lot of activity and my multi-tasking skills were definitely being put to good use. We felt as a family that we not only wanted to live in our community but we also wanted to fellowship in church with a body of cross-cultural believers in our community as well. We tried a few places but nothing resonated with us. I was also actually looking for a building in which to have Kids Club. For various reasons, we needed to move from our location in the building on Turner Street.

I literally went from location to location in our small defined community of Elizabeth Park and nothing seemed to be available to us. I went to the local gym and they said we couldn't have a Bible Club there. We went to a small local church and that didn't work out either. Options were very limited. I love sharing this story because at first it seemed God had no open doors for us, but He wants us to trust Him even when we can't see the plan. There happened to be one more little church by the canal so I called the Pastor, Rev. Paul Jackson II, to see if they would open their doors to the local children for a Bible/Kids Club. Reverend Jackson was more than happy to allow us the use of their church and he even gave me a set of keys—that was a lot of trust.

Sure enough, we started Kids Club at Faith Tabernacle Church of God in Christ. We were so thankful to Pastor Paul Jackson II and his wife, Sister Diane, for extending their hands of connection toward us. The church sat right across the street from the Elizabeth Park community, off Howard and North streets. In order to get the kids there safely we had them meet at my house on Belmont Street and would make several trips in our cars to get them across the street safely. So, Kids Club happened at Faith Tabernacle, where Rodney and I also decided to attend church. It was a small-family, African-American church. We had a lot to learn about the African-American culture but we knew this was the place God would continue His training and humbling in our hearts.

For Friends and Family Day, the pastor encouraged us to *come as you are* to church. So Rodney and I came as we were—shorts and all, and realized that *come as you are* really meant that you didn't have to get too dressed up. Maybe just lose the tie or the hat. Oops!

Our first son Micah was dedicated at Faith Tabernacle, and we just settled in to see what God would do as we immersed ourselves in the African-American community around us. Despite our obvious differences, they loved us and, believe it or not, I even joined the choir. Mother Patterson, who was blind, led the worship with strength and vigor. She could really play and sing! I loved it, even though I had a little bit of a hard time swaying in the right direction with the choir at first, but with time I even got that down too. Not too bad for a white girl without much rhythm. We had to learn, and they were patient. There were times as we grew in relationship that we just had to laugh through our differences, but it was good! God does put the most delightful things together if we let Him.

We met the pastor's son and his wife, Paul Jackson III and Sister Jacque, along with their daughter, Tori. Rodney and I would become very good friends with them all; more than we ever thought or could hope for. Even though we were in an urban part of Akron, the suburban home in which I grew up was close by. It would have been very easy for Rodney and me to continue in a church that was familiar to us because of the close proximity. But we knew we had to follow Jesus' example to tabernacle amongst the people. We needed to live with, go to church with, and do life with people in ministry in order to see a community change from the inside out. Paul and Jacque became those people with whom we did life and eventually ministry as well.

Sister Jacque has a beautiful voice so I asked her if she would come and lead our worship time at Family Night Camp at our house, since at that time in our lives, Rodney and I truly wanted to follow the CCDA model (Christian Community Development Association) set up by Dr. John Perkins. Every year they held a held a conference in a different major American city to encourage urban practitioners like us in their ministries. (They still hold the conference yearly—as I said earlier, you should check it out on their website: www.ccda.org.)

I will never forget listening to a Caucasian man sharing alongside an African-American man and hearing their testimony of committing their lives, friendship, and ministries together in reconciliation. How does the world know God dwells amongst His people? When the people truly love each other across culture, across economics, across what so many called and still do call, the Great Divide. I was so inspired by the talk during which they said, "There is a stink in the room and we have to talk about it."

They continued by saying it is time for believers to come together and "scoop the poop." Not wonderful imagery to think about, but it was time as believers to do what Jesus asked us to do: love God with all your heart, soul, mind, and strength and then go love your neighbor as yourself. I mean really love, really be committed to work through fluff and stuff to get to the real deal of life. That night I prayed asking God to give me an African-American friend who would be that kind of kindred spirit, that kind of sister, someone willing to cross the divide so that we could walk to the edge together.

Sister Jacque Jackson became that friend. She and Paul and Rodney and I all really connected. God gave us each other; brothers and sisters of different cultures, to walk the path of ministry together. Of course, in every relationship there is the honeymoon phase, but true reconciliation takes genuine work, lots of grace and patience, and lots of time to talk. We called them table talks. These were set times Rodney and I, and Sister Jacque and Brother Paul, would sit down even after a long day of work and ministry and try to understand each other the best we could. Sounds easy but there were many late nights talking, debating, praying, laughing, and yes, even crying. During those years, I learned so much about the differences in cultures and how to really love the people with whom you do ministry.

Jodi and Jacque together at the office

One thing we discovered was that not everything we struggled with as individuals or couples always had to do with race, but with our personalities as well. Sister Jacque and Rodney were often on opposite ends of the spectrum from each other, so it got a little interesting at times. Brother Paul and I were a little more in the middle with our personalities, trying to hear what each of us was saying. Don't get me wrong, we loved each other dearly, and still do, but when you do life and run a ministry together there is a lot that you just have to work through. So, what do you do? You pray, pray, and pray, and then you listen and then you communicate some more. Then you do what my dear professor from Moody said so simply: you just see it through! We sometimes had a hard time listening well, but those were times when God moved in all of us greatly.

Jodi and Rodney, Paul and Jacque at an
Urban Vision fundraising banquet

The Jacksons moved into our community into a house that
God's people helped to renovate. It was so cool once again to
see how God provided the resources needed to do that. In fact,
I remember one story of asking for some help from a man who
had some wealth and who loved the Lord with all his heart.
Rodney and I had never asked for this kind of money before,
but we felt that God led us to ask Mr. Paul Tell, Jr. for some help
to see this project move forward. We had an amount in mind to
specifically ask for. As we sat over dinner and began to share the
need with Mr. Tell, who loved Urban Vision and loved the kids
in the neighborhood, he pulled a check out of his briefcase and
handed it to us, saying, "I have been praying about where to
put this money I just received." Wouldn't you know, it was the
exact amount we needed to start the project! I never saw such
generosity, such willingness to give to others with such joy.

Mr. Paul Tell was like that. Although he was a business man
with resources, he always made time to be with the city children
and for people like us who needed someone to bounce an idea
off of. He was a kingdom thinker and loved and supported many
of the local urban ministries in Akron. He would even come from

his downtown office on his lunch break to visit the kids at summer camp. I will never forget him stopping by and letting the kids wrap him in toilet paper; dress pants, shirt, tie, and all. He was one of the most humble men of God I have ever met and we loved him dearly! He since has gone home to be with the Lord but the impact he made on my life and the ministry will never be forgotten. *Precious in the sight of the Lord is the death of his faithful servants* (Psalm 116:15 NIV).

He understood the heart behind the concept of us, as staff, living in the community, and how much his humble gift would impact the lives of children and families around us. The Matthews and Jacksons became neighbors. We had another young white couple, Scott and Sybil Lambert, move into the community later on as well; and also Miss Juliet, a single mom from the community, joined us in the work of Urban Vision. God was working out His plan in all of us. The vision to which God called us started to become a reality right before our very eyes.

I love looking back and seeing what God has done! We are all definitely works in progress. There is an old Bill Gaither song, *He's Still Working on Me* (lyrics by Joel Hemphill), that says,

He's still working on me to make me what I ought to be.
It took Him just a week to make the moon and stars,
The sun and the earth and Jupiter and Mars.
How loving and patient He must be, 'Cause He's still workin' on me.

Isn't that the truth for all of us!

When I first tried to find a place to have Kids Club, it seemed that hardly any doors were open to us. Yet God made a way! When God opens a door, what man can shut it? When God wants to tabernacle amongst His people, He does it!

Within just a few years, God gave us access to practically every facility in the community of Elizabeth Park. People gave us the keys and welcomed us to use their spaces for Kids Clubs or whatever was needed at the time. We met in what the community called the Big Gym for many years. We had Kids Club and started the Afterschool program there as well. For our first fifteen years, Urban Vision never owned its own building. God gave us a vision for a building from day one of the ministry, but it was going to be in God's time and in God's way. Those years without a building taught our ministry to be creative, humble, and willing to connect with others. This was not about our plan but about seeing God's plan played out in and through us.

I will be honest; there were many days in the first years of ministry when I wondered if I had heard God right. Did He really say He would give us a place of our own one day? I knew I heard God, but I couldn't see how that would all come together. I believe God needed to take me through some growing pains before He could entrust such a responsibility to us. We needed to trust God, trust His Word, and stay faithful to what He had given us to do. He who started the work is faithful to complete it. Oftentimes I would go to the words in Habakkuk 2:2–3 and be encouraged with what God spoke to my heart for the waiting time, the times of holding onto His unseen hand.

Then the LORD replied: "Write down the revelation and make it plain on tablets so that a herald may run with it. For the revelation awaits an appointed time; it speaks of the end and will not prove false. Though it linger, wait for it; it will certainly come and will not delay."

I am sure it was hard for people to await the Messiah to come, to live, to die for His people, and then come back as risen King. I am sure in the waiting it could have been so easy to wonder if God had forgotten about them or if they had heard wrong. However, God is a promise keeper. He came and dwelt amongst His people. The incarnation of God made flesh happened not a moment too soon or a moment too late. God has taught me to hold on, stand firm, and wait on Him. He sees, He cares, and He surely has not forgotten any of us. Amen and amen!

CHAPTER 17

SURRENDER...DETOUR AHEAD

Hear my prayer, LORD; let my cry for help come to you.
Do not hide your face from me when I am in distress,
Turn your ear to me; when I call, answer me quickly.
For my days vanish like smoke; my bones burn like
glowing embers. My heart is blighted and withered
like grass; I forget to eat my food...I lie awake; I have
become like a bird alone on a roof...My days are like
the evening shadow; I wither away like grass. But you
LORD, sit enthroned forever; your renown endures
through all generations. You will arise and have
compassion on Zion, for it is time to show favor to
her; the appointed time has come...For the LORD will
rebuild Zion and appear in his glory. He will respond
to the prayer of the destitute; He will not despise their
plea. Let this be written for a future generation, that
people not yet created may praise the LORD
(Psalm 102:1–18 NIV).

This is the prayer of an afflicted man when he is faint and pours out his lament before the Lord. Maybe he speaks of you and me.

After reading this psalm of lament, I wonder if perhaps this man was on a detour on his path to the edge. Though his heart was heavy, we can find hope between the lines; he had not given up on God, who sees both now and into the future generations to come. Although the pain was very real and had an effect on him physically, emotionally, and spiritually, he fell into the arms of a compassionate God who remains throughout all generations. It says in Hebrews 13:8, *Jesus Christ is the same yesterday and today and forever* (NIV).

Detours are just plain inconvenient, especially to all of us "doers of the Word of God" who are on mission and on task and who have to get there on time to stay on schedule. I know I am not the only type A person in the world. We have a goal in mind, and we have our faces set like flint, and we are headed to the mountains determined, like a deer, to get those hind feet to the place where just maybe we can leap a little faster.

Just the other day I was traveling to my mother's house, on my normal route, ready to turn onto a familiar path—and the road was closed off by a detour sign. I didn't want to use the detour, I just wanted to stay on my familiar course, and how dare they close the road and not inform me! No contesting on my part would change that big bulldozer sitting in my path, so I turned, none too happily, onto the detour. As I took the street the detour suggested, my mind began to flood with memories of when I was a little girl taking this very street to go visit my grandma's house on my bike. Before long what had been an inconvenient detour became an enjoyable opportunity to share some memories with my youngest son. If only all detours in our life would be so easy and surprisingly pleasant. Sometimes they can be, but I am pretty confident that if they were all paths of ease, then we would leave our detours unchanged and none the better. Detours are unfamiliar paths, steps into the unknown, and at times they can cause great pain and confusion. Isaiah 42:16 says, *I will lead the blind by ways they have not known; along unfamiliar paths I will guide them* (NIV). I have had a few detours in my life...how about you?

A book that I have grown to love more and more every time I read it is called *Hinds Feet on High Places*, by Hannah Hurnard (Wheaton, IL: Living Books, 1988). Much Afraid is the main character, and I feel great affinity with her. She desires to follow the Chief Shepherd, the Lord Himself, to great heights in order to set her hind feet like a deer. One problem: Much Afraid is severely crippled with fear and doesn't know if she should even attempt such a journey. With much loving encouragement from the Shepherd who assures her that He will assist her in this journey, Much Afraid decides, with great fear and trembling and not knowing what lay ahead, to follow the Shepherd of her soul.

In the beginning of her journey to the high places, she has a close call with Pride, a bully character in the book who tries to keep her from making the journey. Much Afraid makes it past this first little test but to her dismay she is led to a plain; a desert that stretches beyond what the eye could see. Much Afraid soon cries out that she cannot go down there into the desert; most definitely the Shepherd could not mean this for her. Much Afraid knows her goal is to get to the mountains, but she thinks that means going up, not descending and going in the opposite direction. This seems to be an absolute contradiction of all that was promised.

Immediately, she calls the Shepherd to discuss this apparent mix-up and she feels confident that He will set things straight. But to her great dismay, Much Afraid learns that the path leading away from the high places is the detour He has chosen and it is the path she must take. While she is still dazed with confusion, the Shepherd responds to her as quoted in the book: "It is not a contradiction, only a postponement for the best to become possible." The question *Why?* surfaces from the depths of her soul as she feels the anguish of what seems to be a betrayed heart. The Shepherd had chosen for her, as He sometimes does with us, a season of detour leading away from her heart's desire rather than closer to it. The path that leads to the edge often first leads through a detour…a detour in the desert.

Such detours are defining moments in our lives. Will we give up, turn back, lose heart? Yes, sometimes we do, but God knows our frames; He knows that we are only dust. *His compassions never fail. They are new every morning; great is your faithfulness* (Lamentations 3:23 NIV).

Beth Moore, in the updated version of her book *Breaking Free*, (Nashville, TN: LifeWay Press, 2009), says, "God has reserved momentous victories and great rewards for us. But we will never make it to our milestones, [and may I add, we will never make it to the edge] if we can't make it through our moments." Life is filled with moments that require decisions on how to respond to the detours that come our way.

At the time that I first wrote about the detours in my life, I was doing a Bible study with women who had hearts to seek the Lord. My detours right then were that I had bronchitis, two eye infections, a blistered tongue, a burnt hand—small but painfully irritating, car trouble, disappointments, and believe it or not, my wallet was stolen…all in the same week. I realize these are small detours but they are detours nonetheless. I wish I could say I was victorious in all my moments but I wasn't. I am not trying to be insensitive because I know some of you are going through major rerouting of your life and the desert is none too kind a place to be if you have to travel that way for any length of time. God wants you to take heart throughout your detour. Listen to His Word of hope found in Isaiah 43:18–21: *"Forget the former things; do not dwell on the past. See, I am doing a new thing! Now it springs up; do you not perceive it? I am making a way in the desert and streams in the wasteland. The wild animals honor me, the jackals and the owls, because I provide water in the desert and streams in the wasteland, to give drink to my people, my chosen, the people I formed for myself that they may proclaim my praise"* (NIV).

I know it seems hard to believe that praise can flow from our lips even in the detours of life. It is sometimes even incomprehensible to find joy in the wilderness, but I came across something years ago that has literally given me a fresh perspective on the detours I encounter. Pastor David Anderson shepherds a multicultural church in Washington, DC, and spoke at a conference I attended on how we respond to crises in our lives.

I learned that so often we go through our lives, our moments, hemmed in by the circumstances of life. When our circumstances become oppressive, we have different ways of coping with our lives that leave us feeling empty and stuck in a rut. For example, when we have a crisis, some of us shut down emotionally but keep going physically. Some handle a crisis by sleeping the day away or by falling into dark depression. Some turn to temporary comforts that don't fix or change things like alcohol, drugs, binge eating, working too much, etc. Some turn to entertainment and pleasure—always in search of that next adventure so as to avoid facing our realities—some just pick up and leave and say, "I am through." Unfortunately, there are some who end up feeling utterly lost in despair and even taking their own lives. We live life one dimensionally, thinking or hoping to make it through our crisis and in most cases, to face yet another day. However, the cycle then just repeats itself.

Pastor Anderson said that although we live our lives in the horizontal, we cannot take one step further until we praise in the vertical; praise our God who sees and hears our prayer. Psalm 43:5 says it this way: *Why, my soul, are you downcast? Why so disturbed within me? Put your hope in God, for I will yet praise him, my Savior and my God* (NIV). Something supernatural happens when *we get our praise on!* As I begin to recognize a bad moment or a detour, I am learning to say, *This is it. Despite what I feel, despite what I know, I choose to praise You anyway.*

God, through the delivering work of His Holy Spirit who is our Great Comforter, comes directly, vertically down into our hurting, bleeding hearts and fills us up so that we can take one more step in the horizontal. It may just be a small baby step and, depending on the heartache at hand, it may only be a crawl, but God is the one who can fill us up and move us out beyond the moment, through the detour and on to the heights, because we have learned to praise Him even through the unexpected rerouting.

We all know these verses from Habakkuk 3:17–19, but I would like to suggest that they become the theme of our lives: *Though the fig tree does not bud and there are no grapes on the vines, though the olive crop fails and the fields produce no food, though there are no sheep in the pen and no cattle in the stalls....*Though our detours are unbearable and though the suffering never ends, though I face this loss, though I have this burden, and though life is just plain hard...*Yet I will rejoice in the LORD, I will be joyful in God my Savior.*

Praise is not a feeling, it is a choice. And what is the result?

The Sovereign LORD is my strength; he makes my feet like the feet of the deer. He enables me to tread on the heights (NIV).

Trust in him at all times, you people; pour out your hearts to him, for God is your refuge (Psalm 62:8 NIV).

And hope does not put us to shame, because God's love has been poured out into our hearts through the Holy Spirit, who has been given to us (Romans 5:5 NIV).

I love Isaiah 63:9: *In all their distress he too was distressed* (NIV). God is not up in the clouds removed from our pain. He hurts when we hurt: ...*a man of suffering, and familiar with pain. Surely he took up our pain and bore our suffering, yet we considered him punished by God, stricken by him, and afflicted. But he was pierced for our transgressions; he was crushed for our iniquities; the punishment that brought us peace was on him, and by his wounds we are healed* (Isaiah 53:3–5 NIV).

When we ask God to use us and to take us to the heights, we must resign ourselves to every path, including the detours our Sovereign Lord may choose, in order to bring us closer and closer to the edge. Yet our response is crucial. Will I stand stuck in my path or will I surrender to God's way and not cling to my own?

There it is, that word *surrender*, which seems to be the familiar, flashing neon sign as I start on a detour I had no intention of taking. Yet to get where I am going and not miss what was intended, my response to the detours of my life must be to die to self and surrender to God. Life is full of surrenders on many levels. Admittedly, I have a problem with the little and big surrenders from time to time. I just can't stand it that my husband, the love of my life, beats me playing games all the time! I wish I could tell you that all our family game nights have been lighthearted fun, but I think the more accurate term would be: war. I have to surrender to losing to my husband most of the time. I wish I could do it gracefully, but I don't. Thankfully, it hasn't dampened my spirit to at least keep trying.

But seriously, to me the definition of *surrender* was often: to lose. Many times in my past I have connected the word *surrender* too closely to my pride, which skewed my vision of what I have come to know as I have journeyed closer to God's heart. In fact, I have learned quite the opposite on my path to the edge: *surrender* actually means yielding to my will and making more room for God's. In this paradox, I find I gain much more than I could ever imagine.

> *For whoever would save his life will lose it, but whoever loses his life for my sake will find it* (Matthew 16:25).

We all, at times, have to figure out how life will work itself out in our realities. There was one very challenging time in my life when we were starting our family and I was working in ministry, while Rodney took on more responsibility at work and traveled more and more as part of his job. It was summer and I was pregnant with our second son, and Micah, our oldest, was about one and a half years old. I was teaching at a summer day camp at the Elizabeth Park Gym. My mom has always been there for me by watching our boys. It has been a joy to her but even the joys of little boys make for a tired grandma at times. It was one of those hurried, hectic moments as I was trying to get my tired pregnant body moving and my one year old packed up for the day at grandma's. Feelings and emotions were running high as I did what doers, or should I say—moms—just keep on doing. I just did! Moms just keep persevering at all costs. We just suck it up, deny ourselves, and take up our cross—that just seemed like what any good and useful servant of God would do. Balance was hard during those days and I was trying to walk that balance beam of life and ministry. However, the real question that lurked beneath all the *doing* was: *was I really doing anything well?* Uh oh, I think I feel a detour coming on...

So there I was, running late, and the tears began to fall. I was rushing to my mom's house so I could rush right back to tell kids about Jesus. I was tired, frustrated, my attitude was wavering, and my joy was missing. Something was seriously wrong with this scenario. On top of all my other woes, I went into my mother's house and before I knew it we were in a fight. I picked up Micah, whom I had just dragged in, and now dragged him right back out to my van. Poor kid, I had him really confused. I wanted so badly to see this call God had on my life through to the end. I wanted to make things work as a wife, a mother, and the director of a ministry. At that moment, I realized I was wrong and I humbly brought poor Micah back into Grandma's house and apologized for my attitude. Dragging my child back and forth, stressing both myself and my mom out, in no way honored God in my doing for Him. Something had to change. All I could see in front of my life right then was a big sign: *Surrender...Detour Ahead!*

In that moment it became very clear that I needed to lay down control of a vision that was so dear to me. A dream God had given to me, a job for me to do. *Did I somehow hear You wrong, God?* I wondered how in the world resigning my position as director of Urban Vision could possibly be the right path to follow, yet that seemed to be what I was supposed to do. To me, this was not a detour on which I would be pleasantly surprised, but a detour that was like a death process for me. You see, when most people resign a place of leadership they move on to other endeavors. This would not be true for me. God called me to stay in the middle of things, but to give up the title, the position, the money (not that I was in it for the money by any means), the control—give it all up to someone else and submit to their leadership of my dream!

This was tough stuff for me. After letting go of my dream and coming off staff from Urban Vision, I have to admit I felt pretty lost and miserable. No more running things my way, no more having people look to me as the leader, no more having the final say on my dream and my vision. You have got to be kidding me, God! But He was not kidding at all and thus began my detour into the desert where I was made to wander for a couple of years.

I got a phone call not too long after that, which became a huge test for me. Yes, I had submitted on the outside but not so much in my heart. We can walk down God's detours in apparent obedience, but on the inside we may be trudging defiantly into hurtful, unfamiliar territory. On this day, the girls from the UV office called and innocently said, "Jodi, we packed up some of your things and wanted to put them in storage."

What?? So soon? I thought it was a conspiracy! Who do they think they are moving all my things? I'm the founder of this ministry! These were mine—my office, my things, and my dream for that matter! What kind of detour is this? Feeling sorry for myself, I wondered how I could rebuild the age-old foundations and be a repairer of streets to dwell in if I couldn't even finish my laundry or keep up with the needs of my growing family. I felt like my life was packed up in storage and placed on a shelf, and I wondered if God had forgotten the plan or maybe He just forgot about me.

> *The LORD is compassionate and gracious, slow to anger, abounding in love. He will not always accuse, nor will he harbor his anger forever; he does not treat us as our sins deserve or repay us according to our iniquities. For as high as the heavens are above the earth, so great is his love for those who fear him; as far as the east is from the west so far has he removed our transgressions from us. As a father has compassion on his children, so the LORD has compassion on those who fear him* (Psalm 103:8–13 NIV).

In a very short span of time after the phone call, God spoke to me from His Word from John 21. He asked me the same question He asked Peter after he had denied Jesus on the detour he took: *Jodi, do you love me?*

Yes Lord, I love you.

Then feed my lambs.

Jodi, do you love me?

Yes Lord, you know I love you.

Take care of my sheep.

Jodi, do you love me more than these programs, your stuff, and most importantly, more than your dream itself?

Lord, you know all things. You know, Lord, that I will do whatever you want me to do; stay or go, I yield to your plan and release mine.

Jesus said to me, as He says to you, *Follow me.* We can choose to answer: *Even though I walk through the valley of the shadow of death, I will fear no evil, for you are with me; your rod and your staff, they comfort me* (Psalm 23:4 NIV).

I just recently read an old book by David Wilkerson. (He was best known for his work called *The Cross and Switchblade* and was a pastor called to the gangs of New York in the 70s.) This particular book was titled, *Have You Ever Felt Like Giving Up Lately?* (Grand Rapids, MI: Revell, 2012). He made an interesting point that I haven't given a lot of thought to until recently and it has been messing with me ever since. We are all familiar with the account of Jesus' suffering even prior to the cross itself. The interrogations, the beatings, the humiliation, the crown of thorns, and even having to bear the weight of carrying His own cross that led to His crucifixion. As it says in Isaiah 53:7: *He was oppressed and afflicted, yet he did not open His mouth; He was led like a lamb to the slaughter, and as a sheep before her shearers is silent, so he did not open his mouth* (NIV).

Jesus took up His cross but it wasn't long into the journey (maybe we could even call it His detour) to the place called The Skull that Jesus Himself fell beneath the weight of the cross. His body bruised, broken, and mutilated beyond recognition had no more strength to move even another inch with that load. But Jesus Himself said in Luke 14:27, *And whoever does not carry his own cross and follow me cannot be my disciple* (NIV). Is this an apparent contradiction? Is Jesus asking something of us He could not do Himself? Absolutely not. There is a point in taking up the cross and that point is to take it up so we can lay it down.

Jesus knows my weaknesses and identifies with my humanity. He knows how our crosses burden us down to the ground with our face in the dust as we cry, *I can't do this any longer.* He knows the helplessness we feel when our detours in the desert take us to places we don't want to go or even have the strength to go. Wilkerson says that "a cross is any burden or pressure that threatens to break you down and that will hasten a crisis in your spiritual journey."

He reminds us that Jesus was tempted at all points as we are. He continues to say that, "The temptation is not in failing or in laying down the cross because of weakness. The real temptation is in trying to pick up the cross and carry it in your own strength."

You remember that attitude we get—with our teeth gritted and our faces like flint—but it is more like I fall to the ground with teeth in the dust. The lesson of the cross is that we can't carry our own cross. John 15:5 says, *Apart from me you can do nothing* (NIV).

Detours can be crosses we must bear. Surrender is our response. We know the story: Simon of Cyrene stepped in that day and was forced to carry the cross for Jesus. This was Simon's unforeseen detour—one that led his Savior to a hill called Calvary, a detour that I assume changed his life forever. For us, a risen Savior steps in and *for the joy set before him he endured the cross* (Hebrews 12:2 NIV). We can then get up and go on. It is still our cross but now it is on His shoulders, as Wilkerson says.

God has given me many sustaining Scriptures during desert times, but one that kept coming up in my heart frequently is found in John 12:24 and says, *I tell you the truth, unless a kernel of wheat falls to the ground and dies, it remains only a single seed. But if it dies, it produces many seeds* (NIV). Remember how much fruit we want to bear in our lives. Satan wants to sneak in after we have yielded to a detour and rob us of our joy and hope so that we soon lose sight of the vision God has for us. We feel or become like dead men walking. Isaiah 44:20 says, *He feeds on ashes; a deluded heart misleads him; he cannot save himself, or say, "Is not this thing in my right hand a lie?"* (NIV). Have we sold out or bought into too many lies of the enemy whose desire is to keep us wandering in the wilderness just like the people of Israel did for forty years? God takes us on our detours so we can see the end of ourselves and the beginning of what He wants to do.

God used the prophet Ezekiel to prophesy to the stubborn rebellious people of Israel. In Ezekiel 37, God took this prophet to the valley of dry bones and asked this son of man, *"Can these bones live?"* Maybe that is a question you are asking in the middle of your detour into the dry desert. Ezekiel responded by saying, *"Sovereign LORD, you alone know."* Then the Lord said to these dry bones, *"I will make breath enter you and you will come to life....Then you will know that I am the LORD....Come from the four winds O breath and breathe into these slain, that they may live."* Verse 10 continues, *"So I [Ezekiel] prophesied as he commanded me and breath entered them; they came to life and stood up on their feet—a vast army"* (NIV).

Our detours sometimes knock the breath right out of our souls. Or sometimes we take one big giant breath at the start of our detour or crisis and we wait until relief or deliverance comes. We are just waiting to exhale. I have felt like this many times, but God wants to restore to us the joy of our salvation; He wants us to find our hope in Him. We have wept like the prophet Jeremiah over the detours in our lives. He writes in Lamentations 3:19–25: *I remember my affliction and my wandering, the bitterness and the gall. I well remember them, and my soul is downcast within me. Yet this I call to mind and therefore I have hope: Because of the LORD's great love we are not consumed, for his compassions never fail. They are new every morning; great is your faithfulness. I say to myself, "The LORD is my portion; therefore I will wait for him." The LORD is good to those whose hope is in him; to the one who seeks him* (NIV).

Do you see what it says? Because of the Lord's great love for us, we are not consumed. There are days I walk around and say, *I am not consumed...I am not consumed...I am not going to be consumed by this frustration...I am not going to be consumed by my anger...I am not going to be consumed by my pain...I am not going to be consumed by my children...I am not going to be consumed in this moment because I want to make it to my milestone! I am not going to be consumed because my Jesus is the all-consuming One; let us run to Him for our shelter. If anything is going to consume me, let it be like the psalmist says in Psalm 69:9, **for zeal for your house consumes me.*** Let Him be my all in all. Just let Jesus consume me. Just give me Jesus! I trust Him, and even if He consumes me, I am assured he will get me where I need to be in the time I need to be there. David Wilkerson also states that "dryness can only be stopped by the dew of His glory."

We need to cry out and praise God and say, *Come, Breath of Heaven, breathe on me for I am in great need of a resurrection.* In our detours, we come face to face with the One who said in the face of death, **I am the resurrection, and the life: he that believeth in me, though he were dead, yet shall he live** (John 11:25 KJV). He has walked me through some deserts in my life, and I am sure there will be more detours to come, but God is faithful.

I was stuck in a crisis moment one day around the Christmas season. Schedules were tight, between family and ministry there were constant activities. We didn't have our own Urban Vision building and we were using our basement for storage. Generous people donated new gifts for our Christmas Store that literally filled the basement from floor to ceiling with gifts. The phone was ringing off the hook, and those interruptions were mixing in with homework, dinner, and volunteers constantly showing up at my house to transport all these wonderful gifts through the snow and cold. A problem crept up with a staff member that had to be dealt with and I thought I was going to pull my hair out. It was one of those moments. I ran downstairs to try to change up the laundry since the dirty laundry was piled nearly to the ceiling, and I sat down on the pile of clothes and said, *That's it. I can't do it any longer. I'm done. I'm through. God, if only you could give me something to hang onto right now."* And right then I looked up above my washer at the wall of our old dugout basement and I saw a little sun catcher craft my son had made. The phrase was simple but it was exactly what I needed to know in that moment. It said, "He Lives." He Lives. How, you may want to know? One Resurrected Moment at a time! My Jesus lives in my moments, in my detours, and yes, even in my surrenders. He lives in me and He lives in you, if you have made him your Savior. Yes, surrendering is a dying process but not a losing one. Let us be encouraged by what David said in Psalm 27:13–14: **I had fainted unless I had** *believed to see the goodness of the LORD in the land of the living* (KJV). (Not the land of the dying!) We are that vast army of dry bones into which God wants to breathe afresh so that He will inhabit or dwell in the praises of His people, so that others will see and know that we serve a risen Savior and His name is Jesus. Psalm 27:14 concludes, *Wait I say on the LORD: be of good courage, and he shall strengthen your heart: wait, I say, on the LORD* (KJV).

One day on the sidewalk outside my front door I noticed something unusual. A beautiful purple flower had somehow burst its way through the concrete, growing there in all its beauty, looking as if it belonged on display in a beautiful garden instead of in the middle of a broken patch of sidewalk. Surely this could not be the plan for this one small beautiful flower to be surrendered in such a display. We all have heard the phrase, "bloom where you're planted," but I would suggest that the lesson from this little flower is Surrender to the Detour and "bloom wherever God has led you." This could be in fertile soil or in the midst of a concrete patch. Surrender the circumstances to God and just watch the most beautiful flower appear even in the most unlikely places. Here is a portion of a poem I found called A Sign from God by Saundra Snow that still hangs on my kitchen wall as a reminder that God is the God of the impossible and He can do all things well!

A Sign from God
—Saundra Snow

There among the rocks did grow
A flower strong—it did not know
That flowers need a caring hand,
Water, light and fertile land.
It only knew the will to live
And that its purpose was to give.

CHAPTER 18

SEASONS OF THE SOUL

The LORD is exalted, for He dwells on high;
he will fill Zion with justice and righteousness,
and he will be the stability of your times, abundance
of salvation, wisdom, and knowledge;
the fear of the LORD is Zion's treasure
(Isaiah 33:5–6).

I love living in a part of the country that has all four seasons. Spring, summer, fall, and winter are all very obvious in Northeast Ohio. We may not always get enough vitamin D due to lack of sunshine, but at least the seasons are very distinct. There are things about each season I have come to appreciate more and more as time goes on: The freshness of spring with all the blooms and the twigs beginning to burst. The long, hot days of summer when it's a joy to be outside appreciating nature while berry picking or taking long late evening walks. Fall brings its touch of briskness and dazzling golds, deep purples, and brilliant orange colors that stand out in such a majestic display across the canvas of hills and valleys. Warm apple cider and pumpkins and, of course, candy corn, make this season of harvest one of great delight. Then come the short days and cold months of winter when all of nature seems to be tucked away until the first big snowfall covers the ground with glistening snow that makes you want to go build the first snowman of the year.

Yes, there are annoying parts of each season but that is part of the ebb and flow of life. I am certainly not a fan of the rain in the spring, the heat in the summer, the fall warning that winter is coming, or of the bitter cold and death of winter. I like seasons though, because they come and go with such faithfulness; even when a season is not what I hoped for, there's the assurance that sometime soon this season will pass.

We have had many seasons now at Urban Vision throughout this journey to the edge. Each one has included amazing mountain-top joys, but there has also been much time in the valley of weeping. I believe both are necessary to shape us into all God desires us to be. Over time, I have learned to expect both good and hard to come, flowing in and out like the seasons. I have begun to learn to embrace each season for what it is and trust God to see me through.

In the last chapter I spoke about surrender and how various detours from God can be overwhelming. After stepping off staff of Urban Vision for a *season*, I often found myself in a fog, not knowing what was to come. This was a very hard time for me. So many times in my life the next step or the "expected season" had seemed so clear, but this was not one of them. During this part of my faith journey, God was teaching me to trust, not just in the light, but to trust and hold on to God's unchanging hand when the path I walked seemed very, very dark.

> **And I will lead the blind in a way that they do not know, in paths that they have not known I will guide them** (Isaiah 42:16).

When I had stepped off as Director, my coworker, friend, and sister in Christ, Sister Jacque Jackson, took over leading the ministry. These were hard days for both of us as God was prompting Jacque to lead and prompting me to be still. In my pride, I often wondered how God was working out His plan without me (Ha ha) but I learned some treasured lessons during this season in my life. I wish I could tell you that everything was smooth during our transition, but as you certainly know, changes are rarely ever easy—even when they're necessary.

I thank God for Sister Jacque and for what an amazing prayer warrior she is. I drove her crazy at times, but the Spirit in both of us kept us on the path together for a very long time. As iron sharpens iron, so would be my relationship with Sister Jacque.

I can remember sitting with her in the office of an African-American pastor who encouraged us not to give up on our relationship with each other. He spoke of the story in Luke 8: 22–25, when the disciples got into the boat and Jesus said, **"Let us go over to the other side of the lake"** (NIV). Little did the disciples know that they would encounter a very bad storm that threatened the lives of all on board. Not to mention the very interesting fact that Jesus Himself was physically with them; He was there but just taking a little snooze. The pastor encouraged us to remember the Word spoken to the disciples: *let us go to other side,* which inferred that Jesus had every intention of getting them all safely across, storm or no storm. Often in my journey to the edge I have had to remember Who called me in the beginning and what He asked me to do. The entire plan was not laid out in front of me; that would have required no faith at all. Often God calls us to remember His Word and hold on tightly when the way is narrow and dark. Like the psalmist David said: **"Bless the LORD, O my soul, and all that is within me, bless His holy name! Bless the LORD, O my soul, And forget not all his benefits"** (Psalm 103:1–2).

I think that sometimes we give up and give in way too easily. I know I have. We must be careful not to say, *Oh this must not be God's will,* the moment one thing doesn't go our way. God may just be giving us an endurance check to see whether or not we are strong enough to handle what lies beyond the bend. This was very true in Jacque's and my relationship. I longed to see our relationship work out because I really wanted to understand people who were different from me. Not just in color or culture, but different in giftings and skill sets. Can we not learn to get along? Are we not to work together as the body of Christ? How will the world know that God is who He is if we cannot learn to persevere in our relationships one with another? Yes, there are "seasons" in friendships, but let us not be too quick to jump ship when the slightest bump comes our way.

I love Sister Jacque and Brother Paul. They are, in every sense of the words, true friends. A genuine brother and sister in Christ, both across cultures and across personalities. God has used them greatly to help shape and mold the vision of Urban Vision as we worked and ministered together in the same community as neighbors for over fifteen years. Most of the community saw Jacque and me together all the time. Yet, this switch in roles really challenged me to see in the dark with a different set of eyes. No longer the leader, I had to submit to another in the style and way she led. Pride is an ugly thing, every inch of it. I needed God to cleanse me of every thought not surrendered to Him in order to press on to the edge. God's grace poured over us both. God began to teach me, to humble me, to help me trust His heart and who He was and what He was doing, not only in my life but in the lives He so intricately connected me to within the ministry.

There were moments in this season of letting go of my ideas and my plans when I wasn't sure if I would survive, and I thought I might take some hostages with me. Rodney was patient with me during those times; he has loved me through much and I am grateful.

I remember one of those not-so-clear days; actually, it was raining and gloom filled the sky, but mostly at that moment gloom filled my soul. My mom would always say, "When life gets you down, run to Jesus—but then go to K-mart." (Back in her time it was K-mart; now it is Walmart). I am not sure if this works for all God's children, but sometimes meandering around Walmart on a cold rainy day to get my mind off the heaviness of life really helps me.

Off to Walmart I went, feeling pretty low about where I was in my journey to the edge. I even felt at times that maybe God forgot about me, maybe somehow I missed a turn somewhere. Believe it or not, God met me at Walmart that day!

I walked into the front doors in a daze and practically ran into a display for a book by Bruce Wilkinson called *The Dream Giver* (Sisters, OR: Multnomah Publishers, 2003). It caught my attention and I picked up the book and read the back cover which said something about the dreams and plans God has given each one of us and how God will take our broken dreams and make something new. Seriously, I could not believe that God put that book in my life during that season. I have read it many times since then.

In short, the first part of the book tells an allegory about a character called Ordinary who lived in the land of Familiar, in his comfortable house with his comfortable job, day in and day out. Then one day he was called by the Dream Giver to let go of the familiar and pursue the very purpose he had been made for. It was quite a struggle to leave; in fact he was misunderstood by the others who lived in the land of Familiar, but he finally left. The story records his journey past the Border Bullies, through the desert, to a stop at Sanctuary to refresh his weary soul and, eventually, to find his dream.

It was at the part of the book after his Sanctuary stop that got my attention because I felt in many ways Ordinary was telling my story. After he was refreshed and encouraged and spent a brief time with the Dream Giver, he then was asked to do something very unexpected. He was asked to surrender the very dream he was given and let go of it completely.

At this point I knew God was speaking to my soul. God had asked me to do the very same thing. It made no sense to Ordinary and it made no sense to me either. How could God ask such a thing? Was He not the One who gave me this dream to follow? Why let it go now after we have been through so much? I knew, as Ordinary did, that to go on with my dream, to refuse to lay it down, would mean losing the hand of the Dream Giver Himself. I just then began to understand that verse that says, **Whoever seeks to preserve his life will lose it, but whoever loses his life will keep it** (Luke 17:33).

So much whirling around in my heart, yet God clearly confronted me as He has time and time again on this journey. *Lay it down Jodi...let it go!* The moment we actually lay something down, it feels like a dagger to our hearts, but my experience has been that the sting is followed by a sweet release and deep peace. Once surrendered completely to the Master's hands, whether it made sense or not, I have found a refuge like none other.

Taste and see that the Lord is good. I have tasted, so, dream or no dream, I was determined to walk hand in hand with Jesus to the edge—even without the dream itself. This was definitely a season of the soul. There are no words to adequately describe what happened after I left my dream with the Dream Giver. You see, soon after Ordinary surrendered his dream, he found something the Dream Giver had left for Him: his dream back again, but much fuller, much greater, much more extraordinary than he could ever begin to hope for.

Sister Jacque and Brother Paul were called on to another ministry and season of life. After leading for a time, Sister Jacque had a sweet surprise in her forties—God blessed Paul and her with two sons (who joined their already grown daughter). That changed things up, but God in His infinite wisdom and grace was working out His plan in Brother Paul and Sister Jacque as well as in and Rodney and me. Yes, another transition on the horizon...

Sister Jacque and I still keep in touch and meet to pray and talk as God gives us opportunity. Our hearts have been knit together on several levels for which I will always be grateful. She has been a kindred spirit. No matter where we are or in what capacity we're serving God, I thank the Lord He has given me a friend for life. Praise God.

It is kind of funny what God does. I just recently ran into Brother Paul at a hospital where he was waiting with a member of his congregation. You see, Paul and Jacque currently lead and pastor a majority white congregation, continuing to be reconcilers in many ways. We laughed together and said, "See what all those table talks did, getting to know each other. God was equipping us both to learn from each other so that we could each lead others from other cultures in a way that could be received—because we took the time to understand each other's hearts." Not that we are experts by any means, but God helped us build relationships in different cultures through those seasons when God called us to persevere together.

So many people along the way have helped me in this journey to the edge. I cannot mention them all, but they know who they are. People who have lived, worked, and loved intentionally across so many differences are part of the heartbeat of Urban Vision. Many of us differ from one another, but God has used them to grow the ministry of Urban Vision and to encourage and challenge me to get to the edge of where God was leading.

I am also thankful for those dark seasons of my soul because without them I would never be where I am today. Both in ministry and in my life, the view of the edge became clearer than I could ever imagine. My eyes are set on Him, the author and perfector of my faith. The ministry now has grown and taken on such beauty, including people from many cultures; people who have so greatly enriched my life. I am so excited to tell more of God's story here... there's so much to learn, so much to take in.

Please, take a moment to thank Him for whatever season He has you in. Hold on to God's unchanging hand. As my sweet prayer partner/mentor, Miss Clorinda, always reminds me: without a test there is never a testimony...God is faithful to see us through!

Yes indeed, I want to bless the Lord and remember all He has done through the seasons of my soul.

CHAPTER 19

GREAT EXPECTATIONS

Come to me, all who labor and are heavy laden,
and I will give you rest. Take my yoke upon you,
and learn from me, for I am gentle and lowly in heart,
and you will find rest for your souls. For my yoke is easy,
and my burden is light
(Matthew 11:28–30).

One of my favorite quotes is from William Carey, a missionary who is known as the Father of Protestant Missions and who suffered much in his sacrifice to see others reached for Christ. He is famous for a line that I have often thought of as I've continued my journey to the edge: "Expect great things from God; attempt great things for God!"

As I told you, when I was a child, Luke 12:48 fueled my desire to be a doer of God's Word: ***Everyone to whom much was given, of him much will be required.*** I think we should expect much from God because He is a great, magnificent God. Too often I meet people who try to define God and put Him in a box instead of believing Him for all He is and all He can do. Yet the danger for me has always been in putting this expectation on myself in order to perform, instead of leaving the expectation to God and trusting

Him to do the work in and through me. I have struggled with my own expectations over the years, but little by little God has helped me place my hope in Him, the solid rock. Here is a hymn that I love to sing.

My Hope Is Built on Nothing Less
Lyrics by Edward Mote (Public Domain)

My hope is built on nothing less
than Jesus' blood and righteousness;
I dare not trust the sweetest frame,
but wholly lean on Jesus' name.

Chorus:
On Christ, the solid rock, I stand;
all other ground is sinking sand,
all other ground is sinking sand.

When darkness veils his lovely face,
I rest on his unchanging grace;
in every high and stormy gale,
my anchor holds within the veil.

His oath, his covenant, his blood
support me in the whelming flood;
when all around my soul gives way,
he then is all my hope and stay.

When he shall come with trumpet sound,
O may I then in him be found,
dressed in his righteousness alone,
faultless to stand before the throne.

So, just a few years after the surrender of my dream, it appeared that God literally put it back in my hands. There were many changes going on in the Elizabeth Park community during those days. The Hope VI grant was finally awarded to our community which would bring so many changes for Urban Vision and for all of us who lived in the community. There was a massive plan to relocate people and to tear down the projects to build multi-family units. It was quite the difficult season for Urban Vision as we watched many of the children we worked with leave the community to live elsewhere.

Urban Vision had never owned its own building, so during these times of change within the community, we were housed in various places. We moved from our location on Turner Street to the little church on North Street to the Big Gym on North Street, then for a brief season to the AMHA building on North Street, and finally to a little blue house on Belmont Street, right across the street from our own home. And, as they started their new family, Brother Paul and Sister Jacque transitioned to a new season of life and I once again took directorship of Urban Vision.

I was a young mom with kids in elementary school so having our offices across the street worked well for me as I juggled many roles in my life. One hard working young lady named Sarah who was on staff with us carried out the ministry of our little Afterschool Program on the first floor of the blue house. Our offices were upstairs and another dear woman of God named Carol helped us manage the administrative side of things while we all pitched in to do the best we could with the many changes we had to face in our neighborhood.

Carol, Sarah, and I had many sweet times together, referring to ourselves as the three musketeers. We laughed so much in that tiny blue house on Belmont, and laughter is always good for the soul. We must not always be straight-faced on our journeys. If we cannot enjoy good company or a good tease from time to time, we will miss out on the joy of good friends who are connected to our hearts and traveling to the same edge that God called us to. Simply said, we must find joy in serving Christ because the sweet memories of that joy will take us through the rough spots. I found Nehemiah 8:10 to be very true: **The joy of the Lord is my strength** (NIV). And Psalm 28:7: **The LORD is my strength and my shield; my heart trusts in him, and he helps me. My heart leaps for joy, and with my song I praise him** (NIV).

Although I enjoyed the time with my other musketeers, the challenge was in directing, mothering, and being a wife (which at times took a back seat and I knew that needed to change). The feelings of being on overload soon crept in. Many people would often say to me "Jodi, I don't know how you do it." Most of the time I would respond quite frankly that I felt like I wasn't doing it well at all. The ball would eventually drop somewhere and I knew this could not go on much longer. If the expectations from others weren't enough, the even higher expectations I constantly put on myself practically ran me ragged. Once again I wanted so much to do a good job for the Lord so I would prayerfully ask, *God, you have given back the dream, right?*

It wasn't long into this before I realized (once again!) that I can do nothing apart from Jesus and the Spirit of God working in me. The kids were coming to our Kids Club on Saturday mornings and you would be surprised how many children would fit into a 12 x10-foot room. Kids would crowd in and sit on the floor as we sang songs and learned about a Savior who loved and died and rose again for us. Oh, what precious memories!

Yet from lessons gone by I just needed to die to myself, surrender what I could not do, and leave the results with the Lord. So much dying in this process of living. I wondered if I would survive yet once again. (Ha ha, isn't the point that you die daily? So, survival is not an option!)

Our neighborhood was changing, our families leaving, and I was in a place of not being able to handle all that it took to run the ministry. Maybe God really was leading us to let go of the original dream of seeing our little community reached for Christ. I had always held onto the original vision God clearly put on my heart flying back from Dallas many years ago, hearing God speak into my spirit, *Take what you have seen in Dallas and bring it to Akron.*

I was committed to that vision; I was committed to doing whatever it took to see people reached with the gospel of Jesus Christ. Rodney and I couldn't imagine abandoning the idea of living and loving in an urban community of need. Yet a thought crossed our minds during this season that maybe God wanted us to let go of our dream and possibly join someone else's. So we met with another couple, Duane and Lisa Crabbs, whom we loved and for whom we had great respect. They ran another urban CCDA-type of ministry called South Street on the South side of Akron. We were very mindful of God's leading during this time and I believe genuinely that we, as broken and humble servants, wanted to do God's will. If South Street was the place God chose for us, and they were willing to have us, we were willing to go. We attended church there and began looking at buildings and houses that could be potential places to live and do ministry.

I remember driving through the streets of South Akron with our three boys, exploring potential places for our new home. My oldest son, Micah, who was around ten at the time, even offered his suggestion for one of the buildings we passed, "Mom, that would be a great job training center." Micah has always been ahead of most kids his age but I looked at him and took his comment and just pondered it in my heart, *Lord, you have quite the plan for this little guy, don't you?!*

I often found in those times of cloudiness that I held on to a reminder from Elisabeth Elliot who said, "Just do the next thing." Having the plan laid out and clear would be extremely helpful but once again, as always, we are on a faith journey so we must continue to trust God to get us to the desired end. His way and not ours. In ministry and in life we don't always have all the pieces or know the complete plan, but we do what we know to do. Cry out to the Lord, trust Him, walk out loving God and loving others around us, and then see what God will do day by day, moment by moment. Rushing ahead of God doesn't work, neither does lagging behind—but being yoked to the master teacher is where I have learned I need to be.

It wasn't long before God made it clear to all of us that leaving North Akron and Urban Vision behind was not His plan for now. So, what did all of this mean? I still couldn't keep up the pace I found myself in, so I prayed and went to my Board of Directors to let them know how I was doing and to see where things should go from there. After all this surrendering, I literally went into the meeting surrendered with my hands up!

I thought that as soon as I told them my overwhelmed state that they might suggest that I let go and let someone else take over. That's not what I wanted, but I had learned to trust God and see where He was leading. That meeting turned out much better than I could have hoped. None of them told me to pack up and move on or let go, but they did say, "Jodi, for this season you are in, do what you can do, and clearly communicate your plan. We as a Board will be fine with that." I can't even begin to tell you how the burden of expectation rolled off me that evening. I finally could let go and surrender even my *doing* to Him, knowing that God is faithful to complete that which He starts. Praise God for His grace, mercy, and compassion over and over again. God finds us right where we are and continues to keep us on the path if our desire is to follow Him. I have been a witness to this time and time again!

I can specifically remember that my walk felt lighter than it had in a long time. All the emotion of great expectation is a heavy burden to bear; being free of it put a fresh wind in my sails. I was free to be just what I could be in Christ, nothing more and nothing less.

Kids Club that Saturday stood out to be a very memorable and joyful experience. I even remember teaching about Jesus being the light of our lives. I have a vivid memory of what happened that day. It started off as a cloudy and gloomy Saturday, but then a ray of sunshine burst through a crack in the door and spilled across the room onto the children's faces. This little ray of sunshine was a gift to me, a reminder that God loves me and He is ever with me. Jesus is the one who bears burdens, who lifts chins, who takes expectations, and offers freedom. How thankful I was to be in that little room packed with more than thirty children, teaching from experience that Jesus has been my light!

I still have great expectations of God to do great things because He promised He would. ***Truly, truly, I say to you, whoever believes in me will also do the works that I do; and greater works than these will he do, because I am going to the Father. Whatever you ask in my name, this I will do, that the Father may be glorified in the Son. If you ask me anything in my name, I will do it*** (John 14:12–14).

In God's wisdom and with His direction, I still want to attempt great things for Him. Why? Because I love Him and want others to know what a mighty God we serve.

CHAPTER 20

FEAR NOT

Have you not known? Have you not heard?
The LORD is the everlasting God, the Creator of the
ends of the earth. He does not faint or grow weary;
his understanding is unsearchable. He gives power to
the faint, and to him who has no might he increases
strength. Even youths shall faint and be weary,
and young men shall fall exhausted; but they who
wait for the LORD shall renew their strength; they shall
mount up with wings like eagles; they shall run and not
be weary; they shall walk and not faint
(Isaiah 40:28–31).

At this point on my journey to the edge I was beginning to see God move in my heart in fresh ways. I was drawn more and more to God's presence, longing to see more of Him, be with Him, and communicate with Him. What a sweet thing it is to walk this journey with Jesus. I love an old hymn, *In the Garden*, lyrics by C. Austin Miles, that my Grandma Janie used to play on her organ when I was a little girl. Here is the chorus:

"And He walks with me, and He talks with me, and He tells me I am His own, and the joy we share as we tarry there, none other has ever known."

I was very content being in the little blue house on Belmont Street. In spite of all the changes surrounding the tearing down of the projects, the kids in the neighborhood around my house still came and our Kids Club started to grow. Urban Vision started with Kids Clubs, but the need to educate and come alongside kids academically was great. Many children fell through an educational gap and unfortunately would be passed on to the next grade whether or not they mastered their current grade level. This is true even today. Individual kids have so many needs!

Jodi teaching the kids

We understood that if our kids could not succeed academically, the cycle of poverty could never be broken. Thankfully, God brought people to us who could see the needs of the children and could develop programs to make change happen. Our dear friend and mentor, Mr. Paul Tell Jr., was the man who had a heart for the education of the young people of our community. We started our first Afterschool Program in our unfinished home back in 1994 with carpet rolls as chairs and pieces of dry wall for tables. Mr. Tell, along with others, from both outside and inside the community, worked to see change happen educationally from the inside out. My dear friend, Sister Jacque, had a heart for the kids educationally as well, and people like Miss Sarah and Miss Charlotte faithfully provided homework assistance to the children of Elizabeth Park when we were at the Big Gym location. Once we moved to our little location on Belmont Street, we were smaller but Sarah kept things running the best she could while I assisted her with food and such.

It wasn't long into our time there that we began to feel the smallness of the house. Cramming thirty-five to forty children in for Kids Club and literally having fifteen to twenty kids spread throughout the house to do homework, got pretty challenging. We set up our Back to School Store on tables outside of the house. We had a Carnival and Summer Night Camp out there too. We would actually serve food like a drive-through outside the kitchen window. In ministry, as in life, we shouldn't focus on what we don't have, we should simply thank God for what we do have... and then add a little creativity into the mix to carry out the plan. God blessed this little ministry of Urban Vision. We learned that if God was present, He would draw the people and supply all that we needed.

Another Scripture God put on my heart early on in the ministry is found in Luke 12:32: *Do not be afraid, little flock, for your Father has been pleased to give you the kingdom* (NIV).

God delights in taking the small and weak things of this world and using them to bring Him glory. I have been very conscious of His involvement, His provision, and of the need for me to get out of the way and let God do His thing in me, in the people around me, and through this ministry. I would occasionally get the question from the children we worked with asking, "Who's in charge around here?" What a beautiful opportunity to remind the children and myself that most assuredly, God is!

Rodney and I had always hoped to be in full-time ministry together as we journeyed to the edge of God's plan. We intentionally made the decision that having Rodney work at a full-time job was an important example to the community: seeing a mother and father functioning as one, with the Dad providing for the family. Rodney started out in shipping in the manufacturing company, but eventually worked his way up to the position of Chief Operating Officer and being responsible for over 800 employees. He also earned his Master's Degree in Finance from the University of Akron. He did have to do some traveling with his job, which complicated things because even though he had a full-time job, he was also very much involved in the ministry. As time went on, the desire to run Urban Vision together as one started to burn a little brighter in us both.

Our need for space continued to confront us daily. The kids would crowd onto the floor of the front room in the little blue house to listen to the Bible stories—and they'd literally have to tiptoe around each other to get to the only bathroom in the house. The kids themselves started praying with us for a place big enough to have Kids Club. We needed God to provide a place so that more children could come and hear the good news of the gospel. We prayed simple prayers to God telling Him our need and asking if He would please show us the way.

Rodney and I had been looking at various places in the community for a space we could afford with our small budget. There were limited places available at the bottom of the hill, and with all the changes in the Elizabeth Park neighborhood (which was eventually renamed Cascade Village), the greatest needs and most of the children were up the hill. But it wasn't an easy jaunt to get up the Howard Street hill. I have hiked it before and that so-called hill really feels more like a small mountain when you're walking up it.

The hill had always been a natural barrier between our little community at the bottom and the neighborhoods up at the top. Yet the needs within the community at the top of the hill were increasing. Gunshots in our neighborhood still happened from time to time but violence and crime escalated more and more on Akron's North side of the hill. We looked for places to move our office and our center of programming to be in the middle of the community of need. But that meant that we needed a location that would also allow for fairly easy transportation for our current kids, from the bottom of the hill.

Rodney and I are pretty aggressive when it comes to seeking out God's will. You could say we have a tendency to run ahead and then ask God to catch up. However, having done ministry for a little while, we finally learned not to try to outpace God. We looked around and we prayed much about where God was leading and what the next steps looked like for Urban Vision. There was one large United Methodist church building which seemed to have potential, but it proved to be a challenge to connect with those who ran the building. Having finally caught on to relying on God's timing, Rodney and I decided to wait and not get anxious and to just see what God would do. We let it all alone for the time being and simply waited on God's plan to unfold.

We did look at some storefront locations on Cuyahoga Falls Avenue on the hill but nothing seemed right. We checked out another building in the area that seemed to have potential. The rent they were asking was higher than anything we had ever paid before, but we still walked through the building and tried to figure out if this could be the new location for Urban Vision. As we exited, a thought came into my head that had to have come from God, because it wasn't on my radar at all: *Don't settle for Ishmael because Isaac is on the way.* It was one of those times I could not ignore what God clearly put on my heart. I knew we should not commit to that place because the promised location was yet to come.

We all know the story of Abraham and Sarah (check out Genesis 17:15–21). Even in their old age they had a son who was the fulfillment of a covenant God had made with Abraham, promising him that He would make many nations through Abraham's offspring. The fulfillment of the promise came many years after God had made it. Sarah tried to take matters into her own hands (which sounds like me) by trying to fulfill God's promise another way—by giving her servant to Abraham and telling him to have a child with her. (THAT part doesn't sound like me!) According to their culture, the child of her maid servant would be considered hers. Abraham conceded and slept with Hagar, Sarah's maid servant, and Hagar conceived and gave birth to Ishmael. (Talk about family drama! You just can't make this stuff up!) So problem solved, right? Hardly. What a resulting mess of tangled, hurtful relationships just because they refused to wait on the promises of God.

However, God is always a promise-keeper. Clearly Sarah was way past her child-bearing years, yet God visited her and Abraham and said the child was on the way. Of course, Sarah had to laugh and was confronted with the words of God, **Is anything too hard for the Lord?** (Genesis 18:14). God is the only one who can resurrect the dead things and dead situations in our lives. Why? Because He is life, and He conquered sin and death on the cross. Amen!

Abraham and Sarah had their promised child and named him Isaac. Ironically the name Isaac means "He laughs." Yes, God does His work with creativity and sometimes with a sense a humor too! So, when God asked Rodney and me not to settle for the Ishmael, we both knew we should be patient because God promised that Isaac was on his way. Honestly we didn't know when or where, but we waited and put our hope in God.

One day in the early spring of 2007, I ran over to our office to attend to whatever needed to be done…and got an unexpected phone call. Rodney was calling in the middle of the morning on a work day to tell me he was coming home. I wasn't sure what he meant so I asked if he was sick. He said no, but that as of that day he was going to be full time at the ministry. Wow, what a shocker.

We had been praying about when Rodney should start his full-time adventure with Urban Vision but when the "when" suddenly became "now" it seemed quite overwhelming to me. Rodney's company was going through many top management changes and they wanted their own people to take over Rodney's position. So, with a few months of severance pay, our faith walk on the path to the edge seemed quite a bit narrower than it once had.

It is natural to wonder about things like how to provide for our growing family, how to get health insurance, and how to buy boots and other necessities for the kids. Seriously, I worry about the strangest things at times. I know that little fear about boots was very minute but it was still a thought that went through my head.

Rodney came home that day and walked into the office where I was waiting. It was like taking a deep breath and wondering if we would ever breathe the same way again. We were almost afraid to exhale—wondering if the next breath of air would really be there to take.

There have been many times when I have wanted to turn back on my journey to the edge. Fear of the unknown still has potential power over my heart if it is left unchecked. Yet, as God comforted His people of the Bible, so He has comforted my heart and will comfort yours as well. *So do not fear, for I am with you; do not be dismayed, for I am your God. I will strengthen you and help you; I will uphold you with my righteous right hand* (Isaiah 41:10 NIV).

Fear is fear, no matter how large or small, and must be acknowledged and surrendered. God had brought us this far on our journey and would continue to take us the rest of the way. We had to trust Him to provide for all of our needs. Sure enough, one morning I stepped out onto my porch and there was a pair of boots for one of my kids to wear for the next season. How in the world did anyone know this secret fear in my heart? I had never made that known to anyone!

God put those boots on my porch to remind me that He had us covered, boots and all. I still don't know who put them there but someone, by acting in obedience, encouraged me greatly! *Jodi, do not fear. I am with you.*

God meets me where I am and gives me extraordinary surprises on my journey to the edge. And it's a good thing He does too, because a storm was coming on and there was rain in the forecast, so the encouragement those boots brought would sure be needed.

God is good all the time and all the time God is good! Oh, how He cares for me; oh, how He cares for you! Take a moment to reflect on this worship song:

O How He Loves You and Me
Lyrics by Kurt Kaiser.

O, how He loves you and me,
O how He loves you and me.
He gave his life, what more could he give?
O, how He loves you;
O, how he loves me;
O, how he loves you and me.

CHAPTER 21

WHERE GIANTS WALK

*Now faith is the assurance of things hoped for,
the conviction of things not seen*
(Hebrews 11:1).

I love telling the Bible story of Joshua from the Old Testament. Spies, giants, people marching with trumpets, and great shouts causing big city walls to come crashing down, all make for a great plot for any storyteller. There's enough action in Joshua to keep the attention of even the feistiest kindergartner. They love to imagine and act out the great victory of the battle of Jericho.

Joshua had some mighty big shoes to fill as the next leader of the people of Israel after Moses. Yet Joshua's leadership skills didn't just develop overnight. Joshua was on his own journey to the edge. Every step of faith, every day of observing Moses, every opportunity to assist where he could, made him become the leader he needed to be—so he could walk by faith into a land filled with enemies and take over what God was giving him. *I will give you every place where you set your foot, as I promised Moses* (Joshua 1:3 NIV).

What blessed assurance Joshua had in the directions God had given him, but in order to receive the promised land he still had to walk in faith and take the first step. In Numbers 13, twelve spies were sent out to collect as much information as they possibly could about the land and its people. They looked over this new territory that was said to flow with milk and honey. All that was great, but in order to get to the good stuff, they would have to go through people who looked like giants to them. This caused fear in all the spies and the people of Israel except for two, Joshua and Caleb. Caleb, being older and full of faith, said to Moses, **Let us go up at once and occupy it for we are well able to overcome it** (Numbers 13:30). Only Joshua and Caleb stood up against everyone, reminding the people that the Lord was with them; there was no need to fear the so-called giants of the land.

It was very clear to Rodney and me that as we waited for God and His timing to go wherever He called, we must wait with a readiness to move when God said move. Having Rodney leave his job and start his journey as a full-time Urban Vision employee took our faith walk to a whole other level. We knew we needed to be tuned in to hearing God's voice very clearly.

Now that he had some new-found time on his hands, Rodney wanted to make good use of it. He had a passing thought about that large Methodist Church on Blaine Avenue and half-heartedly decided to try one more time to connect with our contact there. We had hoped to at least meet and talk to this contact and see the inside of the church, but it had been a year and a half and we had still never been able to connect with him. Now, waiting that long does not sound like much when you read it, but it felt like forever as we were living it; waiting and waiting for God to make *something, somewhere,* happen. Waiting is not easy; in fact, it just stinks—especially for those of us who can't seem to let the grass grow too much under our feet. It just doesn't feel productive to wait. However, I know it is in the waiting on God that He develops in us a rest, a learned trust that comes when our focus turns from what we're waiting for, to God.

I was still stunned and trying to process all that was happening in our lives. As I heard Rodney make the call to our contact (as he had many times before), it seemed like something sounded different this time. Rodney usually never got beyond talking to the secretary and she would always say she would leave a message for her boss. This time was different—when Rodney asked to speak to this elusive contact, the man was actually there and talked with Rodney that very morning. I could hardly believe it! Waiting is not my favorite thing to do, but when God does start to move, He MOVES and we'd better hold on! All of the sudden, we needed to strap ourselves in and hold on for the ride we were about to embark on.

Rodney got off the phone and told me he had set up a time to see the church on Blaine Avenue. We spent all that time—that whole year and a half—waiting on God. But it wasn't until we took a big step of faith out of our boat of comfort, out of the secure boat of Rodney's job and our own plans, that God moved with great power. It just amazes me!

This journey to the edge continues to be one of walking in faith. This journey requires us to take on the giants that seem to occupy the destination ahead. Yet, if God is for us, who can be against us? Are there any Joshuas and Calebs reading right now? God has called and He has promised. Will you, as His people, believe Him for all He is and all He wants to do in your lives?

God was not just a God of the extraordinary in the past. He is the same yesterday, today, and forever (Hebrews 13:8). He delights to have His children put great faith in Him and walk in places we would not choose to go on our own accord. Great faith starts with even small faith; one step, one acknowledgement, one wholehearted belief that God is faithful. He who promised will bring it to pass (1 Thessalonians 5:24).

Right from the beginning God had given me the vision of a community center like the one I had seen at the Voice of Hope ministry in Dallas when I went to visit all those years ago. Just as

God had told me to, I wrote the vision down so that others who came alongside us could read it and run with it (Habakkuk 2). We had created a ministry plan that included this center, which we were calling the ARC (About Reaching Community). That name never stuck, but the purpose behind the name did.

So, we had an appointment to go see the building on Blaine Avenue. We were so excited to bring members from our Board of Directors and other interested friends and finally step into the building. We had no idea what was going to happen, but God did. This large building had three floors of classroom space, a sanctuary, a kitchen, and even a gym with a stage! Listen, everything—I mean *everything*—we had hoped for in the ministry plan we had written years earlier was there for our eyes to take in. The place was enormous. Rodney and I both knew in our hearts that this had to be the "Isaac" God had spoken of, but there were giants in the land.

The people we took with us to help assess the building were faithful to give us their input, but they had a lot of doubts. They wondered if the building was too big, how we would be able to maintain that size facility, whether or not it was a good idea to commit to such a building. These were all good questions to consider. Not to mention that there were quite a few repairs needed because the building had sat empty for a while. Many of the pipes had burst from the cold Ohio weather, so running water was not even an option in parts of the building. Giants everywhere!

This was a defining moment in our faith journey. The story of Joshua and Caleb came flooding into my mind. I felt like I was walking and spying out the land that God had promised us many years ago. We didn't try to talk people into anything; instead, we began to pray. We prayed, prayed, and prayed some more!

Rodney had his hands full talking to our Board, connecting with the people who owned the church, and checking all the facts to see if this could become a reality for Urban Vision. This was a daunting responsibility for Urban Vision to take on and many of those who counseled us wondered if we were getting in over our heads. We knew it was definitely over our heads, which is the reason we needed to keep listening closely to the Lord's voice and what He was truly leading us to do.

Giants of doubt, giants of lack of resources, giants of fear, all kinds of giants seemed to lurk around every corner. I am thankful that God gave me a partner who loves Him and wants His heart above all. Rodney and I are so good for each other because he is very financially gifted and I have a visionary's heart. God matched us in marriage and in ministry to complement each other for times like these. We didn't want to make a blind leap of faith, but faith would be required to take on such a place and make it Urban Vision's home. We all face giants on our journey to the edge and we need to remember that God is bigger!

I love the story of John Bunyan's *Pilgrim's Progress* (Public Domain). Christian, the main character, encounters many situations along his journey to the celestial city. Because of a poor choice, he got off the right path and wandered into the woods of the Giant of Despair. He and his companion, Faithful, were captured and thrown into Doubting Castle and tortured by the Giant of the land. It wasn't until much later that Christian remembered he held the key of promise the whole time. It was a key of hope and he pulled it out and they escaped, never to leave the right path again.

Giants in our lives can be defeated because we have hope in God, the Creator of heaven and earth! Giants do not have to define us or keep us from doing what God has planned for us. Giants need to be captured. We cannot allow them to dominate our minds or keep us paralyzed in fear. We fill our minds with the truth of God's Word and we stand on the promises despite what we see or feel about the giants on our paths. Walk on, dear sisters and brothers, knowing that your shepherd walks with you!

> **Not by might, nor by power, but by my Spirit, says the LORD of hosts** (Zechariah 4:6).

CHAPTER 22

PREPARE FOR RAIN

For which of you, desiring to build a tower, does not
first sit down and count the cost, whether he has
enough to complete it?
(Luke 14:28).

I love being prepared for what lies ahead. I'd probably make a great Boy Scout! Well, except for the part about having to go camping. In the rain. Or the cold. Or in a place without bathrooms.

Okay, so I might not actually want to go camping in the rain, but if I had to do it, I'd be the most prepared person on the trip. I think this goes back once again to my innate control issues. Being prepared gives me the comfort that I am as ready as I can be for whatever might come my way.

Working with children all my life has taught me one very important lesson: never leave home without Wet Ones®! That's no joke—having Wet Ones® with me has saved me from some pretty precarious situations. Like the time when one of the kids at Day Camp had a bathroom accident out in a park with no running water. Wet Ones® definitely came in handy that day.

Need I say more? Probably not. But seriously, knowing I have done all I can to prepare brings comfort to situations like event planning, teacher preparation, or just about anything in life. Working at Kids Club with over 200 inner-city children at one time has given me more than enough reason to want to be prepared for the unexpected. However, I have also learned that I can be very prepared and still not be able to control my circumstances. *The heart of man plans his way, but the LORD establishes his steps* (Proverbs 16:9), has been a proverb I have quoted often as a reminder to myself that God is in control, not I.

God obviously had His plan in motion, with Rodney's work changing and the simultaneous opportunity to look at the building at the top of North Hill. Once it let loose, it was like the floodgates of heaven opened wide and sent a continual shower of blessings flowing so steadily that there might not be room enough to contain them. That's when Rodney started saying to me, "We need to prepare for rain!"

Rodney actually took that line from a Christian movie called *Facing the Giants*. It's all about a losing football team who had to come together in several ways to face what seemed to be impossible odds against others who were bigger and better. The coach had little to start with, but with a surrendered heart he decided to tell everyone around him that he, as a coach, would prepare for rain. He would plan, coach, and instill character on and off the field and then would leave the results to God. He would do everything he knew to do to prepare the team to be all it could be. Then, at the right time, all the pain and all the hard work of preparation would finally come together to result in fruitfulness in his players as individuals and as a team.

A farmer must do a lot of work to prepare the soil so that it is ready to receive the seed when it is planted. However, the seed will not grow or bear fruit unless the sun shines and rain showers come. If the showers came and the soil was not ready, or no seed was planted, how could anyone expect fruit to result?

Rodney believed with all his heart that if he took the steps he knew God was directing him to take, God would bring the rain and provide all we needed to do His will. During many initial conversations about the building on the hill, numbers in the hundreds of thousands were thrown around as to what was needed to purchase the property. We could have been very discouraged right from the outset with these kind of figures being quoted to us.

But Rodney, knowing we did not have that kind of money, began to believe and pray that as we prepared for rain and readied ourselves to receive a shower of blessing, God would do a miracle. We would pray, keep connecting with God's people, and share the vision for what we hoped the building would become. Rodney kept meeting with people about the logistics of the building, and as he did, I believe the people saw how great his faith was. They began to see the vision we had for this building—the vision of seeing it greatly impact the community as it had many years ago.

The North Hill United Methodist church began in North Hill in the late 1800s and moved to its Blaine Avenue location in 1917. It had a huge pipe organ, beautiful stained glass windows, and a large sanctuary and balcony that could hold over 700 people. Old pictures of the building show that the church was quite packed for many years with people who came from the surrounding community to hear a word from the Lord. In fact, it is recorded in their history book that they had over 1600 people attend two Easter services one year. An addition to the building came in 1928 when they added the gym and more classroom space. In 1967 they added more classroom and office space. Someone had a kingdom vision for this church and the community.

North Hill United Methodist Church building

A garden, when carefully tended, can grow and bear much fruit. But it must always be maintained to make sure that every year, every harvest that comes, will be as productive as it can be. This requires work, it requires assessing needs, and it requires being open to change, which is never easy.

As times changed, so did the people in the community of North Akron. North Akron has always had much diversity; it has gone from being an Italian community, to an African-American community, and now we find that large Asian and Hispanic communities have settled in the area as well. Oh, if the streets could speak, they would share many rich stories of history, culture, and change.

As things change around us, we must continue to share the story of the gospel in ways people can understand and embrace for themselves. This in no way compromises the truth of God's Word, but we must prayerfully seek new approaches to really meet the needs of those in the community. This takes time, it takes a listening ear, it takes humility, and as Isaiah says: **The Lord is exalted, for He dwells on high; he will fill Zion with justice and** *righteousness, and he will be the stability of your times, abundance of salvation, wisdom, and knowledge; the fear of the Lord is Zion's treasure* (Isaiah 33:5–6).

God's timing is always perfect and I am so thankful that as we trust Him, He does direct our steps, our thoughts, and our words. Those few months in the spring of 2007 were crucial in the carrying out of the vision of the ministry. I saw the faith of my husband stand out like never before. My very money-conscious, fact-finding husband was walking to his edge with great faith. He continued to speak boldly to everyone, not with arrogant confidence, but with a deep trust that God would give us the "Isaac" we had hoped and prayed for, by providing the building on the corner of Blaine and Cuyahoga Falls Avenues in North Akron.

Not everyone shared the same confidence. Well-meaning people looking at the facts had a hard time getting behind such an endeavor. It looked impossible to some, and we could understand how they felt. Taking on the building would be a huge responsibility for our little Urban Vision; especially since we had only $4,000.00 in our checking account at the time. Yet God made it clear that we should trust Him.

Rodney met with the insurance man to see what kind of expenses we would be taking on with this facility and what kind of insurance we would need. The agent came right out and asked Rodney how much we would be paying for the facility. For some reason, he thought we were paying about $80k for the building. Rodney confidently answered by saying, "I believe God is going to give us this building."

I am not sure if the insurance man thought that would really happen, but we had an assurance in our hearts that God had led us to this and that He would provide. Don't get me wrong, we were not into the *name it, claim it* method, but God's plans are sure and we have to linger close to Him and walk out what He places in front of us. Understanding His will comes after much time spent in obedience to Jesus and in constant relationship with Him. This was not a lone shot in the dark. This was a promise being fulfilled by God after we had spent many years walking with and hearing from Him and being willing to wait on Him. No magic formula, no 2 + 2 = 4, just an ability to recognize His hand after having held it for such a long time.

We did not have money to purchase the building or to maintain it. Our Board members were rightly concerned that we might get the building and then not be able to use it. There were so many necessary repairs and so much upkeep—did we really want to be responsible for all that? We just humbly prayed that God would open doors and part the Red Sea.

Remember the story about when God led the people out of Egypt out of a life of bondage, toward the Promised Land? They left with joy, but little did they realize they were going by way of the Red Sea. It didn't take long for the hot-headed Pharaoh to regain his composure after the many destructive plagues that touched his people, even the taking of his own son's life, and he decided to pursue the people he had just set free. Pharaoh had agreed to finally let the people go after the many requests from Moses and his brother Aaron. But then he realized he had released all the manpower behind the building of Egypt. Pharaoh and his armies pursued the people of Israel all the way to the Red Sea. There was nowhere for the people to go. They seemed to be trapped. Had God led His most loved people to the beaches of the Red Sea only to let them be destroyed?

Fear spread quickly, but once again God had a plan for His people, as He still does today. God told Moses to take his staff and place it in the sea. With great faith come great results, and the sea opened up, and all the children of Israel walked through on dry ground. (Check out the story in Exodus 14.)

I have told this amazing story to many children over the years. And I knew this was our time to face our Red Sea. God had called us to our promised land, yet we were at an impasse. There were times when I would go out for a run and I'd be praying with tears just streaming down my face as I asked God to part our sea if this was truly of Him. I knew if God was for us who could be against us, but I also realized that we had to know for sure that this was His doing. True, we did not have the money in the bank, and true, our Board was very hesitant to take on such a responsibility. Yet God opens possibilities in situations that seem impossible.

In early June 2007, after much deliberation with the church that owned the building, Rodney received a phone call telling us that they had decided to give us the building. What a day of rejoicing that was for Rodney and me! That phone call was the parting of the sea we needed in order to know that God's hand was in it!

We could not wait to share the good news! Yet in the back of our minds we wondered how people would respond now. I think a lot of our advisers were encouraged by this news but still hesitant to just say yes to this offer. If we didn't have the assurance that God was in this, I think I would have felt like a deflated balloon. Yet deep within my heart I had a peace knowing that God was leading, and I just needed to hold His hand a little tighter, wait a little longer, and then step aside and watch the glory of the Lord go before us!

After our meeting with our Board, Rodney went back to the owners and told them that our Board was hesitant to take this facility, even as a gift. It felt like a deal breaker, but the owners responded back quickly, saying, "We will give you this facility with the understanding that if you don't use it within five years, we will take it back and resume ownership."

Are you serious????!!!! God is so good. He is so patient and understanding. Those words gave the more conservative members of our Board the confidence needed to accept the gift. All the concerns over the daunting responsibility of such a large building were relieved. Rodney and I knew this was the plan God had for us, but He had to reveal it in a way that assured everyone that this was a God thing, a parting of the Red Sea. God caused it all to come together. Just like Moses who encouraged the people not to be afraid but to stand back and watch the salvation of our God: *Fear not, stand firm, and see the salvation of the Lord, which he will work for you today. For the Egyptians whom you see today, you shall never see again. The Lord will fight for you, and you have only to be silent* (Exodus 14:13–14).

Isn't the Lord good?! Our Red Sea opened and we took a step even closer to the edge than ever before. It was a bend in the pathway, and a new view lay before us. It was an exciting time, and I love telling this story because our God still does miracles today; He moves mountains and parts the Red Seas on our journeys to the edge. God had given us the building, and 749 Blaine Avenue in North Hill, Akron, Ohio, became the new home to Urban Vision.

By God's grace, Rodney and I learned to prepare for rain—and God gave us a shower of blessings! When it started to rain, our soil was ready and the seed was planted. Ever since, our prayer has been, *Lord Jesus, bring much fruit as You promised, for Your glory. Bring many in our community to know Your great power and love!*

My dear friends, I believe showers are expected in the forecast—so let's start right now and prepare for that rain! Sing with me...

There Shall Be Showers of Blessings
Lyrics by Daniel W. Whittle (Public Domain)

There shall be showers of blessing:
This is the promise of love;
There shall be seasons refreshing,
Sent from the Savior above.

Chorus:
Showers of blessing,
Showers of blessing we need;
Mercy-drops round us are falling,
But for the showers we plead.

There shall be showers of blessing,
Precious reviving again;
Over the hills and the valleys,
Sound of abundance of rain.

There shall be showers of blessing;
Send them upon us, O Lord!
Grant to us now a refreshing;
Come, and now honor Thy Word.

There shall be showers of blessing;
O that today they might fall,
Now as to God we're confessing,
Now as on Jesus we call!

There shall be showers of blessing,
If we but trust and obey;
There shall be seasons refreshing,
If we let God have His way.

CHAPTER 23

SPROUTING UP

*For as the earth brings forth its sprouts, and as a
garden causes what is sown in it to sprout up, so the
Lord G*OD *will cause righteousness and praise to sprout
up before all nations*
(Isaiah 61:11).

I've never been a gifted gardener. However, there is nothing like putting a seed in the ground and watching the first little green leaf poke its way through the soil. The sprouting up of something new, something with so much potential, causes much joy. One little sprout of something which seems to come from nothing, shouts a message of hope.

So there we were. Urban Vision was in its new ministry home, feeling like a fragile young sprout. I am sure God's people rejoiced after crossing the Red Sea, as we did also. But it didn't take long for reality to sink in and we started to ask the question: *Now what, Lord?*

That whole summer of 2007 was filled with tours and open houses as we communicated to God's people the great vision that lay before us. The first couple of tours were a little exciting because we didn't have electricity, and we had to take people around the building with flashlights. Even though we were in the middle of the city, we had no electricity and no running water in parts of the building. Our spirits were high and hopeful even though much work loomed ahead on our path.

We launched our Isaac Campaign, asking God to provide dollar amounts that we could not even begin to imagine before. God did provide for our needs—above and beyond—and in those first months, it was a challenge to keep up with God. Waiting is hard but sprinting with God is even harder.

Urban Vision looked like a freshly tilled garden with sprouts springing forth in the form of pipes being fixed and gym floors being redone. It was simply amazing how many people God brought alongside us to get the building functioning so we could start programing in the fall. One of the first businesses that jumped in to help in 2008 was willing to resurface the warped gym floor, which had first been built in 1928. We may not have had running water but there was a brand new gym floor with our logo painted in the middle of it.

I actually thought it was quite funny that God made it a priority for us to have a functioning gym for all the children to play basketball on. However, our broken boiler pipe issue was quite an overwhelming task that could not be overlooked for long. Dave Baker, who called himself *The Dyslexic Carpenter*, crawled through ceilings and behind walls and came out covered from head to toe in black soot. It must have been Mr. Baker's love for Jesus that prompted him to tediously go through the entire 34,000-square-foot building, checking and replacing pipes on all three floors. Sure enough, Mr. Baker got us up and running with the help and strength of the Lord. He and his wife Marlene have supported and encouraged both Rodney and me personally and in ministry throughout the years.

This was the first time in fifteen years of ministry that we had a building of our own. But those fifteen years were so beneficial. We learned great lessons about networking with others. We learned how to share space and the importance of communicating with others to reach a common goal. We learned how to stay true to our mission even when some didn't agree. We learned how to work with others to make resources accessible to the people of the community. We learned that a community of many needs requires many people to make a difference, and there is no room to say we have no need of others. We needed to work with many churches and organizations for the good of all. We have not always done this perfectly, but years of having no place of our own made us more dependent on God and His plan and helped us to see the importance of working with others as much as possible. All these lessons made a great foundation for heading into this new phase of ministry.

The vision from so many years ago, the one written in our ministry plan, was literally taking shape right before my eyes. What a joy it is to be called closer and closer to the edge. Glimpses of God; His faithfulness and His provision, began to deepen our faith, and I have never been the same since. It is like Job in the Old Testament who went through so much suffering and waiting yet still held his faith intact and said in Job 42:5, *My ears had heard of you but now my eyes have seen you* (NIV).

Our staff changed as we were shifting into a new season in our ministry. Our dear Sarah had married and was having a little one her own, and she and her family moved away due to her husband's job. And our dear Carol Eberly was also called to move away at around this same time. She had started off as a curious volunteer, not knowing what or how God would use a white woman from the suburbs. She had a humble, teachable spirit, and she brought a sense of fun and joy as she embraced others around her. God gave her a heart to love and walk alongside people in the city, and she continues to reach out to the homeless living on the streets in her new home of Tennessee.

These were exciting yet hard times as I learned to walk through the ebb and flow of life and ministry. I struggled watching others leave because my heart went with these precious people with whom we had labored, cried, and prayed. The edges in all of our lives look different; some are called to go on another path and some are called to remain where they are. I have known for a long time that God has called Rodney and me to live and love in the city; that it was to be our temporary, our earthly, home. I must keep my hand open to God's plan and not try to control things in a tight grasp. That sometimes means letting people go to follow the paths God intends for them. It's about learning to look through the Lord's lens and trusting Him to accomplish everything that concerns us, even when we can't see how it will all work out, as the psalmist says: *The LORD will accomplish what concerns me; Your lovingkindness, O LORD, is everlasting; Do not forsake the works of Your hands* (Psalm 138:8 NASB).

Although Sister Jacque Jackson was now adapting to the arrival of their two sons, Brother Paul worked for us part time helping with our Afterschool Program and transportation for the kids. A couple others joined us as we just took one step at a time to figure out how God was unfolding His plan for Urban Vision.

When we were given the building, we were also given what was in it—office equipment, kitchen supplies, dishes and silverware, tables and chairs. As the transformation of the building started to take place with new paint on the walls, I was grateful for the many items already on-site for us. In His goodness, God not only gave us a building but also many useful things inside of it to help us get started with the children. I often thought of how God gave the people of Israel the Promised Land and they inherited fields and houses and other things that they did not build or grow but that were now theirs to use: *I gave you a land on which you had not labored and cities that you had not built, and you dwell in them. You eat the fruit of vineyards and olive orchards that you did not plant* (Joshua 24:13).

Never having had a place of our own, we had previously always borrowed or rented tables and chairs for events. One time we borrowed ten heavy wooden tables from Akron Bible Church and one of them slid right out the back window of our station wagon in transit. I would often wonder how Moses transported the Tabernacle through the wilderness. I couldn't even get ten tables across town without drama!

We were very mindful that the building God gave us was to be used to continue the work of reaching the community around the building itself. I don't know exactly the vision of the founder of the previous church plant, but I have to believe it involved loving God and loving others and declaring the good news of the gospel. I have over the years seen abandoned churches or buildings become other things like restaurants or even wine cellars and it always makes me a little sad because I think that whoever started the original church would have hoped and prayed that it would continue on as a lasting legacy way into the future.

One elderly woman who had been a longtime member of the previous church stopped by early on after we had the building in our name. She told us how thankful she was that God gave us the building to use for reaching others for Christ in the community. God answers all kinds of prayers as we seek Him for His will and His direction. Not only ours, but prayers that have been prayed long ago; prayers asking that His kingdom come, His will be done in our little corner of the earth, both now and into the future.

There is an old sign that hangs on the wooden fence that surrounds the flower bed that someone put there long ago. It says *Martha's Garden*. I don't know who Martha is but wouldn't she be thrilled to know that others come and care for her garden and that every spring the tulips sprout up and bring beauty to the area around the entrance of Urban Vision. God has had His plan all along. Even if our plans, or the plans of those who came before, haven't always turned out the way we desired, when we surrender to God, He does make all things beautiful in His time. God's Heart is always for people to know and love Him. His plan remains intact. It might just look a little different on the outside.

The soil was tilled, seed had been planted, and the garden was sprouting all around Urban Vision, inside and out. How appropriate is the verse we used at the beginning of this chapter: *righteousness and praise [will] sprout up before all nations*. How we praise Him for all He has done, all that He is doing for His glory and honor, and all that He will continue to do to leave a legacy of love! *He has made everything beautiful in its time* (Ecclesiastes 3:11).

In His Time
Lyrics by Diane Ball

In His time, in His time,
He makes all things beautiful, in His time,
Lord, please show me every day,
As You're teaching me Your way,
That You do just what You say, in Your time.

…Lord, my life to You I bring,
May each song I have to sing,
Be to You a lovely thing, in Your time.

CHAPTER 24

LOVE ALWAYS WINS

So now faith, hope, and love abide, these three;
but the greatest of these is love
(1 Corinthians 13:13).

I never considered myself competitive until I met my dear soul mate, Rodney. Rodney loves to play games and he loves to win. Not just sometimes; he plays to win all the time, and he actually does win most of the time. His philosophy is: why play at all if you're not trying to win?

It's great to have someone on your team who plays to win, but when that person is actually your opponent, family game night can turn into family feud. Although Rodney and I have different skills sets and giftings; his being in business and administration and mine being in vision and compassion, we both were born with high levels of perseverance and determination. Or I guess you could just call it plain old stubbornness. (Rodney would say that he is not stubborn...he is just always right! Ha ha...we will leave that for another discussion.)

When it comes to doing things a certain way, we each have an idea of what that "way" is. It can be something as trivial as where we put the ketchup back in the refrigerator, or as serious as how we discipline our children. Rodney and I have a way of turning something that should be a non-issue into something that becomes real drama just because we cannot figure out what in the world the other is thinking.

At times these debates over words spoken or deeds done have caused us to collide in arguments spewed out for anyone and everyone within ear shot to hear. I am not proud of this, but I am just being real in admitting that this has been a huge struggle in our relationship. I love Rodney and I know he loves me. But throw in life with all its ups and downs, add a lot of ministry to the mix, with a few children and a couple of dogs, some financial challenges, sprinkled with selfishness and pride—and you have a recipe for relationship disaster.

It was early in our marriage that I realized how damaging these encounters were to us and those around us. I had been mentoring a young lady for quite some time and we went to visit her on her college campus. We happened to go out one evening for ice cream with her and the young man she was dating at the time, which sounds simple enough. To be quite honest I am not sure what happened, but our fun, light-hearted conversation turned quickly when one of us got perturbed with a response that we gave the other. We just could not let whatever it was slip by without getting into a pretty contentious argument on who was right and who was wrong. It was tense but thankfully by the grace of God we were able to recover our peace of mind and start acting civilly toward one another. The evening ended on a good note, so we thought, and we all went our separate directions. No harm done, right?

Rodney and I had both gotten what needed to be said off of our minds, but did not realize the trail of devastation we left behind. My friend told me later that her date said to her, "If that is what marriage is all about, I don't want anything to do with it!!!" Ouch!!! What an arrow of conviction directly to our hearts. We acted so thoughtlessly, not realizing the damage we caused in the young couple's perspective on marriage. Oh, how sorry I was to be such a poor example! I wasn't living out in my marriage the truth I proclaimed with my lips. That encounter made Rodney and me very conscious of our struggle. We knew that this issue was not just going to go away but it would have to be confessed to the Lord and daily surrendered to Him.

There was a lot going on during those early years in our new building. We added a couple of staff; Katie Truax joined us for a brief season, followed by Stacey Wahl who had volunteered with us for quite a while working with the children and mentoring the youth in the community. A couple of moms from the community also joined our staff—Miss Janaya Johnson and Miss Sandra Hammonds had volunteered their time at Kids Club back on Belmont Street. They both loved the children and were faithful to walk down our big hill every Saturday morning to assist in any way they could. They both became involved in our women's Bible study as well.

I was always looking for ways to connect with the moms. Loving the kids in our community gave us an open door to encourage and love the parents too. These were some special years at Urban Vision because we needed the parents to jump in and help us work with the kids. I loved partnering with the parents, connecting at the heart and loving the children together. It is so easy in our white culture to want to jump in and fix everything and everyone. Although our intentions might be good, the reality is that we need to humble ourselves and learn to lean on others to accomplish things together.

The most important principle for seeing neighborhoods of need changed from the inside out is the principle of dignity. Change must come from the people who have lived in the community and who understand exactly what the community needs. We are still learning in this area, and I thank God for the many teachers I have met who loved and accepted me so we could walk together. We have made our mistakes, but with God's grace we have gained so much joy and depth of relationship with people who are different from us, simply by taking that step closer to the edge within God's plan.

Interestingly, back when my grandma taught Bible under the bridge all those years ago, Sandra Hammonds and her sister Jeanette were two of her Sunday school students. Then, so many years later, Miss Sandra and Miss Jeanette both had their kids involved in our Kids Club. God has an amazing plan. I would never have imagined that we would have the privilege of teaching the children of people impacted by my grandma so many years ago; in the same community, under the same bridge, sharing the same message of the gospel. Yet God, in His infinite wisdom, was carrying out His story in all of our lives. Praise God—what a Savior we follow!

I was doing the best I could, wearing many hats in my life at that time, including serving as Urban Vision's co-director/partner with Rodney. I have actually had a lot of issues with titles over the years, not really knowing what to call myself. Thankfully, even if I am a little confused about what my role is titled, Jesus knows exactly who I am and what He is trying to do—title or no title! Trying to figure out my new role in ministry, along with being a wife and mother of children who were then seven, ten, and twelve, created some unique challenges for me, both at work in the ministry as well as in my role at home in our family.

God has given me many opportunities to be in leadership positions over the years. Oftentimes, especially early in the ministry, I was one of the few women leaders in our ministry circles. I found at times that it was challenging, but I thank God that Rodney has always given me respect and space to be myself. He had enough confidence of his own not to be threatened by my leadership abilities. In fact, I think he kind of liked them!

It worked great when Rodney was leading at his job and I was leading at Urban Vision. Our dominant sides didn't overlap for the most part. But that all changed when Rodney left overseeing his company of 800 employees to come and be the new boss at Urban Vision, with just a few people to oversee and his wife being one of them. Try to figure out that new equation! All I could think was, *Caution! Explosive material on the path ahead. Potentially fatal if not handled correctly.*

These were difficult times in our marriage and ministry, and to be quite honest, we still bump heads on occasion in our leadership style. I knew God brought Rodney to Urban Vision to help us handle the administrative side of what would soon be an ever-growing ministry. Yes we partnered in every way, but someone had to have the authority to make the final decision. As time went on and the needs of our own family grew along with the needs of the ministry, it only made sense for Rodney to be the Executive Director, but there was a lot of me that had to get out of the way. There is that dying to self once again that feels incredibly difficult. Please don't say, *That was so sweet and submissive of you Jodi,* because that would be far from the truth. I was learning to die but pride and ego take the agonizing slow death. I have grown since then (still working on that) but honestly, I just hated losing, especially to Rodney. Having learned our lesson from my mentee and her boyfriend years earlier, in public we were civil most of the time. We got good at being smilingly sarcastic with one another, leaving our staff wondering if they should laugh with us or call a marriage counselor to referee.

Unfortunately, at home in front of the children, we were not nearly as civil. We needed help, but to whom could we turn? We had a lot of churches supporting us, but we weren't sure where to turn to safely tell our deep marital issues without compromising the work at Urban Vision. Rodney started reading a lot of marriage books and at first I felt a little turned off by that. I didn't want to read a book on how to fix our marriage when I felt our marriage had this unique twist to it. How many people do we know who are married, work together, and lead together in a ministry in which the wife had founded and led for over fifteen years? Now her loving, gifted husband, who thinks quite differently from her, steps in and is given most of the executive duties (which we mutually agreed upon) and suddenly he has the final say about everything.

I was a director/ leader at work in the ministry, still trying to figure out my newly defined leadership role, and then had to put on my submissive wife hat in the home. Talk about role confusion! These were uncharted waters for both Rodney and me, and we felt at times as though we were suffocating the life out of our marriage. We argued, we cried, we prayed, we kept persevering, but it just got worse.

But then one day, Rodney said something that changed our lives: "Jodi, I have been doing a lot of thinking, and as much as I love the thought of working at Urban Vision with you, I would give that up rather than lose your love. You mean more to me than this ministry, and I am committed to you first. If that means you stay and I get a different job, I will do that because I love you."

Rodney was so genuinely sincere that for the first time in a long time I began to lay down my defenses and my offenses and seek the heart of God for what His will was for Rodney and me and the ministry He had entrusted to us. God is so good and so faithful. I praise Him for what Psalm 103:8–12 says: *The LORD is merciful and gracious, slow to anger and abounding in steadfast love. He will not always chide, nor will he keep his anger forever. He does not deal with us according to our sins, nor repay us according to our iniquities. For as high as the heavens are above the earth, so great is his steadfast love toward those who fear him; as far as the east is from the west, so far does he remove our transgressions from us.*

Rodney and I got on our knees by our bed and surrendered everything in our lives and ministry to God and to each other. This changed my heart. There are no substitutes for surrendering all. All means all! Yes, we still have issues from time to time, but I can say with joy that we are not what we used to be.

Since then, Rodney and I and our staff took a DISC test to identify our personalities and gifts and how they function in a group dynamic. Guess who, out of our whole team, had the two top dominant personalities? Yes, Rodney and I were true to form!

I asked the consultant, "What if the two Ds in the group are married?"

His jaw dropped and he looked at me and said, "Well, it would be quite an interesting challenge to run an organization that way."

I quickly responded with, "You're absolutely right. It sure is a challenge—to say the least."

God has a way of helping us die to ourselves in order that He may be seen. Dying in some ways feels like losing, but from God's perspective dying to ourselves and putting others first is the most loving thing we can do. It isn't about who is better or first or in charge or winning or losing. It is surrendering to each other on this journey so that we can complement and encourage those with whom we walk so closely. It is seeing God's team win for His kingdom and His glory!

Rodney and I recognized that we needed to make some changes so we could reflect more of Jesus in our lives and less of us. So we decided to set aside a consistent time together in a safe space, to communicate our hearts about leading the ministry and to learn how to love each other better. We chose to spend one half day every week with each other, shutting out the world. We began to pray more together instead of just having our individual times with God. These practices are still very important to us and we have had to be very intentional about not compromising our time for anything else. There are exceptions from time to time, but for the health of our relationship, family, and ministry we had to be committed to let nothing come between the two of us; not children, not ministry, not our pride, nothing. The truth is, when it comes down to it, love always wins!

If I speak in the tongues of men and of angels, but have not love, I am a noisy gong or a clanging cymbal. And if I have prophetic powers, and understand all mysteries and all knowledge, and if I have all faith, so as to remove mountains, but have not love, I am nothing. If I give away all I have, and if I deliver up my body to be burned, but have not love, I gain nothing.

Love is patient and kind; love does not envy or boast; it is not arrogant or rude. It does not insist on its own way; it is not irritable or resentful; it does not rejoice at wrongdoing, but rejoices with the truth. Love bears all things, believes all things, hopes all things, endures all things. Love never ends (1 Corinthians 13:1–8).

CHAPTER 25

A SAFE PLACE FOR ALL

How precious is your steadfast love, O God!
The children of mankind take refuge in the
shadow of your wings
(Psalm 36:7).

I have always had a heart for people but especially for children. It goes back to those early days bouncing around on the big brown bus, watching my mom and dad love so many of the children they picked up to come to our church. My mom was a kid magnet and I think somehow I inherited that gene in my DNA. My mom always taught me through her example to never tower over the children, but when appropriate to get down on your knees, seeing things from their perspective. Also, be genuinely excited about and interested in what they are doing and experiencing. Doing those things will mean you will always have friends who want to hold your hand, tell you all kinds of stories about anything from the food they eat to the dogs that sleep in their houses.

I love the innocence of children; all they want us to do is love them, teach them, and even set up healthy boundaries that will help them feel safe. I have encountered many children in my life and I can't think of even one I didn't love. I can think of a few who were challenges, but I always tried to find ways to love them too. There have been a few in whose eyes I could see a longing for something to be different in their lives.

My heart has always been to provide a safe place for children in our city. A place to come and just be a kid, free from all the drama that can sometimes invade a child's life. I think of my little friend from Kids Club, many years ago, who always wanted to come over and play with our sons when they were little. Her home life was not easy; her parents battled the vices of drugs, alcohol, and depression, which left my little friend pretty much on her own. I would watch her crawl in and out of the front window of her home and suggested to her that she probably should not do that because she may get hurt sneaking out of the house. It didn't seem to bother her, but it caused a lot of stress for me personally since my standard of safety was set so much higher than hers.

One time when this little girl was over at my house, I wanted to remind her of the importance of being safe. I suggested she needed to always let her mom know where she was at all times. She replied, "It's okay, Mrs. Jodi, because no one really cares for me anyways." Even though her family struggled, I still knew her mom cared. However, my little friend accepted this lie from the enemy of her soul as truth and really believed she was on her own. My heart still breaks from that memory and it spurs me to want as many kids as possible to be off the streets, know that Jesus loves them, and for them to come be a part of a safe place like Urban Vision.

Our Afterschool Program was up and running; we would transport the children from our little community at the bottom of the hill to the top of the hill where we were now located. Our community was still in transition, with all the old vacant houses and the old projects being torn down. Our Kids Club continued on Saturday mornings and started to grow with children attending from the community surrounding our new building.

Kids Club has always been our outreach program, inviting kids to come in for a hot breakfast of pancakes and sausage, a Bible lesson, games, and crafts. Kids have always loved Kids Club. It is a fun, safe atmosphere in which kids learn that there is a God who loves them and that He has an amazing plan for their lives. We have had great volunteers willing to come put the special touches on these Kids Club breakfasts like French Toast Saturday or Strawberries and Whipped Cream Mornings for the children to have their fill. Hugs and high fives are given out frequently and it truly has become a refuge of love in the middle of our community.

My little friend and me at Kids Club

I never know what kind of surprises God has along this path He has called me to. It is simply amazing to be living out the dream that God put in my heart of having so many people come to a place where they could find hope and, ultimately, find Jesus! Recently someone asked me if I could ever have imagined what God would do at Urban Vision and the many different people He would bring there. Absolutely not. But that is what the faith journey to the edge is all about. We start out with a dream and limited vision. And as we continue in obedience and follow His lead day by day, the view becomes clearer.

A few years ago, I ran into a man I knew from high school named Logan Schellenberger. He had been a missionary in China and was now back in the states. He told me about a people group I had never heard of before that now lived in our community as refugees. They were the Karen [*kuh-***ren***] people who once lived in the country of Burma that is now called Myanmar. Many of the Karen people were forced to leave their villages and travel many miles through a jungle and cross a huge river to live in the refugee camps. They had no choice but to flee to Thailand for fear of the Burmese who took their land, took their children as soldiers, and harmed their wives and daughters.

People left in great numbers to escape such violence. Many resettled in camps in Thailand, where there was very little freedom to come and go, limited resources, no jobs, and little food. Many lived in a type of bamboo shelter, grew what little food they could, and cooked on open fires. Many of the Karen people had a Christian background passed along back in the early 1800s when Adoniram Judson went to Burma as a missionary. He translated the Bible into their language. He endured many hardships of his own, but through his efforts, the Karen culture heard the good news and responded to the gospel of Jesus.

Feeling trapped in a place with limited futures for their children, a lot of the Karen people sought and were granted the opportunity to come to America. Many of them were resettled in Akron and the children were enrolled in the public schools. When my former classmate mentioned that there was a large group of children meeting in an apartment, trying to help one another with homework, God tugged at my heart to investigate a little bit further. Logan told me that there were several people who were trying to help with homework when they could, and he invited

Rodney and me to check out what was being done and see if there was a way to help.

One night our whole family went to help with homework, not knowing what kind of situation we would encounter. Upon arriving at the apartment, we saw a pile of shoes—mostly flip flops—that practically filled the front porch. We entered the tiny apartment and found at least twenty-five children with a few Karen adults and a couple of Americans trying to help children with their school work. The Karen adults could barely speak English and the children had no books and very few resources to reference. It was quite overwhelming to say the least.

My sons, even my youngest who was eight, jumped in and made some new friends and we helped the best we could. The Karen moms brought out their food and set it before us and treated us with great love and kindness. I never would have imagined that I would be sitting in this little apartment with all these Asian children trying to communicate the best we could right in the middle of North Akron. It was like being transported to another world as we tried to understand this new culture of people. What an experience that night was. As a family we continued to help out in their home for about a month, and then we suggested that the children come to Urban Vision to get the help they needed. We knew we had resources for them—but the question was: would they come?

One of my favorite verses is Luke 19:10: **For the Son of Man is come to seek and to save that which was lost** (KJV). This verse is in the context of the story of Zacchaeus, a very short Jewish man who collected taxes for the Romans. Zacchaeus was very wealthy, but was probably not too well-loved in the Jewish community. He probably kept a healthy chunk of the change for himself before giving the rest to the Romans. However, he heard that this Jewish Rabbi named Jesus was coming to town and he wanted to see this guy who was healing the blind, the lame, and the deaf. Being too small to see through the crowd, Zacchaeus climbed up in a tree so his view of the Lord would be much clearer. As Jesus approached, Zacchaeus searched the crowded area only to look down and see Jesus stop right in front of the tree he was in. Jesus looked up and asked Zacchaeus to come down because he was going to visit him that day. With heart pounding and his mind racing, he may have wondered why Jesus would stop and talk with a short Jewish tax collector that no one seemed to care about or like. Zacchaeus climbed down that tree as fast as he could.

Jesus knew Zacchaeus was lost and needed to be found. Zacchaeus needed to find refuge not in his money, not in his power, but in a God who loved him very much and saw to the depths of his soul. After meeting Jesus, Zacchaeus was a changed man because the One who truly loved him, sought after him—a man who was lost was now found!

This verse has guided me all these years on my call to the edge. I would never have started my own journey if it had not been for Jesus seeking after me and calling me to come follow Him. I too had been lost and needed a Savior to find me, to guide me, to love me, and to get me to the places and people in my life that could make an impact for all eternity. Jesus beckons you and me to come see what He already sees in us, a completed vessel to be used for His glory. This picture of Jesus seeking me, compels me to keep moving closer to the edge no matter what. As I take each step, I can then begin to take in what God has for me and to see things I never would have seen if I had not been willing to follow Jesus to the edges in my life.

The philosophy of Urban Vision is learning, loving, and living amongst the people whom we are called to serve. I had learned to have a great respect and deep love for the African-American culture and the history of pain and suffering they have endured. From the time I was a child, I also had a love for the Hispanic culture with its great family connections and close-knit community ties. Yet now God was humbling me once again, allowing me to enter and know a group of people from an Asian culture for which I had no reference point at all except limited knowledge from a history textbook. Oh, taste and see that the Lord is good! What an amazing journey I was on and am still on to this day. I could not have made up this plot line on my own even if I had tried. God's plan continues to unfold, and what a plan it has been!

Like any missionary principle, the heart of going to the people and learning from them is imperative. John Perkins, in his movement of Christian Community Development, has often quoted a Chinese proverb (Lao Tzo) that tells us to go to the people; to live among, learn from, and love them where they are. Make what they know the starting point and then walk alongside and build them up from there. So that at the end of the task, the people will own the sense of accomplishment and believe and know they made the change happen!

My boys loved to play hide and seek all the time as they were growing up. They would get creative in choosing their hiding places—in closets, under beds, and even in laundry baskets. It's just so much fun knowing someone is searching for you. Games aside, it is even more impactful for someone who is truly lost to learn that there is One who is intensely looking for them. That thought gives hope, gives a reason to keep on keeping on. Jesus is that someone, that shepherd looking for the one lost sheep. Even though He still had the other ninety-nine safely in the fold, He could not rest until that one little lamb was found. I have always said that the walls of this building cannot define us or hem us in. We must be seekers and continue to reach out in love and in perseverance.

And in the case of our Karen friends, reaching out in love meant going to their apartment and allowing them to get to know us. There had to be a level of trust built in order for the parents of the Karen children to allow them to come to Urban Vision. Like any caring parents, they wanted to know that we had good intentions for them and their families. Finally, after several weeks building trust, we invited them to the Afterschool Program.

Rodney and I had no idea who would show up from our invitation. That first week after we invited them, back in 2008, four of the Karen children walked through the doors of Urban Vision. We were thrilled and honored that our new friends had begun to trust us enough to entrust their precious children to us. As soon as the first four came we practically doubled every evening afterwards. All twenty-five of the children we met in the apartment came, and more! We were so glad to have them come to Urban Vision to get the help they needed to thrive in their new lives in America.

Creation Museum trip with lots of our new Karen friends

Children from everywhere need a safe place to come and be encouraged to grow, to live, to breathe, and to become all that God would have them be. We are thankful that God has entrusted us with the precious, priceless gifts who have walked through our doors and still continue to come today. Whether children from families who have lived in our community for years, or those who have just arrived as our new neighbors—Urban Vision is a safe place for all!

My little friend from years ago was a victim of many things that she never wanted or asked for. Poverty, neglect, and, from her perspective, no one to love or care for her most basic need to feel safe. When she was at my house enjoying moments of care-free childhood for just a short speck of time, she would often ask to do whatever we were doing "just one more time" before she had to go home. Anything from swinging on our swing set to reading a book, it didn't matter. I can still hear her say, "Mrs. Jodi, please, just one more time!"

So I wrote a poem for her and for all the children of the world who need a refuge, a safe place to run to when life just doesn't seem to make sense. I live my life believing and knowing that one day the God who sees all, the God who has intervened with love through the death and resurrection of His Son, Jesus, will make all wrongs right! But in the meantime, as we journey through this life, He is our safe place to run to, a place where there is room enough for all.

Just One More Time
—Jodi M. Matthews

Will you swing with me One More Time
So I can tell you what's on my mind?
My dad is mad and my mom is sad and I am only 5.
I don't know what to do, she sighed;
But swing me high up in the clouds
So I can't hear their shouts out loud.
So will you swing with me Just One More Time
So I can tell you what's on my mind?
Will you play with me One More Time
So I can tell you what's on my mind?
I am so confused I cry, fighting the pain, the wondering why
So if you may, please pray today;
I hope to have my dreams come true
Just One More happy day with you.
So if you don't mind can we play Just One More Time?
Will you read to me One More Time
So I can tell you what's on my mind?
Take me to a story where love does abound;

The one that tells me I was lost but now I am found.
I know Jesus loves me so,
But right now I am scared down here below.
So will you read to me One More Time
So I can tell you what's on my mind?
Will you rock me just One More Time
So I can tell you what's on my mind?
My dad is mad and my mom is sad and I am only 5.
I know I'm too big to rock in your chair
But somehow it stills my biggest of fears.
You see no one really does care for me.
Oh my child that's not true you see
For I know Jesus does and me...
So sit down my child One More Time
And I would love to hear what's on your mind.
I know your dad is mad and your mom is sad and I know that you
are only 5.
You are never alone my child so trust Him in the painful night
And one day God has promised to make all wrongs right.
So hold on my child and know a Savior is close;
He listens to every word you say so pray to Him Just One More Time
Because He cares what's on your mind.

Therefore, as you received Christ Jesus the Lord,
so walk in him, rooted and built up in him and
established in the faith, just as you were taught,
abounding in thanksgiving
(Colossians 2:6–7).

There is a question that keeps resurfacing in our discussions about how best to reach and come alongside people in our community: *Should we go deep with our time and energy; pouring into only a few, or go wide so as many as possible can be reached with the good news of the gospel?*

Both are necessary if we are to see the lasting change we hope for in our sphere of influence. However, to carry out a philosophy of *deep **and** wide* in the context of our urban community requires many resources, a lot of staff, and unlimited time. In the realities of life, it is very hard to do both to the fullest, day in and day out. We are humans with human limitations. So, what are we to do when the need before us is great, but the more involved we get with individuals, the more complicated the problems become?

There are no quick or easy solutions to poverty, generations of brokenness, or habitual addictions. These circumstances can suck the life not only out of the person living in them, but also out of everyone around them, even those who are trying to help them break free. Yet a model of evangelism and discipleship is certainly on the heart of God. In Mark 16:15, Jesus Himself told us to go and preach the gospel to everyone. In Matthew 28:19, He says to go and make disciples (learners, committed followers, students of a teacher). The underlying assumption is clear: one cannot become a disciple unless one has first heard and responded to the gospel.

> *How then will they call on him in whom they have not believed? And how are they to believe in him of whom they have never heard? And how are they to hear without someone preaching?* (Romans 10:14).

Should we be a ministry that just focuses on evangelism, sharing our faith in the Savior whom we know redeems people's lives? Or should we spend our time walking with others for the long haul of discipleship, meeting holistic needs? Once again, both are necessary for the furthering of the body of Christ and for His glory. We know faith without works is dead. Faith alone in Jesus saves us, but our faith is seen and confirmed when we accompany our message of the gospel with deeds of love and kindness. It has always been our desire not just to say Jesus loves you but to demonstrate that love by coming alongside people in physical, spiritual, educational, and social areas of need.

For me it is not a question of whether we should go *deep **or** wide*, it is a question of how do we go *deep **and** wide*? We desire to live out the truth before others in such a way that inspires people to seek the Lord for themselves while He may be found. We have learned much over the years at Urban Vision with the many dear people we have encountered both in the community and those who have served with us. We have learned from our successes and from our failures.

Unfortunately, we have made mistakes, and my greatest regret is that some people have been hurt in the process. Our mistakes have never been intentional, but their outcome is still just as painful. I regret the times when we have helped beyond the point of assisting with an emergency and have created unhealthy dependent relationships that we have had to make right. Not easy at all. I regret that we have sometimes lacked follow through due to lack of resources, and many kids with great potential have been overlooked, with no one to go deep with them. I regret the times we have not relied on God as much as we could have and have allowed self to get in the way.

I have learned much from D. L. Moody, a great preacher in the 1800s, who said, "Keep short accounts with God and man." Moody had an evangelist's heart, desiring many to hear and respond to the good news. Yet he knew that people needed to be trained, men and women alike. Moody recognized the need for both evangelism and discipleship in reaching others and training them to see continued possibilities for expanding God's kingdom. This took time, money, and investment from people who didn't just see the here and now but also wanted to see God's work continue long into the future. As a graduate of Moody Bible Institute, I believe that his vision has carried on, leaving a lasting legacy that is still producing much fruit; fruit that is the result of evangelism and discipleship working together.

Jesus was no stranger to the masses. He loved them and had great compassion for them both spiritually and physically. We see this especially in the story of the feeding of the 5,000 in Matthew 14 and Mark 6. Jesus spoke of His great compassion for the crowd who came to be healed of all their diseases. Jesus said they were like sheep without a shepherd longing for the gentle touch of a shepherd's care. Even though tired Himself, He loved the people and saw past their immediate needs and directly into their hearts. Yes, He would cure them of their diseases and feed their hungry stomachs, but He longed for them to see that He was the Bread of Life, not just to sustain them in the moment but their Sustainer for life, even into eternity.

Yet the Scriptures also show that Jesus saw the importance of pouring a lot of time and energy into those with whom He walked, the twelve disciples. Sometimes He would explain His parables and give in-depth teaching needed for understanding God's heart and purposes. Often, Jesus gave these talks at very practical moments. Even amongst the twelve, Jesus had deeper fellowship time with Peter, James, and John than with the others. They walked with God Himself. Through His life and ministry, both public and private, Jesus gave us His example of how to reach and love people.

Jesus' life and ministry were focused and intentional. He often got up early in the morning to spend time with His Heavenly Father and receive His instructions for the day. I believe this example has helped set my pace in this journey to my edge. Communication with the Father in Jesus' name, as well as listening and being led by His Spirit, are moments I cannot live without. I have learned that there are times when I must present truth to the masses and there are times when I must go and sit, cry, and pray with an individual.

I must be dependent on the Lord's leading in both my personal life and in the life of our ministry as we wrestle with where to put the resources of our time, talent, and treasure. In the recent past, I have often felt misunderstood because many believe that evangelism to the masses is now obsolete. It's true that Kids Club gets a little crazy at times and many could wonder if anything of depth could happen in that atmosphere. With so many children and our rather unique, controlled chaos going on, I keep asking myself if the children are hearing the gospel and feeling loved in this environment. No matter how many kids walk through the doors, I want each of them to know they are seen and loved and welcomed in this place.

With the help of our committed staff and loving volunteers I have seen the impact Kids Club makes on kids, even in a crowd. I know the Holy Spirit goes up and down the rows of kids and speaks to the children's hearts. Some listen, some don't. But if they didn't feel seen and loved, the kids simply would not come back. The good news is that they do come back every week. I know they feel it. I see it in them. I see it as I step into the local elementary school and the kids ask me when Kids Club is. I see it in their smiling faces when they tell me how they love being at Urban Vision. I see it in how quiet the room gets when I teach a Bible lesson and the Word of God comes alive in power and truth, and the story of God's love and forgiveness are spoken before them.

As we have gone deeper with some of the teens by bringing them into our daily Afterschool Program, many of them have told us that their first encounter with Jesus was at Kids Club when they were younger. For us here at Urban Vision that has been the starting point of going deeper. And we must go deeper. While my strength has been on the evangelistic side of the ministry, I have learned that if lasting, sustainable change is going to occur, then we must strive for depth in our kids.

Urban Vision has always had a desire to reach out to children and teens in our community. Kids Club was originally coupled with what we called Teen Night. We would have the teens meet in various places, usually in the homes of our staff members. It was a time to connect with the youth, play games, and have a lesson from God's Word that was applicable to real life situations our youth faced in the city. At times, things could get a little out of hand, especially when we had 3 on 3 basketball tournaments in our yard. One time things got too heated and we had to call the police to help us get the crowd under control. I wasn't sure what was going to happen to Rodney and Jeff Smith in that moment. I hadn't realized how tense basketball could be in our neighborhood, but that day we found out.

We have great memories of sharing our lives and our hearts with these teens, praying that they would see God's plan for their lives. One night Rodney sat in our old station wagon talking with one of the teens who ended up praying right then and there to receive Christ. These were exciting moments. Yet as time went on we realized that just hanging out with our teens was not inspiring the growth we had hoped to see in their lives.

The person who said *life is good* has not seen or heard some of the situations that sometimes confronted us. Life is hard, too hard, and these children and teens were sometimes swept along as innocent victims of life's cruel realities in our community. Yes, some were responding to the gospel, but the pull of the world and our limited follow-through often led them back to making wrong choices and eventually slipping away. Even when we poured a lot of time and energy into a few of them, deep change was still not happening as the norm. Teen pregnancies were still on the rise and the lure of the streets still captured the hearts of too many of our young men. By the time we were in our new building on the hill, we had up to forty teens coming to Teen Night or Teen Club, but we were not seeing the depth we longed for. Something needed to change.

In the summer of 2008, the friends who had originally helped us start Urban Vision, Jeff and Lee Ann Smith, moved back to the states after being missionaries in Turkey for many years. The hard lesson of letting go of good friends was balanced out by the great surprise of learning that sometimes God brings people back. Ministry has always been on the heart of the Smiths and as they moved back here with their two children, Kyra and Tanner, they desired to rejoin us at Urban Vision to walk together to expand God's kingdom work in North Hill.

We love the Smiths; they have been the truest and most sincere friends that Rodney and I have had over the years. Jeff, with his out-of-control, fun-loving style, has won the hearts and trust of many in our community. Lee Ann's kind, caring heart for people and the little ones has added to the quality of what God is doing in and through

Urban Vision. I have known Lee Ann and her family ever since I was a little girl bouncing around on that church bus. Lee Ann's family was one of those my parents would pick up. We have a history together that has made serving together now all the richer. So, the Smith family moved into our community and began asking the questions of how we could best walk with the people of North Hill.

Jeff's focus was to be on the youth of the community and working out a plan that would bring the depth we longed to see in the teens' lives. It didn't take us long to figure out from our perspective that Teen Club could no longer continue the way it was, as just a safe hang-out for teens. So Jeff and Rodney challenged the youth to grow deeper in their relationship with Jesus by coming to our new Leadership Program. Only a third of the teens showed up the first night. We ended up losing a lot of teens who were not interested in going deep. It is not wrong to have a hang-out type of ministry with teens; it provides a safe refuge for kids to be off the streets and in a caring environment. However, with limited resources and wanting to have the greatest impact possible, we decided to put our time and energy into developing teens and not just hanging out with them.

My evangelistic heart struggles often with wanting more and more people to come, but I have learned that if we can go deep with some, then they in turn will reach others. That thought encouraged us as we started our teen Leadership Program. Jeff poured his heart into seeing these few teens develop into men and women who would grow to be kingdom shakers. He even wrote a discipleship study, *What's It All About: 22 Studies for Understanding and Living the Christian Faith*, which we have always called the purple book (Jeff made the cover purple because he loves purple!) These studies address issues of salvation, sin, and mankind's response to a God who loves them. The book is written with fun stories, using characters of real people like themselves, helping them grasp the truths of the Word of God in ways they can understand. It has been a great way to connect the teens to God's Word.

We have seen great things come from these young people as time has gone by. Many of them are now in college (yes, college— they are first generation college attenders!) or some kind of trade school, or are working jobs. We now have some teens and college students who grew up with us who serve as Interns with Urban Vision or volunteer in some capacity. With intense follow-up and educational assistance through the Afterschool Program and the Beacon Christian Learning Center, (which we'll be talking about coming up!), these young people became leaders for the next generation. The ending is yet to be written in their lives, but we can see that switching to the leadership/ discipleship method of reaching our youth has impacted the lifeblood at Urban Vision. We see change and even fruit coming from their lives as many of them share their testimonies and live and give the gospel to their peers.

Many little eyes focus on these teens/young adults as they volunteer in our Kids Club. They are eager to give back, and they love the children in unique ways, having grown up in the neighborhood themselves.

Leadership teens leading their own neighborhood Kids Club:
Top Juvante, Micah, Too Doh Say (Toody),
Eh Kaw Sher Way (Ehki), Joseph

Let me introduce you to a fun-loving, caring, Karen young lady named Ba Bler, otherwise known as Bobbi. Bobbi was one of the first Karen children who walked through the doors of Urban Vision back in 2008. Bobbi has grown up in Kids Club and the teen Leadership Program and has been a part of our Beacon Christian Learning Center. I simply love Bobbi because her heart for Jesus is one that is evident in her compassion toward others, especially the children. She has been an Intern for Urban Vision and puts into practice the things she has learned over the years. She once texted me and asked me to pray for a little girl who was in her group at Kids Club. She said that this girl told her she had no one who loved her. She told me that she told this little girl about God's love and that He was always there for her. How impactful it was for this child to hear this message of love and hope from someone she could look up to and identify with as a young person.
Hear the heart of my sweet friend, Bobbi:

Ba Bler (Bobbi)

What Urban Vision Means to Me

"Urban Vision is where I found my true love, who is Jesus. It is not the kind of love that the world gives. Because, no matter what I am going through, no matter how many times I failed, I know that He will always love me. He loves me with unconditional love. Urban

Vison is the place where I see true, compassionate people and true followers of Jesus Christ. I struggled to love myself because of the way I look and how people view me, but I know that God loves me no matter what because Urban Vision taught me that no one is perfect. God makes me perfect just the way I am and just the way He wants me to be. Urban Vison gives me hope because without it, I would not have known Jesus Christ, who is my Savior and would fall into the lies that the world is telling me. Without Urban Vision's help, I would never be able to live the life that God wants me to live and I would never have a relationship with Him. Without Urban Vision, I don't think I would improve in my academic life, graduate high school, or even go to college. Urban Vision supports, encourages, and motivates me through many things, which are too many to name. Urban Vision gives me the hope, the possibilities, and taught me to believe in myself and that with God I can do anything. Urban Vision is my home. The people there are my family."

We just recently received an essay that one of our UV participants wrote for a school assignment. This young Karen teen has grown up at Urban Vision, has fully participated in Kids Club, is involved in our Afterschool Program, now called S.O.S. (Set On Success), and now is a teen volunteer. She is an amazing young lady who loves God with her whole heart and now gives back in so many ways at Urban Vision. If you saw her in action, how she loves the kids, how patient and loving she is toward others, you would know she is destined for something great in God's plans.

Here are portions of Heh Gay's story:

Hey Gay Moo Brow

"Urban Vision is my treasure, and when we think of treasure we think of gold and money, but my treasure is very valuable to me, and I hold it very dear to my heart. Urban Vision is my treasure because it is my family, it molded me, and it has always taught me the truth.

"I am who I am because of Urban Vision. Urban Vision has taught me a lot of things and one being my personality traits. I have learned valuable lessons such as respect, kindness, patience, love, family, and many more. They even taught me very important life lessons that I am going to use later on in life. God is my first foundation and Urban Vision is my second. They have shaped me for the better.

"One of my favorite things about my treasure is the fact that if I need any help or if I just want to talk, they are always going to be there for me...I love Urban Vision and the people in it. They are there for me and I know I can always trust them."

Heh Gay loves God, loves her family, and loves being around the people at Urban Vision. She closes her essay by saying, "Having one family is great, but having two families (like Urban Vision) is even better!"

These young people are the future of Urban Vision. With their diverse cultural backgrounds, gifts, talents, and their hearts rooted and built up in the Lord, time will tell the great kingdom stories that will come from their lives. God's Word is powerful; it goes deep and wide to accomplish the purposes of the Lord. I have seen some amazing things. As we speak truth into the lives of young people and then walk with them to their edges, they become oaks of righteousness, a planting for His glory (Isaiah 61:3).

We may never have a clear answer on how to go both *deep and wide*. I know we cannot do anything apart from what God wants to do in us as individuals and whatever ministry God has called us to. I know God will accomplish His purposes in us, and the beautiful thing is that when the world just sees a scraggly little tree sprout, God sees a mighty oak flourishing for His glory— deep and wide!

> *For as the rain and the snow come down from heaven and do not return there but water the earth, making it bring forth and sprout, giving seed to the sower and bread to the eater, so shall my word be that goes out from my mouth; it shall not return to me empty, but it shall accomplish that which I purpose, and shall succeed in the thing for which I sent it.*
>
> *For you shall go out in joy and be led forth in peace; the mountains and the hills before you shall break forth into singing, and all the trees of the field shall clap their hands. Instead of the thorn shall come up the cypress; instead of the brier shall come up the myrtle; and it shall make a name for the LORD, an everlasting sign that shall not be cut off* (Isaiah 55:10–13).

CHAPTER 27

UNLIKELY BEAUTIFUL THINGS

But the LORD said to Samuel, "Do not look on his
appearance or on the height of his stature, because
I have rejected him. For the LORD sees not as man sees:
man looks on the outward appearance, but the LORD
looks on the heart"
(1 Samuel 16:7).

I love the stories from the Bible that show how God often chose the most unlikely people to do His work. Gideon hid from his enemies in his winepress. Yet God called him to be a mighty man of valor (Judges 6). Deborah, a wise Jewish woman, taking her position as judge (it was rare to have a female judge in those days), amongst men who would not fight for Israel unless she was with them (Judges 4). Moses, called to lead the people out of Egyptian slavery, with a speech problem that made him feel insecure about going alone even though the great I Am promised to be with him (Exodus 3–4).

One of my favorite characters in the Bible was David, the youngest son of Jesse and a lowly shepherd boy, chosen to be anointed king of Israel by the great prophet of that time, Samuel (1 Samuel 16). Samuel went to Jesse's house knowing he would find the young man that God wanted to replace the disobedient King Saul. Jesse's first son came before the prophet, and Samuel saw his strength and stature and thought surely this must be the one. But God clearly let Samuel know His standards are different from man's. God is always looking at our hearts, never our outward appearance. Seven sons of Jesse passed before Samuel that day but none were God's choice. A little confused, Samuel inquired of Jesse if these were his only sons. Jesse told him of his youngest child, David, who was out watching the sheep. ***Samuel said, "Send and get him; for we will not sit down till he comes here!"*** (vs. 11).

As soon as David came in from the fields, God confirmed that this young man was the chosen one. Then the Word says that the Spirit of God rushed upon David from that day forth. David, the lowly shepherd boy, was now a chosen king of Israel. All that time alone caring for his sheep, protecting them from lions and bears, learning the importance of worship and praise to God, prepared him to be God's heart choice. This ordinary boy who later became a man after God's own heart was chosen for the important task of leading and caring for the people of Israel.

All these people from the Bible were unlikely candidates, just ordinary people called to purposes beyond their understanding, called to the edges of their lives. People just like you and me, whom God desires to have follow His path to places we could not even begin to imagine.

Many times, I have felt so unqualified in my journey to the edge. Why would God choose me to walk this path? So often I would say in my heart, *I am just ordinary Jodi.* I never was super athletic, although I played sports. I never was the first musician, although I played flute, tuba, and cymbals. (Yes, it was quite the odd combination). I never was a valedictorian, even though I got decent grades. I was not gifted enough in any one thing to make me stand out in a crowd. Yet God takes the weak things of this world and uses them for His glory, if surrendered to Him.

In the old devotional *Streams in the Desert*, by L. B. Cowman (Grand Rapids, MI: Zondervan Publishing, 1996), George Matheson was quoted, writing about John the Baptist, highlighting John 10:41–42: ***John did no miracle: but all the things that John spoke of this man [Jesus] were true. And many believed on Him [Jesus] there*** (KJV).

John was the voice crying in the wilderness, ***"Prepare the way of the Lord"*** (Mark 1:3). I would not necessarily categorize John as "ordinary," for I am sure he stuck out with his goat hair apparel and diet of locusts. John did no miracles, yet he used his voice to cause people to think on Christ. Matheson writes, "We are doing more good than we know sowing seed, starting streamlets, giving men true thoughts of Christ to which they may refer one day as the first things that started them thinking of Him."

God wants us to think. God wants us to choose Him by faith, but with clear understanding that our Lord Jesus is the way, the truth and the life (John 14:6). I may be just ordinary Jodi but He has given me a voice to declare the Word of the Lord to the next generation in our little corner of the world. My heart is to let the world know the amazing truth that Jesus loves you and me. Proclaiming the truth at Kids Club may seem simple but it may be the very thing that causes one child to think on Jesus! There are times as I look around at Urban Vision, seeing the children bustling through the halls, that I have thought, *God, thanks for allowing me, just Jodi, to be a tiny part of Your plan.* How grateful I am as I see the vision God put in my heart starting to come into view. It truly was and is a beautiful thing. I love that song, *Beautiful Things* by Gungor, (lyrics by Lisa Gungor and Michael Gungor), that says: *"You make beautiful things out of the dust....You make beautiful things out of us."* Amen!

We have continued to grow from 2007 to the present. We added staff as needed, many of whom had volunteered with us over the years. A young lady named Lauren came on to help us out with our Afterschool Program, as we said, now called S.O.S. for

Set On Success. Lauren also helped us start a ballet program to give our girls a chance to learn and be exposed to the arts. I love watching the girls dance and move with awkward grace as they learn how to twirl and leap. This has grown from our first small class into three levels of about fifty girls learning to love the art of ballet now under the direction of Evie Seifert, a committed staff person. She has appropriately named the ballet ministry In His Steps, encouraging young ladies to worship God through dance. Every time I see them perform it reminds me of the beauty of the Lord in His temple and these are the sweet little ones praising His name before Him. Yes, beautiful ones in the most unlikely places, right in the middle of the city, girls from many cultures declaring together the glory of the Lord! I just can't help but smile and I am sure God does too!

In His Steps ballet girls

There has been growth in programs, growth in staff, growth amongst the many different cultures. Many beautiful things were happening and what a joy it was to be a part of it all. We were able to start a computer lab in which the kids could come and use Rosetta Stone, a language learning software, to learn a different language from their own. A kind-hearted young man named TJ joined our staff, bringing his gifts of math, computers, and art to come alongside the youth of Urban Vision. He helped to put on a drawing contest to design an Urban Vision T-shirt. He and the youth began painting on the walls outside of Urban Vision (in Martha's Garden) to beautify the exterior of our brick wall. He later painted foundational Scriptures on the walls of Urban Vision so that the children who walk the halls can visually take in the Word of God. One verse that he did was Proverbs 29:18, **Where there is no vision, the people perish** (KJV). We want to inspire the children and youth not just to hear and see the Word but to live it out in their own lives.

We recently had more than 137 children attend our summer day camp. It is run mostly by teens under the direction of UV staff member, Jordan Fairfax, and takes place from 9-5 every day. I asked some of our teens what the best thing was about camp and the hardest thing about camp. One of our up and coming young ladies who volunteered almost every day said one simple word. She said the answer to both of those questions for her was most definitely *the kids*. She said, "It was hard, it was long, it was hot, but the kids were worth it!"

2nd and 3rd grade boys at Summer Day Camp 2017

As I went outside before leaving camp one day, I saw a child crying over by the fence, away from everyone else. Before I could do anything about the situation, I saw this same young teen walk across the field and sit down with the hurting child and comfort her. Two girls from different cultures, one Asian and one African-American, connecting at the heart level in God's love and peace, which transcends all barriers and brings grace in a time of need.

Oh, the joy that flooded my soul at seeing a child who herself had grown up at Urban Vision and was now developing into a beautiful servant of God. Without a doubt, love truly was on display in that situation. It was a clear reminder that what we do in Christ makes a difference. No hate, just pure love. Seeing this kind of love in our world today, crossing so many barriers—it's an unlikely beautiful thing!

This girl not only reads the Word on our walls at Urban Vision, she has also embraced the message of the love of Christ in her heart. Beautiful things. Beautiful moments with ordinary people in the most unlikely places.

> *Remember, dear brothers and sisters, that few of you were wise in the world's eyes or powerful or wealthy when God called you. Instead, God chose things the world considers foolish in order to shame those who think they are wise. And he chose things that are powerless to shame those who are powerful. God chose things despised by the world, things counted as nothing at all, and used them to bring to nothing what the world considers important. As a result, no one can ever boast in the presence of God* (1 Corinthians 1:26–29 NLT).

CHAPTER 28

DRIVE-BY PRAYER

Be joyful in hope, patient in affliction, faithful in prayer
(Romans 12:12 NIV).

Prayer has been the lifeline of my relationship with God as I have followed Him in my call to the edge. I am learning to live my life as a prayer and my desire is to stay connected to my Lord and Savior; the One who keeps calling me to Himself. I don't think the verse that says "pray without ceasing" (1 Thessalonians 5:17), means you shut yourself in some room for weeks on end. (Although I once did, unintentionally, come close to that. I was on a retreat and spent some time in prayer and reflection in a small chapel overlooking a beautiful lake. It was really nice, but when I went to exit the chapel, I found that the latch was locked from the outside and I was literally trapped in, giving me the opportunity to try out the whole *pray without ceasing* concept.) I think the verse actually means we are to offer our everyday moments as prayers and be constantly aware of the Lord's presence in our lives. God is not a far-off God; He is up close and personal. I have come to depend on the Lord, knowing that the nearness of God is my good, as the psalmist says in Psalm 73:28: **But as for me, the nearness of God is my good; I have made the Lord GOD my refuge, That I may tell of all Your works** (Psalm 73:28 NASB).

I am thankful for the loving, convicting work of the Holy Spirit in my life. He reminds me right away when I sin and prompts me to quickly confess those sins, knowing He is able to cleanse me from all unrighteousness (1 John 1:9). The Lord calls us to walk in the light and to stay away from the dark shadows (see 1 John 1:5–7 below); His promise is assured. I have great times of fellowship with Him that I surely do not want to miss. Yes, so sweet are those moments when He shows me how very close He is. He speaks to me through His Word, through others, and through amazing sights and circumstances that He has allowed my soul to see on my journey to the edge.

> *This is the message we have heard from him and proclaim to you, that God is light, and in him is no darkness at all. If we say we have fellowship with him while we walk in darkness, we lie and do not practice the truth. But if we walk in the light, as he is in the light, we have fellowship with one another, and the blood of Jesus his Son cleanses us from all sin* (1 John 1:5–7).

Prayer has not always been easy for me. Sometimes I find it very hard to verbally express all that is going on in my mind and heart. Those who know me may think that's not true, since I usually have something to say about most things. But my struggle is real. Journaling my prayers to the Lord has helped me out a lot. When I was in high school, my mentor taught me the importance of prayer, studying God's Word, and journaling. I have always needed time to think, time to process and to gather my thoughts together. As I have gotten older and have learned more about communication with God, I have learned that it is not always what I have to say to God, but it has become more about listening to what He has to say to me.

I would like to share an example of an intimate prayer time with you. I know that some may find fault with this. But I know that if God is responding to me and it does not contradict His Word, then I can rest in knowing that these thoughts coming to me are from the Lord. You'll see below some of my struggle with insecurity, especially regarding my weak eyesight and my weight, which is super personal to me—I don't share this lightly. I have had some great victory in recent years for which I am grateful, but I have to continually remind myself that God's love for me goes much deeper than the natural human eye can see.

Journal entry June 2016

Lord, I have always longed to be accepted. I want approval from others, I want to be liked and looked up to. I have always wanted to be beautiful, wanting so much to be looked upon as special or unique. I have carried with me what I have often called strikes against me (from the world's view) especially with my lazy eye that turns into my nose which causes me to look out of place. No one sees this but me. Hidden away from the view of man I have tried to conceal this secret. (Thank God for contacts even if they are the hard gas permeable kind.) I have also struggled with my weight, being a little heavier than I should be for my height of 5'2". A constant frenzy of working out, an unhealthy obsession with food at times— this has been my struggle. (Sounds pathetic, doesn't it?) Jesus, You have asked me before, "Do you desire acceptance of others more than your completeness in me?" To be quite honest I can't seem to overcome this battle of what I know to be true and what I constantly see in the mirror. Why should all of this matter? How do I change these deadly thought patterns in my life? I want to find wholeness in Your love for me, in Your purpose for me. I know God You made me uniquely me. Yet at times I tell You I don't like me; I don't like what I look like or even worse who I am in this battle. I struggle so much even though You have blessed me more than I could ever hope for with a husband, family, and friends who love me and accept me. What is my problem? (Adapted for clarity.)

In the stillness of my time with God, this was His response to my heart.

Those external looks are not what I see when I see you Jodi. I see your heart for children and love for people to know me. I see your dedication and hard work for your family. I see your joy in knowing me and longing to be with me. I see your faith in my Word, and without faith it is impossible to please me. I see your tender, moldable heart, my child, always seeking the truth. I see your perseverance and your willingness to own up to sin, to make things right in the body of Christ. I see your love that is ever increasing so no child is without the opportunity to know me. No, my child, I do not see those things that you see through your mask. I see much deeper…I don't expect you to show the world all your most intimate weaknesses to prove anything to me. But I would ask that you show to me all of your heart so I can prove to you that is all I have ever wanted. It is beautiful!

I pray that you don't think, *Wow, she just wrote a lot of nice stuff to make herself feel better.* Absolutely not! Yes, it does make me feel better, but the reason I feel better is that the message comes from God Himself. I am His beloved child, flaws and all. His beautiful masterpiece. I have a living relationship with a most gracious, precious Savior and He tells me what He sees in me! I know that unhealthy thoughts consume me way too often. That's the reason that I need to go to God in prayer, tell Him how distorted my thinking is, and ask Him to help me. Then I listen to Him speak Truth into my heart.

When Jesus reminds me of Who He is and what He sees in me, it encourages me to respond with love: **We love because he first loved us** (1 John 4:19). I am learning to love myself in ways that are healthy and God-centered, which means I can then speak into the lives of others who struggle like I do. God is good and although I may not hear Him every time, I am grateful for those still quiet moments when He does gently speak words of life into my soul. I encourage you to try it—take your Bible, a journal, and a pencil, and write your heart to God, and then sit still and listen to what He might have to say to you.

Now, back to the story of Urban Vision...

We continued to add staff as needed, especially in administration to help assist Rodney with office maintenance and grant-writing. McKenzie Baker was one of those young ladies. She was administratively strong, but also loved the kids and worked with our city kids in overnight camp. Evie Seifert who I previously mentioned in regards to ballet, has done amazing work administratively and in helping us write fundraising grants. In 2011, Nate and Jessica Kries joined our staff. They desired to see our vision expand even more. Nate handled our ever-growing S.O.S. afterschool program and coordinated our volunteers and special events like the Christmas and Back to School stores. Jessica also helped with S.O.S.

They both had a heart to see young preschool-aged children in our neighborhood get the help they needed before entering kindergarten. So many of the children in our community are behind before they even get started. With the help of Dee Moore, a woman with many years of experience, they began our On Your Mark program; a readiness program to prepare three- and four-year-olds to embrace the love of learning before entering school. This program has given many children the start they need to be ready to embrace school both educationally and socially.

As we continued to grow and deepen our relationships with children and their families, we couldn't ignore some very difficult challenges faced by our young people, especially our non- English speaking youth. Some of them were involved in our Leadership Program, but they still struggled to read and write. Several of the older non-English speaking students were many grade levels behind where they should have been for their ages. How could they move on with their lives and be successful in any way if they could not speak or communicate in the language of their new home here in the States? Prayerfully, we made it our goal to focus on English development for our non-English speakers, and God gave us the opportunity to come alongside our new friends from Burma in the Karen community. Having the kids for a few minimal hours in our S.O.S. program did not seem to be enough to give the needed help to put our non-English speaking students on grade level. Some of our upcoming middle school students were also being harassed in school, which did not help them learn at all. There were so many obstacles that prevented these students from truly succeeding. Something needed to be done.

After one further incident that needed police involvement, we sought ways to come alongside these children. And that's when the Beacon Christian Learning Center was formed under the leadership of Guida Sweitzer. A beacon is a great light that shines to offer hope in the midst of the storms of life. We wanted to be a light that would shine on the path so that these children and teens could hope for a better future. God tells us in Matthew 5:14, ***You are the light of the world. A city set on a hill cannot be hidden.*** Guida and her husband Dave had been involved from very early on at Urban Vision. Dave has served on our Board of Directors and Guida has been a tremendous resource for educating children. Guida had homeschooled her own six children and had helped provide leadership in a local homeschooling co-op, creating Crown Academy, a school within the co-op itself. She was the perfect choice to come alongside our students at Urban Vision.

Beacon Christian Learning Center students

The school was intended to bridge the gap for some selected children who needed extra help. The plan was for the Beacon Christian Learning Center to work with the students until they were caught up to grade level and could return to public schools. We had twenty-three students. We hired several teachers to assist Guida at the Beacon CLC: Megan Gale, TJ Carrol, and Kaite Marshall. We also had dedicated volunteers (some retired teachers) pouring time into these kids. I will never forget an older retired man the kids called Mr. Jim who came practically every day to be with some of our younger Beacon students. I would occasionally peek in on the class and find Mr. Jim sitting with one of the boys as he read to Mr. Jim. It was no small act of God to keep this particular boy still, but how he loved Mr. Jim. Every now and then the young boy would lean his head on Mr. Jim's shoulder as he did his work. This boy had lost his mother in a house fire and was being raised by Grandma. He learned so much better in this environment, where someone took the time to be patient with this conflicted little boy who had dealt with so much in his young life. It's a great picture of prayer; that dependence on God as we, His children, struggle and yet find a place of rest and comfort near our Savior.

> *O LORD, my heart is not lifted up; my eyes are not raised too high; I do not occupy myself with things too great and too marvelous for me. But I have calmed and quieted my soul, like a weaned child with its mother; like a weaned child is my soul within me* (Psalm 131:1–2).

We were able to do this school under the umbrella of Ohio Virtual Academy. They actually used Beacon as a pilot program for working with non-English speaking youth. We have already had a couple of graduations, and it's a great joy to watch these young adults go forth, equipped with the confidence and the skills they need to pursue college or other vocational work.

Everything that has been done, and everything that will continue to happen, is a result of prayer. As we walk closely with God, our heart becomes His heart. God brings situations or needs to our attention through His Spirit. With His help on our journey to the edge we can begin to see His vision unfold as He gives us the power to enact it in life and ministry. Let us continue to seek His heart, dwelling in the consciousness of prayer without ceasing: **Seek the LORD and His strength; seek His presence continually!** (Psalm 105:4).

Our heart for children has been, and will always be, at the heart of Urban Vision: **Let the little children come, and do not hinder them, for to such belongs the kingdom of heaven** (Matthew 19:14).

Early on in my experience working with children in the city, I saw that so many of them just needed love, attention, and the Truth of God spoken into their lives. I can remember teaching kids in some interesting situations, especially when we did Bible Clubs out in the community in vacant yards, on porches, or just on the sidewalks. There would be loud neighbors, blaring music that drowned out the stories we were teaching, and ambulances or police sirens in the background adding still more distractions. Yet even in all this apparent chaos, the kids would still come and sit down on the blanket and hear a story about Jesus.

The story of Jesus is powerful and all the kids loved the songs, puppets, and the special sticker they would get for saying their Bible verses. Line upon line, precept upon precept, teaching God's Word has taught me that I can do nothing without the Lord. I have learned to cry out to Him frequently, learning to live the *pray without ceasing* attitude. God loves the children. He wants us to love the children in our lives, to speak the truth that He has a plan for them, and then to walk with them to help them discover this plan for themselves.

I wrote this poem expressing that our enemy, Satan, has a plan too. But God's heart is to bring the children to Himself.

Let the Children Come
—Jodi M. Matthews

Satan says I will love the children; you bring them unto me.
For I will fill their minds with junk and I will use their bodies.
Satan says I will love the children, the ones who are alone.
To keep them in the darkest night, just hear their painful groans.
Satan says I will love the children, the ones who I can train
To sell the drugs to make a buck, my evil it will reign.
Then on the scene the living Word stood and spoke so clear.
He placed a child within the midst and He wiped all their tears.
Then Jesus said I will love these children; you bring them unto me.
For I loved them through my life and death when I died there on
that tree.
Jesus then asks do you love these children just as much as me?
For such is the kingdom of heaven for all eternity!

Throughout the years, the movement of God has surely been seen, but in the unseen there were women praying. Women from the community would gather and pray for God's will to be done right here in our little corner of the world. These ladies are strong; they've faced much difficulty over the years, but still they pray the heart and will of God. We need to be surrounded with people like this. There have been seasons in my life when there were not a lot of people who wanted to pray, but it's a great thing when you can find the ones who do. There's no telling what God will do through people seeking Him and praying for His kingdom to come on earth as it is in heaven.

We had also begun a Bible study for women (moms) in the community so that they could also seek God in relationship. We went through many studies together and I started to see some growth in some of them. Yet the enemy is not pleased when we seek God. We went through a very difficult season during which the enemy stirred up some issues at UV. There were times when

I felt that all I did was put out little fires. In the midst of all the mistrust, unkind words, and attitudes, all I could do was cry out to the Lord for His strength. I am not equipped to handle conflict like this. I just want to love people and share the good news.

Of course, God was working on me in the process. I had to learn that it is not so much the fact of what is going on around me as it is how I respond to it. *For our struggle is not against flesh and blood, but against the rulers, against the authorities, against the powers of this dark world and against the spiritual forces of evil in the heavenly realms. Therefore put on the full armor of God, so that when the day of evil comes, you may be able to stand your ground, and after you have done everything, to stand* (Ephesians 6:12–13 NIV). I knew in my heart that enough was enough. A house divided against itself will fall. The action of prayer was needed—9-1-1—I needed Jesus now!

I called my dear African-American friend and mentor, crying out my woes and telling her that all had been lost. She gave me some advice that helps to this day. She said, "Go ahead and cry, Jodi. You will cry for a moment but you will be okay. Jesus got this all under control." She continued with her treasured words of wisdom and added, "You know, sister, I often do the drive-by at Urban Vision, the drive-by prayer every time I pass on by." I told her I was sure she had seen smoke signals of distress coming out from all the explosions inside the building (Ha ha). How thankful I was for these prayers and the voice of truth that came with them. Jesus is the only One who can work it out, and He did. Yes, we were tear-stained and weary, but God works out all things that are surrendered to His will.

These were hard times for all involved and there were scars left behind, but God is our healer. He knows our frames, He knows how fragile and frail we are and how often we don't respond rightly in the moment. I have needed that grace many times over the years. I have made my share of mistakes and have sinned often, but I am thankful God has led us through the fire and the flood, and has made us all the stronger. These verses in Isaiah have often comforted me as God comforts His people of Israel: *But now thus says the LORD, he who created you, O Jacob, he who formed you, O Israel: "Fear not, for I have redeemed you; I have called you by name, you are mine. When you pass through the waters, I will be with you; and through the rivers, they shall not overwhelm you; when you walk through fire you shall not be burned, and the flame shall not consume you. For I am the LORD your God, the Holy One of Israel, your Savior* (Isaiah 43:1–3).

I have often found comfort in just pouring my heart out to the Lord, knowing He sees me and loves me and that He will enable me to get to the edge He calls me to. We may be scarred, bumped, and bruised, but so was Jesus—a man who was definitely acquainted with many sorrows (Isaiah 53:3). God is our great advocate and even prays for me through the Holy Spirit when I can't even utter a word:

> *Likewise the Spirit helps us in our weakness. For we do not know what to pray for as we ought, but the Spirit himself intercedes for us with groanings too deep for words. And he who searches hearts knows what is the mind of the Spirit, because the Spirit intercedes for the saints according to the will of God* (Romans 8:26–27).

Over the years we have had our house and our vehicle in the path of drive-by bullets. We are thankful that in our case, no one was harmed, although that is unfortunately not the case with others in the city. My heart goes out to the innocent ones who have been in the path of someone else's destructive heart. Oh, how we need God in our lives to help us through this journey we are on. Pray, pray, and pray some more! We can never over communicate the power of prayer; but we definitely underestimate it. I am learning to run to Jesus, fall on my knees, cry in my moment, and then rise up with the confidence that He is with me. When we live with a posture of *praying without ceasing*, we can know and experience the presence of God and be ready to respond well to every trial we face, and, as we said at the beginning of this chapter, being **Joyful in hope, patient in affliction, faithful in prayer** (Romans 12:12 NIV).

Drive-by bullets are never wanted, but drive-by prayers are a must! So, to all you prayer warriors out there: drive by and pray on!

Make My Life a Prayer to You
—Melody and Keith Green

Make my life a prayer to you
I wanna do what you want me to
No empty words and no white lies
No token prayers no compromise

I wanna shine the light you gave
Through your Son you sent to save us
From ourselves and our despair
It comforts me to know you're really there

(I want to encourage you to go and listen to the whole song. It has been a blessing to me and I pray it will encourage you too!)

CHAPTER 29

A PLACE CALLED HOME

*So then you are no longer strangers and aliens, but
you are fellow citizens with the saints and members of
the household of God, built on the foundation of the
apostles and prophets, Christ Jesus himself being
the cornerstone, in whom the whole structure,
being joined together, grows into a holy temple in
the Lord. In him you also are being built together
into a dwelling place for God by the Spirit*
(Ephesians 2:19–22).

The word *home* should bring to mind a safe place in which to share life with those you are closest to. I know that this is not always the case for everyone in the world. There are people all around us who may live in a structure they call *home*, but that place is not their safe refuge. I have met some people in that situation over the years, but I have also met people who may not have a lot in their homes, but their homes are filled with love and respect for the people they care for the most. They say home is where your heart is, and if your heart is deeply connected to those in that home, I would say I agree. I am certainly thankful for the home I share with my husband, our three nearly grown sons, and our two dogs (Okay, thankful might not be the right word to use when referencing my dogs since they tend to drive me a little crazy!).

Over the years, we have had the opportunity to be a part of a few different bodies of Christ where we would fellowship and worship with other believers. When I say *different* I mean that they have ranged from conservative to Pentecostal and from small to large, and have been culturally very different. God has met us in each, as we made meeting together with other believers a priority in our lives and ministry. I feel strongly about being part of a body that challenges one another and cares for one another through life's ups and downs. A place in which each person uses his/her God-given gifts to edify the body as a whole. This is described in Hebrews 10:24–25: ***And let us consider how to stir up one another to love and good works, not neglecting to meet together, as is the habit of some, but encouraging one another, and all the more as you see the Day drawing near.***

We attended several churches that had excellent teaching and leadership, but as a couple we never found a church we could really call home. From the very beginning of our ministry I had great hopes that Urban Vision could partner with a local church within our urban community and work together as a team. I imagined that Urban Vision would focus on outreach while the church would focus on shepherding the people in the community who needed someone to walk alongside them for the long haul. I dreamt of a diverse group of people worshipping together across cultural and economic barriers. I wanted us to tear down walls so that 11:00 on Sunday mornings would no longer be the most segregated hour of the week.

Usually, in our homes, we talk like each other and we look like each other, and that makes us feel comfortable. However, I am not convinced that this same-ness should be a part of our church homes. A church in which everyone talks like each other and looks like each other does not represent the kingdom of heaven. Just visualize this scene in heaven…

> *After this I looked, and behold, a great multitude that no one could number, from every nation, from all tribes and peoples and languages, standing before the throne and before the Lamb, clothed in white robes, with palm branches in their hands, and crying out with a loud voice, "Salvation belongs to our God who sits on the throne, and to the Lamb!"* (Revelation 7:9–10).

Simply amazing! Simply beautiful! My heart yearned for a home like this!

Over the years, I have both observed and learned through personal experience that multicultural churches don't just happen. They are grown out of a labor of intentional love when believers in Christ, who look different from one another and come from different backgrounds, are willing to say, *I'm willing to make this church family my home.*

We wanted to be in a church with people with whom we could do life, study God's Word, serve, and see change in the community. This kind of church would take time, relationship building, and much prayer and understanding. Having a home church like that comes at a cost. We each bring in much baggage, which can keep us from truly loving one another. A look into the mirror of God's Word has often revealed sin issues that I chose to hang on to. Issues that kept me from seeing myself and others from God's viewpoint.

Even in the body of Christ, we keep from engaging with one another due to sins of pride, prejudice, misunderstandings, and sometimes even anger or hate wrongly projected onto those who are different from us. Good housekeeping is important in any home, but let's be honest: how many of us really like to do the hard kind of cleaning when a simple gloss over will do? I mean, come on now, who actually dusts anymore? (Okay, I know some of you out there do dust and keep everything neat and pristine, but for me cleaning house is a constant task that takes a lot of time and energy, and I find I am lacking in both. Please don't even get me started about the mounds of laundry in my basement. Don't judge me, just pray for me!)

Since 2012, there have been several young couples who have decided to follow their call to the edge and move into the city to either be on staff with Urban Vision or to volunteer with us on a deeper level. People like Jordan and Rachel Fairfax, who moved their young family to North Hill and came on staff with UV to help develop our donor base and communicate with them our ever-expanding needs. Kaite Marshall continues to work at the Beacon Christian Learning Center and UV, and she and her husband James have purchased a home in the community. Evie and her husband Ian Seifert have been living in the community and have a heart to see our neighborhood change from the inside out. Tom and Fiona Paisley have also started working for UV and are investing their lives in our community. Tom's parents have also moved into the community and are committed to seeing God's kingdom work continue through Boy Scouts for youth and English language learning for adult refugees.

Bruce and Carol Britten have become a beautiful part of the Urban Vision family. They served as missionaries in Swaziland for more than forty years, and when they retired, they chose to settle in North Hill and to continue ministering through the teaching of God's Word and just loving others in the community in a very caring, personal way. They could have moved anywhere, but chose to live life with us. I constantly see the Brittens out in the neighborhood catching the bus and engaging with others around them. They are such great examples for all of us. I want to be like them when I grow up!

These are all testimonies of God working in His people for a greater good. And there have been others whom I have not mentioned who made the commitment to share in a dream of seeing God's people be salt and light. God has used each one greatly, knitting our hearts together with a call to be a part of something bigger than all of us. How exciting it has been to see people catch the vision of seeing our community of need restored.

It is super exciting for me when someone who lives in our neighborhood catches the vision and comes alongside us to help make the vision become a reality. People who are already a part of the community and desire to be a part of the change from within. People like Miss Regina, our dear sister in the Lord, who has two sons in our Urban Vision programming. She started off by sending her boys to Kids Club, and then she began volunteering her time, and now she is on staff. Miss Regina is literally the first person everyone connects with when they walk into the doors of Urban Vision. I often tell her I am so thankful that God put her as the door keeper in this place. God is working in her life as she greets people with a warm smile and welcoming spirit. She genuinely loves all people from all cultures and has a love and giftedness to reach out to those with special needs, stemming from her love for her own son who has special needs as well. We get a glimpse into her heart through this story she told about summer camp:

One little boy was a camper at one of our UV summer camps, and through his mom we learned he was autistic. During meal time, with almost seventy kids in the dining room, the noises would be a bit much for him so I would bring him in the kitchen with me. His distressed look from the noise soon turned into smiles and laughter. We talked and laughed a lot together. On the last day, I spoke to the mom and she said that her son talked of nothing but camp and that was a big deal for this autistic child, because he did not warm up to strangers easily. This little boy asked for a Bible and said that he wanted to stay at Urban Vision forever, even sleep here! That child made me cry. Camp UV definitely made an impact not only on this child and me as a staff member but on his mother as well, as she began to trust us more and more with her precious son.

I can also tell you of another dear African-American woman whose two daughters have been part of Urban Vision over the last ten years.

She is Linda Johnson, and she loves Jesus. She is my prayer sister in the Lord and has been there for me personally in so many ways. She is a true reconciler, willing to bridge the gap. We have been through much together with the women of our community as we have called out to Jesus to lead, guide, and direct us. When God started prompting me to write this book and to start writing and doing Bible studies, she was a great encourager. She has gone with me, prayed for me, and encouraged me when at times I have felt very alone. Linda and another sweet sister, Susie Hayes, both planted in me the seeds of courage I needed in order to begin the process of writing this story down. I have had many true encouragers along the way. They are the beauty I have grown to see, love, and experience in the body of Christ.

Every Tuesday, regardless of rain, snow, sun, or freezing temps, my dear sister in Christ, Clorinda Tucker, walks and prays with me and for me, our families, the ministry, and the community. How I thank God that I have praying women around me to help me run to the throne room of grace where we find strength to face life. That is the definition of a home, where people face life together and find hope to carry on. We have had so much to be thankful for as God has brought people together. When people live, love, and work together to see the community change from the power of the gospel, great things can happen. This can only be a work from God and we give Him all the glory. If anyone wants to shout, *Hallelujah, great things He has done!* with me, just let it go!

Those who have come alongside us share in our vision to see a vibrant unified community transformed by the love and hope of Jesus Christ. Our mission through Urban Vision is:

> To live out the gospel of Jesus Christ in North Hill by coming alongside children and their families as they discover Christ's vision for themselves and their community, through relationships focused on building dignity, inspiring unity, empowering futures, and meeting holistic needs.

This is a work that can only be done through God and the people He draws together to see His kingdom come, His will be done on earth as it is in heaven. This is what we all should call home: a place to love God and to love others wherever He has placed us—so that many come to know the truth of the Word of God. We need the church to be that place of refuge for all, not only for kids but for families from all cultures to come and for young people to return and call this place of worship *home*. A house of prayer for all nations (Mark 11:17).

Being impatient, I wanted Urban Vision to have a church (a place where we could worship together on Sundays) on day one, but I now realize that God had to lead me down a path of humility, teaching me not to focus on my plans but to wait for Him to unfold His. His plan unfolded a lot slower than I'd liked, which was yet another reminder of who is really in charge.

We did a lot of things together at Urban Vision but I also wanted to worship and enter into Sabbath rest with those we loved. Over the last twenty-five years there have been a few attempts to start a church. What humbling learning experiences these were. Things didn't always happen the way I hoped they would, yet God's timing and His ways are always perfect and His grace is sufficient.

I desired a place for the kids to come with their families that wasn't based on what clothes you were wearing or how much money you had or what culture you were from. I desired a place where our teens could have a place of community in Christ so they could stay connected and feel loved. I wanted a place in which the presence of the Lord was felt and no one was concerned about the carpet or the color of paint on the walls, or what we would be serving for potluck dinners. Just a simple place to worship God in spirit and truth. I wanted people from many cultures who truly knew each other like a family.

Forming a church like that doesn't just happen overnight. There were moments on the journey when my hopes were high, but then were dashed, and I just didn't know how or even if it would ever come together. We have all had our share of hurts and disappointments when it comes to being a part of a church home. Why? Because we are each a work in progress, in different places and in different seasons. Oh, how we need Jesus to help us to put all the pieces together!

There was a young girl named Tamara (her name has been changed) who came to our Kids Club a long time ago. She did not have much support growing up, living with a grandma who struggled with alcohol. Tamara went to an overnight church camp one year through a camp sponsorship from Urban Vision and she just loved it. The week away from her difficult environment transformed this little girl. We sang camp songs about Jesus all the way home, and somehow were thinking that she would be warmly welcomed when she got back. This was anything but the case. Tamara walked into a dark, smoke-filled room and found Grandma passed out on the couch. I literally watched the light-hearted, free Tamara change back to the girl filled with oppression, discouragement, and despair. Tamara wanted to return to a home in which someone loved her and wanted to hear stories about her week at camp, but that wasn't her reality.

Tamara's story continued. She tried out several churches, getting involved in any church that opened the doors. She would go to one place for a while and then switch to another, never rooting herself anywhere in particular. Tamara had a beautiful voice and loved to sing. Once, she called me for a ride home from choir practice at one of the churches. She was hopeful for a part in the choir. As I drove, I wondered how long it would take before she moved on, and then wondered if anyone at any of these churches had ever noticed when Tamara stopped showing up. Yet in all the places she went she couldn't find a home, a place of belonging. Are we, the church, so busy *doing* church that we miss opportunities to *be* the church for people like Tamara? The situation prompted to me to write this poem:

Tamara's Song
—Jodi M. Matthews

A little girl on her own came to church one day
And saw the choir sing a song, the pastor preach and pray.
And the choir sings on and on, and the choir sang their song

She saw there in the choir an empty spot to fill,
They said come and join us, and she said, "I will."
And the choir sings on and on, and the choir sang their song.

No one knew this girl, where or how she came.
No one knew the thoughts she had, only that she could sing the same.
And the choir sings on and on, and the choir sang their song.

Her mom on drugs, her life a mess, her grandma didn't care.
She still went to church each week to fill her spot right there.
And the choir sings on and on, and the choir sang their song.

One day the girl was missing for her solo she would sing.
Instead of finding help for her, they just did there thing.
And the choir sings on and on, and the choir sang their song.

The little girl now grown, a teen, is only to be found
Hanging with her street life friends, with trouble all around.
And the choir sings on and on, and the choir sang their song.

Her spot was vacant for a while, no one bothered to see
What happened to that girl that stood there so faithfully?
And the choir still sings on and on, and the choir sang their song.

Well the spot was taken once again by a boy who sang so well,
While the girl who once stood there now stands at the gates of hell.
Yet the choir still sings on and on, yes, the choir still sings their song!

To be quite honest, for me it always took a while before I'd even begin to consider a church to be a home. I had seen too much of what I didn't want church to be, and somehow a bitterness grew in me, and I wasn't even aware of it. The truth is that I had an attitude. Instead of seeing Christ and His church as something that could work together, I saw the church as too broken, too messed up. So many have dealt with hurt and pain from the world, but also from fellow brothers and sisters in Christ. David knew that pain of betrayal from someone with whom he once had sweet fellowship: *Even my close friend in whom I trusted, who ate my bread, has lifted his heel against me* (Psalm 41:9).

Listen, I am not pointing fingers here. We all know the saying that if you find a perfect church, stop going because you will mess it up! And the other saying—if you point a finger, you will find many more pointing right back at you. There is truth in these sayings, but there is also truth and a painful reality in the fact that sometimes innocent people get hurt by others. We are fallen, broken people who don't always operate in the Spirit.

I am not sure why I was so angry. Maybe because I have seen way too many people damaged in the name of Christ. Unfortunately, I may well be amongst those who have done damage to others— through gossip, betrayal, lack of genuine love, and failure to see God's heart for the gospel and true discipleship. Also through caring more for material things than caring for hurting people, and through staying at a surface level of involvement in others' lives. Sometimes we focus more on our agendas than on truly caring for people.

To be honest, the bitter taste in my mouth was something that lingered way too long. Needing something or someone on which to project my hurt and blame, I chose the church. If the church had the love answer to life's questions, then why were so many of God's people hurting and not feeling loved by those who claimed to be transformed by God? It didn't make sense to me and I used that confusion as an excuse to blame the church. Instead of pouring out my disgruntled attitude to God, I became what I thought was a seething pot of righteous anger.

There were some great injustices and hurt happening amongst believers. Many of us have felt that sting way too often. Somehow I thought it was my duty to take up the offenses of others and put the blame on the very institution God has ordained to bring healing to our hurting hearts. In my own hurt and in seeing the hurt of others, I wanted to take matters into my own hands. How tragic and sinful this was of me.

Early in the ministry I went to meet with an associate pastor at a fairly large church to share about Urban Vision, hoping they would want to get behind us in our Kids Club program. As I walked through the large halls with beautiful decorations I felt a little intimidated about sharing our story. It wasn't long into our conversation before the pastor let me know that they did not offer salvation to children under the age of twelve. This comment disturbed me, since I had come to Christ at the age of four, and we had just buried Jessie—the twelve-year-old Kids Club participant who had died. I wondered: *What if he hadn't been offered salvation before the age of twelve?*

All I know is that when the Scripture tells us to *come like a child* and Jesus said *let the children come* I believe it means that children can know and receive the message of truth. We chatted for a little while more, as he had told me how much the church does in the community and how they have been there for many years doing God's work. Before I left, he gifted me with a copy of a book they had just published about the rich history of their church. I left the office with book in hand, feeling sad that their church believed children were not mature enough to understand the gospel.

I did not debate with him, nor was I his judge or jury, but I grieved in my heart because the children I met (some from very difficult backgrounds) needed to know Jesus loved them and invited them to the table too. Life is fragile and never to be taken for granted.

I walked out the door without looking at the book. Later, when one of my prayer partners asked me how it went, I recounted the story with great sadness. Together we opened the book he had given me. It was hard cover, with the name of the church etched into a maroon background. As I began to flip through the pages, I saw that there were no pictures, no words, no page numbers. Somehow that particular copy had been bound with all blank pages. How unlikely to have a whole book with all the pages missing versus maybe a few here and there that missed printing.

I almost dropped it, feeling as if God shot a message straight into my heart. I felt that God was telling me, *You can do a lot of great things and boast of a lot of accomplishments and even be around for a long time, but if you are not seeking my heart, my presence, my love for people, including children, my will in my kingdom plan, and most of all my heart for the church, it's all for nothing.* I felt that the message of that experience was that everything we think we have accomplished shows up as blank pages in God's eyes when done with wrong motives or attitudes. Wood, hay, and stubble burnt up:

> **Now if anyone builds on the foundation with gold, silver, precious stones, wood, hay, straw— each one's work will become manifest, for the Day will disclose it, because it will be revealed by fire, and the fire will test what sort of work each one has done. If the work that anyone has built on the foundation survives, he will receive a reward. If anyone's work is burned up, he will suffer loss, though he himself will be saved, but only as through fire** (1 Corinthians 3:12–15).

To this day I have never shared the name of this church or even hinted who it was again to anyone. That is not my place. Who am I to judge? But I still have that book as a reminder that only what is done for Christ in a spirit of love will last.

Even with all my hang-ups I didn't just want to do church, I wanted to be a part of a real, active extension of Christ. If you asked me if I loved Jesus, the answer was *most definitely yes*, but the church—not so much. Then God clearly confronted me with the truth that love does cover a multitude of sins. How could I love God yet have such issue with how He chooses to express Himself through broken people in the church, even when His children are often disobedient and not willing to do the very things He asks, like loving others no matter what? In my attitude of do-good outreach and strong justice for all, it was easy to slip into my own justified anger, which was just as hateful and destructive as those I criticized for being unloving to the least of these.

One time God clearly confronted me about my lack of love for His church. *Jodi, how can you not love my bride, the one whom I love and died for? Jodi, you are a part of that bride.* As much as I wanted to disassociate myself from the church, the truth burned deep into my soul. I could not be seen as separate from the church body and survive, any more than a hand could live without the arm or the rest of the body as well. *Jodi, you do loving things but you are not loving me in the process. It is just noise to me!* Hear the Word of the Lord:

> **If I speak in the tongues of men and of angels, but have not love, I am a noisy gong or a clanging cymbal. And if I have prophetic powers, and understand all mysteries and all knowledge, and if I have all faith, so as to remove mountains, but have not love, I am nothing. If I give away all I have, and if I deliver up my body to be burned but have not love, I gain nothing** (1 Corinthians 13:1–3).

Scripture is clear that it's possible to do a lot of good things and still miss the point of doing them in love. How tragic my bitterness might have been if God had not confronted me about the need to love His church, His bride, no matter how messed up I thought it might be. God uses the church to execute His will for this world. Somehow He takes our beautiful, and not so beautiful, stories and weaves them into a masterpiece as only He can do. We are the extension of Christ to a hurting, dying world that needs to know the love of Jesus. God began to help me move from focusing on what was wrong, toward getting behind what was right in His church. Instead of a critical, judgmental spirit (which comes so easily for me at times), God began to give me eyes for the hurting church. To be the change we want to see. I needed to be that change, but the bottom line was that Jesus first needed to change me. *Oh God, how truly sorry I am for not loving the very thing You love, died, and rose again for, and will come back for.*

A cleansing flood washed over me as I began to stop *doing love* and started *being love*. I say all this knowing there is still much to look at within the body of Christ. We cannot just say, *Well, God loves the church no matter what* (which is true), *therefore, we can stay in the state we are in.* God forbid! How can we, who know the truth, continue to take advantage of His grace and love (Romans 7)? This is not God's heart or intention for us. Often in Scripture God calls His church, His people, to wake up from our slumber and let Christ shine in us. Wake up, Jodi. Wake up, Believer. Wake up, church, and listen intently to the heart of God on our journeys to the edge.

In September 2015, North Side Open Door Church was formed and started meeting in the Urban Vision building. We are not a large church, but we are a multicultural church family that loves one another deeply. We have families that have participated in Urban Vision who have been faithfully attending. Many of the people on our staff, along with some volunteers and people in the community, come together to study God's Word and worship the Lord together. We have a faithful group of teens and young adults who helped form the church as they expressed a desire for such a place. Appropriately, our founding pastor, Jeff Smith, was the one who has trained our youth through leadership development over the years.

There was one special Sunday during that fall when we first began meeting as a church. The sun was shining, the yellow and orange foliage was stunning, and I just had so much joy as I returned home from church. I went outside and lay down on an old picnic table bench and soaked in that fall sunshine with a huge smile beaming from my soul. A long-awaited dream had become a reality, but even more beautiful to me was the fact that I finally had a place to call home. A home with people I loved, people who were different from me, people who would love and challenge me to pursue the heart of God. Yes, there is no place like home! How thankful I am that God didn't leave me in my sinful state, but led me with His heart to a place where now my heart is too. His beautiful church, my home!

I hope and pray that you have found and are actively part of a church home that really loves God and loves others well. If not yet, here is some advice from a fellow traveler who has learned the hard way: be patient, keep praying, be reflective, be repentant when needed, be humble, and love the bride of Christ—flaws and all. Be the change you want to see! Dear friends, be the church. Amen!

The Stranger among Us
—Jodi M. Matthews

One day a youth stood watching the church folk do their thing. The Deacon prayed, their Preacher preached, the choir would sing and sing.

Nothing too unusual was going on in there; children ran through the hall, when one said, "We don't do that here."

Some were sleeping in the pew while others talked, the news about the woman whose dress was short was the gossip of a few.

There was a light in one or two or three, whose love shone from their eyes. They were in the minority.

The youth happened to notice a stranger at the door, waiting to be welcomed never seen before.

And although most did not see him how he hoped they would so, the stranger walked through the door and quietly he stood.

His eyes full of mercy, his hands were open wide, yet in the hustle bustle the stranger seemed pushed aside.

Truth has stumbled in the streets is what the prophet said, but truth is scarcely to be found in the bride He wed.

So the stranger left the place he thought he would call home, to seek out the ones who would make their hearts Christ throne.

The youth pursued Him out the door, the stranger turned around; His eyes lit up for the hope this youth had found.

Oh my child who showed some love, I will stay with you; let's call the others back to Him, for I do love them too.

Oh how I love My bride, though imperfect may it be. Please welcome back the King of Kings for that stranger once was me.
—Jesus

CHAPTER 30

PATHWAY TO HIS PRESENCE

But the path of the righteous is like the light of dawn,
which shines brighter and brighter until full day
(Proverbs 4:18).

A picture is worth a thousand words. I love family photos taken in years gone by, especially photos of the boys when they were young. I find myself getting lost in the details of every picture. Details like the cute little dimples of Nathanael's baby picture, or the huge smile and sparkling eyes on Joseph's face as he roller skates with his Karen friend, or three-year-old Micah's little legs dangling off the computer chair as he played some strategy game with his dad. Photos allow me to revisit moments in time that are long gone but that remain as memories in my heart.

Micah at three years old, playing a
strategy game on the computer

I love all the photos I have with many of the beautiful children and families I have had the joy of knowing over the years at Urban Vision. I love the picture of our three little African-American neighbor girls playing in a big cardboard box with Micah, all four of them smiling from ear to ear. So many pictures, so many memories. If you walk into my house, you may not find a lot of organization but you will see pictures lovingly displayed on the walls, on the shelves, and of course—all over the refrigerator. (Some of you sweet organized people out there are just cringing at the thought of a million pictures all over my fridge! Isn't that the purpose of the refrigerator anyway? Ha ha!)

A picture is the visual of a memory that will bring different feelings, emotions, and words back to our spirit. It is a way to recapture the past and allow us to dwell on it now, in the present. It is a reminder, a visual representation, of what we have been through, where we have been, and those whom we love very dearly. We all have these snapshots, these unique portraits that stir within us a thousand words of emotions.

Throughout the pages of this book, I have prayerfully tried to display some of these snapshots through words, hoping to stir within you the courage to follow God's call to the edges He has in mind for you. My prayer as I have been writing is that you, as the reader, would see a picture through my eyes; what it has meant for God to call me to my edge on this journey of Urban Vision, and that with a prayer of faith, you too will get a vision to step toward your edge as well. We have had a lot of ground to cover but I pray that every step has taken us closer to following the plans He has for you and for me. Plans to lead us all along the pathway to His presence.

God has given us a picture, a vision, an Urban Vision, that even twenty-five years later is still about reaching the community for Christ, one child and family at a time. Proverbs 29:18 says, **Where there is no vision, the people perish** (KJV). It is very clear from the Word and through seeing ministry before my eyes that we need a vision. We need hope, we need to be able to catch a glimpse of this hope so that we will have enough strength to get up and face one more day. A vision or a hope will carry a person through many things because they are assured through faith in God that He is who He says He is, and one day all will be made right. **Now faith is the assurance of things hoped for, the conviction of things not seen** (Hebrews 11:1).

As the years have passed on this journey to my edge, the fog has lifted and I have had the joy of seeing much of the vision God put on my heart come to fruition. Now, in 2017, God has brought Rodney and me, and the family at Urban Vision, to a place I only dreamed of so many years ago. So many people from so many different cultures from all over the world have now crossed the doorsteps of Urban Vision. Children fill the hallways and rooms of Urban Vision as we try to fill their hearts with the understanding of who they are and encourage them to follow God to the edges He has for each of them. Volunteers representing many area churches come together to make a difference in our little community of North Hill. Partnerships have formed for the good of the community—and God has led us all the way! I praise Him with the psalmist: *Many, LORD my God, are the wonders you have done, the things you planned for us. None can compare with you; were I to speak and tell of your deeds, they would be too many to declare* (Psalm 40:5).

As we have journeyed, we have learned to walk not with eyes on the ground, focused on the step in front of us, but with eyes focused on the One who calls us to step in the first place. We need to keep looking up so a clear vision of God and His glory can be imprinted on our very souls. Oh, to look more and more like Jesus, reflecting His heart—that is what the journey is really about.

I highly recommend A. W. Tozer's book, *The Knowledge of the Holy* (Grand Rapids, MI: Family Christian Press, 2001). Although at times weighty in word, it is so worth the time to dwell on what Tozer writes because he helps us see God's character. We need to see His character, His attributes, in order to get an accurate picture of God and His presence. An attribute is a quality or feature regarded as a characteristic or inherent part of someone or something. His attributes tell truths about God in ways we can understand. Tozer says it well: "An attribute as we know it is a mental concept, an intellectual response to God's self-revelation."

How encouraged we should all be that we have Jesus, God's Son, who came to be a physical presence amongst His people. We have Jesus, an exact representation of God in character and likeness (Hebrews 1:3). Jesus Himself claimed: *Whoever has seen me has seen the Father* (John 14:9–11). Look at His faithfulness, His immutability, His power, His unconditional love, and the list goes on and on. We may not have a portrait of God, but we have His Living Word that works in us, through His Spirit, to reveal the great Triune person of God. The good news is that we get our snapshots not through our camera lens but through the display of His attributes so beautifully captured through the pages of Scripture.

We have everything we need for life and godliness (2 Peter 1:3) because we have the Living Word of God to direct our every step: *Your word is a lamp to my feet and a light to my path* (Psalm 119:105).

In his book, *Experiencing the Presence of God* (Minneapolis, MN: Bethany House, 2014), A. W. Tozer states, "Down through history man has taken many paths in his quest for God's presence, all to no avail. Only one path is correct, and that path is revealed in the Word of God. Only in the Bible do we begin to understand what these inward stirrings are and how to find entrance into the presence of God. A right understanding of the Bible opens to us the only path in the presence of God."

The Word has been a constant in my life. I have learned to long and thirst for it like a cool drink of water on a hot summer's day. When I begin to wander off track, it is the Word that speaks Truth to me and keeps calling me back to Jesus. I have learned to trust this Word, not just in the circumstances that seem in my favor, but even when nothing is going the way I would like. Trust in the Lord has upheld me because I am confident that He who began a good work in you [and me] is faithful to complete it (Philippians 1:6).

I always loved looking through my first King James Bible, a gift from my grandma when I was a child. This old Bible, with its faded cover and loose pages, had pictures in it. I always loved the one showing Jesus holding a child in a warm embrace, and I would imagine that is what he would do for me and for all the children I knew. There were pictures of Daniel in the Lion's den—how did he keep his nerve with the ferocious hungry felines surrounding him? And of Jonah—he must have needed an extreme makeover after sitting in the belly of a fish for three days! But the picture that most attracted me was of Savior Jesus suffering on the cross between two thieves. I looked for the nails, I looked for the crown of thorns, I looked for the blood He shed. There was something about that picture that held my gaze longer than all the rest.

Hebrews 12:2 says, *Fixing our eyes on Jesus, the author and perfecter of faith who for the joy set before Him endured the cross, despising the shame, and has sat down at the right hand of the throne of God* (NASB). And in Colossians 3:1, the apostle Paul encourages us with this word: *Since, then, you have been raised with Christ, set your hearts on things above, where Christ is, seated at the right hand of God. Set your minds on things above, not on earthly things* (NIV). God wants us to have a picture of what is going on up there in the heavenly realm so that we can function down here in the natural. I am not talking about getting so heavenly minded that you are no earthly good. But I am talking about getting a vision of God before us to help us persevere with hope in the daily grind of life.

We can also get a glimpse of God from those in the Bible who recorded their pictures of the glory of God and His kingdom. We can go to Isaiah 6 when God was calling Isaiah to take His message to the stubborn hearts of Israel. We read of the Lord who was seated on the throne, high and exalted, and the train of His robe filled the temple. In verse 3, he spoke of the angels calling to each other saying, *Holy, Holy, Holy is the Lord Almighty; the whole earth is full of his glory* (NIV).

Or we can go to Daniel 7:9–10 and 12–14 where we hear of the Ancient of Days taking His seat on the throne and His clothing was white as snow and His hair white as wool. His throne was flaming with fire and thousands upon thousands were there before Him.

We can recount Ezekiel's vision of God or when Jesus himself was transfigured into His heavenly appearance right before Peter, James, and John, with a declaration from the Father that this was His beloved Son; listen to Him.

In Revelations 1:12–19, the Son of Man is revealed in power and majesty with a robe that went to His feet and a golden sash around His chest. I love that this description, written by John, reflects descriptions in the Old Testament which were written over 1,000 years earlier. This is truly amazing.

I love the account in Exodus 33:12–15, where Moses makes it very clear that If God's presence does not go with Him and the people of Israel, he would not go on without Him. Moses was serious and said something like: *God, don't send me with all these hard-hearted, stubborn, complaining Israelites unless your presence goes with me.* I believe we can assume that Moses could not survive without the picture of His presence, and I love how he wraps this conversation up by asking God, **"Please show me your glory"** (Exodus 33:18).

Over twenty-five years ago God gave me a vision, an Urban Vision, and I can't tell you how many times I had to return to the mental snapshot of that original calling in order to have the courage to take one more step. I remember how badly I wanted, and how much I prayed for, my neighbors and their three girls to know Jesus. I had a vision of what God wanted to do in their lives. God showed me that I could be one of the people who humbly came alongside them and took up the mat just like the mat of the paralytic in the Bible, and together we would carry them to see Jesus.

The faithful mat bearers in the Bible (Mark 2), encountered roadblocks in their struggle to get their friend to Jesus. But praise God for vision! It was vision for Jesus that allowed the creativity to flow, and before you know it they cut a hole in the roof. Nothing was going to stop them from getting their friend to the healing presence of God in their lives!

I had to cling to the vision of the mat bearers through all the times the police showed up on our street, through all the times children ran to our house when they didn't know what to do with their suicidal, alcoholic mother and abusive father. I had to have a heavenly vision despite what I saw in the natural. You see, we have to have a vision of the presence of God in our lives to get us past the muck and mire of the brokenness of life.

I am just wondering if there is anyone reading this right now who needs a little vision to help them get through stress, anxieties, a death or separation of family or friends? Does anyone need a vision of the presence of God for someone who is hurting;

a child, a friend, a spouse, a parent that is suffering from sickness or who is lost in their sin? I am just asking if someone today is ready for the presence of God in their lives.

But there is a problem that has crept between the church pews and has made its way into hearts and minds, subtly and silently, even amongst the children of God; even into my heart as well: We have believed the lies of the enemy and exchanged the truth for a lie and we have begun to lower our view and concept of God in our lives. We have reduced Him to our terms of understanding, not revering Him as we should. In our limited understanding, we have joined with Satan himself, casting doubt on the very Word of God as he did back in the garden long ago when he asked Eve, *Did God really say that? Did God really have your best in mind?* And to all of us, the enemy today asks, *Did God really give you a vision? Did He really say He would never leave you or forsake you? Are you sure He is going to provide for you?*

Tozer states (again, in *The Knowledge of the Holy*), "The heaviest obligation lying upon the Christian Church today is to purify and elevate her [the church's] concept of God until it is once more worthy of Him and of her, the church." Oh, that we can cleanse our lens to see what we do not want to miss—a view of God and His presence!

I am humbled to even be writing these thoughts for you this day; a word I am confident God has put on my heart to share. I agree with Tozer, who said so clearly (again, in *Experiencing the Presence of God*), "I tell you, we cannot keep still about that which we love." I want you to know from the depths of my heart that I love Jesus, I love people, and I love to tell His story. Through all the prayers, tears, pleadings, doubts, and even victories in my life and within the ministry of Urban Vision, I was and am still called to be like John the Baptist, a voice crying in the wilderness: **Prepare ye the way of the Lord!** (Mark 1:3 KJV).

Dear Friends, prepare for His presence because once you are there you will never be the same again.

Prepare for His Presence
—Jodi M. Matthews

Locked up heart no place to see;
Tucked in corners my thoughts to be.
Crowded stuffy, I could not breathe
Because all that filled my life was me.
No room, No room, the inn keeper cried;
No room, No room, I thought satisfied.
Darkness death had settled in,
Surrounded, chained by my sin.
On the out, looking right,
Inward battle, raging fight.
Desperate longing, a truthful look;
A need for Him, a sin forsook.
Yielded, humbled, scarred, yet free.
Jesus, prepare my heart for thee.

If you could only see what I now see here at Urban Vision, you too would rejoice at the many things God has done and is still doing—praise His sweet Name! My heart is overwhelmed and I thank Him for how He has included so many in the process of building His kingdom here in our little corner of the world. Most of all I thank Him for His presence, which resides in the hearts of the many people who love Jesus, and live out the precious story of His Word in our community of North Hill.

Set on Success group photo—many
children representing many cultures

There is so much more for you to see. There's Legacy of Success, the housing program Urban Vision partners with. They restore old homes and then sell them to people in the community at prices they can afford, allowing for home ownership in our neighborhood.

There is also our aquaponics green house, built in back of Urban Vision with the hope to grow fresh food in our community right in the middle of the city. (I know Jesus multiplied the fish in His ministry, but we have had our share of trouble just trying to keep ours alive! But we are learning, praise God! Yet who would have thought fish would be housed at Urban Vision?)

We are still running our S.O.S. and Kids Club programs which have always been close to my heart. I thank God for the many young people and our loving staff who have caught the vision and who do an excellent job of loving the kids there, especially because I don't move as fast as I once did. In fact, I could barely move at all after running up and down the stairs a million times at the last Kids Club (well, it *felt* like a million times…). And worshiping God with the kids is just as strenuous as any aerobic workout class. Yet God gives me strength and I keep moving along.

Some of our kids from the city have been involved with Bible quizzing—memorizing the Word of God and competing with kids from other local churches. They are amazing! We have children learning strategy in playing the game of chess and volunteers teaching children to play instruments like the alto sax and piano. We also have our little Gospel Choir, led by people from the community, teaching the children to praise and worship Him.

There's a little piece of land across the street from us where drugs have often been a problem. Many times the police visited this place of constant bad activity that was not good for the children of the community to see. I'll never forget when some of our youth saw the police and ambulance bringing out the body of someone who overdosed on bad heroine. Something needed to change! A few of us ladies would pray, *Lord, either move the people into Your kingdom or move them off the land.*

The drug house was shut down, the property became available, and we were able to acquire it. Now, this land, which used to be used for bad things, offers its big, beautiful oak trees and green lawns as a safe place for the children of Urban Vision to run and play. We have dreams of using it for sports clinics and community leagues and maybe even a splash pad (the kids voted for that!).

We now partner with a local church and offer adult English classes up on the third floor, in a space we've named The Living Room. (Isn't that a fun name?) Classes are offered almost every day now for people to receive the help they need, in a place of refuge, a place that proclaims the name of Jesus.

We have been able to partner with other organizations to help provide medical care and pregnancy counsel in favor of life, to come alongside under resourced people who are in need of these services in our community. Isn't the Lord good?!

If your head is spinning, know that mine is too! There is so much to take in. It is hard to get my mind wrapped around and communicate it to you. God has led us to this place and the sights are enough to make us say, *Look at what the Lord has done!*

We have by no means arrived at our final destination or seen the end of our journey. There is still much to learn and more people to meet. This all started with a response to the Savior who calls His kingdom people to their edges. It all started with one step, one grain of a mustard seed faith, to begin our journeys to the edge. The path has been arduous lately; despite seeing the great rewards, there are also great trials. Yet sweet are my days, clinging to His presence, facing each day with a deep peace and trust I have never experienced before...

I know who I am. I am a wretched sinner, saved by grace, and set aside for a kingdom purpose—just like you. For He has delivered us from darkness and has transferred us into the kingdom of light. For even though my vision at times is still blurred, the Word reminds me: **For we know in part and we prophesy in part but when the Perfect comes the partial will pass away...For now we see in a mirror dimly, but then face to face. Now I know in part; then I shall know fully, even as I have been fully known** (1 Corinthians 13:9–12).

Praise God!

If I were to interview King David and ask him, *So, King David, what is your secret to being a great king, a fearless warrior, a creative poet, and musician? Is the secret of who you became found in your wisdom, your strength, or your gifts?"* His reply would be this: **One thing I have asked from the LORD, that I shall seek: That I may dwell in the house of the LORD all the days of my life, to behold the beauty of the LORD and to meditate in his temple** (Psalm 27:4 NASB).

David knew who he was and the one thing that made the difference. David's call to the edge started off as a shepherd boy but led him to the palace to be a King of the Jews. David, a man after God's heart (not a perfect man), got himself into the presence of God. That was his secret, which is really no secret at all—it's available to all who pursue the heart of God: *Open my eyes that I may see wonderful things in your law* (Psalm 119:18 NIV).

> *Blessed is the man that walketh not in the counsel of the ungodly nor standeth in the way of sinners, nor sitteth in the seat of the scornful. But His delight is in the law of the LORD and in His law doth he meditate day and night. And he shall be like a tree planted by the rivers of water, that bringeth forth his fruit in his season; his leaf also shall not wither, and whatsoever he doeth shall prosper* (Psalm 1:1–3 KJV).

Scripture is very clear that if we get into the presence of God, we can fill up in Him and go out into a dying, hurting world in need of a Savior. We are not defeated by what is going on in the world but we are overcomers, fruitful kingdom players who know who we are, whose we are, and that we are headed into God's plan for us. A call to the edge has led me into His presence, a place I have learned to abide. It was this pathway to His presence that has made all the difference! I have come to know that I want to be a pillar in the house of my God, never to go in or out. Hear the Word of the Lord:

> *I am coming soon. Hold fast to what you have, so that no one may seize your crown. The one who conquers, I will make him a pillar in the temple of my God. Never shall he go out of it, and I will write on him the name of my God, and the name of the city of my God, the new Jerusalem, which comes down from my God out of heaven, and my own new name. He who has an ear, let him hear what the Spirit says to the churches* (Revelation 3:11–13).

A pillar stays put! It is a part of the supporting structure of the building. We are God's building, and I want to remain in His presence to impact the world around me! ***For we are God's fellow workers. You are God's field, God's building*** (1 Corinthians 3:9).

What a picture it is when lives are touched by the Master photographer Himself. Through His Spirit, He creates the most beautiful displays in the lives of people; allowing the world to see who He is and how God the Father gives a love that knows no boundaries. This is a picture of the pathway to His presence. Yes, this is a Kodak picture moment for everyone!

God includes you and me in this picture; all who choose to follow His call to the edge! Look up, smile, and say, Hallelujah! (Hallelujah is much better than cheese, don't you think? So, are you smiling yet? I sure hope so!)

> ***Now to him who is able to do far more abundantly than all that we ask or think, according to the power at work within us, to him be glory in the church and in Christ Jesus throughout all generations, forever and ever. Amen*** (Ephesians 3:20–21).

The Promise of His Presence
—Jodi M. Matthews

Oh the promise of His presence, Oh the whisper of His Word
That keeps me on the path we trod; His voice I have clearly heard.

I'm watching for the potholes, the pits along the way;
Finally now I get it when you said, "Just watch and pray."

No half a heart would ever do, but a transplant He designed;
Now my heart is wholly His, and His is wholly mine.

Oh the precious promise of His love so ever near;
Hand in hand I walk with Him, I don't have to fear.

I can follow down in the valley or up on mountains high
Because I'm so familiar now with His presence nigh.

I love this sweet communion, this treasure I did find;
Lord, please help me not to run ahead or get too far behind.

Let me be yoked to You; I choose You to stay my course;
Drinking from the Living Water, I find my strength and source.

I've posted some caution signs and cleared the path along the way
To help other pilgrims walk that they might not be led astray.

Oh the joy I have; it's true, I've learned to let things go.
You replaced those things with seeds to plant to watch Your
kingdom grow.

Heaven is much nearer now, in His presence I delight
For though I've walked Your path by faith, King Jesus is now in sight.

For one day when on earth my journey here is through,
No introductions needed; I will know it's You!

For I will see my closest friend with whom I did trod
And fall before the King of Kings, crying, "My Savior and my God!"

Oh the sweet, sweet presence, though we toil and labor long;
One day we will stand and sing, "Holy, Holy, Holy," with the angel
throng.

So, my friends, walk on to find your promise on the Pathway
to His Presence!

CONCLUSION

A Sight to Behold

The heavens declare the glory of God; the skies proclaim the work of his hands. Day after day they pour forth speech; night after night they reveal knowledge. They have no speech, they use no words; no sound is heard from them. Yet their voice goes out into all the earth, their words to the ends of the world (Psalm 19:1–4 NIV).

Those who have spent time with the Lord can understand when the Scripture says in Psalm 34:8, *Taste and see that the LORD is good!* Once you have tasted a good thing, nothing else will quite do. Rodney always gets so annoyed when I tell him how much I *love* good food and at how expressive I am in describing such savory food details. I have spent a lot of hours in the kitchen and I figure if I have to cook food, I want it to be good food! Let's be honest—food that tantalizes our taste buds is a pleasure none of us would like to be without. How boring it would be if everything that we ate tasted bland.

However, I think Rodney wishes I would be more expressive in my words towards him rather than expressing at least five times in one meal how much I love Chicago style, deep dish Giordano's pizza! Okay. I have some food issues but thankfully I have learned not to use the word *love* to describe my obsession with food anymore. I have become quite convicted about using that particular word to describe a pizza in the same way that I describe

245

my dearly beloved hubby. I can see how he could get a little upset over that, so I have tried to amend my ways and not express my appreciation of food in the same way that I express genuine love for people in my life. Words do have meaning, and I should use them more wisely and accurately in my description when referring to things, experiences, or people of great importance. However, in all seriousness, words cannot adequately describe our Lord. Saying *He is good* doesn't do Him justice...in His case, good is definitely good, real good!

John 20 is the story of the resurrection of Jesus after He had been so cruelly crucified on the cross. Although they had heard Jesus Himself say that He would rise on the third day, even His disciples and followers had a hard time getting their minds wrapped around the possibility that He had risen from the grave. Mary Magdalene brought spices to the tomb to anoint the decaying body of Jesus. Seeing the stone rolled away, and that Jesus' body was not there, she rushed back to tell Peter and John who raced to the tomb to see what had happened. Mary left there in sorrow, wondering who had taken the body of her Lord. Even the angels in the tomb didn't seem to faze Mary as she so naturally responded to them asking her why she was weeping. She just wanted to know where they had put her Lord. At this point in the story, she turned and saw a man whom she thought was the gardener and said to him, *"If you have carried Him away, tell me where you have put him, and I will get Him."* Poor girl didn't see the very person she was looking for until this "Man" said her name: *"Mary."* Hearing her name spoken in the way that was familiar to her made her aware that Jesus was right before her very eyes. She cried out *"Teacher!"* and clung to Him with all her might. Jesus told her to let Him go and to go and tell the others that *"I am ascending to my Father and to your Father, my God and your God"* (NIV).

Mary left at once and announced to the disciples, *"I have seen the Lord!"* I am sure there were other words but those were the ones recorded, and how absolutely thrilling that her crucified Jesus, who once was dead, now lives! This truly was a sight for her sore, weeping eyes to look upon! Although I have never seen the Lord the way Mary did, this journey to my edge has led me to see in my soul; so I too have seen the Lord. I guess it is more like I have seen the evidences of this Good God and it has been a sight to behold!

So now I am in my late forties, and I have seen a lot in the twenty-five years since the beginning of Urban Vision. I often revisit the conversation I had with my dad all those years ago out in his shed. You know the question: "Jodi, why is it that you always feel you have to live life on the edge?" I replay it like a recorder in my mind over and over again. At the time, I didn't know the answer. I believe God had to lead me to the answer through a twenty-five year journey of following His call to the edge.

Thankfully my dad is still with me so I can go to him and tell him all these years later that I have the answer now. I can say, "This call to the edge is something I needed to follow out beyond my comfort zone. Although I may not have always understood this call, I can tell you it is much clearer for me now. You see, Dad, the reason I have to live life on the edge is because it is where the most spectacular, the most remarkable, the most magnanimous view of God is that I have ever seen!!!! The view I see from my edge is the view God knew my heart would long to behold. It was a picture that would not just hold my gaze for a moment but it would keep my eyes fixed on Him and His presence until the day when finally I see Him face to face!"

My story is not over. Your story isn't either. God continues to call us beyond where we are today. He implores us to come press in to those places beyond where others may have settled and has called us on to press in closer to the heart of Jesus. In Matthew 26:39, Jesus left HIs beloved disciples to watch and pray while He went "further" as He submitted His will to God, His Father. He cried out to His heavenly Father to give Him the strength to face the impending cruelty of the cross so that in a little further still He would be a part of the glorious resurrection. Oh, the places God wants to take us to and through if we would only trust Him more!

I love Beth Moore's poem, Further Still (from a book by the same title, *Further Still, A Collection of Poetry and Vignettes*, Nashville, TN: LifeWay Press, 2004). I would encourage you to seek out the whole poem in its entirety, but Beth Moore makes the point that getting to your Further Stills in life changes you. She writes:

Life pivots there
In Further Still
Face to the ground
Fighting his will.
Can't choose to return
The same who went
Once Further Still
The old is spent.

May God give us all the courage to follow through to our Further Stills to His call to the edge. In Psalm 40, the writer starts in the muck and the mire and ends up on the rock, firm and secure. God then puts a new song in his heart, a song to sing that will lead many to see, fear, and put their trust in God.

That is my hope! This is my prayer: that you too will get to your edge, take it all in, and behold our radiant King Jesus as never before!

> *He put a new song in my mouth, a song of praise to our God. Many will see and fear, and put their trust in the LORD* (Psalm 40:3).

So, I asked Jesus, *what is my new song?* This was His reply. Amen!

A New Song
—Jodi M. Matthews

Praise wells up from my soul
For all You have done for me me.
Marvelous, Omnipotent, Almighty God
Who Reigns in Victory.

Wonderful, beautiful, stunning You are;
Words that barely will do;
But this is the song, the new one that I sing;
I sing it just for You.

A new song I sing because You have asked;
Oh let me sing my part.
May it add to the symphony of all the earth
That comes from the depths of my heart.

Praise Your Name, Your salvation proclaimed,
Oh what a privilege this is;
Declaring Your glory, Your marvelous deeds,
With joy I know I am His.

I asked, so I sing this new song that You gave
With adoration from deep within.
You're worthy, You're Holy, Righteous are You;
You have cleansed me from all of my sin.

Unworthy, I cry, to sing such a song
To my Savior and my King.
But thank You, dear Jesus, for the song that You gave
So this is the song that I bring.

Chorus:
It's a song that I sing coming straight from my heart;

It's a song that I sing with a brand new start;
It's a song that I sing as a prayer to Your throne;
It's a song that I sing and we made it our own.

It's a song that I sing,
It's a song that I bring;
A New Song...

PERSPECTIVES FROM THE EDGE

*In the year that King Uzziah died I saw the Lord
sitting upon a throne, high and lifted up; and the
train of his robe filled the temple. Above him stood the
seraphim. Each had six wings: with two he covered his
face, and with two he covered his feet, and with two
he flew. And one called to another and said:
"Holy, holy, holy is the LORD of hosts; the whole earth
is full of his glory!" And I heard the voice of the Lord
saying, "Whom shall I send, and who will go for us?"
Then I said, "Here I am! Send me"*
(Isaiah 6:1–3, 8)

I love seeing through the eyes of so many characters in the Bible their perspectives of God. Isaiah's vision and call from God clearly describes His encounter with the presence of the Lord on His throne! What a sight for Isaiah to take in to the point he felt paralyzed in his unworthiness. The good news is that Jesus is a sight to behold but also a sight that is needed to bring healing and purpose to our lives. God doesn't just leave us in our sin; He provides a way to be forgiven and cleansed, and then He sets us on a journey to our edges in life so that others can know and see Him too.

There is always a response to seeing God, and just as God asked Isaiah, **"Whom shall I send and who will go for us?"** He asks us too. For us to see Him in His glory and majesty and not take what we've seen and heard to others would be a great loss indeed. There are many who need to hear how when one life is obedient, God will use them to call and bring others to their edges of obedience. My prayer, as you have read my call to the edge, is that now you will read and see how others' lives were impacted along the way. God is so good to allow us to be a part of His wonderful plan.

As I leave this in your hands I wanted you to read the thoughts of those very close to me and some much younger than me who are learning what it means to follow God to their edges and the impact it has had on their lives. Hear their testimonies, take in the view from their perspective. There is much to be done in the work of the Lord and, seeing Him, we can never be the same. He continues to call us all to keep on going to further edges in our journey with Him. God is not through with me yet, nor is He through with you—He has only just begun! Stop, look, take in the whole view. Don't miss it! See it, hear it! Oh, what glorious things of You, our Lord, are spoken! It makes me want to shout one more time, *Glory Hallelujah, great things He has done!*

Jessika Johnson: 19-year-old, African-American young woman studying to be a teacher at University of Akron. Past participant and current Urban Vision volunteer.

Jessika Johnson

There was a point in my life where I was completely lost. I was constantly trying to figure out who I was and how I identified myself, never looking to God with these problems. I came from a Christian household and my mom was always pouring into my sisters and me about God, but it wasn't until I was around eight years old during a morning church service when I felt God's presence and gave my life to Him.

I didn't really understand what it meant to give my life to Christ, and for years I would just repeat what others said about God without applying it to my own life. I idolized people and devoted my life at a young age to being likable to get attention. The more I pursued the attention of others, the less I thought about God. When I could not get the attention I longed for, I would blame God and turn even further away from Him. There came a point when I hated God and wanted nothing to do with Him. I was convinced that God hated me too, and was the reason behind all suffering, and He enjoyed it. I don't think I ever understood completely God's love for me until I got involved in Urban Vision. I remember walking home from school to avoid going to their building because I was afraid. When my mom saw me, she saw through my lies of "forgetting to go" and would drive me to Urban Vision. As I started going, all my fears started to fade away.

As I got closer to Christ, I was able to open up about some issues which hindered my relationships with people and my relationship with God, which was also affected by these issues. God chose this place for me to start a serious relationship with Him and unpack the pain of my past onto Him. The more I turned to God with these issues, the closer I got to Him. He shifted my view from finding myself in people to finding my identity in Him.

I have seen God move in my life and open doors to do what I would never have thought I was capable of doing. He showed me, and continually shows me, that He will never leave me and how He values the time I spend with Him to grow stronger in my walk with Him. It was never easy but I have always found support in the people who have walked alongside me to keep me focused. I am very thankful to the people who have poured into my life, like Mrs. Jodi and those at Urban Vision, and for what God has done in my life to bring me closer to Him.

Ni Doh: 19-year-old, Karen young man, graduated from Beacon Christian Learning Center 2017. Attends University of Akron. Current participant and volunteer at Urban Vision.

Ni Doh

Hello my name is Ni Doh. I have been involved in Urban Vision ever since I first moved to the United States as an immigrant, which was about nine years ago. I started out being invited by a neighbor of mine who told my parents about Urban Vision, which helps students with their homework and teaches students about God.

After that moment, my life has changed completely. With the help from many volunteers, I was able to accomplish many things. First of all, I was able to read, write, and speak in the span of a short period of time. Urban Vision was one of the first groups of people in Akron who reached out to me with the gospel, the good news. I trusted in the Lord Jesus Christ at the age of twelve after fully understanding the gospel, and the people at Urban Vision have helped me grow not only academically, but also spiritually.

Urban Vision has impacted my life in many positive ways. Beacon Christian Learning Center, which is a part of Urban Vision, has taught me so much in just four years. I was able to take on many responsibilities being part of the school and also volunteering in programs at Urban Vision. Urban Vision has taught me to give what is given to me and to use my talent that is given to me by God. I am very blessed to be part of the ministry of Urban Vision and will continue to be part of many journeys that are to come.

Eh Dah Doe, also known as Doey: 19-year-old, Karen young woman. Recently graduated from Cuyahoga Valley Christian Academy and will attend University of Akron to pursue a Nursing Degree. Current Intern with Urban Vision.

Eh Dah Doe (Doey)

I started coming to Urban Vision when I was in second grade. I've been involved with Urban Vision for a decade now, so it's home to me and I absolutely love every second of it here. Urban Vision has impacted me in many aspects of my life. It has influenced me in the following three ways: spiritually, intellectually, and emotionally.

Spiritually: The people of Urban Vision have walked with me spiritually ever since I made my decision to give my heart to Jesus. They helped me understand Scripture and they keep me accountable. When it's hard, they constantly remind me of the Truth and to keep my eyes on Him. The people at Urban Vision really show the love of Christ, not only through words, but also their actions in the way they serve this community.

Intellectually: The number one reason why I started coming to Urban Vision was that I needed help with my schoolwork since my parents couldn't help me with it. Every day after school, I would walk to Urban Vision to get help with my homework. I have to say, Urban Vision helped me so much that I caught on easily and was given options to go to different schools to further my education. I saw the love of Christ through the people who have helped me with my homework. The patience they displayed towards me and the desire to help some little kid they didn't even know has had a huge impact on me.

Emotionally: The staff at Urban Vision has walked with me through my journey of emotions. From the happy times to the sad, they walked alongside me, helping me go through my journey. What I love about UV is that the staff here is just so willing to be there for you, whether you're in a good situation or bad situation, and that's what makes them really different to me. Most importantly, no matter the circumstance, they pray for me.

These three aspects have really shaped me into the person I am today. Right now, I'm an Intern at Urban Vision, helping with their administrative responsibilities. I graduated high school this year, class of 2017, and I will be going to the University of Akron for nursing. Urban Vision is part of my life, and I am really thankful for this place and the people here.

Nathanael Matthews: 16-year-old, my third son. Attends Cuyahoga Valley Christian Academy. Participant and Intern at Urban Vision.

Nathanael Matthews

Being the son of Rodney and Jodi Matthews, I have been raised in the diverse life of Urban Vision and all of Akron. Our community, filled with an array of ethnicities, has broadened my own worldview. In this book, my mother, Jodi, has illustrated the image of every person's call to the edge. This edge, or the end of our comfort zone, has far greater and deeper boundaries, because of Urban Vision. Urban Vision *is* my life. I was born into it, raised in it, and now I serve with it. My comfort lies within the walls of Urban Vision and its vast cultural entourage. The ministry has called for me to serve Christ and to love others just as He has commanded.

Now, I serve and work at Urban Vision for the good of the mission and the improvement of myself. The community of Christ enables me to grow in Him and to have a place to share my life. The lives we affect today will affect the lives of tomorrow. Hopefully, my mark on the world will not be of a physical or financial success, but of a spiritual change in the hearts of people.

Within my communities I stand out, because of the spiritual and mental training I have been provided with by Urban Vision, my parents, and the gifts invested in me by God. At home, I am the only one not currently planning to taking up the family mantle of missions. Rather, I have decided to pursue a career in engineering. The training and desire for this has come through the education of Urban Vision (S.O.S. and Boy Scouts), schooling, and the ability given by God. In school I remain different since I have a culturally diverse background compared to the middle and upper class white community where I attend. My cultural experiences within my community allow me to share my insights with those who haven't been privileged with a cosmopolitan community. Even at Urban Vision I used to stick out because I was the only white kid or I was the son of people directing the organization. Either way, I felt singled out, but that didn't matter. What matters is that through a variety of backgrounds I have been able to acquire wisdom I couldn't have comprehended in any other life. This wisdom is truly a blessing.

George White: 76-year-old, my dad. Past board member and volunteer. Current supporter and Number 1 Fan. (You're the best!)

I have learned over the years that as Christians we all need to be "living on the edge" with Christ. If we are in His will, there is no safer place to be. Remember, "He hideth my soul in the cleft of the Rock."

And as the old evangelist Oliver Greene used to quote a poem by Elizabeth Cheney: "Said the Robin to the Sparrow, 'I should really like to know, why these anxious human beings rush about and worry so.' Said the Sparrow to the Robin, 'Friend, I think that it must be, that they have no Heavenly Father such as cares for you and me.'"

Rodney Matthews: My husband, soul mate, love of my life. Current Executive Director and Board Member of Urban Vision.

Living on the edge. That is what human eyes see when we are following God's plan for our lives. My journey to the edge began quite soon after accepting the Lord as my Savior in December of 1989. When I met Jodi in January of 1992, while she was asking for help in the urban areas of Akron, I unknowingly found my path to the edge. I knew I wanted to put my faith in action, and I loved working with kids. Now, with Jodi, the boys and my journey keeps us close to the edge as God's direction and faithfulness keeps us from going over it. When we are in Him and not just ourselves, God takes us on a journey where each of us is meant to be.

Many know that God has blessed Jodi and me with different strengths and weaknesses, and He has used them in each of our lives to help us on our journey. We've both learned to listen for Him for direction, which doesn't come naturally to either of us doers. I'm often asked about my decisions to live and work as we do, and I reply there is no better place to be than where God wants you to be.

God bless!

Micah Matthews: 21-year-old, my first son. Studying to be an urban pastor at Moody Bible Institute. Past participant of Urban Vision and current Intern of Northside Open Door Church/Urban Vision.

Micah Matthews

I love my mother. I have vivid images of Mom that delve deep into my past. Singing songs, leading Bible Clubs, getting groceries, and making dinner all came wrapped up in one day. Our lives often pulsed with intensity as we dashed to each place. My mother was the eye of the hurricane, simultaneously the place where the craziness revolved and the place of comfort from it all. Through it all, she lived with integrity, being a follower of Christ as Mom, as well as "Mrs. Jodi." Many moments of laughter, smiles, fun, and comfort all happened through my mom's consistent life at home. Every pancake filled my stomach. Every song filled my ears. Every hug filled my heart.

I wanted to be like my mom, and in a lot of ways, I am. I have no doubt where I get my loud voice, my vision casting, my love of kids, and so much more. I do a lot of what I do because Momma did it best, inside the home and out. However, when looking at Mom climbing to the edge, I quickly decided that I had to do the same. I felt I had to show that I was worthy of my mom's calling, that I could start my own ministry, that I could go where no one dared to go, and I labeled myself as second class if I couldn't. I've since learned that this is not who I am. But my mom would say the same thing as the author of Hebrews does. The great cloud of witnesses do not inspire us to replicate their lives, but rather to fix our eyes on Jesus and live in the life He has given.

Nearly every time I've gone off to college my mother has cried, and though I don't often show it, I hurt, too. I remember that each step I have taken and will take will be because my mother has taken the steps before me. I live into my own call to the edge because of her faithfulness to live in hers, and I cannot wait to stand on eternity's shores with her in the presence of our Lord and together say, "I have fought the good fight. I have finished the course. I have kept the faith" (2 Timothy 4:7).

> I press on toward the goal to win the prize for which God has called me heavenward in Christ Jesus (Philippians 3:14 NIV).

Praise God for all of you following God to your edge! Doxology, from Jude 24–25:

> *Now to him who is able to keep you from stumbling and to present you blameless before the presence of his glory with great joy, to the only God, our Savior, through Jesus Christ our Lord, be glory, majesty, dominion, and authority, before all time and now and forever. Amen* (ESV).

William at the blue house—A smile says it all!

You're invited to check out our website to see what God continues to do at Urban Vision:
www.urbanvisionministry.org
Find your call to the edge at www.ACallToTheEdge.com

CROWN OF CREA
A BIBLE STUDY SERIES

WOMEN
OF
TROUBLED
TIMES

CINDY COLLEY

Books with Class

PUBLISHING DESIGNS, INC.

P.O. Box 3241 • Huntsville, Alabama 35810
256-533-4301 • www.publishingdesigns.com

Publishing Designs, Inc.
P.O. Box 3241
Huntsville, Alabama 35810

All scripture quotations, unless otherwise indicated, are taken
from the New King James Version. Copyright © 1982 by
Thomas Nelson, Inc. Used by permission. All rights reserved.

Publisher's Cataloging-In-Publication Data

Colley, Cindy, 1959-
Women of Troubled Times / Cindy Colley.
(Crown of creation)
160 pp.
Thirteen chapters.
1. Women in the Bible. 2. Bible, O. T. 3. Christian women—
Religious life.
I. Title. II. Series.
ISBN 978-0-929540-63-4
248.8

Printed in the United States of America

To Hannah Colley

who grew up

in America's most troubled time to date,

and, in the process,

developed a faith that continues

to glorify her Father

in the best and worst of circumstances.

CONTENTS

THE UPSIDE OF TROUBLE

CHRISTIANS ARE SAFE REFUGEES!

I like to write positive books that make us feel happy and productive as God's women. That's what I want this book to be. But it's a real challenge to put a positive spin on the era of the judges. The upside of the study has to be what we do with the account rather than the account itself. Hold that thought.

This book opens on a world that is any godly woman's nightmare. It was clearly a society steeped in moral and spiritual subjectivism. In the lives of its women we will see harlotry, deceit, evil desires. Times were much like our own era in many respects. Judges 17:6 records God's terse summation of this era of Israel's history: "In those days there was no king in Israel; everyone did what was right in his own eyes."

TROUBLE FOR MOMS AND GRANDMOMS

It's a challenge to raise godly children. To do so in our present culture of relativism is extremely difficult. Our culture calls the acceptance of sin "tolerance." It calls avarice and greed "success."

"In those days there was no king in Israel; everyone did what was right in his own eyes."

—Judges 17:6

When women forsake their God-given roles in rearing their own children, it's feminism. Homosexuality is love; murder in the womb is abortion. When my children live in a world where blatant immorality is ascribed these most sterile names, it becomes my job, as a mother, to be ever more vigilant in peeling back the devil's deceitful and glamorous facade. As we again evoke Judges 17:6, we know that calling wrong right does not make it right. Neither does its renaming provide any protection from the consequences of wrong. This philosophical diet of moral tolerance must be countered at home with the antitoxin of God's immutable truth. If my son's history teacher is an outspoken advocate of homosexuality and my daughter's theater director is a spiritual universalist, these situations must light a fire under me as their mother! When even conservative religionists tell my children that the New Testament is merely a book of general principles rather than a standard of absolute truth, my job as a Christian mother again intensifies.

Sometimes when I sit back and evaluate this world in which I struggle as a parent, I'm truly amazed at how far society has veered in one generation. Let's notice the digression.

❋ *Government-funded events now include what is vile* (Romans 1:26). When my children were small (1992), I had to shield their curious eyes from witnessing the inaugural parade of our U.S. Presidency because homosexual advocates were given, for the first time, a place of honor in that Presidential procession. Thirty years earlier, when I was small, homosexuality was never mentioned in any honorable public arena.

❋ *Prime time television is filled with sexual innuendo, as well as graphic sexual material.* As a teenager, I can remember when the show "Happy Days" first aired. My parents were amazed at the innuendos that frequently surfaced in this sit-com and we frequently had to turn it off. Typical recent themes would certainly make "Happy Days" seem very benign. These recent themes have included "breast-only orgasms," homosexual and lesbian heroism, and sex-driven competition in amazingly vulgar reality TV.

❋ *The Boy Scouts of America have been forced to sacrifice corporate funding.* Why? Hefty donors like the Levi-Strauss Company refuse to sanction homosexuality in its leadership. The Boy Scouts have faced numerous lawsuits because of this stance. When I was a child, no known homosexual could have successfully led an adult civic club, much less a group of innocent young boys!

❋ *Our federal government offers tax incentives to young working mothers.* Women who choose to have babies and then relegate their care to day care workers are actually rewarded! When I was a preschooler, more than ninety percent of my peers were being daily nurtured at home, with their mothers.

❋ *Popular CDs are rarely curse free, and even more rarely, pure in theme.* I checked the lyrics recently of the top five songs on America's pop charts. Four of the five contained extremely objectionable lyrics. When I was a child, an album with objectionable material was far rarer than an album with decent lyrics.

❈ *Oral sex is the popular pastime of the early teen years.* Several mothers of middle schoolers in an upscale community have filled me in on this current event. When I was in middle school, I had never heard of oral sex. I believe my innocence in this regard was fairly typical at the time.

❈ *Wednesday night ballgames, play practice, club meetings, etc. are all very common in most American communities.* When I was a child there were only very rare Wednesday night Bible study conflicts because entire communities were cognizant of the priority of Bible study in most American homes.

❈ *Less than half of American children now live with both birth parents.* Divorce rates have exceeded marriage rates in America in recent years. When I was in elementary school, there was only one girl in my class whose parents were divorced. In most of our eyes she was an anomaly.

❈ *Over a million babies this year in America will be aborted.* Not one single baby in America had ever been legally aborted until I was fourteen years old. The word "abortion" was defined by Webster's dictionary as "a miscarriage" when I was a child.

The list could go on and on. If you are over thirty-five you could easily reminisce and make your own list. But why? Why have we seen such a rapid and expansive moral decline during the last thirty five years?

Have older women in the class call to mind moral changes they have noted in the past four decades. As they are listed for the class, find scriptures that have been violated in each case, thus causing the moral erosion.

_____

_____

THE TROUBLE WITH TOLERANCE

These women of the book of Judges were raising children in the shadow of national disobedience. Remember, as the tribes of Israel were preparing to enter the promised land, God was clear in instructing them to destroy the peoples of Canaan (Deuteronomy 7:1–2). But they didn't. Instead, they left remnants of these heathen groups. They made treaties with them. They finally intermarried with them. They allowed their sanctified status to become polluted and cowered in compromise to big armies and military might. The first chapter of Judges relates in detail their multiple failures in ridding the land of idolatrous heathen tribes. Now as we study the judges, we find that succeeding generations are left to struggle in a nation plagued by the spiritual pollutants of that idolatry. Tolerance turned to acceptance which turned to conformity.

The point must not be overlooked. The society that was doing what was right in its own eyes did not happen overnight. A nation did not go to sleep one night in compliance with Jehovah and wake up the very next morning in rebellion to Him. Passive iniquity grows into active iniquity in a generation.

> Someone wisely said, "When tolerance becomes the primary virtue of a nation, it is soon the only virtue." How is this true?
>
> _____
>
> _____

So I'm convinced about Israel's problem. They brought it on themselves. But what does that have to do with my struggles as a Christian parent today?

THE TROUBLING CONNECTION

God's nation today, His spiritual Israel, is the church. Just as God told Israel to purge Canaan of the idolatrous heathen, so He tells the church of the New Testament to purge itself of fornicators (1 Corinthians 5:1–7), to withdraw from brethren who walk disorderly (2 Thessalonians 3:6–7), to have no company with those who are not walking the walk (2 Thessalonians 3:11–14), and even to refrain from eating with those who are fornicators, idolaters, covetous, railers, drunkards, or swindlers (1 Corinthians 5:11).

Those who cause division in the body by teaching false doctrines are to be marked and avoided, as well (Romans 16:17).

A study of these passages reveals no ambiguity. God is clear in His command, even calling the admonition a command in 2 Thessalonians 3:6 and invoking the authority of our Lord. But have we done this in the body of Christ? Just as Israel did in Judges 1, we have picked and chosen when we would obey. We have, in most congregations, largely ignored these commands because we find them distasteful, and it seems more peaceable to us just to look the other way when the enemy is in our territory. We had rather make a treaty than to fight the distasteful battle that purifies the church and saves the lost brother. As a result our children often attend worship with people who are living in adultery, have Sunday school teachers who are engaging in impure forms of entertainment, and are associating with friends' families who are putting all kinds of activities before worship of God Almighty. In many congregations, those who are serving publicly in our worship assemblies are profiting from the sale of alcoholic beverages. No wonder it's hard for me as a parent to instill a respect for the absolute truth of God's word in my kids when church leaders take such an irresponsible stance toward the purity of the body of Jesus and the peril of lost brethren. When those who know better ignore sin in the camp, failing both to practice and to preach this purifying process, there will arise a generation that doesn't know any better. It falls as the duty of parents, teachers, and certainly elder's wives to teach, to pray, and to encourage a return to the prescribed method of congregational purity.

> *We have ignored these commands; we find them distasteful, and it seems more peaceable to us just to look the other way.*

You see, Israel wasn't commanded to fix all the problems of the heathen nations. God's people were simply not to co-exist with them in the Promised Land. They were to drive them out or utterly destroy them. While we cannot fix the problems of a society that will not accept biblical teachings of morality, we can, by obeying the New Testament commands to maintain our sanctification, refuse to encourage sin within our own promised land, the church. God's prescribed plan today is not the physical destruction of the immoral and unholy. It is our withdrawal of interaction that is purely social—exclusion from fellowship while sin persists. That is God's method of congregational purity today. If my children see a shepherding leadership and a supportive congregation really working to maintain that purity and enforcing these biblical consequences for blatant, persistent sin, it will impact their moral and spiritual decisions. They will see in a very practical way that every man cannot do that which is right in his own eyes and still be in fellowship with God's holy "called out" people. I wish my children could have seen a lot less tolerance for obvious impenitence and a lot more loving leaders who were willing to work through the difficult process of discipline within the body.

But we cannot go back. Beginning the process of obeying in the case of discipline so long neglected is a Herculean task. It takes leaders of integrity who are committed to stand on the truth of God's word at any personal cost. It takes their families being willing to endure harsh criticism and sleepless nights. It takes churches of people who are willing to have their hearts broken as loved ones are marked and disciplined in love. Once we allow sin to grow within the body as leaven (1 Corinthians 5:4–6), it is much more difficult than it would have been if vigilant elders had been conscientious all through the years. But the fact remains. Loving discipline is a commanded characteristic of the church of the New Testament. No rationalization for its absence excuses the Israel of God today.

What wording in 2 Thessalonians 3:6 invokes the authority of the Lord?

_____

Is a church that ignores the commands of discipline a fully restored New Testament church? Why or why not?

_____

Find and list other New Testament passages that call the church the spiritual Israel of today.

_____

HEALING FOR A TROUBLED LAND

> If My people who are called by My name will humble themselves, and pray and seek My face, and turn from their wicked ways, then I will hear from heaven, and will forgive their sin and heal their land (2 Chronicles 7:14).

We often hear this scripture used as a plea for a return to the religious and moral principles upon which the United States was founded. What a blessing it would be if our nation could experience a moral cleansing and turn back to a recognition of God as the source of good government. But, in reality, the true Israel of our day is not America. It is the church! (Romans 9:6–33). We, as the body of Christ, are the people who are called by His name: Christians (Acts 11:26), the church of Christ (Romans 16:16), the house of God (1 Timothy 3:15). We are the ones who are called to humble ourselves. We are the ones to whom the avenue of prayer is available. We are the ones who, because we are in Christ and have contacted His blood, may be forgiven. We are the ones who can truly claim this healing.

> *The true Israel of our day is not America. It is the church!*

Remember that thought you were holding? Well this is the upside. This is the great potential for good that can come from our study. This is the positive tack we must use in studying these often desperate women. This is the hope for our day found in the hopelessness of theirs.

So be not dismayed. We will find applicable, positive, and objective truth for our day. We will be better as we study. And we will find ways to encourage our leaders to be better as well. We will learn that His way is always best and we will develop faith to do life His way. Our inner resolve will grow and our circles of influence will widen. We can be a part of the healing in our corners of the world.

As we focus on being the sanctified spiritual people we should be in the new Israel, let us remember that, as nations crumble around us and even as America will one day fall, the holy nation of God is eternal. Our truest citizenship is in a country that is not of this world.

Study our citizenship from Hebrews 11:13 and Philippians 3:20. Does the fact that our citizenship is in heaven mean we should remain politically inactive in this life? Why or why not?

⇐ *Cindy's Reflections* ⇐

Your Truest Citizenship

Will there still be an America when you have grown to be
Big enough to fight for her? Will she still be free . . .
Still one nation under God, from sea to shining sea;
Or will she be a pretty part of an aged memory?

Will the flag to which we pledge be waving in the breeze?
Will Liberty still hold her torch o'er great Atlantic seas?
Will the Bible grace her courtrooms? Will coins still bear His
name?
Or will they go the way of prayer—at school and at the game?

I cannot promise you, my child, that she can yet be saved;
That Lady Liberty will glow . . . the flag can still be waved.
But I'll show you a country where you can plant your heart,
And in a million years your dreams will still be at their start.

If you will be a soldier in the service of its King,
"My Country 'Tis of Thee" forever you can sing.
This country won't be terrorized, demoralized, defeated,
Nor plundered by the enemy when armies have retreated.

No emergency management or militia in this heaven,
No reserves, no disasters, no wars or 9-11,
No revolts against the system, no assassinations,
No threat of nuclear holocaust, no evacuations.

God has a welfare system that operates in the black,
His courtroom system is flawless, His judgment is exact.
His right-hand-man is Jesus and righteous are His laws.
And you can be a citizen, a soldier for His cause.

And this homeland security has never been undone
If all else fails, He still prevails. The battle He has won.
So work and pray for the USA and wave the red, white and
    blue.
But remember where your home is. To that kingdom, first, be
    true!

THE CURSING WOMAN

MICAH'S MOTHER

Have you ever even heard of her—this cursing mother? She may be obscure to Bible students, but she packs a powerful lesson about the depravity of a nation walking away from God. In a series of lessons about women of confused and troubled times, the mother of Micah in Judges 17 is a fitting character to study first. Although we do not definitively know where she fits in chronologically, it appears that she actually lived before the time of the judges. This seems to be the case since, at the time of the account of Micah, the Danites had not received all their land allotment (Judges 18:1). They fought for and obtained this land in the days of Joshua (Joshua 19:40–48).

She was a troubled woman in a troubled world seeking peace in all the wrong places.

It is appropriate to begin this series with the story of Micah's mother because she animates for us in one persona the national state of spiritual confusion and despair that led to the days when "every man did that which was right in his own eyes" (Judges 17:6). She raised her son during a time when the national security threat was always at the red level. While attacks from without were imminent, the state of immorality within Israel left the people purposeless and vulnerable. She was a troubled woman in a troubled world seeking peace in all the wrong places. A part of her wanted to please Jehovah God, but she was ignorant of His will for her life. Since she was uninformed about God's specific will for her life and worship, was her disobedience palatable to God? Let's find out.

THE MOTHER WHO CURSED

I once knew a Christian family who received a small inheritance from the grandmother who had passed away. The inheritance was so small, in fact, that the father in this good family had placed the money in an envelope in his sock drawer, just until he decided on something sentimental to purchase with the money—something special by which the family could remember Grandmother. By and by, when the father went to retrieve the money, he discovered it was missing. Upon investigating, he found that the money had been stolen by his oldest son. When I first heard about this event, how sad I was for this good family. Oh, it wasn't that the missing money made any appreciable difference to them at all. But the hearts of those godly parents were broken. It was such a little inheritance; how could they have raised a son who would stoop to thievery from his own parents?

That's exactly where this mother of Mount Ephraim found herself. Eleven hundred shekels of silver were missing. That was no small sum. (Notice it was the same amount offered to Delilah for her betrayal of Samson in Judges 16:5.) Her reaction was to curse over the lost money. And her son, Micah, heard his mother cursing.

Have your children heard you cursing? I am still shocked when I hear moms in Wal-Mart yelling and cursing at their innocent children, some still young enough to be strapped in the infant seats of grocery carts. It is inexcusable for dads to curse in front of their children. But it is nauseating for me to hear mothers—the ones who are to tenderly nurse and nurture those tiny babies; the ones who are called to have meek and gentle spirits (1 Peter 3:4)—shouting profanities and obscenities in the hearing of those souls so fresh from heaven itself.

THE SON WHO CONFESSED

> And he said to his mother, "The eleven hundred shekels of silver that were taken from you, and on which you put a curse, even saying it in my ears— here is the silver with me; I took it." And his mother said, "May you be blessed by the Lord, my son!" (Judges 17:2).

From this verse and others that follow, it seems that Micah's father was either dead or missing in action. Furthermore, it seems that his mother hadn't the slightest notion of how to be an effective godly parent. How many children do you know who have grown up in this scenario? They are all around us.

One single mother moved to a new apartment to get her daughter in a better school system. She described the woes of battling the culture while trying to put morality in her daughter's character. Then she casually wondered out loud as to whether she, herself, should continue a relationship with a man who had recently come into her life. As she began to tell about this relationship, someone asked a pointed question: "Have you had sex with this man?"

Her answer: "Yes, several times."

So what on earth is she thinking! Does she believe that her thirteen year old is oblivious to and protected from the influence of her on-going illicit relationship? After all, it is occurring right in her own house. Does she

think the influence of a "better" public school is going to trump the promis-
cuous influence of her mother at home? The casualties of missing fathers
and weak mothers are all too often children who grow up clueless about
morality, destined to continue the tragic cycle of promiscuity and children
in spiritual and moral—not to mention, economic—jeopardy.

So Micah's mother gave her son the money he had stolen in the first
place reserving only enough to introduce him to idolatry.

AND BOTH WERE CONFUSED

This mother was religious. She blessed the Lord (Judges 17:3). She had
at least acknowledged Jehovah in previously dedicating the silver to Him.
She was inclined toward some form of worship. But this mother had little
knowledge of the Word of the Lord. She obviously had very little exposure
to the law which strictly and expressly forbade the making of any silver
images (Exodus 20:4, 23). The law she violated when she took the two hundred shekels to the foundry (17:4) was the second of the Ten Commandments.
She didn't venture into the grey area of judgment here. She leaped into the
blackest of heathen practices in the name of Jehovah.

How can one's religion become so convoluted? How can one who has
access to the scriptures travel so far from her moorings? How can a human
potentate sit in an ornate but man-made chair and proclaim he is speaking
for deity? How can a mother carry a baby to a basin of water, have a man
in a robe sprinkle that tiny forehead, and then walk away believing she has
affected that baby's eternal destiny? How can an entire world of religionists
decide that baptism, the point of contact with the blood of Christ (Romans
6:3–4), has nothing to do with washing away sins? How can a man convince
himself that all heartfelt worship is pleasing to the same God who destroyed
Nadab and Abihu for a small departure from the God-prescribed details of
worship? (Leviticus 10:1–7). How can we believe that everyone who cries
out to the Lord for salvation will be saved, when the Lord himself stated the
opposite? (Matthew 7:21).

The answer: We can do it only when we stop studying the Word for
ourselves. If you want to be spiritually comfortable in this life, get out of the
Word. Go to church. Pray. Give to the poor. Look around you for community standards of morality. Talk about values. Teach your children the gold-
en rule. But *do not* study your Bible! It's kind of a fun way of life. Other
people respect you because you are religious. Your children can be popular

because they are accepting of all "people of faith." They can participate in all of the activities of their peers, because God wants them to be happy. Your god is a god of pluralism—a god who is accepting of all good and sincere hearts. There are few pangs of conscience because the verses you are violating don't pop into your unstudied head. There are no real rules of religion, but it sure makes you feel good to be religious.

And all is well with you and your household—until the Judgment Day.

> Many will say to Me in that day, "Lord, Lord, have we not prophesied in Your name, cast out demons in Your name, and done many wonders in Your name?" And then I will declare to them, "I never knew you; depart from Me, you who practice lawlessness!" (Matthew 7:22–23).

The trouble with Micah's mother was not that she left God out of her life. It was not that she failed to worship. It was not that she didn't make sacrifices or teach her son to be a religious man. The trouble was, there was a revelation from God; a detailed prescribed plan complete with commands and prohibitions for the people of God. God had called Moses into a mountain to deliver a law written by the very hand of God (Exodus 19–20). He had given detailed instructions about the preservation of this law in a traveling temple called the tabernacle (Exodus 25–27). He had been, and always would be, serious about both the spirit and the details of this law. He instructed his people to put these laws into the hearts of their children (Deuteronomy 6:4–7). And Micah's mother lived and worshiped as if there were no written law.

Give at least two other Bible examples of worship that displeased God. In each instance, explain why it was not pleasing.

_____

_____

Give examples from modern church history of seemingly small departures that ultimately led to false religions.

_____

THE CONTINUING CONSEQUENCES OF A MOTHER'S CONFUSION

In Judges 17:4 we find that Micah's mother had two statues made for the house of Micah. How sad! Have you ever encouraged your child to give allegiance to some idol of our world today? One mother wants her to daughter to be a cheerleader. She wants her daughter to dress immodestly and move seductively, even though she knows that will hinder her faithfulness to God. Another mom is all about her son being a star ball player. She encourages him to bow down to the American god of sports on Wednesday nights instead of being faithful to the Lord in Bible study. One mom makes beauty the god in her home. She spends mega-bucks to keep her daughter on the pageant circuit while giving very small token amounts to the work of the local church. And another mother has enshrined academics in her home. Studying for tests at school is obviously more important than studying the Word of God since her children both have a 4.0 GPA at school, but come to Bible class ill-prepared and with lazy attitudes.

What began as two little idols grew into a house of idols.

But notice the very next verse. What began as two little idols grew into a house of idols. Idolatry finally grew in the heart of Micah to the point where he felt comfortable installing his own personal priest, a man not even belonging to the priestly Levite tribe!

The man Micah had a shrine, and he made an ephod and household idols. He consecrated one of his sons, who became his priest (Judges 17:5).

How short-sighted are mothers who fail to see the long-term consequences of putting the idea in the hearts of our children that *any* earthly pleasure is worth compromising faithfulness to God! When that beautiful sixteen year old daughter is fifty-four, will it matter whether she was a cheerleader in high school? Will it matter whether she learned that true success is living her life and going to heaven? Will it matter when that son is out in the business world whether he played in the district tournament on that Wednesday night when he was fourteen? Will it matter whether or not he learned to be faithful to God? When that beauty queen has married and had three babies, will her children need to see the trophies to think she is pretty? Or would they think she was beautiful if they could see God in her?

Some of us need to get a spiritual eye exam. Lots of us need a new prescription for long-distance vision. Think of a young girl, just out of high school for one year. To those of you who are just preparing to do those middle and high school years, let me tell you a secret. One year out of high school, it will matter very little to your daughter whether she was in the "in group" or the "not-so-in group." She'll likely have a whole new group of friends. One year out of high school she will view proms and dances and high school parties as really very insignificant events in the scheme of life. She will have moved on quickly from high school responsibilities and high school drama—it *is* a very dramatic world in high school.

But she will not have moved on from her responsibilities to God. For which are you preparing her? That football star moves quickly from being a big fish in a small high school pond to being a little fish in a big collegiate sports sea. The glamour of stardom fades quickly. How will he fare in running that race that has eternal consequences? Micah's mother prepared him for a life of allegiance to material things which quickly pass. She encouraged him as he pledged allegiance to passing interests that competed for his very soul.

CONFUSION'S CONSEQUENCES

Micah's mom was religious, but she was religiously confused. She had a heart for service, but she failed to do the research. Since she was trying to please God and since she sacrificed a good portion of her recovered treasure, God spared her the consequences of disobedience. Right? Wrong! Notice the future departures of her posterity. As you see the great depths into which we can slowly wade as we make small worship and lifestyle departures, think about the number of people affected. Think about the ruin that eventually ensued. Think about how different things might have been if this one woman had searched out God's truths and followed them.

❄ Her son, Micah had a house of idolatry (Judges 17:5).

❄ Her grandson was appointed by Micah as a priest in spite of his lack of scriptural qualifications (Judges 17:5; Deuteronomy 18:1–5).

❈ Micah then hired a Levite to "serve" as his personal priest in the house with the molten and carved images, believing God would bless him if he had a Levite priest (Judges 17:10–13).

❈ Micah's images were stolen and his priest defected to the Danites, who enticed him with more goods, power, and prestige (Judges 18:1–21).

❈ The entire tribe of Dan set up the images and polluted their worship with Micah's gods until the time of captivity (Judges 18:30–31).

Micah thought hiring a Levite priest would make his worship and his life acceptable. Discuss some false doctrinal positions Martin Luther (or other religious leader) opposed while clinging to religious traditions foreign to Scripture.

_____

_____

_____

_____

Make a list of people from the Scriptures who disobeyed in sincerity.

_____

_____

Discuss the consequences of religious confusion in hearts motivated by a sincere desire to please God. What can be done to alleviate confusion in these sincere hearts?

_____

List some practical ideas we Christian women can use to engage our sincere but unsaved friends in Bible study.

_____

_____

_____

_____

_____

Moms, you are making a multigenerational difference. You may be affecting other families for generations. You may not even know your personal Danites, those families who will ultimately be affected by the decisions you are making in your homes today. Is your house free of idolatry? Is your Bible opened every day? Are you keeping your home free of religious confusion? Is your total allegiance to God? Is Christ your only high priest? Do your children know that all competing interests are a distant second to obedience to God? Any idol of your heart may still be in existence long after you've left this life, just as this woman's images existed until the captivity of Israel. Get it right while you have the time. Confusion breeds sin. Sin, when it is finished, brings death (James 1:15).

⇐ *Cindy's Reflections* ⇐

A House That's Truly Clean

I'm not a clutter person . . . I put things away.
I constantly remind the kids . . . "It's easier that way."
"When every item has a place and every item's in it,
It really saves a lot of time and we need every minute!"

I'm also big on hygiene. "Be sure to brush and floss!"
Everyone has check-ups, no matter what the cost.
Once the kids came home from school infested with head lice.
We quickly bought the remedy and did full treatments...twice.

The bed sheets are changed weekly. The floors are daily
    swept.
The vanities are shining and the bedrooms neatly kept.
When the baby had a virus, I scrubbed and disinfected.
For other kids were in the house and they must be protected!

No raw meat on the counter, no raw eggs in the cream.
No drinking after others or swapping helmets with your team.
I take the baby wipes for our booth at Burger King
And we wouldn't touch that toilet at the Y for anything!

But do I live a cluttered life in a more important way?
I mean, do I make sure there is time for God inside my day?
Do I save a place for Him in conversation and in prayer?
When my children watch my schedule, are they impressed that
    He is there?

While I'm so concerned that they are clean, and getting good
    nutrition,
Am I feeding them the Bread of Life? What of the soul's
    condition?
I lose my sanity when they come home from school with lice.
But they turn on the TV, and none of us think twice.

As all the world's pollutants nestle snugly in their heads,
The lies, the cursing and filth remain, when I tuck them in
    their beds.
I kiss their sparkling foreheads and their freshly shampooed
    tresses,
I am not the least concerned about those mental messes.

The startling contradictions they must be thinking through
The difference in what's said at home and what's taught in
    Sunday school
The things that made Mom mad today, the things she rushed
    to do
And maybe even sadder still . . . the things Mom didn't do.

We didn't learn my memory verse. Our Bible time we missed
We didn't check on Sister Smith, but she's still on our list.
In fact I can't remember if we even said a prayer.
Oh yeah, Coach said one on the field . . . at least we made it
    there!

Kids know the stuff you think is neat. They see what makes
    you tick.
They know when you missed Bible class, you really weren't
    that sick.
They see what makes you happiest. They wait for your
    applause.
They know when you are angry and they contemplate the
    cause.

And so they're off to sleep, their teeth are brushed and clothes
    laid out,
And Mom has just a moment to see what Daddy's all about.
He's glad to finally have a rest . . . a client made him late
He hasn't had his dinner yet and, my, it's half past eight!

He asks about that virus . . . if Timmy's finally fit.
He asks about the practice . . . Did Johnny get a hit?
He talks about his business deal, the merger he controls.
He talks of money, men and might, but not about their souls.

He says, "Are the kids asleep yet? You might want to close
    their door."
I want to turn the TV up. Tonight's the final four!
He gets worked up at the referees, but when the game is done
He says, "Did you get my shirts starched? I think I'm down to
    one."

Clean shirts, clean cars, a clean bill of health. It's just the way
    we live.
We never stop to think of the impression that we give.
Those tiny hearts tucked into bed can see right through the
    clean.
They see misplaced priorities. They know just what we mean.

So when I grab that Pine Sol to wipe up those greasy
    splatters.
I say a prayer that He will help me see what really matters.
To know that in the scheme of things, these messes are so
    small.
For if I've made a mess of living, I have lost it all.

I thank him for the blood that is the cleanser for my soul.
I pray for wisdom as I let His purpose take control.
It's on the One who washes white as snow that I must lean
If I ever hope to live inside a house that's truly clean!

TOUCHED BY AN ANGEL

MRS. MANOAH

WHEN GOD OPENS THE WOMB

Mrs. Manoah was one of several Bible women who, after an extended time of trying to conceive, were blessed directly by God with children. Sarah, Rachel, and Hannah all come immediately to mind. In each of these cases, it is almost as if God is preserving a specific womb for a specific purpose. When He opens that womb and releases that little life He has prepared, it's almost as if in each case, He breathed an extra measure of His power when He breathed into that man-child the breath of life. There was Isaac whose young life would be spared on Mount Moriah, then Joseph, the dreamer-turned-ruler who brought Israel into Egypt; and Samuel, the powerful prophet to the kings.

Samson, the promised Nazirite child of Judges 13, would be no exception. Little did Mrs. Manoah know that the tiny hands in her womb would one day slay lions and destroy a great temple. But deity was about to unleash its power when she gave birth.

While God's power within our children today is not miraculous in nature, be assured that with the breath of life in every baby He gives opportunities for His glory. I am convinced that His greatness in our world today can be seen, not so much through the vastness of His universe and the awesome wonders of nature as by the fulfilled ideals of humble mothers who purpose to give tiny lives to Him. In giving Him our children, their ambitions, their talents, and the might of their bodies and minds we display His awesome power to the world: "Praise the Lord! Blessed is the man who fears the Lord, who delights greatly in His commandments. His descendants will be mighty on earth; the generation of the upright will be blessed" (Psalm 112:1–2).

Assign someone to research scientific evidences that show there is life in the womb. Why do you think God has a purpose for my unborn child?

FROM THE WOMB

All abortion advocates who profess any allegiance to God should notice Judges 13:5: "For behold, you shall conceive and bear a son. And no razor shall come upon his head, for the child shall be a Nazirite to God from the womb; and he shall begin to deliver Israel out of the hand of the Philistines."

Was Samson more than a mass of fetal tissue when in his mother's womb? Was he as the passage says, "a child"? Was he a Nazirite placental mass or a person under a vow to God?

Scriptures and ultrasounds, logic and biology all identify the preborn as living. How absurd is a legal system in this enlightened era which fails to acknowledge the overwhelming evidence of life in the womb!

The tiny hands in her womb would one day slay lions and destroy a great temple.

GOD'S WORD TO THE WOMAN

It is interesting to notice that God's angel first came to the lady of Manoah's house: "And the Angel of the Lord appeared to the woman and said to her, "Indeed now, you are barren and have borne no children, but you shall conceive and bear a son" (Judges 13:3).

These tidings, along with some specific instructions about the upbringing of Samson, were delivered directly to Samson's mom. It was her job to reveal this wondrous prophecy to Manoah. Sometimes today, not because of direct revelation but because of my exposure or study, I may, as a wife understand the gospel or its injunctions before my husband has been taught. What a blessing for a wife who has a new-found faith to be able to share this knowledge with her husband! Surely Mrs. Manoah was excited to tell her husband of God's plan for them.

SPECIFIC AND SIMPLE DIRECTIONS

Notice the specificity of God's word as revealed to Samson's mother:

Now therefore, please be careful not to drink wine or similar drink, and not to eat anything unclean. For behold, you shall conceive and bear a son. And no razor shall come upon his head, for the child shall be a Nazirite to God from the womb; and he shall begin to deliver Israel out of the hand of the Philistines (Judges 13:4–5).

I love the simplistic language with which our God makes His will known. There is nothing ambiguous about His directions to Mrs. Manoah.

She surely understood them well as she was able to repeat them almost verbatim to her husband in verse 7. She certainly was not confused about who her prenatal dietician was and how to follow His orders. We, like Mrs. Manoah, can understand God's simple commands for our lives today. We surely need help to misunderstand passages such as these:

—He who believes and is baptized will be saved; but he who does not believe will be condemned (Mark 16:16).

—Then Peter said to them, "Repent, and let every one of you be baptized in the name of Jesus Christ for the remission of sins; and you shall receive the gift of the Holy Spirit" (Acts 2:38).

—There is also an antitype which now saves us—baptism (not the removal of the filth of the flesh, but the answer of a good conscience toward God), through the resurrection of Jesus Christ (1 Peter 3:21).

—And now why are you waiting? Arise and be baptized, and wash away your sins, calling on the name of the Lord (Acts 22:16).

Yet millions today claim confusion about the requirements of salvation, how to have sins remitted, what it is that saves us, and exactly what washes sins away. Don't you think that most any third grader—even one who has never been exposed to religious dogmas of our day—can fill in the blanks about salvation without confusion? I will never understand the present-day chaos over salvation's requirements. Perhaps it is a result of not receiving truth rather than not being able to understand it. The resulting delusion in our modern world, whatever the cause, is eternally tragic.

> . . . and with all unrighteous deception among those who perish, because they did not receive the love of the truth, that they might be saved. And for this reason God will send them strong delusion, that they should believe the lie (2 Thessalonians 2:10–11).

Give examples of New Testament teachings that are very clearly taught, yet have been confused by modern theologians.

THE POWER OF A PRAYING HUSBAND

Be impressed with Manoah's quick response to his wife's news: "Then Manoah prayed to the Lord, and said, 'O my Lord, please let the Man of God whom You sent come to us again and teach us what we shall do for the child who will be born'" (Judges 13:8).

One of the greatest blessings I have enjoyed as a Christian wife is the blessing of a praying husband. Wives, if your husband is oblivious to your need to pray with him, by all means ask him to pray with you. Ask him daily. Ask him humbly, but ask him. Your Christian husband should not have to be asked to pray for you. But if you ever wonder if you're in his prayers, then ask. Ask if he's praying for you. If he is, express your gratitude. If he's not, beg a place in his prayers. Ask him to lead you as together you lift your children up to God in prayer. Talk with Him about specific needs of each child, needs of which he may be unaware. After all, dads are generally at work all day. What a blessing of cohesion this shared prayer life brings to a family!

Suggest some ways wives can encourage husbands to be more prayerful without nagging or usurping authority.

_____

_____

List your favorite prayers for unborn children and/or grandchildren.

_____

_____

Manoah's prayer is exemplary to all parents today, both because of its content and because of its timing. We should surely beg the Father's guidance in parenting. The proper time to start praying for direction in parenting is prior to the births of our children. We should begin then to pray for:

—wisdom as mothers (James 1:5).

—resources from which to learn (Titus 2:3–5).

—the physical well-being of our children.

—the education and mental development of our children.

—spiritual strength for ourselves and avenues to build this faith within our children (2 Timothy 1:5).

—faithful Christians for our children's spouses.

This list is not exhaustive, of course. The greatest resource of any Christian parent is prayer!

ENTERTAINING ANGELS UNAWARES

Do not forget to entertain strangers, for by so doing some have unwittingly entertained angels (Hebrews 13:2).

Often we assume that this New Testament admonition refers to Abraham and Sarah's visitors in Genesis 18, but it could well be a reference to Samson's parents in Judges 13. Notice verses 15–16:

Then Manoah said to the Angel of the Lord, "Please let us detain You, and we will prepare a young goat for You." And the Angel of the Lord said to Manoah, "Though you detain Me, I will not eat your food. But if you offer a burnt offering, you must offer it to the Lord." (For Manoah did not know He was the Angel of the Lord.)

Hospitality has always characterized the people of God. In fact, it is a requirement of New Testament Christianity (1 Peter 4:9). The faithful practice of hospitality in our rushed society takes a great deal of effort. In such a society, Christian women who work to be hospitable are set apart from the world. Hospitality is just one of many distinguishing earmarks of Christianity. May we all be women who glorify God through hospitality.

List four New Testament passages that encourage Christians to be hospitable.

_____

List three secrets of true hospitality. Be creative in thinking of ways to minister in and from our homes.

_____

_____

HUMILITY

I am stricken with a feeling of incredible awe when I think that there were actually many human beings in earlier eras of world history who found themselves tangibly and physically in the presence of heavenly beings. I think about Mrs. Manoah on the morning of this angel's visit. Perhaps she had that queasy feeling in her stomach that often attends early pregnancy. Surely, after her barren years, she was preoccupied with "baby" plans, and anticipation of motherhood. Like all mothers-to-be, she probably wondered if he would have his father's features, and she was likely thinking of possible names.

And then "the man" appeared again. This was certainly no ordinary man-child in her womb, for even in early pregnancy, the intervention of deity in the little life was recurring. This time she was going to be sure that Manoah saw the mysterious visitor too. She ran in haste to her husband, who had prayed for the return of this visitor and together they witnessed a series of events they would never forget.

> And God listened to the voice of Manoah, and the Angel of God came to the woman again as she was sitting in the field; but Manoah her husband was not with her. Then the woman ran in haste and told her husband, and said to him, "Look, the Man who came to me the other day has just now appeared to me!" So Manoah arose and followed his wife. When he came to the Man, he said to Him, "Are You the Man who spoke to this woman?" And He said, "I am." Manoah said, "Now let Your words come to pass! What will be the boy's rule of life, and his work?" So the Angel of the Lord said to Manoah, "Of all that I said to the woman let her be careful. She may not eat anything that comes from the vine, nor may she drink wine or similar drink, nor eat anything unclean. All that I commanded her let her observe." Then Manoah said to the Angel of the Lord, "Please let us detain You, and we will prepare a young goat for You." And the Angel of the Lord said to Manoah, "Though you detain Me, I will not eat your food. But if you offer a burnt offering, you must offer it to the Lord." (For Manoah did not know He was the Angel of the Lord.) Then Manoah said to the Angel of the Lord, "What is Your name, that when Your words come to pass we may honor You?" And the Angel of the Lord said to him, "Why do you ask My name, seeing it is wonderful?" So Manoah took the young goat with the grain offering, and offered it upon the rock to the Lord. And He did a wondrous thing while Manoah and his wife looked on—it happened as the flame went up toward heaven from the altar—the Angel of the Lord ascended in the flame of the altar! When Manoah and his wife saw this, they fell on their faces to the ground. When the Angel

of the Lord appeared no more to Manoah and his wife, then Manoah knew that He was the Angel of the Lord (Judges 13:9–21).

It is valuable to notice Manoah's reaction to the visitor in verse 17 before he was aware that he was an angel. He wanted to give him honor. Compare this reaction to the one given in verses 20–21 when he became aware of the presence of heaven's messenger. Notice also that this reverence was shared by Mrs. Manoah. I believe these two passages serve succinctly as a prescription for success in our relationships. Here is that prescription.

1. *We should honor one another.*

   "Be kindly affectionate to one another with brotherly love, in honor giving preference to one another" (Romans 12:10).

   "Let nothing be done through selfish ambition or conceit, but in lowliness of mind let each esteem others better than himself" (Philippians 2:3).

   "Honor all people. Love the brotherhood. Fear God. Honor the king" (1 Peter 2:17).

2. *We should reverence God.*

   "By faith he forsook Egypt, not fearing the wrath of the king; for he endured as seeing Him who is invisible" (Hebrews 11:27).

   "By faith he kept the Passover and the sprinkling of blood, lest he who destroyed the firstborn should touch them" (Hebrews 11:28). Like Moses, we should fear the wrath of God on the disobedient more than the wrath of any powerful man.

   "He has sent redemption to His people; He has commanded His covenant forever: Holy and awesome is His name" (Psalm 111:9).

3. *We must, in our souls, be prostrate before Him.*

   "It happened as the flame went up toward heaven from the altar—the Angel of the Lord ascended in the flame of the altar! When Manoah and his wife saw this, they fell on their faces to the ground" (Judges 13:20).

"He went a little farther and fell on His face, and prayed, saying, 'O My Father, if it is possible, let this cup pass from Me; nevertheless, not as I will, but as You will'" (Matthew 26:39). This humility to His will is spiritual victory. It is eternal exaltation by the only One who has eternal glory at His disposal.

"Therefore humble yourselves under the mighty hand of God, that He may exalt you in due time" (1 Peter 5:6).

"Humble yourselves in the sight of the Lord and He will lift you up" (James 4:10).

Regardless of the posture of my body, I must, in my soul, be prostrate on the ground before Him, just as were Manoah and his wife as soon as they sensed His presence through His angel. I recall that even my Lord, when facing the ultimate challenge of all ages, fell to the ground as well. His words echo in my heart when I face my most difficult challenges.

Find at least three examples from Scripture of those who fell down before deity or before angels.

_____

_____

_____

PARENTAL WEAKNESS

So Samson, the promised baby, grew up to be the promised deliverer. But somewhere along the way, he rebelled. When Samson grew to maturity and began looking for female companionship, he didn't look among the people of God. He looked among the idolatrous Philistines. He found the woman, a woman void of moral character, and demanded that his parents get her for him.

Then his father and mother said to him, "Is there no woman among the daughters of your brethren, or among all my people, that you must go and get a wife from the uncircumcised Philistines?" And Samson said to his father, "Get her for me, for she pleaseth me well" (Judges 14:3).

Approach the subject of family to groups of mothers and grandmothers, and you will find that the Samson scenario is very common. Mothers burdened with grief relate stories of their children's rebellion as teens, subsequent marriages to non-Christians, and ultimate lost conditions. While we must sympathize and grieve with families in such cases, we should also, for the sake of parents of younger children, teach biblical parenting skills that help prevent teen rebellion. I am quite certain that Samson's determination to marry the girl of Timnath was not the first occasion of defiance in Manoah's household. Although we are not given details about Samson's childhood, we may safely assume that this oppositional behavior did not begin when Samson decided whom to marry. Here are several evidences.

1. *Samson's associates were not wholesome influences.* Samson was not befriending the people of God. He was instead running with the heathen, a rowdy partying crew who enjoyed gambling and feasting. Samson's wife was not his friend. She was willing to betray him to preserve her own interests. Parents should guard their children's friendships from very early ages.

2. *Samson was unwilling to listen to the wisdom of his parents.* His response to their pleas was not one of respect and reason. He was blunt and insolent in attitude. His hardness of heart was likely cultivated by a lack of restraint during the tender years. Hearts must be molded while they are still pliable.

3. *Samson's parents apparently cowered to Samson's demands.* Not only did Samson marry the girl, but his parents attended the feast. How amazing to see parents who know full well that their children are running with the wrong crowd. So their children fall in love with the wrong people. The parents encourage and often fund the dating process. The children become engaged to the wrong people. The parents give showers and gifts to the couple. The children marry the wrong people. The parents pay for the wedding. The children and grandchildren are lost. The parents grieve.

As you can see, something is very wrong with this picture. We cannot wear blinders throughout our children's early years and adolescence and then expect no surprises when they become adults. The smallest inconsistencies in childhood should be addressed, the tiniest rebellion quickly disciplined, the childhood friendships guarded, and the future surrendered to Him in prayer.

One woman, now in her late 80s, is still grieving over her lost adult children. She is hesitant to even discuss spiritual matters with her own children because of the distance it seems to put between them. How should she address eternal matters with her daughter? Why is it painfully obvious that these spiritual barriers between parent and child result not from any single decision on the part of the child to abandon the Lord, but rather years of ignoring smaller steps the child takes in the direction of the world? Sometimes a mother wakes up too late, but it is never too late to influence a new generation. Heed the words of an eighty-seven-year-old Christian soldier: "Just because my children have chosen to reject God is no reason for me to quit winning souls. I will keep hoping that they will repent, but I must keep encouraging today's youth."

We cannot wear blinders throughout our children's early years and adolescence and then expect no surprises when they become adults.

Mothers, be passionate about your children's faith. Be firm and consistent in discipline while they are young. Be constantly in prayer for them. Spend time knowing needs, planting seeds, and pulling weeds in the soil of their young and tender hearts.

These admonitions are intended, not to pour salt in painful wounds of mothers whose adult children are lost, but to make those whose children's destinies are yet undetermined to think—to think about the eternal importance of every parental decision, every reaction to every instance of rebellion, yea, the countless responses to the myriad of situations in which I can show my children a living and sacrificial faith.

Read Hebrews 11:23–28. Notice the decisions Moses made as an adult. What description of his parents in these verses may have helped mold these courageous characteristics?

One family faced a sticky circumstance which turned into an opportunity for placing a stone in their daughter Bailey's faith foundation. Students from a private school planned an extended field trip to New York City. Bailey was excited that she was asked to go. One of the members of the congregation where Bailey worshiped was chaperoning the trip. She asked detailed questions regarding all activities, church attendance while away, and other pertinent details. Her parents were satisfied that the trip was a wholesome adventure for Bailey, and encouraged her to work to save her money. She cheerfully saved and made significant, non-refundable deposits. Shortly before the departure date, the plan changed. Bailey was informed that the group would spend all day Sunday touring and shopping and visiting the Statue of Liberty. All kinds of compromises were proposed as alternatives to worship, from visiting a cathedral to having a short devotional before the day's activities.

> *It is only when a family's Christianity is obviously distinctive that other families will begin to see Christ.*

But Bailey's parents had not invested fifteen years of prioritizing spiritual concerns in vain. Bailey decided she had rather remember her commitment to God. She decided not to go with the group. Her parents applauded her choice. One day, she will look back and remember a decision of commitment rather than a decision of compromise. Her statement at the time was, "I really want to go to New York, but not as badly as I want to go to heaven."

A young mother's oldest child Taylor is an enthusiastic basketball player in a community league. Taylor was discussing upcoming games with one of her neighborhood friends, a fellow-player in the league. When Taylor's young friend found out that Taylor was going to miss an upcoming game because it was on a Wednesday night, she reacted with shock. "Don't you ever miss church for anything?" she asked.

Taylor recalled having been sick and missing worship, but other than that, she explained, they never missed. Her friend was astonished and began to give her somewhat of a hard time for being so dedicated to attend Bible classes. The little girl's mother (not a Christian), overhearing her daughter's taunting said, "Leave Taylor alone. Their lifestyle is completely different from ours."

What a profoundly wonderful compliment this non-Christian paid this godly Christian family. It is only when my family's Christianity is obviously distinctive that other families will begin to see Christ. It is in the very practical differences that my sanctification can be noticed by the world. This sanctification begins with little decisions God gives us. He gives us opportunities to build character. Let us seize them. They are priceless.

LESSONS LEARNED

1. God empowers godly people through their children.

2. God recognizes preborn humans.

3. God often leads men through the influence of women.

4. God's commands are not hard to understand; sometimes they're just hard to keep.

5. Women who have praying husbands are rich wives.

6. We should pray for our preborn children.

7. Hospitality is characteristic of all faithful Christians.

8. The heart must always be prostrate before God, regardless of our physical posture.

9. We should train children whom to marry before they enter the dating years.

Cindy's Reflections

If . . .

If I could put my preferences aside and see His cross . . .
If I could sacrifice for Him and count it all but loss . . .
If everything I do could be for Him and not for me . . .
If I could look at people through His eyes and really see
That the most important things in life are not mere things at
    all;
The thing of life is being still and listening to His call . . .
I'd spend less time in worry and more down on my knees.
I'd talk less about money and more about His peace.

I'd fret less about my house and focus more on His.

I'd take less time for TV and more for my prayer list . . .

Less time in front of the mirror and more in front of the
Word . . .

I'd have a lot more compassion for those who haven't heard.

My life would be a lot simpler. I'd discover less is more.

I'd be a little farther from this world . . . A little closer to
heaven's shore.

LESSON 4

A DOOMED MARRIAGE

MRS. SAMSON

PICKING A PARTNER FOR MARRIAGE

I am quite convinced that rarely does any young person contemplating marriage really realize the seriousness of that decision. Future successes or failures, the plights of generations to come, and the destinies of souls can all be determined by the choices we make about marriage. I was twenty years old when I married. I had dated Glenn for a year and a half when we made our vows. We were both faithful Christians having been raised in Christian homes. Glenn was already preaching the gospel on a regular basis. We were serious about spiritual things. Yet I am now convinced that I could not, at that vulnerable point in my young life, have fully comprehended the vast consequences of that one decision.

Focusing on the eternal import of choosing the right mate is especially hard in modern America, a society in which the media puts so much emphasis on outward beauty and material success. A recent TV viewing season had all of America, it seems, engrossed in a couple of reality television dramas in which groups of people were paid large sums of money to participate in marriage competitions; contests in which some "lucky" contestant would marry the supposed millionaire. As a culture we are sending the wrong message to our children about the marriage vows. We are cheapening the sacred and desecrating the holy union of marriage when we convey that the one who gets the glamour guy with the most money is the winner. Marriage is a God-ordained institution and should never be relegated to being the grand prize at the end of a game show.

Samson's mother and father were understandably disappointed with his choice of a mate. After all, he was promised by an angel, set apart with a Nazirite vow for the purposes of God, and moved by the Holy Spirit of God. This incredible young man had found his wife-to-be among the uncircumcised Philistines.

> So he went up and told his father and mother, saying, "I have seen a woman in Timnah of the daughters of the Philistines; now therefore, get her for me as a wife." Then his father and mother said to him, "Is there no woman among the daughters of your brethren, or among all my people, that you must go and get a wife from the uncircumcised Philistines?" And Samson said to his father, "Get her for me, for she pleases me well" (Judges 14:2–3).

Samson's wife was not of the chosen people of God (v. 3), she ran with a rowdy crowd of gambling heathen folks who cared nothing about her (v. 15), and she had no sense of loyalty, even to her own husband (v. 17). Samson's parents naturally protested his marriage to her. But he was determined and insisted that his father get her for him. Samson, much to his own detriment, got his way.

While I know that we as parents cannot fully control—nor do we want to—the choices our children make when it's time to date and marry, I believe we can do some things beginning at very early ages to encourage our children to be extremely selective when the marrying years roll around.

Consider these suggestions.

1. When your child is old enough to talk at all, begin making this statement to him/her: "When I marry, I'm going to marry a—" Do this daily with even your two-year old. Elicit the response "Christian." As your child matures, accompany the statement with an elicited definition of what a true Christian is. A Christian, by definition is a follower of Christ. This means more than being a member of some church. This means patterning his/her life after Christ in all practical areas.

2. Well before your child begins to date, come up with a list of characteristics or qualifications for which to search in finding this Christian. When we did this at our house we made little wallet sized cards, laminated them, and called them our "dating check cards." They look like this:

DATING CHECK CARD FOR GIRLS

☐ Does he speak respectfully to and about his parents?
☐ Does he pray in the restaurant?
☐ Is he careful in his entertainment choices?
☐ Does he avoid physical compromises in our relationship?
☐ Does he like to talk about the scriptures?
☐ Is there someone he is trying to convert to Christ?
☐ Does he sing out in worship?
☐ Does he take notes during the sermon?
☐ Does he like to sit toward the front in worship?
☐ Does he avoid alcoholic beverages?
☐ Does he control his anger and avoid profanity?
☐ Is he a faithful Christian?

DATING CHECK CARD FOR BOYS

☐ Can she be happy when she is not the center of attention?
☐ Does she speak respectfully to and about her parents?
☐ Is she careful in her entertainment choices?
☐ Does she avoid physical compromises in our relationship?
☐ Does she like talking about the scriptures?
☐ Is there someone she is trying to convert to Christ?
☐ Does she sing out in worship?
☐ Does she take notes during the sermon?
☐ Does she like to sit toward the front in worship?
☐ Does she avoid all alcoholic beverages?
☐ Does she dress modestly?
☐ Is she discreet about sexual matters?
☐ Is she a faithful Christian?

Remember, it's too late to say or do any of these things once your son or daughter has fallen in love and decided whom to marry. While you should still do all you can to help your child avoid marrying someone who will endanger his/her eternal salvation, the time to begin is well in advance of the teen years. If your child can walk and talk even a little, get busy!

What are some additional ways in which our society cheapens marriage?

_____

What additional characteristics would you add to the list of qualities of a potential mate?

_____

Someone has said, "The best time to get a divorce is before you marry." What are some societal pressures that make it difficult today for an engaged couple to heed warning signs when the marriage is destined for trouble?

_____

How can we help our children watch for and heed these "red flags" before it is too late?

_____

Betrayal in Marriage

So Samson's father relented and Samson married the wrong woman. How many of your friends and mine are today singing another verse of this same song? It is almost weekly that I grieve with some parent whose adult child has been either led from faithfulness or betrayed by an ungodly spouse.

As we might expect, Mr. and Mrs. Samson's honeymoon was over all too quickly. Betrayal in marriage never brings happiness. Here's how the trust unraveled in Samson's house.

Samson put forth a riddle to the men of Timnath at the wedding feast:

> "Let me pose a riddle to you. If you can correctly solve and explain it to me within the seven days of the feast, then I will give you thirty linen garments and thirty changes of clothing. But if you cannot explain it to me, then you shall give me thirty linen garments and thirty changes of clothing." And they said to him, "Pose your riddle, that we may hear it." So he said to them: "Out of the eater came something to eat, and out of the strong came something sweet." Now for three days they could not explain the riddle (Judges 14:12–14).

Samson's wife's unsavory friends threatened to burn her and her father's house if she didn't find the riddle's answer so they could win the bet. (Who needs enemies?) You know what I would do if my friends asked me to betray my husband? I'd go straight to him and tell him what these "friends" had asked of me and we would handle the situation as a team. After all, we are one flesh (Matthew 19:6). I especially hope I would have thought to enlist the help of my husband had I been married to someone who could whip them all with a little jawbone. But this marriage was not built on trust.

Then Samson's wife wept on him, and said, "You only hate me! You do not love me! You have posed a riddle to the sons of my people, but you have not explained it to me." And he said to her, "Look, I have not explained it to my father or my mother; so should I explain it to you?" Now she had wept on him the seven days while their feast lasted. And it happened on the seventh day that he told her, because she pressed him so much. Then she explained the riddle to the sons of her people.

What are four practical ways to build trust in a marriage?

_____

_____

MANIPULATION IN MARRIAGE

We all know how to manipulate in marriage. We selfishly attempt to get our way using our tears, our tricks, our lies, our begging, or, if all else fails, the withholding or exchange of our sexual favors. It's hard not to do it, because it works! As children, we learn that sometimes—maybe not with Mom, but certainly with Aunt Ruthie—crying or pouting really works. We learn that if we catch Dad off guard, he might not listen too well to the question, and he may answer yes without really knowing he said yes. But these tricks are for kids—you silly rabbit!—and when we become mature enough for marriage, we must be mature enough for total honesty. Besides, I'd much rather get the petition I'm asking because he loves me than to have my way because I pouted until he gave in or because I tricked my way into it. Ladies, we really don't want husbands who are weak enough to be manipulated, so why do we often seem to try so hard to wear them down?

Samson's wife mastered the evil art of manipulation. She got her way. But was she happy? Well, let's see. In the next few verses, her husband left her and murdered thirty of her kinsmen, her father picked out a new husband for her, her sister was offered to Samson to be his wife, and Samson burned up the farms of her countrymen who, in turn, burned her up along with her family. Great manipulative success for Mrs. Samson. An overall win, right?!

We never win when we manipulate in marriage. Rebekah manipulated Isaac and lost her favored son and the respect of her husband (Genesis 27). Herodias manipulated Herod and gained her place in history as the one who beheaded the beloved forerunner of the Messiah, John the Baptist (Matthew 14:3–12). We are winners when we reverence our husbands (Ephesians 5:33), for it is then that we win the favor of the one who is truly able and willing to make us happy.

Describe a typical modern-day scenario in which a wife might manipulate her husband. Why are the consequences never good in the long run?

_____

Find other examples of Bible women who manipulated their husbands.

_____

A Second Marriage

Samson's riddle was exposed. His fellows had gotten the best of him by consorting with his wife and he was not a happy camper. In fact, he left the camp, killed thirty men of Ashkelon, paid the debt, and went home to his father.

> So the men of the city said to him on the seventh day before the sun went down: "What is sweeter than honey? And what is stronger than a lion?" And he said to them: "If you had not plowed with my heifer, You would not have solved my riddle!"
>
> Then the Spirit of the Lord came upon him mightily, and he went down to Ashkelon and killed thirty of their men, took their apparel, and gave the changes of clothing to those who had explained the riddle. So his anger was aroused, and he went back up to his father's house (Judges 14:18–19).

Samson's father-in-law reasonably assumed it was all over between Samson and his daughter and, as heathen customs would allow, gave her to one of Samson's friends for his wife. (Again, who needs enemies?) But this young woman's second marriage was going to be more tumultuous than her first and almost as short-lived.

Samson soon came back to reconcile with his wife. He brought a young goat, our modern-day equivalent of roses and candy, and assumed she would be available. Samson was not pleased when her father met him at the door with this response: "I really thought that you thoroughly hated her; therefore I gave her to your companion. Is not her younger sister better than she? Please, take her instead" (Judges 15:2).

When Samson got mad, he typically found some people to kill or some property to destroy using some outlandish means. This time was no exception.

Then Samson went and caught three hundred foxes; and he took torches, turned the foxes tail to tail, and put a torch between each pair of tails. When he had set the torches on fire, he let the foxes go into the standing grain of the Philistines, and burned up both the shocks and the standing grain, as well as the vineyards and olive groves (Judges 15:4–5).

When the Philistines traced Samson's fury and their resulting loss to the household of Samson's father-in-law, their furor was intense.

Then the Philistines said, "Who has done this?" And they answered, "Samson, the son-in-law of the Timnite, because he has taken his wife and given her to his companion." So the Philistines came up and burned her and her father with fire (Judges 15:6).

List the responses of anger exhibited by Samson throughout his life. Then find New Testament passages that teach us the proper way to deal with anger.

_____

_____

Thus, we come to the tragic end of the short life of Samson's only wife. This pretty face became a nightmare in the reckless life of Samson. In a much abbreviated lifetime she was a great grief to Samson's parents, to Samson, to her countrymen, and to her family. She literally contributed to the deaths of hundreds. Today we would say, "She's trouble with a capital T." But troublemakers are troubled people. She likely never experienced any real contentment.

God can take the weakest of character and use even the most troubled lives to accomplish His purposes. In the saga of Samson and his wife, we see the Philistine people, perhaps the most powerful nation of the world, slowly coming to its knees before God's Israel. God controls, even through the weaknesses of humanity in ways that are beyond our scope of comprehension.

⇜ *Cindy's Reflections* ⇝

My Superman

He doesn't have a long red cape
Or a fear of Kryptonite.
He can't stop a locomotive
Or set a falling building right;

But when he dons that big red towel
And flies down the nursery hall,
When he coaches my personal favorite team:
The Rascals in pee-wee T-ball;

When he bursts through the door with a rose in his mouth
And Chinese take out in his hands;
When he vacuums the den after game night
Or winks at me up in the stands;

When he rescues me bravely from laundry
Or just gently reaches out for my hand;
When he kneels at our bedside and talks to his God,
In these times, he's my Superman!

THE WOMAN OF THE NIGHT

THE HARLOT OF GAZA

BEFORE MIDNIGHT

Twenty years had passed since the marriage saga of Samson's young life. In the interim, Samson had repeatedly amazed both friend and foe with incredible strength from God. He could snap like a thread any cord that bound him. On one occasion he killed a thousand men with the jawbone of an ass. Then one night he saw a prostitute. All of Samson's strength was physical. He had no spiritual prowess. His character was repulsively weak.

> Now Samson went to Gaza and saw a harlot there, and went in to her. When the Gazites were told, "Samson has come here!" they surrounded the place and lay in wait for him all night at the gate of the city. They were quiet all night, saying, "In the morning, when it is daylight, we will kill him" (Judges 16:1–2).

Prostitution is a grievous plague of any society. America today is ridden with terrible consequences resulting from harlotry and its attending vices. There are areas of all major American cities in which poverty, disease, drugs, crime, and death—all associated with prostitution rings have literally transformed desirable middle-class neighborhoods into ghettos of hellish horror.

According to Prostitutes Education Network, over one million Americans today have worked as prostitutes. The average American city spends 7.5 million dollars annually on prostitution control. Studies show that seventy percent of American men have engaged a prostitute at least one time. A London study revealed that fifty percent of males who have bought the services of a prostitute were married or co-habiting at the time of their involvement. In a study of street prostitutes, eighty percent of prostitutes were found to have been physically assaulted. It is estimated that street prostitutes are often raped eight to ten times annually with only four percent of these rapes being reported to police. Today in larger American cities, between twenty and thirty percent of prostitutes are reported to be male.

While these statistics are alarming, they are not of the utmost concern to me. What is most disconcerting about prostitution today is the ever-growing push by prostitution advocates in our society to mainstream prostitution as a legal and recognized profession. Advocacy groups are focusing on our legal system as the avenue through which they intend to make harlotry just another career with all attending rights and restrictions. This push involves the legal changing of the name "prostitute" to "sex worker."

Groups of supporters are advocating not only the legality of this sex work, but the protection of its workers from unhygienic working conditions, and the use of communal needles for contraceptive purposes. They are actively lobbying for paid holidays, unions, shorter workdays, compulsory HIV testing, and social security benefits. We are not hearing a lot about this from the media, but, rest assured, it is occurring under our noses. We must educate and push for legislation that protects society from the legalization and protection of prostitution.

As early as 1949, the United Nations passed a resolution to decriminalize prostitution. This resolution has been ratified by fifty nations. The United States is not among those who have ratified it! The National Organization for Women has passed its own resolution seeking and supporting the decriminalization of harlotry in the United States.

It is difficult to imagine that standards of morality in heathen nations, such as the Philistine, were any more immoral than the current standards in the United States. Bible believing people will continue to deplore the sin of harlotry and vocalize their objections to any legislation that would decriminalize this sin against which God's warnings have always been clear.

Proverbs 7 is devoted to warning the naive young man about the cunning nature of whoredom. Notice the difference in what she offers and what she delivers. Her offer: "Come, let us take our fill of love until morning; Let us delight ourselves with love" (Proverbs 7:18). What she delivers: "For she has cast down many wounded, and all who were slain by her were strong men. Her house is the way to hell, descending to the chambers of death" (Proverbs 7:26–27).

"For she has cast down many wounded. . . all who were slain by her were strong men. Her house is the way to hell."

—Proverbs 7:26–27

Samson was a strong man. But the harlot's house was on his way down the road to the chambers of death. While it is true that he had a few more stops to make before that terrible day of death, this house of harlotry was clearly on a destructive path that Samson was too weak to resist. He was yet to display some amazing feats of physical strength, but he was headed for a bitter end and it would be his weakness for wicked women that would, in the end, be his undoing.

Why did Samson's own people bind him in Judges 15? At this point in his life who were Samson's loyal friends? Why is it that when we sacrifice our morality, we often sacrifice our true friends?

_____

_____

_____

How many Philistines had Samson slain by the end of Judges 15? ____

Assign research on prostitution statistics in your city or state. What are attending crime problems in your area? (For general information use this web site: bayswan.org/stats.html.)

_____

MIDNIGHT MADNESS

> And Samson lay low till midnight; then he arose at midnight, took hold of the doors of the gate of the city and the two gateposts, pulled them up, bar and all, put them on his shoulders, and carried them to the top of the hill that faces Hebron (Judges 16:3).

Samson must have known he was surrounded by Philistine foes, for he arose from the harlot's bed and walked to the gate of the city. Undaunted by the Philistines that surrounded him, he picked up the gate of the city with its bars, likely made of iron, and with the entire apparatus hoisted across his shoulders, proceeded to carry it to a nearby hilltop. These city gates were massive, typically built to keep out invaders and secure the city. No Philistine was about to try to tangle with this man who carried such a load. All he would have to do to slay any man is just drop his load on him. Imagine the Philistines on the hilltop at dawn trying to figure out how to return the gate to the defenseless city!

I wonder how the ruthless Philistines treated the harlot the next morning when they viewed the bare entrance to the city, realizing her client had demolished their city's grand entranceway. At any rate, the morning after a night of sinful sex is generally not very pleasant. She must have been a very pitiable woman, having been used by Samson and then left alone at midnight to deal with the angry band of humiliated Philistines.

Read the following passages:

Proverbs 7:1–27   Proverbs 9:13–18
Proverbs 2:10–22   Proverbs 5:1–23

Have half the class members make a list of the characteristics of a harlot from these passages. Then have the other half list the consequences that come to those entrapped by her. Why are these consequences apparent in areas where prostitution rings are prevalent?

THE MOTHER'S NIGHTMARE

Gena is the mother of two young teen girls. Too late, she realized that she needed help in dealing with the fourteen-year-old who was sexually active with her boyfriend. But the saddest part of Gene's saga is her daughter's loss of innocence. This child of fourteen invites others to watch her as she has sex with her boyfriend. She charges admission to her classmates and to internet viewers who patronize her sex show.

Don't you weep for this mother? How could life go on in your world if this was your fourteen-year-old daughter or granddaughter? How would you face each morning knowing that your very young girl had slipped into a devil's grasp that, at best, would never fully release her? What counselor would be able to reach into such a mixed-up heart and untangle the complicated web of guilt, the future haunting of relational insecurities and the fear of disease possibly already inflicted on that beautiful young person?

The devil is merciless. He attacks the most vulnerable and devours the unsuspecting without warning. It would be so very nice if he set up a roadside warning and yellow lights for adults before he messes with our children.

CAUTION

SATAN'S CREWS
AT WORK AHEAD
PROCEED WITH
EXTREME CARE

But he often has our children in the ditch before we are even aware that his crews are erecting the safety hazards.

The warning signs are apparent only when we really know our kids. They come up in unplanned conversations. The yellow lights blink only when we are spending large amounts of time talking to our kids and really knowing what they are about. Being home when they come home from school is important. Knowing and conversing with their teachers and coaches is essential. Having the privilege of being the adult chaperone when they are with their friends is something you should covet earnestly. Your house should be open to their friends and your table always the one around which they gather for pizza or popcorn. Your family Bible time should be inviting and interesting to their friends. If their boyfriends or girlfriends are watching the movie at your house, then you are there baking the cookies.

Teen years rush by. All these chances to know your teenager will soon be gone. Is parenting a teen a major time commitment? Oh yeah! But I have a hunch that Gena would love the chance to turn back the clock and put in a little more time with her teen.

I pray that some mother who is reading this still has time on her side. Leave this classroom determined to get to the heart of the matter and observe the warning signs before you approach the danger zone.

Have a prayer time for all of the children of those in the class or discussion group. Take each child's name before God's throne and pray for each mother to be able to communicate effectively with her children so their lives will be better insulated from the devil's deception.

What potential effect will the decriminalization of prostitution have on scenarios faced by moms like Gena? Research legislation in your state. How can you voice opposition to the legalization of prostitution?

_____

_____

Cindy's Reflections

Don't Kiss Toads

Toads are really nasty creatures.
With totally boogey-eyed warty features.
They're lazy and they eat gross stuff,
Until their throats and bellies puff.
They don't mind slime or mud or muck.
Sometimes, they hop in a pick-up truck!
If you grab one, you don't have him long.
He wriggles and squiggles and slips out. He's gone!
And you are left with slimy fingers
And a swampy smell that's putrid and lingers.
And Grandma says you may get warts,
Cuz' "that's what happens to a toad's cohorts."
Maybe you're okay with walking out on that log
Reaching in the "yuck" and grabbin' that frog.
'Cuz you've heard that tale about how you can change him…
Clean him up spic, teach him tricks, rearrange him.
You're not worried at all. You're a girl with good sense.
So you go ahead and kiss him and then he's your . . .
. . . Toad!

MISTRESS OF MANIPULATION
DELILAH

Immortalized as one of history's most famous couples, the names of Samson and Delilah can be found in poetry, in pop songs alongside the likes of Romeo and Juliet, and in international folklore. The reality of immortality, though, is the most tragic part of the story of Samson and Delilah. Somewhere today their souls are agonizing in torment or euphoric in bliss. The eternality of immortality is larger than finite minds can comprehend. Samson and Delilah, having been in one of these two places for several thousand years, have not completed any fraction, however small, of the total time they will exist in this place. We cannot go there in our minds. The concept is surreal to us; and yet, it is extremely real to each of us. Sixteen verses in Judges 16 complete the earthly narrative of Delilah. Yet she still lives. She still regrets the choices she made in the valley of Sorek on the now distantly removed planet earth.

How is the narrative of your life coming along? Its brevity in comparison with eternity is mind boggling. Get busy getting ready for a place far removed from this temporary planet earth.

Find and discuss three New Testament scriptures that emphasize the brevity of life and the spiritual implications of the shortness of life.

_____

Read the account of the rich fool in Luke 12:16–21. The length of life is an unknown variable to us all. How should this unknown affect our decisions about material goods? What will happen to all our material goods on the last day? Cite a scripture to support your answer.

_____

_____

HER MOTIVE WAS MONEY

And the lords of the Philistines came up to her and said to her, "Entice him, and find out where his great strength lies, and by what means we may overpower him, that we may bind him to afflict him; and every one of us will give you eleven hundred pieces of silver" (Judges 16:5).

Is money one of the key driving forces in your life? Delilah was willing to sell relationships, personal integrity, and ultimately heaven for eleven hundred pieces of silver. Oh, eleven hundred pieces of silver was no small reward; it was about two talents. It only took about twenty-nine talents of gold for the completion of the entire holy place in the tabernacle (Exodus 38:24). The Philistines wanted this man of iron and they were willing to use Delilah's greed to get him. The amount was enticing. It might be added that it was significantly larger than the price given for the betrayal of Christ.

But Delilah thought she was selling a man. It never occurred to her that the materialistic choice she made in that conference room with the Philistines had eternal consequences for her own soul. Do the eternal consequences of our financial decisions occur to us? Are we sometimes willing to sell our souls?

I have good friends who are currently in the process of moving to another state. Mike is a corporate lawyer. His income is enviable to most of those around him. He has decided to forfeit that income to take a much less lucrative position teaching law at a Christian university.

"Entice him. . . find out where his great strength lies. . . that we may bind him to afflict him; and every one of us will give you eleven hundred pieces of silver."

—Judges 16:5

When discussing this move with his wife Jenny, I asked her about the reason for this major life change. She said, "We are learning that the hours away from home that are required in Mike's job are taking too much valuable time away from our kids during formative years. He is not getting to put the time into the local work of our congregation that he wants to devote. Most importantly, we don't want our children to be negatively influenced by the affluence that seems unavoidable in this position and place. We want them to grow up with an appreciation for blessings and not be around so many kids who experience daily instant gratification. We want to choose spiritual prosperity over what we see as material consumption."

Jenny was on target and the move, though difficult in many ways, will be remembered by the children as a spiritual crossroads where eternity loomed larger than life on this earth. It's reminiscent of Abraham and Lot and the choices that determined destinies in Genesis 13. Don't let the pieces of silver get in your way of heaven.

❋ When the choice is a tournament game or a worship service of your congregation, ask yourself, "Which is just a piece of silver?"

❋ When the decision is an on-the-job raise with Sunday hours or passing on the raise so you can worship, ask, "Which is a piece of silver?"

❋ When the choice is a home in an affluent area that's far from the church meeting place or a smaller house that will facilitate faithfulness, ask, "Which is a piece of silver?"

❋ When the choice is to stay at home and raise your own kids or the pursuit of a career which will provide a more luxurious lifestyle, ask, "Which is a piece of silver?"

❋ When you compare the amenities of your lifestyle with the amount you purpose to give to God each Sunday, ask, "Which investments are just pieces of silver?"

Many older Christians are agonizing over lost children and grandchildren. They have figured out at last how to identify pieces of silver. Their bank accounts reflect their many good financial decisions. But their children and grandchildren are spiritually bankrupt. They would give those bank accounts in a heartbeat if they could purchase one of those lost souls for heaven. But when we choose the silver, we often forfeit for ourselves and for others that street of gold.

Discuss some materialistic choices people make today. What pleas should we include in our prayers to help us focus on what's really important and avoid the materialistic mindset that consumes the society around us?

_____

_____

Her Method Was Manipulation

When I speak to young married women about submission to husbands, Delilah is my biblical example of manipulation. There was something she wanted: the pieces of silver. There was something Samson wanted: Delilah. So Delilah was willing to resort to whatever subtle, coercive methods at her disposal to get what she wanted. She asked, she enticed, she pouted, she pressed, and she urged until she took away the physical strength of the man who loved her. It took her several days to do it, but she finally got what she wanted. What she wanted, however, didn't turn out to be what she wanted at all. What good did a bag of silver do her as the great temple of Dagon crushed her body or, at the very least, destroyed the civilization in which she lived?

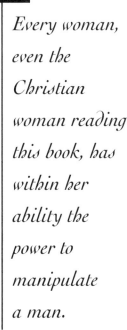

Every woman, even the Christian woman reading this book, has within her ability the power to manipulate a man.

Can we exercise such power over men today? Of course. Jezebel did it (1 Kings 21). Tamar did it (Genesis 38). Herod's wife did it (Matthew 14). Potiphar's wife did it (Genesis 39). You can do it, too. Every married woman, even the Christian women reading this book, has within her ability the power to manipulate a man.

But may I suggest to you that a woman's real strength is in the ability to resist the temptation to manipulate, rather than in the power of manipulation itself. When you think of a woman of strength, which comes to mind: Mary the mother of our Lord who submitted in all things or Mary the mother of James and John who was out to manage her family's position into the limelight of the kingdom? (Matthew 20:21). Which comes to mind, the great woman of Shunem who served Elisha (2 Kings 4) or Sapphira who had a plan for her own prestige? (Acts 5). You see, the women of character were no less able to manipulate the men around them, but they were strong enough to mold their own wills into submission. Submission to God and His delegated authorities demands a great deal more strength than manipulation.

Discuss woman's power of manipulation. Cite biblical examples to show that God's will always involves human restraint as opposed solely to human action.

_____

_____

You know how to manipulate. You, too, can ask, cry, pout, lie, entice, withhold sex, or make sex less desirable. You can, with body language, tone of voice, tears, or sullenness elicit all sorts of responses in your husband. Some of these responses may tempt him to forget his spiritual responsibility to guide your home. You know how to accomplish selfish purposes. But are you willing to put the harness on your great powers in order to allow your husband to be the man God wants him to be? Just as Delilah stripped Samson of his physical strength, our husbands lose their spiritual strength when they allow us to manipulate them. Men of God are strong enough to care for the emotional needs of their wives while refusing to relinquish godly leadership roles. Women of God are strong enough to give the reins of leadership to their husbands. Just as Delilah's silver quickly became an irrelevancy as the temple tumbled, so are our temporal victories unsatisfying when gained by manipulation.

HER MAN WAS MACHO

And that was it. There was no strength of character, no depth of perception, no loyalty to purpose, and no spiritual cognitive skills. The man was massive and muscular. He was stronger than any man alive. He definitely stood out in any crowd. And he always had his way with women—until now. Delilah was different—or was she?

As the mother of two children who, at the time of this writing, are in the dating stage of life, I am probably in overkill mode as I write about the importance of looking beyond the physical characteristics and even beyond the attractive personalities to the character of spirit. The popular people are not always the poor in spirit or the pure in heart (Matthew 5:3, 8). The fun girls don't always have faith's fundamentals down. The tough guys are challenged to develop tender hearts of submission to God. The guy who makes you laugh may not be the one who can lead you to heaven. The girl who stops traffic may be the obstacle in a guy's path to heaven.

So the questions should be asked early on in the relationship. Is this somebody with whom I could entrust my very soul? Would this person ever sell out for any price? Can I go to sleep every night knowing that I will never waken betrayed and without God on my side? Bottom line: Can this person help me and our future children go to heaven? Delilah severed Samson's link to God's strength. Many mates are still in the shaving business today.

List and discuss all of the "things" Delilah shaved from Samson when she shaved the locks.

_____

Notice the phrase "that the word of God may not be blasphemed" in Titus 2:5. Where was the word of God being "made a mockery" or blasphemed in this account of Delilah? How can we cause the word of God to be blasphemed today by failing to adhere to the standards of Titus 2:3–5? Be specific. Name some celebrities who are making fun of these principles today.

_____

_____

_____

_____

HER MASTERY WAS MOMENTARY

For a short moment in time, Delilah had conquered. She had conquered her lover. She pressed, urged, and vexed until he sacrificed the secret of his strength on the altar of her lap (Judges 16:16–19). Little did Samson know that he was actually sacrificing the strength of Israel itself at the feet of the false god Dagon. Sometimes it's that way. Sometimes in the privacy of a bedroom or boardroom or in some secret relationship we can sacrifice important eternal commodities. The eleven hundred pieces of silver were prized by Delilah. But they were nothing compared to the victory Samson was placing in the hands of the Philistines. For a fleeting moment, she had the silver, the favor of her kinsmen, and the prestige of having brought low the great man of Israel. Samson was but a blind man grinding grain in a prison, and occasionally the object of sport among the boasting Philistines. The Scripture even says that Samson became the focal point of praise to Dagon (Judges 16:23). When we, as God's people, sacrifice to and compromise with the forces of evil in our world, we promote false religions and bring dishonor to truth.

But God was still on the throne. It was just a matter of time until the house of Dagon was to crumble, crushing three thousand festival participants (Judges 16:24–31). Remember how you felt when our nation, 285 million in number, lost 3000—one-thousandth of one percent of our total population—in the terror attack on the World Trade Center? How do you suppose the Philistines felt when their much smaller nation lost 3000?

Was Delilah there? Did she perish at the hands of this blind man who had once gazed on her with desire? Or, perhaps worse still, did she live on for some years, knowing that her betrayal and deceit had resulted in this unforgettable scene of terror? Did she attend the funerals of those who were crushed? Do you think she enjoyed the purchases made with the betrayal silver?

You see, as long as God is on the throne, sin always turns out worse than the sinner can imagine. If, as you study this lesson, you find yourself in between the commission of some sin and the resulting eternal consequences, find a space of repentance. While you may not be able to escape all of the earthly consequences of your sin, you can still escape the terror of that final scene on the Judgment Day. If Delilah was looking on as the house of Dagon fell, surely she cried out in horror and regret. But it was too late. God was on the throne and His purposes would be accomplished. Remember His sovereignty as you prepare for the day when all temples to idols, pleasures, and material riches will burn and crumble.

Research the god Dagon. How could Samson's capture and torture have been an act of worship to this god?

_____

Cindy's Reflections

If I Love You

If I love you, I'll believe you
Though what you've pledged is far away.
What you say about tomorrow
Is what's real for me today.

If I love you, then I long
To hear your strong, assuring voice.
I will trust you with my secrets;
Honor you in every choice.

If I love you, I'll defend you
When others ridicule your name.
If all the world denies you, still
I'll endure the shame.

If I love you, I will be there
Whenever you're expecting me.
I will love whatever you love.
Where you are, I'll long to be.

If I love you, I will trust you.
All my hopes on you rely.
But should faith and hope be passing,
Love abides to never die!

And now abideth faith, hope, and love, these three,
but the greatest of these is love.

If you love me, keep my commandments.

A WOMAN WHO WENT TO PIECES
THE LEVITE'S CONCUBINE

WHAT IS A CONCUBINE?

What is a concubine, anyway? As a child I confused concubines with porcupines; they do get some seemingly good men into some very prickly situations. David had ten of them who were used to shame him (2 Samuel 15:16; 16:22; 20:3). Solomon had three hundred of them who, along with his seven hundred wives, proved to be his undoing (1 Kings 11:1–8).

A concubine was a secondary wife. While some sources tend to legitimize the master/concubine relationship, it seems to me that the concubine relationship was tantamount to society-accepted adultery.

There were laws regulating maidservants (Exodus 21:7–11), but a maidservant was not always a concubine. (Remember Hagar was a maidservant long before she ever had a sexual relationship with Abraham in Genesis 16.) I can find no scripture in which God condoned the taking of concubines, and it appears that they were simply sexual servants of their lords. Furthermore, in Scripture, their roles generally were degenerative in the overall scheme of events.

> Have someone do research on the concubines of the Bible. What good things, if any, arose out of concubine relationships?

So why did this Levite, a man of the priestly tribe who certainly knew better, take a concubine of Bethlehem-Judah? (Judges 19:1). Because, as we shall surely see, he lived in a society in which "every man did that which was right in his own eyes" (Judges 21:25). Remember once again, that the heathen nations had been left in tact in opposition to what God had commanded in Deuteronomy 7:1–6. Now several generations have passed since the time of the Israelites' entrance into Canaan. These idolatrous nations have grown and are wielding an untold influence for evil on Israel. So, as always occurs when we leave the morality prescribed by Jehovah, the plot darkly thickens.

The newly situated concubine was apparently less than pleased with this relationship and found other sexual interests rather quickly: "But his concubine played the harlot against him, and went away from him to her father's house at Bethlehem in Judah, and was there four whole months" (Judges 19:2).

The Levite still wanted the concubine, so he prepared gifts for her and went to ask her to come back home.

> Then her husband arose and went after her, to speak kindly to her and bring her back, having his servant and a couple of donkeys with him. So she brought him into her father's house; and when the father of the young woman saw him, he was glad to meet him (Judges 19:3).

We really don't know if the young woman was happy to see him or not. Supposition alone leads one to believe not. Would you be happy to see a man who wants a sexual relationship with you, but doesn't want to give you the rights of wifehood?

Why was the concubine in this story not totally innocent of all wrong doing? Discuss her night of torture. Was it her own fault?

But, alas, her father was very happy to see the Levite and even enjoined him to stay around and visit for three days. Perhaps the girl's father needed the time to try to convince his daughter to give this relationship another chance. Maybe he thought her chances of marrying after having been a concubine and an adulteress were slim. At any rate, he was favorable toward the Levite.

Get Up and Go!

After three days of feasting and merriment, the Levite got up on the fourth morning to return home. But the damsel's father talked him into staying for breakfast, and as they engaged in merriment once more, the day wore on and night fell once again and they had still not begun the trip home.

On the fifth morning, expediency demanded that they depart early, so they could arrive at a place of relative safety before nightfall. But once again, the Levite let his lack of initiative get the best of him. He once again got busy eating and talking, and the morning wore on to afternoon. Once again the girl's father asked him to spend the night, but this time, the Levite, firm in his resolution to go toward home, said his goodbyes and went on his way. His journey, because of his repeated procrastination, was to be a treacherous one.

Could we pause here to make a spiritual application? When you decide to go toward home, go! Do not procrastinate; do not allow others to convince you to engage in a little more of the world's merriment before your departure. Get on the road to heaven immediately. I'm thinking of a man who had decided to become a member of the Lord's church. He had even set a date for his immersion into the body of Christ. He had told others of his plan and family members were anxiously awaiting the arrival of the date when he planned to give his life to Christ. But, for him, the day never came. The date he had set aside for this obedience found his body in the cold earth!

Of course, one might procrastinate her obedience and still mercifully be given the chance to go home. But there is always loss in procrastination. There is loss of influence, loss of opportunity, and many times, there are spiritual casualties as a result of the wait. I am thinking of another man who died seven years ago as a faithful and godly man. He is now enjoying the bliss God has reserved for the saved. But he will never see his children again. He will never walk the street of gold with his grandchildren. There is great loss at his doorstep. For, you see, though he had decided to go home, he waited. He waited in merriment until his children were grown and had left his sphere of influence. How he grieved in his later years because of the spiritual loss of his children caused largely by his procrastination! Don't let this happen to you. Get up in the morning of life and get started toward home!

LOOK WHO'S RUNNING THE CAPITAL!

And so it was afternoon when they started toward home. At nightfall they had come to Jebus. History tells us that Jebus was the portion of Jerusalem that was occupied and controlled by the Jebusites, a group of idolatrous people who should have been destroyed two hundred years earlier. Interesting, isn't it? The people who were allowed to dwell beside God's people are now in control of Israel's primary city! We had better "come out from among them and be separate" (2 Corinthians 6:17) or the ungodly will soon be in charge of our centers of control, as well! If we give sin a place to dwell within us, it slowly gains control of our lives and our congregations.

Is There Safety among the Brethren?

The Levite's servant was tired and suggested that they turn in for the night among the Jebusites. But the Levite insisted that they lodge among brethren, rather than among strangers. Surely he thought they would be more warmly received among the Israelites. So they traveled on to Gibeah, a city of the Benjamites. As we shall see, this town was certainly no center of hospitality, and it seems the Levite and company were resigned to sleep in the streets of Gibeah, since no one had offered them accommodations. Finally, though, there was one older man who, as he passed by the weary troop on his way home from working in the fields, invited them to stay in his house for the evening. His hospitality was complete, including food for man and beast as well as merriment.

But the night of feasting was blackened by the shadow of sin. No sooner did the news get out about the visitors than the corrupt homosexuals of the city surrounded the house demanding the surrender of the Levite for their sexual pleasure. This event, reminiscent of that horrible night in Sodom (Genesis 19), was occurring right in the town of Gibeah. These offenders were Israelites. This shows us the complete penetration of the evils of the heathen into these Benjamites. Again, it cannot be overemphasized that these men of Benjamin were products of multiplied sin whose original factor is found in Judges 1:21: "But the children of Benjamin did not drive out the Jebusites who inhabited Jerusalem; so the Jebusites dwell with the children of Benjamin in Jerusalem to this day."

Just as the Benjamites were no beacon to the Jebusites among them, neither can I be the "light of the world" if I, myself, am living in the darkness.

Isn't it sad that, while the Levite was hesitant to stay in the camp of the stranger, it was in the city of the Israelites where real danger lurked? Sometimes, as a parent, I easily become frustrated that, while I encourage my children to make their closest friendships with those who are from Christian homes, the standards of morality are higher in certain non-Christian homes than they are in certain "Christian" homes. Just as the Benjamites were no beacon here to the Jebusites who were dwelling among them, neither can I be the "light of the world" if I, myself, am living in the darkness (cf. Matthew 5:14–16).

Parents must realize the depth of the plunge the church has made into worldliness. They can no longer feel secure in knowing their children are associating with other church families. No longer is church membership a guarantee of morality in daily living. It is each parent's personal responsibility to insure that the children's influences are wholesome, even at the risk of hurting someone's feelings who should know better than to be engaging in some immoral activity or form of entertainment. Have you had the unsavory responsibility of explaining to other parents who are fellow church members that your young son or daughter could not go to the movies with them because of the rating of the chosen film? While taking such a position is uncomfortable, it is right, and it is the duty of a Christian parent.

But isn't it sad?

She was abused so wretchedly, that when the new day dawned, she was only able to drag her wounded body to the threshold.

What's Inside the House?

The master of the house where the Levite was staying went out to try to appease the lusty crew of homosexuals. He offered both his own daughter and the concubine for their sexual pleasure, if they would but leave his Levite guest alone. "Look, here is my virgin daughter and the man's concubine; let me bring them out now. Humble them, and do with them as you please; but to this man do not do such a vile thing!" (Judges 19:24).

I must confess that I don't comprehend the strange reasoning behind this proposal, particularly as made by a father in reference to his own daughter. I failed to understand how Lot could have the same proposal in Genesis 19:8 and it still escapes me in Judges 19. It is of little consequence, however, when we see that the vile men were not interested in bargaining for the daughter. They were angered by the proposal and responded by taking the concubine who was subjected to physical and sexual abuse throughout the hours of darkness. She was abused so wretchedly, that when the new day dawned, she was only able to drag her wounded body to the threshold of the house where her master was lodging. Then she collapsed and awaited her passage to eternity.

Where was the Levite during her night of extreme abuse and torture? Where was the one who had brought the presents to her only five days earlier? We should recall that he was in the midst of merry-making at the time of the interruption by the vile men. The next thing we know, it's morning and he rises up from his bed of rest and makes his preparations to leave for home. It is only when he opens the door to load his asses that he notices her now lifeless body lying in the doorway. He, unaffected by her obviously ruffled condition, instructs her to get up and get going.

> When her master arose in the morning, and opened the doors of the house and went out to go his way, there was his concubine, fallen at the door of the house with her hands on the threshold. And he said to her, "Get up and let us be going." But there was no answer. So the man lifted her onto the donkey; and the man got up and went to his place (Judges 19:27).

This Levite is on the verge of showing what is likely the most graphic portrayal of wrath over sin that can be found in scripture. Yet we must marvel at his inconsistency. Had he not used this woman solely for the fulfillment of his sexual desires? Had he not displayed an extreme lack of interest in her well-being even during her last few desperate hours?

Sometimes while I may be enraged and outraged at sin in the lives of others, I can become quite comfortable with my own. After all, just as this man was a Levite, a member of the priestly tribe, so I am a member of the priestly tribe today, the church of Christ. And my sins? Well, they, just like his treatment of the concubine, are not so vile as the sins of others. In fact, my sins are only the ones that are quite accepted in the society around me. I can, just like the Levite, rest quite comfortably in my sins, for there are so many people who are much more vile than I.

But just as the casualty of his evening of repose was lying at the door in the morning, there are casualties of my indifference about my sin. There are those around me who will pay big prices when I claim to be a priest, but continue to excuse my own sin. When I act as if I am appalled at the vileness of this society and yet I am inconsistent in my personal devotion, there will be lost souls at my own doorstep. By the time I wake up and call to them, it may be too late. They will likely not hear me.

I know several teens who suffer from eating disorders, drug addictions, and pornography addictions. They attend church regularly with their parents.

But in each case, the daily devotion in the home, the time spent as a family in God's word, and the rich prayers of godly parents in the hearing of tender hearts have been long missing. The outward picture is one of a Christian home, but at home, the Christ is crowded out by busy schedules and misplaced priorities.

This Levite is about to mount a very public campaign against a terrible wickedness. But to those who know him best, his inconsistencies must be glaring.

Why did the Levite attempt to avenge her death? Was he feeling pangs of guilt for his mistreatment of her or was he so impacted by society that he felt perfectly upright in his relationship with her? Defend your answer.

_____

_____

List the similarities between the events of Genesis 19 and those of Judges 19.

_____

YOU'VE GOT MAIL!

When he entered his house he took a knife, laid hold of his concubine, and divided her into twelve pieces, limb by limb, and sent her throughout all the territory of Israel . . . All who saw it said, "No such deed has been done or seen from the day that the children of Israel came up from the land of Egypt until this day. Consider it, confer, and speak up!" (Judges 19:29–30).

So he dissected her corpse, packaged her pieces. and had a package delivered to each of the twelve tribes. Let your mind grasp for a moment the reality that occurred. Someone from each tribe actually did open the package containing body parts. Imagine the horror. Imagine the stench. Then imagine reading the letter explaining why you got the package. Imagine showing it to the other tribal leaders and imagine calling those massive assemblies to display this horrible package to the people.

The whole of Israel was outraged at this abuse committed by its own. They called upon the Levite to testify publicly against these Benjamites.

Then they demanded the release by Benjamin of those who had terrorized the concubine that they might be executed for their crimes against her. But the men of Benjamin protected these lawless men and thus invited the whole of Israel to battle.

First in Battle

The children of Israel went up to the house of God to inquire of Him: "Which of us shall go up first to battle against the children of Benjamin?" The Lord said, "Judah first!" (Judges 20:18).

God's choice is significant, especially when we look back at Judges 1:8 and see that Judah had originally taken Jerusalem. Judah conquered it, set it on fire, and continued south to fight the Canaanites in Hebron without driving out the Jebusites.

Benjamin first moved into Jerusalem (Judges 1:21). Benjamin should have completed Judah's unfinished business, but instead they took the path of least resistance and merely made neighbors of the remaining Jebusites. Notice the failure to exterminate the Jebusites from Jerusalem by these two tribes as they entered Canaan:

> Now the children of Judah fought against Jerusalem and took it; they struck it with the edge of the sword and set the city on fire . . . But the children of Benjamin did not drive out the Jebusites who inhabited Jerusalem; so the Jebusites dwell with the children of Benjamin in Jerusalem to this day (Judges 1:8–21).

Surely if the Benjamites of Judges 1 could have met the wretched homosexual Benjamites of Judges 19, they would have refused to make treaties with the Jebusites. But they were far too short-sighted, and they failed to take advantage through faith of their friendship with the Omniscient One who knew the future—the consequences of their decisions.

Have a class member tell the account of the ensuing civil war between Israel and Benjamin. Why will the side which truly seeks the counsel of the Lord always be victorious in the end?

_____

_____

Now the two tribes are set to do battle, each tribe destined to lose many soldiers. All of these losses were because of unfinished business a couple of generations back. If only we could see the grave consequences of disobedience. But many times we are just as short-sighted as were they.

Casualties were high on both sides. Of Israel's 400,000 fighting men, about 40,000 were killed as the Lord allowed Benjamin to prevail on the first two days of battle. But on day three, Benjamin was sorely defeated as 25,000 of their 26,700 warriors were defeated, all but wiping out the relatively small tribe. This amazing battle is chronicled in Judges 20.

Sometimes when we forget the commands of our Omniscient Friend we really wage war against ourselves. Faith is not faith until we are called upon to do the things that are very difficult to do. If I submit only when it seems to me to be the smart thing to do, then in whom am I placing my trust? The tribe of Benjamin fell this day, not because of some powerful invasion by a mighty conqueror, but because of degeneracy within, caused by a failure early on to trust the one who knew the future. Great nations, great people, and even those of us who are just making our way humbly through days of normalcy must realize the secret of continued and true success: unconditional submission to the great I AM.

≈ *Cindy's Reflections* ≈

By the Field

I went by the field of the lazy man, and by the vineyard of the man devoid of understanding; and there it was, all overgrown with thorns; its surface was covered with nettles; its stone wall was broken down. When I saw it, I considered it well; I looked on it and received instruction: a little sleep, a little slumber, a little folding of the hands to rest; so shall your poverty come like a prowler, and your need like an armed man

— Proverbs 24:30–34

I can't preserve the good seed
If I'm not bearing fruit.
I'll never yield a glorious tree
If I have no depth for root.

If I am overgrown
With nettles of care and stress,
I rob tomorrow's harvest
Of a little loveliness.

If my soil goes untended
And covered by many a thorn,
I'm just a sad reminder
Of the fruit I could have born.

I may have a wall around me,
Hiding ruin that lies inside.
Folks may think the secret garden
Glories still in stately pride.

But one day my walls will crumble
And the ruin will be laid bare.
I have wasted precious harvests.
Now I've nothing left to share.

MULTIPLE WEDDINGS
WIVES FOR THE BENJAMITES

While the Elvis Wedding Chapel of Las Vegas boasts availability of multiple couples marrying in the same ceremony at reduced prices, I'm not sure that even this chapel would be prepared to accommodate the six hundred Benjamites who married foreign wives in the closing chapters of the book of Judges. This dramatic era of Israel's history closes with the same sad social commentary that was given several times throughout the book: "In those days there was no king in Israel; everyone did what was right in his own eyes" (Judges 21:25).

This closing saga from the book of Judges serves to show us the depths of degradation to which we plunge when we do "that which is right in our own eyes." It paints for us a sad self-portrait of the face of humanity gone terribly awry. It gives us an invaluable gift: the ability to see what happens when we collectively remove God from the picture. But the account is of positive significance in our lives only if we allow its lessons to impact our decisions in a culture that is ever moving from its original spiritual moorings.

Israel was immediately and decisively united in its call for capital punishment of the men involved in the sin against this woman.

TRIBE IN TROUBLE

Recall the Levite's concubine who had been abused throughout one horrible night while the Levite was visiting in Gibeah. Remember that, when they finished with her, she was found, in an unresponsive condition, on the threshold of the house. The text says she came to the house at dawn and fell down on the threshold. Perhaps she died in the next moments as her master was rising from his sleep and preparing for his trip. Or maybe she died shortly after she was discovered by the Benjamite. Whatever the case, her last hours were full of the kind of pain and humiliation that we can hardly bear to contemplate.

So then the Levite, who had given his concubine to the ruthless Benjamites in the first place, laid the corpse on his donkey and took it home, he carried the body into the house and cut it into twelve pieces and mailed her into all the territory of Israel.

Now, I don't know about you, but I think if I got a Fed-Ex package like this one, I would take notice. I would call authorities. It would end up on the six o'clock news. CNN's election coverage would give place to this top news story. It would be in the papers and tabloids. High powered lawyers would be volunteering to handle the case for publicity. We would be talking about it constantly, except during dinner table conversation.

And that's what happened in ancient Israel except, of course, it was a long and drawn-out process, since the packages were likely delivered by Donkey-Express—imagine the stench—and the coverage was in public assemblies and on parchment. But the effect was the same: national outrage.

Israel was immediately and decisively united in its call for capital punishment of the men who were involved in the sin against this woman. "So all the men of Israel were gathered against the city, united together as one man" (Judges 20:11).

> Then the tribes of Israel sent men through all the tribe of Benjamin, saying, "What is this wickedness that has occurred among you? Now therefore, deliver up the men, the perverted men who are in Gibeah, that we may put them to death and remove the evil from Israel!" But the children of Benjamin would not listen to the voice of their brethren, the children of Israel (Judges 20:12–13).

Notice here that the people of Benjamin could have averted the deaths of over twenty-five thousand men, not to mention thousands of women and children, if only they had been willing to surrender the guilty to Israel for punishment. But they were not. At this point, the children of Benjamin became accessories to the multiple rapes and murder of the woman. At this point, they appeared willing to risk their own lives, wives, and children for a few rapists. They had to be aware that they were outnumbered sixteen to one (vv. 15–17). Perhaps they were underestimating the passion of the enemy in this battle. Perhaps they were forgetting that Israel was receiving counsel from God Himself in their treatment of this fallen tribe (vv. 18, 23, 27–28). How do people become so aloof to impending doom? How do they get priorities so askew? (The answer reverberates yet again from the last verse of the book. Today's America needs to examine this answer.)

Examine the unwillingness of the Benjamites to surrender their guilty kinsmen. Sometimes today there are those who will stand firmly against a sin until family members become involved in that sin. What specific problems are prevalent in some churches today because leaders have become weak in fighting sins within their own families?

_____

_____

Make a list of the snowballing consequences of sexual sin in our society. Have someone bring clippings from the local newspaper during the next week reflecting this snowball effect.

_____

_____

RUN TO THE ROCK!

Through a series of skirmishes, highway chases, battles, and burnings cited in Judges 20, the tribe of Benjamin was effectively destroyed. Only six hundred soldiers remained having fled to a rock called Rimmon in the outlying wilderness. At the end of the day, 25,000 fighting men of valor and all the women and children were dead. Sexual sin snowballed into the literal destruction of tens of thousands of people. Sexual sin still has that snowball effect.

But what of those who fled to the rock? They lived there for four months, likely without proper provisions and unable to properly mourn the loss of their families and friends. They had no cities to which to return and no rescue mission to help them get back on their feet. They were, in short, desperate, destitute men.

COMPASSION IN CHAOS

And the children of Israel grieved for Benjamin their brother, and said, "One tribe is cut off from Israel today" (Judges 21:6).

Now that a woman has been raped multiple times, murdered, and cut into pieces, war has been made, women and children have been killed and six hundred men have been living in the cleft of a rock for four months, a glimmer of compassion shines in the blackness. (The ESV actually says they "had compassion for Benjamin their brother.) Notice here that the compassion of Israel was not pure compassion because pure compassion finds its direction from the will of God. Pure and true compassion restores order from chaos. Compassion rescued the great leader, Moses, from the Nile in his infancy (Exodus 2:6). Compassion settled the dispute over the living son in 1 Kings 3:26. Compassion offered the rich young ruler an ordered set of priorities in Mark 10:21. Compassion through evangelism pulls people out of the fire to safety (Jude 23). Compassion pulled the whole world to safety at Calvary (Hebrews 5:2–3). Is your world tumultuous and chaotic? Are you a truly compassionate person?

The children of Israel wanted to rebuild the tribe of Benjamin. Recall that Benjamin was the baby of the original family (Genesis 35:16–19). Recall that when the brothers were traveling to Egypt, Jacob was extremely hesitant to allow Benjamin to leave the safety of home (Genesis 42–43). Perhaps the leaders of the tribes of Reuben and Judah reviewed this rich heritage of the tribe of Benjamin remembering that the original fathers of their tribes had offered to give precious lives in exchange for Benjamin's should any evil come to him. At any rate, they were moved to try to save the tribe of Benjamin.

Some believe compassion involves overlooking sin. Prove biblically that, while a forgiving spirit must always prevail, sin must be reckoned with and forgiven, rather than overlooked.

Bringing Benjamin Back

But they were now in a precarious position. Upon hearing of the crimes against the concubine, they had all sworn with oaths that they would not allow their daughters to marry Benjamites. All of the Benjamite women were dead. Six hundred men remained but, upon their deaths, the tribe would be extinct. So Israel had to set its collective cogs turning to find a way around the oath against Benjamin. The resulting question is in Judges 21:8: "What one is there from the tribes of Israel who did not come up to Mizpah to the Lord?" And, in fact, no one had come to the camp from Jabesh Gilead to the assembly.

Oops! Extremely bad and short-sighted decision on the part of Jabesh Gilead. They thought they would take their ease while God's people were fighting the Benjamites. Perhaps they thought their presence would be insignificant and their absence unnoticed. Maybe their leadership was weak and had discouraged their faithfulness. Perhaps there were some who saw the need to go and really wanted to go; but because none of their friends were going, they decided to stay home, too. Whatever the case, Easy Street is a very short street, intersecting in the end with the Way of Destruction. Notice the intersection for the people of Jabesh Gilead:

> So the congregation sent out there twelve thousand of their most valiant men, and commanded them, saying, "Go and strike the inhabitants of Jabesh Gilead with the edge of the sword, including the women and children. And this is the thing that you shall do: you shall utterly destroy every male, and every woman who has known a man intimately" (Judges 21:10–11).

Are you living on Easy Street? When the people of God come together to accomplish His purposes, are you there? Are you offering Him your resources in the fight against wickedness? Is your zeal easily overcome by your compulsion for convenience? In short, have you shown up at your modern-day Mizpah?

Jabesh Gilead was promptly attacked by Israel. The only ones spared in the attack were four-hundred virgins, destined to be given to the Benjamites for wives. You may be wondering why the virgins could not have been given to the Benjamites without the bloodshed of their mothers and fathers, brothers and sisters. Would not the mere taking of these four hundred have been punishment enough for the failure to show up at Mizpah?

> Looking for the easy or most convenient way to live is incompatible with Christianity. Why? When will Christians get a "rest"?
>
> _____
>
> _____

But the leaders of Israel were calculating. How would your husband react if someone came into town and took your daughter away, along with three hundred ninety-nine of her friends, to go and marry men who, at least indirectly, had supported the rape and murder of a concubine, had been a part of a coup against the national leadership, and had run to hide in a rock in the thick of battle? My husband would be risking life and limb to protect our daughter from such a fate. Her older brother would be saying, "Over my dead body will you take her to the sons of Benjamin!" So that's how it was. It was "over their dead bodies" that the girls were taken to the altar. The Israelite leaders knew it had to be that way or not at all.

Four hundred young maidens had no chance to return home and mourn the loss of their families.

Four hundred young maidens had no chance to return home and mourn the loss of their families—no time to honor those fallen by the sword. They were taken to Shiloh and presented to those men who had been hiding in a rock for four months. Talk about some unexpected reversals in life—some major factors on the stress level index! Even taking into account the ancient customs of prearranged marriages, these women had to be at risk for mental and emotional breakdown! But we are reminded yet again of the chaotic state of affairs when people do "that which is right in their own eyes."

THE DANCING DAUGHTERS

It's kind of interesting to think about the scenario now. The six hundred Benjamites are called to Shiloh where they are presented the four hundred obviously distraught women of Jabesh Gilead. How were these women distributed? Did the men get to pick? If so, how did they determine order? How long did it take the Benjamites to notice that there were not enough to go around? Were there any of the women who traded husbands or vice versa? These are questions that just beg the imagination, the answers to which we cannot know. What we do know is that these were real people with real emotions. And how those emotions must have been reeling at the end of this day!

When the wives were all handed out, the supply was a bit short of demand. Two hundred single Benjamite men remained wifeless. The Israelite leaders remained firm in their adherence to their original oath. They said,

There must be an inheritance for the survivors of Benjamin, that a tribe may not be destroyed from Israel. However, we cannot give them wives from our daughters, for the children of Israel have sworn an oath, saying, "Cursed be the one who gives a wife to Benjamin" (Judges 21:17–18).

But what to do? In their most creative ploy of the whole account they issued Plan B:

Therefore they instructed the children of Benjamin, saying, "Go, lie in wait in the vineyards, and watch; and just when the daughters of Shiloh come out to perform their dances, then come out from the vineyards, and every man catch a wife for himself from the daughters of Shiloh; then go to the land of Benjamin. Then it shall be, when their fathers or their brothers come to us to complain, that we will say to them, 'Be kind to them for our sakes, because we did not take a wife for any of them in the war; for it is not as though you have given the women to them at this time, making yourselves guilty of your oath.'" (Judges 21:20–22).

Did any of the single men, or any leader of Israel voice any objection to the whole sordid "catch a dancing daughter" process?

Looking for a Loophole

But wait a minute! These men of the Bethel Highway, the fathers of these targeted daughters had made the same oath that all the rest of Israel had made. Their daughters were no more eligible for marriage to the Benjamites than any other women of Israel. Wasn't a father naturally going to be a tad bit peeved when he went down to the feast and realized that his innocent daughter had been snatched away by some Benjamite who just popped out of the woods, picked her out, and grabbed her? It's hard for me to imagine containing the wrath of my husband in any similar situation.

Now this scene really begs the imagination. Were some of the ones who were issued wives in the first place disappointed because they didn't get to play this catch-a-wife game? I can just hear them saying, "Wait! I didn't know there was going to be a door number two when I took this woman of Jabesh Gilead." Did any of the single men, or even a single leader of Israel, rise and voice any objection to the whole sordid "catch a dancing daughter" process?

Apparently the only thing which concerned them was what to do about the angry fathers and big brothers of the dancing girls once they became aware that their daughters had been stolen. We're not really told what the reaction of these brothers and fathers was, but I cannot imagine its being a pleasant one. They must have risen with one voice of outrage and said something like this: "None of you were willing to give your daughters to these black sheep of the house of Israel, so you come over to our feast and steal our virgin daughters!"

But any objection made by the time the angry fathers knew just what was occurring was likely too late to avoid the marriages. The Israelite leaders were prepared, at least in theory, for the objections of the fathers and brothers.

> Then it shall be, when their fathers or their brothers come to us to complain, that we will say to them, "Be kind to them for our sakes, because we did not take a wife for any of them in the war; for it is not as though you have given the women to them at this time, making yourselves guilty of your oath" (Judges 21:22).

They were simply going to explain that since the men of Shiloh were unaware of the marriages of their daughters, they were thus not accountable to the oath; an obvious dodge, a breach of integrity, a selfish way to keep their own oaths (and daughters) while stealing these daughters of Shiloh.

Foolish vows are foundations for some of the cruelest things people do. Jepthah's daughter paid for a foolish vow with her life (Judges 12). Daniel was thrown in the lions' den at the behest of an ill-devised vow (Daniel 6). John the Baptist lost his head because of the vow of a wicked king (Matthew 14). If you've promised to do something sinful, break your promise. Call upon your integrity and the wisdom from above to give you boldness to repent of your vow and do the right thing before God and your peers. And as for swearing by God, or by the heavens, or by earthly things, take some advice from the book of James: "But above all, my brethren, do not swear, either by heaven or by earth or with any other oath. But let your 'Yes' be 'Yes,' and your 'No,' 'No,' lest you fall into judgment" (James 5:12). Let your intentions be well-considered and reasonable; then let your actions reflect your integrity.

LITTLE LESSONS

Benjamin finds himself starting over; back at square one. With six hundred fighting men left of the twenty-six thousand they had only days ago, their spirits must have been humbled in the presence of Israel's four hundred thousand men of war. To say the least, they had experienced a vivid lesson on how to quickly become team players. Totally dependent now on God and their Israelite brethren for sustenance and defense, they went back to their cities to rebuild.

From this tiny tribe came the first king of Israel only a few decades hence (1 Samuel 9:21). Many decades hence, from this re-born tribe came the mouth of the gospel to the Gentile world, the apostle Paul (Romans 11:1; Philippians 3:5). I, for one Gentile, am very thankful for Paul the Benjamite. Our God is limitless in his resources. He can take the tiniest things and magnify them through His power for His glory. He can take even me and my meager abilities and funnel them, in his own time and through His abundant mercies, for some eternal good. But, as the tribe of Benjamin learned the hard way, I must learn to humble myself under His mighty hand. "Therefore humble yourselves under the mighty hand of God, that He may exalt you in due time" (1 Peter 5:6).

David said it best in Psalm 68:26–27: "Bless God in the congregations, the Lord, from the fountain of Israel. There is little Benjamin, their leader."

What eventually happened to the tribe of Benjamin after the kingdom divided? With which major tribe did Benjamin become aligned?

_____

_____

≈ *Cindy's Reflections* ≈

When I Throw Up My Hands in Despair

When the plumbing is broken; the kids have the flu;
When money is tight and there's too much to do;
My insurance was canceled; my floor needs repair . . .
I finally just throw up my hands in despair!

Why all of this stress, Lord? I know there's a reason
Why it all seems to happen in the same dismal season.
I know that You know, Lord. I know that You care
When I finally throw up my hands in despair.

Then it just seems when I cry from my soul,
That You take my hands, Lord, and You take control.
And just like a father You pity my plight.
When life seems the darkest, You show me Your light.

I think of Your Son with no place to call home
When He left the splendor of Your side to roam
Where people were dying and life wasn't fair.
I wonder if His hands went up in despair.

I remember that it was my weakness and loss
That held Jesus' hands to that old Roman cross.
My mind sees those hands that were pierced through and
    bleeding
And I know where this road of despair may be leading.

I realize my troubles are really so small
As you steady my hands and I hear your blessed call:
"Come ye who are weary." My soul sheds its doubt,
And instead of my whining, You make my heart shout!

I praise You for broken things, and broken people, too;
That make me see I'm so dependent on You.
I thank you for stretching Your hand out to me;
For Golgotha and the Garden of Gethsemane.

Keep holding my hands, Lord, till You've seen me through.
Then gently release them. There's work they must do.
My soul is at rest, but my hands must be there
For another whose hands have gone up in despair.

FROM BITTER TO BETTER

NAOMI

I well remember a visit with a ninety-one year old man in a nursing home. In the aftermath of many reversals in his lifetime, he lay there, fully conscious and quite able of mind, albeit very hard of hearing. I knew that this now frail body had experienced life at its hardest. The son of a share-cropper, he had learned the value of material things early on. He had experienced emotional loss when his young bride became unfaithful to him and their marriage ended in divorce. I also knew that in this difficult time in his life, he had walked away from the Lord. I knew that a faithful church of God's people had withdrawn fellowship from him according to the instruction given in 1 Corinthians 5. I knew this man had never been reconciled to this faithful church and I knew that the day when he would meet His maker was not too many days away. So in tones that I'm sure all the staff could hear, I talked with him about his soul. I told him how very simple it would be to make his life right with his family in Christ and with his God. I volunteered to write a note for him and take it to the elders of this church and ask for the forgiveness of the church and for their prayers for him as he prepares to leave this world. Absolutely nothing but his own pride could stand in his way of being certain of His eternity with God.

When you cannot feed your family properly, you kick into survival mode and live, not for the joy of the day, but in hopes of better times.

His reaction was one of willful stubbornness. He made me know in no uncertain terms that he was neither humbled nor penitent. I'm confident he will go to his grave having sealed his own doom. He let the reversals of life make him a very bitter person.

The following afternoon, my husband and I visited an eighty-six year old sister in another nursing home. She, too, was widowed several years ago. She has lost her sight. She has no children and only one brother. She had to forfeit all her familiar surroundings and finally acquiesce to life in one tiny little room in the lonely hall of that home. She doesn't make the trek down the hall anymore to the dining room because of her inability to see the food on her plate and because of the tremor in her hands. She eats quietly in her room, so she won't embarrass herself as she clumsily struggles to get the food from her plate to her mouth. Only a few Sundays before our visit, this sister had made her way down the aisle of the church auditorium. The wife of one of our elders hurried to help her to the front pew. She confessed to the church that sometimes she had allowed her disabilities to keep her from worship. She asked for forgiveness and prayers. Now, in spite of blindness and shaking and having to rearrange meals that she misses in the home, she climbs on that church van every Lord's Day and faithfully offers her best to the Lord. Her smile was huge and her eyes still twinkled as she told us how very happy and blessed she is. She grabbed our hands with fervor as we prayed with her. She made us happy and blessed, too.

How can two children of the same loving Father end their lives so differently? What is the hardening agent that can cause a man to turn deaf ears on the pleas of those who love him to make things right before death? What is the tenderizer that opens blind eyes to the beauty of God's grace even in the darkest hours of life? Both of my friends are shortly to meet the Lord. In piercing tones my deaf friend will hear the words "Depart from me, you who work iniquity." My blind friend will see His face with clarity as He ushers her into bliss.

BECOMING BITTER

Naomi had really seen some hard times. She was one of God's people. She had been brought up to rely on the promises of God. And God had conditionally promised that this land of Canaan in which she and her husband and their two sons lived would be a land of wheat, barley, vines and figs; a place of pomegranates, olives and honey (Deuteronomy 8:8). But, alas, it was that wicked period of judges in Israel; a time when the people digressed over and over into idolatry. It was a time when "every man did that which was right in his own eyes" (Judges 17:6). The land of milk and honey had become a land of famine. I know some women who have faced times of famine in their lives. When you are unable to feed your family properly, you kick into survival mode and you live, not for the joy of the day, but in hopes of better times. Life was hard for Naomi as she and her husband, Elimelech, set out on the 120 mile journey from Bethlehem to the land of Moab, a place of unfamiliarity and isolation from family and friends. It was not the happiest chapter of life for Naomi, but at least there was food in Moab for the four of them.

When she left her homeland of Judah, Naomi knew the people in Moab would have different customs and speak a different language, but she also knew that two people of God bound to each other in the sacred union of marriage can conquer almost anything together. Then Elimelech died.

Often, as the weaker vessel in this union, I have praised God for my brave and godly husband who willingly serves as my buffer from the harshness of a spiritually foreign and often cruel society in which we live. I take comfort in knowing he is there to take the responsibility of big decisions from me. He is protective and providential. I am secure in his leadership. But suddenly, Naomi had lost her partner, her shield from the harshness of a foreign world.

In what ways do godly husbands shield their wives and children from the harshness of our society? How is this part of God's plan for the care of the weaker vessel? Find a passage that calls woman the "weaker vessel."

By and by, her two sons married women of Moab. It should be parenthetically noted here that our boys will likely marry some of those women to whom they are introduced through the circumstances of life; circumstances which often result directly from parental decisions. When our children approach marrying age, it is important that we consider their potential future mates as we choose locations, congregations, colleges, and social circles. Naomi's sons, Mahlon and Chilion, married Ruth and Orpah, respectively, and lived in Moab for ten years.

Then, in another wave of tragedy for Naomi, both of her sons died. I'm sure Naomi woke up in the mornings trying to convince herself that this was all a bad nightmare. A mother who had lost an adult child said "I don't really know how I am doing. I just make it from day to day because I have to." Surely Naomi must have persevered daily through this kind of helplessness.

Often a widow will find that leaving the place of her husband's death provides a place and space of renewal. Naomi soon planned to return to Bethlehem. Surprisingly, her Moabite daughters-in-law decided to accompany her to the land of Israel, where the famine was now over. As we read Ruth 1:8–18, we are touched by the devotion of Ruth and Orpah. Both obviously loved their mother-in-law. What a rare and precious blessing it is to find this relationship between mother-in-law and daughter-in-law. Surely in desperate times, Naomi found great comfort in their devotion. She had to marvel at the respect Ruth showed for her and for her God.

But Naomi seemed to have a knack for focusing on the negative. Listen to her answer to Ruth and Orpah as they tried to gather their belongings, leave the land of their births, and follow this woman they loved back to Bethlehem:

> Turn back, my daughters, go—for I am too old to have a husband. If I should say I have hope, if I should have a husband tonight and should also bear sons, would you wait for them till they were grown? Would you restrain yourselves from having husbands? No, my daughters; for it grieves me very much for your sakes that the hand of the Lord has gone out against me! (Ruth 1:12–13).

Orpah returned to her people, and Ruth went to Bethlehem with her mother-in-law, Naomi. Ruth was a widow, too. She had likely left her blood family behind in her homeland and was going to a land she had never seen. The only familiar person in her brave new world would be Naomi. Naomi was soon to introduce Ruth to a kinsman who would change both of their lives. But for now, Naomi had to just stop and take time for what we might call today a pity party.

But she said to them,

> Do not call me Naomi; call me Mara, for the Almighty has dealt very bitterly with me. I went out full, and the Lord has brought me home again empty. Why do you call me Naomi, since the Lord has testified against me, and the Almighty has afflicted me? (Ruth 1:20–21).

Why do we have pity parties? Why do we allow the circumstances of this life to impede our progress toward the next? Let me offer a few reasons. Perhaps these can help us to be prepared for pity party invitations and just RSVP in the negative every time. There is always something better on the agenda.

❋ *Sometimes we forget we are not alone.* Our God is described as the ever present source of strength (Psalm 46:1). He has promised that He will never leave or forsake us (Hebrews 13:5). The *never* of this passage is actually a double negative word adding emphasis to the assurance of His presence.

❋ *Sometimes we forget that Christians see in 3-D.* Many times, those who are newly converted to Christianity have difficulty in correcting the one-dimensional vision that characterizes worldliness. The focus of their existence has always been on themselves. Every decision has been based on "What's in it for me?" This inward obsession is simply and sadly characteristic of our society. To begin to have an upward focus and really care about what God thinks is a challenge for ladies coming out of the world. Then to develop an outward focus, noticing and responding to the needs of others is just a whole new dimension of vision that the new Christian must really work to maintain. Symptoms of the problem are evident. A new Christian may think the fellowship meals are for her, never stopping to think to prepare food and bring it to an activity. A new Christian may have a different problem she wants you to help resolve each time she sees you at worship while she may rarely express interest in the problems of others or take the time to pray for them. She may tell you how busy she is and how little time she has for activities of the church, listing all of her job demands, sports activities, and hobbies, never even thinking that those who are faithful and involved have tough schedules every week as well. She may expect to be visited or called without once thinking of visiting someone herself.

But these ladies are babies in the faith. We must remember that babies are all about themselves. All of us who are moms understand that babies are not thoughtful of the needs of others. The focus is definitely inward. But for those of us who have been Christians for years, the focus should no longer be one dimensional. Stopping the self-absorption while becoming absorbed in the Word and in fervent, practical prayer have the ironic effect of self-fulfillment. Likewise, when we see and minister to the desperate needs of the people around us, we ourselves are lifted up. We begin to be great when we begin to serve (Matthew 23:11).

❋ *Sometimes we stop walking and have a seat.* Idleness is the devil's work-shop. Sometimes I see widows who go home from the funeral, close the door, and resolve never to be happy again. Other times I see widows who, for a very long time, have been unable to do much else besides care for an invalid husband. But once the long hours of caretaking are over, these godly women immerse themselves in programs of the church, ministry to the needy, and the development of godly friendships. These widows are some of the happiest Christians I know.

While I was in my thirties, I had a dear friend named Annie. I was amazed at what Annie could accomplish for the Lord. She visited several nursing homes weekly, taking little goody baskets to several patients. She had a tiny gift for every single child of the congregation at each holiday. (She was the Dollar Tree Queen!) Her four and five's classroom was amazing as her husband lugged a big box of visuals and activities every Sunday morning and Wednesday night. She remembered birthdays and anniversaries and took the time to keep children when their parents were sick or just needed a little time away. She brought computer-made banners to the building for us all to sign so they could be posted in a lonely hospital or dorm room. She prepared welcome signs and goody baskets for the hotel rooms of our visiting preachers and teachers. In short, she was "ready to every good work" (Titus 3:1). Some people thought Annie was just a great person with lots of spare time to do great stuff for other people. Annie was, in truth, a cancer patient, having already had several surgeries with several more to come. She was raising a child with a disability, caring for a mother-in-law who was in poor health, and struggling with severe back problems. I actually remember her attending our Wednesday night ladies' class and lying in the back of the classroom on a table because sitting in a chair was both painful and harmful to her back. Annie simply chose not to stop and sit down when life hurt. She chose to keep walking toward heaven. She chose not to have a pity party!

When we see and minister to the desperate needs of the people around us, we ourselves are lifted up.

❊ *Sometimes we forget who fills our tank.* Sometimes when I am driving a long distance, I am frustrated because I have to stop and pump gas. I hate to pump gas. I especially hate to pump gas at night. I abhor pumping gas at night when the price of gas is three times what I paid only two years ago. I can get in a bad slump over pumping gas. When I do start feeling frustration at the pump, it only takes me a minute to think about the primary reason this frustration builds. It's because pumping gas is a pretty rare occurrence for me. See, I have a husband who will go out of his way to pump gas for me under normal circumstances. It's only when I travel alone that I am forced to deal with the bite of the chilling air, the smell of gas on my fingers, and the pinch of the price gouge.

Naomi said, "I went out full, and the Lord has brought me home again empty" (Ruth 1:21). It is true that Naomi had experienced devastating losses while in Moab. But she, like so many of us today, was quick to blame God for the losses while failing to credit Him with the sustenance, strength, and even the lessons that come with trials. She could have used a quick lesson from the book of Job: "Naked I came from my mother's womb, and naked shall I return there. The Lord gave, and the Lord has taken away; blessed be the name of the Lord" (Job 1:21).

❊ *Sometimes we like to broadcast the problems and keep the blessings a big secret.* Listen to Naomi's homecoming statement in full:

> Do not call me Naomi; call me Mara, for the Almighty has dealt very bitterly with me. I went out full, and the Lord has brought me home again empty. Why do you call me Naomi, since the Lord has testified against me, and the Almighty has afflicted me? (Ruth 1:20–21).

—She said, "Don't call me by my old name. I would like to be called 'Bitter'."

—She said, "God treated me very bitterly."

—She said, "God emptied me."

—She said, "God testified against me."

—She said, "God afflicted me."

I believe Naomi had thought ahead about this little speech. I believe she was ready to get a few things off her chest when she got back to her family and friends. Perhaps it was not the first time she had delivered it. But the indictment of the Almighty God, who is the giver of every good and perfect gift (James 1:17), was a pity-party theme that borders on blasphemy. Thankfully, the party was brief and she soon had an outward focus once again. Broadcasting our problems in a spirit of bitterness serves to feed that spirit. It is a call for reinforcements for all that is negative in our lives. Sometimes Mom's words, "If you can't say something positive, then don't say anything at all," make a lot of sense.

What decisions can widows consciously make to help them overcome grief and live productive lives? Offer helpful experiences or suggestions from Christian widows.

Why should the grieving person allow some time to elapse after the loss of a loved one before major decisions are made?

Compose a list from the Psalms that emphasize partnership with God to be used when you are all alone.

What are some polite ways to help constant complainers develop a knack for looking at the bright side?

What can you do to help a bitter person become a better person?

Sometimes widows feel like a "fifth wheel." What specific activities in your congregation can you help to develop that will involve widows? Brainstorm and be sure there are activities occurring in your church to make widows feel included.

BECOMING BETTER

The first chapter of Ruth doesn't paint a very vibrant picture of Naomi. We leave her there at the beginning of barley harvest—a poverty-stricken, desperate, bitter woman. I'm glad Ruth was still hanging in there with Naomi. Ruth had an idea in chapter 2 that was to turn it all around for the two widows of Bethlehem.

> There was a relative of Naomi's husband, a man of great wealth, of the family of Elimelech. His name was Boaz. So Ruth the Moabitess said to Naomi, "Please let me go to the field, and glean heads of grain after him in whose sight I may find favor." And she said to her, "Go, my daughter" (Ruth 2:1–2).

Life was about to get better. By the end of the book, Naomi had become the blessed nurse of Obed, King David's grandfather (Ruth 4:21–22). Obed was to be a restorer of life to Naomi and a nourisher of her old age (Ruth 4:15). She was to come to understand that this faithful daughter-in-law was better to her than seven sons (Ruth 4:15). Triumph over reversals is guaranteed in the end to all of those who are faithful unto death (Revelation 2:10). Sometimes we need an innovative idea or two from our faithful friends, but we can still choose.

The dark times of life can make us bitter, or they can make us better.

The dark times of life—and we all have them—can make us bitter, or they can make us better. Bitterness keeps getting more and more bitter. Beware! Bitterness can usher us into a place where we will hear with clarity the weeping and gnashing of teeth. But becoming better is a never-ending process as well. Where does the path of "better" lead? To the gates of pearl and the street of gold. And it doesn't get any better than that!

Make a list of popular hymns that describe the victory of those who faithfully persevere through difficult times. Take the time to sing one of these.

_____

_____

⪦ *Cindy's Reflections* ⪧

When It's Hard

If I submit when it's easy . . .
When it makes sense to me,
Doing God's Will when I think it best,
Then I'm not really obeying . . .
Not submitting at all
When it's difficult . . . there lies the test.

When the culture screams one thing,
The Word whispers another,
When I can't understand that command;
When I wriggle and wrest
But I know His way's best,
That's the time when I'm under His hand.

Faith is not faith when
You see why it works.
When you know why each move you are making.
The steps that will lead me
To heaven with Him
Are the ones I don't know why I'm taking.

He's saved all His best
For His children of faith,
But the best is not yet for beholding.
When my eyes are too weak
For the heaven I seek
I just trust in the Hand I am holding.

A WOMAN WITH PULL

RUTH

Entreat me not to leave you, or to turn back from following after you; for wherever you go, I will go; and wherever you lodge, I will lodge; your people shall be my people, and your God, my God. Where you die, I will die, and there will I be buried. The Lord do so to me, and more also, if anything but death parts you and me (Ruth 1:16–17).

These words that you've likely heard at several weddings were actually spoken by a daughter-in-law to her mother-in-law. Both found themselves at new low points of life in widowhood. Both were searching for some security and purpose. Both had unanswered questions and unfilled potential.

Naomi had decided to go back to Bethlehem. The famine that drove her from the homeland had subsided. Her family was back in Israel. Although she figured she was too old to remarry (v. 12), she still longed to go back to the place where people knew her (v. 19). She was looking for a comfort zone.

Ruth, though, was a different story. Her own mother lived in Moab. Her childhood acquaintances were there. Her husband's grave was there. Moab was her comfort zone.

And yet, we see in Ruth a fierce loyalty to Naomi. What is it in the dynamics of this relationship that prompted Ruth to promise to partner through this life with her mother-in-law?

> Have young wives give suggestions to older women about how to make the relationship of mother-in-law to daughter-in-law more comfortable and fulfilling. Then have the older women give the younger women suggestions.

First, we have to credit Naomi as we read between the lines of the first chapter of Ruth. She had captured the hearts and loyalties of two foreign daughters-in-law whose husbands were no longer in the picture. That is no easy feat! Problems with in-laws always make the top five in any expert's list of common marriage problems. It's easy for moms to resent the girls who dethrone them in the hearts of their sons. It's easy for wives to resent the positive comments that husbands make about the great dumplings Mom made—especially if the wife doesn't even know what a dumpling is!—or the way Mom brought Dad his slippers when he came home from work. There are just some hidden, but very deep potential pitfalls in the relationship of in-laws, especially female in-laws! The applied teachings of Christ can navigate us to harmony in these relationships. Naomi had obviously been good and kind and protective of Ruth and Orpah.

Second it had to be the case that Ruth was devoted, not only to Naomi, but primarily to Naomi's God, Jehovah. She was leaving her mother's house (v. 8), her most logical (from a human standpoint) prospects of marriage, and ultimately her sister-in-law, Orpah. I believe it was the case that Ruth was already in love with Jehovah God and His people.

When one of my dear sisters in Christ married a gospel preacher, she asked me to be her matron of honor. Having grown up in a non-Christian home, Terri doesn't get a lot of support from her family as she determinedly lives for Christ. I tried to decline this request politely, suggesting that she ask her own sister to attend her. I said, "Don't you think it's important to include your family?"

Her response was "I *am* including my family. You are my real, forever family." Ruth must have been thinking along these lines. We too should grow to think of our family in the Lord as our truest kinship. I often see congregations struggle through the cliquishness of little family groups within the church

Problems with in-laws always make the top five in any expert's list of common marriage problems.

that are constantly planning all of their activities together to the exclusion of those who may not have any relatives in the church. Sometimes I see new Christians spending lots of time alone because their old friends don't fit into their new Christ-like lifestyles and, sadly, their new Christian family is unconsciously keeping them at arm's length. If you are blessed to have your blood family members in the congregation with you, please work to have an outward focus. Eternity is not all about your blood kin! It's all about your family in Christ. There will be no private parties in heaven.

A large congregation witnessed the baptism of their new brother, Phil. He looked like a stereotypical homeless person. His hair was long and scraggly; his beard was unkempt. His face was somewhat disfigured and he was tall and very lean. But Phil was not homeless. He lived alone in an apartment. Phil was a very hard worker. He did not have a glamorous job, but it paid the bills. Shortly after Phil was baptized, the congregation learned that he had no physical family. How touching to find out that one of the couples in this congregation included him in a large family Thanksgiving gathering! The good woman who made sure this happened is related to no fewer than twenty people in the congregation. But she has an extended view of family. It is a view we all should adopt.

Ruth, like Terri and Phil, had grown to understand that, in Jehovah, there was a family that, although still largely unknown to her, was the eternal family. She was willing to take big risks to be a part of that family. Boaz later described the amazing metamorphosis in Ruth's life. With much kindness he credited her decisions to her trust in the Lord:

> It has been fully reported to me, all that you have done for your mother-in-law since the death of your husband, and how you have left your father and your mother and the land of your birth, and have come to a people whom you did not know before. The Lord repay your work, and a full reward be given you by the Lord God of Israel, under whose wings you have come for refuge (Ruth 2:11–12).

PULLING UP STAKES

So Ruth left it all behind. She left the familiar comfort zone for the unknown. She pulled away from the heathen to go to Israel. At the crossroads of her adult life she passed on the routine and headed for new horizons.

Let's not let the lesson escape us. While, there is a comfortable stability in putting down roots and raising our families at one familiar address or in one hometown, there are times when God's providence provides greater opportunities for service in unfamiliar places.

—Noah did something "crazy" in the middle of his adult years.

—Abraham had a huge travel adventure at God's calling in his mature years.

—Jacob moved to Egypt when he was an old man.

—Moses switched "careers" mid-life when he encountered God in a burning bush.

—Caleb conquered a mountain when he was eighty years old.

—David went from the sheepfold to the palace when called by the Lord.

—Jonah went on an amazing whale-sighting cruise when he really wanted to stay home.

—Esther went from captive to queen overnight.

—Peter and John switched from catching fish to catching men.

—Paul went from persecutor to preacher.

What might you be able to do for Him if your eyes are always open to opportunity and your heart is always open to change?

A preacher once called my husband to ask if he knew of a town with an open pulpit where he might be able to move, along with his young family, to preach the gospel. My husband knew of a great church in need of a preacher and he recommended this congregation to the young man. The young man immediately responded that his wife would never want to move to that particular area. He went on to explain why she would not like living in that town. While it's not necessarily wrong for us to look for cultural "fits" and examine all of the pros and cons of important decisions, to dismiss out of hand a congregation because of a mere preference seems a bit self-focused.

—"What vision do the elders have?"

—"Are there great influences there for my children?"

—"Would I be able to better support my family and give more to the work of the Lord?"

—"Would there be more evangelistic opportunities in this place?"

—"Is worldliness a larger or smaller concern in this area of the country?"

—"Is there, in general, a greater potential for service to the kingdom in this place?"

None of these questions were verbalized, but I believe at least some of them should have come to mind.

Often we are absorbed in external preferences for our lives. Sometimes we become more attached to family, surroundings, or situations than we are to the Lord. Remember, Jesus said, "He who loves father or mother more than me is not worthy of me" (Matthew 10:37). Sometimes the job, the paycheck, the situation in this life is the first concern and the afterthought is, "is this situation conducive to serving my God?" If that is the case, we have the cart before the horse. We need to switch the eternal priority from afterthought to forethought.

Providence is always seen better when we look back than when we look around.

I learned this lesson the hard way. When I was a young mother, my husband got a call from a congregation in a faraway place. In this congregation, the needs were great, the fields were ripe, and the blessings for our little family were abundant. But it was a great distance from my parents, the small town in which I was enjoying raising my family, and all the friends with whom we shared deep bonds. I followed my godly husband to this place, moving into a house I had never seen until the day we moved in. My three-month-old had colic and cried constantly. My three-year-old was, let's say, extremely busy.

Shortly after moving, I found out that my mother, now hours and hours away, was terminally ill. I remember thinking (and probably voicing), "What is this all about? What on earth do we think we are doing?"

I do not wonder why we did that any more. Providence is always seen better when we look back than when we look around. I know a man with whom my husband studied while we lived in that town who was baptized shortly after we left. Now he serves as an elder in the Lord's church. I know a young man whose major life's decisions we have been able to influence because of the early association he had with our family while we lived there. I met a mom one day at a library story hour in that particular town. I was able to study with her and she is now an elder's wife. But the one I know best is a preacher's wife (me!) whose baby and toddler are now adults. These two kids were blessed to have a mom and dad who learned to depend on a Christian family in an unfamiliar setting. That little family learned in times of loneliness and separation from family to lean on the Lord. That marriage grew stronger when the preacher and his wife learned to depend on each other and grow together in the absence of an extended physical family.

It may not always be best to pull up stakes and move across the country. The culture in which you find yourself may be the one in which your maximum potential can be reached for His glory. But the spiritual ramifications of every decision should be examined when we come to the crossroads. Every significant temporal decision should be closely examined in light of the fact that the temporal is swiftly giving way to the eternal. We should daily ask for wisdom in the choosing. Then once we are there we must not forget the primary purpose of a Christian's life in any situation on any spot of the globe.

Ruth could not yet see Boaz. She could not yet know about the son she was to bear who would bear the father of the most famous king in the history of Israel. She could not know that her son would be in the lineage of the Messiah. (Let's see. That would put her in that lineage, too!) Who knew? But she decided on one fateful day to make Naomi's God the Lord of her life. The rest is history. Who is your god and are you willing to pull up stakes—to take risks—to follow him?

> Give examples of modern-day comfort zones that are hard to leave. How do these comfort zones impede our progress in evangelism?
>
> _____
>
> _____

PULLING HER WEIGHT

I can't read the second chapter of Ruth without being impressed with the work ethic of Ruth. She suggested the gleaning and she suggested that she be the one to do the work. She went, she gleaned, she asked, she continued, she reaped, she bowed, she beat the barley, and she took it up. We would say she worked her fingers to the bone. But at the end of the day she had food to eat, a meal plan for the future and the acquaintance of a kinsman who would change her world.

Hard work has its own benefits. You may not have the 401K, the hospitalization insurance, the company car with mileage, or the private cubicle, but if you are a woman in His service, you work hard and the benefits really are "out of this world." Even the casual observer of the virtuous woman in

Proverbs 31 cannot but stand in awe of the daily accomplishments of this woman of God, achievements made possible because she ate "not the bread of idleness (Proverbs 31:27)."

God cares about your work ethic. The devil bombards us daily with temptations to waste time. The internet calls us via email and home shopping and social networking sites to squander minutes that turn into hours. Our televisions are often thieves of valuable time. When "American Idol" or any other obsession of pop culture takes the time that we should be devoting to Bible study and prayer, then it truly has become our twenty-first century American idol. If we have time to watch daytime—or night time—drama and vote on cultural icons, but we don't have enough time to make it to Wednesday night services, something is dangerously askew. We must redeem the time!

Here are a few things that have helped me work to be a better steward of time. (I still have much work to do!)

1. Keep a planner, with the important stuff circled. That way, it's easier for me to focus each morning on what I really hope to accomplish during the day.

2. Pray for the wise use of my time.

3. Avoid getting online at all before noon. That way, I at least have a half day before I become aware of the jillions of correspondences I need to answer. I'm far less tempted to spend a lot of time surfing or exploring eBay if I wait till later in the day to even check my email.

4. Don't turn on the TV during the day.

5. Do the worst first. What do I dread doing? For example if I clean the bathrooms first, it makes me hurry to get to the more "fun" stuff— writing!

6. Remind myself constantly of the reality that my small houseguests are just that, and that all of those fingerprints, cluttered rooms, and postered walls will keep replenishing themselves until one day they will stop. (Clutter-free clean is not ultimately all that important!)

7. Save the sitting jobs—writing thank you notes, organizing recipes or mending—for times when my family wants to watch a movie together

or when we travel. Hotel rooms are great for catching up on these jobs. Multitasking is also very helpful.

8. Adopt the phrase: "my candle goes not out by night" when my husband is out of town for a week. I try to work extra hard while he is gone so I will have more time for him when he is home.

9. Learn that everybody is more efficient when there is a daily quiet time. (For me the time is for a power nap.) Someone said, "Nothing is wrong with a woman that a nap can't fix." That is often true for me.

10. Get Bible study done early in the morning before the telephone-ringing-bustle begins.

It should be noted here that not all work is pleasing to God. In order for my work to please Him, it must result from a proper motivation. Why do I want to work hard and achieve a particular goal? Is it because of vanity? Do I want to look good in the eyes of my peers? Am I motivated by material things? Do I want to accumulate more and more, so that I might fill my barns and build bigger ones? (Luke 12:16–21). Am I doing this desk job because it's easier than staying at home with my toddlers? Some of these questions may be difficult to ponder, but the motivation behind work determines its real value.

Why do I want to work hard? Do I want to help others? Am I motivated by material things? Do I want to accumulate more?

I may be working, as Ruth was, to provide for truly needy people who are dependent on me. I may be working hard all day long in my home to provide the spiritual and emotional haven that my children and husband need. I may be working as a volunteer to ease pain and suffering in society. I may be working in a particular career in my early twenties so that when I reach my early thirties I can have the nest egg I will need to be able to commit to godly motherhood. I may be working in a mission field to advance the cause of Christ.

Reasons matter. If what's driving me fits into Matthew 6:33, the rewards will come.

Secondly the characterization of my work is important. Even if I have good reasons to work, the type of work itself may be counterproductive to my Christian influence or my spiritual growth. If this is the case, then the work is not pleasing to God. I counsel teens to avoid working in restaurants in which alcohol is served. My son was an entertainer for a part of his young adulthood, and he would not play in restaurants that served alcohol; he would not play at parties that included dancing. Teens who are not responsible for their livelihoods should avoid working during hours of worship, and adults who have a choice in the matter should, as well. If my job is characterized by any requirements that draw me away from God or hinder my influence for Him, I should be actively seeking an alternative. If there are long hours or extended trips away from my husband, I should be seeing red flags. If there is someone at work who tempts me to infidelity, I should get out of that situation yesterday!

> *Don't rob your children of true wealth by your materialistic example.*

Thirdly, the dispensation of the funds or benefits derived from my work is important to God. Simply stated, I'm accountable to God for how I spend money earned. Matthew 6:33 again gives me the simplest guideline for the heart of stewardship. By being in prayer, in the Word, and around His people I cultivate a passion for His work and for lost souls. I purpose in my heart to give to the kingdom on every Lord's Day. When given the choice to help support a missionary or purchase some superfluous gadget or luxury amenity, I want to do the "spirit" thing rather than the "flesh" thing. This is the cultivation that I daily oversee in the hearts of my children. This is the lesson that only parents can teach. And it cannot be taught by rhetoric. It's only when parents relegate material things to their proper and relatively unimportant perspective that children can develop spiritual priorities. Don't rob your children of true wealth by your materialistic example. Ask yourself some tough questions:

�֎ Do I avoid purchasing items that are sinful within themselves such as cigarettes, alcoholic beverages, pornography, impure entertainment items?

❋ Have I ever chosen to go on the mission trip rather than the vacation?

❋ Do I spend more money on fashion or hospitality?

❋ Would I sacrifice a Saturday of "hobby" for a ladies day of "holiness"?

❋ Have my children, when receiving monetary gifts, learned to lay aside money immediately for giving to the kingdom on Sunday?

❋ Do I diligently keep records of earnings and gifts and be sure that I am giving a liberal percentage to the church?

❋ Do I have unnecessary credit debt that hinders my ability to support missions?

❋ Am I willing to decline social invitations—eating out or going to the movies—to be sure that financial problems don't put undue stress on our family?

❋ Have I prayed this week that God would help me never to place the material blessings He gives in the way of faithful service?

❋ Am I willing in my heart to relinquish material blessings if they get in my way of heaven?

Review the three important factors of acceptable work. Give biblical examples of how each of the following can make our work unprofitable:

1. Working for the wrong reason. _____

2. Doing the wrong kind of work. _____

3. Spending earned funds in an irresponsible or ungodly way.

_____

Pulling with the Program

Now I don't know about you, but had I been Ruth when Naomi made the following suggestion, I think I would have taken her for an evaluation.

Now Boaz, whose young women you were with, is he not our relative? In fact, he is winnowing barley tonight at the threshing floor. Therefore wash yourself and anoint yourself, put on your best garment and go down to the threshing floor; but do not make yourself known to the man until he has finished eating and drinking. Then it shall be, when he lies down, that you shall notice the place where he lies; and you shall go in, uncover his feet, and lie down; and he will tell you what you should do (Ruth 3:2–4).

"You want me to what? Well, this is just about the most incredulously forward thing I can imagine doing! If you want someone to lie at this man's feet, it's going to have to be you! After all, you are a widow, too."

But Ruth's answer was one of complete compliance: "All that you say to me I will do" (Ruth 3:5).

The now archaic Jewish tradition of lying at the foot of the bed of a kinsman must have seemed strange to Ruth, the Moabitess. But she was a team player. When she had said "thy people shall be my people," she obviously was determined to adapt to the culture of the Israelite people. She understood the levirate law which provided for the marriage of widows to the nearest kinsman of the deceased (Deuteronomy 25:5–10). This suggestion from Naomi surely was a test of Ruth's virtue. It took some inner fortitude to summon the boldness required to lie down at the feet of this powerful man and then ultimately ask him to "spread his skirt" over her, the equivalent of a proposal. But Ruth had summoned great courage before and she was up to the awkward challenge.

For all the people of my town know that you are a virtuous woman.
—Ruth 3:11

It must have been an interesting afternoon for Ruth and Naomi; deciding what to wear when you are going to propose to a man, deciding what fragrance to use and just how much, listening to mother-in-law as she counsels as to when exactly to make an entrance into the volatile situation of lying at the foot of Boaz's bed. I've talked about some pretty personal things with my mother-in-law, but I think concocting a scheme like this one would put a blush in the cheeks of both of us!

But it worked seamlessly! Boaz was startled when he felt something at his feet. I don't think Ruth had to be awakened by this man when he was lighting his candle to see what man or beast had invaded his chambers, do you? He blessed her for "following not younger men." But the greatest blessing, for me, would have been his next words: "And now, my daughter, do not fear. I will do for you all that you request, for all the people of my town know that you are a virtuous woman" (Ruth 3:11).

All the city knew she was a virtuous woman. Can that be said of all those who know me? Virtue is moral courage. It is the accumulation of many conscious decisions to do the right thing, even if it costs me in popularity, money, time, emotions, or affluence. I want people to know me as a morally courageous person. But people know me by my fruits. The first chapter of 2 Peter gives us an excellent "to do" list for the development of virtue in our lives. We often call the list in verses 5–7 the Christian virtues.

> But also for this very reason, giving all diligence, add to your faith virtue, to virtue knowledge, to knowledge self-control, to self-control perseverance, to perseverance godliness, to godliness brotherly kindness, and to brotherly kindness love (2 Peter 1:5–7).

Notice in verse 4 that these are the characteristics we add to our lives after we have made a decision to become partakers of the divine nature, after we have escaped the corruption that is in the world, after we have decided to make life changes based on the exceeding great and precious promises of Jehovah. Does that sound a little like Ruth's decision when she left the Moabite world and made that life-changing decision to believe in the promises of Naomi's God?

Then notice the verse following the list of virtues. If these things are in us they make us so that we are not barren or unfruitful. There are some obvious outward signs—things people can see in our lives—of these inward virtues. Ruth's moral courage was characterized by fruit that was easily seen by Boaz.

Finally, notice the entrance that God gives us in verse 11. It is an entrance into an everlasting kingdom. So here's the sequence.

1. God promises us amazing things if we will escape the old world of corruption.

2. When we come out of that world we must work (give diligence) to add virtues to our lives.

3. When we add these inner qualities, we bear fruit that the people around us will notice.

4. We gain an entrance into the everlasting kingdom.

Ruth escaped the land of Moab because she believed in the promises of God. Ruth worked diligently to add virtues to her life. She was rewarded when Boaz saw the fruits of this effort. She gained an entrance into the kingdom of Israel, even becoming the great-grandmother of her greatest king, David. We can spiritually parallel or simulate the transition of Ruth from a Moabite widow to a woman of great honor in the kingdom. But it all begins with a decision to escape our spiritual Moab. Have you decided His promises will control your destiny?

Discuss each of the fruits found in 2 Peter 1:5–7. Give examples from your congregation of each of these fruits being developed.

_____

_____

_____

_____

PULLED FROM OBSCURITY

Prior to her encounter with the people of God, Ruth was just a Moabite maiden. Through a series of events that were sometimes painful, and a series of choices that were always honorable, Ruth became a mother of kings. She bore a child who bore a child who bore the most respected king in the history of the Jewish people. She, in fact, became a mother in the lineage of the King of kings, Jesus Christ (Matthew 1:3–6; Luke 3:32–33).

Perhaps you sometimes feel that your life is going nowhere. God can pull you from that "nowhere" through your own contact with His people and His plan today, to a position of honor in the family of God. You can be in the royal family (Romans 8:16–18) and one day sit down by the throne of the King of kings for all of eternity. Choose carefully. Work diligently. Be willing to take risks for the kingdom. You, too, can find a place of honor. You can gain an entrance into the everlasting kingdom.

What is our modern-day Moab? How do we leave Moab today? At what point do we enter our everlasting kingdom?

_____

_____

⮞ *Cindy's Reflections* ⮜

If Not Me, Who?

You were seated next to someone who shared with you a
    sorrow.
You met a woman in the mall whose surgery is tomorrow.
Someone on your son's team needs a ride home from the game.
And that woman on your email list needs prayer . . . what *was*
    her name!
The coach said you could have a devo if someone would just
    plan it.
There's a booth uptown to hand out tracts if someone could
    just man it.
Your neighbor has a new baby. She could use some help with
    dinner.
She's really not religious . . . there's a chance that you could
    win her.
There were visitors last Sunday. They sat just across the aisle.
But when you'd gathered up your things, they'd left; that took
    a while.
You pray for missionaries who are in the "foreign fields."
You ask Him to guide, guard, direct, and keep you in his Will.
You prayed along in worship that God would open up a door.
Can you not see them all ajar? What could God do more?
There are places He will lead you with His providential hand.
Times when there's a cause and only you can take a stand.

There are moments that are ripe for showing some lost soul the
   way;
Situations . . . conversations . . . words just you can say.
Sometimes, the task is obvious, the job is yours to do.
The question begs of each of us, "O Lord, If not me . . . who?"

IT MIGHT HAVE BEEN

ORPAH

Orpah is the one who almost did, but didn't; the one who must have thought about what might have been; the one who faded into obscurity even as her sister-in-law, Ruth began her ascent to the royal lineage. Sometimes I think we are too hard on Orpah in our reflective judgment. Any number of reasons may have been on her mind as she gave Naomi and Ruth those final hugs and tearfully walked back from the unknown to the familiar: family sickness, romantic attachments, financial opportunities, or her own weak emotional nature. We just don't know why Orpah changed her mind at the last moment and opted to stay with her family in Moab. Whatever the reasons, we can learn, from her reluctance to take the "road less traveled by," some simple, yet profound lessons about the way we should view our own decisions.

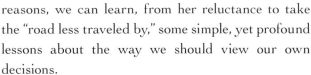

We tend to look at two paths through short-sighted spectacles. We make our choices based on what we see right now.

LOCATION IS EVERYTHING

I recall when moving to Huntsville, Alabama, I went on-line prior to actually traveling to Huntsville to house shop. I saw a beautiful antebellum-like, two-story estate enveloped by a large plot of well-groomed land all nestled inside a gated privacy fence. The best thing was the price which was very comparable to the newer houses built in tightly packed subdivisions. I knew I wanted to see this house.

You've already guessed the rest of the story. When I asked the realtor to show me the house, he began in earnest to try to talk me out of looking at that house. He explained that there was a reason for the tall fence and very secure gate that outlined the property. At my insistence, he finally drove me to the neighborhood and pointed out the "adult" business establishments and bars. He told me about the drugs and crime, the all-night sirens, and the fear I would have for my children to leave the house. He reminded me that Glenn was often out of town and that I would not be comfortable in that part of town. "Location," he said, "is everything."

It's true in real estate and it's true when we consider our most *real* estate—our spiritual estate. Sometimes the temporal beckons us to a particular location or situation in life. Naomi threw out a logically persuasive argument in an attempt to get Ruth and Orpah to return to their people.

> Turn back, my daughters, go—for I am too old to have a husband. If I should say I have hope, if I should have a husband tonight and should also bear sons, would you wait for them till they were grown? Would you restrain yourselves from having husbands? No, my daughters; for it grieves me very much for your sakes that the hand of the Lord has gone out against me! (Ruth 1:12–13).

Orpah apparently was convinced that her most secure future lay in Moab. Eligible bachelors were there. Familiar faces of her childhood and teen years were there. Moab was her comfort zone. So she turned back. Whatever her motives for returning, we must concede that she failed to see the bigger opportunities that rested with the people of God in Bethlehem. She overlooked the fact that, in choosing the Moabite lifestyle, she was choosing to live among the idolatrous, she was severely limiting her marital prospects to men without faith, and she was committing to raise any prospective children in a culture void of God.

Who was the father of the Moabites? Locate the land of Moab. Where is it in reference to Bethlehem-Judah?

Sometimes when we come to a crossroads in our own lives, we look at the two paths. On the one hand there is the path that looks well-trodden, smooth, and convenient. On the other hand, there is the narrow and difficult path that really seems so uninviting (Matthew 7:14). We tend to look at the two paths through our short-sighted spectacles. We make our choices based on what we can see right now—on what looks to be the easiest path for today. We fail to realize that the path of least resistance often leads to the place of least reward. And so we give a thumbs-down to the road that leads to life's most abundant blessings, opting instead for an easy road with a dead end. Think about some of the location choices that we must carefully make. As we make our decisions, we must be wise enough to make far-sighted choices rather than seeing only the immediate comfort of the most enticing path.

When we choose our places of residence or career, we should allow the respective spiritual atmospheres of the various places under consideration to play a very important role in our choices. Is there a great church there? Are there good spiritual influences for my children? Can I convert people to the Lord in this place?

When we choose our children's venues of education, we should consider their spiritual development as the most important of all their areas of growth.

※ Is this school conducive to spiritual excellence?

※ Is this teacher a good moral example?

※ Will the rules prohibit language and behavior that will constantly be a stumbling block to my children?

※ Will this administration be respectful of our family's spiritual choices?

※ Does this atmosphere promote materialism and brand-name worship in the children?

※ Should I choose another option such as home education or private instruction?

When we decide about college for our children, we need to be thinking about more than a degree or a job.

※ Which atmosphere will be most supportive of my child's faith?

※ Which choice will provide the most prospective Christian mates?

※ In which atmosphere will my child likely be more involved in a local congregation?

※ Are the local congregations around this university sound and faithful churches?

※ Are there abundant evangelism or missions opportunities at this location?

❄ Should I choose a better spiritual atmosphere even if the monetary costs are higher?

❄ Should I keep my children home with me for a bit longer before I put them in this situation?

When we choose the placement of our time, we should consider which activities will bring the most glory to the kingdom here on earth. Service clubs, fitness clubs, and social interaction with non-Christians are all well and good, as we are exerting godly influence on the non-believing world around us. But we should pause and once again ask questions.

❄ Is there a service program in the church that would accomplish the same good as this community club and, if so, would it bring more glory to God if I accomplished this benevolence in the name of the church?

❄ When I am participating in this sport or entertainment venue, do I constantly interject the name of the Lord—in a good way—before my non-Christian friends or is this golfing group or work-out program nothing more than a mere physical and social exercise?

❄ Do I take along tracts and invitations to the services when I interact with this group that takes so much of my time?

The word *allocation* contains the word *location* and indicates that I am placing my time and talents in a particular location as I walk through my days. Is that location the very best one to promote my Christianity and help others go to heaven? Location is everything.

I could have chosen to live in the big house with the gate. I'm sure I would have enjoyed the amenities. The pool would have been fun. The huge front porch would have been relaxing, except for the sirens. The extra room for company and kids would have been wonderful. But there would have been dangers lurking—constant threats to my physical well-being. Often that's how it is spiritually. The place that is most comfortable and appealing is the most dangerous. There is a way that seems right to a man, but the ends thereof are the ways of death (Proverbs 16:25).

Give practical spiritual experiences or applications of the "location is everything" principle.

_____

_____

Decisions Determine Destinies

"Captain Obvious." That's what my daughter calls me when I make glaring understatements like "decisions determine destinies." We all intellectually grasp the evident truth of the statement; yet, sometimes we go about the seemingly mundane choices of our days without giving much thought to the huge implications of the successions of choices we are making. Ruth and Orpah serve as testimonies to the importance of one decision made on one ordinary day in the course of regular events. Ruth made decision A and became a key figure in the royal lineage of the King of kings. Orpah made decision B and thus ended her brief appearance in the annals of history, fading back into a culture that failed to recognize Jehovah. Perhaps Lot would have decided differently on that day when he "pitched his tent toward Sodom" (Genesis 13:12), if he could have seen the flames of destruction, the pillar of salt, and the ensuing immorality. Perhaps there would have been some dissenting votes in the brotherhood of jealous men who decided to sell Joseph into slavery in the pasture that day (Genesis 37) if they could have seen themselves bowing before him in his royal quarters in Egypt. Maybe David would have just looked the other way from that rooftop in Jerusalem the instant he saw that pretty woman bathing (2 Samuel 11:2). Maybe Judas would have decided not to pilfer in the treasury that very first time (John 12:6). And the list of deeply regretted decisions goes on.

Satan loves to promise an instant heaven, knowing full well he intends to deliver an eternal hell.

And the list goes on today. A sister in Christ decided one night to go to a bar and have a drink. Someone put something into that drink and the next day she awakened, unsure of any of the night's events. It was only later that she discovered that pictures of her in compromising situations had been posted online. Bad choice for that evening. Bad consequences for a very long time.

Another young man was a member of a congregation whose godly elders had asked the teens not to participate in the local high school prom. But he decided to attend anyway. That night on the way home, he was involved in a fatal car crash. He died in rebellion to the request of those shepherds. Was that a good decision?

Almost all the young men I know are presented with a seemingly small choice at some very young age. The choice is usually presented online. The decision just "pops up" as a result of an innocent click or the accidental opening of an unknown email. And there it is: the first exposure to pornography. The decision to look away or to investigate is one that too many of our sons are unprepared to make. Too many times we've failed to warn them about this likely temptation and too many boys are making that initial wrong choice. Decisions, decisions!

> Suggest ways that parents and mentors can give our children the heads up early to spare them this pornography addiction. (Go to www.ultima-teescape.org and research this problem in our churches. Note: Author does not endorse all material on this website.)
>
> _____
>
> _____

The devil loves to get us into the moment of decisions. At that moment he loves to promise an instant heaven, knowing full well he intends to deliver an eternal hell. We tend to minimize the importance of those "small" single decisions. But the ripple effect of those choices affects the courses we chart to eternity's shore.

Bitter People Give Bad Advice

As we've already seen, Naomi went through a very angry and bitter period of life. It was in the throes of this resentful period that she advised her daughters-in-law to return to their families in Moab. Orpah was a devoted daughter-in-law. It seems from the text that they were well on their way to Judah when Naomi made her speech declaring that "the hand of the

Lord is against me." Orpah had packed her things and begun the life-changing journey with Ruth and Naomi. But the ill-timed, acidic advice of Naomi convinced Orpah to return to the land of her birth.

Orpah was not a native Israelite. Her position at the time of Naomi's insistence to return was similar to the status of new Christians—babes in the body—today. May I suggest that if you have a gripe about the elders, a complaint about the preacher, or a general tendency to be negative in your disposition, refrain from sharing that negative attitude with the babes in your congregation?

In Naomi's words they are saying, "Turn again; just don't be so serious about the Lord and His people."

Having worked extensively with those who are newly converted to Christianity, I have learned to be passionate about their protection and positive growing space in the kingdom. It is extremely disheartening for me to spend long hours teaching them about faithful attendance, going to pick them up for services when they do not have transportation, and finding area services that meet around their work schedules, only to have those who have been Christians for twenty-five years show them that it's "no big deal" to miss the gospel meeting or Bible study for a ballgame, a school fundraiser, or a concert. In Naomi's words they are saying, "Turn again; just don't be so serious about the Lord and His people."

One young mother was counting the cost before her baptism. She had all kinds of questions about the time she would need to put into this new commitment she was making. But the Scriptures convinced her of the relatively small sacrifices we make in this world when we commit our lives, our time, and our children to the service of God. She and her husband were baptized, and they immediately made major life changes. Their kids were in Bible classes on Wednesday nights, even when they were missing ball practices or games. They adjusted their kids' bedtimes to accommodate evening activities. They meant business about the Lord and His people, that is, until his people began to show them that there were things of this world that were "more important" than the church. Today this family is very sporadic in attendance and unfaithful to the commitment they originally made. Why are they rapidly falling away? I believe the reason is that "those who ought to be teachers have need that someone teach them the first principles of the oracles of God."

Katelyn was a brand new Christian. Ladies of the congregation had studied with her, met for "encouragement lunches," and helped her through times of crises; sister Martin had spent many hours just being there for Katelyn. She was growing by leaps and bounds. She was never missing a service and she was even bringing others to study with us, one of whom was soon baptized. She became very close to the entire Martin family. The father in that particular family became upset at the elders because of difficult judgment decisions they had made. This family decided to boycott the evangelistic effort of this church because they "just didn't care for the guest speaker." The worst part of the story is that they encouraged Katelyn to just stay at home with them. They poisoned her mind about the preaching, which was very biblical. They took this baby in the Lord and deprived her of the spiritual milk she needed so desperately while feeding her toxins that put her spiritual life in danger. Thankfully, when the elders spoke to this good family; they realized their mistake and repented of it. They turned their bitterness into "better-ness." Katelyn is out of the spiritual intensive care unit and back on the sincere milk of the Word (1 Peter 2:2).

Lukewarm members easily become bitter members. When people are on fire for the Lord they speak of "what we are doing in our congregation," and it's usually a lot of good things. When people become complacent they tend to speak of "what they are doing over there at the church," and it's almost always not so great. Sometimes I think it would be better if we just petitioned off a section of our worship areas for those who are lukewarm or embittered in their dispositions. That way we could direct the babes in Christ to avoid that section and sit among the happy, encouraging zealous Christians. If we really did such an absurd thing, I hope that section would be very small and I hope its pews would soon be empty as its "regulars" grew to be zealous participants rather than casual and often vinegary observers. As long as we are thinking out of the box, though, let's make it personal:

If your auditorium were so divided, where would you sit?

One day the congregation will be divided. That day is the Judgment Day. But I want to think about where I sit *now*, while there is time to change seats, don't you?

Read Naomi's counsel to Ruth and Orpah when she was struggling with bitterness. Then read aloud Naomi's request that those around her call her name Mara. Why are bitter people sometimes more vocal in their bitterness than faithful people are in their zeal?

Suggest ways that mature Christians can "rescue" babies in the Lord who may be struggling on life-support. What kinds of supportive things can women do for babes in Christ?

IT'S NOT AN ILLUSION

One more thing. I often hear that so-and-so fell away because she just became disillusioned with Christianity. Perhaps our common usage of the word *disillusioned* could describe some members who become discouraged. But if we think literally, doesn't the very word itself imply that there were positive hopes and visions one had upon becoming a Christian and that these hopes and dreams were later found to be unrealistic? When one becomes disillusioned with something, the unbelievable expectations are stripped away and reality sets in.

I believe it is impossible for true Christians to become disillusioned, at least in the literal sense of the word. Upon becoming Christians, God promises us blessings above all that we can "ask or imagine" (Ephesians 3:20). He promises us the abundant life (John 10:10). He promises us a heaven that is far above and beyond our scope of imagination. But these things are not illusions. They are real. We can give up the real for the plastic of this life. But if we turn our backs on the Lord, we have not set aside our illusions. We have set aside the reality of eternal life. Faith is the underpinning of our spiritual imaginations. If we have faith, we may become discouraged. We may become weak at times. But we really don't become disillusioned, because the end of our faith is salvation (1 Peter 1:9), and heaven is not an illusion.

Cindy's Reflections

In Training

Two hours at the gym on Tuesday and Friday,
The neighborhood walk with the weights;
A multi-vitamin every night before bed
And watching what goes on our plates;

Small servings, less carbs, more peelings, less fat,
Raw veggies and more fresh picked greens;
More herbs in my garden and more in my tea,
More fiber and balanced proteins.

More time and more slope on my treadmill today;
No elevator . . . I'll take the stairs.
A much higher number on my pedometer today
And much less time spent in my chair.

Green teas and garlic to keep my heart pumping,
My friend Echinacea on the shelf;
Eight hours of sleep and lots of hydration
I'm just taking care of myself.

I'll feel better, live longer, if I just stay in shape.
I'll be happier if I keep my heart fit.
But, still, when this life's workout finally is done,
My heart rate will slow and then quit.

So what of the heart that must all be for Christ . . .
The one that will go on and on;
The soul that, if tended, will never run down
But will finish one day at His throne?

Am I keeping it fit? Is it exercised daily?
Am I devoted to its fitness training?
When this routine is over, what then? Is there more?
Is there something of me that's remaining?

Am I feeding my spirit a well balanced diet,
Ingesting the milk of His Word?
Do I see the Great Physician when my soul becomes
    weak.
Or when some injury's been incurred?

Are there rituals of exercise; things I must do
For the heart that will never stop beating?
Do I keep its rate up? Do I measure its pulse,
Taking care to supply what it's needing?

There's a fountain of life; living waters in streams.
Am I drinking from these every day?
Do I hunger and thirst for my Lord's righteousness?
And what price am I willing to pay?

For there's sweat in the workout. There's toil in the run.
It takes a real will in this gym.
But the yoke is still easy, the burden is light
When I am in training with Him.

His payoff is heaven. His finish is grand;
A victorious soul's celebration.
The training complete, I'll sit at His feet,
For he made my soul fit for salvation!

CHAPTER 12

TABERNACLE TRAUMA

HANNAH

THE PROVOCATION

The problem of multiple wives just keeps on rearing its ugly head. This time the wounded women are Hannah and Peninnah, wives of Elkanah, one of many Levite priests of the chaotic period of the judges. From the beginning the plan of God was one man for one woman, for life (Genesis 2:23–24). Situations of bigamy and polygamy were not in the original blueprint for happy marriages. I believe they were a part of the "times of ignorance God overlooked" (Acts 17:30). But ignorance is not bliss in such situations. In fact, in every biblical case of polygamy I can recall, in which any detail of relationships is given, this departure from God's original plan was disastrous. Hannah finds herself in the painful position of penalty for this departure as the book of 1 Samuel opens. Take a moment to read the first six verses of the book. Notice particularly verse 6: "And her rival also provoked her severely, to make her miserable, because the Lord had closed her womb" (1 Samuel 1:6).

> What are some examples of wife rivalry and barrenness from the book of Genesis?
>
> _____

The original language indicates that Peninnah was viewed as a rival and that she irritated Hannah to the point of anger and weeping because of her initial inability to bear children. (This certainly calls to mind a couple of situations from Genesis.)

It's interesting to note that this taunting on the part of Peninnah intensified when they made their big yearly trip to the tabernacle to worship and sacrifice (1 Samuel 1:7). Isn't that just the way it still happens today? The devil loves to get damaging tongues going full speed in the middle of the work of the church. If he can get people to be blessing God and cursing men with the same tongue (James 3:9), he knows he weakens the strength of the service to God. It's also interesting to see that the provocation didn't seem to go away, even after years of the same old hurtful words. James really got it right when he spoke of the amazing destructive power of acerbic words (James 3:1–10).

Hannah was faithful in times of provocation. There was a day in Peninnah's life when being in the "normal" crowd was hugely important to her psyche. Looking down her nose at Hannah was her step-stool to self-exaltation. I can imagine some of her sarcastic comments to Hannah as they got ready for the feast day.

"I'm sorry you don't have any gifts for the holiday" . . . or

"Come on, all of my sweet children. Let's get ready to go" . . . or

"Doesn't anyone want to sit with poor, lonely Hannah on the way?"

Are you bitter in your soul about something over which you have no control?

When Peninnah and Hannah climbed aboard the caravan to travel to Shiloh, certainly Hannah was pitied by the majority of those who looked on. To be barren was to be plagued. Remember, we have the twenty-first century vantage point. How many of us could recall the name Peninnah before we began this study? But I venture that all of us have been inspired over and over by the details of the life of Hannah. How many baby girls have been born lately in your community and given the name Peninnah? How many people in your community wear the beautiful name of Hannah? Society's applause is very short lived. So is persecution. Faith abides!

THE PRAYER

Something was terribly wrong in the life of Hannah. Somebody was terribly wrong in her treatment of Hannah. Hannah had real issues with which her husband seemed unable to help. She could have brooded her way to a lifetime of bitterness. At some points in the narrative, it seems she was well on her way. But notice that her bitterness of soul was accompanied by prayer: "And she was in bitterness of soul, and prayed to the Lord and wept in anguish" (1 Samuel 1:10).

Are you bitter in your soul about something over which you have no control? Do you weep over a condition or circumstance that is beyond your power to change? If so, do you spend time each day in prayer about that situation? James 5:16 has been a mental bridge to me on many occasions spanning the chasm between despair and hope. It says, "The effective, fervent prayer of a righteous man avails much."

What is the message this verse shouts to you? To me it is this: there is no hopeless situation for His children. While those around me may say, "There is absolutely nothing I can do about this," I try never to say those words. There is one thing I can always do. Do you know the best part? That *one thing* is the most effective action known to this world. I can pray to the one who is in total control of the minute details of my existence (Matthew 10:30); the one who has all power to affect all outcomes (1 Thessalonians 5:24); the one who wills my best interests into the workings of this universe (Romans 8:28).

I love the fact that Hannah's prayer was uninhibited. She could have gone into a secret place, but she seemed oblivious to all that was occurring around her. She had one petition on her mind and one object of devotion. The public nature of her prayer was not motivated by a desire to have the praise of men, for it rather brought the initial contempt of the priest. Sometimes I come to a place in my life in which prayer is all that matters. In these times of my life, I really don't care where I am or what I am doing. At these times, I may fail to accomplish much else in my day, but I pray!

"The effective, fervent prayer of a righteous man avails much."
—James 5:16

One day, not very long ago, I was out on a vigorous walk in my neighborhood . . . and I was praying. I was praying aloud pretty vigorously, too. After all, it was early morning and no one seemed to be stirring yet in the whole neighborhood. I became so absorbed in my prayer that I really became pretty oblivious to my surroundings. Suddenly, I looked up and found myself almost nose to nose with a neighbor who was also walking vigorously. There I was, nose to nose with her and just talking away! I said, "Hello" as she hurried past me, but, to this day, I think she tells my other neighbors that I talk to myself!

Hannah's prayer life was obviously unreserved. That's how it should be with the God who knows all about us and all of our needs before we even approach him. We should speak to God as she did:

❋ *With reverence*—She addressed God as the Lord of hosts.

❋ *With submissive spirits*—She called herself his maidservant.

❋ *With personal petitions*—She begged for a son.

❋ *With promises of devotion*—She promised to give her child to the Lord.

Make a biblical list of reverent ways to address God in prayer.

_____

_____

Who else termed herself the Lord's maidservant? Cite scriptures.

_____

We should speak from the overflow of righteous hearts: "Out of the abundance of my complaint and grief I have spoken until now" (1 Samuel 1:16).

THE PRAISE

The first ten verses of chapter 2 contain the amazing prayer of praise from Hannah, the exultant mother of Samuel. Do you encourage young mothers to praise Him from that hospital bed on the day you were given that beautiful son or daughter? Is there a better way to begin on the path of parenthood?

A brief study of Hannah's praise will help us to formulate prayers of deeper praise before the throne of the Lord of hosts. What can we learn from Hannah's prayer?

1. *Give God the glory for personal blessings* (1 Samuel 2:1). Do you do that? When God puts to silence the unjust critics or visits you with blessings in the extreme, do you verbally give Him the glory?

2. *Exalt God above all* (v. 2). Do you verbalize to Him your knowledge that there is none to compare with Him?

3. *Praise the knowledge of God* (v. 3). Do you thank Him and praise Him for originating all truth and imparting it to us through His Word? Do you even understand what a blessing it is to be able to make

practical life decisions based on the imparted knowledge of the one who knows every answer to every quandary?

> Look at Hannah's words in 1 Samuel 2:3. Do you think this arrogance of speech is a reference to Peninnah's taunting? Why or why not?
>
> _____

4. *Praise Him as the Great Equalizer* (vv. 4–8). Do you understand that true greatness lies in submission to Him and that ultimate success is in His service? Have you quit struggling to be enthroned as the mightiest, the richest, the healthiest in physical terms, or the most respected among peers? Have you started focusing on the throne of glory? Do you say this to Him?

5. *Praise Him for keeping your feet* (v. 9). Have you done this? He wants you to acknowledge that your feet can't find their way home to heaven without His direction and He wants you to praise Him for providing the direction. He wants you to acknowledge that you see the difference between the light and the darkness in which the wicked walk.

6. *Praise Him for the ultimate future victory* (v. 10). Do you think about that last day when the trumpet will sound and the dead will rise? Do you contemplate how it will feel to fly through the clouds with Jesus? Do you think about the look on His face and the sound of His voice saying, "Well done"? Have you told Him about your anticipation? Have you praised Him for the victory that has already been won?

Too many times we ask and ask and ask some more without ever communicating our praise and thanksgiving. As a parent, I grow weary if my kids are always asking and never thanking. Does God grow weary with you and me?

> Choose an Old Testament psalm of praise and list the specific things for which praise is given.
>
> _____

THE PROBLEM

I've thought a lot about Hannah's decision to allow Samuel to grow up in the temple at Shiloh with Eli. Some of my earliest memories of Sunday school were lessons about Hannah and the little coats she took year by year to Samuel as he grew up in the temple with Eli. I know that God used these boyhood experiences of Samuel to groom him to be the great prophet he became. I know that the first time God spoke to and through Samuel was right there in Shiloh, where Hannah had placed him when he was very young.

But I confess I cannot wrap my mind around the decision Hannah made to allow Eli to raise Samuel. I just cannot reconcile what she and Elkanah chose to do with Samuel with the very personal responsibilities of parenthood given in Deuteronomy 6:3–7. They relinquished their parenting responsibilities to someone who was unfaithful as a parent. I believe it was a mistake conceived in a good, but misled heart. I believe it was a mistake God used for His purposes. I can see His providence at work. But make no mistake. There was sorrow in the outcome of this child-rearing choice.

The first time God spoke to Samuel was right there in Shiloh, where Hannah placed him when he was very young.

Hannah knew Hophni and Phinehas were at the temple (1 Samuel 1:3). These two acting priests did not even know God and were called the sons of Belial (2:12 KJV). They were using the sacrifices of the people to fulfill their own selfish desires and their sin was very great (2:17). They even committed fornication with the women who assembled at the door of the tabernacle (2:22).

They would not listen to Eli when he urged their repentance (2:25). Eli continued to allow this immorality to occur right under his nose in the house of God. He kicked at the sacrifices of God and honored his sons above Jehovah (2:29). God implied that Eli's behavior showed that he actually despised (failed to esteem) God (2:30). Eli knew full well that his sons were vile and yet he did not restrain them (3:13).

And this is the foster home Hannah chose for her small boy, Samuel. How much of the sexual sin was Samuel observing? While we are not told, it must have been difficult to avoid all knowledge of it, since the Bible says he was serving in his linen ephod (2:18) and the fornication was apparently occurring at the tabernacle door. Did he witness the abuse of the sacrifices and the rebellious spirit they had toward Eli? Surely his innocent heart was broken on many occasions.

I don't know the extent of Hannah's knowledge about this exposure. She went to the tabernacle yearly, so she surely was aware of the unfaithfulness of these priests. I do know that by choice or by default, Hannah exposed young Samuel to immorality and blasphemous worship. I believe her intent was pure; her motivation, one of spiritual devotion. Perhaps, like many parents today, she just tried not to think about the damaging influences and hoped for the best. When we allow our children to be exposed to immorality, we make a grave mistake.

I believe the modern mistake is worse than Hannah's because it is often motivated by worldliness and facilitated by a lack of concern about things spiritual. When we purchase tickets to inappropriate movies, we leave our children with Hophni and Phinehas. When we let them listen to those blatantly perverse CDs, we are leaving them in the care of the rebels. When we fail to limit and monitor television, we are leaving them in Shiloh. Oh, I understand we cannot control everything to which our children are exposed, but we can control our homes and our own pocketbooks!

Hannah paid a price for her decision. May I suggest that there is always a price to pay when we relinquish our parenting responsibilities? In this case, the first words of God to the young prophet Samuel were words of judgment against Eli and his sons (3:11–14). Surely this first miraculous revelation must have impressed young Samuel with the serious nature of the sin he had witnessed. But apparently the parenting example of Eli had taken its toll on Samuel.

> Now it came to pass when Samuel was old that he made his sons judges over Israel. The name of his firstborn was Joel, and the name of his second, Abijah; they were judges in Beersheba. But his sons did not walk in his ways; they turned aside after dishonest gain, took bribes, and perverted justice. Then all the elders of Israel gathered together and came to Samuel at Ramah, and said to him, "Look, you are old, and your sons do not walk in your ways. Now make us a king to judge us like all the nations" (1 Samuel 8:1–5).

Certainly, my primary parenting school is the home in which I was raised. Cycles can be broken and new beginnings can change future generations, but breaking the chain of poor parenting is a formidable challenge.

Samuel's sons were a lot like Eli's sons. The people of Israel even used the wickedness of Abijah and Joel as an occasion to rebel against God and demand a king.

I am surely not a perfect parent. But I am the best mother God had for Caleb and Hannah. No parent could ever love them more than their father and I. No mentor could care more about their eternal destinies. As long as there was life within us, we were determined not to give over the joys of parenting those kids to any daycare center or long-term babysitter. Similarly, we would not trust their souls to the guidance of anybody else. The price was just too high.

In the final analysis, Hannah did some great things. But Hannah's grandchildren were lost. I think I've always dreamed about my grandkids way too much to have ever left Caleb and Hannah at Shiloh.

In what ways can God use bad situations to achieve His ultimate purposes? Give biblical references to support your answers.

_____

_____

⇐ *Cindy's Reflections* ⇒

Forgive Me
("Goodbye to Hannah")

Forgive me if I'm just a little bit sad.
I really shouldn't be.
This is what we raised you for.
Today we set you free.

Forgive me when I shed a tear
As I walk out that door.
Tearful prayers have brought you here,
So I may cry once more.

Forgive me if I worry
When I crawl in bed at night.
Forgive the calls and emails
Just to make sure you're alright.

If you ever want to phone me
Even if it's late at night;
Or if you need a place to come
Where we've left on the light . . .

If you need my arms, a home-cooked meal,
Or a weekend shopping buddy,
A proofreader, dress mender, washer, or maid
Or just a quiet place to study . . .

Home is open . . . even on Sundays.
We do laundry, ironing and meals.
We still change oil and gas up your car.
We'll wash it and balance your wheels.

It's amazing how we spent the past 7000 nights
Trying to get you quiet and in bed.
And now that your bedroom is silent and dark.
We wish it was noisy instead.

Funny how we tired of that telephone ringing.
You constantly tied up our line.
But, honey, if you need to tie it up now.
I think it will probably be fine.

So don't hesitate if you need us.
We're available 24/7.
And telling our story and your bedtime prayer
Is still closest in this life to heaven.

Chapter 13

When Girls are the Bullies
Peninnah

The reader might wonder at this last juncture, "Now just what amazing eternal truth am I going to learn from this woman, who is mentioned all of two times in all of Scripture?" God's Word is timeless, though, and as I look for the lesson in Peninnah, I am once again amazed at its relevance for our day.

Peninnah was the taunting wife. God revealed nothing of her except that she was married and bore children to Elkanah, the priest, and she used her words to berate Hannah, while elevating herself. She used another person as a stepstool to make herself stand a little taller in the company of those who chose to be impressed by pompous facades erected by self flatterers.

What was Hannah's perceived handicap? What other choices might Peninnah have made in dealing with this inequity between her and Hannah? What are some ways Peninnah might have helped Hannah deal with the pain? List some Proverbs to follow when dealing with those who have a sorrow.

_____

_____

_____

A PICTURE OF THE TYPICAL BULLY TODAY

It's not the huge muscular gang member who goes around knocking the little bookworms into the lockers. It's not even the cool football player who throws his weight around in gym class or taunts the water boy. Most often, the bully today is thin, wears sparkly nail polish, flawless make-up, hoop earrings, and heels. She's a middle school cheerleader, a majorette, a high school honor roll student, or even a college homecoming queen. She's popular and often parent/teacher approved. She's sometimes in line for scholarships. She might win pageants and she's admired. She may be very religious or given to volunteer in worthwhile causes. She may even use these causes as arenas for wreaking havoc in the lives of the innocent.

The bully weapon is not a club, a gun, or even a fist. The weapon is words; words that can often leave marks for a lifetime. They are intimidating, taunting, cutting, and cruel. They include making fun of body sizes and features, clothing, parents and families, and material class or status. They often contain vulgar descriptive terms and crude jokes at the victim's expense. They include invitations to parties with the purposeful exclusion of the victim and/or tricking victims into socially embarrassing situations. They are spoken to the victim and about the victim. They are whispered, passed in notes, and written in graffiti.

And modern technology has only exacerbated the problem of girl bullying. Now it's easy, safe from adult detection, and effective to do the Peninnah job on the computer. Instant messaging, social networking sites, and email have all become centers for middle school sabotage. It's called cyberbullying.

Experts tell us there is generally a "head bully." This girl—Peninnah, we'll call her, although she is often called the "queen bee" or the "RMG": really mean girl—is usually loud, crass, often funny, and fully "in charge." You can easily pick her out in almost any class or large teen activity. She takes command of the room she enters and directs her "crew" as to where they are to sit or stand. The girls in the "crew" are weaker. They actually could alternately be the perpetrators of bullying or the victims thereof. But since it's much safer to be on Peninnah's side than to be Peninnah's adversary, these girls generally remain loyal to Peninnah. They may secretly feel for the victim. They may even admire the integrity of the victim. But they remain outwardly true to the bully because that's simply the safe side of the relationship street.

Most often, the bully today is thin, wears sparkly nail polish, flawless make-up, hoop earrings, and heels.

Sadder still is the fact that many of the Peninnah girls' moms are oblivious to the destructive force within their homes. They may even be subconsciously promoting the behavior by constantly catering to the material desires and enabling the social prominence of the bully. I even heard recently of one mom who went on-line incognito. This mom pretended to be a popular teenage guy at her daughter's school. She made her daughter's rival, the victim, feel attractive and pursued by this much-admired guy. Then she abruptly ended the relationship, breaking the girl's heart and contributing to her depression and ultimate suicide.

Fifty-eight percent of kids admit someone has said something mean or hurtful to them online. Cyber-bullying is dangerous for many reasons, but one is that girls can "multiply themselves" by using fake names and/or repeating damaging information about a victim in a hundred different places with the click of one key. How can parents capably monitor what is occurring online in their homes? How can parents pay more attention to what is occurring in the teen worlds of their children? How can moms develop better listening skills?

Experts tell us that moms tend to underestimate the seriousness of teen-bullying. We're tempted to dismiss it as a phase of drama that all teen girls experience. How does the Golden Rule influence our parenting when our girls are bullies or victims of bullying?

In what way are girls who are in "the crew" also victims of bullying? How important is their role in the whole process? How can we teach our girls to be leaders for good in social situations rather than putting themselves in positions of peer dependence?

HOW CAN THIS HAPPEN?

How can people, even respected and religious people, get involved in such cut-throat, vicious behavior? Well, it doesn't happen all at once; sin never does. And it has to do with the seeming innocence of words. I asked a teen class recently, "Why do you think girls are so apt to sabotage each other with words?" Their candid answers went something like this.

—"Sometimes they are just jealous. Maybe they want your friend or your boyfriend and so they try to tear you down in that person's eyes."

—"They want to use a weapon that will hurt for a lifetime instead of healing quickly like a body wound."

—"Sometimes it's easier to use words as a weapon, because you will get suspended from school if you get in a fist fight."

—"They are insecure and they feel more 'confident' when they are putting other people down."

May I suggest to you that they were right? Do you think Peninnah was jealous of Hannah? Oh yes. Hannah was the wife who was most loved; the one who was given the larger portion of the family treasure. Do you think Peninnah was using the weapon that would be less detected by Elkanah and, at the same time, hurt Hannah the most? Oh yes. I think the wrath of Elkanah would have quickly found its target in Peninnah had Hannah showed up at the tabernacle with big bruises and broken bones. But words were far easier to get by the authority; in this case, the shared husband. Did the taunting of Peninnah make her feel a little more validated in her own mind and, perhaps, in the minds of their maidens? Oh yes. Did Peninnah long for the affection of Elkanah that Hannah already possessed? Do you think she imagined if she could make Hannah look a little less worthy of that love that perhaps she could have a larger share of it herself? I say yes again.

What Does God Think about a Bully?

We can conclude that "Peninnah behavior" usually springs from common motives. Let's list these and notice what the Lord thinks of each:

1. *Envy.*

—"For where envy and self-seeking exist, confusion and every evil thing are there" (James 3:16).

—". . . envy, murders, drunkenness, revelries, and the like; of which I tell you beforehand, just as I also told you in time past, that those who practice such things will not inherit the kingdom of God" (Galatians 5:21).

—"A sound heart is life to the body, but envy is rottenness to the bones" (Proverbs 14:30).

So the Peninnah sabotage starts with a girl who is seeking something for herself. But soon she creates a scenario of confusion; one in which good and evil become blurred and the consequences of evil speaking become less obvious. Finally evil and destructive behavior that she would have never contemplated before the envy consumed her are no longer off limits. She is fully engaged in a sin that will keep her from inheriting the kingdom of God and it all sort of sneaked up on her like a cancer in her bones. Once she has influenced others to promote her agenda of destruction, it becomes very hard to get rid of the cancer.

2. *Vengeance*—The Peninnah girl lives to "pass along the pain." Perhaps she has been unfairly treated by parents or peers. Perhaps she never received the attention or discipline of godly parents. Maybe someone who has received these blessings becomes her target. She feels the need to capture the lacking attention at the expense of the innocent. In a sense, she is getting back at the world for giving her a raw deal.

> Beloved, do not avenge yourselves, but rather give place to wrath; for it is written, "Vengeance is Mine, I will repay," says the Lord (Romans 12:19).

At some point, we all have to hand over the vengeance department to God. Living in a world that says, "Don't get mad, get even," and "She can take a dose of her own medicine," it's difficult to finally surrender the totality of the vengeance department to the One Who is divinely capable of overseeing it. It is with perfect justice and grace that God will bring into account the actions and attitudes of those who have made life unfair for me or who may have selfishly robbed me of the time and discipline that would have made such a difference in my life. When I determine, in my mind, that I am but a victim of the behavior of others, I will begin to look for other victims and multiply my propensity to cause pain in the lives of others. Instead, I must resolve to stop the pain cycle, leave the vengeance to God, and take responsibility for my own actions. Sometimes it takes a mature Christian counselor to help me take this giant step.

Peninnah had been given a raw deal in her marriage to Elkanah. He had another wife for whom he exhibited more love. Peninnah hurt, so she passed along the pain.

3. *Tongue-over-Fist Disease*—Do we operate under the delusion that "what I say will not hurt"? Sometimes those of us who would never strike a physical blow will quite handily use the far more damaging little tongue to do a person in.

> Even so the tongue is a little member and boasts great things. See how great a forest a little fire kindles! And the tongue is a fire, a world of iniquity. The tongue is so set among our members that it defiles the whole body, and sets on fire the course of nature; and it is set on fire by hell. For every kind of beast and bird, of reptile and creature of the sea, is tamed and has been tamed by mankind. But no man can tame the tongue. It is an unruly evil, full of deadly poison. With it we bless our God and Father, and with it we curse men, who have been made in the similitude of God. Out of the same mouth proceed blessing and cursing. My brethren, these things ought not to be so (James 3:5–10).

What happens before the guys in the locker room get into that fist fight? Words happen every time. What happens before I go to see an inappropriate movie with my friends? Words happen. We make plans with our tongues. What happens before a single Christian girl becomes sexually involved with her boyfriend? Again, it's almost always words. Words lie. Words cheat. Words berate. Words intimidate and manipulate. No wonder the Holy Spirit tells us that if we can just control that little slippery organ of the mouth, we can control our whole bodies! We get ourselves in deep trouble when we underestimate the power of the tongue. Peninnah didn't control her tongue.

4. *Not Enough Christ Esteem*—Did Peninnah consider that Hannah was one of God's people? Obviously she did not hold to the conviction of Joseph who fled temptation because he could not sin against God. Do we count the cost of our mistreatment of friends, family, and fellow Christians?

> Then He will also say to those on the left hand, "Depart from Me, you cursed, into the everlasting fire prepared for the devil and his angels: for I was hungry and you gave Me no food; I was thirsty and you gave Me no drink; I was a stranger and you did not take

Me in, naked and you did not clothe Me, sick and in prison and you did not visit Me." Then they also will answer Him, saying, "Lord, when did we see You hungry or thirsty or a stranger or naked or sick or in prison, and did not minister to You?" Then He will answer them, saying, "Assuredly, I say to you, inasmuch as you did not do it to one of the least of these, you did not do it to Me." And these will go away into everlasting punishment, but the righteous into eternal life (Matthew 25:41–46).

Sometimes we have just not fallen deeply in love with Jesus. While I hurt the Lord when I mistreat anybody, this is especially applicable when I mistreat those who are in His kingdom. When I harm or neglect the people of God, I mistreat the Lord. I cannot think for very long about those people who gave Jesus vinegar when He cried out of thirst on the cross. I cannot bear to think about the palms of big human hands striking my Lord as they mocked Him in that blasphemous fake trial. To think about some human sinner spitting on the Lamb of God turns my stomach. I struggle to avoid the haunting images of the hands that jerked the whip that mutilated His back or the rough hand that held His wrist to the cross as they prepared to put that spike through His hand. But I may not hold the same contempt for someone who would willfully inflict torture and pain in the life of one of his brethren. I fail to remember that Jesus also feels that pain. He feels every jeer, every crude remark, every embarrassment, and every demeaning exclusion.

WHATEVER IT IS, IT'S JESUS!

Think of any Christian summer camp. The classes are excellent: Bible filled and interesting. The rules are conducive to morality and spiritual growth. A lot of the staff has been there for decades. Many of the campers have grown up going each year since before they can remember. They know old camp jokes and legends and share favorite memories. But every year there are a few new people, kids who come to have a great spiritual experience and grow in Christian fellowship.

Can it be a subtle temptation of the devil for the veteran campers and counselors to exclude the new kids on the block from their fun memories? Sometimes, when older campers recall memories and voice lifelong appreciation for one another, the newcomers feel a little left out. More often than not, it makes them feel a *lot* left out. This is just one scenario of many in which the devil can catch God's veteran soldiers "feeling their rank" at the expense of tender souls. Sometimes it's the new convert who sits alone in the assembly. It may be the member who lives far away from family who eats every meal alone. Maybe it's the teenager who is being raised by a grandparent and doesn't have the trendy clothes that most kids in the youth group are able to afford. Maybe, as in the account of Hannah and Peninnah, it's the young married woman—the one who has no children—who is left out of the outings with her sisters in Christ. Whatever it is, it's Jesus! Study His teachings. Commit His "blessed are ye" verses to memory (Matthew 5:3–12) and fall in love with the one who died for you! You will come to recognize and abhor the Peninnah spirit.

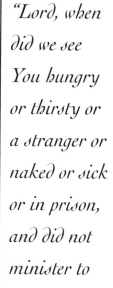

"Lord, when did we see You hungry or thirsty or a stranger or naked or sick or in prison, and did not minister to You?"

—Matthew 25:44

We call it low self-esteem, that deficient inner self that constantly struggles to gain attention and approval from the popular and admired. I think it is more accurately termed low Christ-esteem. When I get into the Word and come to an appreciation of the price laid upon Christ for my redemption, I learn the worth of my soul. In fact, I learn the worth of every soul. When I move the focus from "what's in it for me?" and direct it to seek His honor, I become so interested in the welfare of other souls that I cannot seek their harm. I am automatically transformed into protector and provider for souls around me. I am seeking their salvation and that goal is oppositional in every way to the Peninnah spirit. Peninnah, even as she journeyed to the house of God, carried a spirit of low God-esteem. How does your esteem measure up as you interact in the house of God?

A WORD TO TEEN GIRLS

If you are popular and admired, beware! Take a look at your world and be sure you are popular because of good qualities: honesty, integrity, benevolence, kindness, and adherence to the golden rule. Examine your friendships. Have you pursued any of these relationships because of status involved in hanging out with this person or group? Take a close look at any enemies as well. If you have enemies—people who don't want to be in the same room with you—is it because you have mistreated or excluded them, or is it because they are excluding and reviling you? Think about Luke 6:22–23. Where do you fit in? Are you the persecutor or the persecuted?

> Blessed are you when men hate you, and when they exclude you, And revile you, and cast out your name as evil, for the Son of Man's sake. Rejoice in that day and leap for joy! For indeed your reward is great in heaven, for in like manner their fathers did to the prophets (Luke 6:22–23).

And one more thing. Always remember that you are too valuable to be used for evil by anyone. Don't let some popular person draw you into an exclusive circle of self-aggrandizing followers of Peninnah. (You probably call them snobs.) You will inflict pain on the innocent from this circle. You will be tempted to be worldly in this circle. You will disappoint your Savior in this circle. Then finally, you will reach adulthood realizing you have robbed yourself of the most real friendships a girl can have, because you chose the plastic ones. Anyone who will use you to build fences around her own popularity is not your real friend.

Discuss the pitfalls of popularity. Why isn't it always a bad thing to be popular? What special temptations may come with popularity?

_____

_____

Assign one or two class members to research the following web sites and give a report:

❀ www.opheliaproject.org

❀ Glover, Scott, *Alleged MySpace 'cyber-bully' indicted in teen's suicide*, Los Angeles Times, May 16, 2008

❀ ABC News, *Primetime*, http://absnews.go.com/Primetime/Story id=2421562

❀ Argosy University, www.pioneerthinking.com/ara-meangirls, *Mean Girls: How to Combat Bullying*, p. 2

AND A WORD TO MOMS

I certainly don't know all the answers about the problem of teen bullying, but I do know the Peninnah scenario doesn't occur overnight. There are some things we can do to help prepare our teen girls for the barrage of materialistic pursuits that will tempt them in their most volatile time of life. Consider the following preventive suggestions for their early years:

- Relegate material things to a position far below the spiritual priorities in your home and family as your children are growing up. Let them see you make financial sacrifices to help missions. Let them see that time spent with them is more important than career.

- In your family Bible times, examine passages like James 2:1–9 and role play modern situations in which the James 2 principle is violated.

- Include your children in your benevolent actions. Be sure you are not "picky" when it comes to choosing the people you befriend and help.

- Take your children—especially teens—on a mission trip to a Third World country. They will come home with a different view of material things.

- Don't cater to brand-name requests. This can develop into a dangerous form of materialism that will hamper Christianity through adulthood.

- When entering a playground or story hour, encourage your children to pick out someone who looks lonely and might need a friend. Then sit beside this person and teach your children how to talk to this person. Teach your children the joy in lifting up others.

- Never compromise your family's standards in order to preserve a friendship. If another family or friend is inviting you to do something that is against your standards, always decline with love and a biblical reason for your absence.

- Don't let your children set their sights on worldly activities for the teen years. Teach them in the early years that immodesty—including cheerleading and majorette teams—immorality in entertainment and sports activities that require unfaithful attendance are not "dreams" to be encouraged.

❄ Teach your children from the pre-school years to look for newcomers at every church assembly, and invite them to sit with you.

❄ Open your home to those who may not get lots of invitations to dinner. Make your children comfortable around those with physical disabilities or mental handicaps.

Dr. Dallas Jackson, professor of educational leadership at Argosy University in Tampa, Florida, recommends the following plan of action for those who may be victims of relational aggression. Discuss these, and notice how biblical the principles are. Perhaps you will want to share these with your children.

1. Get an adult involved immediately.

2. Do not associate with friends who require things or favors of you as a condition of friendship.

3. Do not participate in gossip. This includes being a third party message conveyor.

4. Assess your situation by knowing who is good and who is not in your circle of friends.

5. Maintain an open and honest relationship with your parents and family to maintain a support system in trying times.

Cindy's Reflections

OP-portunity

If there's a conversation
    that will wound another—DROP IT!
Some word of gossip tries
    escaping from your lips, just—STOP IT!
A bubble that excludes
    a lonely misfit, won't you—POP IT?
Is there a fence to jump
    and comfort some outsider?—HOP IT!
Some kindness you showed yesterday?
    Today's brand new, so—TOP IT!

ACTES NOIRS
série dirigée par Manuel Tricoteaux

CAUCASE CIRCUS

DU MÊME AUTEUR

LA CHASSE AU RENNE DE SIBÉRIE, Actes Sud, 2008.

Titre original :
Niyazbek
Editeur original :
AST Publishers, Moscou
© Julia Latynina, 2005

© ACTES SUD, 2011
pour la traduction française
ISBN 978-2-7427-9477-5

JULIA LATYNINA

Caucase Circus

LA TRILOGIE DU CAUCASE 1

roman traduit du russe
par Yves Gauthier

ACTES SUD

Telle une corde blanche, la route sillonnait le flanc de la montagne, bordée en contrebas d'une forêt à la verdure éblouissante émaillée de rochers rouges. Un vieux Tchétchène était assis au-dessus du vide, près d'une glissière bricolée de ficelles, vêtu d'une chemise longue, la face ridée comme une noix. L'air triste, il tenait un pare-chocs entre ses mains.

Il y eut comme un grondement d'obus qui souleva une volée d'oiseaux effarouchés, puis un convoi apparut de derrière un éperon rocheux. Un véhicule blindé ouvrait la colonne, suivi de deux camions Oural, d'une citerne et d'un Geländewagen semblable à un cercueil noir. Un autre blindé fermait la marche.

Pneus bruissant, le Geländewagen s'arrêta, et le vieux Tchétchène vit sauter dans la poussière de la route un homme en treillis qui portait un pistolet-mitrailleur en bandoulière. L'homme était très jeune pour ces montagnes. Sous ses yeux noirs et vifs foisonnait une barbe noire et frisée qui allait moutonnant à ses lèvres charnues.

— *Salam aleïkum*, Kharon ! Tu as l'air bien triste…

— *Vaaleïkum assalam*, Arzo ! Ma voiture est partie sans moi, et j'avais vécu avec elle plus d'années qu'avec ma dernière femme. Il y a de quoi être triste.

— Et elle est tombée loin ? demanda Arzo.

— Tout au fond, soupira le vieux.

— C'était quoi comme voiture ? lança un troisième en sautant du blindé, tenue camo et arme à l'épaule, comme l'autre.

— Une Volga. De la belle bagnole, ça. Ta mère était encore grosse de toi, Arzo, quand ton père et moi l'avons transportée dedans jusqu'à l'hosto.

9

Arzo Khadjiev se mit à l'extrême bord de la route et glissa un œil au fond du précipice comme s'il espérait y voir cette Volga vieille de trente-deux ans avec toute l'époque soviétique qu'elle avait entraînée dans sa chute... usines automobiles, champs de tabac et soviets ruraux aux bâtisses pavoisées de drapeaux rouges les jours de fête. Mais il n'y vit rien que des écheveaux de barbelés qui revêtaient la paroi rocheuse presque verticale à cet endroit, et le massif boisé qui montait du fond de l'abîme.

— Monte, dit Arzo ; si c'est à Sekhol que tu veux aller, je t'y dépose.

Mais Kharon de secouer la tête :

— Non. Je préfère rentrer chez moi. Et puis j'avais de la confiture dans la voiture. De la confiture pour le père. Je ferais mieux de descendre la chercher. Des fois qu'elle aurait tenu le choc...

Haussant les épaules, Arzo revint au Geländewagen et ouvrit la ridelle. Le coffre était empli de sacs. Il en creva un, d'où il tira trois liasses de roubles russes.

— Voilà pour ta nouvelle voiture, Kharon. Et laisse ta confiote tranquille. Elle est en bouillie là-dedans. Demande plutôt au père s'il n'a pas besoin d'un Russe pour garder le bétail. Je lui ferai un bon prix.

L'instant d'après, le convoi ne laissait plus derrière lui qu'un nuage diaphane de poussière jaune. Le vieux Kharon était toujours assis au bord de la route, le pare-chocs dans une main, les billets de banque dans l'autre. Des coupures toutes neuves. Vraies ou fausses, Kharon ne savait trop. Pour les fusils-mitrailleurs d'Arzo, pas de doute : c'étaient bien des vrais ; mais pour les billets de banque, il n'y avait guère de chance.

Quand le convoi fut passé, Kharon se leva, déposa le pare-chocs auprès d'une pierre, jeta un dernier coup d'œil sur le gouffre qui venait d'avaler sa Volga soviétique et allongea le pas en direction de chez lui.

Le soleil était déjà haut dans le ciel quand la colonne pénétra dans un long village de montagne enroulé comme une liane autour de sa rue unique. Les Oural et le Geländewagen franchirent un haut portail noir. Les blindés stationnèrent au-dehors.

Les compagnons d'Arzo déchargèrent leurs morts et sortirent les sacs de billets. Au fond du coffre gisait un homme aux bras scotchés derrière son dos. Jeté à terre, il se laissa choir comme un tas de feuilles mortes, et l'une des poules qui grouillaient dans la cour vint picorer le sang qu'il avait à sa manche. Du sang, il y en avait tant ici que même les poules en connaissaient le goût.

L'homme qu'on avait transporté dans le Geländewagen ouvrit les yeux vers quatre heures de l'après-midi. C'était un type jeune plutôt malingre en tenue camo, mais qui n'avait pas l'air d'un soldat. Par son âge, d'abord, parce qu'il faisait dans les vingt-sept ou vingt-huit ans. Et puis ses mains fines aux doigts longs semblaient plutôt celles d'un pianiste que d'un combattant. Prunelles grises, cheveux roux foncé, son visage présentait la molle rondeur qu'ont souvent les enfants des élites, sérieux certes, mais quand même à l'abri des problèmes de la vie.

La cave où l'on avait jeté le prisonnier était une cellule insalubre et basse, empuantie par la pestilence insupportable d'une fosse d'aisances creusée dans le coin droit. Le long des quatre murs couraient des planches, trop courtes pour qu'on s'y tienne allongé sans plier les jambes, et trop étroites pour qu'on puisse les plier. Quelques rais dorés de lumière s'insinuaient dans ce trou par un étroit soupirail.

Un morceau de rail avait été scellé dans du béton au milieu de la cave, auquel étaient soudées quatre chaînes si courtes qu'il était impossible d'atteindre la fosse d'aisances du coin opposé, d'où l'utilité d'un seau en plus de la fosse. La présence de ce seau donnait à penser que la cave avait été bien étudiée pour les prisonniers, comme une bonne maîtresse de maison l'aurait fait pour ses conserves.

Le captif aux yeux gris n'était pas seul dans la cave. Trois autres lui tenaient compagnie.

— Vladislav, se présenta le Russe.

— Gamzat, dit l'un des prisonniers.

— Gazi-Mahomed, dit un autre.

Le troisième ne dit mot : il était couché sur le dos, la face grouillant de mouches.

Gamzat avait dans les vingt-cinq ans : svelte, mince, les yeux noirs incroyablement grands, un petit menton triangulaire hérissé de poils. Sans ce menton disgracieux, on aurait dit un ange. Gazi-Mahomed devait avoir huit ans de plus. C'était un gros brun au visage rêche et gris, l'air un peu bébête. Vladislav pensa que les deux types ne moisissaient pas là depuis bien longtemps : ils étaient encore sans barbe, et l'autre n'avait rien d'un efflanqué.

— Vous êtes tchétchènes ? demanda Vladislav.

— Non, répondit Gamzat, nous sommes rutules. Si un Tchétchène enlève un autre Tchétchène, il faudra qu'il s'explique. Mais pour celui-là, pas besoin d'explication.

Et de pointer le menton sur l'homme aux mouches.

— Qu'est-ce qu'il lui arrive ?

Gazi-Mahomed répondit :

— Ils l'ont sorti d'ici en lui disant : Voilà une chienne, si tu la sautes on te relâche. Eh bien, il l'a sautée. Devant tout le monde. Mais elle était en chaleur et le truc s'est coincé. Une fois dedans, pas moyen d'en ressortir. Le soldat gueulait, la chienne aussi, les Tchétchènes se marraient. Surtout, s'ils te font sauter une chienne, n'y va pas. De toute façon, ils ne te relâcheront pas.

Vladislav plissa les yeux. Quand il les rouvrit, le rai cuivré du soleil qui marquait le sol avait disparu, ne laissant plus que le pâle reflet des chaînes.

— Il est russe ? demanda Vladislav, les yeux posés sur l'homme saigné par le chien.

— Oui, dit Gamzat.

Et Gazi-Mahomed ajouta :

— Crois-tu qu'ils feraient le coup à un Rutule ? Ou à un Lezghe ? Ou à un Avar ? Un Rutule, toute sa tribu l'aurait vengé. Mais un Russe, dis-moi un peu, qui vengera un Russe ?

Quand vint le soir, on fit sortir Vladislav de sa cave. Le village pleurait ses morts, et l'on chargea le jeune homme aux yeux gris d'enlever les corps de deux soldats russes exécutés pendant le rite funèbre.

Il y avait eu des rafales de PM. On faisait mijoter de la viande dans des marmites assez grandes pour la cuisson d'un homme entier. Maintenant, ordre était donné de jeter aux chiens ce qu'il restait des Russes.

Lorsque le prisonnier eut fait son travail, un Tchétchène le poussa du bout de sa mitraillette.

— Par ici.

Un blindé sous un auvent. Arzo, l'homme à la barbe frisée, trônait dessus. On mit le Russe à genoux devant le Tchétchène.

— Comment t'appelles-tu ? demanda Arzo.

Il parlait un russe à l'élocution tranquille, étonnamment pure, à ceci près que d'une consonne à l'autre sa parole (la parole d'un homme ayant passé la moitié de son existence dans la ville russe de Grozny) semblait rebondir sur les rochers d'un torrent, comme ceux de l'impétueux Terek.

— V-Vladislav. Vladislav Pankov.

— Soldat ?

— Euh... non. Je convoyais juste la marchandise. Les wagons, je veux dire.

— Kagébiste ?

— Non. Je... je travaille pour la Banque centrale. Je suis financier de formation, j'ai tous les papiers sur moi...

— Tu as tiré sur mes hommes ?

Machinalement, Vladislav porta la main à la racine de son nez marquée d'une blessure horizontale. Au moment de sa capture, la crosse d'un PM lui avait enfoncé le pont de ses lunettes entre les deux yeux : le garçon portait des verres de moins quatre.

— Oui, dit-il.

— Tu n'es pas financier pour deux sous, dit Arzo. Kagébiste, ça oui. Si tu as fait tes études à Harvard, c'est parce que tu es le fils d'Avdeï Pankov. Du ministre Pankov. Je savais que tu devais convoyer la marchandise. On m'a demandé de rendre un service très spécial : de zigouiller le fils du ministre Pankov. On m'avait prévenu qu'il y aurait de l'argent dans le convoi. Beaucoup d'argent. Deux mille milliards de roubles, qu'ils disaient. Et mille milliards pour moi, qu'ils disaient.

Le captif aux cheveux roux tressaillit. Il avait trouvé ça étrange, dès le début, que les boïéviks à peine entrés dans Grozny foncent droit sur la gare où stationnait depuis deux heures le convoi de cash alloué à la reconstruction de la Tchétchénie.

13

— Sauf que les wagons étaient vides, dit Arzo.

— Impossible ! J'ai moi-même…

— La belle affaire ! On charge deux mille milliards de cash dans un train en partance pour la Tchétchénie. Et où est passé l'argent ? Volé par les boïéviks ! Or moi j'y ai laissé trois de mes hommes. Au nom de quoi ? Qu'est-ce que je vais dire à leurs mères ?

Vladislav n'ouvrait pas la bouche.

Un jeune boïévik surgit dans son dos, un caméscope à la main.

— Parle, dit le Tchétchène.

— Je dis quoi ?

— Que tu es entre les mains d'Arzo Khadjiev. Que tu es bien traité. Que les wagons ne renfermaient que cinq sacs et que ceux qui t'ont envoyé dans ces wagons voulaient que je te tue. Tu diras aussi que, si ton père veut que tu vives, il devra retrouver les sacs perdus. Il est ministre des Finances, oui ou non ?

Quand le malheureux Russe aux yeux gris fut emmené par ses gardes, Arzo réécouta la vidéo et la fit enregistrer sur un magnétophone. Puis il composa un numéro par téléphone satellitaire. Au lieu de saluer son correspondant, il mit en marche le magnétophone.

— D'après toi, dit-il à la fin de la bande, mieux vaut que je récupère l'argent ou qu'Avdeï Pankov récupère cette bande ?

Le soldat saigné par le chien mourut dans la nuit et Vladislav, au réveil, constata qu'il avait la tête appuyée contre celle d'un mort.

— Et vous, pourquoi êtes-vous là ? demanda-t-il aux deux autres.

— Nous possédons une distillerie à Torbi-Kala, dit Gamzat. Et nous lui avons emprunté de l'argent.

— Cinq millions de dollars, précisa Gazi-Mahomed.

Que le barbu à la mitraillette puisse faire un prêt à quelqu'un parut étrange au jeune diplômé de Harvard :

— C'est Khadjiev qui vous les a prêtés ?!

— Oui, pourquoi ? Mais quand il a fait son carnage à Botchol, nous n'avons pas pu le rembourser.

— Si nous l'avions remboursé, le FSB nous aurait accusés de financer les terroristes, précisa Gazi-Mahomed.

Vladislav marqua un silence. La chose le laissait songeur. Un vrai casse-tête juridique : quand un créancier se lance dans le terrorisme international, le remboursement de ses créances tombe-t-il sous le coup du chef d'inculpation "financement du crime" ? Au vrai, Vladislav doutait que ces deux-là aient renoncé à payer leurs dettes pour éviter pareille accusation. Ils avaient profité de l'occasion, tout simplement.

— Et que va-t-il faire de vous ? demanda-t-il.

— Difficile à dire, répondit Gamzat. Tant que nous n'aurons pas payé, il ne nous relâchera pas.

— Mais tant que nous serons là, nous ne pourrons pas récolter les fonds, ajouta l'autre tristement.

Le lendemain et le surlendemain, on célébrait encore la mémoire des morts. C'étaient des gens connus et, à la nouvelle de leur disparition, on n'hésitait pas à faire le déplacement. Il y en avait même deux qui débarquaient de Moscou.

Au matin du troisième jour, on coupa un doigt à Pankov. Cette fois, il n'y eut pas d'enregistrement. On le fit sortir de la cave et on lui donna l'ordre d'appeler son père. Quand répondit le sobre baryton du fonctionnaire, Arzo furieux frappa le rouquin au visage, le traîna à terre comme une peau de bête puis lui sectionna l'auriculaire. Ça faisait moins mal qu'un coup à la mâchoire.

Au soir du troisième jour, deux quatre-quatre argentés, bourrés d'hommes en armes, s'engouffrèrent dans la cour de la propriété d'Arzo par le portail grand ouvert.

L'homme qui commandait la bande était beaucoup moins âgé qu'Arzo. Haut de taille (une bonne demi-tête de plus qu'un Tchétchène), il se mouvait avec la belle plastique d'un lutteur ou d'un karatéka. A la différence de l'autre, il était rasé de près avec une coupure de lame étrange et fraîche en travers de sa face juvénile et joufflue piégée par un menton d'acier. Prunelles et cheveux de la même couleur qu'un canon de Kalachnikov. Contrairement à ses hommes, il n'avait pas l'arme à la main mais à l'épaule, au bout d'une longue bandoulière, comme la sacoche du facteur.

Le visiteur donna l'accolade au père d'Arzo avant de se rendre sous l'auvent où se trouvaient le chef de guerre et son frère. Arzo se leva pour aller à sa rencontre.

— Tu as kidnappé mes frères de tribu, Arzo. C'est une faute. Rends-les-moi.

L'homme ne lui parlait pas en tchétchène, comme tous les autres, mais en russe, comme le font toujours les montagnards du Caucase d'ethnies différentes. Et son russe était plus rustique que celui d'Arzo, peut-être impeccable d'un point de vue grammatical et syntaxique mais si guttural que chaque consonne paraissait grattée au papier de verre.

— Ils me doivent cinq millions, Niyazbek, répondit Arzo, et deux de plus pour préjudice moral.

Les yeux de Niyazbek, couleur de Coca-Cola, scrutaient la cour comme un adversaire à battre sur le ring ou une voiture à plastiquer. Ils fouillaient les moindres recoins, passaient tranquillement, avec une égale indifférence, de la flaque de sang d'une brebis égorgée à la traînée rouge imprimée sur le portail, juste entre deux clous, et ce n'était certes pas un mouton qu'on avait crucifié là.

— Ton chiffre est juste, Arzo. Je reconnais la dette. Ils te la rembourseront jusqu'au dernier kopeck. Mais ces hommes-là sont mes frères de tribu. Et personne ne peut se vanter d'avoir enlevé mes semblables.

— Je vais libérer Gamzat par égard pour toi, dit Arzo. A lui de collecter les fonds. Gazi-Mohamed restera comme otage.

— Ils me les faut tous les deux.

— Alors c'est toi qui feras l'otage, renvoya l'autre avec un sourire. Tu séjourneras chez moi pendant que ton beau-frère ramassera l'argent.

— Je n'ai jamais été otage de qui que ce soit et je ne risque pas de le devenir, dit Niyazbek. Il peut m'arriver d'enlever des gens, mais pas d'être enlevé. Ils te rembourseront, je te donne ma parole.

— Ta parole, répondit le Tchétchène, j'aurais du mal à la tuer ou à lui couper les oreilles. Ces deux larrons sont vils et voraces, tu le sais aussi bien que moi. Pour peu que ça tourne mal… Apporte-moi l'argent toi-même si tu tiens tant à les récupérer tous les deux.

Quand le maigre jeune homme se réveilla, le lendemain matin, il était tout seul dans sa geôle à l'exception du mort. De Gamzat et Gazi-Mahomed, plus une trace. Là-haut, dans le ciel, le soleil dominait déjà le village. Au loin meuglaient des vaches, un mollah lançait son appel à la prière. Assis près du soupirail à barreaux, un garçon d'une dizaine d'années fixait ses yeux de mûres sauvages sur le prisonnier exsangue.

— Moi, c'est Arbi, dit le gamin. Et toi ?

— Vladislav, répondit le Russe.

Debout sur les planches, on pouvait glisser un œil au-dehors : il n'y avait plus ni Oural ni Geländewagen dans la cour. Seuls deux montagnards étaient assis près du portail, dont les Kalachnikov brasillaient au soleil. Arbi remarqua le regard du captif aux yeux gris et lui dit :

— Mon père est parti. Toi, tu resteras là jusqu'à la rançon.

— Et si la rançon ne vient pas ? demanda Vladislav.

— Mon père n'aime pas les Russes, dit Arbi. Ou plutôt si, il aime bien les égorger. Pour le reste, il est très fâché contre eux à cause de ce qu'ils m'ont fait.

— Et qu'est-ce qu'ils t'ont fait ?

Arbi fit demi-tour et prit le chemin de sa maison. Alors seulement Vladislav constata que le garçon n'avait plus de jambes. Il se déplaçait sur une petite planche à roulettes, les mains appuyées au sol.

On le tira si vite de son trou qu'il ne se réveilla que dans la cour. Vladislav vit alors le disque rond de la lune au beau milieu du ciel, et le corps étendu d'un garde parmi les ombres lunaires. Celui-ci avait la gorge tranchée d'une oreille à l'autre. Un deuxième garde était ventre à terre, le canon d'un PM appuyé sur sa nuque.

Deux hommes sortaient une vieille Niva du garage. Jeté genoux en terre, Vladislav leva les yeux sur un homme haut de taille qui se mouvait avec la grâce féline d'un lynx. Il était rasé de près, les prunelles pareilles à deux morceaux de nuit.

17

— Où sont Gamzat et Gazi-Mahomed ?

Vladislav mit quelques fractions de seconde à comprendre la question, tant le parler rocailleux de cet homme différait de l'accent tchétchène auquel il avait eu le temps de s'habituer durant les trois derniers jours.

— Qui êtes-vous ?

— Tu n'as pas répondu à ma question.

— Ils ne sont plus là. Les boïéviks les ont emmenés.

L'inconnu empoigna Vladislav et, du haut de sa taille, le jeta sur la banquette arrière de la Niva. L'instant d'après, on lui flanquait sous les jambes un vieux Tchétchène aux cheveux blancs. Le jeune Russe comprit que c'était le père d'Arzo. Puis l'un des ravisseurs se mit au volant et le portail glissa lentement devant la voiture.

La traversée du village se fit sans encombre. En ces temps de guerre, les voisins assagis par l'expérience ne se posaient guère de questions sur le manège nocturne des voitures qui allaient et venaient chez le père de l'un des chefs armés les plus influents.

Les véhicules ne stoppèrent que dans une gorge abrupte, à l'endroit même où le vieux Kharon, deux jours auparavant, s'était lamenté sur la perte de sa Volga. Deux Land Cruiser argentés stationnaient là parmi des hommes en armes. Vladislav fut jeté dans le Cruiser avec le père d'Arzo. Niyazbek monta devant en portant dans ses bras le petit garçon de dix ans qui n'avait pas de jambes.

Dix minutes plus tard, les roues faisaient cogner le tablier d'un pont qui enjambait la gorge. Niyazbek sortit pour échanger quelques mots avec les soldats descendus d'un mirador, après quoi les voitures se garèrent et Niyazbek composa un numéro de téléphone.

— *Salam*, Arzo, dit Niyazbek. Te souviens-tu de ton dernier échange d'otages ? C'est là que je t'attends avant l'aube. Quand tu m'auras rendu Gamzat et Gazi-Mahomed, tu pourras récupérer ton père et ton fils.

La réponse grésilla dans le combiné.

— Si tu exécutes mes hommes, reprit Niyazbek, je passerai le téléphone à ton fils. Il te racontera la mort de ton père avant de mourir à son tour.

Vilaine réputation que celle du poste de contrôle choisi par Niyazbek. C'était là qu'on venait payer les rançons ou chercher les ravisseurs. De jour, on y voyait tant de voitures et d'intermédiaires qu'on pouvait se croire au marché.

Mais on était de nuit et l'endroit paraissait désert, hormis les soldats en faction, les snipers de Niyazbek et un char retranché qu'un engagé plein de zèle camouflait de pivoines et de courges.

Trois heures plus tard arrivait Arzo Khadjiev dans un cortège de quatre véhicules, non sans avoir disposé ses propres snipers sur l'autre rive du torrent. Niyazbek et Arzo descendirent de voiture et s'exposèrent à la vue des tireurs embusqués, gageant leur propre vie pour garantir l'échange.

Cela dura trois minutes. Quand les hommes de Niyazbek eurent mis les deux frères en voiture, il dit :

— Ils sont lavés de leurs dettes maintenant. Toutes leurs dettes, je les prends sur moi. Reprends-les si tu y tiens.

Silence d'Arzo.

— Rends-moi plutôt le Russe, dit le Tchétchène, et nous serons quittes.

— Quittes, nous le sommes de toute façon. Si tu m'avais cru sur parole, tu aurais touché ton argent. Mais tu m'as dit que ma parole ne valait rien. Donc tu n'auras rien.

Alors Arzo fouilla dans un vide-poche et en sortit un petit paquet en plastique qui contenait un auriculaire.

— Tu donneras ça au Russe de ma part, dit-il.

Trois heures plus tard, les véhicules s'arrêtèrent à un tournant. L'aube pointait à peine. La boule rouge du soleil, incandescente, émergeait des crêtes. Une légère brume matinale montait de la terre sèche. La route, d'un blanc éclatant, pareille à une ficelle qu'on aurait jetée sur la pente, filait en serpentant vers une ville empoussiérée qui formait comme une faucille autour d'une baie.

A droite du virage se profilaient quelques maisons blanches derrière des buissons semblables à des rouleaux de barbelés, l'une d'elles surmontée d'un drapeau russe qui pendillait mollement, faute de vent. L'aube sentait la mer, la chaleur et la liberté.

D'un bond leste, Niyazbek se posa sur l'herbe brûlée. Il fit un signe et les autres passagers descendirent à leur tour.

— Vois-tu le poste de la milice ? dit Niyazbek en désignant la bâtisse au drapeau. Vas-y et téléphone à ton père.

— Et que dois-je lui dire ?

— La vérité : qu'on t'a enlevé et que tu t'es évadé.

Gamzat s'agita :

— Niyazbek ! Mais ce type-là n'est pas un soldat ! C'est une huile ! Et de la Banque centrale ! Tu ferais mieux de nous le confier, et bonjour la rançon.

Sans mot dire, Niyazbek frappa le Rutule d'un coup de crosse à l'abdomen, si fort que l'autre alla valser dans les ronces du bord de la route.

— Allah m'est témoin, Gamzat : encore un conseil de toi et j'oublie que tu es mon beau-frère. Tu vis en parasite, tu empruntes sans rembourser, tu ramasses tout ce qu'il y a de merde sur la route, et ensuite tu vas pleurnicher. Je te le dis devant tous : si tu mets encore un pied dans la mouise, je t'étripe de mes propres mains ! Voilà que, à peine tiré du trou, tu en creuses déjà un autre pour les copains !

Gamzat se dépêtrait des ronces comme il pouvait, le blanc des yeux vitreux de haine et d'humiliation.

Niyazbek se tourna vers l'otage aux yeux gris et aux cheveux roux :

— Va, que je te dis.

— Attendez, Niyazbek, vous m'avez sauvé la vie. Dites-moi au moins qui vous êtes...

— Je suis le chasseur et tu es la proie, répondit l'autre. Va, le Russe. Avant qu'on t'enlève une deuxième fois.

C'était en juin 1999. Vladislav dînait avec des amis dans l'un des meilleurs restaurants de Moscou quand il entendit une porte claquer. Il avisa du coin de l'œil des hommes en treillis. Une main ferme se posa sur son épaule, et une voix s'exclama avec un léger accent gazouillant :

— Tiens donc ! Mais c'est l'autre blanc-bec de la Banque centrale !

Vladislav leva les yeux et reconnut Arzo. Le Tchétchène n'avait pas changé. Pantalon noir et sous-pull noir, une veste par-dessus. Il était encadré d'hommes armés en tenue camo.

Le Tchétchène s'affala sur une chaise restée libre, face à l'autre. Il avait l'air bien aviné.

— Nous l'avons enlevé à la gare de Grozny, entonna le Tchétchène à la cantonade. Avec des sacs de cash. Cinq sacs. Il était enfermé chez moi avec un type nommé Nikita. D'ailleurs, il lui est arrivé une drôle d'histoire, à ce Nikita. J'avais une chienne dans ma cour, Machka qu'elle s'appelait. Elle était en chaleur. J'ai dit à Nikita que je le relâcherais s'il tringlait la chienne. Eh bien, il l'a tringlée.

Visages pétrifiés des hommes en treillis qui accompagnaient Arzo.

— Or, une chienne, quand c'est en chaleur, ça… Bref, il s'est retrouvé coincé. Et rien à faire pour se décoincer. Le temps qu'il se délivre, il était déjà à moitié bouffé.

Arzo éclata de rire, montrant avec les mains ce que la chienne avait bouffé du Russe.

— Et ça c'est qui ? demanda Vladislav à Arzo en regardant les hommes en treillis.

— Ça ? C'est le groupe Alpha, dit le Tchétchène. Ils sont là pour ma garde rapprochée. Tu vois, on prend soin de moi. Parce qu'on ne sait jamais… (Puis, se tournant vers l'un de ses gardes :) Dis donc, major, si je t'avais enlevé, tu aurais tringlé ma chienne ou pas ?

On aurait dit que l'homme en question avait avalé un poteau.

D'une bouteille prise à la table de Pankov, Arzo se versa du vin et leva haut son verre :

— Buvons à la chance que tu as eue. Je n'avais jamais relâché un Russe vivant, et sais-tu pourquoi ?

— Parce que nous avons mutilé ton fils.

— Eh bien non, ce n'est pas pour ça. C'est parce que le pire tort qu'on puisse causer à l'ennemi n'est pas d'en faire un mort, mais un infirme. Un mort repose sous terre et personne ne le voit, alors qu'un infirme fait la manche dans le métro. Voilà pourquoi, le Russe, je bois au nez et au membre qu'on t'a laissés intacts.

Pankov fit une ablution fébrile. Le Tchétchène poussa un rire de rogomme et laissa rouler sa tête sur la table.

Deux hommes du groupe Alpha le prirent sous le bras et le traînèrent prudemment vers la sortie. Le major restait de pierre. Seules ses mains tordaient une fourchette qui se trouvait là sur la table.

— Qu'attendez-vous pour lui fourrer une balle dans la peau ? lança soudain Vladislav d'une voix qui tremblait.

— Il nous faut des ordres et nous ne les avons pas, répondit le major.

I

L'AFFECTATION

Le mois de juin tirait à sa fin. Les rhododendrons de Hyde Park donnaient des fleurs blanches et rouges, les taxis de Piccadilly Circus, pareils à des coccinelles, s'éternisaient dans les embouteillages, et le *Nobu* du Hilton avait deux hommes à déjeuner qui s'étaient installés dans un coin près d'une baie vitrée : Vladislav Pankov, chef adjoint de l'Administration présidentielle de la fédération de Russie, et son vieil ami Igor Malikov, représentant de la Russie à la Banque mondiale.

Ils se connaissaient depuis une dizaine d'années, du temps où Malikov était député à la Douma, mais leur amitié s'était nouée plus tard, à Washington.

Revenu de sa terrible mésaventure tchétchène, Vladislav avait passé six mois dans une clinique autrichienne, puis son père l'avait envoyé aux Etats-Unis pour le poste qu'occupait désormais Malikov. Ce dernier avait été son adjoint.

Lequel avait été le premier à constater que son chef divaguait : il se présentait au travail avec d'étranges lueurs dans les yeux, ricanait aux réunions, et le jour était venu où Igor l'avait trouvé nu dans son bureau, assis sur le rebord de la fenêtre en train de manger une orange avec sa peau.

Malikov ne tarda pas à comprendre que son chef se piquait. Mais, au lieu de se comporter en bon carriériste soviétique (en balançant son boss aux services spéciaux), il prit un autre chemin en s'arrangeant avec un ami pour placer Pankov dans une villa de luxe dans le Maryland.

Ceci fait, il força son patron à poser ses congés et l'enchaîna à son lit avec des menottes. "Tant que tu ne seras pas guéri, tu feras tes besoins dans ton froc", lui dit Malikov.

Deux jours plus tard, Pankov parvint à se traîner jusqu'au téléphone. Par bonheur, il n'appela pas la police mais son dealer que Malikov accueillit sur le seuil de la maison en lui faisant la peau.

Igor passa deux mois en compagnie de Pankov sous la surveillance d'un médecin particulier qu'il avait engagé spécialement pour cela. Il était le seul à connaître le fond de l'histoire. Parfois, il l'entendait crier dans la nuit : "Non, Arzo, non !" mais jamais les deux hommes ne parlaient du Caucase.

Que le vrai prénom d'Igor fût Ibrahim, Pankov ne l'apprit qu'à deux mois de son retour en Russie. Il apprit aussi que l'autre était né dans les montagnes à quatre-vingts kilomètres du village où il avait été enfermé dans une cave ; et que son nom de famille – Malikov – ne se prononçait pas avec l'accent tonique sur la première syllabe mais sur la deuxième parce qu'il tenait son origine non du russe *malenki* ("petit"), mais d'un mot arabe signifiant "roi".

La conversation entre les deux grands commis de l'Etat tournait autour de vétilles comme on s'en raconte entre amis. Ils en avaient déjà fini avec la morue en marinade et le crabe à chair tendre quand Pankov, devant la deuxième bouteille de saké qu'on venait de vider, dit ceci :

— J'aimerais te proposer un nouveau poste.

— Dans l'Administration présidentielle ?

— Non. Je quitte l'Administration. Je serai nommé demain premier commis du Kremlin dans le district fédéral du Caucase. Je te propose le poste de président de la république régionale d'Avarie-Dargo-Nord.

Igor marqua quelques secondes de silence.

— Je croyais que tu ignorais que j'étais de l'ethnie des Avars.

— J'ai consulté ton dossier confidentiel.

— Je ne peux pas accepter ce poste.

— Pourquoi ?

— Combien de temps as-tu passé dans le Caucase, Slava ?

— Trois jours.

— Et combien de temps passé à te faire soigner ?

— Un an, si je compte Washington.

Igor eut un petit rire amer, et ses lèvres étonnamment délicates furent coupées d'une sévère strie verticale.

— J'y ai passé non pas trois jours, mais dix-sept ans. Quand j'avais onze ans, mon oncle a tué sa sœur pour une liaison qu'elle avait eue avec un type. C'était un meurtre plein de sagesse. Il disait : J'ai une fille qui grandit, comment est-ce que je vais la marier ? Les gens diront que sa tante est une débauchée. Tout le monde a pensé que mon oncle avait agi comme un homme doit le faire. Quand j'avais seize ans, mon oncle a été tué d'une balle par le type qui avait fréquenté ma tante. Et un jour que j'étais député à la Douma – j'avais alors trente-deux ans –, j'ai eu la visite de mon petit frère. Il m'a donné l'accolade et m'a demandé de l'accompagner à un anniversaire. Sur-le-champ ! Nous voilà aussitôt en voiture. Les flics n'arrêtaient pas de nous contrôler, comme toujours en ces temps mouvementés. Je montrais ma carte de député, et hue cocotte ! Avenue Roublev, nous avons obliqué dans un bois. J'ai demandé : Et l'anniversaire ? Il m'a répondu : C'est plus loin. Puis la voiture a stoppé dans une clairière et mon frère a ouvert le coffre. Eh bien, ce putain de coffre était plein d'armes. Il avait eu besoin de mon laissez-passer pour les transporter à travers Moscou. Ensuite, on m'a fait changer de voiture et mon frère m'a proposé de dîner dans un resto de mon choix. Je suis européen maintenant. Il m'a fallu vingt ans de ma vie pour arrêter de me demander qui était le beau-père de qui, ou combien payer pour telle ou telle fonction.

— C'est bien pour ça que je veux te voir président de la république d'Avarie-Dargo-Nord. Parce que tu ne te soucies plus de savoir qui est le beau-père de qui.

— Je ne veux plus de ce cirque.

Pankov, après un silence :

— Ces derniers jours… je me suis intéressé de près à la situation dans le Caucase. Je savais que les choses allaient mal. Mais je n'imaginais pas à quel point. Seule certitude : si ce cirque est tenu par des chacals, le Caucase se détachera bientôt de la Russie.

— Mais si je me retrouve aux commandes du cirque, je me ferai tuer.

— Attends…

— Non. Jamais de la vie. Autant demander l'asile politique à l'Ouganda.

Pankov laissa filer un soupir.

— Soit. Peux-tu au moins me rendre le service de faire un saut sur place ? Juste pour m'aider de tes conseils ?

— Pour te dire qui est le beau-père de qui ?

Pankov acquiesça.

— D'accord, je viendrai.

Ils se quittaient déjà à la porte de l'hôtel où les avait déposés une longue Mercedes noire de l'ambassade quand Igor dit soudain :

— Il y a une autre raison pour laquelle je ne peux pas accepter ton offre.

— Laquelle ?

— Ta vieille histoire d'enlèvement. Tu as été libéré par un gars nommé Niyazbek.

— Je sais. Mon père a voulu le retrouver. Six mois plus tard. Il a été tué dans une échauffourée.

— Il n'a pas été tué, coupa Igor. Il s'appelle Niyazbek Malikov. Et c'est mon frère cadet.

Mahomedsalih Salimkhanov, ministre des Travaux publics de la république d'Avarie-Dargo-Nord, cassait la figure à Salaoudin Bamatov, vice-président ("vice-speaker") de l'Assemblée législative.

A coup sûr, les grandes chaînes sportives auraient pu se faire un plaisir d'assurer la retransmission du duel parce que le ministre était double champion du monde de wushu et que le vice-président du Parlement avait le titre de triple champion du monde de pentathlon.

Au vrai, les chaînes sportives avaient de fortes chances de se procurer ces images parce que le ministre réglait son compte au vice-président devant le siège du gouvernement, et que ce captivant spectacle était filmé par trois caméras – pas une de moins – dépêchées sur place à l'occasion d'un forum économique. Outre les caméras, le duel était suivi par les gardes du corps des combattants, une bonne vingtaine de députés, le ministre de l'Intérieur et une statue de bronze de deux mètres à l'effigie du président Aslanov, érigée au beau milieu de la place.

Par feinte, le ministre simula un coup de pied. L'autre, en l'esquivant, le reçut dans les côtes. Puis volte-face du ministre qui lui ajusta dans la foulée son talon à la tempe d'un mouvement impeccable.

Le vice-président de l'Assemblée législative s'écroula sur les dalles de granit qui ceignaient le monument. Le ministre fondit sur lui, l'empoigna par la cravate et entreprit de l'étouffer. C'est alors que le cercle des députés fut rompu par un haut fonctionnaire russe qui surgit devant le piédestal. Trente-cinq ans environ, costume noir, plastron immaculé strié d'une cravate rouge bordeaux à deux cents dollars, l'homme était blanc de peau et roux de cheveux, et ses yeux gris paraissaient amenuisés par les verres épais de ses lunettes d'écaille.

— Suffit maintenant ! lança le binoclard.

L'air étonné, le ministre se redressa. Il dépassait l'importun d'une bonne tête et faisait penser par sa corpulence à une statue réincarnée de Michel-Ange (plutôt Goliath que David).

— Tu es qui, toi ? dit le ministre étonné.

— Je suis le nouvel homme du président, déclara le fonctionnaire aux cheveux roux.

A cet instant le vice-président de l'Assemblée législative se leva de terre et, profitant de l'occasion, prit ses jambes à son cou.

— Je vais le tuer comme un chien, s'écria Mahomedsalih en s'élançant à sa poursuite.

L'un des gardes du corps de Salaoudin Bamatov tenta de lui barrer la route. Un coup de feu retentit, et le garde roula par terre, l'épaule transpercée.

Le vice-président du Parlement escalada une grille de fer forgé qui séparait la place d'un jardin aménagé côté droit. Au pas de course, il enfila une large allée de sable jaune, bordée de chênes, avec le ministre à ses trousses. Lorsque le représentant de la branche exécutive du pouvoir eut constaté que la branche législative courait plus vite que lui, il hurla :

— Fuyard de mes deux !

Là-dessus, il leva un Beretta argenté et se mit à tirer. Le vice-président du Parlement zigzaguait entre les arbres comme un vrai lapin. On sentait bien que, dans un passé sportif encore proche, il avait su magnifiquement dominer les obstacles.

Quand le parlementaire eut disparu derrière les arbres, Mahomedsalih Salimkhanov haussa les épaules et posa les yeux sur son Beretta qui renfermait encore une ou deux cartouches : à tout hasard, il les déchargea sur une caméra qui filmait l'ouverture du forum économique. En homme délicat qu'il était, Mahomedsalih se sentait troublé par les caméras.

De nouveau surgit Pankov :

— Mais on se croit tout permis ! hurla-t-il. Arrêtez-le ! Et vite !

Les convives du forum ne savaient plus sur quel pied danser.

— Pour quel motif ? fit le ministre de l'Intérieur qui venait de reparaître.

Pankov indigné pointa le doigt sur le Beretta coupable.

— Comment pour quel motif ?! C'est un forum d'investissement ou un stand de tir ici ? On était en droit de s'attendre à un débat économique de bonne tenue !

— Qu'est-ce que j'ai fait de spécial ? demanda le ministre des Travaux publics. Ce salopard nous a sucré trente pour cent du budget !

— Arrêtez-le, ordonna l'homme du président. (Puis, levant les yeux sur le ministre de l'Intérieur :) Quant à vous, Arfi Abussovitch, vous en répondez personnellement, c'est vu ?

Le ministre acquiesça d'un air navré.

— Entendu, dit-il. Viens, Momo, on y va.

Le soir même, toutes les chaînes de télévision faisaient part du succès du forum économique qui se tenait dans la ville de Torbi-Kala, sur le littoral nord de la Caspienne. L'envoyé spécial de la première chaîne mit à l'antenne une intervention du premier commis (ambassadeur) du Kremlin qui se félicitait de l'amélioration du climat d'investissement dans le Caucase-Nord. Il précisa, sans entrer dans les détails, que le débat avait revêtu une acuité toute particulière entre le vice-président du Parlement et le ministre des Travaux publics.

Prévue pour onze heures, l'ouverture du forum économique fut repoussée d'une quarantaine de minutes en raison d'un échange de vues improvisé entre deux fonctionnaires de haut rang.

Vladislav Pankov siégeait au bureau de l'Assemblée avec à sa droite le président de la république d'Avarie-Dargo-Nord Ahmednabi Aslanov, et à sa gauche, sir Jeffry Olmers, ami de longue date et patron de l'une des plus grandes compagnies pétrolières au monde. Pankov avait appâté Olmers au forum en lui faisant valoir que le pétrole léger de la côte et la situation maritime de Torbi-Kala, tout à fait exceptionnelle, faisaient de la région un site idéal pour la construction d'une nouvelle raffinerie.

A la soixantaine bien tassée, le président de la république d'Avarie-Dargo-Nord paraissait plus jeune que son âge. Tiré à quatre épingles, les cheveux chenus, portant beau, la voix mâtinée de bronze et le regard d'acier, il avait la prestance propre aux dictateurs ou aux majordomes.

Il présenta à l'assistance le nouveau premier commis du Kremlin en poste dans le district fédéral du Caucase en exprimant l'assurance que l'homme œuvrerait à l'éradication de la pauvreté, du terrorisme, de la servilité et de la flatterie.

— Il n'a pas cessé de pleuvoir de toute la semaine passée, dit le président. Avec votre venue, le soleil s'est levé sur la république. Ce soleil, c'est vous, Vladislav Avdéïevitch !

Sur le coup de midi, Pankov s'éclipsa aux toilettes. A son retour, il fut accueilli à la porte par un Koumyk petit de taille et bien en chair qui avait les yeux noirs, joyeux et vifs comme freux au printemps.

— Arsène Isalmahomedov, se présenta-t-il. Juste une petite minute, Vladislav Avdéïevitch. C'est à propos du ministère des Travaux publics.

— Mais encore ?

— Si je comprends bien, le fauteuil est libre à présent. Eh bien je veux vous dire que mon frère a toujours voulu s'occuper de travaux publics. Si nous pouvions discuter de la chose un peu plus tard, au banquet…

Sans mot dire, Pankov tourna les talons et regagna la salle.

Il y avait eu quelques changements dans le bureau de l'Assemblée pendant ce temps. Le président de la république d'Avarie-Dargo-Nord s'étant absenté pour une heure – nul ne savait où –, sa place avait été prise par un cinquantenaire trapu à la face mate et aux pommettes larges qui contrastait fortement avec le bleu profond de ses yeux.

— Charapudin Ataïev, lui souffla-t-il à l'oreille ; je suis le maire de Torbi-Kala. (Une pause, puis il ajouta dans un filet de voix :) Vous venez de commettre un acte très courageux. Je veux parler de Mahomedsalih. C'est du n'importe quoi ! Savez-vous seulement combien d'hommes il a tués ?! Il a des liens de sang avec les Tchétchènes. Le procureur de l'arrondissement Rive droite aussi. Mais vous risquez gros : il se fiche pas mal que vous soyez l'homme du Kremlin. Vous avez besoin de soutien. Si vous nommiez mon fils ministre des Travaux publics, alors...

— Alors quoi ? coupa Pankov.

— Un million, dit Charapudin Ataïev.

Durant la pause de cinq minutes qui fut faite entre deux allocutions, Pankov reçut encore deux requêtes relatives au portefeuille ministériel, toutes les deux concrètement chiffrées.

Mais la contrariété la plus forte survint à cinq heures, alors que le forum touchait à sa fin et que le président Aslanov regagnait sa place à la tribune.

— Je crois que je vais y aller, dit sir Jeffry Olmers à voix basse en rangeant ses papiers.

— Attendez un peu ! Nous avions prévu de visiter le chantier...

— J'ai changé d'avis, dit le chef du plus gros consortium pétrochimique mondial. Le fond de ma pensée, c'est qu'à la place d'une usine vous feriez mieux de construire quelque chose de plus... approprié. Un chapiteau, par exemple.

Le président de la république d'Avarie-Dargo-Nord annonça la clôture du forum et, tout sourire, s'approcha du bureau de l'Assemblée. La foule se pressait autour du Moscovite aux cheveux roux.

— Eh bien, Vladislav Avdeïevitch, c'est un beau début ! dit-il. Je vous félicite. Après une bonne journée de labeur, un peu de réconfort ne vous fera pas de mal. J'ai pris des dispositions pour la suite, dans un cadre tout à fait informel... Je dois dire que le poisson sera exceptionnel. J'imagine que vous avez un creux...

— Un grand creux, en effet, dit Pankov. Où est la cafétéria ?

Il était huit heures du matin quand le chef du gouvernement de la république d'Avarie-Dargo-Nord entra dans l'ex-maison de santé du Comité central du Parti communiste de l'Union soviétique où était descendu Vladislav Pankov. Il eut une conversation d'une demi-heure avec le premier commis du Kremlin, formant le vœu que celui-ci saurait venir à bout de la pauvreté, du terrorisme et de la corruption. Il fit aussi une proposition concrète visant à améliorer le fonctionnement de la machine gouvernementale. Il s'agissait de scinder en trois le ministère des Travaux publics : un ministère pour la construction des écoles et autres services subventionnés par la collectivité ; un deuxième pour les bâtiments industriels dans le cadre de programmes d'investissements fédéraux ; et un troisième réservé aux besoins du monde rural. Tout cela, selon lui, pour endiguer la corruption, puis renforcer le contrôle exercé sur chaque ministre en l'empêchant de se comporter en racketteur.

— Et maintenant, dit le chef du gouvernement, venons-en à des choses plus agréables : au nom de l'ensemble de notre peuple et du président de la République à titre personnel, j'ai le plaisir de vous souhaiter un bon anniversaire et...

— Mais ce n'est pas mon anniversaire, dit Pankov.

Visage perplexe du Premier ministre.

— Comment ça, ce n'est pas votre anniversaire ! Nous vous avons même préparé un cadeau...

— Quel cadeau ?

Le chef du gouvernement fit un geste de la main. Pankov s'approcha de la fenêtre et aperçut une somptueuse Mercedes blindée garée sur un carré de goudron devant le pavillon qu'il occupait. La voiture était ornée d'un ruban rose et Sergueï Piskounov, chef de la garde personnelle du premier commis du Kremlin, flairait le capot comme un chat une boîte de Whiskas.

— Sergueï, cria Pankov, combien coûte ce joujou ?

— Quatre cent vingt mille dollars ! répondit l'autre du tac au tac.

— Y a-t-il des orphelinats dans la république ?

— Oui.

— Vendez-la et versez la recette au profit d'un orphelinat. Et retenez bien ceci, Saïghid Ibrahimovitch : ce n'est pas mon anniversaire aujourd'hui. Qu'on se le dise !

Quand le chef du gouvernement quitta la maison de santé, il avait le moral à plat.

— C'est curieux, dit-il, lorsque le procureur général nous a rendu visite, c'est tombé tout de suite sur son anniversaire.

Quant au précédent premier commis du Kremlin, c'était carrément tous les mois qu'il fêtait son anniversaire.

Ahmednabi Aslanov, président de la république d'Avarie-Dargo-Nord, fut très étonné d'apprendre comment l'ambassadeur du Kremlin avait accueilli le cadeau du chef du gouvernement.

— Peut-être qu'il préfère les quatre-quatre ? s'interrogea le président.

— Quelle drôle d'idée d'offrir un quatre-quatre blindé ! Les vraies blindées, ce sont les berlines, n'importe quel enfant te le dira. Parce que, en cas d'attentat à l'explosif, l'onde de choc va de bas en haut.

Ayant lui-même réchappé de trois attentats à l'explosif, le fils d'Ahmednabi Aslanov se considérait comme un grand expert en la matière.

— En tant que Russe, il y a des choses élémentaires qu'il ne peut pas comprendre, dit son frère. Mais s'il insiste pour un quatre-quatre, il faut lui offrir un quatre-quatre.

Vladislav Pankov monta en voiture à neuf heures du matin. Fleurant bon l'eau de toilette de premier choix, il passa près de dix minutes devant la glace à choisir sa cravate. D'habitude, c'était le travail de sa femme, mais celle-ci avait pris des vacances à Saint-Tropez. Pankov tenait à ce que sa cravate s'accordât parfaitement à son costume. La voiture démarra en douceur et il prit son téléphone.

— Igor, c'est Slava. J'ai limogé le ministre des Travaux publics. Il a tiré sur quelqu'un en ma présence. On me propose de scinder son ministère en trois. Pourquoi ?

— Pour que le président reçoive de l'argent de trois ministres au lieu d'un en échange de leur poste.

— Le Premier ministre a-t-il des liens particuliers avec le président ?

— Il est marié à sa nièce.

— Putain ! Tu viens quand ?

— Vendredi.

Cinq minutes plus tard, le tirage papier du rapport d'écoute téléphonique se trouvait devant le président de la République et ses deux fils.

— Voilà pourquoi il a refusé la voiture ! dit le fils cadet du président.

— Il veut le nommer à la tête de la république ! s'écria l'aîné.

Ahmednabi Aslanov, président de la république régionale d'Avarie-Dargo-Nord, attendait Vladislav Pankov dans la résidence du prédécesseur de ce dernier, une somptueuse villa nichée au bord de la mer.

Un sol dallé de marbre. Partout, dans toutes les salles de bains, des vécés plaqués or. Les vécés plaqués or étaient au nombre de dix-sept.

Le précédent premier commis du Kremlin commandait le groupement des forces armées de Tchétchénie et s'était illustré en 1999 par l'écrasement d'une incursion tchétchène dans le territoire de l'Avarie-Dargo-Nord, exploit militaire éminent accompli à l'horizontale, une bouteille de cognac à la bouche.

Edifiante histoire que celle de la résidence en question.

Lors de sa prise de fonction, le prédécesseur de Pankov avait jugé que son logement de fonction attribué par les fédéraux ne correspondait pas à son rang, un malheur dont il fit part au fils du président. Son calcul était que celui-ci lui offrirait l'une de ses villas de bord de mer. Au lieu de quoi l'homme emmena le Moscovite dans sa voiture et lui fit visiter une bonne douzaine de demeures. L'hôtel particulier sur lequel l'ex-premier commis arrêta son choix appartenait au ministre de l'Agriculture.

Le fils du président proposa donc au ministre de lui vendre sa villa pour cinquante mille dollars. "Je dois faire un cadeau à quelqu'un de bien", lui expliqua-t-il. Indigné, le ministre en exigea un million. Le marchandage dura jusqu'au jour où le ministre sauta sur une bombe posée par des wahhabites, ou présumés tels, après quoi la famille orpheline s'empressa de vendre la maison.

L'hôtel particulier fut donc offert au premier commis du Kremlin qui s'enticha tellement du lieu qu'il n'en sortit plus jamais. Toutes les rencontres officielles se déroulaient dans les murs de la résidence.

Le président Aslanov était déjà installé dans sa salle à manger d'été. Avec ses cheveux blancs et son costume impeccable, l'homme ressemblait plus à un lord anglais qu'à un ex-secrétaire du Comité central du parti communiste revenu au pouvoir après la pérestroïka. Au vrai, comme nous l'avons suggéré, les présidents Aslanov étaient au nombre de deux.

L'un d'eux faisait un mètre soixante-quinze et pesait cent dix kilos. Au moment dont nous parlons, il attendait le premier commis du Kremlin pour un léger breakfast de vingt-huit plats. L'autre faisait deux mètres quatre-vingts et pesait près de trois quintaux. Il se dressait sur un socle en granit aussi grand que lui devant le siège du gouvernement, saluant d'un geste large les flots bleus de la mer Caspienne et le peuple qui gravissait l'escalier venant du littoral.

Le premier était un joyeux drille et boute-en-train qui adorait ses trois enfants et sept petits-enfants. Le second ne quittait jamais son poste, le doigt pointé vers un avenir radieux.

Ce n'était pas le seul monument de la république. Quand on entrait dans la ville par la route de Bakou, on tombait juste après un barrage de police sur un marbre blanc à l'effigie de Sapartchi Aslanov, célèbre pour ses œuvres de civilisation parmi les Tcherkesses, les Lezghes et les Avars. Il y avait aussi, sur le front de mer, près de la mairie, un monument en l'honneur d'Asludin Aslanov qui fut en son temps, jusqu'en 1937, premier secrétaire du Parti communiste de la république, et un autre dédié à Gazi-Mahomed Aslanov devant son théâtre éponyme dont il fut le metteur en scène de 1961 à 1965.

Mais le monument le plus intéressant célébrait un certain Ramzan Aslanov. Agé de trente-deux ans quand éclata la Seconde Guerre, Ramzan travaillait dans un kolkhoze comme simple ouvrier agricole. Jusqu'en 1997, on ignora tout de lui sinon qu'il était mort à Stalingrad en 1943. Quand Ahmednabi fut élu président, une gazette de Torbi-Kala publia un article relatant un exploit héroïque de son grand-père qui, à lui seul, avait anéanti un char fasciste. Deux mois plus tard, correctif : deux chars au lieu d'un ; trois mois plus tard, il s'avérait que les chars étaient au nombre de quatre. Un point final à la controverse fut posé lorsque le célèbre historien et député Muhtar Meïerkulov révéla dans une revue scientifique, trois ans avant les faits dont il est ici question, qu'il s'agissait en vérité de huit chars. A la suite de quoi le héros Ramzan Aslanov eut droit à un monument en granit de six mètres érigé sur un flanc du Torbi-Taou, et Muhtar Meïerkulov devint vice-speaker du Parlement.

Les portes s'ouvrirent, et le premier commis du Kremlin – cheveux roux, prunelles grises – fit irruption dans la salle à manger. Le président de la République se dit en lui-même que le Moscovite avançait presque en sautillant non pas d'un train de haut fonctionnaire, mais plutôt tel un chaton courant après sa pelote. Ahmednabi Aslanov se leva de son fauteuil, l'allure digne, puis l'embrassa et l'étreignit à l'orientale.

— Vous n'imaginez pas à quel point je suis heureux de votre nomination ! dit le président de la République. Parce que le pays est en proie à l'arbitraire ! Le wahhabisme est en marche ! Des terroristes se promènent impunément dans les rues, pas une semaine sans qu'une bombe n'explose ! Il y a plus d'explosions chez nous qu'en Tchétchénie, et qui peut les arrêter sinon les fédéraux ? Et que fait l'armée ? Rien. Et que faisait votre prédécesseur ? Rien que boire. Par caisses entières, permettez de le dire. Des caisses, vous dis-je !

Le président de la République n'exagérait pas le moins du monde. Une caisse de cognac était livrée tous les jours à la résidence du premier commis du Kremlin, de la marque Torkon, une entreprise d'Etat tenue par le neveu du président.

— Tenez, vous avez eu le cran d'arrêter Mahomedsalih Salimkhanov parce qu'il battait le vice-speaker devant les caméras de télévision. Savez-vous que cet homme a attaqué un barrage de contrôle fédéral ? Et ce dans la voiture d'un boïévik notoire ?

— Quand cela ?

— Il y a deux semaines. Figurez-vous qu'un cortège armé a franchi le barrage à la frontière de la Tchétchénie. Trois véhicules, dix hommes, quinze fusils. Avec, notamment, le terroriste numéro un de la république, contre lequel de nombreux avis de recherche ont été lancés. Un individu soupçonné de plusieurs dizaines de meurtres. Eh bien, un capitaine des forces de l'Intérieur arrête le cortège et le terroriste lui propose de l'argent pour s'en débarrasser. Le capitaine redoute un échange de coups de feu parce qu'il n'a pas plus d'hommes avec lui que l'autre dans son cortège. Aussi prend-il cet argent tout en alertant le poste suivant pour qu'il se tienne prêt à bloquer le cortège. Et que croyez-vous qu'il advînt ? Voilà le cortège qui passe le deuxième barrage ! Et qui fait demi-tour jusqu'au premier ! Là, ils désarment les miliciens ! Ils leur arrachent toute la recette de la journée ! Ils les enferment dans leur guérite et leur disent : Vous allez tous brûler, bande de mouchards ! Et Mahomedsalih est de ceux qui frappent le capitaine de la milice, qui lui brisent les côtes et lui disent : Si tu portes plainte, tu es mort !

— Et pourquoi n'ont-ils pas tué les miliciens ? s'étonna le Moscovite.

— Ce n'est que partie remise ! Cet homme-là, ce n'est pas les mains mais les dents qu'il a dans le sang ! Jusqu'à la racine ! Il fait un trafic d'hommes avec les boïéviks tchétchènes. Une fois, il a même enlevé mes fils !

— Quand donc ?

— Il y a neuf ans. A l'époque, je n'étais pas encore président de la République, et mes fils prospéraient dans les affaires. Une belle réussite, et sans aucune aide de ma part. Et cet homme n'arrêtait pas de les terroriser, de leur extorquer de l'argent ! Il pouvait venir les réveiller à trois heures du matin et les tirer du lit à coups de mitraillette ! "L'argent ! l'argent !…" Il n'avait que ce mot à la bouche. Comme ils étaient honnêtes en affaires, mes fils ont refusé de payer. Alors il les a fait enlever par un Tchétchène nommé Arzo Khadjiev qui réclamait sept millions de dollars !

— Quel rapport avec le premier bandit ?

— Le rapport, c'est qu'Arzo et lui étaient de mèche, et que ce bandit a soi-disant libéré mes fils ! Un coup monté. Pour que la rançon lui revienne à lui plutôt qu'aux Tchétchènes !

Le Moscovite observa un silence, puis :

— Comment s'appellent vos fils ?

— Je vais vous les présenter, dit le président avec flamme en faisant un signe au chef de la garde.

Aussitôt s'ouvrit une porte par laquelle entrèrent les fils du président. Le cadet avait près de trente-cinq ans. Malgré la chaleur, il portait une veste beige clair avec une cravate de perles. Sa petite tête perdait ses cheveux par le front, exhibant ainsi des rides précoces et des oreilles en pointe.

Il roulait des yeux inquiets à la manière d'une poule pico-rant un grain. L'aîné portait un costume à rayures bleues. Il avait beaucoup grossi depuis la dernière fois que Pankov l'avait vu. Le souffle rauque à chaque mouvement du corps, il passait son temps à s'éponger le front. Enfoncés de chaque côté d'un nez bourgeonné rouge cerise, ses gros yeux s'étaient embrumés. Des doigts si boudinés qu'il n'aurait pu fermer le poing.

— Gamzat, fit le président en présentant le cadet, prési-dent du directoire de la Banque nationale avare. Figurez-vous que les banques n'arrêtent pas d'éclater comme des bulles de savon ! J'ai dû placer mon fils pour endiguer les fuites de budget. Il est pourtant surmené de partout : député de l'Assemblée législative, président de la Fédération des sports équestres et j'en passe. Chef de ma garde personnelle !

Le premier banquier et premier garde de la république lui tendit, à l'européenne, une main froide aux phalanges fines.

— Gazi-Mahomed, dit le président en se tournant vers son aîné, directeur général de PétrogazAvarie, consortium d'exploitation des hydrocarbures de la république. C'est fou la pagaille qui règne dans la région ! Ça frelate de partout ! Il a donc fallu que je mette un homme de confiance. Du feu, des coups, de la poigne, voilà ce qu'il faut ! Dieu merci, les temps sont révolus où le premier bandit venu pouvait ra-cketter mes fils à coups de flingue !

— Le bandit, comment s'appelle-t-il ?

— Niyazbek, répondit le président.

— Un sombre type, ajouta Gamzat, un terroriste !

— Et votre femme, comment va-t-elle ? demanda Pankov à Gamzat.

L'autre marqua un tressaillement.

— Quelle femme ?

— La sœur de ce terroriste. Rappelle-toi : quand tu lui as dit qu'il fallait m'enlever, il t'a frappé et t'a fait taire. Il t'appelait son beau-frère à l'époque.

Le mince visage de Gamzat prit la couleur d'une patate pas cuite. Le président de la République leva les yeux sur ses fils. Il ressemblait de plus en plus à un bronze.

Pankov se leva brusquement et quitta le salon.

La matinée du vendredi commença par une séance élargie du Parlement de la république régionale. Assis à la droite du président de l'Assemblée, Pankov écoutait le ministre de l'Intérieur faire son rapport sur les succès de la lutte contre le terrorisme.

Or, des succès, il y en avait. La nuit passée s'était déroulée une opération réussie. Un commando des forces spéciales de l'Intérieur avait encerclé dans les montagnes une bande de boïéviks commandée par Wahha Arsaïev, fameux terroriste. Cinq heures durant, on les avait attaqués au lance-grenade et au fusil d'assaut. Deux corps étaient restés sur le champ de bataille, l'un d'eux identifié avec une quasi-certitude comme celui d'Arsaïev. Et le ministre d'annoncer fièrement l'extermination totale de la bande.

Pankov écoutait d'une oreille distraite : ces sept derniers mois, Arsaïev avait été tué huit fois. Son meurtre se faisait avec la régularité d'une vidange de voiture.

Ce qui intriguait surtout Pankov, en tant qu'économiste de formation, c'était que la république régionale produisait chaque année un million de tonnes de pétrole léger d'excellente qualité, dont la moitié au moins partait dans des camions-citernes.

Pour autant qu'il pouvait en juger d'après les rapports qu'il avait devant lui, aucune citerne n'avait brûlé durant les six derniers mois sur le territoire de la république régionale. Les jeeps de la milice brûlaient souvent, les casernes aussi. La semaine passée, quelqu'un avait même arrosé d'essence et brûlé le siège du procureur de Chouguinsk (l'incendie – caractérisé comme un acte de terrorisme – ayant détruit cinquante dossiers d'instruction), mais les camions-citernes sillonnaient la région aussi tranquillement que dans l'Etat du Kansas.

Si Pankov avait été terroriste, il aurait brûlé les citernes, pas les flics, mais Arsaïev agissait autrement et cela le taraudait.

Du présidium où il siégeait, Vladislav Pankov écoutait le rapporteur en jetant d'incessants regards sur sa montre. Une heure quarante. L'avion Moscou-Torbi-Kala devait se poser d'un instant à l'autre, et le cortège personnel de l'ambassadeur du Kremlin attendait déjà Igor Malikov à l'aéroport.

L'avion de Moscou qui transportait Igor Malikov se posa conformément à l'horaire de la ligne. De la passerelle, Igor avisa une Mercedes noire blindée qui portait une immatriculation fédérale.

Il mit le pied sur le tarmac blanc, véritable poêle à frire. Des chardons blanchâtres s'échappaient d'entre les plaques de béton. Au-delà se dressait la tour à balancier d'un puits de pétrole sous laquelle se dandinait un gros dindon rouge poursuivi par une femme en robe jaune difforme, un fichu blanc sur la tête. Le soleil frappait en pointage direct, et la moirure brûlée de la mer, dans le lointain, se fondait aux cimes brûlées de montagnes pelées. Malikov se crut un instant devant l'image de l'enfer, puis il se souvint que c'était là son pays natal.

— *Salam aleïkum*, Ibrahim ! Tu vas devenir président, à ce qu'on dit !

Igor se retourna. Une file de fonctionnaires et d'hommes d'affaires se pressaient déjà sur la passerelle à la sortie de l'avion, bloquant le passage aux femmes en noir qui ployaient sous leurs balluchons. Nombre d'entre eux avaient félicité Igor pendant le vol, les autres le faisaient maintenant.

— Ibrahim Adievitch, soupira le ministre des Communications, vous n'avez pas idée de la situation qui règne dans la république…

Poliment mais fermement, la garde personnelle du premier commis du Kremlin écarta Igor de ses solliciteurs. L'instant d'après, celui-ci plongeait dans le cocon climatisé d'une Mercedes blindée. Il eut alors le tympan frappé par l'*adhan* : une station de radio grand public annonçait l'heure du *namaz* sur 105.2 FM.

Roustam était dans sa Lada Jigouli près d'un passage à niveau quand retentit la sonnerie brève de son téléphone. "Compris", répondit-il. Puis il descendit de voiture.

Le passage à niveau – ou plutôt ce sillon ferroviaire qui, coupé par la route, menait aux terminaux pétroliers – avait toujours été considéré comme un lieu bien choisi.

D'abord, les voitures devaient inévitablement ralentir à son approche. Ensuite, l'enceinte du port maritime commençait à cinq mètres de là, offrant au tireur un retranchement idéal. On y comptait bien une demi-douzaine de fusillades, et les gens de Torbi-Kala disaient pour rire qu'il était grand temps d'y planter un panneau : *Danger, tueurs à gages !*

Cette fois tout était plus simple. Roustam n'avait même pas besoin de tirer. Il s'étendit sur un sol craquelé par la canicule et tâta un fil relié à un détonateur de type classique, comme on en trouve à l'armée. Il portait un pistolet-mitrailleur à l'épaule, mais sans utilité pour le moment. Le PM servirait peut-être plus tard.

Le soleil pilonnait la route. Le point blanc d'une barque se mouvait au large. Par les vitres grandes ouvertes de la Jigouli, qui était garée près de l'enceinte à cinq ou six mètres de là, Roustam entendit à la radio l'appel au *namaz*. Il se renfrogna. C'était un grand péché que de sauter la prière du vendredi.

Les voitures apparurent au bout de cinq minutes. Il y en avait deux. Une Mercedes blindée de couleur noire, et un Cruiser d'escorte argenté.

Quand la première eut ralenti à l'approche du passage à niveau, Roustam appuya sur le bouton.

Le ministre de l'Intérieur achevait son rapport quand un han ! lointain se fit entendre à la fenêtre, faisant tomber du plafond quelques écailles blanches.

Pankov tourna la tête. Le speaker Hamid Abdulhamidov, assis à sa droite, marqua un signe d'inquiétude et quitta la salle. Il revint une minute plus tard en glissant un papier sous les yeux du rapporteur.

Le ministre de l'Intérieur en prit connaissance, s'éclaircit la voix et annonça :

— Camarades ! Comme je le disais à l'instant, notre ministère a remporté des succès notables dans la lutte contre le terrorisme. Cent quarante-cinq irréguliers en armes ont été arrêtés ces derniers temps. Deux cents kilos de littérature subversive ont été saisis. Par là même, nous avons déjoué plus de cent quarante actes de terrorisme. Mais l'ennemi veille toujours ! Un acte odieux vient d'être commis à l'instant même par des terroristes qui sèment le sang et la haine dans notre république. Par une charge d'explosifs qu'ils ont posée en plein jour sur la route de Bakou à la sortie de l'aéroport, ils ont anéanti un cortège de cinq voitures !

La nouvelle mosquée de cinq mille fidèles se dressait au croisement des avenues Lénine et Chamil, près de la route de l'aéroport. Comme tous les vendredis, elle était noire de monde. A un mètre de l'entrée priait un homme de haute taille en blue-jean et chemise blanche à manches longues.

La déflagration retentit à trois kilomètres de la mosquée et fit sortir de nombreux fidèles, mais l'homme ne tourna même pas la tête. Une minute plus tard, son ami nommé Djavatkhan venait le voir pour lui dire :

— Ton frère a été tué.

L'homme continuait de prier.

— Ton frère a été tué, répéta Djavatkhan.

Alors, entre deux *rakats*, l'homme tourna la tête et dit :

— Mais Allah est vivant.

Et de poursuivre le *namaz*.

Quand le premier commis du Kremlin arriva sur les lieux de l'attentat, une mauvaise odeur de chair et d'acier brûlés flottait encore au-dessus de la route. Un bouchon interminable s'étirait d'un côté comme de l'autre. Le ministre de l'Intérieur, tout vibrant de zèle, rapporta à l'homme du Kremlin que la voiture des terroristes avait été retrouvée, carbonisée elle aussi, près de l'ancienne mosquée.

Vladislav Pankov avança d'un pas précipité.

L'onde de choc avait disloqué la Mercedes blindée comme une vulgaire boîte de conserve, la faisant éclater en deux parties. Les restes humains, carbonisés, avaient volé en l'air avec les sièges et le moteur. Igor Malikov était un homme de haute taille, presque deux mètres. N'en restait plus qu'un vague tison d'un mètre en travers de l'asphalte, telle une grande poupée noire, et Pankov n'aurait su dire s'il était face contre terre ou inversement.

Le passage à niveau était troué d'un cratère de trois mètres. Le Cruiser de l'escorte, un peu plus loin, achevait sa combustion avec une Moskvitch blanche. Un relief de treillis se profilait près du quatre-quatre.

Pankov se mit à genoux près de Malikov et constata qu'il n'était pas mort que de ses brûlures : un éclat de blindage déchiré par l'explosion lui avait tranché le cou et saillait de sa chair meurtrie.

Une éternité se passa avant que le Moscovite aux cheveux roux ne levât la tête. Le véhicule de l'escorte ne fumait plus maintenant, et le soleil s'était rapproché de la mer. Derrière Vladislav un homme était debout, vêtu d'un blue-jean et d'une chemise blanche à manches longues. Il portait à l'épaule un PM à large bandoulière de toile, comme la sacoche d'un facteur. Vu du sol, l'homme à la mitraillette semblait encore plus grand que neuf ans auparavant. De ses doigts forts marqués par les ronds blancs de ses ongles, il tenait négligemment son arme par le chargeur. Par-dessous la manche de sa chemise, qui n'était pas de saison, Pankov vit jaillir l'éclat d'une montre de valeur. Il avait des traits réguliers avec des sourcils noirs et épais, un nez qu'on eût dit brisé, une face rasée de près où saillaient des lèvres humides et charnues. Son visage ne paraissait pas tant vieilli que durci, plus grossier qu'autrefois, avec un menton aussi fort qu'un piège d'acier au-dessus d'un cou désormais traversé d'une longue cicatrice qui plongeait dans le col de sa chemise.

Alentour régnait un silence assourdissant. Tous les hommes des services accourus sur les lieux de l'attentat se tenaient à deux bons mètres du cadavre, du commis du Kremlin et de l'homme au PM.

— Tu voulais le nommer président ? demanda Niyazbek.

Son accent des montagnes n'était pas moins rugueux : il enfonçait les consonnes les unes dans les autres, comme avec un marteau.

— Non.

— Tout le pays savait que vous étiez amis. Tout le pays savait que tu avais signé la demande. Même les brebis colportaient la rumeur par monts et par vaux.

— Il avait refusé. Un non catégorique.

Niyazbek le fixa des yeux, et Vladislav fit une découverte étonnante. Ils étaient de la même couleur que ceux d'Arzo. Pas tout à fait noirs : plutôt brun foncé comme de l'onyx ; et dans le tréfonds de ses yeux, comme dans les abîmes de l'océan, il y avait des éclats d'étincelles rouges.

— Tu l'as tué, dit Niyazbek, j'ai sauvé ta peau et tu l'as tué tout autant que ceux qui ont payé le *killer*. Dommage qu'Arzo ne t'ait pas épinglé à son herbier.

Il tourna les talons et partit.

Ibrahim Malikov fut enterré dans les montagnes auprès de son père et de son grand-père : tel était le vœu de Niyazbek. On emporta le corps sur-le-champ. Selon la coutume musulmane, l'inhumation devait se faire avant l'aube, et le village se trouvait à cent vingt kilomètres de là par une mauvaise route escarpée.

Après une courte engueulade avec son service de sécurité, Pankov se rendit sur place en hélicoptère. L'unique rue du village était encombrée de voitures, un vrai bouchon engorgeait le serpentin de la route à perte de vue. Ibrahim n'avait pas mis le pied dans le pays depuis vingt ans, et l'on venait manifestement moins pour lui que pour son frère cadet.

Le premier commis du Kremlin s'étonna de ne voir aucune voiture blindée. On lui expliqua par la suite que les routes de montagne étaient presque inaccessibles à ce genre de véhicules. Quand les hommes de pouvoir allaient dans les hauteurs, ils s'avançaient d'une cinquantaine de kilomètres dans leurs limousines, puis continuaient dans des quatre-quatre. Pankov se demanda ce qu'on aurait vu si Malikov avait été enterré à la ville ; et il se dit que l'affaire aurait pu provoquer de grands troubles.

Il monta au cimetière dans un cortège d'hommes et s'y recueillit un moment, ne sachant où mettre ses mains quand les autres faisaient leurs adieux au défunt sous la psalmodie arabe de l'imam. En regardant les tombes, il remarqua que les stèles ne portaient pas les noms de famille : rien que les prénoms des pères. Du cimetière, qui surplombait le village, on voyait les cimes voisines et les tables dressées sur le parvis de la mosquée.

Plus tard, on rapporta à Pankov que le cortège du président de la République, pendant ce temps, était entré dans le village. Entouré de ses hommes, Niyazbek lui avait enjoint de faire demi-tour. "Je jure Allah que ce n'est pas moi", avait dit le président ; à quoi l'autre avait répondu : "Demi-tour, sinon je tire." Et le président était reparti.

Après le cimetière, Pankov se rendit chez les Malikov. C'était une maison à l'écart du village, neuve, toute en pierre, avec une enceinte pareille à un rempart derrière lequel on s'étonnait de découvrir un modeste pavillon à deux étages. L'intérieur était vide et tranquille, toute la foule se pressant dans la cour. Seuls deux molosses tenaient l'entrée, qui s'ennuyaient près d'un râtelier à fusils-mitrailleurs.

Passant devant eux, Pankov entra dans un salon aux tapis rouge-vert où il aperçut Niyazbek. L'homme priait en direction de La Mecque, sa Kalachnikov à large bandoulière grise posée sur une couchette recouverte d'un tapis. La table était garnie de vivres sans prétentions : galettes, herbes aromatiques, tomates rutilantes, grosses parts de viande bouillie.

Quand il eut fini sa prière, Niyazbek se leva, roula son tapis et enfila ses chaussettes. Puis il s'assit sur la couchette.

Pankov prit place devant lui.

— Tu l'aimais ? demanda Vladislav.

— C'était mon frère, répondit patiemment Niyazbek, comme si le Russe avait posé une question puérile. (Puis, après un temps de réflexion :) Il m'a élevé. Il était de sept ans mon aîné.

— Tu le voyais souvent ?

— La dernière fois, c'était il y a neuf ans. A Moscou. Il pendait la crémaillère avec ses amis et le directeur de son institut. C'est là qu'il a commencé à me faire la morale devant tout le monde. Il disait qu'il était député, qu'il avait un appartement, un chauffeur, et que son ancien employeur, c'est-à-dire l'institut, le payait cinq cents dollars par mois rien que pour des consultations. On peut vivre correctement sans tuer personne, qu'il disait.

Niyazbek se tut. La balafre qu'il avait au cou se gonfla comme le capuchon d'un cobra.

— Je suis sorti de chez lui avec le directeur de l'institut. Un palier plus bas, je l'ai frappé comme un chien en lui disant : Je te donne deux mille dollars, pourquoi n'en laisses-tu que cinq cents à mon frère ?

— Que s'est-il passé ensuite ?

— Mon frère est sorti dans l'escalier pour accompagner son directeur parce qu'ils étaient amis. Il a entendu la scène. Alors il est descendu et m'a demandé : L'appart aussi vient de toi ? J'ai répondu que oui. Un mois plus tard, il partait pour l'Amérique. Je ne l'ai plus jamais revu.

— Et... le directeur, tu l'as frappé fort ?

— Moins qu'il ne le méritait.

Il y eut un silence de quelques secondes. Au-dehors crépitaient des rafales de PM en l'honneur du défunt.

— Le chef régional du FSB jure ses grands dieux qu'il a été tué par les boïéviks de Wahha Arsaïev. Même mes propres... experts n'excluent pas la chose, articula Vladislav.

Niyazbek poussa un petit rire moqueur.

— Les tueurs ont abandonné les armes, et d'une. Ils ont brûlé leur voiture, et de deux. Pourquoi Wahha aurait-il abandonné ses armes ? Tous les flics connaissent son signalement. S'ils l'attrapent, ils ne le garderont pas vivant dix secondes. Une arme, c'est une chance de survie. Wahha brûler sa voiture ? Mais pourquoi ? Comme si les flics n'avaient pas ses empreintes ! Abandonner ses armes, c'est la signature d'un tueur à gages, pas d'un wahhabite. Wahha aurait gardé et le flingue et la caisse. Il n'a pas d'argent à jeter par les fenêtres, lui.

— Mais...

— Tu te fais encore des illusions ? Ibrahim Malikov est ton ami, et son frère a sauvé ta peau. Que doit penser le président d'Avarie-Dargo-Nord quand le Kremlin te nomme premier commis ? Que doit-il penser quand il t'invite à dîner et que tu demandes où est la cafèt' ? Quelle est la première aspiration de tout un chacun, Vladislav ?

— Garder sa place ? fit le fonctionnaire.

Niyazbek ne put s'empêcher d'éclater de rire.

— C'est vivre, Vladislav. Le président Aslanov ne survivra pas plus d'un mois à son éviction, il en est parfaitement conscient. Et ses enfants, pas plus d'un jour. Ne te leurre pas, le Russe. Dans le Caucase, on le paie de sa vie.

La porte grinça, laissant paraître une jeune fille drapée de noir dont on ne voyait que la face et les mains délicates. Elle posa sur la table un grand plat de porcelaine où de blancs raviolis appelés khinkals nageaient dans un bouillon.

— Mange, dit Niyazbek.

Vladislav comprit alors qu'il avait très faim. Il n'avait pas mangé depuis la veille au soir, une espèce de betterave en salade à la cafétéria du siège gouvernemental. Il aurait bien pris un verre de quelque chose mais, pour une raison x, on n'avait pas mis d'alcool sur la table.

Servis chauds, les khinkals se révélèrent délicieux. Vladislav vida le plat entier et termina par un morceau de saucisson bien sec.

— A l'époque, il y a neuf ans, j'ai fait une longue maladie, dit-il. Je vais t'étonner, mais certaines personnes ont des trucs fragiles. Les nerfs, ça s'appelle. J'ai fait trois jours de geôle et six mois de cure. Puis deux ans aux Etats-Unis pour représenter la Russie à la Banque mondiale. Quand j'ai tenté de retrouver un certain Niyazbek, on m'a dit qu'il avait été tué.

D'un air distrait, Niyazbek triturait un morceau de khinkal du bout de sa fourchette.

— Les médecins m'ont dit d'oublier le Caucase, poursuivit Vladislav, et je l'ai oublié. Une fois nommé représentant du Kremlin, j'ai appris quelque chose d'amusant. Votre nouveau président a été élu en 1998. Cinq mois après que tu m'as tiré de ma geôle. Ses fils s'appellent Gamzat et Gazi-Mahomed. On m'a dit qu'ils faisaient beaucoup de business, et d'une vilaine façon. Ils avaient l'art et la manière de s'attirer les problèmes. Ils oubliaient de rembourser leurs dettes. Sans l'un de leurs amis, nommé Niyazbek, ils n'auraient jamais tenu le coup, et le président Aslanov ne serait jamais devenu président, parce que ce sont les hommes de Niyazbek qui, la mitraillette à la main, lui ont assuré le juste compte des suffrages au soir de l'élection. J'ai appris aussi que, une semaine après que le président Aslanov avait remporté les élections, la voiture de Niyazbek a été pulvérisée par un obus. Histoire de ne plus être en dette avec lui. Qu'as-tu l'intention de faire, Niyazbek ?

Le montagnard le darda de sa prunelle marron-noir et lui dit :

— Rien que je puisse avouer au représentant du président de la fédération de Russie.

Vladislav observa un temps de silence pour recouvrer ses esprits, mais à cet instant une porte claqua et plusieurs hommes firent irruption dans la pièce. Robustes, bruns, les uns en chemise noire, les autres en tenue camo. Ils donnèrent à tour de rôle l'accolade à Niyazbek qui se retourna et présenta le premier :

— Djavatkhan.

Djavatkhan avait la physionomie d'une olive étonnamment avenante encadrée d'une courte barbe noire. D'après les normes locales, il aurait pu exceller avec un égal succès comme ministre ou bandit, voire les deux à la fois.

— Khizri.

Khizri s'appuyait sur l'épaule de Djavatkhan, et Pankov découvrit soudain qu'il avait une prothèse à la place de la jambe. Une maigreur maladive. Des yeux noirs comme un film insolarisé lançaient des éclairs sur une face grise et terreuse.

— Wahha.

Wahha avait dans la quarantaine. Souple, solide comme une chaîne, les cheveux poivre et sel frisés, un regard dur éclairé par des yeux d'un bleu étonnamment profond pour un enfant du Caucase.

Le quatrième visiteur se retourna pour dire bonjour mais Pankov sentit sa main prise d'un violent recul comme s'il la mettait dans un four.

C'était Arzo Khadjiev.

Le chef de guerre avait beaucoup vieilli. Son visage fraîchement rasé présentait tant de rides qu'il semblait porter les marques d'une grille brûlante qu'on lui aurait jetée à la face. La manche gauche de son treillis était vide, agrafée à sa ceinture. Trois étoiles ornaient ses épaulettes. Pankov savait que Khadjiev était passé chez les Russes depuis cinq ans et qu'il commandait désormais le Youg, une unité spéciale du FSB, cependant que son frère représentait la Tchétchénie au Sénat russe, le Conseil de la fédération. Le premier commis du Kremlin savait que tôt ou tard il rencontrerait Khadjiev. Mais il se sentit pétrifié et posa sur le Tchétchène un regard effrayé comme si l'autre allait le frapper.

Khadjiev éclata de rire, découvrant des dents jaunes et fortes, puis il passa sa main valide, la droite, autour du Moscovite.

— Il faut que j'y aille, dit Vladislav.

Personne ne le retint, et Pankov comprit qu'il faisait bien. Ces cinq-là devaient se parler, et quand bien même ç'aurait été en russe (or ce devait être en russe puisque Arzo était tchétchène), aucun Russe n'aurait pu comprendre ce qu'ils allaient se dire.

Dans l'entrée, Pankov tomba sur la jeune fille en noir. Comme elle portait une casserole pleine de viande, il lui demanda :

— Un coup de main, peut-être ?

La jeune fille balaya les lieux d'un regard effarouché, et Pankov découvrit soudain un visage régulier d'une surprenante beauté, avec des sourcils sombres et soyeux, comme ceux de Niyazbek, au-dessus des deux lacs noirs de ses yeux. Même le drap trop flottant dont elle était vêtue ne pouvait cacher la grâce de ses formes. Elle considéra d'abord le Russe aux yeux gris dans son costume taillé sur Savile Row, puis les hommes armés en faction dans l'entrée (plus nombreux désormais), et balbutia d'une voix à peine audible :

— Non, non. Vous n'avez pas le droit. Vous êtes un homme, voyons.

Là-dessus, elle se coula dans la porte du salon. Vladislav la suivit des yeux.

Il faisait déjà nuit quand l'hélico s'éleva dans les airs. Le bouchon qui s'étirait sur la route escarpée brillait de tous ses phares. L'homme du Kremlin ferma les yeux. Il ruminait en pensée la conversation qu'il venait d'avoir. Soudain, comme par l'effet d'une décharge électrique, il sursauta.

— Quelque chose ne va pas ?! demanda le chef de la sécurité aux abois.

Se fermant les yeux de la main, Vladislav revit comme en vrai les visages des visiteurs de Niyazbek. Il avait cédé au choc de sa rencontre avec Arzo, et n'aurait pas dû. Djavatkhan, Khizri, il ne les connaissait pas. Soit. Il lui semblait cependant avoir vu Khizri au forum économique. Mais le visage de celui qui s'était présenté comme Wahha ne lui était pas inconnu. Ils ne s'étaient jamais vus – et n'auraient pu se voir – mais c'était bien ce visage qu'il avait aperçu dans le dossier d'instruction de Wahha Arsaïev, terroriste numéro un de la république, dossier ouvert dès 1997 quand l'homme, flanqué de sept têtes brûlées armées jusqu'aux dents, avait détourné l'avion Torbi-Kala-Moscou.

Le lendemain des obsèques d'Igor Malikov, Pankov convoqua une réunion des principaux responsables des forces de l'ordre. Sur les neuf présents, six étaient de la famille du président, le septième étant Pankov lui-même et les deux autres venant du FSB : le chef de l'antenne régionale et son adjoint, le colonel Chebolev.

Une figure légendaire que ce dernier, dont la carrière avait commencé dix ans plus tôt quand il s'était rendu personnellement à des pourparlers avec Wahha Arsaïev et qu'il avait abattu personnellement deux terroristes, donnant ainsi le coup d'envoi de l'assaut. Après quoi Chebolev avait quitté le territoire de la république pour n'y revenir que trois mois plus tôt : sa nomination avait le même instigateur que celle de Pankov. "Agissez de conserve", leur avait-il préconisé.

Le colonel Chebolev était un homme haut de taille, plutôt corpulent, au visage charnu et aux manières de rhinocéros. Il supportait mal la chaleur et n'arrêtait pas d'éponger son front rose et sa calvitie précoce cernée d'une couronne de cheveux jaunâtres.

Chebolev vint trouver Pankov avant la réunion et lui demanda à mi-voix :

— Vous étiez aux condoléances, paraît-il. Que dit Niyazbek ?

— Et vous, pourquoi n'y étiez-vous pas ?

— J'aurais été refoulé. Vous sous-estimez le fait qu'on vous y ait toléré, Vladislav Avdeïevitch. Avez-vous vu là-bas ne serait-ce qu'un seul Russe à part vous ?

— Demandez un compte rendu à Arzo, suggéra Pankov. C'est un homme à vous désormais. Vous êtes son maître.

La réponse du colonel ne se fit pas attendre :

— Arzo m'a offert un loup. Pour mon anniversaire. Il est en cage à présent, et je suis son maître. Mais je ne sais pas ce que mon loup a dans la tête, et je suis incapable de lui parler.

— Pourquoi le gardez-vous alors ?

— Pour qu'il soit en cage. Et pas dans les bois.

Chef de la commission parlementaire d'enquête sur la mort d'Igor Malikov, le député-rapporteur n'était autre que le président du directoire de la Banque nationale d'Avarie et patron du service de la sécurité présidentielle : Gamzat Aslanov.

— Le plasticage du véhicule du premier commis du président de la fédération de Russie, dit Gamzat, a été réalisé au moyen d'une bombe à fragmentation de type FAB-250 utilisée dans l'armée de l'air. C'est une mine qui représente une masse de deux cent cinquante kilogrammes. La commande se fait par des fils. Au moment de l'explosion, la bombe se trouvait au niveau du coffre de la Mercedes. Le véhicule a été retourné comme un gant, et tous ses occupants tués sur le coup. Le quatre-quatre d'escorte a été détruit par le même choc. Deux gardes ont réussi à s'en extirper, mais ont été exterminés à l'arme automatique. Trois autres voitures ont été sérieusement touchées. Dix mètres de voie ferrée sont hors d'usage, une vache a péri qui paissait près de là dans son troupeau.

Pankov ne quittait pas des yeux le vernis de la table. Niyazbek avait raison. D'entrée cette enquête tournait à la farce. Le meurtre du président potentiel était instruit par le fils du président en exercice.

— C'est l'explosion la plus forte qui ait eu lieu dans la république depuis cinq ans, continua Gamzat, mis à part l'attentat perpétré contre le siège d'Avarie-Transflotte avec un camion chargé d'une demi-tonne de TNT. A noter surtout qu'une telle bombe ne peut être installée en une heure ou deux, notamment sur une route aussi fréquentée. D'après les premiers éléments de l'enquête, elle aurait été enfouie à trente centimètres de profondeur durant les travaux de remise en état du passage à niveau, il y a près de deux semaines.

Pankov leva la tête. Voilà qui le déconcertait.

— A-t-on des informations sur l'origine de la bombe ? demanda-t-il.

C'est le général Razgonov, chef du bureau régional du FSB, qui répondit pour Gamzat :

— Nous vérifions partout, dit-il. A vrai dire, il n'y a que deux sites concernés. Tous nos soupçons se portent sur la base aérienne de Bargo. Une inspection totale est en cours.

— Force est de constater, ajouta le ministre de l'Intérieur Arif Talgoïev, que l'explosion a dépassé en puissance le calcul des terroristes. L'onde de choc a détruit le mur de béton derrière lequel s'était abrité le terroriste. Près de son retranchement, nous avons trouvé des traces de sang, des lambeaux de peau et un fusil-mitrailleur abandonné. L'homme a été blessé, peut-être même étourdi. Ses camarades l'ont aidé à s'enfuir. Leur voiture était une Jigouli 06 immatriculée П3273A. Son propriétaire a été mis en garde à vue, il est en train de déposer.

Pankov marqua un silence.

— Le meurtre d'Igor Malikov, dit-il, est un acte terroriste sans précédent. Par son ampleur, son audace, le nombre des victimes. Un acte qui révèle de criantes insuffisances au sein du pouvoir régional. Comment se fait-il que la commission d'enquête soit conduite par le fils du président de la République ?

Il y eut des échanges de regards.

— Gamzat Ahmednabievitch, dit le procureur Makhriev, est un homme d'expérience respecté dans la république. Un bon juriste. Un brillant spécialiste. Nous espérons qu'avec son influence...

— C'est inutile, dit Gamzat à mi-voix, et le procureur se tint coi.

— Vladislav Avdeïevitch, reprit le fils du président, veut dire par là que ce meurtre pouvait profiter à notre famille. Telle est la thèse des ennemis de notre famille. De notre tribu. Or, la bombe tueuse a été enfouie sous les rails voici deux semaines. Personne ne savait alors qu'Ibrahim viendrait chez nous. Personne ne savait alors que vous-même viendriez, Vladislav Avdeïevitch. Je jure Allah que ni mes parents ni moi-même ne sommes impliqués dans cet attentat. Je me fais un point d'honneur d'apporter la preuve que je ne suis pas coupable de cette mort. Il en va de la sécurité de ma famille. Voilà pourquoi j'ai pris la tête de la commission et je ne m'en cache pas.

Pankov regardait Gamzat en silence. "Et s'il avait raison ?" pensait-il.

La réunion finie, Pankov fit un signe à Chebolev.

— Que pensez-vous de cette commission ? lui demanda-t-il.

— J'en pense qu'elle aura du mal à trouver la vérité, répondit l'autre en faisant glouglouter un filet d'eau minérale dans son verre.

— Estimez-vous comme d'autres que le fils du président est impliqué dans cet attentat ?

— Je n'ai pas été nommé pour estimer, répondit le colonel. J'ai été nommé pour savoir. Ce que je sais, c'est que des bombes ont disparu de la base aérienne de Bargo. Et quand nous avons voulu parler au chef du dépôt, lui aussi avait disparu.

— Depuis longtemps ?

Chebolev remplit encore son verre d'eau minérale et s'épongea le front.

— La base aérienne de Bargo est un site où tout disparaît. Une espèce de triangle des Bermudes, en quelque sorte. Depuis hier que nous sommes en train de l'inspecter, l'idée nous a pris de vérifier le carburant. Il est stocké dans des gros machins, des réservoirs de deux mille tonnes chacun. Et savez-vous quoi ? La réserve est de quatre mille tonnes d'après les pièces comptables, mais des petits malins ont bricolé un cylindre qui va de haut en bas à l'intérieur des cuves. Quand on y met la jauge, le carburant est bien là. Et pourtant il n'est plus là depuis longtemps. Il y a donc des choses qui sont là sans y être. Et d'autres qui s'y trouvent sans devoir s'y trouver.

— Par exemple ?

— Par exemple, une distillerie clandestine qui fabrique de la vodka.

Pankov sursauta.

— Vous plaisantez...

— Pas le moins du monde. Qui plus est : dès que nous avons pêché le coupable par les ouïes, j'ai reçu un appel d'un député qui est son cousin. Et quand je l'ai envoyé promener, le coup de fil est venu du ministre des Finances qui est de la famille de sa femme. Quand enfin nous avons mis la main sur le chef du dépôt des carburants-lubrifiants, mon supérieur a eu un appel du Premier ministre en personne dont le chef du dépôt est le petit-neveu, laquelle parenté, bien sûr, doit lui conférer l'immunité diplomatique.

— Il n'en reste pas moins que votre mission concerne le vol des bombes et non la fabrication de vodka, dit Pankov.

— Incontestablement ! Si je vous parle de la vodka, c'est pour deux raisons. Premièrement, pour vous dire que n'importe qui pouvait sortir les bombes de l'entrepôt. Par exemple, celui qui est venu prendre livraison de la vodka ou du carburant de contrebande. Quant au chef du dépôt que nous recherchons, il y a peut-être longtemps qu'on l'a noyé dans la Caspienne pour lui faire porter le chapeau parce que les flics de la région, comme dit le proverbe, ne vont pas chasser les souris plus loin que derrière le poêle. Deuxièmement, je veux vous dire que Gamzat Aslanov n'est pas en mesure de mener l'enquête même s'il n'est pas l'auteur du meurtre de Malikov. Comment pourrait-il instruire le dossier quand on sait que tous les suspects ont des frères, des cousins, des oncles, des grands-pères et des beaux-pères maternels de la troisième génération ? Je n'ai jamais vraiment coupé les ponts avec cette république, Vladislav Avdeïevitch, et je sais de quoi je parle.

Assis devant l'homme du Kremlin, Chebolev haletait comme un gros saint-bernard tourmenté par la chaleur, et Pankov remarqua que l'homme en bras de chemise dans sa tenue d'été avait la peau des mains brûlée et couverte de squames blanchâtres.

— Voulez-vous un simple exemple ? poursuivit l'officier russe. Les circonstances ont voulu que je sois à l'origine de la capture d'Arsaïev il y a huit ans. Wahha était un fils de bonne famille, de père akkien tchétchène qui dirigeait la première faculté de médecine où les admissions ne se faisaient que sur pots-de-vin. Pour blanchir Wahha, on m'a proposé un demi-million. Puis un million. Ensuite Wahha a écopé de vingt-cinq ans de camp où il a été transféré dans un compartiment spécial avec deux convoyeurs, tous les deux célibataires parce que les mariages coûtent cher dans la contrée et que les jeunes ne peuvent pas se le permettre. Au premier arrêt, les deux garçons sont allés boire un thé, laissant Wahha sans ses chaînes. L'autre a quitté le wagon pour monter dans une Jigouli venue le chercher, et bye-bye. Et les deux convoyeurs, comme de juste, n'ont pas tardé à se marier.

Pankov écoutait sans piper.

— Si vous voulez vraiment lutter contre le terrorisme dans la république, enchaîna Chebolev, vous devez former un groupe spécial au sein du FSB. Un groupe qui n'aurait de comptes à rendre à personne. Un groupe ayant le pouvoir de capturer qui bon lui semble pour ce que bon lui semble quels que soient les coups de fil et les menaces.

— Dans le genre du groupe Youg, persifla Pankov.

Chebolev découvrit ses dents et serra brutalement son poing droit comme s'il tirait sur une chaîne imaginaire.

— Arzo, dit-il, nous le tenons en laisse. Et malheur à ce loup s'il ouvre la gueule pour planter ses crocs dans une poule qui ne le mérite pas. Je le taillerai en pièces.

Le ministre des Travaux publics Mahomedsalih Salimkhanov n'appréciait pas du tout d'être aux arrêts pour "tentative de meurtre", et encore moins que l'affaire, eu égard à son importance, soit instruite sous la conduite personnelle du procureur de l'arrondissement Rive droite, Bagaoudin Arifov.

Parce que, trois ans auparavant, Mahomedsalih Salimkhanov avait tué le fils d'Arifov dans les conditions que voici :

Mahomedsalih, Ali Arifov et quelques autres individus de l'entourage de Niyazbek faisaient des affaires dans le pétrole. On chargeait des camions-citernes dans les raffineries et l'on transportait les cargaisons en Avarie du Sud, république régionale voisine, par le tunnel aux Moutons. On rentrait par le même tunnel avec des cargaisons d'alcool. Il arrivait qu'on charge le pétrole non dans les raffineries, mais par des branchements sauvages pratiqués sur les oléoducs. Dans un cas comme dans l'autre, le pétrole voyageait sans les papiers *ad hoc*.

Le business marchait si fort dans le pays qu'on avait même fait élargir et goudronner deux cents kilomètres de route jusqu'au tunnel aux Moutons, malgré quoi l'on voyait de-ci de-là des camions-citernes carbonisés au fond des précipices parce que les chauffeurs s'endormaient au volant ou se prenaient pour Schumacher.

Un jour qu'on chargeait du pétrole dans une raffinerie, une inspection commando débarqua de la procurature. Mahomedsalih ne prit guère la chose au sérieux et s'en fut trouver Ali. "Tire-nous de là, lui dit-il, nous paierons s'il le faut." L'affaire fut étouffée. Il leur en coûta cent cinquante mille dollars, ce qui n'était pas rien.

Quelque temps plus tard, on mit la main sur deux citernes qui se ravitaillaient à un oléoduc. C'étaient les camions de leur compère Sergueï. Comme celui-ci n'avait pas de quoi payer l'enterrement de l'affaire, Ali s'engagea à tout arranger en échange de parts dans le business de Sergueï.

Il y eut cinq ou six cas du même acabit dans l'année, jusqu'au jour où Murad se fit prendre : un associé de Mahomedsalih.

Il fut accusé du meurtre d'un foreur. Mahomedsalih s'en vint trouver le fils du procureur pour lui demander d'enterrer le dossier, et celui-ci répondit qu'il en voulait deux cent mille dollars. "Il ne les a pas", dit Mahomedsalih. "Que veux-tu que j'y fasse ! renvoya l'autre. Il l'a tué, oui ou non ? Il s'en est même vanté devant tout le monde ! S'il n'a pas d'argent, il n'a qu'à céder son business. Il a cinq camions-citernes ? J'en veux deux."

Mahomedsalih revint chez lui songeur. Son copain Murad avait bel et bien tué le foreur qui s'était permis de monter une affaire avec ses propres camions, mais il n'avait jamais ébruité la chose. La seule fois où il avait vendu la mèche, c'était dans une boîte de nuit entre copains. On avait bien picolé, mais Ali Arifov moins que les autres, et Mahomedsalih le revoyait en train de questionner Murad sur le mort.

Après réflexion, Mahomedsalih se dit que, à chaque prise, les flics savaient d'avance où étaient les camions, comme si un indic les tenait informés. Il se dit aussi que ces prises avaient eu pour conséquence de faire tomber son business de quarante pour cent, et d'accroître la part d'Ali de soixante.

Là-dessus, il prit sa pétoire, monta dans sa voiture et se rendit chez Ali Arifov. Il était trois heures du matin. Ali lui ouvrit en bâillant comme une huître. Il avait des tongs aux pieds et une serviette de bain nouée à la taille. Ils passèrent dans la cuisine et Mahomedsalih aperçut, par la porte grande ouverte, une prostituée qui dormait ivre dans la chambre à coucher. Il lui dit ses quatre vérités, exigeant la restitution de sa part de business et la libération de Murad. Il exigea aussi trois cent mille dollars. Les cent cinquante mille touchés par Ali, plus autant pour préjudice moral. Ali éclata de rire :

— Tu es bandit, je suis fils de procureur. C'est moi qui décide.

Mahomedsalih tira son pistolet de sa ceinture et dit :

— Par Allah, tu vas tout me rendre et demander pardon à Murad.

— Un flingue comme le tien, ça ne rigole pas. D'après toi, tu vas écoper de combien ?

L'instant d'après Mahomedsalih tira. L'affaire ne fut pas élucidée, mais le procureur de l'arrondissement Rive droite savait qui avait tué son fils. Tout le monde le savait. "Si ça avait été Sergueï ou Khizri et pas Mahomedsalih, disait-on partout, ils auraient tué aussi la prostituée qui dormait dans la pièce à côté. Seul Mahomedsalih pouvait la laisser en vie dans une situation pareille."

Niyazbek rendit visite au premier commis du Kremlin deux jours après le meurtre de son frère. De sa fenêtre, Pankov vit surgir dans la villégiature qui faisait office de résidence une colonne de quatre-quatre d'où débarquèrent de grands gaillards bruns armés de mitraillettes.

Il entra dans le bureau du représentant du Kremlin avec trois de ses compagnons. Malgré la chaleur, il portait une chemise à manches longues. Il fleurait bon l'eau de toilette de premier choix, comme la fois précédente, mais son visage avait quelque chose de changé. Pankov mit plusieurs minutes à comprendre que Niyazbek ne s'était pas rasé depuis deux jours.

Pankov reconnut tout de suite deux des compères de Niyazbek. C'étaient le boiteux Khizri et le bronzé Djavatkhan, l'homme à la barbe noire. Le troisième se présenta comme étant Mahomed-Rasul.

Mahomed-Rasul dirigeait un service de réparation de machins et bidules, et Djavatkhan était vice-ministre en charge de la collecte fiscale. Quant à Khizri, il était Khizri, tout simplement.

— J'ai quelque chose à te demander, dit Niyazbek. Relâche Mahomedsalih.

— C'est exclu.

— Tu commets une erreur. Mahomedsalih est mon ami.

— Je sais qu'il est ton ami. Je ne doute pas qu'il avait ses raisons de faire ce qu'il a fait. Et des raisons de taille. Peut-être que le vice-speaker a dit du mal de son chat, ou peut-être que la maman du vice-speaker n'a pas voulu servir à boire à la grand-mère de Mahomedsalih. Mais je me fiche pas mal de toutes ces raisons. Voilà quelqu'un qui a provoqué une fusillade devant la moitié du Parlement, et sous les objectifs de trois caméras ! Si ça ne suffit pas pour l'arrêter, alors qu'est-ce qui suffit ?

— Des fadaises tout ça, lâcha Djavatkhan. Il faisait de grandes choses, et on l'arrête pour une bagarre. De quoi a-t-on l'air ?

Les yeux du fonctionnaire du Kremlin devinrent couleur de mercure liquide.

— Etes-vous en train de me dire qu'il vaudrait mieux l'arrêter pour meurtre ? Je peux vous arranger ça.

— Ecoute-moi, dit Niyazbek, c'est un type bien. Il n'est peut-être pas aussi intelligent que toi, mais il est brave et honnête. Il n'a que vingt-sept ans. Dans deux semaines, c'est le championnat du monde de Tokyo. Laisse-le gagner. A son retour, il se rendra de lui-même en prison. Je te le garantis.

— Non, dit Pankov.

Niyazbek se leva.

— Bon, fit-il, mais tu n'iras pas dire après que je ne te l'ai pas demandé.

Pankov raccompagna les visiteurs dans la salle d'attente.

— Dis-moi, Niyazbek, lui glissa-t-il à l'oreille, que t'a dit Wahha ?

— Quel Wahha ?

— Wahha Arsaïev. Que tu as rencontré le jour des obsèques.

— Tu as dû te méprendre, répondit Niyazbek. (Puis, après un silence :) Laisse tomber ça.

— Quoi ça ?

— Tu exiges l'élucidation du meurtre de mon frère. Ne fais pas ça.

Silence de Pankov. Enfin, il demanda d'une voix encore plus basse :

— Pourquoi n'es-tu pas rasé ?

— De quoi ?

— On m'a dit que chez vous… euh, que les gens se laissent pousser la barbe quand ils font le vœu d'une vengeance de sang. Tu te laisses pousser la barbe, ou quoi ?

Distraitement, Niyazbek se passa la main sur le visage.

— Hou là là, me voilà pire qu'un balai-brosse. Trois jours que je suis debout. Je vais me raser.

De la résidence du premier commis du Kremlin, Niyazbek se rendit chez un certain Daoud. En entrant dans sa cour, il vit plusieurs voitures dont il reconnut les plaques, un détail qui n'échappa pas au maître de maison. Quand ils se furent donné l'accolade, Daoud lui dit :

— Il voulait te parler.

Niyazbek haussa les épaules et monta les marches sur les talons de Daoud.

Les gardes du corps se pressaient aux portes du salon dans lequel se trouvait, solitaire, assis devant une table bien garnie, Gazi-Mahomed Aslanov dont les phalanges en saucisses serraient une bouteille à moitié vide. Son visage bouffi ruisselait de sueur.

Comme dirigeant de PétrogazAvarie, consortium d'exploitation des hydrocarbures de la république, Gazi-Mahomed Aslanov était, en termes formels, le plus grand patron du pays qui extrayait annuellement près d'un million de tonnes d'un pétrole léger d'excellente composition, sans addition de soufre, d'une qualité supérieure à la marque Brent et proche de Basra Light. Il y avait trois façons d'exporter le pétrole de la république.

La première était l'oléoduc, avec cinq ou six branchements sauvages tous les kilomètres.

La deuxième consistait à charger des barges qui allaient en mer et vendaient la marchandise à des tankers. Lesquels tankers auraient pu très bien s'approvisionner au port, mais alors le pétrole eût été de cinquante pour cent plus cher parce que régulier.

La troisième façon était d'exporter le pétrole vers la république voisine d'Avarie du Sud par le tunnel routier du col aux Moutons. Les citernes transportaient des hydrocarbures de contrebande dans un sens, et de l'alcool de contrebande dans l'autre sens. Le tunnel était gardé par un commando de montagnards dont la mission était d'empêcher le passage des extrémistes et des terroristes. Le commando prenait cent dollars par camion-citerne.

C'était un business dans lequel se retrouvaient toutes sortes de gens. Certains possédaient des dizaines de citernes, mais il y avait aussi des montagnards qui entretenaient un seul camion pour deux ou trois familles. Ceux-là achetaient le pétrole à des postes de distribution et payaient des droits de passage à qui en réclamait.

Au bout du compte, le consortium extrayait près d'un million de tonnes de brut alors que son directeur général

Gazi-Mahomed, fils du président Aslanov, ne contrôlait la distribution que de deux cent mille tonnes au grand maximum. Niyazbek en contrôlait beaucoup plus.

Voyant Niyazbek entrer, Gazi-Mahomed tenta bien de se lever, mais il pesait trop lourd et cuvait trop d'alcool.

— Toutes mes condoléances, Niyazbek, dit-il. Est-ce que je peux quelque chose pour toi ?

— Oui, répondit Niyazbek, tu pourrais arrêter de boire comme un porc et cesser d'être la honte de ton père.

Là-dessus, il tourna les talons et sortit.

Gazi-Mahomed le suivit des yeux, le visage perlant de sueur. Et de larmes.

La première fois que Gazi-Mahomed vit Aïzanat, feu sa fiancée, elle avait sept ans et allait à l'école dans la même classe que son petit frère Gamzat. Il ne la revit que douze ans plus tard quand son frère et lui furent empêtrés dans une sale histoire et qu'ils vinrent remercier Niyazbek de son aide. Gazi-Mahomed avait déjà beaucoup trop d'embonpoint, et son frère n'arrêtait pas de le traiter d'imbécile. Son père non plus ne le portait guère dans son cœur. "Fais ce que dit ton frère", commandait-il.

La première fois que Gazi-Mahomed voulut gagner beaucoup d'argent, c'était après avoir vu Aïzanat. Et il décida d'agir sans son frère. Il ne tarda pas à connaître un certain Micha qui fut tout excité d'apprendre que le père de l'autre était l'ancien premier secrétaire du Parti communiste de la république, et qui lui proposa quelque chose de très simple : faire la tournée des banques et souscrire des crédits. C'était l'enfance de l'art. Micha l'introduisait dans un bureau et Gazi-Mahomed disait des mots appris par cœur. Sur quoi le contrat était signé.

Ils totalisèrent bientôt en crédits pour cinq millions de dollars. Gazi-Mahomed se disait qu'il apporterait la somme à Aïzanat qui, du coup, ne le trouverait plus aussi gros. Il ne lui était même pas venu à l'esprit que l'argent n'allait pas dans sa poche, mais dans celle de Micha. Et sans doute ne l'aurait-il jamais compris si Micha, un beau jour, ne l'avait pas emmené à un anniversaire.

C'était l'anniversaire d'un bandit très influent à qui tout le monde offrait des montres, des téléphones portables et même des voitures. Quant à Micha, il posa modestement la main sur l'épaule de Gazi-Mahomed et dit :

— Moi, je t'offre le crétin que voici. Il a déjà rapporté cinq millions de dollars et devra en rapporter au moins autant parce qu'il n'a plus le choix.

Après quoi l'on descendit Gazi-Mahomed dans une cave où il passa deux semaines à signer des papiers. Au bout de la deuxième semaine, la porte s'ouvrit sur Niyazbek qui le ramena à la lumière du jour. Quand ils passèrent devant le maître de la datcha, l'autre se mit au garde-à-vous et tenta même de baiser la main de Niyazbek.

Le lendemain, ils regagnèrent Torbi-Kala. Gazi-Mahomed était tout penaud. Il dit à Niyazbek qu'il aimerait lui donner sa part de business, mais ce dernier se récria :

— Inutile. Je n'accepte aucune part venant de la famille. Ma sœur va épouser ton frère.

Gazi-Mahomed ne se maria que deux ans après la mort d'Aïzanat. Il avait encore pris vingt kilos et n'était plus qu'un pochard fini.

La matinée du mardi commença par des troubles sociaux sur la place de la mairie. Quelque deux cents personnes se massaient au pied de la statue d'Asludin Aslanov en arborant des banderoles – "Charapudin est un voleur !", "Touchez pas à Rasul !", etc. Quand la milice vint disperser les manifestants, l'un d'eux laissa échapper une grenade qui, par bonheur, n'explosa pas, mais dont le propriétaire fut embarqué comme terroriste dans un panier à salade et libéré au bout de deux heures seulement après qu'on eut établi que l'homme était un lointain cousin du chef adjoint de la police de la route de l'arrondissement Bechtoï. Une circonstance qui, apparemment, valait alibi.

Puis la foule passa de la mairie à la résidence du représentant du Kremlin, et Pankov exigea des explications.

Vieux de trois jours, les faits se révélèrent d'une extrême simplicité. A deux cents kilomètres au large de Torbi-Kala, où était basée une bourse pétrolière clandestine, un tanker de la compagnie d'Etat Avarie-Transflotte avait été approvisionné en carburant par une petite barge. Ladite compagnie était dirigée par un certain Sapartchi Telaïev.

Sans qu'on sût pourquoi, le capitaine de la barge monnaya ses services plus cher que la fois d'avant. Du coup, le commandant du tanker s'emporta et refusa tout net de le payer. Il s'en serait lavé les mains si la barcasse avait été celle d'un imbécile heureux. Mais la barcasse appartenait au maire de Torbi-Kala, Charapudin Ataïev, et elle était commandée par le petit-neveu de ce dernier.

Le neveu du maire se lança à l'abordage du tanker avec des hommes armés et s'empara de la somme demandée. Il rafla en prime la totalité de l'argent et des armes qui s'y trouvaient, mais n'eut pas la présence d'esprit de dégrader les appareils de transmission.

Il en résultat qu'au moment où la barcasse s'amarra au port, elle y était attendue. Les vainqueurs furent roués de coups, on leur prit armes et argent. Il y eut même un petit échange de tirs, mais comme personne n'alla s'en plaindre à la milice, celle-ci fit comme si de rien n'était.

Deux heures plus tard, le cortège du maire de Torbi-Kala se présentait devant la maison de Telaïev. Le maire assura au patron d'Avarie-Transflotte qu'il ne permettrait pas à son neveu de faire payer son pétrole plus cher qu'auparavant, mais exigea la restitution des armes et de l'argent. A quoi Sapartchi Telaïev répondit que c'était un trophée obtenu de haute lutte et que le maire ne verrait rien de plus que le cul d'un âne.

Il s'ensuivit un échange de tirs un peu plus important, mais la milice étant habituée aux rafales de mitraillette dans la cour de Sapartchi Telaïev, elle préféra faire comme si de rien n'était.

Vexé, le maire donna des instructions. A son réveil, Sapartchi constata que sa villa était privée d'électricité, de chauffage et même d'eau courante. Flanqué d'une poignée d'hommes, il s'en fut crier justice auprès du chef du service des Eaux. On était encore en pleine conversation quand une grenade fut tirée d'un lance-roquette RPG-7 dans le portail du siège, mais dans la mesure où le chef s'abstint de porter plainte à la milice, celle-ci préféra ne pas noter l'événement.

La conversation finie, le chef du service des Eaux fit rétablir le branchement de la villa bien que le maire le lui eût interdit strictement tant que Sapartchi n'aurait pas rendu armes et argent. Le maire de la ville s'en trouva contrarié. Le chef du service des Eaux fut renvoyé.

Or c'était un homme très respecté. Qui plus est, il appartenait à l'un des clans les plus nombreux de la république. Indignée par ce limogeage, toute sa famille descendit dans la rue et la chose tourna à la manifestation.

Les deux camps en conflit se présentèrent à la résidence de l'homme du Kremlin deux heures plus tard. Entre-temps la foule s'était épaissie sur la place, telle une soupe qu'on aurait laissée trop longtemps sur le feu, bientôt grossie d'individus qui tapotaient leurs mitraillettes comme un concierge, son balai. A voir l'ensemble, on aurait pu penser aux préparatifs du tournage d'un film sur la prise du palais d'Hiver.

Quand le premier commis du Kremlin sortit de son bureau, tous les acteurs de la rencontre étaient en place. Le maire faisait les cent pas devant la porte, ses deux yeux bleus brillant sur sa face mate comme deux becs de gaz dans la nuit. Ataïev avait les yeux de sa mère cosaque, et le faciès large de son père nogaï.

Accoudé à la table de réunion, Sapartchi Telaïev était vêtu d'un maillot noir moulant qui sculptait avantageusement ses épaules et ses muscles. Pankov n'avait rien vu de tel depuis *Terminator 2*. Pour être ainsi taillé, le patron d'Avarie-Transflotte devait passer toutes ses journées de travail en salle de musculation. C'était à se demander quand il trouvait le temps de diriger une compagnie d'Etat.

— Dis donc, faisait Sapartchi, ton bonhomme touche pas une bille dans le business ! Il me fait payer un plein de brut au prix de l'essence !

— Il te fait payer le prix que tu paies à Gamzat, renvoya le maire. Pourquoi ne mets-tu pas Gamzat et moi au même tarif ?

— Parce que tu n'es pas le fils du président ! A-t-on jamais vu ça qu'une tonne de brut achetée au maire vaille autant qu'une tonne achetée au fils du président ?!

— Mais tu me paies moins qu'à Niyazbek ! s'écria le maire.

A cet instant Telaïev, à bout de patience, s'écarta de la table par la force des bras et Pankov découvrit horrifié que ce drôle de Schwarzenegger était en fauteuil roulant, les jambes couvertes d'un plaid de laine à carreaux.

— C'est ma flotte ! Je paie ce que je veux à qui je veux !

— En vérité, coupa Pankov, ce n'est pas votre flotte, mais celle de l'Etat.

— Ben oui, fit Telaïev étonné. Celle de l'Etat. Donc, la mienne.

Geste impuissant de Pankov : les bras lui en tombèrent.

— Vladislav Avdeïevitch, déclara Telaïev, je veux que vous sachiez que cet homme est un tueur. Il a payé deux millions de dollars au fils du président pour son poste de maire. Comme la ville de Torbi-Kala avait déjà un maire, Sapartchi a dit : "Et comment allez-vous supprimer le maire ? – Supprime-le toi-même", qu'on lui a répondu. Et cet homme a tué le maire de la ville ! Il a tué le directeur de la centrale électrique ! Il a tué le directeur de l'usine radiotechnique ! Il tue tous ceux qui le gênent !

— Tueur toi-même ! para le maire. Raconte-nous un peu comment tu es devenu le compagnon de sang de Niyazbek ! Le commerce des hommes que tu faisais en Tchétchénie ! Les voyages que tu allais y faire !

— Quand j'allais en Tchétchénie, répliqua le patron d'Avarie-Transflotte, tout le monde y allait à part le rabbin des Tats ! Toi-même y allais !

— J'y allais peut-être, mais toi tu y vivais !

— Suffit, messieurs, lança Pankov pour couper court à la querelle. A qui sont ces gens qui manifestent dans la rue ?

— A moi ! répondirent en chœur les deux hommes d'Etat.

— Eh bien, vous avez dix minutes pour les faire déguerpir. Sinon, c'est commission fédérale. Et bye-bye à votre fauteuil.

Le représentant du Kremlin tourna les talons et sortit du bureau.

Pour avoir assisté lui aussi à la mémorable réunion tenue dans la résidence du premier commis du Kremlin, Arif Talgoïev, ministre de l'Intérieur de la république d'Avarie-Dargo-Nord, comprenait parfaitement que le premier qui éluciderait le meurtre d'Ibrahim Malikov en sortirait grandi aux yeux des fédéraux.

Aussi agissait-il à une vitesse inouïe. Il convoqua le chef de la section de lutte contre le terrorisme et le chargea d'élucider l'affaire dans les trois jours.

Fort d'une telle habilitation, l'homme engagea une action rapide et bien ciblée. Il se fit apporter la liste de ceux qui avaient été formés dans les camps de Hattab et sélectionna cinq individus qui, de retour au pays, n'y faisaient rien de spécial. A noter que ces cinq-là n'avaient ni amis ni parents influents.

Il donna donc cinq adresses à visiter, d'où l'on ne tarda pas à lui ramener cinq personnes dont quatre figuraient sur la liste. Comme le cinquième n'était pas chez lui, on avait pris son neveu à sa place.

Ceci fait, le chef de section fit arrêter un certain Mahomed à qui appartenait la Jigouli blanche abandonnée par les terroristes. L'homme avait soixante-sept ans. Ancien maçon dans le Grand Nord, il était rentré huit années auparavant avec une femme russe et sa Jigouli achetée grâce aux primes allouées dans le cercle polaire. Mahomed affirmait qu'on lui avait volé sa voiture, mais il ressortait d'une enquête de voisinage qu'il avait manifesté l'intention de la vendre.

Alors le chef de section se fit amener Mahomed, le mit sur une chaise menottes aux poings et posa cinq photos devant lui :

— Tu as vendu ta voiture à l'un des cinq, lui dit-il. A qui ? Avoue !

— Je ne l'ai pas vendue, on me l'a volée.

Le chef de section le frappa si fort que l'homme de soixante-sept ans roula par terre. C'est alors qu'entra le général Talgoïev qui portait l'uniforme et tous ses attributs.

— Salaud ! lança le vieux. Camarade major, il me frappe !

N'ayant jamais eu affaire ni aux flics ni aux militaires, le vieux se mélangeait les pinceaux dans la taille des étoiles.

— Je ne suis pas major, mais général-major, répondit Talgoïev, et il ne te frappe pas. C'est toi qui piques de la tête dans ses bottes. A peine debout, tu retombes aussitôt. Tu te relèves et encore boum.

Il fallut trois bonnes heures pour mettre Mahomed en condition. Après quoi le vieux, criblé de coups et couvert de sang, avoua qu'il avait vendu sa voiture blanche par procuration, et désigna comme acheteur l'un des cinq individus dont on lui montrait les photos.

L'homme s'appelait Kazbek et avait vingt-cinq ans. Six ans plus tôt, on donnait cinq cents dollars à quiconque s'entraînait dans les camps de Hattab alors que le chômage sévissait dans la république. De plus, c'était prestigieux de s'entraîner chez les boïéviks. Ça plaisait aux filles. Kazbek fit une année d'entraînement. Il apprit à tirer, à plastiquer, à prier. Il fit la guerre dans le détachement de Guelaïev. Ce dernier tué, Kazbek pria dans un coin et décida de revenir à la vie civile. Il travaillait depuis trois ans comme gardien à l'usine radiotechnique.

Kazbek fut présenté au chef de section qui lui dit :

— Tu as été reconnu par le vieux à qui tu as acheté la Jigouli. Vas-y, raconte. Où as-tu dégoté la bombe et qui sont tes complices dans le meurtre de Malikov ?

Kazbek dit qu'il n'en savait rien. Alors on le battit comme un chien avant de le jeter au trou. Quand il revint à lui, on le fit remonter dans le bureau du chef de section.

— Je ne sais rien, dit Kazbek.

On le mit ventre au sol, on lui enfonça un tube de fer dans le derrière et l'on y glissa un barbelé. Puis l'on ôta le tube et l'on fit des mouvements de va-et-vient avec le barbelé.

— Je ne sais rien, dit Kazbek.

Alors on fit entrer dans le bureau la femme de Kazbek, enceinte de sept mois. On lui arracha jupe et corsage et on la coucha sur une table.

— On va tous la sauter, dit le chef de section. A la fin de la tournante, on lui mettra le tube dans le bazar et on ramonera jusqu'à la sortie du bébé. Dis voir, Chapi, as-tu jamais pensé que tu ferais un jour un avortement à une jolie dame ?

— Laissez ma femme tranquille, dit Kazbek, et je ferai tous les aveux qu'il vous faut.

Il était dix heures du soir quand le téléphone sonna dans la chambre à coucher de Pankov.

— Vladislav Avdeïevitch ? Ici le général Talgoïev. Nous avons élucidé le meurtre d'Ibrahim Malikov.

Un gamin, ce boïévik. Assis sur sa chaise, l'air brisé, il avait les yeux rivés au sol. On avait passé ses mains menottées derrière le dossier. Une ampoule ornée de ferrure brûlait au plafond, le plancher sentait le chlore et le sang.

— Admirez le spécimen, dit Talgoïev. Kazbek Mahomedgaziev. Vingt-cinq ans. A fait la guerre de Tchétchénie dès dix-neuf ans. Rompu aux armes et au feu à l'école de Hattab. Travaillait depuis trois ans pour Arsaïev qui lui a commandité le meurtre de Malikov. A lui de vous raconter la suite.

Sur sa chaise, le terroriste ne disait rien. Noiraud, maigrichon, il semblait étonnamment vulnérable, et pourtant Pankov se rappelait bien que c'étaient des gars comme lui, efflanqués, dégourdis, jeunes, qu'il avait vus dans les montagnes autour de Niyazbek.

— Pourquoi as-tu fait ça ? lui demanda l'homme du Kremlin. Et sur ordre de qui ?

Le terroriste ne sortait toujours pas de son mutisme. Soudain, d'un geste brutal, le milicien qui se tenait derrière lui leva le menton.

— On regarde droit devant soi et on répond aux questions posées, fit le flic d'un air menaçant.

Le terroriste déglutit.

— La cible n'était pas Malikov, dit Kazbek. La cible, c'était le représentant du Kremlin qui devait accueillir une huile à l'aéroport, d'après Wahha. Pas besoin d'une bombe pour tuer Malikov ! On s'attendait à tout un cortège. On s'attendait à dégommer une trentaine d'hommes. Des fédéraux.

— D'où venait la bombe ?

— J'ai un vieux copain de classe à la base de Bargo. Arsène. J'ai livré des patates à la base, et j'en suis ressorti avec la bombe.

— Avec quoi ? un camion ?

— Non. J'ai une IJ. La version fourgonnette. On peut sortir n'importe quoi de cette base-là. L'an dernier, on a fauché un moteur d'hélico.

Après un long silence, Pankov ordonna :

— Tout le monde dehors.

Les flics se regardèrent.

— Sortez, dit Pankov, il est menotté. Qu'est-ce que je risque ?

D'un pas réticent, le général Talgoïev finit par se retirer, flanqué de ses deux molosses. Le terroriste se trouva seul devant le haut fonctionnaire, ce rouquin taillé dans une allumette. Inerte, vissé sur sa chaise, le garçon bougeait sourdement les lèvres. Pankov comprit alors qu'il était en train de prier.

— Sais-tu qui je suis ? demanda Pankov.

L'autre fit non de la tête sans lever les yeux. Ses lèvres continuaient de bouger.

— Je suis le représentant du Kremlin, Vladislav Pankov. Voulais-tu vraiment me tuer ? Es-tu vraiment de la bande d'Arsaïev ?

Nouveau signe de la tête. Cette fois en forme d'acquiescement.

— On t'a torturé ? Tu ne mens pas ?

L'instant d'après Kazbek fit un bond en l'air. Sa menotte brisée pendillait à sa main gauche. De la droite, il tenait par le pied sa chaise en métal. L'arête en acier du dossier entailla la face de Pankov, le précipitant au sol. Mais le terroriste ne songea pas à finir la besogne. Au coup suivant, le cadre vétuste de la fenêtre vola en éclats. Kazbek lâcha la chaise et plongea dans l'embrasure.

La porte du bureau s'ouvrit à grand fracas et les flics s'y engouffrèrent pistolet au poing. Trop tard. Ils accoururent à la fenêtre juste à temps pour voir l'homme tomber du troisième étage et défoncer de la tête la vitre d'une voiture de patrouille garée près d'un parterre souillé de mégots.

Assommé, Pankov se contorsionnait sur le plancher. "Vivant ?" s'inquiétait un agent trapu qui aidait l'homme du Kremlin à se relever. Le général Talgoïev pestait à la fenêtre.

— Enfants de putes ! hurlait-il. Je l'avais pourtant bien dit ! Qu'il y ait des barreaux à toutes les fenêtres !

II

COMMENT DEVENIR DÉPUTÉ

Khizri Beïbulatov, directeur adjoint des cimenteries de Cham-khalsk, passait pour l'un des hommes les plus dangereux de la république.

Son père était natif du même village que Niyazbek, mais Khizri avait vu le jour à Chamkhalsk, bourgade à cheval sur l'Avarie-Dargo-Nord et la Tchétchénie, rendue célèbre par lesdites cimenteries et par un taux de chômage exception-nel dès l'époque soviétique. Sa fratrie comptait quatre gar-çons et cinq filles. Il avait perdu sa mère à l'âge de six ans. Dès lors, son père avait sombré dans l'alcool.

Depuis tout petit, Khizri savait qu'il devait chercher le salut dans le sport pour s'échapper de cette ville à ras de terre dont les cimenteries bordaient une rivière aux eaux troubles et tumultueuses. A onze ans, il gagna un tournoi de lutte libre ; à quatorze, un championnat du monde de juniors.

Une fois qu'il était revenu passer l'été à Chamkhalsk, à quatorze ans et demi, son père ivre mort manqua un vi-rage de montagne au volant de sa Jigouli. L'auto fit un vol plané de cinquante mètres. Son père mourut sur le coup. Khizri s'extirpa de la banquette arrière et remonta le pré-cipice en rampant.

A la nuit, il atteignit la route où il fut ramassé au petit matin. Trois jours plus tard, on l'amputait d'un pied à hau-teur de la cheville, et d'une jambe au-dessous du genou. C'en était fini de sa carrière sportive.

Khizri fut placé chez un oncle de Torbi-Kala, doyen de l'université qui faisait du business à côté et qui, étant nul en affaires, se faisait voler l'argent que les étudiants lui

payaient pour leur admission. Khizri non plus n'y entendait pas grand-chose en affaires et ne voulait pas faire d'études. Quant à l'univers de la force – le seul qu'il eût compris,
connu et aimé –, cet univers lui était interdit à tout jamais.
En plus de son handicap, son accident se rappelait à lui par
de féroces douleurs à la tête et au dos. Ses anciens camarades, devenus champions du monde et d'Europe, rendaient
parfois visite à ce garçon squelettique et diminué pour lui
conter les mille feux de Paris, les paillettes des hôtels de
Djeddah et les boîtes de nuit de Moscou, tandis que l'autre
restait chez lui à regarder la télé et à boire de la vodka.

Un jour, son oncle reçut la visite d'un partenaire tchétchène. Khizri se trouvait assis devant celui-ci quand son
petit-neveu entra dans la pièce, un garçonnet de cinq ans.
"Comme il est mignon ! fit le Tchétchène en caressant le
petit. J'aimerais bien savoir quelle rançon me paieraient tes
parents si je t'enlevais." Tels furent ses derniers mots : Khizri,
qui avait dégainé, l'abattit sur place.

Le Tchétchène fut enterré, et l'on ignora longtemps le nom
de son meurtrier.

Un ou deux mois plus tard, un fonctionnaire parvenu
acheta un terrain contigu à celui des Beïbulatov et entreprit
de reconstruire la maison. Au vu des cadastres, il constata
que leur clôture débordait d'un demi-mètre. Aussi exigea-
t-il le déplacement de la clôture sous peine de plainte à la
procurature. Khizri le tua par balle le soir même avec ses
deux fils. Blessé, le cadet eut le temps de s'échapper par la
fenêtre et de gagner l'hôpital. On lui fit une opération, puis
on le plaça dans une chambre avec deux autres malades.
Khizri s'y rendit clopin-clopant dès le lendemain et l'abattit
sur-le-champ.

On ne tarda pas à parler de lui. On le prit en estime. Les
frères du Tchétchène assassiné, qui avaient entrepris de le
tuer, disparurent à tout jamais. L'oncle de Khizri lui céda
ses affaires, lesquelles, du coup, se mirent à prospérer parce
personne n'osait plus tromper son neveu.

Si célèbre qu'il fût, Khizri continuait de trop boire. Un soir
qu'il fêtait son anniversaire avec ses hommes dans un restaurant, il se querella avec le fils du procureur de la République. Il sortit son arme comme de juste mais fut maîtrisé
par les gardes et ne recouvra ses esprits que sur la paille

d'un cachot. Craignant pour son fils, le procureur l'inculpa non seulement de violence publique, mais aussi d'une bonne vingtaine de meurtres dont il n'avait pas commis la moitié. Comme Khizri ne voulait rien avouer, il fallut bien le rendre un peu plus bavard en lui arrachant tous les ongles et en lui sciant toutes les dents. Peine perdue, il ne lâcha rien.

C'est alors que son oncle, Mahomed-Hussein, appela Niyaz-bek à l'aide.

— S'il te plaît, fais quelque chose, lui dit-il, ce garçon a vingt et un ans et il est handicapé, amputé des deux pieds, malade des vertèbres... On l'accuse de vingt meurtres et on lui fait des trucs tellement atroces qu'il n'y a pas de mots pour le dire. Et tout ça pour une querelle avec le fils du procureur.

— Ton neveu est un tueur et un ivrogne, répondit Niyaz-bek. A vingt et un ans il a déjà du sang jusqu'au cou et nul ne peut dire qu'il n'a jamais tué que ceux qui le méritaient.

— Mais comme handicapé, rétorqua l'oncle, il ne peut frapper personne. Il ne peut que tuer. Au nom de feu ton père et de tous les gens du village, fais quelque chose pour lui !

Niyazbek réfléchit trois jours durant. Au quatrième jour, il alla rendre visite à Khizri en maison d'arrêt. L'autre se trouvait à l'isolement par une chaleur de quarante-deux degrés. Son visage n'était plus qu'un énorme hématome. On lui avait confisqué ses prothèses et des asticots grouillaient dans ce qu'il lui restait de jambes.

Après l'avoir nettoyé de ses asticots, Niyazbek lui demanda :

— As-tu avoué quoi que ce soit ?

— Non.

Alors Niyazbek lui tendit une cruche d'eau. Au moment où Khizri voulut étancher sa soif, l'autre lui dit :

— C'est de l'eau pour tes ablutions.

Ils firent ensemble le *namaz*, puis Niyazbek commanda :

— Jure-moi de renoncer à boire et je te tire de là. Mais je jure Allah que, à la première cuite, je te descendrai de mes propres mains.

Deux semaines plus tard, Khizri était libre. Le procureur n'avait pas voulu le relâcher parce qu'il craignait pour son fils, mais quand Niyazbek eut fait monter les enchères à un demi-million de dollars, la cupidité l'emporta. Niyazbek paya la somme de ses propres deniers, allongeant même quarante mille dollars supplémentaires pour la clinique viennoise où Khizri se fit soigner.

Depuis qu'il était sorti de prison, Khizri ne buvait plus une goutte. Il priait cinq fois par jour et ne tuait plus jamais de son propre chef. Il ne tuait plus qu'à la demande de Niyazbek, ou quand il sentait que Niyazbek n'y verrait pas d'inconvénient.

Sapartchi Telaïev, directeur général d'Avarie-Transflotte, s'en vint trouver Niyazbek Malikov une semaine avant la nomination de Pankov au poste de premier commis du Kremlin. Quand ils se furent donné l'accolade, Sapartchi dit :

— Niyazbek, j'ai besoin de ton aide.

Le visage de Niyazbek s'assombrit parce que Sapartchi était un personnage insaisissable et déloyal, et qu'il préférait ne pas avoir affaire à lui. On n'avait encore jamais vu qu'il n'eût pas vendu quelqu'un qu'il pût vendre. Niyazbek avait même l'intime conviction qu'il avait vendu son propre fils.

— Je voudrais être élu député de la circonscription de Chouguinsk, mais je n'ai guère de chance sans le soutien de Khizri.

L'ancien député avait été tué un mois auparavant. Un nouveau scrutin devait avoir lieu prochainement, auquel Khizri Beïbulatov était candidat. D'aucuns le désignaient même comme l'auteur du meurtre, mais ceux-là ne portaient guère Khizri dans leur cœur.

— Et pourquoi pas dans une autre circonscription ? demanda Niyazbek.

— Il n'y a pas d'élections en vue dans les autres circonscriptions, répondit Sapartchi, et puis mon gendre est de Chouguinsk. Si je fais enregistrer sa candidature, nous aurons deux fois plus de temps de parole et ses proches travailleront pour moi.

Niyazbek ne disait plus rien.

— Aide-moi, s'il te plaît, reprit Sapartchi. Je suis prêt à rembourser tous les frais de campagne de Khizri.

Khizri avait engagé deux cent mille dollars, somme payée en totalité de la poche de Niyazbek qui, en pareil cas, offrait toujours son aide.

— Je vais tenter quelque chose, dit Niyazbek, mais cesse de m'abaisser avec ces histoires d'argent.

Le jour même Niyazbek se rendait à Chamkhalsk où Khizri possédait une belle maison qui dominait le Terek à cinq kilomètres de la frontière de la Tchétchénie. Ce n'était pas la seule maison de Khizri : il en possédait une autre à Torbi-Kala, avec une deuxième épouse. Le bruit courait aussi qu'il avait une troisième femme à Moscou, mais nul ne savait exactement s'il l'avait épousée, comme le font les bons croyants, ou s'ils partageaient simplement le même lit, comme le font les Russes.

La femme de Khizri dressa la table, puis courut à l'étage où braillait un enfant.

— Sapartchi Telaïev veut être élu député de Chouguinsk, dit Niyazbek, et j'ai décidé de l'aider.

— Pourquoi ne pas lui donner une autre circonscription ?

— Parce qu'il s'agit d'un scrutin partiel et que les députés des autres circonscriptions sont tous en vie.

— Voilà un malheur qui peut s'arranger facilement, dit Khizri.

Niyazbek laissa la réplique sans réponse. Quelque chose tomba par terre à l'étage, et les pleurs de l'enfant reprirent de plus belle.

— Et pourquoi Sapartchi a-t-il déposé la candidature de son gendre en même temps que la sienne ? demanda Khizri.

— D'après ce qu'il dit, c'est pour doubler son droit de parole et pour faciliter la tâche des proches de son gendre.

— D'accord, dit Khizri, je n'en meurs pas d'envie mais je vais retirer ma candidature par égard pour toi.

Khizri raccompagna le visiteur jusqu'à son troupeau blindé de voitures, et Niyazbek lui demanda :

— A propos, cette Larissa, à Moscou, qu'est-ce qu'elle fricote avec toi ?

— Elle m'aime, dit Khizri, et moi aussi.

— Eh bien si elle t'aime, qu'elle se convertisse à l'islam pour t'épouser. Tu as déjà commis trop de péchés pour vivre avec une femme en concubinage.

Il fallut près d'une heure à Niyazbek pour couvrir les cent soixante kilomètres qui séparaient Chamkhalsk de Torbi-Kala. Bien calé sur le dossier de la banquette arrière, il regardait défiler les mirages de l'été où s'entrecoupaient salins et roseaux.

Jadis fertile, la bande côtière perdait chaque année des milliers d'hectares de terres. Moscou allouait annuellement cent cinquante millions de dollars aux travaux d'assèchement des marais et de désalinisation des sols, et le fauteuil de directeur général de SA Avarie-Bonification, occupé depuis trois ans par le fils du président Aslanov, était l'un des plus enviés de la république.

Si Niyazbek Malikov avait choisi de ne pas se brouiller avec Sapartchi Telaïev, c'était pour la simple et bonne raison qu'il ne voulait pas quitter ce bas monde sans avoir récupéré toutes les dettes qu'on lui devait, et qu'il ne voulait pas non plus voir grandir le cercle des endettés.

Son grand frère ayant été tué, Niyazbek n'hésita pas le moins du monde sur ce qu'il allait faire, de même qu'une graine mise en terre ne se demande pas si elle doit pousser ou non. Elle pousse sans se poser de question.

Niyazbek savait qu'il devait tuer le président de la République et ses fils.

Niyazbek le savait depuis longtemps, depuis la mort de sa sœur, mais la chose eût alors semblé par trop précipitée. Toute sa vie durant, il n'avait jamais fait que ce qu'il devait faire au moment où il devait le faire. Il méprisait ceux qui, au lieu d'agir, s'ingéniaient à expliquer pourquoi ils n'agissaient pas.

Tuer Gazi-Mahomed Aslanov, le fils aîné du président, ne présentait guère de difficulté. Certes, sa villa de trois étages en plein cœur de Torbi-Kala était cernée de caméras et de clôtures, certes son escorte l'accompagnait partout, mais sa garde ne surpassait pas celle de Niyazbek : à titre d'exemple, il s'était rendu chez Daoud avec seulement trois véhicules.

Tuer le président serait plus compliqué. A elle seule la garde fédérale comptait près de deux cents hommes dont certains dépêchés par Moscou et par le FSB sans parler, dans certains cas, de la milice et de l'armée.

Mais le pire n'était pas là. Il y avait aussi le service de la république régionale, fort de quelque cinq cents hommes et que dirigeait le fils du président, Gamzat Aslanov : la cible la plus difficile. Le député Gamzat Aslanov ayant sur la conscience plus de morts que quiconque dans le pays, il ne se déplaçait jamais autrement qu'avec une horde de janissaires.

Au Parlement, son cabinet se trouvait non pas dans les étages mais dans les sous-sols, avec sas d'accès et barrage de contrôle à portes de verre blindées pour empêcher toute tentative de pénétration, et gardes armés disposant de détecteurs d'explosifs.

Le bureau du député Gamzat Aslanov était passé du deuxième étage au sous-sol après qu'il eut essuyé un tir direct de roquettes antichars. Circonstance salvatrice, le fils du président venait de s'absenter pour parler au speaker. Mêmes mesures de protection pour son bureau de président du directoire de la Banque nationale d'Avarie.

Au vrai, Gamzat Aslanov ne mettait guère les pieds au Parlement ou à la banque. Parfois, son cortège fonçait dans les rues de la ville, précédé par une brigade de sapeurs qui sondaient le terrain à la recherche d'éventuels explosifs. Les miliciens, ruisselant de sueur, bouclaient alors la circulation, des tireurs d'élite se postaient sur les toits des immeubles, des servants de lance-roquettes se déployaient dans les cours, on faisait pleuvoir des coups de téléphone sur les hauts fonctionnaires de la république en les convoquant dans la demi-heure au bureau de l'élu du peuple. Mais quand ils arrivaient au siège du Parlement, Gamzat n'y était pas. On les faisait monter dans des voitures qui les conduisaient chez lui. Le cortège, les tireurs sur les toits… neuf fois sur dix tout ce tohu-bohu n'était qu'un subterfuge, un ballon d'essai.

Un subterfuge qui, une fois au moins, sauva la vie de Gamzat Aslanov le jour où une bombe à fragmentation explosa au poste de contrôle du siège du gouvernement, à l'endroit où les voitures devaient ralentir pour slalomer entre des blocs de béton. L'un de ces blocs était la bombe à proprement parler : on l'y avait coulée dans le béton deux jours avant l'explosion à l'occasion d'une "remise en état" du barrage. Le véhicule blindé du fils du président fut alors déchiqueté comme une vesse-de-loup trop mûre, mais d'Aslanov, pas une trace.

Nul ne savait à l'avance ni où ni quand se ferait le prochain déplacement de Gamzat qui n'assistait presque jamais aux cérémonies officielles et dont le cortège stationnait toujours dans la cour, prêt à transporter n'importe qui, n'importe quoi : le député lui-même, son ombre, du vent…

La plupart du temps, Gamzat recevait ses visiteurs dans sa résidence personnelle, laquelle se trouvait dans l'enceinte de l'ex-parc Lénine, à la périphérie ouest de Torbi-Kala. Un chemin de ronde bordait le périmètre extérieur du domaine où des maîtres-chiens ne cessaient de patrouiller ; du côté intérieur s'étalaient des champs de mines et des écheveaux de barbelés. L'enceinte se présentait comme une muraille de cinq mètres de haut balayée par un système d'alarme et de télésurveillance. Elle renfermait trois bâtisses : l'une d'elles de style arabe avec un mobilier et des finitions importés spécialement d'Arabie Saoudite ; une deuxième à l'identique de la villa de Madonna près de Los Angeles ; et la troisième érigée par un architecte hollandais sur le modèle du château de Glenmore à échelle réduite. L'un des pavillons servait à l'hébergement des visiteurs, les deux autres étant pour les deux femmes de Gamzat. Quatre chambres par maison, dans lesquelles il dormait d'une façon imprévisible sans que personne – ni ses femmes ni ses gardes – ne le sache à l'avance. On comptait aussi cinq maisonnettes réservées aux amis, aux parents et aux petits profiteurs de passage.

Bref, le domicile de Gamzat Aslanov était mieux défendu que la base de la section spéciale du FSB Youg ou que la résidence du Premier ministre britannique.

Seul un cercle très restreint d'élus se voyait invité chez Aslanov, mais pareille invitation était tenue pour un insigne honneur. Assister à une réception chez le président de la République était infiniment plus facile que d'aller chez son fils. C'était là, dans cet ancien parc de loisirs, que se tenaient des fêtes qu'on se racontait à voix basse, les uns envieux, les autres horrifiés. C'était là aussi qu'avait disparu après un concert une chanteuse nommée Aïcha, étoile montante des variétés russes. Le maître de maison avait exprimé le désir de coucher avec elle, mais en des termes si crus que la fille, piquée au vif, le gifla devant tout le monde. On retrouva son corps trois jours plus tard, dans un tel état que le prédateur sexuel et *serial killer* Tchikatilo en eût rendu les tripes. Il n'y eut pas d'instruction, la chanteuse fut portée disparue.

Là, sur ces quarante hectares, le maître pouvait tout se permettre. Il pouvait ordonner à ses gardes de faire des sauts périlleux, et ils faisaient des sauts périlleux. Il pouvait leur ordonner des exercices de funambulisme, et ils faisaient du funambulisme. Il pouvait convoquer un ministre ou un député et lui ordonner de faire des sauts périlleux, et le ministre ou le député faisait des sauts périlleux devant Gamzat qui tapait dans ses mains. Et si le visiteur lui plaisait, il pouvait décrocher le téléphone pour exiger telle ou telle chose, généralement des fonds budgétaires. Du reste, les minauderies et les sauts périlleux n'étaient d'aucune utilité au visiteur si celui-ci n'avait pas promis d'avance le tiers de ces fonds à Gamzat lui-même.

Le système de protection de Gamzat Aslanov ne présentait que deux faiblesses.

La première était Gamzat lui-même, qui traitait les gens comme des insectes ; or, quand on traite les gens comme des insectes, ils peuvent répondre à coups de dard.

Sa deuxième faiblesse était le golf.

Le fils du président de la république d'Avarie-Dargo-Nord avait à cœur d'améliorer le climat d'investissement dans la région, raison pour laquelle il fréquentait assidument les forums mondiaux consacrés à la question : Los Angeles, Londres, Nagasaki. Grâce à quoi il fit un jour ce pertinent constat : dans tous les pays à forts taux d'investissements étrangers, on jouait au golf.

D'où Gamzat inféra que, en aménageant un terrain de golf en république d'Avarie-Dargo-Nord, celle-ci deviendrait propice aux investissements.

De retour à Torbi-Kala, il créa une société d'Etat par actions appelée Golf-Club et se fit octroyer à cet effet cent vingt hectares de terres côtières adossées aux contreforts du Torbi-Taou. C'était une zone marécageuse envahie de roseaux avec, à flanc de montagne, un vestige de forêt primaire. Gamzat fit venir un spécialiste du nom de Rittelsmann qui avait déjà réalisé des travaux de ce genre au Japon, en Norvège et en Amérique. On appelait *turf managers* les gens de sa profession.

A l'examen des roseaux et du sanctuaire forestier, Rittelsmann décréta que la zone requérait un réaménagement de fond en comble. Il fallait assécher les marécages, faire un drainage et procéder à un épandage de sable avec des machines spéciales. Pour que l'herbe y pousse, ce devait être un sable particulier : pas celui des mers, trop grossier et graveleux, mais celui des rivières, plus fin. Renseignements pris, Gamzat sut qu'on en trouvait dans une carrière située à l'ouest de Torbi-Kala.

Le lendemain, Gamzat s'y rendit avec toute son escorte et ordonna son chargement. Vu l'importance de l'affaire, il s'en occupait personnellement. Sur ces entrefaites arriva le chef d'exploitation qui exigea le paiement de la marchandise.

Alors Gamzat lui asséna un coup de crosse sur la tête et déclara :

— Comment oses-tu te rebiffer ? Il nous faut la carrière pour l'aménagement d'un terrain de golf, et il nous faut le terrain de golf pour l'amélioration du climat d'investissement dans la république ! A moins que tu ne sois contre les investissements étrangers ?

Sur ce, le chef d'exploitation fut jeté dans un fossé et battu comme un chien, et la garde de Gamzat, fortement indignée, cribla de balles les pneus des camions qui travaillaient dans la carrière. Elle emporta tout le sable qu'elle pouvait.

Le jour suivant, Gamzat revint chercher du sable parce que l'affaire était d'importance et qu'il s'en occupait personnellement. Aux abords de la carrière, il vit que plusieurs quatre-quatre en barraient l'accès, occupés par des hommes en armes. Le chef d'exploitation l'attendait de pied ferme, pistolet-mitrailleur à la main.

Ne trouvant pas la chose à son goût, Gamzat envoya chercher le directeur de la carrière.

Lequel directeur fut reçu dès le lendemain dans le bureau de Gamzat, et le fils du président lui expliqua que le golf contribuait à l'amélioration du climat d'investissement. Le directeur de s'incliner en disant :

— Pas de problème, je vous donnerai autant de sable que nécessaire. Et par respect pour vous, cher Gamzat Ahmednabievitch, je vous le donnerai gracieusement.

— Rien que le sable ? Donne-moi plutôt la carrière entière.

Le directeur de la carrière tenta bien de protester, mais Gamzat lui frappa le nez de la crosse de son pistolet, ajoutant :

— Comment oses-tu te rebiffer ? Il nous faut la carrière pour l'aménagement d'un terrain de golf, et il nous faut le terrain de golf pour l'amélioration du climat d'investissement dans la république ! A moins que tu ne sois contre les investissements étrangers ?

Là-dessus, on frappa le directeur jusqu'à lui faire signer tous les papiers nécessaires à l'amélioration du climat d'investissement dans la république.

Le jour suivant, Gamzat revint chercher du sable à la carrière parce qu'il attachait une attention toute personnelle au problème des investissements étrangers, et quelle ne fut pas son indignation de constater qu'il y avait deux fois plus d'hommes en armes et qu'aux pistolets-mitrailleurs s'étaient ajoutés des lance-grenades. Il se renseigna et apprit que la carrière ne fonctionnait pas en régime autonome. Elle appartenait à Torstroï, une société de bâtiment.

Il apprit aussi que ladite société possédait, outre la carrière, une usine de matériaux de couverture, une verrerie, soixante-dix mille mètres carrés de surface habitable dans le centre de Torbi-Kala et trente-sept unités en construction. Gamzat téléphona au patron pour le convoquer dans sa résidence.

Le patron de la société fut reçu dès le lendemain dans la résidence de Gamzat qui lui expliqua personnellement que le golf contribuait à l'amélioration du climat d'investissement. Le directeur de s'incliner en disant :

— Pas de problème, prenez la carrière. Et par respect pour vous, cher Gamzat Ahmednabievitch, je vous la donnerai gracieusement.

— Rien que la carrière ? Donne-moi plutôt Torstroï ! dit Gamzat.

Le patron de la société tenta bien de protester, mais Gamzat lui frappa le nez de la crosse de son pistolet, ajoutant :

— Comment oses-tu te rebiffer ? Il nous faut ta firme pour l'aménagement d'un terrain de golf, et il nous faut le terrain de golf pour l'amélioration du climat d'investissement dans la république ! A moins que tu ne sois contre les investissements étrangers ?

Là-dessus, on jeta le patron de la firme dans une cave de la résidence où on le tint enfermé jusqu'à lui faire signer tous les papiers nécessaires à l'amélioration du climat d'investissement dans la république.

Quand, le jour suivant, Gamzat vint chercher du sable à la carrière, il vit que les hommes armés de mitraillettes et de lance-grenades avaient reçu le renfort d'un blindé sur lequel était juché le maire de Torbi-Kala. Il s'avéra, renseignements pris, que le patron de Torstroï était le gendre du maire. Outre Torstroï, le maire possédait trois restaurants dans le centre de la ville, une brasserie, deux marchés et le centre sportif olympique où s'entraînaient quatre cents gaillards bien baraqués.

Après réflexion, Gamzat convoqua dans sa résidence un homme nommé Charapudin Ataïev, très respecté dans la république. Quand ils eurent causé un brin, Ataïev toussota prudemment en ajoutant :

— J'ai ouï dire que je pourrais devenir maire de Torbi-Kala moyennant la somme de deux millions de dollars.

— Voilà des dires parfaitement justifiés, dit Gamzat.

— Et que va-t-il advenir de l'ancien maire ? demanda Ataïev.

— A toi de voir, répondit Gamzat.

Deux semaines plus tard, le maire fut abattu devant son domicile et Charapudin Ataïev remporta les élections au poste de nouveau maire.

Le lendemain de cette victoire, Gamzat se rendit à la carrière et n'y trouva personne. Il ordonna aux ouvriers de charger ses camions de sable pour le futur terrain de golf. A peine sept mois plus tard les travaux étaient finis, et l'on vit surgir un club de golf de niveau mondial sur le versant ouest du Torbi-Taou entre une mer bleu profond et de noirs rochers sans neige.

Le fils du président de la République inaugura personnellement le club et donna même, à cette occasion, une interview au journal télévisé fédéral. "J'ai consacré sept mois de mon temps à ce projet, déclara-t-il. Je n'en tire évidemment aucun bénéfice personnel, nous faisons cela pour améliorer le climat d'investissement dans la république."

Toujours est-il que, une fois construit le terrain de golf, le président Ahmednabi Aslanov se mit à y passer une bonne part de son temps et qu'à son exemple tous les fonctionnaires se lancèrent dans le golf. Quiconque voulait faire preuve de son estime jouait au golf. Gamzat y jouait aussi.

Quand Niyazbek et ses hommes évoquèrent le sujet, Djavatkhan dit : "Un sport d'homme, ça ? Tu parles !" Et Khizri de constater : "Il n'existe aucun sport qui permette à qui le pratique de parcourir cent vingt hectares en toute sécurité."

Vladislav Pankov s'absenta pour deux jours. Il était en Tchétchénie, où tous ceux qu'il voyait remerciaient les Russes de ce qu'ils faisaient pour la république et stigmatisaient les suppôts de l'étranger qui ne parviendraient pas à faire échouer le processus de paix. On lui fit même visiter un village qui célébrait des noces.

Au moment de repartir, il avisa une fillette qui jouait à la poupée près de sa voiture.

— Et pourquoi manque-t-il un bras à ta poupée ? demanda Pankov.

— C'est parce que son bras a été arraché par une mine, répondit sérieusement la petite. (Puis, montrant un nounours en peluche :) Lui, il n'a perdu que son pied.

Le colonel Chebolev accueillit le premier commis du Kremlin à l'héliport. La route de la ville avait été bouclée, et les flics rendaient les honneurs au cortège. Pankov était pressé : il avait rendez-vous à deux heures avec le mufti de la république parce que les douanes venaient d'intercepter un livre arrivé d'Arabie Saoudite avec pour titre *Riyad as-Salihin*. Sachant que telle était l'appellation du groupe de Bassaïev, l'ouvrage avait été saisi comme d'inspiration wahhabite. "Parce qu'il n'est pas d'inspiration wahhabite ?" s'était fait préciser Pankov au téléphone par un adjoint du mufti, et l'autre d'expliquer très prudemment à l'impie que le livre se présentait comme un recueil de hadiths et qu'il datait du XIIIᵉ siècle. D'un autre côté, on pouvait comprendre les douaniers : on attribuait à leur chef un revenu mensuel de deux millions de dollars, il fallait bien qu'ils confisquent quelque chose.

— Que s'est-il passé en mon absence ? demanda Pankov.

— Le frère d'Isalmahomedov a sauté sur une bombe.

Ce nom de famille lui disait quelque chose.

— Quel Isalmahomedov ?

— Arsène Isalmahomedov, le président d'Avarie-Céréales.

— Et qui l'a fait sauter ?

— Les Ataïev.

— D'où le tient-on ?

— Ben, quand il est apparu évident que Mahomedsalih serait limogé du ministère des Travaux publics, Ataïev a voulu le poste pour son fils, et Isalmahomedov, pour son frère. Ataïev a payé un million et demi au fils du président, et l'autre autant. C'est là qu'on vous a proposé de créer trois portefeuilles de ministre. Et quand vous avez refusé, Gamzat est allé voir ces deux-là pour leur dire : "Arrangez-vous." Ils se sont donc arrangés.

Pankov soupira.

— Quoi d'autre ?

— Mahomedsalih s'est évadé.

— Comment ça ?!

— Il a été interrogé à la procurature sur la castagne qui a éclaté au forum, et deux ou trois cadavres ont refait surface pendant l'interrogatoire. Niyazbek est arrivé avec ses hommes, il a donné dix mille dollars au juge d'instruction en disant : "Laisse-nous causer cinq minutes." Et le juge a quitté la pièce. Ils ont descellé les barreaux, sauté par la fenêtre et filé dans les montagnes. Le ministre de l'Intérieur a appelé pour demander quoi faire. Il n'était pas chaud pour ouvrir une enquête.

— Qu'il fasse comme bon lui semble, dit Vladislav.

D'abord considérée comme l'évidence même, la nécessité d'évincer Mahomedsalih Salimkhanov de son poste de ministre semblait fondre d'heure en heure. Il apparaissait clairement que, à trop faire traîner sa nouvelle nomination, on verrait que le nombre de cadavres causés par la venue du nouveau ministre dépasserait le nombre de cadavres imputables à Salimkhanov. Il n'y avait qu'une seule personne capable de venir à bout d'un tel foutoir. Elle s'appelait Ibrahim Malikov. Et il était mort.

Après son rendez-vous chez le mufti, Pankov prit le chemin de sa résidence où il arriva très vite. Il trouva sa femme, Alissa, en train de faire sortir des caisses dans la cour, et la petite Nina, neuf ans, qui ne se sentait plus de joie parmi les gardes en armes.

La première épouse de Vladislav était morte dans un accident de voiture sept ans auparavant. Il en gardait au cœur un trou noir de brûlures et de meurtrissures. Il pensait alors qu'il ne se remarierait plus, mais il avait changé trois fois de femme au cours des quatre dernières années. Alissa était une blonde somptueuse un tantinet vulgaire, qui venait d'Ouglitch.

Absorbé par la paperasse, Pankov ne comprit pas tout de suite où on l'amenait.

Quand il eut compris, il en resta coi.

Alissa lui avait bien dit au téléphone qu'elle avait repéré une autre résidence, mais il s'était contenté de marmonner "Comme tu veux", pour qu'elle lui fiche la paix. Jamais pourtant il n'aurait imaginé que cette autre résidence serait une villa de quatre étages avec une jolie tourelle surplombant la mer et une courette en marbre au milieu de laquelle murmurait une fontaine mauresque.

— C'est quoi ça ? demanda-t-il à Alissa.

— Ça, c'est notre nouvelle résidence, dit Alissa.

Bien qu'établie à Moscou depuis déjà cinq ans, Alissa n'en continuait pas moins de prendre les *a* pour des *o*, particularité d'élocution de la plupart des provinciales russes. Dans le bain guttural ambiant de l'accent caucasien, sa prononciation semblait complètement décalée.

— Et d'où ça sort ? demanda l'homme du Kremlin sans forcer la voix, et ses yeux gris parurent se glacer de givre.

Sourire d'Alissa qui se lança dans des explications. On l'avait très bien accueillie à l'aéroport. Il y avait même deux ou trois ministres, elle ne savait plus trop : "Tous plus noirauds les uns que les autres, et qui n'arrêtent pas de rauquer, ainsi qu'un charmant petit gros qui s'était présenté comme le fils du président. Il parlait un russe très convenable (dit Alissa en faisant vrombir ses *o*), mais bonjour les gardes du corps. Toute une légion !"

Le charmant Gazi-Mahomed la conduisit à la résidence du premier commis du Kremlin, laquelle ne fut guère du goût d'Alissa. Alors il lui dit qu'il y avait d'autres possibilités, et lui fit visiter une vingtaine de villas. Elle finit par arrêter son choix sur celle-ci. Elle avait craqué pour le télescope au sommet de la tour et pour le mobilier blanc à dorures dans les chambres à coucher.

— Et ça appartient à qui ? s'enquit Pankov.

La villa appartenait au directeur de l'Inspection des pêches, ici présent, dont le salaire officiel était de sept cents dollars par mois. C'était un Balkar de petite taille au visage retors encadré d'une courte barbe blanche.

— N'ayez aucune inquiétude, dit le Balkar. Je l'ai fait construire pour mon fils qui vit actuellement à Moscou. J'étais justement en train de la vendre.

— Eh bien vendez-la à quelqu'un d'autre, lui décocha froidement Pankov.

Alissa le regarda comme un enfant à qui l'on aurait confisqué ses jouets sous le sapin de Noël.

— Mais pourquoi ? dit-elle. Ces gens ont agi de bon cœur pour nous être agréables ! Ce Khazi, là, euh... ce Kozi... il me l'a bien dit : "Je n'attends rien du représentant du Kremlin ni ma famille non plus, mais quelqu'un de bien doit vivre dans un endroit bien."

La femme qui était assise en face de Niyazbek avait peut-être dans les trente-cinq ans, mais elle en faisait beaucoup plus. Elle portait une longue jupe noire et un foulard noir qui lui couvrait la tête. Seules les manches de sa blouse noire, achetée pour deux cents roubles dans un marché de Moscou, étaient enjolivées d'une dentelle synthétique.

Niyazbek l'écoutait d'une oreille attentive et sans l'interrompre. Comme il jugeait inconvenant d'être seul avec une femme qui n'était pas la sienne, il y avait aussi dans la pièce, assis sur un divan bas, Mahomedsalih Salimkhanov.

Elle s'appelait Ella Oumarova. Depuis que son mari, un sous-officier des transmissions, avait sauté sur une mine, elle vivait sous le toit de son frère.

Elle élevait son fils et soignait sa mère grabataire. Elle faisait aussi des ménages chez deux employeurs différents. La fatigue la prenait si tôt qu'elle n'avait plus la force de regarder son émission favorite à la télévision. Une émission de la chaîne publique qui avait pour titre : *Ce que veulent les femmes*.

Le frère d'Ella, Rasul, travaillait comme serveur dans un site confidentiel appelé Clairière-1, autrement dit : le club de golf. Rasul était plus qu'un simple serveur. Jadis, il s'était produit comme jongleur de cirque. Quand Gamzat eut vent de l'histoire, il exigea un numéro de démonstration. Depuis lors, il ne venait jamais au golf sans crier "Rasul !", et Rasul le divertissait selon son bon vouloir, ce qui lui valut d'être promu chef adjoint. Parfois, Gamzat lui envoyait cent dollars qu'il attrapait à la volée. Bref, Rasul occupait un poste important dans la hiérarchie de ce petit monde qu'on appelait terrain de golf, ce qui lui permit de placer le fils d'Ella, un gamin de neuf ans nommé Boussik, comme caddie, c'est-à-dire porteur de clubs.

Un jour que Gamzat jouait contre le procureur de la République, il advint que la balle de ce dernier atterrit à deux doigts du trou alors que la sienne se trouvait à un mètre cinquante. Gamzat s'approcha de la balle du procureur et lui dit :

— Vois ça, comme j'ai visé juste !

Naturellement, le procureur n'osa rien dire. C'est le gamin, comme un nigaud, qui montra la balle de Gamzat en disant :

— La vôtre, la voilà !

Furibond, Gamzat leva le club et assomma Boussik qui s'écroula. Rasul accourut, informé de l'histoire, mais la garde l'arrêta en disant : "Le petit fait du chiqué, on s'en charge."

— Non, non, de grâce ! s'écria Rasul, mais Gamzat lui glissa deux cents dollars et lui dit :

— Dégage, imbécile.

Comme Rasul avait jeté l'argent par terre, la garde le roua de coups et emporta le petit. Mais toujours pas de gamin le lendemain, ni le surlendemain. Au quatrième jour, Ella porta plainte à la milice en consignant par écrit les circonstances de la disparition de son fils. Lecture faite de la plainte, le milicien de service prit un air grave et quitta le bureau. Y entra bientôt un major qui lui dit : "Votre plainte est irrecevable." Ella se mit à crier et fut flanquée dehors illico.

Le soir même, Ella recevait la visite d'un garde de Gamzat qui lui demanda ce qu'elle voulait.

— Rendez-moi mon fils mort ou vif, dit Ella.

Alors le garde jura Allah que le garçon, de peur d'être puni, avait sauté de la voiture en marche, et que Gamzat ferait tout son possible pour le retrouver.

— En attendant, il te demande d'accepter mille dollars à titre de modeste consolation, dit le garde.

— C'est mon fils qu'il me faut, pas votre argent, répondit Ella.

Le garde revint le lendemain :

— Vingt hommes sont à la recherche de ton fils et je te jure qu'ils le retrouveront, dit le garde. En attendant, Gamzat te demande d'accepter cinq mille dollars à titre de modeste consolation.

Ella se jeta sur lui et se mit à lui arracher les yeux. L'autre la frappa et partit sans demander son reste. Le jour suivant, dix miliciens étaient chez elle pour une perquisition. Ils mirent tout sens dessus dessous et l'emmenèrent au poste. Là, elle fut placée avec cinq autres femmes dans une cellule où l'on introduisit bientôt un homme en tenue de camouflage qui dit :

— Oui, c'est bien elle.

Puis entra un deuxième homme qui dit la même chose.

On leur fit signer un procès-verbal d'identification, et Ella fut conduite dans une pièce à part où l'attendait un major de la milice qui lui annonça en ricanant qu'il y avait du nouveau pour elle. Son fils avait été renversé par une voiture parce que sa mère ivre lui faisait traverser la route. Deux passants avaient vu la scène, qui s'étaient précipités pour le secourir, mais l'autre ivrogne les avait écartés en disant : "Je me débrouillerai toute seule." Elle était partie avec l'enfant dans les bras.

Après quoi le major sortit la plainte d'Ella et lui dit :

— Dis donc, chienne, qui t'a mis dans le crâne d'aller faire du chantage au fils du président de la République ?

Ella subit cinq heures d'interrogatoire. On n'arrêtait pas de lui demander ce qu'elle avait fait du corps de son fils. Au bout de cinq heures, elle vit entrer dans le bureau le même garde que l'autre fois.

— Gamzat sait ce que tu manigances, et il sait que tu n'agis pas seule mais à l'instigation de ses ennemis. Et pourtant il te pardonne, sotte femme que tu es. Tu peux prendre les vingt mille dollars que voici et rentrer chez toi, comme tu peux rester ici pour nous expliquer ce que tu as fait du corps de ton fils parce que deux témoins ont vu qu'il vivait encore quand tu l'as emporté après l'accident.

Alors Ella prit les vingt mille dollars et rentra chez elle. Elle cacheta les billets dans un papier qu'elle cousit de fil et s'en fut trouver sa cousine dont le mari était de la famille de Mahomedsalih.

— Je dois voir Niyazbek, lui dit-elle.

Niyazbek et Mahomedsalih écoutèrent Ella, et Niyazbek lui demanda :

— Que veux-tu ?

— Je veux qu'on me rende le corps de mon fils, dit Ella.

— Et qu'en dit ton frère ?

— Il tremble pour sa place. Voilà trois fois qu'il m'assure que Gamzat a bel et bien relâché le petit. Quand quelqu'un a peur pour sa place, on peut lui faire avaler n'importe quoi. Mon frère peut penser ce qu'il voudra. C'est un faible et il fera ce que notre mère et moi dirons. Or elle et moi voulons la même chose.

Niyazbek marqua un silence, et Mahomedsalih demanda :

— Qu'as-tu fait de l'argent qu'ils t'ont donné ?

Ella sortit la liasse de son sac et la posa sur la table.

— Je l'ai accepté pour qu'ils ne se doutent de rien, dit-elle. Donnez-le à la mosquée.

Niyazbek fit non de la tête et lui dit :

— Reprends cet argent et dépense-le au vu et au su de tous. Si tes voisines te posent des questions, tu n'auras qu'à répondre : Jamais je n'aurais cru qu'on puisse gagner autant d'argent pour un cancre pareil. Ne reviens plus jamais nous voir. Nous saurons où te trouver.

Quand Ella fut partie, Mahomedsalih se leva et ficha un tel coup de pied dans le divan qu'il le cassa. D'un naturel fougueux, il préférait exprimer ses émotions par des gestes plutôt que par des jurons qu'il considérait comme la marque des impies. Ce qui, au bout du compte, avait fait de lui un champion de wushu. Et de s'écrier :

— Il l'a tué sur place, c'est sûr ! Il l'a tué avec cette fichue canne, sinon ils auraient rendu le corps ! (Puis il enfonça un poing rageur dans le mur et dit :) Et toi, que penses-tu de cette histoire, Niyazbek ?

— J'en pense, répondit Niyazbek, qu'il faut commencer par vérifier qui elle est.

Vladislav Pankov, premier commis du Kremlin, était sur le départ du dix-septième trou, tenant à la main un superbe club en titane incrusté de diamant, modèle exclusif.

Alissa se trouvait près de lui. Quant à la petite Nina, elle gambadait plus loin sous les yeux bienveillants d'un homme armé d'un pistolet-mitrailleur. A trente mètres du départ, le terrain était coupé d'un vrai précipice d'une largeur d'environ soixante-dix mètres qui offrait un superbe obstacle naturel avec une petite cascade aménagée par le *turf manager.*

La balle passait sans peine d'un bord à l'autre du gouffre, mais le trou avait ceci de vicieux que, pour l'atteindre en trois coups au lieu de quatre, il fallait faire un tir diagonal et non transversal ajusté sur une bande étroite comprise entre le déversoir de la cascade et une longue pièce de sable aménagée plus à gauche. De là, au coup suivant, on arrivait au green.

En Amérique, Pankov avait été plutôt bon golfeur (avec un handicap personnel de trois coups), et il ne doutait pas qu'il passerait le précipice. Pour autant, il craignait que la balle ne chasse à gauche et ne finisse sa course dans le bunker placé là pour piéger les joueurs trop sûrs d'eux.

Il se demandait encore s'il avait bien fait de venir ici. Les tentatives de corruption de la part de la famille Aslanov se répétaient avec une ingéniosité croissante et il ne se passait pas de semaine sans qu'il soit approché par des gens qui lui proposaient de l'argent contre un poste.

Le cas le plus critique était survenu quinze jours auparavant par suite de l'enlèvement du directeur du port maritime, une fonction qui relevait de l'administration fédérale. Trois personnes différentes lui proposèrent aussitôt un million chacune pour leur recommandation à ce poste. Pankov les éconduisit, puis se rendit avec sa femme à la cérémonie d'anniversaire du président du Parlement. Alissa portait une belle robe verte assortie d'un collier vert qu'il ne lui connaissait pas. "Alors, où en est-on ?" lui demanda, désinvolte, l'un des candidats qu'il venait d'éconduire.

— Sortez-le de là, fit Pankov à ses gardes cependant qu'on le poussait déjà à l'écart.

C'est alors qu'il entendit sa protestation indignée :

— Ma nomination, elle est au cou de sa femme !

Au retour, Pankov fit un furieux scandale à sa femme. Le collier vert fut renvoyé à l'expéditeur. Le directeur du port, soit dit au passage, fut bientôt de retour chez lui, expliquant vaguement qu'il s'était absenté à Piatigorsk. On classa l'affaire sans suite, mais on voyait bien que l'homme n'en menait pas large et qu'il paraissait même rapetisser de moitié en la présence de Niyazbek.

Bref, Pankov n'était pas chaud pour jouer au golf ce jour-là, mais un haut responsable humanitaire de l'OSCE venait d'arriver, et la vue d'un bout de champ vert émeraude perdu dans les roseaux l'avait fait frémir au sortir de l'aéroport, de là sa question :

— *Isn't this a golf course ?*

Lord Cobbleham se révéla un fin connaisseur de golf, et voilà maintenant qu'ils étaient trois à fouler la pelouse : l'Anglais, Pankov et Gamzat Aslanov.

Pankov ajusta le tir puis posa son club et s'essuya le front. La température de l'air était d'au moins trente-cinq degrés, ils jouaient depuis bientôt quatre heures et l'endurance du Britannique avait de quoi surprendre.

— Au fait, dit Alissa, il faut que je rentre à Moscou. Nina doit aller à l'école. Sans parler de la chaleur qu'il fait ici.

— En effet, dit Pankov, Nina doit aller à l'école, et j'ai déjà décidé qu'elle irait à Torbi-Kala.

— Ici ? Dans le Caucase ? s'affola Alissa.

— Le président russe m'a placé à la tête du Caucase et je n'ai pas l'intention de réduire mon travail à un programme de déplacements. Si le chef de la région ne s'autorise pas à faire vivre ses enfants sur place, de quel droit obligerait-il les autres à vivre ici ?

— Mais ce sont des sauvages !

— Si ce sont des sauvages, pourquoi acceptes-tu leurs cadeaux ?

— Mais ce sont des bandits !

— Si quelqu'un répond de sa parole tout en exigeant la même chose des autres, rétorqua Pankov, je ne crois pas que ce soit un bandit. J'ai parfois l'impression que c'est quelqu'un de normal.

Sur ce, il frappa la balle. Elle survola le précipice, et Pankov dépité vit se produire ce qu'il avait redouté : déportée sur la gauche, la balle atterrit dans le bunker de sable.

Des hauteurs du Torbi-Taou, Niyazbek en position couchée scrutait à la jumelle le bas de la montagne. De là-haut, on ne distinguait bien que huit trous : du premier au troisième, puis du quinzième au dix-huitième. Les autres étaient cachés par la forêt. Plus loin, près de la côte, on apercevait deux bandes herbeuses aux extrémités terminées par des cercles tondus court.

Au fond de lui, Niyazbek avait toujours considéré qu'un terrain de golf était une espèce de tatami, mais un tatami de cent hectares. Or – surprise – il n'y avait pas de terrain à proprement parler. Il y avait des bandes décousues d'herbe tondue à ras qui se faufilaient entre les arbres, les plans d'eau et même un précipice, avec des chemins pour les relier l'une à l'autre. Quand ils avaient joué un trou, les golfeurs passaient au suivant par un petit chemin, le jeu consistant, comme le comprit Niyazbek, à faire le moins de coups possible par trou.

Depuis quatre heures qu'il était couché là, les joueurs avaient fait le tour du terrain pour revenir auprès du précipice. Le premier coup fut donné par Pankov qui de rage laissa tomber son club. Vint le tour de Gamzat, vêtu d'un long short à carreaux et d'une chemise à col. Et bien que sa balle eût atterri tout près de la précédente (pour autant qu'il put en juger), son coup fut applaudi. La balle du troisième finit son vol dans la cascade, et Niyazbek s'en trouva même piqué de curiosité : comment allait-il jouer, maintenant, le malheureux ? Ou c'était la même chose qu'un K.-O. ?

Après quoi les joueurs passèrent de l'autre côté du précipice par un petit pont de pierre pavé de gros galets gris. Ils avançaient de conserve, les trois joueurs et les trois garçons porteurs de sacs de clubs. La garde leur emboîtait le pas.

Niyazbek se disait que plus bouffon que ça, comme sport, ça n'existait pas : non seulement les joueurs marchaient au lieu de courir (en faisant porter leur matos à d'autres, par-dessus le marché), mais il avait vu, de ses yeux vu l'Anglais sortir une flasque pour y faire des libations, et il aurait juré que ce n'était pas de l'eau !

D'un coup direct, Pankov envoya sa balle dans une zone bien lisse où pointait un drapeau blanc, et Gamzat en fit autant. S'agissant du troisième joueur, la curiosité de Niyazbek fut bientôt récompensée. Pas de K.-O. du tout : imperturbable, l'Anglais s'approcha du précipice où se dressait une espèce de piquet rouge, mesura deux longueurs de canne et mit une balle neuve sur l'herbe.

Quand les trois balles se retrouvèrent dans un cercle tondu très court comme il y en avait à chaque trou, un petit gars costaud d'environ seize ans, celui-là même qui portait les clubs de Gamzat, enleva le drapeau et les golfeurs ramassèrent leurs balles. Ne restait que celle de l'Anglais, la plus éloignée de toutes. Gamzat se planta entre l'Anglais et le trou pour passer un savon à l'un de ses gardes mais Pankov le toucha à l'épaule et l'autre fit un pas à l'écart. L'Anglais poussa sa balle qui alla rouler à côté du trou.

Sans attendre la fin du jeu, Niyazbek ramena ses jumelles vers le pont de pierre.

Niyazbek n'avait plus revu Ella Oumarova, mais il avait très soigneusement vérifié son histoire. Ses hommes s'étaient entretenus avec les voisins et les flics. On avait même dégoté l'un des "témoins" payés pour reconnaître celle qu'on accusait d'avoir emporté son enfant renversé par une voiture.

Ce n'était pas la première fois qu'on lavait Gamzat d'une telle affaire. Loin de là. Niyazbek ne le savait que trop.

Quant au petit garçon, il n'était pas que l'enfant unique d'Ella. Il était aussi le neveu unique de Rasul qui n'avait pas d'enfant du tout, chose rare par les temps qui courent : Niyazbek, par exemple, en avait quatre, et Khizri, sept, en comptant celui qu'il avait eu de Larissa la Moscovite.

Donc, Niyazbek n'avait plus jamais revu ni Ella ni son frère, mais quelqu'un avait frappé la veille à la porte de Rasul : un gars d'une vingtaine d'années, un visage rond aux oreilles en feuilles de chou, des mains de bûcheron.

Niyazbek porta ses jumelles plus à gauche, là où la cascade, le gazon et le *golf house* situé en contrebas cédaient la place à une enceinte en béton de trois mètres de haut elle-même protégée par des rouleaux de barbelés et des capteurs de mouvement. Le long de ce mur, des hommes montaient la garde avec des fusils-mitrailleurs.

Sur le toit du bâtiment, Niyazbek avisa un sniper.

Si bien défendu qu'il fût, le dispositif de sécurité du terrain laissait entrevoir une faille, et une faille au sens propre du mot : le précipice et sa chute d'eau qui séparait le terrain entre les deuxième et dix-septième trous. L'architecte avait placé le *golf house* au bord du précipice, permettant aux visiteurs de marque installés sur la véranda de poser leurs yeux enchantés sur les rochers couverts de mousse, la cascade et le pont de pierre mouillé par une poussière de gouttelettes.

Sans doute était-ce très judicieux du point de vue de l'architecte que de placer le bâtiment au cœur de l'endroit le plus pittoresque. Et sans doute était-ce très judicieux du point de vue des golfeurs que de commencer et de terminer le jeu aux abords du *golf house*.

Mais quelle bêtise du point de vue de la sécurité que de couper une partie du terrain, comprenant un grand nombre de gardes, de l'autre partie, qui en comprenait peu ; et de relier ces deux parties par une passerelle de pierre qu'aucun joueur ne pouvait éviter pendant le match.

Niyazbek venait d'établir une chose capitale. Les golfeurs se déplaçaient ensemble. Cela voulait dire qu'au premier tournoi officiel où joueraient immanquablement le président Ahmednabi Aslanov et son fils Gamzat, ils passeraient le pont tous en bande.

Gazi-Mahomed n'en serait sûrement pas, mais on pourrait toujours l'éliminer plus tard. Le peu de temps qu'il passait sans boire, il préférait le consacrer à ses enfants et à ceux de son frère, et il ne représentait guère d'autorité ou de danger pour quiconque.

L'explosion suivante survint le 20 août à quatre-vingts kilomètres de Torbi-Kala, sur la frontière tchétchène, dans le village de Karagatchinskaïa où se trouvait une base du Youg, unité spéciale du FSB. Nichée à flanc de montagne au-dessus des habitations, la base était protégée d'une triple barrière de barbelés avec bande de contrôle surveillée et champs de mines.

Drôle de dispositif pour une base installée en territoire ami, sachant surtout que la plupart des combattants de l'unité provenaient de ce même village.

Naturellement, ces hommes allaient souvent au village, seuls ou par deux, parfois dans des voitures ordinaires. Mais vint le moment où ils se firent piéger par des explosifs, les uns par des mines antipersonnel, les autres par des charges posées sur la route. Toutes les explosions se produisaient dans un espace où la route débouchait des entrailles de la forêt, plongeant dans la vallée et devenant visible de la montagne d'en face noyée dans la verdure.

Il était clair qu'un terroriste se nichait là-bas et qu'il actionnait la mise à feu dès qu'il apercevait sa proie.

Un officier de la base, le major russe Kononov, prit un transporteur blindé avec dix hommes pour passer au peigne fin les bois du versant opposé. C'était un piège. Les mines et les bombes n'avaient d'autre but que de débusquer le commando de sa base par la ruse en le mettant sur la fausse piste d'un boïévik certes téméraire mais passablement cinglé. A peine engagé sur la vieille route d'un village abandonné, le blindé sauta sur une FAB-250 identique à celle qui avait tué Ibrahim Malikov.

Le transporteur fut fendu en deux moitiés restées jointes, mais retournées à l'opposé l'une de l'autre comme une feuille de papier minutieusement coupée et pliée : avant contre arrière et arrière contre avant. Un cratère d'une profondeur de cinq mètres se forma dans la route.

Quand Pankov se rendit sur les lieux, les corps n'étaient toujours pas levés. L'un des hommes, projeté par l'onde de choc, gisait en travers de la route, les yeux vitreux rivés dans le ciel vespéral, les cheveux renvoyant une rebutante odeur de roussi. L'agitation se calma autour de l'homme du Kremlin. Il faisait plus de trente degrés, le goudron désagrégé semblait sorti d'un four mais Pankov en nage fut pris soudain d'un frisson glacé.

— T'as pas peur ? fit une voix dans son dos, empreinte d'un vague accent.

Le fonctionnaire aux cheveux roux se retourna. C'était Arzo Khadjiev dont la manche gauche du treillis, vide, battait au vent.

— C'est peut-être un piège ça aussi, enchaîna Khadjiev. Une vieille pratique. On fait sauter une charge et, quand les chefs arrivent, rebelote. T'as pas peur de te retrouver comme lui ? (Arzo de pointer le menton sur le mort qui n'avait plus que de courtes pattes de poulet à la place des jambes.)

— Est-ce que tu parles en connaissance de cause ?

— Oui, acquiesça Arzo d'un air indifférent.

Il y eut près de là un cri sauvage de femme, et Pankov se dit que la base comptait beaucoup de gars du village et que leurs mères et leurs sœurs n'allaient pas tarder à monter. Un vieux Tchétchène était assis près du cratère, secoué de sanglots. Arzo s'accroupit, ramassa une tige brisée par l'explosion et se mit à battre distraitement la poussière de la route.

— Les gens, pour toi, qu'est-ce que c'est ? demanda Pankov de but en blanc.

Le Tchétchène le darda de ses yeux anthracite.

— De la chair, dit Arzo, de la chair brûlée, en l'occurrence. Même pas besoin de la faire griller.

Et de planter le bout de sa tige dans la chair du mort, cuite avec son treillis.

Il y eut des bruits de pas, et le représentant du Kremlin vit approcher un groupe d'hommes en tenue camo. Le colonel Chebolev, chef adjoint du FSB régional, marchait en tête avec le ministre de l'Intérieur Talgoïev sur ses talons. A la vue de Pankov, une expression sincère de stupeur se peignit sur la face du ministre : il ne pouvait croire qu'un fonctionnaire russe de ce niveau se fût déplacé sur les lieux d'un acte terroriste. Il était arrivé que le précédent premier commis du Kremlin reste au lit les jours d'attentat et même, une fois, tout le temps d'une guerre qu'il était censé commander.

— Ce type qui a sauté par la fenêtre l'autre jour, Kazbek Mahomedgaziev, il est mort, non ? demanda Pankov.

— Il est mort, le diable, répondit Talgoïev. Après deux jours de souffrances, il a fini par crever.

— Mais nous mettrons quand même le grappin sur ses complices, promit l'adjoint de Talgoïev, un colonel d'une cinquantaine d'années, haut de taille et bedonnant.

— Pas évident, dit Pankov. (Mine renfrognée du ministre de l'Intérieur.) Je me rappelle très bien les dires de ce Kazbek. Il prétendait avoir transporté la bombe dans une minifourgonnette. Une bombe, pas deux. Si le gars avait vraiment décidé de collaborer avec les enquêteurs, il aurait parlé de toutes les bombes dont il avait connaissance, et pas seulement de celle dont nous avions déjà connaissance, vous ne trouvez pas ?

Le séant dans la poussière, affalé contre la carcasse éventrée du transporteur, Vladislav Pankov regardait le couchant rouler derrière la crête blanche de la montagne.

Une telle chaleur dans l'air qu'on y eût fait cuire un œuf.

Il pensait à deux choses. Un innocent était mort deux jours auparavant dans d'atroces souffrances après avoir sauté par la fenêtre sous ses yeux, et par suite d'un ordre qu'il avait donné. A dire vrai, c'était peut-être un boïévik et un meurtrier. Mais il n'avait pas tué Igor. Dans le cas contraire, ce jeune homme brisé aurait parlé de la deuxième bombe. Deuxièmement, Pankov se disait qu'il devenait difficile de soupçonner la famille du président d'avoir éliminé Malikov. Parce que les deux bombes, à l'évidence, avaient été posées et actionnées d'une manière analogue, et qu'il ne serait pas venu à l'idée du président de tailler en pièces les troupes fédérales. Même pour se faire un alibi.

A deux mètres de là, un vieux Tchétchène au visage ridé comme un carton gaufré enveloppait un mort dans un sac.

— Sale endroit, dit le Tchétchène.

— Quoi ? fit Pankov.

Il avait le cœur barbouillé. L'homme du Kremlin aux cheveux roux et à la peau blanche supportait mal la chaleur qui ne lui laissait aucun répit ni de jour, ni de nuit. Son seul salut était le climatiseur, faute de quoi l'on aurait pu tirer un verre de sueur de sa chemise essorée.

— Sale endroit, répéta le vieux. Il y a neuf ans, ma voiture est tombée dans le vide ici même. Il n'en restait plus que le pare-chocs. Aujourd'hui c'est mon neveu qui est tué.

Pankov sentit une main sur son épaule. Il se retourna et vit le colonel Chebolev.

— Arzo t'invite, dit le chef adjoint du FSB régional.

— A la base ?

— Non. Au village. Chez lui.

Pankov fut pris d'un frisson.

— Et... il vit ici depuis longtemps ?

— Depuis toujours, dit Chebolev.

Pankov crut sentir sa sueur se changer en glace.

Le lourd portail de fer n'avait pas changé en neuf ans. Toujours le même auvent avec le même modèle de blindé garé dessous, à la différence près que celui-ci portait une immatriculation fédérale d'ailleurs couverte de boue.

Mais la cour avait changé de fond en comble. Plus de terre battue : un joli dallage courait du portail à la maison, le tout sous un auvent. A ciel ouvert, il y avait une piscine à l'eau bleutée. Derrière la piscine, les femmes s'affairaient à dresser la table.

Pankov descendit de voiture et passa derrière la maison, là où jadis était le hangar qui abritait le soupirail et l'entrée de la cave. Du hangar, il ne restait plus rien. Une maisonnette en brique à deux étages l'avait supplanté, dont les fondations muraient le soupirail. Le potager commençait là, avec un haut grillage derrière lequel grattaient des poules.

Il fit le tour de la maison à la recherche de l'entrée mais se retrouva soudain dans une petite cour. Sous une tonnelle frisée de vigne, contre le mur blanchâtre de la maison principale, un garçon de seize ans était assis dans un fauteuil roulant. Un plaid le couvrait jusqu'à la ceinture, d'où sortaient deux chaussures jaunes bien cirées. Un pistolet-mitrailleur était posé en travers du fauteuil.

Accroupi devant le garçon, Arzo lui relaçait ses chaussures vides. Avec une main unique, ce n'était pas facile.

Alerté par un bruit de pas étrangers, Arzo se retourna vivement. Il reprit sa mitraillette au garçon et se leva.

— Comment va ta santé, Arbi ? demanda Pankov.

Arzo répondit pour son fils :

— On fait aller. Trois bras et deux jambes pour deux, ce n'est pas si mal, pas vrai, Arbi ?

Le garçon se fendit d'un sourire sans joie et sans défense. De sa main unique, Arzo invita Pankov à le suivre, et il quitta l'auvent.

— Est-ce que je peux vous aider ? demanda subitement Pankov.

— Non, dit Arzo. Il est de ces choses pour lesquelles tu ne peux rien de plus que dans la cave où je te faisais croupir.

Pankov ne s'attarda guère chez Arzo : une demi-heure plus tard, il partait déjà en compagnie du colonel Chebolev.

— Où en est votre enquête ? demanda Pankov.

Chebolev observa un silence de quelques secondes.

— Quelle enquête ? Celle du meurtre d'Ibrahim Malikov est bouclée. L'exécutant de l'attentat est Kazbek Mahomedgaziev, et le commanditaire, Wahha Arsaïev. Le ministère de l'Intérieur s'accroche à cette version des faits. Gamzat

Aslanov aussi. Ma hiérarchie n'a pas envie d'en découdre avec lui.

La mâchoire du colonel claqua d'une manière agressive comme le couvercle d'un coffret, et Pankov remarqua que Chebolev avait encore cuit au soleil. Les poils roux de ses bras replets revêtaient l'aspect décoloré d'un champ de sel.

On roulait en silence. La route, raide, tricotait dans la montagne et levait le cœur de Pankov. Quand on l'avait transbahuté par cette même route, neuf ans plus tôt, poings scotchés, c'était par une chaleur d'août aussi pesante qu'aujourd'hui.

— A propos, dit-il, qu'est-ce que c'est que cette histoire de sang entre Niyazbek et Sapartchi Telaïev ? Vous savez, le patron d'Avarie-Transflotte ?

— Niyazbek a tué son fils, répondit Chebolev.

— Comment ?!

Le colonel prit l'exclamation pour une question et répondit :

— A coups de Stetchkine, le pistolet.

— Il y a longtemps ?

— Il y a cinq ans. Niyazbek venait d'arriver dans un resto de Moscou. En descendant de voiture, il a ouvert la portière si brusquement qu'elle a heurté l'auto d'Arsène. Le gars a fait un esclandre. Alors Niyazbek lui a dit : Qu'est-ce que tu veux ? Y en a pour cinq dollars de carrosserie. Tiens, en voilà deux cents. Arsène, bien éméché, l'a frappé au bras et l'argent est tombé dans la gadoue. Ils ont fait du foin, les flics ont rappliqué. L'autre était tellement cuité qu'ils ont voulu l'embarquer. Mais Niyazbek a ramassé l'argent dans la boue pour le leur donner en disant : Entre gens du même pays, on saura se réconcilier. Sur quoi les flics sont partis et Niyazbek est entré dans le resto. Il y a passé une heure et demie avec des Russes. Il en est ressorti vers deux heures du matin. Arsène l'attendait dehors avec trois autres types. Aussitôt, il lui a tiré dessus. Touché au ventre et au cou, l'autre est tombé. Arsène et ses hommes ont fait feu sur les Russes. C'est là que Niyazbek s'est réveillé : il a roulé sous une voiture et s'est mis à tirer à son tour. Il en a tué trois, le quatrième s'est sauvé. Alors Niyazbek s'est hissé dans une auto en y chargeant un Russe à la force des bras, et en route pour l'hôpital. Le Russe est mort, Niyazbek a survécu.

Pankov digérait l'information sans piper.

— Donc, Sapartchi veut tuer Niyazbek ?

— Allez savoir ce qu'il veut, le diable lui-même n'y retrouverait pas ses petits, commenta Chebolev. Ces gens-là, on ne pourra jamais les comprendre. Ils se sont réconciliés, à ce qu'on dit. Un cheik les aurait rabibochés dans les montagnes. Niyazbek l'aurait même soutenu aux élections.

— A quelles élections ?

— A celles de Chouguinsk. On y a tué le député. Un ami de Niyazbek nommé Khizri s'y est présenté avant de se désister pour Sapartchi. A la demande de Niyazbek.

— Et qui a tué le député ?

— Allez savoir. D'aucuns disent que c'est Khizri. Comme d'habitude : quand on ne sait pas qui est le tueur, on montre toujours du doigt soit Arsaïev, soit Khizri.

L'élection du député de la circonscription de Chouguinsk à l'Assemblée devait avoir lieu le 5 septembre, mais elle était jouée d'avance. Sur les cinq candidats en lice, deux ne jouissaient d'aucun soutien, et le gendre de Sapartchi représentait le même clan que Telaïev.

Le cinquième candidat aurait pu concurrencer Telaïev. Natif de la circonscription, le médecin-chef de l'hôpital n° 1 jouissait de l'estime générale. Sa grande faiblesse, toutefois, était de ne pas disposer d'hommes armés indispensables à la victoire. Au dépouillement des votes, en effet, un pistolet-mitrailleur posé sur la tempe d'un membre de la commission électorale valait un millier de voix. Lucide, le médecin-chef retira sa candidature et reçut de Telaïev, en échange, deux cent cinquante mille dollars.

A une semaine du scrutin, c'est Telaïev lui-même qui se désista. En faveur de son gendre.

La nouvelle fut annoncée à la radio à deux heures de l'après-midi. Le hasard avait voulu que Khizri Beïbulatov se trouve alors au volant de sa voiture à l'écoute des infos. Il freina si fort que la grenade posée à toutes fins utiles sur le siège avant du véhicule vola au sol avec les journaux qui la recouvraient. Khizri se gara sur le bas-côté, descendit de voiture, ouvrit la portière droite et ramassa la grenade.

Il resta quelques secondes solidement campé sur ses prothèses au bord du précipice, dans la poussière, puis dégoupilla la grenade, étira le bras et la projeta dans le vide. La gorge était si profonde qu'elle éclata en plein vol, et l'écho se mit à ricocher d'une montagne à l'autre.

Le 1er septembre, Vladislav Pankov conduisit sa fille à l'école. C'était l'école n° 1 de Torbi-Kala, en plein centre-ville, et, tout le temps qu'il resta dans la cour ornée de fleurs, Pankov put noter la singularité de cette école de privilégiés par rapport à celles du même genre qu'on trouvait à Moscou : toutes les voitures qui venaient là étaient blindées et chacune ne déposait pas moins de deux, trois ou quatre enfants. Pankov figurait parmi les rares hommes présents. Les écoliers étaient accompagnés par leur mère ou leurs gardes du corps.

Nina supportait la chaleur mieux que son père. Assailli par les maîtres, le représentant du Kremlin fut contraint de dire quelques mots, ce qu'il fit en tiraillant sa cravate. Il eut bientôt le cou cerné de boutons roses par l'effet de la sueur, du soleil et du déodorant, et l'envie le démangeait de relâcher le nœud. Enfin, n'y tenant plus et faisant fi des convenances, il arracha sa cravate, se retourna et fut cloué sur place.

A deux petits mètres de lui se trouvaient deux femmes en jupes de deuil, coiffées de foulards arrangés avec soin. L'une d'elles, plus replète et plus âgée, portait un nourrisson qui clappait délicieusement de la bouche. Un gamin de huit ans s'agrippait à la seconde, et deux autres enfants se tenaient devant elles : un gamin de onze ans et une fillette plus petite. Un peu plus loin, Mahomedsalih bavardait avec un garde. La seconde femme – élancée, fine, la tête nouée d'un foulard finement liseré de dentelle blanche – était cette même jeune fille que Pankov avait vue dans la maison de Niyazbek.

Elle tourna la tête, renvoyant à Pankov l'image de son visage blême et délicat aux yeux de cerise et aux sourcils soyeux qu'elle n'épilait pas. Elle laissa courir sur ses lèvres un sourire timide. Planté là devant elle, il la regardait d'un air béat, comme un soldat prosterné devant le poster d'une star au fond de sa caserne. Rien ne flétrissait sa beauté, ni sa tenue noire, ni ses sourcils trop fournis, ni ses ongles trop courts sur ses doigts fluets d'enfant. Ainsi vêtue, elle semblait une perle dans sa coquille, et Pankov se sentit pris du désir exaspéré d'écarter les valves de ce coquillage pour en posséder la perle.

— Vous ne vous souvenez pas de moi ? lui demanda Pankov, sa cravate pendouillant à la main.

Il maudit la terre entière quand il comprit que cette fichue poussée de boutons roses se voyait à travers son col ouvert.

— Si. Il n'y avait guère de Russes chez nous ce jour-là.

— Moi... c'est Vladislav. Vladislav Pankov. Et vous ?

— Aminat.

— Et vous...

— C'est Farida, dit la jeune fille en montrant la femme au nourrisson, la femme de Niyazbek. Moi, je suis sa sœur. Et voilà ses fils. Chamil et Djamolidine.

Pankov ne put réprimer un soupir de soulagement. Il avait craint que la jeune fille ne fût aussi l'épouse de Niyazbek. La moitié des mariages se faisait ici d'après la charia, sans la moindre régularisation à l'état civil. N'importe quel personnage fortuné pouvait "prendre" une deuxième femme, voire une troisième, comme ça lui chantait.

— Que faites-vous dans la vie ? demanda Pankov.

— Doctorante à l'université de Torbi-Kala. En logique mathématique. Au départ, j'étais analyste-programmeur.

"Niyazbek sait-il seulement ce que logmath veut dire ?" faillit dire Pankov qui se mordit la lèvre à temps. Après tout, Niyazbek ne portait ni l'antique tunique caucasienne ni la chemise à cartouchières. Il savait même très probablement se servir d'un ordinateur.

L'un des gardes toucha Mahomedsalih à l'épaule et lui dit quelque chose à voix basse. L'autre se retourna vivement.

A cet instant, Pankov crut le voir pour la première fois. Pas l'Abrek, pas le ministre (fût-il ex-ministre), pas le sportif. Non. L'homme.

Il vit un garçon superbement bâti, à la peau mate, aux muscles saillants sous une chemise blanche à manches courtes et à col ouvert, un garçon éclatant d'une beauté masculine implacable. Même son nez restait d'une pureté intacte malgré l'extrême cruauté du sport qu'il avait choisi. Célibataire, bien sûr, sans quoi Niyazbek ne l'aurait pas envoyé à l'école pour accompagner sa famille… et la fille magnifique et non mariée qu'il avait pour sœur.

D'un geste énergique, Pankov fourra la cravate dans la poche de sa veste et boutonna le haut de sa chemise. Il se sentit étranglé par son col trop serré.

— Bonjour, Mahomedsalih, dit le représentant du Kremlin, et ce championnat ?

— Je l'ai remporté, répondit l'ex-ministre des Travaux publics.

Et Pankov se rappela pourquoi il n'avait pas le nez cassé. "Parce que je n'ai jamais permis à personne de taper dessus", avait-il expliqué dans une interview.

Le 4 septembre, Pankov se rendit au club de golf. La chaleur était retombée, l'éruption rose résorbée, et il joua six trous en se relaxant et en oubliant toutes les misères du monde dans la splendeur magique du paysage et des rochers entrecoupés d'une pelouse impeccablement tondue.

Au sixième trou, il était attendu par le ministre de l'Information. Depuis que le président Aslanov et son fils jouaient au golf, toute l'élite de la république s'y était mise. Le ministre de l'Information pesait cent cinquante kilos et ne se déplaçait jamais autrement qu'en golfette électrique d'un trou à l'autre, mais il jouait aussi au golf.

Ils discutèrent quelque temps les détails du prochain tournoi fixé pour le 17 septembre entre le club de Moscou et l'équipe de la république régionale. A ce propos, le ministre moucharda à l'oreille de Pankov : l'on s'était demandé en Conseil des ministres qui du président ou de l'homme du Kremlin devait gagner le tournoi, et l'on avait décidé que le vainqueur serait le président.

Une fois le jeu fini, Pankov prit une douche et monta à la terrasse du club. L'endroit était désert : un barman en noir, semblable à une mante religieuse, s'ennuyait au comptoir, et une ribambelle de jeunes filles, derrière une table, se distrayaient de papotages.

A la vue de Pankov, elles se turent et se retournèrent. C'est alors qu'il reconnut Aminat. Elle était vêtue plus modestement que les autres d'une longue jupe noire liserée d'un ornement rouge avec une blouse du même goût, mais ses cheveux, découverts cette fois, bordaient en vagues drues l'ovale de son visage. C'était la première fois qu'il voyait ses cheveux, s'étonnant de la ressemblance d'Aminat avec sa défunte épouse.

— Vous savez jouer au golf ? demanda Pankov.

Aminat parut gênée, mais une autre fille en pantalon vert et blouse blanche répondit en riant :

— Non. Mais vous allez nous apprendre.

A cet instant deux jeunes gens apparurent sur la terrasse avec des cocktails pour les dames. L'un d'eux natif du pays, mais l'autre était russe, incontestablement, avec ses cheveux couleur de blé, ses taches de rousseur étalées sur sa face rose et ses muscles bien gonflés qui débordaient des manches courtes de sa chemise de sport griffée Hugo Boss.

Pankov se rendit à l'étage supérieur pour un rendez-vous avec des Karatchaïs. Une demi-heure plus tard, quand il redescendit, il aperçut à sa gauche une aire d'entraînement.

Le garçon aux cheveux de blé montrait à Aminat l'art de la frappe, et force était de reconnaître qu'il faisait pâle figure. Pankov jouait beaucoup mieux. Le golf était sans doute le seul sport, à l'exclusion des échecs, qui lui donnait ses chances dans le Caucase. Le gars débitait les balles l'une après l'autre.

Pankov s'approcha de l'aire d'entraînement. Il se sentait comme l'aiguille d'une boussole près de laquelle on aurait branché un aimant électrique.

— Mahomedsalih n'est pas contre ? demanda-t-il en montrant des yeux le Russe blond comme les blés.

Des étincelles de malice s'animèrent dans les prunelles sombres de la jeune fille.

— Mahomedsalih ne sait pas jouer au golf, dit Aminat.

— Votre ami non plus. Serez-vous là demain ?

— Non. Je pars demain pour Moscou.

— Il est vrai que moi aussi, dit l'homme du Kremlin. A trois heures. Je peux vous prendre en avion.

Aminat n'appela ni dans la soirée, ni dans la matinée du lendemain, mais, quand le cortège de Pankov s'arrêta devant le Yak-42 gouvernemental, l'homme du Kremlin avisa devant la passerelle une Mercedes noire à l'immatriculation familière.

La portière de la Mercedes s'ouvrit en grand, laissant apparaître Niyazbek. Pankov crut apercevoir, au fond de la limousine, la silhouette sombre de Mahomedsalih.

— Mais où est... se hasarda Pankov.

— As-tu l'intention de te convertir à l'islam ? demanda Niyazbek.

— Je crois que non.

— Es-tu marié ?

— Ben oui, je...

— Alors touche pas à ma sœur.

Pankov se posa à Moscou à cinq heures de l'après-midi. Après l'atterrissage, il se trouva en butte à une histoire passablement désagréable. Quand sa garde eut sorti son imper et sa mallette, elle se mit à décharger de drôles de boîtes.

— C'est quoi ? demanda-t-il.

— Votre femme nous a demandé de transporter ça, répondit Sergueï Piskounov, chef de la sécurité.

Pankov fit ouvrir l'une des boîtes. Elle contenait deux bocaux de trois litres pleins de caviar. Les autres renfermaient du cognac. Pankov fit le numéro du portable d'Alissa qui était à Paris. A la voix de son mari, elle se mit à pépier joyeusement.

— Alissa, dit l'homme du Kremlin, je viens d'atterrir à Moscou. On m'a chargé d'un tas de caviar. As-tu commandé du caviar ?

— Oh ! c'est ce garçon si sympathique, tu sais, Khamza... ou Gamza... j'oublie toujours leurs prénoms à la con... bref, le fils du président, je ne lui ai rien demandé du tout, c'est lui qui me l'a proposé.

— Et le cognac ?

— Il y a aussi du cognac ? Oh ! comme c'est chouette ! Vladislav, mon petit Slavotchka, dis-lui un grand bonjour de ma part, je vais passer une petite semaine à Paris, d'accord ? Ne te fâche pas, mon trésor...

— Tu peux rester à Paris tout le temps que tu voudras, coupa Pankov. Nous divorçons.

Ibrahimbek Sultygov, *alias* Quoi-d'Neuf, chef du comité de lutte contre les stupéfiants, comprenait parfaitement qu'il ne jouissait pas des mêmes prérogatives que le ministère de l'Intérieur ou le FSB régional. La mission assignée à son administration était fort limitée : éradiquer la prolifération de la drogue. Au vrai, il ne savait même pas comment s'y prendre.

Il avait fait toute sa rude carrière dans la police de la route, décrochant le grade de capitaine à l'âge de quarante-sept ans. On ne pouvait pas parler de carrière ratée pour cause de fautes ou de manquements graves. Non. Ni fautes ni manquements à son passif, mais aucun succès non plus.

Ibrahimbek faisait le même job que les autres flics de son service. Cela consistait à bloquer la circulation pour laisser la voie libre au président de la République et aux membres du gouvernement ; et, le reste du temps, à arrêter les camions-citernes sur la route de Chouguinsk pour les faire banquer, faute de papiers en règle.

Comme tout le monde il prenait des bakchichs, mais, en homme probe et en bon voisin qu'il était, il ne taxait jamais les gens natifs de son village ni les parents de sa femme. Comme tout le monde il rétrocédait une partie de sa recette à la hiérarchie, mais quelle ne fut pas sa stupeur le jour où le bureau de l'arrondissement Rive droite de son service de police fut perquisitionné par la section de lutte contre le crime organisé aux cris de "Tous à terre !". Il s'avéra que le colonel Gannouchkine, supérieur immédiat d'Ibrahimbek, organisait la régularisation à grande échelle de véhicules volés de toutes provenances. Et qu'il n'y allait pas avec le dos de la cuillère : rien qu'en Mercedes, on comptait plus de deux cents faux certifs. Si l'affaire avait fait surface, c'était parce qu'un général de la maison briguait la place de Gannouchkine pour son neveu.

— Deux cents certifs ! Une paille ! faisait Ibrahimbek ahuri.

Ce disant, il sirotait le thé du soir dans son minuscule deux-pièces de la banlieue de Torbi-Kala. Sa femme était là qui comptait la recette de la journée, ce qu'elle faisait en morigénant à voix basse son vaurien de mari. Originaire de la tribu des Cosaques du Terek, du genre opulent et fort en gueule, c'était elle qui tenait la baraque.

Quand elle avait recompté sa recette et fait les poches de sa veste en quête d'un petit pécule secret, son mari recevait cent roubles en retour pour aller boire une bière et tailler le bout de gras avec les collègues et les copains sur un banc de la cour, à l'ombre d'un orme. C'étaient les moments qu'il préférait dans la vie. On jouait aux *nardy*, on buvait de la bière, et, comme les femmes aux fenêtres veillaient à ce qu'on ne dise pas de cochonneries, Ibrahimbek Sultygov parlait politique. Il était question de la Russie, de la nécessité d'éradiquer la corruption.

— Deux cents Mercos, c'est dingue ! Ça ne l'empêchait pas de nous faire casquer cinq cents roubles chacun par jour. Aboule cinq cents par jour, qu'est-ce qu'il te reste pour vivre ? La voilà, la corruption en marche !

La vie du capitaine Sultygov changea du tout au tout par une belle journée ensoleillée où sa fille, étudiante en deuxième année à l'université, décréta qu'elle allait se marier (comme on a pu le voir d'après l'exemple de la bière, sa famille n'était guère à cheval sur les traditions musulmanes et la jeune fille jouissait d'une relative liberté).

L'élu de son cœur était un veuf de trente-deux ans, Gamzat Aslanov, qui avait fait sa connaissance à l'inauguration de la bibliothèque universitaire. Le fils du président avait offert la bibliothèque à l'université, et Tamara lui offrait des fleurs au nom de l'université.

Deux mois après les noces, le colonel Ibrahimbek Sultygov était nommé à la tête du comité de lutte contre les stupéfiants. Il considéra sa prise de fonction avec tant de sérieux qu'il contrôla personnellement l'inventaire des chaises de son cabinet. Il fit un scandale effroyable au vu de la disparition d'une petite cuillère dans la salle de repos, lequel scandale ne tarda pas à porter ses fruits : la petite cuillère fut retrouvée (en vérité, on venait d'en racheter une autre au magasin d'à côté mais, cela, Sultygov l'ignorait). Il inspecta personnellement sa nouvelle Mercedes et constata l'absence d'extincteur. Il s'apprêtait même à verbaliser son chauffeur quand il se rappela qu'il jouissait désormais d'un autre statut.

— Et le réseau des agents, allez-vous le recevoir ? lui demanda son adjoint à la fin d'une journée de travail bien remplie.

— Les agents ? s'étonna Sultygov. (Un capitaine de la police de la route n'avait pas de réseau d'agents.) Bien sûr que oui ! Je veux tous les voir demain dans mon bureau à dix heures pétantes !

— Mais...

— Y a pas de mais ! cingla-t-il à la face de son adjoint. Je vais faire le ménage, moi, dans ce bordel. Même les petites cuillères fichent le camp, ici...

Le colonel Sultygov consacra ainsi deux semaines à passer en revue les petites cuillères et les agents de renseignement mais, à la troisième semaine, il comprit que quelque chose clochait. Car enfin : son prédécesseur vivait dans une villa de quatre étages derrière un mur d'enceinte de cinq mètres et roulait en Mercedes blindée ; même l'esprit le plus distrait pouvait en conclure que le poste de président du comité de lutte contre les stupéfiants rapportait des pépètes, et beaucoup. Or le colonel Sultygov n'en trouvait nulle part la moindre trace. Il avait même ouvert tous les coffres et les tiroirs de son cabinet, pour voir, mais toujours pas d'argent pondu.

A la fin de la troisième semaine, n'y tenant plus, Sultygov demanda à son prédécesseur comment pondre de l'argent dans cette maison. L'autre le dévisagea d'un œil morne et lui dit :

— Vois-tu le tiroir du haut ? Je convoque un adjoint dans le bureau, je lui demande : Quoi de neuf ? et j'ouvre le tiroir. Il y met l'argent et s'en va.

La simplicité de la procédure sidéra Ibrahimbek Sultygov. Le lendemain, il ne fit ni une ni deux et convoqua un adjoint. "Quoi de neuf ?" lui demanda-t-il en ouvrant le tiroir. "Rien à signaler", répondit l'adjoint qui tourna les talons et sortit. Etonné, Sultygov fit venir un deuxième adjoint. "Quoi de neuf ?" (Il ouvrit le tiroir.) Même réponse de ce dernier qui sortit à son tour. Un mois passa. Ibrahimbek avait beau convoquer ses adjoints, il n'y avait toujours pas d'argent dans le tiroir.

Et deux mois plus tard, ce fut son gendre qui l'appela pour lui laisser entendre que la famille c'était bien joli, mais que le président de la République attendait toujours l'argent de la nomination. Pas moins d'un demi-million de dollars.

— Mais pourquoi, fit Ibrahimbek effaré, nous sommes de la famille, non ?

— C'est pour le principe, répondit Gamzat. La république doit savoir qui est le maître chez elle.

— Mais je n'ai pas tant d'argent ! s'exclama Ibrahimbek les bras au ciel. Je leur ouvre un tiroir tous les jours en leur demandant : Quoi de neuf ? et ils n'y mettent jamais rien.

— Quel tiroir ? articula Gamzat interloqué.

Dès lors l'histoire fut mise au grand jour. Six mois durant, la république en rit, et le général Sultygov fut affublé du sobriquet de Quoi-d'Neuf qui lui colla à la peau.

Trois ans bientôt que le général Sultygov était en place. Tant bien que mal, il avait fini par prendre ses marques, parvenant même à faire banquer les deux plus gros narcotrafiquants d'héroïne de la région.

Il comprenait qu'il n'aurait jamais les lauriers des services de l'Intérieur et du FSB qui enquêtaient sur l'attentat terroriste de la route de Bakou. Mais c'était quand même vexant : la milice avait déjà mis la main sur le *killer* et son complice qui lui avait vendu la Jigouli ; le FSB régional avait battu la charge à la base de Bargo ; et lui, Sultygov, n'avait encore trouvé personne.

Aussi convoqua-t-il l'un de ses subalternes, le colonel Abdulkadyrov, et lui ordonna :

— Gazi ! Envoie tes hommes sur la route de Bakou à la sortie de la ville. Arrêtez toutes les voitures qui transportent des hommes armés. D'après nos renseignements, une grosse cargaison de stups est en route. Et ceux qui font le coup sont les tueurs d'Ibrahim Malikov.

Le groupe d'intervention du comité anti-stups, posté sur la route de Bakou à quatre kilomètres de la ville, comptait quatre hommes armés conduits par le capitaine Ahmedov.

La première voiture arrêtée fut une Merco blindée noire. L'officier lui fit un signe de la mitraillette, une vitre teintée se coula dans la portière et Ahmedov vit trois hommes armés en compagnie d'une jeune fille aux lèvres fardées de vert.

— Vos papiers, dit frileusement Ahmedov.

Le conducteur poussa un petit rire bref et lui tendit sa carte d'agent opérationnel du FSB.

— Lâche-nous les baskets, lui lança-t-il.

Ahmedov soupira et leur lâcha les baskets.

Le véhicule suivant fut une BMW série 7 avec Khizri Beïbu-latov au volant. Un PM traînait sur le siège avant et une autre pétoire – un Stetchkine – dépassait de son ceinturon.

— C'est quoi ? lâcha Khizri.

Ahmedov avala sa salive. Tous les flics savaient que, pour avoir osé arrêter le cortège de Niyazbek, des miliciens avaient été passés à tabac ; et tous savaient que Khizri en était.

— Ben, fit Ahmedov, contrôle des véhicules... recherche d'armes interdites...

— Où vois-tu des armes ici ? s'enquit froidement Khizri.

Ahmedov posa les yeux sur le PM qui occupait la place avant et poussa un profond soupir.

— Vous avez un permis de port d'arme ?

— Cent *bucks*, ça te va ?

Ahmed opina du chef.

— Alors ouvre le coffre et sers-toi.

Une fois levé le coffre, Ahmed et un autre patrouilleur découvrirent un sac en plastique plein de coupures de cent dollars. Certaines en liasses, mais la plupart en vrac, comme du linge sale. Les yeux rivés sur le magot, Ahmedov sem-blait envoûté. Puis, la main glissée prudemment dans le sac, il y puisa une poignée.

— Qu'est-ce que j't'ai dit ? aboya Khizri qui observait la scène dans le rétroviseur. Cent billets !

Avec un soupir de regret, Ahmedov prit cent dollars et fit claquer le coffre. Khizri mit les gaz. Les pneus de la série 7 envoyèrent un nuage de poussière à la face des narco-flics.

La troisième voiture qui passa fut un tacot blanc sale des usines Moskvitch. Ahmedov exaspéré leva le bâton. Il avait déjà compris qu'il n'arriverait jamais à saisir de vraies armes à des gens dangereux. Il ne lui restait plus qu'à en fourrer en douce à qui n'en avait pas. La Moskvitch blanche conve-nait à merveille. Pour sûr, les occupants d'une guimbarde pareille n'avaient ni carton du FSB ni sac de billets dans le coffre.

La voiture freina trop tard. Elle dépassa le poste d'une ving-taine de mètres et fit lentement marche arrière. Elle stoppa à trois mètres mais personne n'en descendit, ce qui parut louche au capitaine Ahmedov qui s'avança en rectifiant fer-mement la prise de son PM.

L'instant d'après, un patrouilleur nommé Chapi lâchait une rafale de pistolet-mitrailleur sur ses collègues. Ahmedov et un autre agent furent tués sur le coup. Le troisième qui s'était approché de la portière gauche fit le geste de se retourner. Un coup de feu parti de la Moskvitch le jeta sur le bitume.

Chapi tourna le dos aux boïéviks, ouvrit le coffre de la voiture de patrouille et, s'arcboutant, sortit un sac d'armes. Celui-là même que les narco-policiers avaient prévu d'utiliser au besoin comme fausse pièce à charge.

— Prenez ça, dit Chapi, ça pourra toujours servir.

Le sac fut jeté dans le coffre et Chapi dit :

— Logez-moi une balle dans la jambe et partez.

— C'est trop risqué, répondit le conducteur de la voiture, ils vont te démasquer.

Chapi opina, se baissa pour ramasser le PM de l'un de ses camarades qui venait d'être tué. Encore une seconde, et la Moskvitch démarra en trombe, emportant trois terroristes et leur complice qui travaillait dans l'anti-stups.

A huit heures du soir commença le dépouillement des votes de la circonscription de Chouguinsk. Un cordon de la section de lutte contre le crime organisé avait été déployé autour du siège de la commission électorale afin d'éviter toute provocation, à quoi Telaïev ajouta sa garde personnelle.

Une foule d'un ou deux milliers de personnes s'était rassemblée devant le cordon : environ deux cents membres de la tribu de Telaïev, les autres pékins ayant été alléchés par la bouffe à gogo. Les moutons étaient saignés sur place, devant le siège de la commission. L'odeur de sang frais se mêlait à celle de viande rôtie, et des gens faisaient la chaîne avec des pancartes de format identique aux slogans identiques : *Vive Kassim Zaguirov, l'espoir et le rempart de Chounguinsk !*

Au premier étage du siège de la commission électorale, deux grosses dames déversèrent sur la table une montagne de bulletins, et un vieil homme sec à lunettes se mit à les lire à voix haute en les classant par piles.

"Zaguirov, Zaguirov, Zaguirov, Mahomedkhanov, Zaguirov, Zaguirov, Boulatov..."

Sapartchi Telaïev observait la scène dans son fauteuil roulant avec, derrière lui, un grand jeune homme aux épaules étroites et aux pupilles anormalement dilatées. Un rang serré d'hommes armés de PM montait la garde autour des Telaïev.

"Zaguirov, Zaguirov, Boulatov, Boulatov, Zaguirov", psalmodiait le président de la commission électorale.

D'un œil de voleur, le jeune homme chercha une porte par où sortir. Un garde voulut le suivre mais Sapartchi le retint d'un mouvement imperceptible du menton, sachant que son gendre était toxico et qu'il avait besoin d'être seul un instant.

La pile des Zaguirov était déjà trois fois plus haute que les autres. Une nouvelle urne fut renversée sur la table. Alors Telaïev, d'un geste puissant de la main, poussa son fauteuil jusqu'à la table et, dans la seconde qui suivit, mit en tas tous les bulletins en disant :

— Zaguirov.

Le vieux aux lunettes soupira et poursuivit le dépouillement. A neuf heures du soir, il sortit sur le perron devant les caméras de télévision, salua la foule de la main et dit :

— A l'heure où je vous parle quatre-vingts pour cent des bulletins ont été dépouillés. Quatre-vingt-quinze pour cent des électeurs ont donné leurs suffrages à Kassim Zaguirov. Vive Kassim Zaguirov, l'espoir et le rempart de Chouguinsk !

— Hourra ! cria la foule.

Sapartchi Telaïev entendit le cri, consulta sa montre et fronça les sourcils. Son gendre se faisait attendre. Il ne manquait plus qu'on l'hospitalise la nuit des élections pour une prise d'héroïne pourrie. "O Allah, se lamenta Telaïev, pourquoi m'as-tu pris mon fils et pourquoi ai-je laissé ce vaurien approcher ma fille ?" Il rongea son frein pendant cinq minutes, puis souffla un ordre à l'oreille d'un garde.

L'homme acquiesça et sortit de la pièce. Pas une âme qui vive dans le corridor obscur. Déserts aussi les vécés insalubres. Le garde enfila le couloir en secouant une à une les portes fatiguées, verrouillées, ornées d'écriteaux fanés. La cinquième à gauche céda. Il entra et découvrit Kassim Zaguirov.

Celui-ci gisait sur un plancher vert sombre, les yeux vitreux fixés au plafond. A l'évidence, la cause de sa mort n'était pas une prise d'héroïne mal coupée : Kassim avait le front percé d'un petit trou d'où s'échappait un filet de sang.

III

COMMENT ENLEVER UN INVESTISSEUR

Djavatkhan Djaparovitch Askerov, vice-ministre de la Politique et de la Collecte fiscale, était un homme fort respecté dans la république.

Une fois nommé à ce poste, il s'en fut faire la connaissance du président. Il se présenta en tennis blanches et chemise noire dont le col bâillait sur une chaîne en or. Afin de ne pas être pris pour un chrétien, Askerov avait mis à la chaîne une médaille d'or remportée au championnat fédéral (clandestin) de combat libre. Il aurait pu porter trois médailles du même métal, mais il était modeste et ne voulait pas ressembler à un caniche d'exposition.

Pour que le tableau soit complet, il conviendrait d'ajouter que Djavatkhan Djaparovitch avait oublié de laisser au vestiaire son Stetchkine préféré dont la crosse striée dépassait de sa ceinture.

Le président dévisagea le nouveau vice-ministre et lui dit :

— Djavatkhan Djaparovitch, êtes-vous bien sûr de pouvoir collecter l'impôt ?

— Absolument, répondit Askerov, j'ai une expérience colossale en la matière. Mes camarades et moi ne faisons que cela depuis au moins cinq ans. A une époque où personne ne se préoccupait encore de lever les taxes, nous les prélevions déjà.

— Et pour le compte de quelle administration ? s'enquit le président.

— Oh ! c'était une entreprise privée, répondit modestement Askerov.

Choqué par la prestation du ministre des Travaux publics, sir Jeffry Olmers, président du consortium pétrochimique Escoil, avait quitté le forum sans même un au revoir.

Une semaine plus tard arrivaient des représentants de la firme autrichienne IG Färben. L'un des plus gros groupes pharmacologiques au monde s'intéressait à une usine construite à la fin des années 1980, fleuron de la branche, qui n'avait encore jamais fonctionné. La motivation majeure de IG Färben était que l'usine avait été livrée clés en main par les Autrichiens et qu'elle s'insérait parfaitement dans leur cycle technologique.

Après un mois d'intenses tractations, Martin Raffensneider, patron du groupe, atterrit à Torbi-Kala le 8 septembre. Il venait de Moscou où il avait assisté à un sommet germano-russe : le chef de l'Etat fédéral, dans un allemand impeccable, lui avait promis toute son aide dans la cause du redressement économique du Caucase-Nord.

Deux jours durant Pankov trimbala Raffensneider dans Torbi-Kala, jouant au golf avec lui et le faisant baigner dans la mer. Ils visitèrent l'usine ensemble (qui aurait pu avoir plus fière allure, soit dit au passage). Faute d'hôtel de classe internationale, l'Autrichien était descendu à la résidence du premier commis du Kremlin.

Au troisième jour, Raffensneider fut enlevé.

Djavatkhan Djaparovitch Askerov, vice-ministre de la Politique et de la Collecte fiscale, n'avait pas l'intention d'enlever Martin Raffensneider, président du consortium IG Färben. Mais bon, les circonstances en avaient décidé autrement.

Quand, ce matin-là, Djavatkhan se rendit à la plage avec ses amis, ils découvrirent un périmètre de sécurité gardé par les hommes des forces spéciales avec deux tours de surveillance démontables de part et d'autre du périmètre. Les hommes dirent à Djavatkhan d'aller se baigner ailleurs, la plage étant prise par un type venu d'Autriche.

La chose le contraria légèrement mais, sympa de nature, Djavatkhan ne fit pas d'esclandre.

Au lieu de quoi il s'en fut voir les gardes-frontière avec ses copains pour leur demander un hélico, le temps d'une balade. Mais les gardes-frontière répondirent que les hélicoptères étaient réservés par le représentant du Kremlin qui devait faire un tour dans les montagnes avec un type venu d'Autriche. Représentant du Kremlin, aux yeux des gardes-frontière, ça voulait dire quelque chose. Djavatkhan eut beau tenté de les bakchicher, rien n'y fit.

La chose le contraria un peu plus mais, sympa de nature, il ne fit pas de grabuge. Il n'allait tout de même pas menacer des gardes-frontière d'une inspection fiscale. Quant à sortir les flingues pour une misère pareille, c'était *too much*.

Le soir venu, Djavatkhan se rendit à l'*Eldorado* mais les abords du restaurant étaient occupés par les voitures du premier commis du Kremlin, sans parler de la garde fédérale. On lui expliqua que le resto était réservé pour une soirée spéciale. Sur quoi vinrent les vigiles de l'établissement qui le firent entrer avec des ronds de jambe.

En fait de soirée spéciale, il n'y trouva que la clientèle ordinaire à l'exclusion, peut-être, des wahhabites les plus radicaux. Une longue table était dressée près de la fenêtre où festoyait l'Autrichien, un blond aux yeux bleus entouré de fonctionnaires de l'antenne du Kremlin. A la droite de l'Autrichien se tenait une interprète, ce qui mit Djavatkhan dans tous ses états.

D'abord, l'interprète portait une robe à manches courtes. Or Djavatkhan Askerov ne supportait pas que les jeunes musulmanes portent des robes à manches courtes. Deuxièmement, l'interprète riait et plaisantait avec l'Autrichien qui lui servait du vin dans un haut verre à pied. Or Djavatkhan Askerov ne supportait pas que les jeunes musulmanes boivent du vin avec des étrangers. Troisièmement, l'interprète était sa cousine au troisième degré. Or cela ferait jaser la ville entière dès le lendemain et il ne pouvait laisser dire que la cousine du vice-ministre de la Politique et de la Collecte fiscale avait bu du vin avec un étranger. Il ne tolérerait pas que pareilles médisances le salissent.

Quand l'orchestre se mit à jouer quelque chose de langoureux et que l'étranger se leva pour une danse avec l'interprète, Djavatkhan s'approcha de Narijat :

— Rentre à la maison.

La jeune fille effarouchée battit des paupières et l'étranger toisa Askerov d'un œil méprisant, ses puissantes épaules, sa coupe de cheveux ras et sa mâchoire carrée que le rasoir n'avait pas touchée depuis l'avant-veille.

— *Was ist das ?*

En homme subtil qu'il était, Djavatkhan s'abstint de répondre à l'injure par un scandale public. Il préféra attendre quelques secondes avant de filer aux toilettes. En passant devant une table tenue par des gardes, il donna un ordre à voix basse.

Il dut patienter une bonne vingtaine de minutes. Enfin l'étranger entra, qui sifflotait joyeusement. A la vue de Djavat-khan, il eut un signe de méfiance mais, se rappelant sans doute qu'un bataillon entier l'attendait derrière la porte, il ouvrit grande sa braguette. L'autre s'approcha de lui à pas de velours et lui colla le poing sous la mâchoire. L'étranger s'écroula. Askerov lui ôta sa veste de lin pour lui en lier les poings, fit sauter les barreaux de la fenêtre et l'y poussa. Des types attendaient dehors qui le chargèrent illico dans une voiture.

La nuit même, l'étranger fut transporté dans un village de montagne à la frontière de l'Azerbaïdjan. Le village natal d'Askerov. La moitié des habitants étaient de sa famille. Il allait s'y cacher chaque fois qu'il se passait de vilaines choses. En cinq ans, il n'était jamais arrivé que les villageois laissent approcher les flics si Djavatkhan était recherché.

L'étranger ne revint à lui qu'à l'aube. Il se mit aussitôt à gigoter des jambes.

— Comment osez-vous ! Savez-vous qui je suis ? lança-t-il à Djavatkhan.

Pour quelqu'un d'aussi bête qu'un étranger, il se débrouillait pas mal en russe, même si un gamin qui n'aurait pas encore fait l'armée parlait beaucoup mieux que ça.

— Et qui es-tu ? demanda Djavatkhan.

Il n'avait pas eu le temps de se renseigner la veille, et la question, on s'en doute, l'intéressait au plus haut point.

— Je suis président et coactionnaire du consortium IG Färben ! Sais-tu quel est le budget de ta république ? Deux milliards de dollars ! Et sais-tu combien coûte ma compagnie sur le marché ? Quarante milliards !

Djavatkhan compta jusqu'à quarante dans sa tête et poussa un sifflement.

— Tu veux dire par là qu'on me donnera vingt milliards de dollars de rançon contre ta libération ?

Le premier commis du Kremlin convoqua son monde pour sept heures du matin.

Etaient présents : Arif Talgoïev, ministre de l'Intérieur, le colonel Guennadi Chebolev, chef adjoint du FSB régional, Kamil Makhriev, procureur de la République, le maire de Torbi-Kala, les fils du président Aslanov, Niyazbek Malikov et un huitième homme nommé Daoud Gazikhanov. Ce dernier, triple champion olympique de lutte libre, était l'un des hommes les plus respectés de la république, convoqué ce matin-là parce qu'il devait ses premiers millions au commerce des hommes avec la Tchétchénie.

— Qu'on me rende l'Autrichien ! tonna Vladislav. Et vite ! Je me fiche de savoir qui a fait ça et pourquoi. Mais si ça dégénère en scandale international, j'anéantirai le coupable. Ai-je été clair ?

Il y eut des échanges de regards. Le ministre de l'Intérieur avait les yeux suspendus à la bouche de Pankov comme s'il voyait en sortir non pas des mots, mais des billets de banque. Niyazbek se balançait sur sa chaise, appuyant sur le vernis de la table des phalanges longues et fermes cerclées d'ongles rapaces.

— C'est clair, dit Niyazbek, mais tu as oublié la formule magique : *s'il vous plaît.*

Le jour suivant tomba sur un dimanche, et Vladislav Pankov accepta l'invitation de Niyazbek, qui faisait un chachlik, avec le secret espoir d'y trouver Aminat. Espoir déçu quand il vit les tables dressées sous une tonnelle de vigne, avec une kyrielle de gars costauds.

Ça n'en finissait plus d'arriver. Le portail à peine franchi, Arzo jura ses grands dieux qu'il n'avait pas enlevé l'Autrichien. Vint ensuite Khizri qui se mit à proférer des trucs en langue avare. Et Pankov sentit son moral descendre dans ses chaussettes quand il vit entrer Mahomedsalih Salimkhanov à la peau mate, lisse et régulière, ni brûlée ni boutonneuse, plus haut que lui d'une bonne tête et de dix ans plus jeune, ce qui le mit dans une crise noire de jalousie, aussi aiguë qu'une appendicite. "Et pourtant elle préfère les blonds", se consola le Russe contre toute logique.

Son humeur s'assombrissant de minute en minute, Pankov était sur le point de partir quand Niyazbek apparut sous la tonnelle avec un long tapis à l'épaule. Il se mouvait comme toujours avec aisance et légèreté. Ses cheveux courts et fraîchement lavés brillaient au soleil en renvoyant des éclats de charbon.

— Nous connaissons tous et apprécions Vladislav Avdeïevitch, dit Niyazbek, et nous savons qu'il n'a jamais pris le moindre pot-de-vin. Il a refusé la voiture qu'on lui offrait. Il a refusé la villa. Il a fait renvoyer le collier qu'on avait offert à sa femme. Longtemps je me suis demandé quel cadeau lui faire qu'il ne désapprouve pas, et je me suis décidé pour ce modeste présent.

Sur ce, Niyazbek posa à terre le tapis enroulé.

Pankov se leva d'un bond furieux.

— Attends voir… lui lança-t-il.

Niyazbek imprima une légère secousse au tapis qui se déroula aux pieds du Moscovite. L'instant d'après, Pankov vit en sortir, passablement hirsute mais indemne, le businessman autrichien. Durant quelques secondes l'homme promena son regard sur l'assemblée, puis le fixa sur le premier commis du Kremlin.

— C'est quoi, une plaisanterie, *Herr* Vladislav ?

Pankov devint rouge comme un feu du même nom.

— Qui est le ravisseur ? tonna-t-il. Hein ?

— Nul ne le sait, répondit Niyazbek.

— Comment ça ?! s'indigna l'Autrichien. Le ravisseur c'est lui !

Et son doigt de se ficher sur Djavatkhan Askerov.

L'autre eut l'air d'un gamin surpris avec un pot de confiture dans le buffet de sa grand-mère.

— Doucement, dit Mahomedsalih, sais-tu qui tu accuses ? Tu accuses un haut fonctionnaire, bougre d'Autrichien ! Le vice-ministre de la Collecte fiscale, tu entends ?

— Tiens donc ! fit l'Autrichien. Et vous… vice-ministre aussi ?

— Ministre, renvoya fièrement Mahomedsalih qui ajouta cet aveu après un instant de réflexion : Ex-ministre.

— *Donnerwetter !* s'écria l'Autrichien.

Quelqu'un à table ricana mollement. Khizri Beïbulatov jeta dans son assiette l'os de mouton qu'il était en train de ronger, se cura les dents du bout de l'auriculaire et dit d'un ton blasé :

— Dis donc, l'ami, qu'as-tu à pestiférer ? As-tu été maltraité ? Battu ? Prends l'exemple de Slava : Arzo lui a coupé un doigt du temps où il le tenait enfermé dans sa cave. Il jetait des Russes en pâture aux chiens sous ses yeux.

Et de pointer le doigt sur Arzo Khadjiev.

L'Autrichien leva les yeux sur le Tchétchène aux cheveux grisonnants dont la manche vide était agrafée à la ceinture, puis sur Khizri à la peau basanée et aux dents en or qui remettait son doigt à la bouche pour en extraire un bout de nerf coincé.

— C'est vrai ça ? fit l'Autrichien abasourdi.

— Bien sûr que non, répondit Pankov ; le colonel Khadjiev est le chef d'une unité spéciale du FSB. Un officier des forces fédérales.

Ce disant il sentit sa voix trembler, mais l'Autrichien, qui était tout à son malheur, ne remarqua rien.

— Incroyable, *unmöglich* ! En arrivant chez vous, je me suis cru dans un pays normal. Mon portable marchait aussi bien qu'à Vienne. Mes appartements étaient de standing européen. J'ai même joué sur un terrain de golf magnifique ! Et voilà qu'on m'a traité comme un objet, pas comme un homme ! Un objet qu'on peut voler ! Un objet qu'on peut offrir en cadeau ! Le comble, c'est que mon ravisseur n'est pas un bandit, mais un haut fonctionnaire. Et dans la finance, par-dessus le marché ! Et qui s'imagine que si le capital social d'une société fait quarante milliards de dollars, elle peut en donner vingt en échange de son patron. De la bêtise finie...

— Ohé ! le Fritz, lança Niyazbek, on t'a relâché trop tôt, je crois. Si on t'avait gardé plus longtemps, t'aurais donné des conférences. Encore un peu et notre Djavatkhan aurait fini par s'y connaître dans le marché des titres.

A ce moment Pankov revint à lui, prit l'Autrichien par la main et l'entraîna loin de la table vers les voitures garées sous l'auvent.

Le Learjet privé atterrit à Vienne à seize heures trente avec Martin Raffensneider à son bord. L'Autrichien appela aussitôt Pankov sur son portable personnel.

— Vladislav ? C'est Martin. Vous devez comprendre que, si je porte plainte, vous n'aurez plus de visa pour aucun pays de l'Union européenne. Je veux dire vous, personnellement. Vous comprenez ?

Pankov ne disait mot. Il n'y avait rien à répondre à cela.

— J'ai longtemps réfléchi, reprit l'Autrichien. J'ai décidé que ma société n'avait rien à gagner à faire du tapage. J'ai décidé de me taire. Naturellement, il ne saurait être question d'investissements ou de contrats. Savez-vous pourquoi ? Pas à cause de mon enlèvement. Mais parce que mon ravisseur est vice-ministre des Impôts ! Et que, en occupant ce poste, il s'imagine en toute bonne foi qu'une compagnie qui pèse quarante milliards peut en débourser vingt ! Et dire que ce type aurait été en charge des comptes fiscaux de mon usine ! Rien que d'y penser, j'en ai la chair de poule ! M'entendez-vous, Vladislav ?

— Je vous entends, Martin. Combien de temps avez-vous passé dans les montagnes ?

— Une journée !

— Eh bien moi, c'est tout l'été que je passe à ce régime-là.

Djavatkhan rendit visite à Pankov le lendemain, amené par Niyazbek à la demande du représentant du Kremlin. Le jour se levait à peine. Le Moscovite s'enfilait des goulées de café brûlant en parcourant des piles et des piles de dossiers avec, à ses côtés, le colonel Chebolev.

Pankov dévisagea Djavatkhan Askerov sans un bonjour et lui montra une photo. On y voyait le jeune Djavatkhan assis entre Bassaïev et Hattab, tous les trois bras dessus, bras dessous, et contents l'un de l'autre.

— Un montage ? demanda Pankov.

— Non, répondit l'autre.

L'image suivante montrait Djavatkhan près d'un soldat russe qu'on égorgeait. Il le regardait avec une expression coupable mêlée de compassion.

— Pourquoi l'a-t-on égorgé ?

— Parce qu'on manquait de cartouches, répondit Djavatkhan.

Sonné par la réponse, l'homme du président se tut quelques instants. Puis, sèchement :

— Je continue ? J'ai là tout un album de famille. Papa, maman, Hattab…

Niyazbek, bien calé dans un fauteuil, fit non de la tête avec un nuage de moquerie sur les lèvres qui horripila Pankov. Le Russe bondit en brandissant pêle-mêle photos et dossiers :

— Vous me le paierez ! hurla-t-il. L'un comme l'autre ! Pour Zaguirov aussi ! Et pour le directeur du port ! Il y a là de quoi te coffrer pour vingt ans ! Putain de toi ! Ça manque de cartouches, que ça dit !

Djavatkhan attrapa la main du premier commis du Kremlin en lui écrasant les doigts, puis la leva d'un coup sec. Pankov eut l'impression d'être broyé par une presse de fonte, il s'affaissa et poussa un cri de douleur.

— Pas de jurons devant moi, dit Djavatkhan, personne ne se le permet jamais.

Niyazbek se leva de son siège d'un mouvement impétueux qui tenait du percuteur frappant l'amorce.

— Nous ne sommes pas venus ici pour entendre des insultes, dit Niyazbek.

Il tourna les talons et sortit. Djavatkhan lui emboîta le pas.

Pankov resta planté quelques instants au beau milieu de la véranda, secouant la main, puis il se jeta au-dehors. Niyazbek montait déjà en voiture.

— Et c'est tout ce que tu peux me dire ? demanda Pankov.

Niyazbek toisa le Russe. Il avait la face rouge de rage, la cravate stricte mais de guingois, la chemise blanche sortie de son pantalon. L'un debout sur les marches, l'autre les pieds à terre devant sa voiture, et leurs deux têtes à hauteur égale.

— Djavatkhan n'était pas le seul à vouloir enlever son Autrichien, dit Niyazbek après un silence.

— Comment ?!

— Le type était filoché. Les hommes de Djavatkhan l'avaient déjà constaté sur la plage. Et Djavatkhan, il a eu de la visite. Un gars du FSB. L'Autrichien, qu'il disait, est un espion de l'Ouest, et puisque les labos pharmaceutiques sont dans les toxines et que les toxines c'est le terrorisme, c'est qu'il achète l'usine en vue d'une opération terroriste. Il a dit qu'il paierait cent mille dollars contre les aveux de l'Autrichien devant une caméra. Et aussi il a proposé de vendre le bonhomme à la Tchétchénie. Il a dit : "Tu gâches notre affaire, empoche le fric et casse-toi."

Du coup, Pankov n'avait plus mal à la main. Niyazbek était on ne peut plus sérieux. Le Moscovite aurait juré qu'il ne le faisait pas marcher.

— Le commanditaire ? demanda le Russe.

Niyazbek, d'un geste impuissant des bras :

— Y a rien de secret dans c'te ville. Fais la tournée des popotes et renseigne-toi.

Niyazbek avait dit vrai. Comme put l'établir le colonel Chebolev, l'Autrichien avait bel et bien fait l'objet d'un contrat passé par Gamzat Aslanov à un major russe du FSB, chef d'un service de moyenne importance. Ce qui frappait surtout le premier commis du Kremlin, c'était que le major n'était pas plus conscient de ses actes que Djavatkhan Askerov. Une fois l'argent en poche, il s'était empressé d'aller démasquer l'espion étranger dans l'espoir sincère de décrocher de nouveaux galons.

Quand le colonel Chebolev eut éclairé son collègue sur le danger d'un scandale international et du recul des investissements, l'autre exhiba un rictus de mépris en disant que la grande Russie se passerait des miettes qu'on voulait lui jeter en aumône, et qu'un officier sous serment ne pouvait transiger avec les intérêts stratégiques de son pays, fût-ce contre la promesse de placements impurs effectués par des saboteurs potentiels. Alors Chebolev lui montra une photo sur laquelle l'"espion étranger" dont il avait eu la charge embrassait le président de la Russie. Du coup, le major blêmit, rougit, oublia aussitôt ses élucubrations sur les intérêts stratégiques et les menées des services étrangers et s'écria : "J'ai été manipulé !"

Bref, le major était à côté de la plaque ; mais pas Gamzat. Le fils du président comprenait parfaitement ce que signifiait pour la région le rachat de l'usine pharmaceutique par une firme autrichienne. Et si le fils du président voulait le faire échouer, c'était parce qu'au fond de l'usine désaffectée, dans l'un de ces ateliers qui prenait de plus en plus des allures de catacombes, un businessman à sa botte avait monté un labo d'héroïne en partenariat avec des affairistes turcs ou afghans, qu'importe.

L'homme du Kremlin convoqua le fils du président dans son bureau et lui cria dessus si fort que les vitres menacèrent de sauter. Ceci durant une dizaine de minutes. Quand Pankov s'arrêta pour reprendre son souffle, Gamzat arbora le plus innocent de ses sourires et lui dit en le regardant droit dans les yeux :

— Mais n'oubliez pas, Vladislav Avdeïevitch, que je n'ai rien fait de mal. Le FSB régional non plus. On a eu un message d'alerte. Un message d'alerte, ça se vérifie. Il faut être vigilant en toute chose, on ne peut pas ouvrir une région aussi explosive à n'importe qui. Quant au ravisseur de votre Autrichien, c'est un bandit de la plus pure espèce, membre actif de groupes armés clandestins. Vous avez le dossier de Djavatkhan Askerov. Je pourrais y verser d'autres pièces.

— Et pourquoi cet homme est-il devenu vice-ministre avec un dossier pareil ? demanda Pankov.

— Le ministre a fait l'objet d'intimidations, répondit Gamzat d'un geste désolé. De la part de Djavatkhan et de ses protecteurs.

A quoi Pankov ne pouvait rien rétorquer.

De tous les amis de Niyazbek, Djavatkhan Askerov était le plus modeste. Un garçon doux d'un mètre quatre-vingt-quinze et de quatre-vingt-deux kilos.

Il avait grandi dans un village de montagne à trois cents kilomètres de Torbi-Kala, sans électricité, ni gaz, ni téléphone. La seule conquête du pouvoir soviétique arrivée jusqu'à ce village, c'était la poudre de fraise soluble en sachets qu'on trouvait au magasin. Les grands jours de fête, Djavatkhan en buvait.

Au village vivaient une femme nommée Mariam et un homme nommé Chapi. Lequel avait voulu l'épouser, mais elle se maria avec un autre. Les choses de la vie firent que le fils unique de Mariam quitta sa montagne au début des années 1970 et n'y revint jamais pour cause de prison ou de mort violente, on ne savait pas trop. En 1993 mourut son mari. Peu après, Chapi fut nommé à la tête du village.

Un certain jour, peu de temps après son service militaire, Djavatkhan alla faire les foins et vit Chapi, le maire du village, en train de charger la remorque de sa Jigouli 2104 d'une meule apprêtée par Mariam. Djavatkhan s'approcha et dit :

— Que faites-vous là, mon cher ? C'est le foin de Mariam.

Sans s'arrêter, Chapi paya le garçon d'un vilain regard en lui disant :

— Fiche le camp, morveux.

— Je ne peux pas ficher le camp parce que cette femme est seule et qu'elle n'a personne pour la défendre. Si vous lui volez son foin, elle n'aura plus rien à donner à sa vache.

Alors Chapi, brandissant sa fourche :

— Pourquoi prends-tu sa défense, petit ? Tu n'aurais pas des visées sur elle, par hasard ? Alors dépêche-toi de l'épouser, parce que ta fiancée va bientôt mourir de vieillesse.

Là-dessus, il continua de charger le foin.

— Ce foin ne te portera pas bonheur, dit Djavatkhan qui frappa la voiture du pied.

Un coup de pied si puissant qu'il défonça l'aile et faussa l'axe du moteur. Voyant cela, Chapi courut au coffre, l'ouvrit et sortit son fusil. Mais il manqua son premier coup et n'eut pas le temps d'en tirer un deuxième parce que Djavatkhan lui arracha son arme et, de cette arme, lui réduisit le crâne en bouillie.

La nouvelle parvint à la connaissance des autorités qui le firent arrêter au bout d'une semaine. Une fois transféré à Torbi-Kala, il fut placé dans une cellule de quarante prisonniers.

Au soir, on amena Djavatkhan dans le bureau du directeur de la prison. Il y avait près de lui un petit bonhomme à la trogne rusée de renard.

— Est-il vrai, dit le directeur, que tu as faussé un moteur d'un seul coup de pied ?

— C'est vrai, dit Djavatkhan.

— Laisse-toi guider par cet homme, lui ordonna le directeur.

Durant les deux mois qu'il passa en prison, on le conduisit une fois par semaine à des combats libres, proclamés "sans règles", que Gamzat Aslanov organisait dans son club.

Djavatkhan n'avait jamais appris à se battre, mais il était si fort qu'il remportait la plupart des duels. Au bout de deux mois, il fut déféré au tribunal où il écopa d'une peine de dix ans pour le meurtre du maire du village. Le soir même, on l'amena chez Gamzat qui lui dit :

— Pour le verdict, ne t'inquiète pas. J'ai payé pour qu'un autre purge ta peine à ta place. Toi, pendant ce temps, tu iras te battre dans des clubs de Moscou. Mais, d'abord, on t'apprendra la vraie bagarre.

Pendant quatre mois, un coach l'entraîna au combat comme on entraîne un chien à la chasse au renard. Au bout de quatre mois, le coach dit à Gamzat :

— Je n'ai jamais vu un lutteur comme lui. Si ce Lezghe pouvait se battre sous son vrai nom, il serait champion du monde dès demain.

Mais Djavatkhan ne pouvait pas se produire sous son vrai nom parce que ce vrai nom-là purgeait une peine de dix ans dans un camp de Syktyvkar. Aussi Djavatkhan fut-il transféré à Moscou.

Le premier combat qu'il y disputa fut plié en deux minutes par Djavatkhan qui mit son adversaire K.-O., grâce à quoi les patrons du club gagnèrent cinq cent mille dollars ce soir-là, bien qu'ils en eussent gagné beaucoup plus s'ils n'avaient pas été aussi méfiants : son adversaire était quand même champion d'Europe de kickboxing.

Le combat terminé, Djavatkhan partit pour l'appart qu'on lui louait au volant d'une Samara 09 aux vitres teintées, un cadeau du patron du club. On lui avait donné aussi cinq cents dollars de récompense.

Il était près de deux heures du matin et le sol se drapait de neige comme si Moscou se trouvait haut perchée dans les montagnes. Une fille en jupe courte se tenait sur le bord de la route, qui leva le bras à la vue de la voiture.

Djavatkhan stoppa. Quand la fille vit ce Caucasien de deux mètres au crâne rasé, elle tressaillit.

— Je te dépose quelque part ?

La fille monta à l'arrière et se fit toute petite.

— Où va-t-on ? reprit Djavatkhan. C'est que je ne connais pas Moscou.

— Ben, je n'ai nulle part où aller, dit la fille qui se mit à pleurer.

— A l'hôtel alors ?

Pour l'hôtel, elle était d'accord. Mais de là surgit une nouvelle difficulté : Djavatkhan ne savait pas ce qu'il y avait comme hôtels à Moscou ni où ils se trouvaient. Il stoppa devant un poste de contrôle pour expliquer son problème. L'agent le toisa, fit hum ! et l'envoya au *Métropole*.

Djavatkhan se rendit donc au *Métropole* où il prit une chambre pour la fille. A tout hasard, il la prit pour trois nuits. Les cinq cents dollars y passèrent, mais Djavatkhan avait sa fierté et ne voulait pas perdre la face devant la demoiselle.

— Voilà pour toi, lui dit-il en lui tendant la clé. Et dépêche-toi de te trouver un travail. Parce que si tu traînes dans les rues à deux heures du matin, Dieu seul sait ce qui peut t'arriver. On n'est pas dans les montagnes, ici, pour errer impunément à deux heures du matin. On est à Moscou, ici.

Djavatkhan parti, la demoiselle s'en trouva comme deux ronds de flan.

Il vivait à Moscou depuis un mois et demi quand le patron de son club lui donna l'adresse d'un bureau, rue Tverskaïa, avec la consigne d'aller y chercher de l'argent, lui disant que ces gens-là lui devaient dix mille dollars en réparation d'une voiture accidentée.

— Mais sois prudent, ajouta le boss, ces bouffons-là sont fichus d'appeler les flics.

Djavatkhan nota l'adresse sur un bout de papier et s'en fut chercher l'argent avec le papier dans une poche et une grenade dans l'autre. Le bureau en question se trouvait au deuxième étage d'un immeuble ordinaire. Etrange pour le siège d'une société : il était gardé par deux jeunes types au crâne rasé, tout vêtus de noir avec une croix gammée rouge et blanche à la manche. La même croix gammée figurait sur le drapeau qui ornait le mur dans le bureau du chef.

Rappelons ici que Djavatkhan n'avait rien de l'apparence d'un Moscovite ou, disons, d'un Chinois. Presque deux mètres à la toise, des yeux noirs, des cheveux noirs coupés ras, un maillot noir d'où s'échappait une chaînette en or offerte à l'issue d'un tournoi.

Quand Djavatkhan entra, l'homme assis à un gros bureau en chêne sous le drapeau à la croix gammée se rembrunit et dit :

— Qu'est-ce que tu viens foutre ici, espèce de cul-noir ?

— Stanislav Grigoriévitch a dit que vous lui deviez de l'argent. Dix mille billets pour une aile défoncée.

— De quoi ? fit l'autre ahuri.

Il n'eut pas le temps de continuer. Djavatkhan, comprenant que ça tournait mal, lui allongea un coup de poing par-dessus le bureau. Le chef glissa de sa chaise, inerte. Alors le montagnard sortit la grenade de sa poche, noua un fil à la goupille, fourra le projectile dans le pantalon du bonhomme, le remit sur sa chaise.

— Ton bureau est mastoc, lui dit Djavatkhan quand l'autre sortit de sa torpeur. Cette grenade, c'est une Diakonov-33. Portée de frappe très limitée. Si je tire sur le fil, il ne m'arrivera rien. Mais, toi, on te ramassera en pièces détachées. Alors donne-moi le fric et je me tire.

Le bonhomme qui était assis avec une grenade dans le froc à un bureau en chêne massif du Canada sous un svastika rouge et noir décrocha le téléphone en demandant :

— Et combien te doit-on ?

Il se trouva que, faute de dollars, on dut remettre à Djavatkhan un grand sac en plastique plein à ras bord de roubles russes. Comme le sac était transparent, Djavatkhan arracha l'oriflamme du mur pour y enrouler le tout. Dehors, tout le monde se retournait sur son passage parce qu'on ne voyait pas souvent un Caucasien de deux mètres marcher rue Tverskaïa avec un balluchon emballé dans un drapeau du parti nationaliste russe. Djavatkhan apporta la somme au patron du club et lui dit :

— Ils n'avaient pas de dollars. Ils ont payé en roubles.

Stanislav Grigoriévitch dénoua le balluchon, puis examina le drapeau.

— Où étais-tu ?

— A l'adresse indiquée. Bâtiment jaune, escalier 2, deuxième étage.

Le patron partit alors d'un rire tonitruant parce que Djavatkhan avait tout confondu : l'immeuble était bien le bon, mais pas l'escalier.

Vint un soir, encore deux mois plus tard, où Djavatkhan se retrouva devant une table bien garnie après une victoire qu'on fêtait entre copains. Il sentit quelqu'un se couler sur la chaise voisine, et une voix de jeune fille lui dit :

— Salut, me reconnais-tu ?

Djavatkhan se retourna et vit une blonde en bas résille noirs et jupe plissée. La jupe commençait plus bas que le nombril qu'elle avait percé d'un anneau à pierre. C'était la demoiselle que Djavatkhan avait placée à l'hôtel *Métropole*. Il la regarda et se mit à rougir copieusement, puis croisa les jambes pour que la petite ne voie pas sa... ou qu'il... enfin bref, chacun sait ce qu'un jeune type peut ressentir après plusieurs mois d'abstinence quand il se retrouve près d'une jeune fille à bas résille dans une jupe qui ressemble à une rose.

Notons ici que Djavatkhan n'était pas bête. Il était simplement bon, ce qui n'est pas la même chose.

— Oui, dit-il. Tu es une prostituée, ou quoi ?

— En fait, quand tu m'as mise à l'hôtel, j'ai eu beaucoup de chance. Parce que de prostituée je suis devenue top-modèle.

— Où est la différence ?

— Viens avec moi, je vais te la montrer.

Djavatkhan se colla à la table. Il n'aurait pas fallu qu'à Dieu ne plaise la jeune fille entrevoie l'objet de sa honte. Puis il dit :

— Non. Chacun chez soi. Vois-tu, je n'ai pas l'intention de pécher avec une fille qui n'est pas ma femme, et je ne vois rien chez toi qui me fasse envie de t'épouser.

Mais c'était plus facile à dire qu'à faire. La petite blonde multiplia ses visites au club, et il advint que Djavatkhan, un beau soir, l'amena chez lui. Puis il lui loua un appart. Sveta aimait bien qu'on dépense de l'argent pour elle et réclamait tantôt ceci, tantôt cela. Elle n'arrêtait pas de lui dire qu'on le mésestimait. Après qu'elle se fut pris le bec avec le patron du club, Djavatkhan toucha dix mille dollars par combat, puis vingt mille.

Encore un mois de passé. Différentes personnes l'associaient désormais à différentes tâches. Un jour, Stanislav appela Djavatkhan, lui donna un jerricane d'essence et lui dit :

— Connais-tu le café du passage Mamonov ? Vas-y demain à sept heures du soir, entre par le local de service, monte au premier étage et mets-y le feu.

Le café brûla la nuit suivante.

Le boss convoqua Djavatkhan pour lui dire :

— J'avais dit : sept heures du soir ! Pas dans la nuit, nom d'un chien !

— Je suis arrivé à sept heures du soir, mais il y avait du monde. Des femmes, des enfants. Je n'allais tout de même pas brûler tous ces gens avec le café ! Qu'est-ce qu'ils ont fait de mal ?

Alors le boss leva la main pour frapper Djavatkhan, mais le montagnard lui attrapa l'avant-bras en disant :

— Personne n'a le droit de me battre en dehors du ring.

— Si tu recommences ne serait-ce qu'une seule fois, tu seras bon pour finir ta peine en Sibérie.

Après cette conversation, Djavatkhan alla chercher Sveta. Il la trouva dans une boîte de nuit, assise avec des copines à la table d'un type nommé Serguéï qu'il connaissait bien. C'était l'un de ses fans, un habitué des tournois. Serguéï, à ce qu'on disait, possédait la moitié de l'aluminium de la Russie.

Ça manquait bougrement d'air là-dedans, et la musique faisait un boucan de Boeing au décollage. Djavatkhan et Sveta sortirent dans le couloir.

— Ecoute-moi bien, lui dit-il. Je veux rentrer dans les montagnes et t'emmener avec moi. Je veux que tu te convertisses à l'islam, que tu te maries avec moi, que tu portes un foulard sur la tête et plus jamais de jupe qui s'arrête plus haut que les cuisses et plus bas que le nombril. Avec l'aide d'Allah, je trouverai bien de quoi nous faire manger, nous et nos enfants.

Sveta éclata de rire et l'embrassa de ses lèvres mouillées de vodka. Puis elle ajouta :

— Je préférerais Nice.

Trois jours passèrent. Un soir qu'il prenait du bon temps dans un café avec elle, quelqu'un s'assit à sa table. Djavatkhan leva la tête et reconnut Niyazbek Malikov, surnommé la Chouette, un nom qui ne jouissait pas encore d'une grande réputation, mais qui n'était pas inconnu non plus. Tout le monde savait qu'il avait seul survécu à l'extermination de sept Avars près du Bolchoï, et tout le monde savait qu'il avait vengé les morts et pris sur lui toutes leurs dettes, bien qu'ils n'eussent rien d'autre que des dettes.

— Qu'est-ce que c'est que cette histoire de café qui n'a pas été brûlé de jour ? demanda Niyazbek.

— Je ne vois pas de quoi tu parles, répondit Djavatkhan.

— Tu es un mec bien, articula Niyazbek, dommage que tu te sois mis avec une pute. Le jour où ils te planteront, appelle-moi.

Là-dessus, il lui tendit son numéro de téléphone, et Djavatkhan partit chez sa petite amie en sa compagnie.

La semaine suivante devait avoir lieu un nouveau combat contre un Malaisien. Une enveloppe de quarante mille dollars était promise à Djavatkhan. Or, quand le patron du club analysa les paris, il comprit qu'il ne gagnerait pas gros dessus parce que tout le monde misait sur lui. A une heure du coup d'envoi, il appela le montagnard.

— Ce combat, tu dois le perdre.

— Allah seul décidera.

— Dans ce club, c'est moi qui remplace Allah, dit Stanislav Grigoriévitch.

Le Malaisien était un adversaire de poids, mais les circonstances firent que Djavatkhan le battit. Quand il arriva au club le lendemain, il y trouva le patron seul. Il se confondit en excuses, mais l'autre eut un geste désabusé de la main.

— Ne te bile pas, dit le boss. Ce n'était pas pour moi, mais pour Sergueï, l'amant de Sveta.

— Que dis-tu là ?

— Comme si tu ne savais pas que Sveta était la maîtresse de Sergueï. Tiens, en ce moment, il doit y être.

Djavatkhan quitta le club et s'en fut à l'appartement qu'il louait pour Sveta. En montant l'escalier, il vit deux gardes du corps russes qui poireautaient sur le palier. Seulement deux, s'étonna-t-il. Il les empoigna par l'encolure et les entrechoqua front contre front, puis ouvrit l'appart et les traîna à l'intérieur.

Ayant entendu du bruit dans l'entrée, Sergueï montra le nez juste au moment où Djavatkhan traînait les gardes dans l'appartement. Il se précipita dans la chambre où il avait laissé son pistolet avec le reste de ses habits, mais le Lezghe lui donna un coup dans les dents, et Sergueï vola au tapis d'un côté, sa denture de l'autre. Ceci fait, Djavatkhan enfourcha Sergueï au sol et l'aurait étranglé si les autres gardes n'avaient pas accouru dans l'entrée à cet instant.

Voyant que ça ne tournait pas à son avantage, Djavatkhan arracha un pistolet à un garde et sauta par la fenêtre. La garde ouvrit le feu mais ne le blessa que légèrement au bras.

Comme on le voit, Djavatkhan n'était pas bête. Quand il pensait, il pensait juste, simplement avait-il la fâcheuse habitude de cogner d'abord et de penser ensuite. Maintenant, il comprenait que le patron du club n'avait pas parlé de Sergueï comme on parle pour ne rien dire, mais pour se venger du combat gagné. Après réflexion, Djavatkhan composa le numéro de téléphone que lui avait donné Niyazbek.

— Il faut que je quitte Moscou, dit Djavatkhan.

Une semaine plus tard, il se trouvait déjà aux Emirats avec un faux passeport. De là, il se rendit à La Mecque.

Il y passa deux semaines, puis encore deux mois en Azerbaïdjan d'où il revint en Tchétchénie avec un détachement de moudjahidin. On lui faisait savoir que Niyazbek n'était pas très content de sa décision, mais Djavatkhan dit : "Les combats sans règles, j'en ai soupé. Maintenant je veux me battre pour Allah. Je vois bien que les infidèles commandent aux musulmans, et que de là viennent tous nos malheurs."

Et puis Djavatkhan avait des comptes personnels à régler avec les Russes. Le patron du club qui l'avait planté était russe, Sveta était russe, russe aussi Sergueï.

Djavatkhan fit la guerre pendant près d'un an. Il fut blessé, soigné à Bakou, puis la guerre s'acheva et Djavatkhan, une fois rétabli, débarqua à Grozny.

Il y fut accueilli avec tous les honneurs, rencontra le président de l'Itchkérie, rendit visite à la garde chariatique et, un soir, répondit à l'invitation d'un vieux compagnon d'armes. Vaïnakhs, Avars, Lezghes, Adygués... ce fut une vaste rencontre à laquelle assista aussi Niyazbek. Tous les convives étaient attablés ensemble dans une salle immense où dansaient pour eux des fillettes de treize ans. Le vieux compagnon de Djavatkhan en prit une par la main qu'il mit sur les genoux de son hôte.

— Cette petite, dit-il, nul ne l'a encore jamais touchée. Nous l'avons préparée pour toi.

Djavatkhan écarta la fillette et aperçut Niyazbek assis près de lui.

— De quand date ton dernier séjour à Moscou ? demanda Djavatkhan.

— C'était il y a deux mois, répondit Niyazbek.

— Sais-tu quelque chose de Sveta ? Est-ce qu'elle travaille toujours *Aux Lueurs de la Nuit* ?

Niyazbek marqua un silence, puis répondit :

— Elle a fait des pieds et des mains pour que tu ne sois pas inculpé. Serguéï n'a jamais porté plainte. Apparemment, elle tenait à toi plus qu'elle n'en avait l'air. Ensuite, on ne l'a plus revue.

Niyazbek promena son regard sur les faces avinées des convives et dit en soupirant :

— Que penses-tu de tout ça ?

— J'en pense que je suis un combattant d'Allah mais que j'ai l'impression d'être retombé dans le milieu des combats sans règles. Et que les dés sont beaucoup trop pipés. Je ne sais plus quoi faire.

— Si tu ne sais plus quoi faire, pourquoi ne pas rentrer au village ? dit Niyazbek.

Djavatkhan quitta Grozny le lendemain matin. Il prit sept de ses plus proches compagnons et s'en fut acheter des armes au marché de la ville. Pour pas cher, il en remplit un plein coffre, tel un kolkhozien remplissant sa remorque de pommes de terre.

Le voyage ne lui prit que huit heures. La paix était de retour dans le Caucase et personne ne lui chercha noise. A certains barrages, il donnait de l'argent. Quand ça pinaillait trop, il se recommandait de Niyazbek.

Il faisait encore jour quand il arriva au village. La guerre n'avait pas touché ce coin perdu de montagnes à la frontière de l'Azerbaïdjan. Les jeeps passèrent un col et Djavatkhan aperçut au loin les jardins verts de la vallée, des brebis éparpillées sur des brûlis pentus, et les couronnes blanches des cimes sous la voûte bleue du ciel.

Une demi-heure plus tard, il stoppait devant un grand portail. Le portillon se laissant ouvrir, il le poussa et entra. Les traces nettes d'un balai marquaient la cour. Une grille à volière partait de l'angle de la maison, derrière laquelle cacardaient des oies blanches. Et dans la cour, sous une tonnelle défraîchie par le temps, une jeunette à foulard et jupe longue était en train de langer un enfant.

Djavatkhan s'arrêta. Il portait une tenue camo turque et de lourds brodequins de montagne. Kalachnikov à l'épaule, poignard et grenade à la ceinture ; un autre poignard – au manche coulé de plomb – à la tige de son godillot. La face mangée d'une barbe de dix-huit mois. Une blessure de guerre lui élançait l'épaule, souvent.

Planté là, il regardait la cour qui l'avait vu grandir, la jeunette et son enfant, les pentes blanches dorées par le soleil, et il se rappela Moscou, le club, les tournois de combat libre et cette nuit d'enfer qu'il avait vécue près de Pervomaïka quand il s'était jeté avec d'autres volontaires dans un fossé qu'on croyait miné, mais les Russes avaient eu la flemme de le faire. Il se disait que, tout ce temps, il aurait pu le passer au village à prier Allah, et qu'alors ces deux-là auraient pu être sa femme et son enfant.

La jeunette se retourna, et Djavatkhan reconnut Sveta. D'abord, il n'en crut pas ses yeux. Puis elle lui dit en souriant :

— Je ne savais pas où te trouver, alors j'ai pensé que tu finirais par revenir au village. Ça s'est bien passé entre ta mère et moi. Et je suis heureuse à l'idée que ton fils ne grandira pas sans son père.

IV

LES RÈGLES DU GOLF

Une troisième explosion se produisit le 15 septembre à deux heures du matin sur la voie ferrée Torbi-Kala-Akhol. Même procédé d'enfouissement de la bombe que la première fois : sous la ligne d'un passage à niveau qu'on venait de refaire, à ceci près que la cible n'était pas une voiture mais un train de marchandises. Comme en application du mode d'emploi, on avait activé l'engin en milieu de convoi, à hauteur du dixième wagon. Le onzième était chargé de munitions pour la Tchétchénie. Le souffle de l'explosion fut d'une force telle que les fenêtres de deux pâtés de maisons volèrent en éclats le long de la voie. Le convoi comprenait au total six wagons d'explosifs qui, par chance, avaient été disposés dans le strict respect des consignes : un plein, deux vides. Les autres déraillèrent sans exploser.

La bombe annihila deux cents mètres de voie ferrée. Pas de victimes humaines. La thèse de l'implication des dirigeants de la république dans l'assassinat d'Ibrahim Malikov fut enterrée à jamais sous les décombres du train.

— Qu'on le veuille ou non, dit le colonel Chebolev à Pankov, c'est votre voiture que les terroristes ont plastiquée, et elle seule. Ils vous croyaient dedans. C'est la signature type des attentats dans la région. Leur cible, ce sont les fédéraux, les miliciens, les troupes, jamais la population locale (intentionnellement du moins). Le convoi de munitions, le transporteur blindé des forces spéciales, la voiture du premier commis du Kremlin, voilà ce qu'ils visent. Ibrahim Malikov s'est trouvé là par hasard à votre place.

Pankov écoutait sans piper, les yeux accrochés au vernis de la table.

— Dis-moi, Guennadi, pourquoi Arsaïev ne fait-il jamais sauter les camions-citernes ?

La question le taraudait depuis le premier jour de son entrée en fonction.

— De quoi ?

— La moitié du pétrole de la république passe par le col aux Moutons. Pourquoi ne fait-il pas sauter les citernes ?

— Parce qu'il a sa part sur chaque camion qui passe.

— Niyazbek aussi le paie ?

— Même le clan des Aslanov le paie.

— Et les flics ? On les paie eux aussi ?

— Plus on les fait sauter, moins on les paie.

Drôle de système économique où le président payait le premier terroriste du pays pour que son fils puisse voler tranquillement du pétrole, et où l'on flinguait les flics pour qu'ils ne fassent pas concurrence à ce même terroriste dans la cause édifiante du racket pétrolier. Pankov avait beau tenter d'en cerner la logique, ce n'était pas évident.

— Nous devons renforcer votre garde, dit Chebolev. J'insiste pour que vous fassiez venir de Moscou un minimum de huit officiers du service d'ordre fédéral. Tant que vous ne le ferez pas, vous serez gardé par les forces spéciales du Youg. Les gens d'Arzo.

— Ce n'est pas la première fois qu'Arzo me garde, lâcha Pankov. Il m'en reste un souvenir inoubliable.

Le soir même Pankov appela Niyazbek pour demander à le voir. L'autre répondit qu'il était au club de sport.

Attenant au vieux stade qui accueillait désormais un souk, le nouveau club avait plutôt fière allure avec son bâtiment nickel à trois étages et à plafonds hauts. Deux ados aux pieds nus gardaient l'entrée, accroupis, avec chacun une mitraillette en bandoulière.

A cette heure tardive, l'intérieur était calme et désert. Les pas ramollis par un sol de mousse, Pankov et ses gardes défilaient devant des salles vides où des appareils d'entraînement semblables à des engins de torture ou à des sculptures futuristes se reflétaient dans de grands miroirs.

Dans la seule salle éclairée, ils trouvèrent une quinzaine de gars assis par terre devant Niyazbek en duel contre un adversaire. Myope comme il était, Pankov n'aimait déjà pas beaucoup la bagarre au cinéma mais, là, pas moyen de suivre : les lutteurs évoluaient trop loin de lui, et pas de gros plans. Tout au plus remarqua-t-il que Niyazbek surpassait nettement son rival sans le ménager pour autant, sans faire les choses à moitié. Au bout d'une minute, déjoué par une feinte, le type fit un pas en arrière et reçut un coup en pleine face. K.-O.

Il resta un temps étendu sur le tatami, inerte, puis revint à lui et se leva, aidé par Niyazbek qui lui tendit la main.

— Retiens bien une chose, dit Niyazbek au perdant, ne recule jamais. Si tu reçois un coup par feinte, tu peux toujours aller de l'avant. Ou faire un pas à l'écart. Mais, à la première reculade, ton adversaire t'achèvera.

Niyazbek se tourna vers Pankov. De la sueur perlait de ses cheveux noirs coupés court, et deux auréoles mouillées marquaient son kimono sous ses aisselles. Son col, défait par le combat, laissait voir que sa cicatrice qui partait du cou allait presque jusqu'au cœur. Pankov vit aussi que Niyazbek avait les pieds massifs, de forme ovale, aux orteils déformés, mal remis d'innombrables fractures.

Niyazbek descendit du tatami et serra la main du Moscovite.

— Apprends-moi à me battre, dit subitement Pankov. Montre-moi au moins comment me défendre.

Niyazbek sourit.

— Pour quoi faire ? fit-il avec un étonnement sincère. Tu es comme une femme. Tu n'as à répondre de rien.

Puis ils se rendirent chez Niyazbek. Un dîner les attendait sur une table dressée près de la piscine, comme toujours sans vin ni vodka. Pas un Russe à table hormis Pankov, assis à la droite du maître de maison. En face était Khizri.

Le boiteux exhibait un vilain sourire. De ses lèvres fines et humides, il attrapait des morceaux de saucisson sec à la pointe du couteau. De le voir ainsi sourire donnait la chair de poule à Pankov qui repensa à un dialogue rapporté par le ministre de l'Intérieur. Arif ayant reçu Khizri dans son cabinet lui avait demandé qui était le tueur du gendre de Telaïev. "Moi, avait répondu l'autre sèchement. – Et pourquoi ? – Comme si la réponse ne coulait pas de source. – Mais tu dois comprendre que je suis dans l'obligation de t'arrêter ! – Essaie toujours", avait renvoyé Khizri avec un sourire ostensible.

Niyazbek et Mahomedsalih ne mangeaient rien. De temps à autre crissaient des pneus de l'autre côté du portail, et la garde faisait entrer un nouveau visiteur qui se mettait à table ou s'entretenait avec Niyazbek dans un coin d'ombre épaisse au bord de la piscine.

Pankov observait attentivement le va-et-vient des femmes qui faisaient le service de la table. Quand la silhouette d'Aminat se profila sur le seuil de la cuisine, le Moscovite se leva comme si de rien n'était, s'assura que Niyazbek parlementait avec un visiteur du côté des voitures et allongea un pas de promeneur sur les dalles de la cour.

Lorsqu'il eut atteint la cuisine, il vit Khizri à l'entrée. Le boiteux souriait de ses quatre dents en or. Le tissu de son maillot mouillé de sueur faisait saillir ses côtes maigres et, plus bas, les crosses de ses calibres.

— Fichue chaleur, se plaignit Khizri.

— Tu l'as dit, acquiesça Pankov. J'aimerais bien trouver… les vécés.

Khizri s'étira comme une vipère au réveil et prit un pistolet de sa ceinture. Clic, il sortit le chargeur, en vérifia les cartouches, remit le chargeur en place et montra le chemin à Pankov de la pointe de son arme.

— Les chiottes, c'est par ici, fit-il laconiquement.

"Quel effronté, pensa Pankov. Un vrai *killer*." Jamais, six mois auparavant, il n'aurait pu s'imaginer assis à la même table que ces hommes en maillots noirs et pantalons de survêtement, chacun champion du monde – ou d'Europe à la rigueur – de telle ou telle variété de cassage de gueule. Certes, ces types-là ne manquaient pas en Russie non plus. Mais là-bas ils taxaient les marchés de fringues et de quincaille ou vendaient des stups ; ici, ils étaient l'élite de la société, ils s'achetaient des fauteuils de ministres à coups de fric ou de menaces. C'était donc qu'il y avait quelque chose dans l'air de ces montagnes qui les distinguait foncièrement de leurs collègues russes. Pankov ne voulait pas s'avouer à lui-même que ce quelque chose était la foi en Allah. Et que ce quelque chose distinguait les hommes de Niyazbek non seulement de leurs collègues russes, mais aussi de la bande qui se disait de la famille du président Aslanov.

Irrité de n'avoir pu parler à la jeune fille, Pankov regagna sa place à table et se mit à grignoter une confiserie gorgée de sucre.

Près de lui, Mahomedsalih jouait aux échecs avec le fils aîné de Niyazbek, un garçon de onze ans. A regarder le jeu de plus près, Pankov se dit avec amertume que, décidément, le golf était bien le seul sport dans lequel il pourrait battre le jeune Avar. La partie gagnée, Mahomedsalih se leva et clac ! coucha le roi adverse.

— Coup de grâce ! s'exclama Mahomedsalih.

Deux semaines auparavant Mahomedsalih Salimkhanov avait été nommé directeur adjoint du port maritime, et Pankov brûlait de lui demander quel était le lien avec l'éphémère disparition du directeur qui avait fait tant de bruit dans Torbi-Kala.

Entre-temps Niyazbek avait pris congé d'un nouveau visiteur venu en Audi blindée. Quand la voiture se fut éloignée, il s'approcha de Pankov.

— On cause un peu ? dit-il.

Ils montèrent au premier étage par un escalier extérieur et se retrouvèrent dans un vaste salon à tapis et divans. Un énorme écran plat trônait dans un coin.

Agacé, Pankov songea qu'on lui faisait là un grand honneur : si tous les autres visiteurs avaient eu droit à un entretien près d'une voiture ou à la table commune, on daignait le recevoir, lui, à la maison : il faut ce qu'il faut. Puis il jeta un œil au sol et comprit qu'il avait oublié de se déchausser. Le tapis bordeaux foncé portait les traces de ses chaussures, et l'homme du Kremlin se sentit tel un sauvage européen dans un foyer musulman. Il rougit, s'approcha du seuil et se déchaussa.

Quand il revint, Niyazbek était déjà enfoncé dans un lourd fauteuil de cuir. Ses habits larges aplanissaient quelque peu ses muscles, une expression de quiétude mâtinée de fatigue irradiait de ses yeux de chouette marron noir. Sous le feu d'un tel regard, le grand commis de Moscou éprouva de la gêne. La question qui lui vint subitement à l'esprit était sans rapport avec le sujet prévu :

— Niyazbek, pourquoi ne t'achètes-tu pas un poste à responsabilités ? Tu as bien payé à Djavatkhan un fauteuil de vice-ministre de la Collecte fiscale, pourquoi pas à toi ?

— C'est *harâm*, dit Niyazbek. Interdit.

— Qu'est-ce qui est *harâm* ?

— Les impôts, les douanes, tout ça. *Harâm*. Un musulman doit payer la *zakât* et rien d'autre. Comment pourrais-je prélever à d'autres musulmans de l'argent qu'ils ne doivent pas payer ?

— Etre banquier aussi c'est *harâm* ?

— Bien sûr.

Pankov se rappela soudain une vieille bravade de Niyazbek qu'on lui avait rapportée la semaine d'avant. C'était l'époque où Gamzat Aslanov, aujourd'hui tout-puissant cardinal gris de la république, n'était encore que businessman et beau-frère de Niyazbek. Gamzat avait pris un crédit dans une banque et, naturellement, s'était assis dessus. Niyazbek s'était donc présenté à la banque pour proposer le remboursement de la moitié de la dette. L'autre moitié devait être oubliée. Devant le refus de la banque, Niyazbek et ses hommes avaient plaqué les hommes au sol, forcé le coffre-fort à coups d'armes à feu et brûlé tous les papiers qu'il contenait, à commencer par les attestations de crédit. C'était au début des années 1990 où les copies informatiques n'existaient pas encore. Résultat, la banque était morte. Du point de vue de Niyazbek, il n'avait rien fait de mal en se contentant de punir les auteurs d'un sacrilège : donner de l'argent contre intérêts.

— Donc, collecter l'impôt est *harâm*. Et tuer les hommes ?

Bref silence de Niyazbek.

— Un musulman, finit-il par dire, a cinq devoirs. Croire en Allah et son prophète Mahomet, que béni soit son nom, prier cinq fois par jour, faire le *hajj*, respecter le jeûne et payer la *zakât*. Où est le devoir de ne pas tuer dans ces cinq piliers-là ?

— Etre président, c'est aussi *harâm* ? demanda brusquement Pankov.

— Non. A condition de ne pas prendre de pot-de-vin. Et de ne pas piller les musulmans.

Pankov se tut quelques secondes. Le montagnard au front haut et à la mâchoire de mule le dardait de ses yeux rapaces et sombres, et l'homme du Kremlin fut pris d'un frisson. Il imagina Niyazbek Malikov à la tête du pays. "Pire qu'Aslanov, se dit-il soudain. Pire que Gamzat avec ses orgies, ses cadavres de chanteuses. Même pire que Wahha Arsaïev."

— De quoi voulais-tu me parler ? demanda Niyazbek. Tu n'es pas venu me parler des douanes, tout de même.

— Non. De l'attentat d'aujourd'hui. Sur la voie ferrée.

Niyazbek opina du chef mais ne dit rien.

— Restes-tu dans l'idée que le meurtre d'Igor est signé Gamzat Aslanov ?

Silence de Niyazbek.

— Alors argumente. J'ai besoin de t'entendre.

Pas un mot en réponse.

— Ecoute-moi bien, Niyazbek, tu es le frère d'Igor, je suis son ami. Et je ne me fiche pas de savoir qui l'a tué. Je n'ai pas l'intention de pardonner à ces gens-là. Mais quatre bombes ont disparu de ce putain d'entrepôt. L'une d'elles a mis en pièces un blindé plein de fédéraux. Une autre a fait sauter un train de munitions. La troisième a tué Igor. Même signature, même style. Dois-je en conclure que le président de la République ou son fils s'amusent à plastiquer des blindés sur leur propre territoire ? Je veux bien admettre que le président soit capable de faire liquider quelqu'un, ou que Gamzat, pour redorer son blason, s'ingénie à fabriquer un attentat à la noix pour l'élucider aussi sec, genre plasticage d'un tacot des usines GAZ ou deux cents grammes de TNT dans une poubelle. Mais anéantir un groupe spécial du FSB ? Dynamiter un train de munitions ?

— Alors qui voulait-on tuer à la place de mon frère ?

— Moi. Dans la voiture, ils croyaient que c'était moi. Je suis coupable de la mort d'Igor, Niyazbek. Regarde la vérité en face. Si tu cherches des coupables, tue-moi. Ça te soulagera.

Le montagnard souriait.

— Que t'a dit Wahha ? demanda Pankov.

— Quel Wahha ?

— Ne te paie pas ma tête. Wahha Arsaïev. Tu l'as rencontré à l'enterrement de ton frère. Il t'a fait gober un tas de bobards, je parie. Il t'a fait croire qu'il n'avait pas tué Igor. Mort de trouille, il était. C'était l'ambassadeur du Kremlin qu'il voulait tuer, un Russe que personne n'aurait pu venger, or voilà qu'il a fait pisser du sang entre lui et toi ! Alors il t'a menti : c'est pas moi, c'est le clan des Aslanov. Il a eu le culot de venir te voir et tu l'as laissé partir. Comprends-tu que tu as relâché le meurtrier de ton frère sous l'empire d'une haine aveugle pour Aslanov et fils ? Qu'as-tu à voir avec Arsaïev hormis les droits de péage que tu lui verses ?

— Je n'ai rien à voir avec lui.

— Le cherches-tu au moins ?

— Oui.

— Alors que vous êtes-vous dit, Niyazbek ? Comment liquider ensemble le président de la République ? Quoi que tu fasses avec lui, tu le fais de mèche avec le tueur de ton frère, comprends-tu ça ?

— Je n'ai pas vu Arsaïev.

— Jure au nom d'Allah.

— On ne jure pas au nom d'Allah pour des fadaises pareilles, Slava.

Là-dessus, Niyazbek quitta le salon en lançant un regard au couteau sur les traces de chaussures qui souillaient le tapis.

En rentrant chez lui, Vladislav Pankov était d'une humeur massacrante. Il avait pensé que, en s'invitant chez Malikov, il le ferait parler. Car, bon sang, n'importe quel dirigeant de la république serait flatté d'avoir la visite de l'homme du Kremlin. Tout le monde se réclamait des traditions de la juste foi et de la montagne, tout le monde glosait sur l'honneur et la fierté mais, quand il s'agissait d'une audience chez le premier commis de Moscou Vladislav Pankov, ils étaient tous prêts à faire antichambre jusqu'à plus d'heure !

Pankov ne connaissait personne dans la république, président compris, à qui la venue de l'ambassadeur du Kremlin n'eût fait boire du petit-lait.

Et Niyazbek ?

Et Niyazbek Malikov ne lui avait consacré que dix minutes, autant qu'à un petit vieux rabougri venu le voir dans sa Jigouli déglinguée, autant qu'à deux Tcherkesses en Geländewagen. Tout le reste du temps, le premier commis du Kremlin l'avait passé à la tablée commune avec des types en pantalons de survêt. Ou plutôt : avec des ministres en pantalons de survêt.

Car enfin que savait-il de l'homme nommé Niyazbek Malikov ?

Que cet homme lui avait sauvé la vie.

Arzo avait enlevé Pankov et Niyazbek l'avait sauvé.

Mais Niyazbek était-il si différent d'Arzo ?

Niyazbek sillonnait les montagnes de Tchétchénie avec des gardes armés. Il circulait librement là où les fédéraux n'étaient pas admis. Il parlait librement avec ceux qui n'adressaient la parole aux fédéraux qu'en faisant parler la poudre. Il poussait la porte de leurs maisons, banquetait à leurs noces, pleurait leurs morts. Il était là-bas chez lui. Et que fallait-il faire pour qu'Arzo te considère comme l'un des siens ?

Niyazbek le voleur, il ne s'en cachait même pas. Niyazbek le tueur, aucun doute là-dessus pour Pankov : il y avait au moins deux hommes dans son entourage que l'on désignait comme des *killers* patentés. Pas comme des bandits ni comme des boïéviks, si extensible que fût ce terme dans une contrée où même les ministres se faisaient passer tranquillement pour des boïéviks. Non. Comme des *killers*. Des pros. Des vrais. Des champions de l'explosif et du fusil à lunettes.

Igor Malikov n'avait jamais parlé de son frère à Vladislav. Qu'aurait-il pu lui raconter sinon l'histoire (anodine aux yeux des gens d'ici) d'un stock d'armes transporté à travers tout Moscou grâce à un sauf-conduit de député ?

Une fois le Moscovite parti, Niyazbek Malikov descendit dans la cour vers la table garnie de victuailles. Il se versa de l'eau mais, levant les yeux vers le soleil dont un coin émergeait encore au loin dans la mer, reposa son verre et s'assit.

— C'est qu'il a raison, dit Khizri.

Il avait suivi toute la conversation derrière la porte.

Niyazbek se balançait dans son fauteuil de plastique blanc, sa main caressant la lanière de son PM. Le tournoi de golf entre le club de Moscou et la sélection de la république régionale devait avoir lieu le surlendemain, auquel tournoi le président Aslanov jouerait en tandem avec son fils Gamzat.

— On aura l'air bête si on ne tue pas le coupable, dit Khizri.

Niyazbek se leva sans un mot et rentra chez lui. A l'intérieur, il déroula un petit tapis et se mit à prier.

Quand il revint à la table, il y trouva plus de monde. Deux neveux de Niyazbek étaient arrivés avec le frère cadet de Mahomedsalih. Le mois du ramadan n'était pas encore arrivé mais, dans cette maison, on observait le jeûne deux mois durant et l'on attendait le coucher du soleil pour manger.

— En route, dit Niyazbek. Il faut qu'on parle à quelqu'un.

Cinq minutes plus tard, la Merco blindée de Niyazbek s'immobilisait devant le mur relativement bas d'un pavillon privé.

Ironie du destin, la maison se trouvait sur la route la plus surveillée de la ville : c'était par là que Gamzat Aslanov se rendait au Parlement. La maison de pierre à deux étages faisait corps avec une enceinte haute de deux mètres. Un portail de fer donnait directement dans le garage. Une caméra de vidéosurveillance chapeautait le portillon. La propreté du trottoir, le long de la façade, témoignait du passage minutieux d'un balai. Deux belles jardinières à fleurs rouges encadraient la sortie des voitures. Il est vrai que toutes les maisons de la rue avaient la même allure à l'exception d'une vieille bâtisse en bois, en face : le siège du tribunal.

La Merco s'avança d'un demi-mètre devant le portail et s'arrêta, barrant le passage. Niyazbek descendit de voiture. Mahomedsalih voulut en faire autant, mais l'autre lui ayant dit : "Bouge pas", il claqua la portière.

Le quatre-quatre de l'escorte attendait à trois mètres. En sortirent deux gardes armés de PM qui firent quelques pas indécis, puis remontèrent en voiture sur un signe de Niyazbek.

Ne restait donc que Niyazbek. La nuit arrivait à grands pas. Le soleil s'était abîmé dans la mer où l'eau revêtait les couleurs du feu, et le vent qui se leva d'un coup fit rouler des papiers de Snickers et des tiges d'herbes sèches. Le parterre de fleurs qui s'étalait devant le siège du tribunal flamboyait de rouge, de bleu et de blanc. Niyazbek s'approcha du portail, leva les mains grandes ouvertes comme pour montrer à la caméra qu'il était sans armes, et appuya sur le bouton de la sonnette.

Du premier étage de la maison, qui surplombait le portail, deux types observaient la Merco avec horreur. Ils étaient vraiment très jeunes : l'un avait seize ans, l'autre dix-neuf et demi. C'étaient deux frères qui se ressemblaient en tout point : grandeur d'échalas, maigreur juvénile, maillots défraîchis par la sueur, pantalons crasseux – treillis sur l'un, survêt sur l'autre.

— Diables de Russes ! murmura le plus jeune, prénommé Kassim.

— Non, dit l'autre, c'est… c'est… ô Allah, mais c'est Niyazbek !

— Va réveiller Wahha, articula Kassim.

— Comment a-t-il su ?…

A cet instant, Niyazbek pressa le bouton de l'interphone, et le trille alarmant de la sonnette retentit dans la pièce.

— Qui est là ? demanda Kassim d'une voix enrayée par la peur.

— Je dois parler à Wahha.

— Quel Wahha ?

Dans la seconde qui suivit, un boïévik penché à la fenêtre arrosa l'asphalte d'une rafale d'arme automatique. Niyazbek réagit en un éclair dès qu'il eut aperçu la silhouette à l'embrasure : il se faufila derrière sa voiture avec l'agilité d'un poisson tout en sortant son pistolet. Une pluie de balles s'abattit sur la Mercedes et les jardinières aux fleurs rouges. Les vitres du Land Cruiser volèrent en éclats : les gardes de Niyazbek tiraient de l'intérieur, jugeant que des bris de verre valaient mieux que des crânes percés. Deux rafales de PM balayèrent les fenêtres ouvertes du premier étage et le boïévik, penché trop bas, poussa un cri, lâcha son arme et tomba à son tour.

D'un bond, Niyazbek se plaqua contre le mur. Une seconde plus tard, Mahomedsalih qui était au volant enclencha la marche arrière et braqua. Les cinq tonnes de la Merco emboutirent par le coffre le portail de fer en le faisant sauter de ses gonds. Les portières de la voiture s'ouvrirent, d'où jaillirent Djavatkhan et Mahomedsalih.

Là-haut, à l'étage, Wahha Arsaëv fit irruption dans le salon un PM au poing. Au lit comme ailleurs : tout habillé, tout armé. Il observa d'une façon quasi automatique que la Merco blindée avait barré la sortie du garage, puis aperçut la plaque du Land Cruiser, notant au passage combien les attaquants étaient peu nombreux. "Si Niyazbek était venu pour tuer, songea Wahha, il aurait pris une centaine d'hommes avec lui."

— Qui a tiré ?! hurla-t-il.

Trop tard : de l'autre côté de la rue, un homme s'était propulsé hors du Land Cruiser pour sortir du coffre une "mouche", lance-grenade à un coup. Wahha, presque sans viser, tira sur le type qui s'écroula sur place. Kassim était au sol, sur le séant, blessé à la jambe.

— On se replie, ordonna Wahha. (Puis, le doigt pointé sur Kassim :) Toi, tu nous couvres.

Cinq minutes plus tard, après une échauffourée brève mais sévère, Niyazbek et ses hommes surgirent à l'étage. Rien, personne. Seul Kassim était assis près de la fenêtre, mort, qui souriait à ses propres tripes grandes ouvertes. On découvrit bientôt dans la cave un passage souterrain qui semblait s'enfoncer vers le siège du tribunal. Nul ne s'y aventura de peur d'un guet-apens. On devait comprendre plus tard qu'Arsaïev et deux autres boïéviks avaient enfilé le passage secret jusqu'à deux pâtés de maisons plus loin. Là, ils avaient sauté dans une voiture prévue spécialement à cet effet, et bye-bye.

Niyazbek sortit du pavillon juste au moment où les voitures à gyrophares commençaient d'affluer. Le colonel Chebolev fut le premier arrivé. A la vue de Niyazbek, il comprit tout et s'écria :

— Bouclez le quartier ! Mais bouclez le quartier, bon sang !

— Trop tard, dit Niyazbek. Le comité du Parti a mis la clé sous la porte. Ils sont tous au front à l'heure qu'il est.

— Et il n'y a plus personne ?

— Celui qui reste est HS, articula Niyazbek, la main sur la portière de sa Mercedes.

Une demi-heure plus tard, ils étaient déjà de retour après un passage à l'hôpital. Un petit-neveu de Niyazbek (celui-là même qui avait voulu jongler avec un lance-grenade au nez et à la barbe des boïéviks retranchés dans la villa) était grièvement blessé au ventre, et Mahomedsalih souffrait d'une lésion superficielle à l'épaule. (Il refusa l'hospitalisation, se fit administrer un anesthésique et panser sa plaie, puis repartit sans demander son reste.)

Malikov gara sa Mercedes dans la cour. Il s'apprêtait à monter à l'étage quand Khizri l'apostropha :

— Niyazbek ! Nous avons un cadeau pour toi.

Il se retourna.

Khizri ouvrit le coffre de la Mercedes, et Mahomedsalih en sortit un jeune blondin au maillot rouge et au jean fripé.

— Ils le tenaient enfermé dans le garage, expliqua Mahomedsalih. Dans la fosse de visite.

Le gosse était gris de peur. Une puanteur pestilentielle s'infusait lentement dans la cour. Quand Mahomedsalih l'avait recueilli dans le garage, il avait fait sous lui. Apparemment, il avait remis ça dans le coffre.

— Livre-moi aux flics ! Livre-moi aux flics, Niyazbek ! s'écria le garçon.

Niyazbek secoua la tête.

— Les flics ont assez de boulot comme ça, dit-il. On ne va pas les surmener.

Pankov avait établi sa résidence dans un petit pavillon à deux étages situé place de la Trinité, à l'ouest de la ville. Si la place portait ce nom, c'était parce qu'une vieille et petite mosquée faisait vis-à-vis à une église nestorienne et qu'il y avait aussi, tout près de là, une synagogue.

Habité, ce quartier l'avait été dès le XVIIᵉ siècle mais, curieusement, s'était vidé à l'époque soviétique, investi par des entrepôts. Ceux-ci rasés, ils cédaient maintenant la place à l'un des quartiers résidentiels les plus attrayants de la ville. De la colline où il s'était établi, Pankov pouvait embrasser du regard la villa à quatre étages du procureur de la République, celle, attenante, du chef du bureau judiciaire et même, en diagonale, le toit rouge de la villa de Niyazbek, quatre pâtés de maisons plus loin.

Pankov sortit sur le balcon. En cette soirée de vendredi, les hommes avaient repris le chemin de la mosquée ; dans la ruelle qui menait à la synagogue s'alignait une file de vieillards aux chapeaux à larges bords, leurs mains tenant des cierges. Deux calicots publicitaires étendus en travers de la rue ondoyaient mollement au vent. L'un d'eux vantait le top des ventes de la saison : un anti-explosif par brouillage radio *made in Russia*. L'autre annonçait pour le surlendemain le tournoi de golf entre le club de Moscou et la sélection de la république.

Le disque rouge du soleil, vaporeux, avait sombré dans la mer, la lune s'imprimait timidement dans le ciel comme une image naissant sur un papier photo, une volée de mômes s'agitaient dans le jardin d'à côté entre des draps à l'étendoir, et Pankov remarqua dans les mains d'un bambin une mitraillette en jouet, du moins l'espéra-t-il.

Il se rappela soudain ces gosses tchétchènes qui jouaient avec des poupées sans jambes. "Je n'accepterai pas une chose pareille dans cette république, jura-t-il. Je ne l'accepterai pas quoi qu'il m'en coûte parce que cette terre est un morceau de Russie et que la Russie n'existe pas sans cette terre."

Puis il vit une femme qui courait. Elle venait de la gauche, débouchant d'une ruelle qui menait à la maison de Niyazbek. Elle traversa la place, se tailla un passage parmi les fidèles qui allaient à la prière et bientôt se coula dans le portail en fer forgé de la résidence.

Il descendit les marches quatre à quatre. Comme dans de nombreuses villas de la région, les deux étages tenaient l'un à l'autre par un escalier intérieur, mais aussi extérieur : celui qu'il dévala. Quand il atteignit l'allée de gravier sur laquelle lévitaient les boules jaunes des réverbères dans un air encore lumineux, le portillon s'ouvrit en grinçant, par où surgit, si frêle devant le molosse en faction, essoufflée, ébouriffée, des chaussons aux pieds, Aminat.

La jeune fille se jeta sur Pankov, s'agrippa à sa manche et serait tombée dans les graviers s'il ne l'avait retenue à temps :

— Sauvez-le ! Il n'y a que vous ! Je vous en supplie, vous seul pouvez...

— Moi ? fit Pankov le cœur rempli d'un secret espoir.

Aminat éclata en sanglots. Elle sanglotait, étouffée par ses mots et ses larmes à travers lesquels Pankov crut comprendre ce qui suit. Aminat avait un ami, ancien camarade de fac, ce garçon aux cheveux de blé qu'il avait vu au golf. Il s'appelait Serguéï, et Niyazbek n'avait jamais caché qu'il n'en voulait pas comme beau-frère. Il avait dit un jour à Aminat que le jeune était lié aux milieux séparatistes. Après avoir reçu deux avertissements, Serguéï avait disparu la semaine d'avant. Aminat accusait son frère de l'avoir enlevé, mais Niyazbek jurait sur Allah que non, ce n'était pas lui.

Or aujourd'hui, peu après le départ de Pankov, Niyazbek s'était absenté. Il venait de rentrer avec Serguéï. Aminat l'avait vu, ses hommes et lui, sortir le garçon du coffre et le rouer de coups de pied dans la cour.

Elle s'était sauvée avant qu'on ne repense à elle, vêtue comme elle était, en chaussons, sans foulard, et si près de Pankov qu'il voyait ses longs cils collés par les larmes, ses lèvres criblées de morsures et son sein si jeune, gonflé, prêt à jaillir du bonnet de son soutien-gorge sous son maillot blanc.

— Vladislav Avdeïevitch, aidez-nous ! Il va le tuer !

A cet instant le chef de la garde de Pankov, Sergueï Piskounov, sortit en trombe de la maison.

— Vladislav Avdeïevitch, criait-il, prenez le téléphone ! Niyazbek et ses hommes ont tué Arsaïev !

L'instant d'après Pankov occupait déjà la banquette arrière d'un quatre-quatre qui partait sur les chapeaux de roues.

A peine quarante minutes de passées depuis le raid de Niyazbek contre la maison de l'avenue Lénine, et déjà une demi-douzaine de voitures de police postées autour de son pavillon. Il y avait aussi des gars de sa bande – toute une meute groupée dans sa cour –, mines sombres, tignasses noires, bodybuildés, et Pankov sentit son nez piqué d'une mâle odeur de violence, de sueur, de canon lubrifié.

Niyazbek accueillit Pankov dans le salon où il se trouvait en compagnie de Djavatkhan et de Khizri autour d'un guéridon, presque tête contre tête. Il se redressa tranquillement à l'entrée du Moscovite, alla à sa rencontre en le regardant du haut de sa taille et en lui tendant une main large aux ongles longs sous lesquels caillait du sang.

— Ton conseil était plein de bon sens, dit Niyazbek.

— Où est Sergueï ?

— Quel Sergueï ?

— Le boïévik que vous avez coffré chez l'autre.

Niyazbek posa sur le Moscovite les deux olives marron-noir de ses yeux.

— Je ne comprends pas, dit Niyazbek.

— J'ai eu la visite d'Aminat aux abois. Encore heureux qu'elle soit venue. S'il te plaît...

— Sais-tu seulement pour qui tu plaides ? articula Niyazbek d'un ton à hérisser le poil.

Là-dessus, il tourna brusquement les talons et quitta la pièce, invitant Pankov à le suivre d'un mouvement du menton.

Le garçon croupissait dans la cave, menotté à un tuyau, ses cheveux de blé gélifiés de sang. Plus une trace des taches de rousseur que lui avait connues Pankov lors de leur dernière rencontre. Face grise, front boutonneux, nez saignant qu'il essuyait sans cesse de sa manche gauche laissée libre. Au bruit de la porte, il leva la tête et ses yeux s'écarquillèrent quand il vit entrer dans la cave, sur les talons de Niyazbek, le fonctionnaire chétif aux lunettes d'écaille et à la veste mal ajustée.

— Comment t'es-tu retrouvé chez Wahha, raconte un peu, ordonna Niyazbek.

— J'ai été enlevé, Vladislav Avdeïevitch, je ne suis pas de leur camp, ils m'ont enlevé et jeté dans une fosse…

— Et pourquoi t'a-t-on enlevé ?

— On m'a enlevé parce que tu l'as exigé ! C'est Wahha lui-même qui me l'a dit. Si tu es là, qu'il m'a dit, c'est grâce à Niyazbek.

Niyazbek se tourna vers Pankov et lui dit d'un ton impassible :

— Tu voulais que je t'apprenne à frapper ?

Pankov sentit sa paupière trémuler.

— Dans un combat libre, reprit Niyazbek, il y a deux coups interdits. Dans les couilles et les doigts dans les yeux. Si tu veux frapper, fais-le la main ouverte. Dans les yeux et plus bas. Comme ça. Même toi tu pourras.

L'épine nasale de Sergueï craqua comme une paille sèche quand Niyazbek le frappa au visage du plat de la main. Sa nuque heurta le mur. Niyazbek l'empoigna par ses cheveux trop longs et, d'un coup sec, leva son menton souillé de morve et de sang.

— Ton père, comment s'appelle-t-il ? demanda Niyazbek.

— A… alkadi.

Sergueï s'efforçait de reprendre ses esprits. On aurait dit qu'il avalait avec ses dents la moitié des mots. Il y avait quelque chose d'étrange dans sa prononciation, avec sa façon de prendre les *r* pour des *l*.

— Il est russe ?

— Oui.

— Alors quelle mouche t'a piqué d'aller faire la guerre aux Russes ?

— A l'époque, tout le monde faisait la guelle aux Lusses.

A ce moment, Pankov comprit tout : Sergueï avait l'accent liquide des gens de Grozny, le même qu'Arzo. L'accent d'un garçon qui avait grandi parmi les Tchétchènes ; d'un garçon qui partageait les mêmes valeurs que les jeunes Tchétchènes ; d'un garçon qui voulait coûte que coûte devenir le premier d'entre deux.

— Et maintenant, raconte ce que tu as fait plus tard, dit Niyazbek.

Bruit de bouche, bruit de nez, Sergueï cherchait de l'air. Son visage n'était plus qu'un masque de larmes et de sang.

— Non ? alors c'est moi qui raconte, gronda Niyazbek. Il a été pris les armes à la main, mais la famille de son beau-frère a payé la rançon. Un mec bien, son beau-frère, quoique tchétchène. Mais ça n'a pas effacé son dossier judiciaire. Il y a deux ans, les flics ont remis la main dessus pour le faire condamner, mais ils ont fini par le relâcher. Après quoi il s'est lié d'amitié avec le fils du directeur de l'usine radiotechnique, lui fournissant armes et littérature. Les flics ont coffré le fils du directeur et son père a dû payer deux cent mille dollars pour que son dossier judiciaire soit classé sans suite, plus cent mille dollars qu'il continue de payer mensuellement. Après, Sergueï devient doctorant et se lie d'amitié avec le fils du doyen de la fac d'économie, lui fournissant armes et littérature. Les flics le coffrent à son tour, et son père débourse trois cent mille dollars pour le classement du dossier, sans compter cinq admissions gratuites qu'il a dû faire à l'université. Après, Sergueï se lie d'amitié avec le fils du directeur de l'aéroport, et il en coûtera trois cent cinquante mille dollars à son père. Ensuite, il se met à faire la cour à ma sœur.

— C'est vrai tout ça ? demanda Pankov.

— J'ai pas voulu la recluter ! hurla Sergueï. Je l'aime !

— C'est vrai, renvoya Niyazbek, tu ne l'as pas plantée, pas fou à ce point. Ton calcul, c'était que je te fasse blanchir par les flics.

— C'est vrai ? redemanda Pankov.

— Non !

Niyazbek sortit son arme de son dos et la braqua sur le crâne de Sergueï.

— Tu vas me signer un papier, dit Niyazbek, pour expliquer comment, sous les ordres des boïéviks, tu t'incrustais chez les gosses de riches, et comment tu les livrais à Arif. Et Vladislav repartira avec. Demain, tu seras inculpé. Tu en prendras pour cinq ans. Ça te va ?

Le garçon ensanglanté tenta de se soustraire à la menace du pistolet. Pankov secoua la tête :

— Je ne marche pas, dit l'homme du Kremlin.

Le coup de feu retentit comme un coup de tonnerre. Pankov eut la chemise éclaboussée de cervelle et de sang. C'était la deuxième fois qu'on tuait quelqu'un sous ses yeux. La première fois, il l'avait vu faire par la main d'Arzo.

Il lui sembla que le temps avait suspendu sa course. Il vit flotter la main de Niyazbek, légèrement secouée par le recul ; il vit aussi chavirer le mort. Il se sentit soudain du coton dans les jambes, fit un pas en arrière, trébucha et se laissa tomber sur un siège métallique qui était là derrière lui.

Niyazbek remit son pistolet à la ceinture et dit en souriant :

— Voilà qui est fait. Puisque tu n'as pas voulu passer par la justice…

— Tu es fou, dit Pankov. Que vais-je dire à Aminat ?

— Tu n'as rien à lui dire, répondit Niyazbek. Allons chez toi ensemble, je la ramènerai. Tu ne t'imagines tout de même pas que ma sœur va passer la nuit sous le toit d'un homme inconnu ? Ou veux-tu que je sois obligé de te tuer comme ce petit salopard ?

Gamzat Aslanov se rendit chez Pankov à huit heures du matin. Pour un homme qui passait son temps enfermé chez lui comme silure en eau profonde, c'était faire acte de bravoure. Mais quand il sortait de son trou, il le faisait sans sommation. Ainsi se présenta-t-il chez le premier commis du Kremlin, sans s'être annoncé.

Pankov venait à peine de se lever, ses fonctionnaires n'ayant pas osé le déranger au téléphone.

Quand Gamzat entra dans la véranda où le Moscovite prenait son café matinal, il lui tendit un mince dossier.

— De quoi s'agit-il ? demanda Pankov.

— Une expertise dactyloscopique. Le pistolet-mitrailleur abandonné par le meurtrier d'Ibrahim Malikov parce qu'il était blessé, vous souvenez-vous ?… Il portait des empreintes digitales. On a trouvé les mêmes dans la maison d'hier.

— Ce sont celles des morts ?

— Non. Dans la cuisine, sur une tasse, et dans le garage. Il y avait tout un labo d'explosifs. Ce type-là en a laissé un peu partout. Il a dû fuir avec Arsaïev, ou peut-être avant.

Le Moscovite marqua un silence.

— Soyons francs, reprit Gamzat, vous ne portez guère notre famille dans votre cœur. Il faut vraiment avoir une dent contre quelqu'un pour obliger sa femme à lui renvoyer des cadeaux offerts de bonne grâce. Mais vous avez tort de penser que ce meurtre nous était profitable. Vous avez beau être le représentant du président fédéral, ce n'est pas vous qui décidez qui sera promu à la tête de la république. Ces choses-là se décident au Kremlin. Votre avis pèse lourd, certes, mais il ne suffit pas. Vous n'aviez guère de chance de placer Ibrahim Malikov à la tête de la république, et savez-vous pourquoi ?

— Pourquoi ?

— Question d'argent. Ni lui ni vous n'aviez les moyens d'acheter la place, et il n'aurait jamais sollicité Niyazbek.

Pankov sentit le sang lui monter au visage.

— Le meurtre d'Ibrahim Malikov devait d'abord profiter aux séparatistes, dit Gamzat, parce que sa disparition est à l'origine d'une situation anormale dans la république. Une situation dans laquelle le premier commis du Kremlin Pankov déteste le président Aslanov, et cette détestation réciproque court-circuite le bon fonctionnement du pouvoir. De cela, Niyazbek Malikov est parfaitement conscient. Il n'a pas le moindre doute sur la véritable identité du meurtrier de son frère. Mais il préfère monter sur ses grands chevaux de preux caucasien au nom de la famille, de l'honneur et de la gloire. En vérité, il est comme nous tous. Il se fiche pas mal de savoir qui a tué son frère. L'important, pour lui, c'est de régler ses comptes avec mon clan et moi-même.

Pankov ne disait mot. Wahha Arsaïev avait quand même fait le déplacement pour les condoléances. L'autre reprit :

— Et croyez-vous que ces comptes soient à ce point édifiants ? Pour l'enlèvement, c'est vrai, nous avons menti à notre père. Arzo nous avait enlevés pour de bon. Mais pourquoi

pensez-vous que nous n'avons pu lui payer nos dettes ?
D'après vous, où cet argent est-il passé ? Niyazbek et ses hommes maraudaient autour de nous jour et nuit ! Ils venaient me
voir à quatre heures du matin, à cinq heures, pour me rouer
de coups ! Niyazbek disait : Nos gars ont un championnat,
aboule le fric. Par reconnaissance, ils m'ont nommé entraîneur. Un jour, un garçon dont j'étais l'entraîneur déclaré a
gagné les Jeux olympiques et le comité d'Etat aux Sports lui
a alloué une prime de cinquante mille dollars. C'est moi qui ai
touché cet argent parce que j'étais son entraîneur officiel et
que je l'avais accompagné au Kremlin. Résultat, ils m'ont enlevé à la sortie de l'avion. Croyez-vous qu'ils se soient conten-
tés de me faire recracher les cinquante mille ? Vous n'y êtes
pas ! Deux cent mille, qu'ils m'ont fait cracher. Pour préjudice
moral, humiliation, ceci, cela. Et Niyazbek n'a même pas tiqué !
(Gamzat fit la grimace.) Ma garde ne vous plaît pas, Vladislav
Avdeïevitch ? Vous la trouvez trop nombreuse ? C'est parce
que j'ai juré que personne ne m'enlèverait plus jamais ! que
personne ne me traînerait plus jamais dans la boue ! que personne n'entrerait plus jamais chez moi à quatre heures du
matin ! C'est vrai, je ne suis pas aussi fort que Niyazbek ! Je ne
peux pas tuer un homme d'un seul coup de poing ! Ce qui fait
de moi un imbécile aux yeux de Niyazbek et de ses hommes !
A vos yeux aussi ?

Gamzat eut un mouvement vers la sortie. A cet instant,
Pankov avisa le colonel Chebolev sur les marches de la véranda. Sans doute était-il là depuis quelques minutes. Il avait
un dossier plastique à la main.

— *Salam aleïkum*, Gamzat Ahmednabievitch, dit Chebolev.

Gamzat maugréa, toisa le colonel de la tête aux pieds et
quitta prestement la véranda.

Chebolev s'approcha, salua le Moscovite et consulta les
feuilles laissées par Gamzat.

— Que m'apportes-tu là ? fit Pankov en pointant le menton sur le dossier.

— La même chose que Gamzat.

— A-t-on vérifié les empreintes des morts ?

— Oui.

— C'est donc que l'individu a pris la fuite ?

Chebolev laissa la question sans réponse.

— En vérité, il y a une troisième possibilité.

— Laquelle ?

— Il y avait un autre zèbre dans la maison.

Pankov sentit son sang se glacer. Non, pensa-t-il au bout d'une seconde, ce n'est pas possible. Sergueï était ce qu'on voudra, mais pas un professionnel dans les explosifs.

— Il y avait un autre zèbre, continua Chebolev, et tout me fait dire qu'il était détenu dans une fosse. Je ne pense pas qu'on l'ait simplement enlevé. Sans doute était-il de mèche avec les boïéviks, mais on lui reprochait quelque chose.

— Cet homme-là ne pourra plus jamais parler, dit Pankov.

Le colonel fronça le sourcil.

— Tiens donc ! Auriez-vous vu le cadavre ?

Pankov posa sa tasse de café sur la table, et ses mains se mirent à trembler.

— Hé ! hé ! fit le colonel.

— Quoi hé ! hé ! Qu'est-ce que tu veux dire par là ?

Le cri du Moscovite était celui d'un oiseau blessé.

— Rien de spécial, dit Chebolev. Je suis étonné que les choses se soient passées aussi vite. Je pensais que Niyazbek, en pareil cas, n'était guère enclin à… euh… à des moyens aussi expéditifs.

A ces mots, le premier commis du Kremlin courut à la balustrade, d'où il renvoya son petit-déjeuner.

La commission de lutte contre le terrorisme se réunit en séance extraordinaire à deux heures de l'après-midi dans la Maison sur la Colline. Outre les chefs des plus grandes autorités administratives, y assistaient aussi le président de la République avec son fils cadet, le speaker, Arzo Khadjiev et Niyazbek Malikov.

Le général Razgonov, chef du FSB régional, fut le premier à rendre compte au premier commis du Kremlin des succès remportés dans ce domaine.

— Hier, dit le général, au terme d'une longue et minutieuse enquête, nous avons fini par localiser la planque de Wahha Arsaïev. Avons mis en œuvre une opération pour le neutraliser. Deux de ses complices sont morts. Arsaïev a réussi à s'enfuir mais, d'après nos informations, il serait mortellement blessé.

Telle était la version officielle des événements de la veille, aussitôt retransmise par tous les bulletins d'information. En vérité, bien sûr, même les trous du terrain de golf savaient ce qu'il en était vraiment.

— Les services de l'Intérieur ont élucidé jusqu'au bout les circonstances de l'attentat terroriste perpétré contre Ibrahim Malikov, déclara le ministre et général Arif Talgoïev. Bien que l'exécutant se soit suicidé, nous avons pu établir l'identité de ses complices.

— En ces jours où la république fait la cible d'attaques massives de l'extérieur, dit Ibrahim Aslanov, chef des Douanes et cousin du président, une mission particulière échoit aux services douaniers. Au cours du seul dernier trimestre, nous avons pu saisir sept tonnes de littérature toutes langues confondues, dont le livre du fameux wahhabiste An-Nâwawî *Riyad as-Salihin* – même titre que l'appellation du groupe armé de Bassaïev.

— Je tiens à souligner l'exploit de mes collaborateurs, déclara le chef du comité de lutte contre les stupéfiants Ibrahimbek Sultygov. Lors d'un raid, ils ont accroché une voiture de terroristes qui transportaient de la drogue. Bien que moins nombreux, mes hommes leur ont livré un combat inégal. Trois d'entre eux ont été tués, le quatrième, grièvement blessé, a été enlevé par les scélérats. Il y a fort à parier qu'il ait été torturé et assassiné. Je propose de présenter tous les hommes de la patrouille à des distinctions *post mortem*.

Le président fut le dernier à prendre la parole :

— Voilà des succès notables, j'insiste là-dessus, que nous avons remportés sous la sage férule de Vladislav Avdeïevitch. Disons-le franchement : sans son soutien, sans ses conseils, nous n'aurions jamais eu la force de tenir tête à ces nervis et terroristes qui étranglent notre peuple pacifique du garrot de l'extrémisme. Notre république vient d'entrer dans une ère nouvelle. Que Vladislav Avdeïevitch en soit remercié !

Toute l'assistance applaudit et Pankov ne put s'empêcher de jeter un œil en coin sur Niyazbek. Celui-ci seul n'applaudissait pas. Renversé comme à son habitude sur le dossier de sa chaise, il appuyait ses doigts longs et puissants sur le revêtement verni de la table, et son visage de carnassier aux traits réguliers, au nez légèrement écrasé et aux yeux couleur de roche du mont Torbi-Taou – son visage était de statue.

— N'as-tu rien à ajouter au rapport du général Razgonov ? demanda Chebolev à Niyazbek.

— A savoir ?...

— Il y avait là-bas un boïévik mis au trou par ses propres camarades. Il avait dû faire quelque chose de dérangeant. Quoi au juste ? Et qu'est-il devenu depuis ? Tu ne veux pas nous le dire ?

— Tu as bien entendu ce qu'a dit ton chef, répondit Niyazbek : je n'étais pas dans la maison. Comment pourrais-je savoir qui est passé où ?

Gamzat Aslanov échangea un regard avec son père. Une chenille passa sur ses lèvres en guise de sourire.

Pankov se leva.

— Je vous ai réunis, messieurs, pour faire l'annonce que voici. Dès avant ma nomination à ce poste, nous avions envisagé au Kremlin la refonte de plusieurs autorités administratives en une seule et même organisation dotée de pouvoirs exceptionnels, une organisation non subordonnée au gouvernement de la république régionale. Il y a deux heures, le président de la fédération de Russie a signé l'ordre de créer un état-major antiterroriste qui sera la principale autorité de la région. Je suis nommé à la tête de cet état-major. Mon premier adjoint devient le général Guennadi Chebolev, nouveau chef du FSB régional. J'aurai aussi pour adjoints le général Akromeïev, désormais ministre de l'Intérieur, et le général Stroutchkov, commandant en second du district militaire du Caucase. Le général Sultygov et le procureur Makhriev, ici présents, sont démis de leurs fonctions. Le groupe d'intervention spéciale du FSB Youg a désormais sa base dans la ville à dater de ce jour. Il est habilité à accomplir toutes les opérations avalisées par l'état-major. D'ici deux heures, l'aérodrome de Torbi-Kala recevra les premiers avions-cargos transporteurs de troupes des forces de l'Intérieur. Cinq mille agents du groupe d'intervention spéciale et de la section de lutte contre le crime organisé sont attendus dans la république, ainsi que des chars et des engins lourds.

Pankov s'assit. Le silence se fit tel qu'on eût entendu le murmure d'une chasse d'eau, deux étages plus bas.

Le premier à réagir fut le général Sultygov. Il leva les bras au plafond, rougit et dit enfin, les yeux embués de larmes :

— Mais alors... et dire que... j'avais déjà présenté mes gars aux plus hautes distinctions...

Le procureur Makhriev, qui devait disputer le tournoi de golf du lendemain en tandem avec Pankov, battait bêtement des paupières. Ahmednabi Aslanov affichait la dignité de sa propre statue. Niyazbek, la tête inclinée, payait Pankov du regard souriant d'un tueur.

— Pour les plus durs de la comprenette, dit Pankov, j'ajoute autre chose. Si jamais quelqu'un s'avise de faire crépiter des mitraillettes dans les rues de la ville (je pense être clair, Gamzat Ahmednabievitch), ou de lancer ses propres sbires dans des opérations spéciales (n'est-ce pas, Niyazbek Adievitch ?), ceux-là se verront pris en charge directement par l'état-major antiterroriste. Hier c'était hier. Et aujourd'hui c'est aujourd'hui. Y a-t-il des questions ?

A ce moment le silence de plomb de la salle fut rompu par des battements de mains espacés mais réguliers. C'était Niyazbek dont les yeux marron-noir de faucon continuaient de sourire et dont les mains sonnaient comme des gifles. Pankov fut soudain pris de panique. "Je suis chef d'état-major, se dit-il à lui-même, je tiens sous mes ordres le FSB et le ministère de l'Intérieur, cinq mille agents des forces spéciales, les nervis de Khadjiev et deux bataillons de blindés. Que peut faire Niyazbek avec ses Abreks et sa mitraillette en bandoulière ? – Il peut tuer un homme du plat de la main, se répondit le Moscovite à lui-même, alors que tu n'es pas fichu de lever la main sur quiconque."

L'ambassadeur du Kremlin se leva brusquement et quitta la salle en invitant le général Chebolev à le suivre d'un mouvement du menton.

Ce n'était pas le triomphe attendu. Il avait lu de la panique dans les yeux des pontifes, ministres, sous-ministres et présidents de tous poils. Il avait lu de la panique jusque dans les yeux du président de la République. Mais rien dans ceux de Gamzat Aslanov ou de Niyazbek Malikov, rien d'autre qu'un sourire patenté de tueur devant un gosse qui les menacerait d'un pistolet à eau. Pankov, quelque part, n'avait pas su s'y prendre.

La nouvelle se répandit comme une traînée de poudre. Quand Niyazbek quitta le siège du gouvernement, les députés faisaient des messes basses devant leurs Mercedes. On aurait dit des abeilles vibrionnant autour d'une ruche saccagée. La dernière fois que Niyazbek avait été le témoin d'un tel spectacle, c'était quand les sbires de Wahha Arsaïev avaient abattu un député nogaï après que celui-ci eut insulté Aslanov en pleine séance parlementaire. Tout le monde donnait raison à Gamzat mais la chose faisait jaser parce que les basses œuvres avaient été exécutées par Wahha, et non par le service d'ordre d'Aslanov offensé.

Niyazbek se fraya un passage à travers la foule aux abois et regagna la voiture où l'attendait Djavatkhan.

— Est-ce vrai qu'on nous envoie les troupes ? demanda Djavatkhan.

— Oui, répondit Niyazbek.

— Alors que fait-on demain ?

— La même chose que prévu.

Djavatkhan marqua un silence de quelques secondes. Il aurait pu en dire des vertes et des pas mûres à la face de Niyazbek. Il aurait pu lui dire qu'ils avaient eu l'idée d'abattre le président parce qu'à l'époque on le croyait responsable du meurtre d'Ibrahim mais que, maintenant, plus personne n'en savait rien sauf peut-être le tueur lui-même. Il aurait pu lui dire que massacrer la famille du président de la République le lendemain de l'arrivée des troupes, c'était carrément chercher des crosses aux fédéraux. Il aurait pu lui dire aussi que lui-même – Niyazbek – avait passé les bornes : s'il n'avait pas logé une balle dans le crâne d'un type enchaîné à un radiateur sous les yeux de Pankov, il n'était pas sûr que l'autre aurait sonné la mobilisation des troupes.

— Tu perds la tête, dit Djavatkhan. Si la famille Aslanov est la seule zigouillée, passe encore. Mais imagine un peu qu'on en zigouille une centaine...

D'un œil indifférent, Niyazbek regardait la voiture louvoyer entre les blocs de béton qui balisaient l'accès au barrage.

— Vois-tu, dit Niyazbek, j'ai donné ma parole à cette femme. Je tiens toujours ma parole.

Le match qui devait opposer le club de golf de Moscou à la sélection de la république régionale était prévu pour le 17 septembre. Dans la mesure où, *de facto*, une situation d'urgence avait été décrétée la veille, les préparatifs s'accompagnaient de mesures exceptionnelles de sécurité.

Quarante flics écumèrent les dix-huit trous du parcours avec des détecteurs de métaux, passant même au peigne fin la pelouse intacte du terrain. Suivirent vingt maîtres-chiens à la recherche d'explosifs. On mit un soin particulier à vérifier les lignes de départ et les greens.

Vingt-quatre heures avant le match, le périmètre du parcours fut encerclé par les services de patrouille de l'Intérieur, et dès qu'une unité de la section de lutte contre le crime organisé eut débarqué de Krasnoïarsk, à une heure de l'après-midi, elle fut transférée de l'aéroport au terrain de golf. A la mi-journée, le chef de la sécurité de Gamzat, un nommé Chapi, décida de faire installer des miradors près des deuxième et douzième trous.

Le soleil amorçait déjà son plongeon dans la mer quand Chapi et ses hommes virent accourir à la véranda où ils se trouvaient, à huit heures et demie du soir, l'un des managers du club. Il s'appelait Rasul.

— Là-bas, dit Rasul essoufflé, là-bas…

"Là-bas", c'était la passerelle située entre les deuxième et dix-septième trous : un petit pont en parfaite harmonie avec le paysage entièrement habillé de jolis galets – balustrade et tablier. Or, ce tablier avait été balayé d'une rafale de pistolet-mitrailleur, et les éclats frais de granit brillaient sous les rayons du couchant comme des tessons brisés.

Chapi et ses hommes échangèrent des regards. Ils avaient certes entendu un tir, une heure ou deux auparavant, mais n'y avaient guère attaché d'importance. Trop tard désormais pour démêler qui des hommes de Krasnoïarsk ou des gens du coin avait donné ce coup de griffe à la magnificence du décor. Ce qui comptait, maintenant, c'était que les compétiteurs passeraient forcément par là le lendemain (ils n'allaient tout de même pas voler dans les airs) et qu'ils verraient cette horreur. Si Gamzat se contentait seulement de leur donner le bâton, passe encore. Mais s'il les fichait carrément à la porte ?

Agacé, Chapi téléphona à l'atelier qui avait travaillé la pierre. Une demi-heure plus tard arrivait un vieil artisan nommé

Ali. L'homme examina le revêtement en présence des gardes et s'engagea à le refaire pour le lendemain matin. En soi, ces galets-là n'étaient pas un matériau introuvable : le parvis du siège du gouvernement en avait été pavé deux mois auparavant (vu le coût des travaux, on aurait même pu penser que les galets étaient d'or).

Puis Chapi se tourna vers Rasul :

— Accompagne-le et rapporte ce qu'il lui faut. Et que ce soit fini à l'aube.

Il était déjà dix heures du soir quand Rasul et Ali arrivèrent à l'atelier. Ils firent les préparatifs jusqu'à onze heures et prirent le chemin du retour dans la nuit noire. Des feux passèrent dans le ciel : un avion gros comme une baleine se positionnait pour l'atterrissage.

— Un transporteur, dit Ali.

— Deux milliers d'hommes arrivés par avion dans la journée, commenta Rasul. Ils sont logés dans les gymnases, à ce qu'on dit.

De nombreuses patrouilles sillonnaient la ville. Cela faisait six mois que les miliciens ne circulaient plus la nuit. Ils se retranchaient dans les postes. Quand ils sortaient, ils ôtaient leurs gilets pare-balles pour en revêtir leurs véhicules de service. Autrefois, un patrouilleur achetait sa place deux mille dollars ; maintenant, ceux-là mêmes qui avaient déboursé pareille somme préféraient démissionner.

Cette nuit-là, ils furent arrêtés trois fois, et toujours par des patrouilleurs russes. Les Russes avaient l'air timoré.

— Dis donc, mec, dit un sergent russe qui les avait arrêtés sur l'avenue du Cheik-Mansour, où est-ce qu'on peut trouver des filles par ici ?

Rasul leur montrait le chemin du port quand son téléphone sonna. Rasul dit "Allô", écouta le message et perdit brusquement ses couleurs. Le milicien n'y vit que du feu.

— Qu'y a-t-il ? demanda Ali.

Rasul hocha la tête et redémarra. Ils roulaient déjà rue Bolotov quand Rasul dit :

— Je vais passer chez ma mère. Il faut que je prenne à manger.

— OK, consentit Ali.

Rasul gara son tacot devant le portail d'une vieille maison sans le faire entrer dans la cour.

— Attends-moi ici, dit Rasul.

— D'accord, fit l'autre en haussant les épaules.

Il passa le portillon. Moins qu'une maison, c'était une espèce de hangar aux murs lézardés, étayés çà et là d'une botte de foin. Le portail donnait sur un auvent délabré qui abritait une antique Moskvitch toute rouillée. Rasul avait beau ouvrir l'œil, il ne put distinguer les hommes qui se cachaient derrière. Or ils étaient bien là, aucun doute là-dessus.

Il poussa la porte et tressaillit.

Une pièce à la fenêtre soigneusement occultée baignait dans une lumière blafarde, dans laquelle étaient assis trois hommes : Niyazbek, Djavatkhan et un jeune type d'une vingtaine d'années à la tête ronde et aux bras musculeux courts. A la porte entrouverte de la cuisine se profilaient des ombres.

Il y avait sur la table, face à Niyazbek, une vingtaine de pavés identiques à ceux que les balles venaient d'ébrécher.

Pétrifié, Rasul les fixa du regard. Une seule pierre évidée pouvait contenir une livre de TNT indétectable à la sonde magnétique parce que cet explosif ne renfermait aucun projectile métallique. Les éclats du pavé remplaçaient les projectiles. A lui seul le choc explosif pouvait suffire à anéantir tous ceux qui passeraient le pont à ce moment-là.

Rasul sentait bien que ce n'était pas tout. Le troisième homme n'était certes pas disert, mais qu'il fût kagébiste, sapeur ou boïévik, on voyait bien qu'il calculerait l'onde de choc pour précipiter le pont entier dans ce gouffre étroit de deux cents mètres au fond duquel murmurait un ruisseau.

De voir Niyazbek en chair et en os stupéfiait Rasul. Depuis que sa sœur était allée lui parler, ni ses hommes ni lui-même n'avaient cherché à le rencontrer. Des gens étaient venus qui disaient des choses apprises par cœur et repartaient aussitôt. Rasul pensait d'ailleurs que Niyazbek avait confié la tâche à Wahha, lequel disposait d'experts parfaitement qualifiés en explosifs.

— Pourquoi n'as-tu pas garé la voiture dans la cour ? demanda Niyazbek. C'était pourtant convenu. Les hommes planqués dans la cour devaient écarter Ali du véhicule pour laisser sa place à l'autre, le taiseux.

Rasul, avalant sa salive :

— Vois-tu, Niyazbek, je ne peux pas tenir ma parole. Il vient de m'arriver un malheur. Mes parents et ma sœur viennent de disparaître. C'est la voisine qui me l'a dit au téléphone à l'instant même.

— Te fais pas de bile, répondit Niyazbek, ce sont mes hommes qui ont enlevé tes proches et les ont placés en lieu sûr. Ceci pour t'empêcher de changer d'avis et qu'ils ne soient pas inquiétés quand l'enquête sera mise en route.

Rasul, articulant avec peine :

— Tu les as pris en otage.

— Je te promets que mes hommes leur prodigueront tous les égards dus aux aînés. Va rejoindre l'homme qui t'attend dans la voiture et gare-la dans la cour.

Un temps immobile, Rasul dit en baissant les yeux :

— Tu le savais depuis le début, non ?

— De quoi ?

— Personne n'a tué mon neveu, dit Rasul. Gamzat et Chapi l'ont pris en otage, tout simplement. Chapi a manigancé toute cette histoire pour te pousser dans un piège. Le genre de blague qu'il aime bien, Chapi.

Djavatkhan leva les yeux sur Rasul, et Rasul pensa : vivement la mort. Il aurait dû tout dire à Niyazbek dès le début. Car alors Niyazbek l'aurait aidé. Tout le monde savait que Niyazbek aidait les gens. Il y avait beaucoup de monde, dans la république, qui aidait les amis. Seul Niyazbek aidait les gens. Au lieu de quoi Rasul avait empoché le fric – vingt mille dollars – et vendu l'homme qui aurait pu l'aider.

— Et combien t'a donné Gamzat ? demanda Djavatkhan.

— Ce n'est pas une question d'argent. Je n'ai pas de fils ! Je n'ai qu'un neveu. Et me voilà contraint de choisir entre tous mes proches et mon neveu !

Ali attendit une bonne demi-heure dans la voiture. S'il avait été russe ou *a fortiori* américain, il aurait tout plaqué depuis longtemps, mais Ali était né dans le Caucase où le temps passait autrement. Aussi patienta-t-il une demi-heure avant de se poser des questions, malgré tout, parce qu'il s'agissait d'un travail urgent et que, s'il n'était pas fait à l'aube, on risquait de leur trancher carrément la tête. Donc, au bout d'une demi-heure, Ali descendit du tacot et frappa doucement au portillon.

Pas de réponse. Il poussa le portillon et se glissa à l'intérieur de la cour. Un chemin pavé de briques menait à la baraque, bordé d'herbes folles. Une Moskvitch pourrissait sous un auvent rouillé. Une seule et unique fenêtre à rideau rouge épais laissait paraître un peu de lumière, près de la porte.

Ali gravit les marches du perron, frappa encore une fois et se coula par la porte. Une entrée minuscule, puis la pièce unique avec une grande table de chêne au beau milieu. Rasul était là, qui mangeait des khinkals à un plat fumant. Il y avait près de lui un type d'une vingtaine d'années à la tête ronde et aux bras musculeux courts.

— Ali, dit Rasul, assois-toi et mange. On n'aura pas le temps de casser la graine avec tout ce boulot.

Le match amical entre le club de golf de Moscou et la sélection régionale devait commencer le dimanche à dix heures du matin. Pankov s'y rendit directement de l'aéroport où il venait d'accueillir deux camarades moscovites.

Des mesures de sécurité sans précédent avaient été prises. Plantés tous les cent mètres, les miliciens formaient une haie de poteaux télégraphiques de plus en plus serrés à mesure qu'on se rapprochait du terrain de jeu où ils ne faisaient plus qu'un cordon continu. Deux blindés montaient la garde à l'entrée du club. Là, l'un des amis moscovites de Pankov siffla en le tirant par la manche :

— Non mais, vois-tu ça ? Un vrai perchoir à sniper !

Pankov lui-même s'en étonna. Un mirador amovible se dressait à une centaine de mètres du club-house, et plus loin, près du littoral, il en aperçut un autre.

— Non, dit Pankov en scrutant l'installation. C'est un dispositif anti-sniper. Au laser. Ça brûle la rétine de qui surveille le terrain dans sa mire.

D'après les appariements initiaux, le président devait jouer en tandem avec son fils, et Pankov, avec le procureur Makhriev. Ce dernier n'aurait pas dit non, mais il s'était retrouvé à l'hôpital avec une crise cardiaque à l'annonce de son éviction. Résultat, les joueurs furent redéployés par trois, et Pankov fut placé dans la même troïka que le président et Gamzat.

Quand Pankov entra en jeu, attendu par Gamzat et son père au premier trou, le coup d'envoi était déjà donné. La zone était bouclée comme une place au plus fort d'une manifestation.

Debout sur la ligne de départ, ses jambes maigres sortant d'un ample short à carreaux, Gamzat s'appuyait sur son club. Ahmednabi Aslanov – pantalon blanc et chemise crème à col – donna bienveillamment l'accolade à Pankov. La perspective de jouer dans le même trio que le président ne souriait pas du tout à l'ambassadeur du Kremlin : ses gardes avaient un trou spécial à la poche par lequel ils pouvaient remettre une balle en jeu en cas de coup raté.

Le premier trou fut simple à jouer. Pankov le fit en trois coups réglementaires, là où il en fallut cinq à Gamzat. Aslanov junior avait le trac, état forcément néfaste dans un sport comme le golf.

Au deuxième trou, les choses empirèrent. La balle de Gamzat s'abîma dans le gouffre, et il fit mine de n'en rien voir. Une fois le coup tiré, il eut un aparté avec le chef de sa propre sécurité. Pankov fut étonné de constater que les gardes avaient doublé : ils s'agglutinaient au pont comme des mouches. Soudain, Gamzat se tourna brusquement et envoya une gifle à la face de Chapi.

A ce moment, surprise, Pankov aperçut Niyazbek. Vêtu d'un maillot blanc et d'un jean, il marchait sans escorte sur un chemin de sable. Lorsqu'il se fut rapproché, le Moscovite remarqua son Makarov à la ceinture.

Niyazbek atteignit la ligne de départ où se trouvaient le président de la République et son fils. Le voyant, Gamzat devint tout gris. Son œil droit trémula légèrement.

— Niyazbek, lança Pankov, quel bon vent ? Tu te mets au golf, toi aussi ?

— Oui, répondit-il, j'ai envie d'essayer. Vous avez là, à ce qu'on dit, un garçon porteur de clubs... un...

— Caddie, dit Pankov.

— Non, Boussik, rectifia Niyazbek. Ce Boussik n'a qu'à m'apporter des clubs.

Sur ce, il leva les yeux sur Gamzat.

— Je ne fais pas partie de la valetaille, dit Gamzat dont le visage se figea.

Niyazbek haussa les épaules et s'approcha d'un sac de clubs qui appartenait à Pankov. Un sac rouge mastoc, monté sur deux roues, à rayure de daim blanc. Il choisit le club le plus long enveloppé d'un étui de laine Winner's Cap et mit à nu une magnifique canne en titane. L'Avar la fit tourner dans ses mains comme s'il essayait de distinguer le grip du shaft.

— Je vais m'exercer, dit-il d'une voix pleine de calme et de courtoisie. Ce Boussik-là n'aura qu'à porter les clubs derrière moi.

Mentalement, Pankov tenta de mettre en rapport la présence de Niyazbek avec les mesures de sécurité inédites (même à l'échelle de la république) qui venaient d'être prises, et sa conclusion ne fut pas du tout de son goût.

— Expliquez-vous ! exigea-t-il sèchement.

Gamzat faisait des yeux en coulisse à Pankov et à Niyazbek. Le Moscovite crut un instant qu'il allait s'emporter, mais Aslanov eut soudain un sourire désarmant. D'un mouvement du menton, il appela le chef de sa garde.

— Chapi, dit-il, trouve-moi ce Boussik et fais porter des habits convenables à notre hôte pour qu'il ne déshonore pas la république devant ces messieurs de Moscou. Parce que notre hôte ne sait pas encore qu'on ne joue pas au golf en jean et en chemise sans col.

Dix jours déjà que l'état-major antiterroriste était en place, et Pankov sentait que la fébrilité des premiers moments se transformait en quasi-euphorie.

Aucun meurtre de haut fonctionnaire n'avait eu lieu durant ce temps ; aucun règlement de compte à l'arme automatique ; aucune manifestation suscitée par la mise à l'écart ou l'arrestation d'un tueur de renom.

La moitié des grands commis de la république, redoutant les contrôles de police plus encore que les *killers*, avaient remisé leurs voitures blindées. On en vit même qui se mirent à marcher.

La nuit où l'état d'urgence fut décrété, un détachement de l'OMON de Saratov arrêta deux miliciens qui transportaient une bombe à fragmentation dans une Jigouli 2106 volée. Ceux-ci prirent peur et mirent les gaz. Les patrouilleurs ouvrirent le feu, le véhicule fit un tonneau et la bombe explosa. L'un des deux miliciens, qui eut le temps de s'extirper, échappa à la mort. Il ressortit de ses dépositions que les terroristes étaient étrangers à l'affaire : la bombe avait été commandée par le chef du comité d'Etat à la Pêche, et le milicien en question était le petit-neveu de son adjoint.

Les Sibériens du groupe d'intervention spéciale Condor eurent pour mission d'inspecter les vieux taudis du sud-est de Torbi-Kala. Des occupants les accueillirent à coups de feu. Le groupe attendit des renforts, fit monter trois hommes sur le toit et s'engouffra dans le logis en faisant sauter la porte avec un cordon détonant.

Grave erreur. Le repaire se révéla parfaitement équipé pour ce genre de situation, avec un passage dérobé à travers deux logements jusqu'à la cage d'escalier d'à côté. Quand les Sibériens eurent fait sauter la première porte en bois, bringuebalante, ils en trouvèrent une deuxième, mais blindée. Celle-ci à peine démontée, une puissante explosion fit sauter la moitié de la bâtisse. Cinq Sibériens furent tués, trois blessés, contre un seul mort du côté des boïéviks (celui-là même qui avait essuyé une balle au premier contact). Tous les autres avaient miné la baraque et pris la fuite par les logements voisins.

Le lendemain, ces mêmes Sibériens tombèrent dans une souricière à l'intérieur d'un nouvel immeuble de dix étages. Cette fois, ils se gardèrent bien de jouer les gros bras. Après avoir fait sortir tous les occupants, ils anéantirent l'appartement avec le canon d'un char. Parmi les cadavres, on découvrit le corps d'un gamin de dix ans. Blotti près d'une fenêtre, il serrait dans ses mains un fusil de précision plus grand que lui.

Choqué par la nouvelle, Pankov convoqua le commandant du groupe pour le chapitrer.

— On se croit tout permis ?! tempêta-t-il.

— Ben… pour sauver mes gars, je suis prêt à faire péter une dizaine de leurs baraques, à ces bachi-bouzouks.

— Ça veut dire quoi, à ces bachi-bouzouks ? Vous vous croyez en territoire occupé ? Vous n'êtes plus en Russie, ou quoi ? Chez vous aussi, à Krasnoïarsk, vous allez pilonner les immeubles à coups de char maintenant ?

— Je n'ai pas le souvenir d'avoir vu des lardons de dix ans avec des fusils à Krasnoïarsk, répondit le colonel.

Se distingua tout particulièrement le groupe des forces spéciales Youg.

Pankov s'était opposé catégoriquement à faire des hommes d'Arzo le bras armé de l'état-major antiterroriste. Et pourtant

Guennadi Chebolev avait su le convaincre du contraire en disant :

— Si les montagnes sont nettoyées par Arzo, on détestera Arzo. Si les montagnes sont nettoyées par les Russes, on détestera les Russes. Je préfère qu'on déteste les Tchétchènes.

L'argument sentait fortement l'Italie médiévale – "divisez pour mieux régner" – mais il était plein de justesse. Doté de blindés et d'hélicos, le groupe d'Arzo déferla sur la république en délogeant les boïéviks de leurs villages et en les débusquant du fond des gorges à coups de roquettes sol-sol NURS.

Arzo s'en prit alors à l'un des hommes de main d'Arsaïev qui travaillait depuis trois ans comme chef adjoint du service de sécurité du ministère de l'Intérieur. C'était d'ailleurs dans sa voiture, murmurait-on, qu'Arsaïev se déplaçait impunément dans Torbi-Kala. Le type prit le maquis dans les montagnes. Voyant cela, Arzo captura toute sa famille et menaça de tuer ses fils un à un tant qu'il ne se rendrait pas. Le gars se rendit dans les six heures qui suivirent. A peine eut-il franchi le seuil de sa porte qu'on l'exécuta.

Le lendemain, Pankov découvrit dans son bureau une cassette VHS amateur acheminée par coursier du ministère de l'Intérieur avec la mention *Urgent*. Il la glissa machinalement dans son magnétoscope. Il lui fallut plusieurs secondes pour comprendre ce qu'il voyait. Quelques années auparavant, le premier commis du Kremlin auprès de la Tchétchénie avait été enlevé à sa descente d'avion sur le tarmac de Torbi-Kala. La vidéo montrait la suite. Du début (son transfert dans les montagnes) à la fin (sa mort par strangulation).

Que la cassette eût été acheminée par vaguemestre officiel produisit sur Pankov une forte impression. Le lendemain matin, il envoyait sa fille en Angleterre.

Le 25 septembre, quand Pankov monta dans sa voiture pour se rendre à l'aéroport, il remarqua une femme assise à la grille de sa résidence. De loin, elle ressemblait à un sac à ordures. Dès que le véhicule eut passé le portail, elle se dressa et se mit à crier des choses dans son dos.

— Faites-la venir, dit Pankov.

Une minute plus tard, elle était devant le premier commis du Kremlin.

Une folle, se disait-il. Il en avait rencontré une légion de ce genre dans sa précédente carrière de fonctionnaire russe. Elles accusaient les gérants d'immeubles de voler leur pension, se plaignaient des voisins qui faisaient leur lessive à trop grand fracas dans leur salle de bains, voire carrément des extraterrestres qui irradiaient des rayons à travers les murs.

— Que vous arrive-t-il ? demanda Pankov.

— Rendez-moi mon fils, dit la femme.

— Qui est votre fils ?

— Il a été arrêté hier. Il allait au marché vendre du raisin. Des hommes masqués l'ont stoppé en route et l'ont emmené dans leur propre voiture qui n'avait même pas de plaque. Au premier barrage, ils ont montré des cartes du FSB en traitant mon fils de terroriste. Tout le monde dit que c'est vous qui avez donné l'ordre d'enlever les terroristes sans procès ni jugement.

— En effet. On ne soigne pas un cancer avec de l'aspirine.

— Mon fils n'est pas wahhabite. Il a dix-huit ans, il fait son droit à l'université. Il s'est battu voilà deux mois avec le fils d'un chef adjoint du FSB régional. A cause d'une fille. C'est pour ça qu'on l'a pris.

— Tout le monde me dit la même chose. Il y a seulement une semaine, il ne se passait pas de nuit sans un attentat à la bombe. Des villages entiers servaient de base arrière aux boïéviks. En juillet, cinq miliciens sont allés faire un pique-nique dans les montagnes. On les a retrouvés en bouillie dans la carcasse de leur voiture : il a fallu plusieurs jours pour racler tout ça. Mais chaque fois qu'on met la main sur quelqu'un, la famille appelle, ça réclame, ça pleure. Même s'il y a des empreintes sur les lieux de l'attentat, cent cinquante personnes de son village attesteront par écrit qu'il était chez lui ce jour-là !

— Mon fils cadet n'est pas un boïévik, dit la femme, mais je jure Allah que mes autres fils le deviendront si vous ne faites pas la lumière sur cette affaire.

Pankov consulta sa montre. Son adjoint à l'état-major, le tout-puissant général Chebolev, chef du FSB régional, assistait à la conversation sans y participer.

— Emmène-la et enquête à fond, lui ordonna Pankov. Tu me feras ton rapport à mon retour.

— Monte là-dedans, dit Chebolev à la femme en lui montrant son Geländewagen de service.

La femme se tenait parfaitement droite. Elle semblait ne craindre ni les Russes qui l'entouraient, ni les agents du FSB, ni les gardes du représentant du Kremlin. Elle avait été très belle dans sa jeunesse. Aujourd'hui encore, malgré le deuil qu'elle portait, elle n'avait pu s'empêcher de marquer une touche de coquetterie : son foulard noir à demi transparent voilait moins ses cheveux qu'il ne soulignait la grâce de ses jolies mèches autour d'un visage fier aux lèvres pulpeuses et aux pommettes bien dessinées.

— Combien avez-vous d'enfants ? demanda Pankov.

— Huit. Et six d'entre eux sont des hommes, répondit la femme.

Pankov revint de Moscou deux jours plus tard, et sa première question fut pour la femme de l'autre fois. Au fond de lui-même, il se disait que le garçon n'était pas blanc comme neige, mais Chebolev lui fit une tout autre réponse :

— Kassim Chakhbanov faisait partie de nos réseaux d'indics. Le garçon a été enlevé dans une Niva blanche sans plaque d'immatriculation, et ses ravisseurs ont bel et bien produit des cartons du FSB au barrage de contrôle. Pour autant, nous n'y sommes pour rien. Qui pis est, c'est le quatrième cas de ce genre, et ce n'est pas la première fois non plus que cette Niva blanche se fait remarquer. Nous avons ouvert une enquête et sommes bien décidés à la faire aboutir.

— Un coup des séparatistes ?

— Ou des gus des élites locales qui ne veulent pas admettre qu'ils ont fait leur temps. Mais le plus triste n'est pas là. Vous souvenez-vous de l'histoire du chef du comité d'Etat à la Pêche ? Que son adjoint avait tenté de tuer ?

— Oui.

— Eh bien le *killer* a parlé. Nous sommes allés arrêter le commanditaire un dimanche en pleine nuit, et figurez-vous qu'il avait déjà été embarqué. Par des types en Niva blanche qui se disaient du FSB.

Fin septembre, près d'un mois après le meurtre de son gendre, le patron d'Avarie-Transflotte Sapartchi Telaïev rencontra Arzo Khadjiev, colonel du FSB.

La rencontre eut lieu dans une boîte de nuit qui appartenait à Sapartchi, et Arzo eut droit à tous les honneurs. Quand on se fut bien restauré, bien rincé le gosier et bien relaxé, Sapartchi dit :

— C'est une très bonne chose que tes hommes fassent la guerre aux boïéviks. Ces boïéviks, ils nous rendaient la vie impossible. Et sais-tu à quoi je pense : que tu devrais faire la peau à Khizri. Parce qu'il prête la main aux boïéviks et que c'est un sale type.

Arzo fixa Sapartchi des yeux :

— C'est une très bonne chose que tes hommes transportent du pétrole. Tu devrais m'offrir ce petit tanker de trois mille tonnes que tu viens de faire réparer. Ce tanker ne vaut pas plus cher que la tête de Khizri.

Sapartchi aurait préféré payer en argent, mais Arzo s'entêta. Alors ils topèrent.

Khizri jouait aux *nardy* chez lui quand il eut la visite d'un gars de son village.

— Ta grand-mère est tombée et s'est cassé le col du fémur, dit-il à Khizri. Elle demande à te voir.

Khizri n'avait d'aïeuls que la vieille Tamum qui vivait au village. Aussi prit-il deux hommes avec lui, et en route pour les montagnes.

A la sortie de Torbi-Kala, il tomba sur le cortège de Niyazbek. Ils s'arrêtèrent et se donnèrent l'accolade.

— Où vas-tu ? demanda Niyazbek.

— J'ai eu la visite du vieux Momo qui m'a dit que ma grand-mère Tamum s'était cassé la jambe. Je vais la mettre à l'hôpital.

— Eh bien je t'accompagne. Les temps ne sont pas sûrs. Les barrages russes risquent de te chercher noise. Face à nous deux, ils auront plus de mal.

Niyazbek et Khizri partirent à deux voitures. Eux dans le Land Cruiser, les trois autres dans une Niva, avec des PM. En tout et pour tout, ils avaient cinq pistolets-mitrailleurs, deux Stetchkine et deux chargeurs par PM. Ils firent la route en près de quatre heures. En traversant le village, Niyazbek remarqua quatre inconnus en armes qui mangeaient des glaces sur les marches du magasin.

Le hameau où vivait la grand-mère de Khizri se trouvait à deux kilomètres du village à proprement parler : quatre maisonnettes adossées l'une à l'autre et tenues par des murs au bord du vide. Khizri freina et sauta de voiture. C'est alors qu'il vit sa grand-mère nonagénaire, bon pied, bon œil, tirer de l'eau au puits. Niyazbek se souvint des quatre militaires qui mangeaient des glaces devant le magasin et dit :

— C'est un piège, Khizri, et un piège tendu par quelqu'un d'important. Quelque chose me dit que la famille de ce Momo qui t'a apporté la nouvelle a été prise en otage.

A ce moment Khizri se retourna et vit que deux blindés les rattrapaient par la route avec des soldats dessus. Impossible de faire demi-tour. Impensable aussi d'aller de l'avant parce que la route était dans la mire du blindé à perte de vue.

Niyazbek et Khizri sautèrent dans les voitures et vroum ! mirent le pied au plancher par une ruelle étroite et courte qui menait à la montagne et venait mourir dans le lit d'un torrent de printemps. Comme on était en automne, on ne voyait là que des amas de pierres hérissés de fanions métalliques balisant des champs de mines. Lesquelles mines avaient été entraînées depuis longtemps par l'eau et la boue, les unes ayant fait long feu, les autres ayant explosé, mais toutes encore marquées d'un fanion.

Ils roulèrent jusqu'au torrent, abandonnèrent leurs véhicules et se mirent à gravir la pente.

Khizri peinait à marcher sur les pierres avec ses jambes de bois et Niyazbek le percha sur ses épaules comme un gosse.

— On est foutus, dit Khizri. Laisse-moi là que je brûle mes dernières cartouches.

— Arrête tes âneries, coupa Niyazbek.

La ruelle du hameau était si étroite que même les quatre-quatre de Niyazbek avaient eu du mal à s'y faufiler. Les blindés s'y taillèrent un passage, bien sûr, mais avec tant de peine qu'ils durent entamer les murs des maisons d'un bord comme de l'autre, à quoi ils perdirent beaucoup de temps.

Quand ils arrivèrent au torrent, leurs proies étaient déjà loin.

Au moment où les hommes d'Arzo sautèrent de leurs blindés, ils reçurent une pluie de tirs qui tombait d'en haut, où le torrent décrivait un coude. Ils se virent alors plutôt mal en point. La gorge montait à pic avec un gros rocher d'au moins deux mètres au beau milieu du lit, le tout à portée de fusil. Un Tchétchène dit :

— Qu'on fasse rouler ce fichu roc et un blindé pourra enfiler la gorge. En face, ils n'ont pas de lance-grenade.

Tant bien que mal on finit par faire basculer le rocher, ouvrant ainsi la voie au blindé qui monta jusqu'au premier tournant. Au passage, l'engin écrasa la Niva comme un paquet de clopes et emboutit le Cruiser dans la paroi rocheuse avec un pommier sauvage qui poussait là depuis une trentaine d'années.

Mais déjà Niyazbek, Khizri et ses hommes avaient atteint un deuxième coude du torrent auquel le blindé ne pouvait accéder.

On se tirait dessus depuis une dizaine de minutes quand Arzo arriva sur place. Pas un mort, parce que les uns s'étaient embusqués derrière un rocher, et les autres, derrière le blindé. Seul un combattant d'Arzo souffrait d'une légère blessure au bras.

— Qu'est-ce que vous fichez là comme une épine dans un trou du cul ? tonna Arzo. Prenez-les à revers.

Entre-temps Niyazbek et Khizri avaient laissé un homme pour les couvrir au tournant avant de continuer leur ascension. La gorge se faisait de plus en plus abrupte et Niyazbek savait que, pour mener à bien le plan qu'il avait en tête, il fallait s'écarter du torrent et gravir une paroi, chose accessible à un homme agile dans la force de l'âge, mais inimaginable pour Khizri.

Ils parvinrent à un nouveau détour où Khizri remarqua que l'endroit se présentait comme une fortification naturelle inespérée. L'eau avait creusé dans la roche une mini-tranchée d'où un tireur aguerri pouvait se défendre tant qu'une grenade ne l'atteignait pas.

Khizri sauta dans la tranchée en disant :

— Laissez-moi une demi-douzaine de chargeurs et décanillez.

A y regarder de plus près, Niyazbek constata que Khizri pourrait y loger entier s'il dégrafait ses prothèses.

— Mauvaise idée, dit Niyazbek. Enlève plutôt tes jambes de bois et niche-toi là-dedans. Si les Tchétchènes passent sans te voir et que tu arrives à redescendre au village, tu seras beaucoup plus utile.

Khizri retira ses prothèses et se glissa comme il put sous la roche, puis Niyazbek le recouvrit d'une grosse pierre plate.

Pendant ce temps, Arzo avait emmené vingt hommes dans les montagnes par une autre route qui partait à un kilomètre du village, route empruntée au XIXᵉ siècle par les naïbs de Chamil en guerre contre la Kakhétie, et qui depuis lors n'avait guère été entretenue. Encore quarante minutes de perdues. Quand ils atteignirent le point le plus haut, ce fut pour constater qu'il n'y avait plus personne en contrebas. Arzo prit son émetteur-récepteur et ordonna aux combattants restés près du blindé de continuer leur ascension.

Déjà Niyazbek et les trois hommes qui lui restaient avaient gravi la paroi rocheuse et se trouvaient presque à la cime d'une crête montagneuse qui faisait penser au squelette d'un osciètre. Il y avait là quelques maisons de pierre. Niyazbek escalada prestement un mur, entra dans une maison et se mit à y gratter le sol à mains nues. Quelques secondes plus tard, il tomba sur un anneau enfoui sous terre. Il tira dessus avec une force telle qu'il faillit arracher la trappe d'une cave. C'était une planque aménagée par Niyazbek cinq ans auparavant. Il s'était battu pour obtenir d'un Tchétchène le remboursement de ses dettes. L'autre avait dit qu'il ne pouvait pas payer en argent, mais en armes. Niyazbek s'était donc vu remettre dix "mouches" (les lance-grenades), une vingtaine de PM et tant de pistolets qu'on en avait bourré un sac et qu'on en distribuait en veux-tu en voilà.

Le commando du Youg avait perdu beaucoup de temps à contourner sa cible. Quand les Tchétchènes débouchèrent de l'autre côté du versant, complètement déboisé à cet endroit, Arzo avisa une paroi escarpée de roches rousses qui offrait un perchoir à quelques vieilles maisons de pierre serrées flanc contre flanc comme rayons en ruche. Une antenne relais inachevée dominait l'ensemble aux couleurs de Beeline, opérateur de téléphonie mobile. Perplexité d'Arzo : à tous les coups Niyazbek et ses hommes s'étaient embusqués dans ces maisons mais, bon sang de bois, comment avaient-ils fait pour monter Khizri tout là-haut ?

A ce moment jaillit un éclair du haut de l'escarpement, aussitôt suivi d'un impact de grenade à cinq mètres d'Arzo. Un combattant fut tué, un autre blessé. Tous se jetèrent ventre à terre dans une vieille ornière d'un demi-mètre de fond, seul abri qui fût sur ce mont pelé.

— On s'y prend comme des pieds, dit Arzo. Quelle idée d'aller chercher l'ours dans sa tanière.

Dix combattants se tapirent dans les plis de la route, les autres rampèrent vers un rocher rouge. Il y avait là une trentaine d'attaquants contre les hommes de Niyazbek qui ne pouvaient être plus de huit avec rien d'autre que des armes, c'est-à-dire sans eau, ni nourriture, ni médicaments. Malgré l'altitude, le soleil tapait sans pitié, et Arzo faisait d'incessantes libations à une gourde plate qui contenait de l'eau vitaminée.

Les échanges de tirs durèrent encore une demi-heure sans faire davantage de morts, les combattants d'Arzo étant très expérimentés. Quand le groupe Youg eut cerné les maisons, Arzo rampant se mit hors d'atteinte et ordonna à son aide de camp de déployer l'antenne satellite.

— *Salam* Sapartchi, dit Arzo quand le téléphone fut en place, te rappelles-tu notre deal ?

— Bien sûr que oui, répondit Sapartchi.

— Je ne crois pas que ce soit possible. Nous avons traqué notre proie dans les rochers d'Ulgo, mais il est en compagnie de Niyazbek. Ils ont un arsenal d'enfer, il y a déjà trois morts dans mes rangs. Un pétrolier pour une histoire pareille, ce n'est pas assez. Il m'en faut deux.

— Comment oses-tu ? protesta Sapartchi. Nous sommes amis !

— Amis peut-être, mais j'ai déjà trois cadavres sur les bras, et j'en aurai dix quand tout sera fini. Le moment viendra où je devrai expliquer à leurs familles pourquoi ils sont morts. J'aurai moins de peine à le faire avec deux pétroliers qu'avec un seul.

— D'accord, dit Sapartchi, je te donne un autre tanker, d'un millier de tonnes, mais c'est le dernier, quel que soit ensuite le nombre de cadavres.

La conversation finie, Arzo noua un chiffon blanc au canon de son fusil, le leva en l'air et se dirigea vers les maisons. Ainsi marcha-t-il sans un coup de feu jusqu'à mi-pente, puis il sortit un talkie-walkie de sa chemise, le posa sur une pierre, y planta un drapeau et se retira. Bientôt apparut un neveu de Niyazbek. Il ramassa le talkie-walkie et le remonta à son repaire.

— Vois-tu, Niyazbek, dit Arzo quand son ennemi fut en possession de la radio, c'est le hasard qui t'a embringué dans cette histoire. Il me faut Khizri. On m'a promis deux tankers en échange. Si tu me livres Khizri, il y en aura un pour toi.

— Si on t'a promis un tanker en échange de Khizri, je doute que l'offre vienne du ministre de l'Agriculture, renvoya Niyazbek.

— En quoi ça te concerne, Niyazbek ? Pour toi c'est soit un pétrolier, soit une balle en pleine tête. Tu as peut-être assez d'armes, mais tu n'as ni eau ni moyens de transmission. D'ici une heure j'aurai de quoi déglinguer ta baraque à coups de lance-roquettes.

— As-tu peur de me faire la guerre au point de renoncer à un tanker ?

— Ohé, Niyazbek, ne me nargue pas s'il te plaît. Ni toi ni moi n'avons plus à prouver que nous sommes des hommes, et depuis longtemps. Ce serait dommage que quelqu'un comme toi crève à cause d'un salopard comme Khizri. Qu'en dis-tu ?

— J'en dis que tu aurais dû te battre avant de marchander. Regarde plutôt ce qui vient d'en bas.

Arzo rampa jusqu'au bord de la route et regarda en contrebas. Une foule noire montait du village. Vu de loin, on aurait dit un magma de mouches agglutinées sur un morceau de lard.

— Quelque chose me dit que cette opération ne me vaudra ni les médailles des Russes ni le pétrole de Sapartchi, dit Arzo. Fichons le camp !

L'ordre était plus facile à donner qu'à exécuter. Arzo et son groupe se trouvaient coincés entre Niyazbek et la foule des villageois, tous armés, les uns d'antiques pétoires, les autres de mitraillettes. Le Tchétchène discerna même un ou deux lance-grenades. Certes ces paysans n'avaient pas le cuir aussi épais que les combattants du Youg, et Arzo ne doutait pas que son groupe les eût traversés comme une balle un carton. Mais il y avait longtemps qu'Arzo n'était plus un boïévik tchétchène. C'était un colonel du FSB venu au village avec deux blindés pour arrêter des séparatistes et leurs acolytes. Il n'aurait pas été en mesure de rendre compte à l'ambassadeur du Kremlin Vladislav Pankov d'un pareil massacre perpétré dans le village de Niyazbek.

Finalement, les Tchétchènes furent ramenés à leurs blindés, toujours stationnés au fond de la gorge, et Niyazbek descendit de la montagne avec les villageois. Il annonça son intention de repartir dans l'un des deux blindés, disant qu'Arzo pouvait le suivre une heure plus tard dans le deuxième.

— Parce que je ne veux pas qu'on nous rattrape ou qu'on prévienne qui que ce soit de notre retour à Torbi-Kala, dit Niyazbek.

Arzo demanda :

— Eh quoi, tu nous voles un blindé ?

— Point du tout ! Juste un échange : je prends ton blindé et tu récupères mon Cruiser à la place.

Quatre heures plus tard, Niyazbek se présenta en blindé à la villa de Sapartchi située dans les quartiers ouest de Torbi-Kala. Comme les gardes, à la vue de l'engin, oublièrent d'ouvrir le portail, il fallut bien passer au travers. Le blindé s'engouffra dans une cour dallée de carreaux bleus et verts, et l'on ne peut pas dire que le carrelage n'en ait pas souffert. Une fois la machine arrêtée devant la maison, Niyazbek mit lestement pied à terre près d'une fontaine. Une table était dressée là, à laquelle Sapartchi Telaïev et sa jeune épouse prenaient le thé.

La femme poussa un cri et s'enfuit. Niyazbek s'approcha de Telaïev, s'assit en vis-à-vis et demanda :

— Pourquoi as-tu embringué les Tchétchènes dans cette histoire ?

— Si j'avais mes deux jambes, je n'aurais pas été chercher de l'aide ailleurs.

— C'est juste, consentit Niyazbek. Mais est-ce bien à moi d'arranger les choses ? Ne dois-je pas plutôt les confier à Khizri ?

Khizri pendant ce temps était dans le blindé. En ôtant ses jambes de bois, dans la montagne, il avait endommagé les fixations et, depuis, plus moyen d'ajuster une prothèse. C'était lui qui avait levé les villageois après s'être rendu, ou plutôt traîné au village.

Sapartchi réfléchit longtemps, les yeux posés tantôt sur le blindé, tantôt sur la fontaine où nageaient des poissons noirs et blancs à longues queues.

— Mieux vaut que tu arranges ça toi-même, lâcha-t-il, parce que si Khizri s'en occupe, les poissons de cette fontaine seront bientôt remplacés par des cadavres.

— Tu vas faire de Khizri ton adjoint, dit Niyazbek.

— Si je le fais, il me tuera pour mettre la main sur Avarie-Transflotte, objecta Sapartchi.

— Pas besoin d'attendre ce moment-là. Dès que tu l'auras nommé adjoint, tu donneras ta démission en désignant Khizri comme directeur général par intérim.

Entre-temps Khizri, enfin rabiboché avec sa prothèse, s'était extrait du blindé cahin-caha. Il clopina vers Sapartchi, la face blanche de rage. Mais quand il comprit ce qui se disait, il marqua le pas et s'arrêta à un demi-mètre de Sapartchi.

Sapartchi réfléchit longtemps ; lorsqu'il se retourna, il vit Khizri qui le dardait du regard comme s'il prenait sa mire.

— On dirait, dit Sapartchi, que c'est devenu une tradition : des directeurs culs-de-jatte pour Avarie-Transflotte.

Vladislav Pankov eut vent de cette histoire par la bouche du vice-speaker de l'Assemblée législative, lequel l'avait accompagné à une réunion de la CSCE où l'ambassadeur du Kremlin devait présenter un rapport sur la stabilisation de la situation dans le Caucase-Nord.

Dès après son rapport, Pankov s'envola pour Torbi-Kala où, à peine posé, il convoqua Niyazbek et Arzo.

Khadjiev se présenta au chef de l'état-major antiterroriste en tenue de soldat : treillis-rangers. Niyazbek portait un pantalon clair et une longue chemise blanche au col griffé Valentino. Soigneusement peigné, le visage massif, le front haut, le menton volontaire, il affichait un calme olympien.

— Qu'est-ce que ton groupe fichait dans les montagnes d'Ulgo ? demanda Pankov au Tchétchène.

— Nous avons été alertés sur la présence d'hommes armés dans le village, répondit Arzo. Des boïéviks, apparemment.

Le temps qu'on mette les choses au clair, ça a légèrement canardé.

— Et toi, qu'en dis-tu ? demanda Pankov à Niyazbek.

L'autre haussa les épaules.

— Je pensais avoir les hommes d'Arsaïev à mes trousses. Heureusement qu'on a éclairci l'affaire. Parce qu'on aurait pu en faire, du grabuge.

Pankov regardait ses Caucasiens en silence. Version crédible si n'était sur son bureau un papier signé Sapartchi Telaïev. Non que le chef d'Avarie-Transflotte s'y plaignît des événements, que nenni ; simplement nommait-il par ce papier Khizri Beïbulatov directeur adjoint, et tout le monde avait parfaitement compris, dans la république, le pourquoi de cette étrange décision.

Le Moscovite leva lentement la tête. Arzo était là debout devant lui dans son treillis crasseux, la face labourée de rides, fendue d'un vilain sourire, et Pankov se rappela soudain leur première rencontre. Arzo affichait alors un visage lisse et jeune mais il le regardait comme maintenant, de haut en bas, ses yeux sombres de glands de chêne dénotant le même mépris des Russes, à cette différence près que, de prisonnier, Pankov était devenu son supérieur hiérarchique.

— Si tu portes plainte, Niyazbek, il sera dégradé, dit Pankov.

— Loin de moi l'intention de porter plainte, dit l'Avar.

— Et pourquoi donc ?

— Chez nous autres montagnards existe une superstition : les balles de qui porte plainte se mettent à voler moins vite qu'avant.

— Tu peux disposer, Arzo, dit Pankov. Niyazbek, reste un moment.

Le Tchétchène tourna les talons et, sans dire un mot, sortit du bureau. Niyazbek resta campé crânement sur ses jambes en position "repos", le regard tout aussi impénétrable que celui du Tchétchène. A cet instant se dessina aux yeux de Pankov une solution d'une limpidité mathématique en réponse au problème qui le taraudait depuis qu'il avait doté le groupe Youg de prérogatives spéciales.

— Vois-tu, Niyazbek, ça ne peut pas durer éternellement. Dans un Etat civilisé, on ne peut pas faire ce que tu es capable de faire sans être investi d'un pouvoir. Je n'ai pas besoin d'Arzo. Qu'il aille où ça lui chante. Veux-tu que je te nomme commandant des forces spéciales à sa place ?

— Pourquoi ça ?

— Parce que tu ne prendras pas de pots-de-vin pour tuer du monde en échange.

— C'est vrai, acquiesça Niyazbek dont les yeux couleur de miel brûlé jetèrent un éclat de mépris. Mais qui t'a dit que j'accepterais de faire la chasse à mes frères musulmans pour la seule raison que c'est dans l'intérêt des Russes ?

Il fit demi-tour et quitta le bureau.

V

LA BATAILLE DE KHARON-YOURTE

Dix jours s'écoulèrent sans excès particuliers. Khadjiev voyait bien que le premier commis du Kremlin ne pouvait pas l'encadrer et qu'il cherchait un prétexte pour le mettre à mal. On rapporta à Pankov ces mots d'Arzo : "Si j'avais su qu'il m'en ferait baver autant à cause d'un malheureux petit doigt de coupé, je l'aurais descendu aussi sec en gare de Grozny."

Mais Arzo comprenait aussi qu'il avait fait des bêtises, de grosses bêtises. Il ne se montrait plus guère à Torbi-Kala maintenant, préférant courir les montagnes après les rebelles comme un chien enragé après les puces.

Cinq hommes de perdus en deux semaines de combats, et deux grosses bandes de piégées. Pankov lui-même baissa les bras quand on lui rapporta une histoire survenue à Chamkhalsk. Les combattants d'Arzo y avaient débusqué deux bandits des bois, deux frères qui dévalèrent une rue à toutes jambes. L'un d'eux fut abattu, l'autre se jeta dans un café où l'on vendait des glaces, dégoupilla une grenade, criant à tous de ne pas approcher. Le café faisait vis-à-vis à une école, c'était l'heure de la récréation et la moitié de la clientèle se composait d'enfants.

Les combattants d'Arzo cernèrent le café, lui-même criant au garçon de libérer les enfants pour régler l'affaire entre hommes. Le boïévik, qui n'avait guère plus de dix-neuf ans, hurla qu'il relâcherait les gosses si Arzo entrait seul et sans armes.

Au mépris de toutes les règles écrites et non écrites, Arzo se montra à la porte du café trente secondes plus tard. Les gamins prirent la poudre d'escampette, le gars s'affola. L'un des serveurs se jeta dessus pour lui arracher sa grenade. L'autre le frappa et la grenade vola en l'air. L'instant d'après, Arzo plaquait le boïévik. Tomba d'abord la grenade, puis le boïévik par-dessus, puis Arzo qui le cloua au sol. Le gars eut les tripes en compote, mais personne d'autre ne fut atteint, Arzo compris. Belle bagarre tout de même pour un colonel de quarante ans privé de son bras gauche, d'autant que nul ne connaissait le modèle de la grenade. Eût-ce été une F-1 au lieu d'une RGD qu'Arzo n'eût pas manqué d'y laisser des plumes.

Jour après jour, les coups portés par Arzo contre les bases des boïéviks se faisaient de plus en plus précis. Les forces de l'Intérieur venues de Saratov ou d'ailleurs n'auraient pu l'égaler, non seulement parce que les hommes de Saratov ou de Krasnoïarsk se repéraient moins bien dans les montagnes (ils n'arrivaient même pas à respirer, que dire alors de leur sens de l'orientation !), mais aussi parce que Arzo faisait parler les prisonniers avec des méthodes inaccessibles aux Russes.

Aussi Pankov ne fut-il pas étonné ni alarmé d'apprendre au soir du 10 octobre que le groupe de Khadjiev avait traqué un gros gibier : un vrai combat faisait rage près de Kharon-Yourte, village de montagne, et le Youg appelait les troupes fédérales en renfort.

Ça tombait mal : il y avait un avis de tempête sur Torbi-Kala, des trombes d'eau se déversaient sur les montagnes et les héliports ne donnaient aucune autorisation de vol. Puis Arzo se ravisa de lui-même au prétexte qu'il craignait encore plus d'être exposé à un feu ami.

Tout fut fini à l'aube. Pas un boïévik n'en réchappa parmi ceux qui s'étaient retranchés sur une hauteur entre la frontière géorgienne et le village de Kharon-Yourte. Le général Chebolev débarqua dans la journée en hélicoptère avec une caméra. Il repartit avec les blessés. Le soir même, la télévision fédérale diffusa des images d'archives militaires : reliefs de treillis en lambeaux sur une terre détrempée, douilles brûlées de lance-grenades.

L'état-major antiterroriste se réunit à neuf heures du matin. Grande nervosité de Pankov : un agenda surchargé, deux rendez-vous à la résidence, une rencontre à Moscou à seize heures.

Etonnamment, la rencontre ne concernait en rien le travail. Dans l'une des somptueuses villas de l'avenue Roublev, un vieux camarade fêtait son anniversaire, l'un des rares businessmen d'envergure qui soit pour lui un ami sincère. Pankov n'avait pas assisté à une partie de ce genre depuis le mois de juin, et jamais il n'aurait pensé que ça puisse lui manquer à ce point.

Mais maintenant il brûlait de quitter cette chaleur insupportable qui n'avait rien d'automnal pour la fraîcheur et l'espace d'une salle à miroirs où des femmes en robes de soirée et des hommes plastronnant avec un verre de rouge à la main parlaient de tout et de n'importe quoi : de la dernière mise en scène au Bolchoï, de leur été à Saint-Tropez, du club le plus chic de la saison... de tout sauf de cadavres, de coups de feu, de condoléances, des avantages de la berline blindée sur le quatre-quatre blindé.

Arzo Khadjiev était présent, imperturbable, tiré à quatre épingles. Pankov fut épaté par son allure : sans les cernes noirs qu'il avait sous les yeux, on n'aurait pu imaginer que cet homme avait passé la nuit d'avant sous un torrent de pluie et de feu.

— Le groupe du colonel Khadjiev, rapporta le général Chebolev, a anéanti vingt-quatre boïéviks. A en juger par leur aspect physique, deux d'entre eux sont des instructeurs venus de pays arabes. On a pu recenser sur le champ de bataille dix-neuf pistolets-mitrailleurs, trois fusils à lunette, un fusil de haute précision, sept lance-grenades et cinq jeux de munitions assortis. La planque que les boïéviks cherchaient à atteindre recelait cent quinze kilos d'explosifs, des détonateurs et autres systèmes de mises à feu, vingt lance-grenades avec une cinquantaine de jeux de munitions. Il y a tout lieu d'affirmer que l'opération d'hier a permis de prévenir plusieurs dizaines d'attentats terroristes. Au vu des résultats, je demande que le colonel Khadjiev soit présenté à l'ordre du Courage.

Distraitement, Pankov faisait tourner dans ses mains les photos prises sur le théâtre des opérations. Le cadavre d'un boïévik gisant ventre à terre ressemblait à un tas de feuilles mortes. On avait aussi photographié un seau. Un seau ordinaire, de ceux dont les simples femmes tiraient de l'eau au puits, mais qui était plein d'explosifs truffés de billes d'acier.

Deux semaines auparavant, un seau identique avait été laissé près de sa résidence privée. Son service de sécurité l'avait repéré à temps.

Il se plaisait à penser que ce seau-là ne serait jamais laissé nulle part.

— J'approuve cette citation, dit le représentant du président.

Pas le moindre geste d'Arzo, et Pankov se dit qu'il se fichait tout autant des médailles russes que des balles russes neuf ans auparavant.

Pareille à un corbeau noir, une femme apparut sur le coup de midi au portail de la résidence du premier commis du Kremlin. Bientôt, il y en eut cinq. Pendant que Pankov, de sa fenêtre, regardait les gardes aux prises avec elles, une Jigouli arriva sur la place, d'où descendirent encore trois autres femmes.

Lorsque le portail glissa devant la voiture qui emmenait Pankov à l'aéroport, elles étaient déjà une bonne douzaine qu'il entendait piailler comme des freux effarouchés même à travers les vitres blindées.

Les gardes tentaient de les écarter quand Pankov ouvrit la portière arrière de la voiture et descendit.

— Qu'y a-t-il ?

Les femmes se turent un instant. Puis elles se jetèrent dans les filets de la garde, comme poussées par une onde de choc, et l'une d'elles hurla, grosse, ébouriffée, les cheveux noirs crasseux, la jupe noire graisseuse :

— Rends-moi le corps de mon fils !

— Qui est ton fils ?

— On l'a trouvé hier à Kharon-Yourte ! On a même montré son visage à la télé ! Et maintenant on me refuse le corps sous prétexte qu'il est terroriste !

— C'est la loi, de ne pas rendre le corps d'un terroriste à la famille.

— Mais il n'est pas terroriste ! se récria la femme. Il a été enlevé par les hommes d'Arzo en vendant des pommes de terre au marché ! Parce qu'il avait tué un Tchétchène ! Si bataille il y a eu, que faisait là-bas le corps de mon fils ? Arzo l'a enlevé le 17 septembre !

Pankov sursauta comme s'il avait reçu un coup. "Impossible, pensa-t-il, Chebolev m'en aurait rendu compte." Mais la grosse femme fut poussée à l'écart et il se retrouva nez à nez devant Patimat Chakhbanova, la belle femme de l'autre fois, aussi grande, magnifique et élancée que trois semaines auparavant, avec le même foulard de dentelle coquettement posé sur ses cheveux bouclés, mais ses boucles avaient complètement blanchi depuis lors.

— Tu as vendu mon fils pour vingt-cinq mille dollars ! s'écria Chakhbanova. Rends-moi au moins son corps !

— Moi ?!

— Nous avons vendu notre voiture pour rassembler la somme ! Nous avons vendu notre maison ! Et voilà que le corps de mon fils est montré à Kharon-Yourte ! Tes généraux le traitent de terroriste !

A cet instant, une femme jeta une pierre sur Pankov. La garde réagit instantanément. Son chef Sergueï Piskounov le poussa au fond de la Mercedes et le chauffeur appuya sur le champignon. Les gardes se jetèrent sur les femmes qui furent traînées à terre à coups de clés de bras.

— Quelle mouche vous a piqué de descendre de voiture ? hurla Piskounov. C'est de la provoc ! Et si vous aviez reçu une grenade au lieu d'un caillou ?

Le cortège passa en trombe de l'avenue Lénine à l'avenue Chamil, et Pankov aperçut un milicien au garde-à-vous qui bloquait la circulation, la main à la visière du képi.

— A gauche, dit Pankov.

— L'aéroport c'est à droite, s'étonna Piskounov.

— Nous allons à Kharon-Yourte, répondit Pankov.

Cent kilomètres les séparaient de Kharon-Yourte, qu'ils couvrirent en une heure et demie. La route longeait une gorge qu'elle enjambait de temps à autre, et Pankov fut tellement ballotté dans sa Merco blindée qu'il demanda à changer de voiture avec son escorte.

Une fois dans le quatre-quatre, il se sentit un peu mieux. Il se mit à l'avant malgré les protestations de ses gardes et, recroquevillé, laissa courir son regard sur les montagnes indifférentes et les ronces squelettiques qui bordaient la route. A un détour, il vit briller un gazoduc à l'assaut d'un escarpement.

Il regretta une bonne dizaine de fois de ne pas avoir pris le chemin de l'aéroport. Comme chef en titre de l'état-major antiterroriste, il était le troisième homme de la région après Allah et le commandant en chef et pouvait parfaitement disposer d'un hélico auprès des gardes-frontière. Mais la météo faisait toujours des caprices et le vent du large arrivait en rafales. De plus, s'il avait pris un hélicoptère, sa décision d'aller à Kharon-Yourte aurait fait le tour de la place en moins de temps qu'il n'en fallait pour le dire.

Le réseau mobile disparut à cinquante kilomètre de Torbi-Kala, à quoi Pankov trouva plus d'avantages que d'inconvénients. Personne ne pourrait faire pression sur lui à Kharon-Yourte.

Un gros village que ce Kharon-Yourte. Les gamins envahissaient la route au passage de cet étrange cortège et les femmes, fagotées de jupes et de tabliers mal taillés, se faisaient statues en l'accompagnant du regard. Plusieurs dizaines de personnes se pressaient sur la place du village, près du magasin. Des Land Cruiser et des Niva stationnaient là, avec des hommes armés à l'intérieur. Sautant de voiture, le premier commis du Kremlin ne fut pas étonné de reconnaître parmi eux Djavatkhan Askerov, vice-ministre de la Politique et de la Collecte fiscale. Son chargeur de secours, de couleur orange, était collé à l'autre chargeur par un scotch bleu, d'où son aspect rayé qui lui donnait un air de marinière.

— Que fais-tu ici ? lui demanda Pankov.

Askerov pointa le menton vers les hauteurs. Passé un cimetière, un petit sentier bordé d'épines montait vers le ciel.

— Mon neveu est là-bas, répondit Djavatkhan.

— Et pourquoi pas toi ?

— J'attends des amis.

Pankov haussa les épaules et allongea le pas vers le sentier, suivi de Piskounov et de Djavatkhan.

Ascension plus rude que prévue. A cette altitude, il faisait plus frais que sur le littoral mais le thermomètre ne devait guère être en dessous des vingt-sept degrés. Conséquence des pluies de la veille, un brouillard lévitait entre les montagnes, et la chaleur, humide, collait au visage et aux aisselles. Pankov en nage tomba la veste, puis marqua un arrêt pour dénouer sa cravate, le souffle court, la face écarlate. Et cette montagne, là-haut, qui n'en finissait pas...

En se retournant, il se vit suivi non seulement de ses gardes et des hommes de Djavatkhan, mais aussi, plus loin, du peuple des villageois. Presque tous les hommes qu'il avait vus sur la place s'étiraient maintenant sur la sente en file indienne, et Pankov remarqua aussi une Niva qui stoppait à l'orée du bourg. Trois hommes en sortirent qui parlementèrent avec des gens du coin et s'empressèrent à leur tour d'enfiler le chemin.

Vingt minutes passèrent, et Pankov se sentit mal pour de bon. Ruisselant de sueur, les lunettes embuées, le cœur cognant avec la force d'un métronome, il souffrait aussi, pardessus le marché, d'une soif irrésistible. Il vit soudain comme un mirage : la villa de l'avenue Roublev, les dentelles vitrées de la véranda, une cerise dans un verre de martini et les filles en robes flottantes... S'il était parti pour Moscou, il y serait déjà, pas sur cette foutue montagne au milieu de nulle part – ni Avarie ni Géorgie.

Le manque d'oxygène le faisait étouffer. Drôle à voir de l'extérieur, sans doute : tout rouge, débraillé, baignant de sueur. On ne marche pas dans les montagnes en pantalon Armani. Même ses gardes, près de lui, avaient la respiration courte et pénible. Djavatkhan et ses hommes, discrètement, dépassèrent les Russes et se mirent à donner la cadence.

Passé la crête, le sentier piquait. Il traversait des éboulements de pierres et gagnait en largeur. Pankov s'arrêta et sortit un coin de chemise de son pantalon pour en essuyer ses lunettes. Djavatkhan lui tendit une gourde.

Cinq minutes plus tard, le sentier tournait à droite et débouchait sur un espace presque plan entre deux hauteurs. Plus loin, le chemin fourchait. Là-bas, une dizaine d'hommes assis, en treillis, regardaient descendre tout ce monde d'un œil inquiet.

Un vieux montagnard s'approcha de Pankov et se mit à lui parler en tendant le bras vers le haut, du côté droit, dans un si mauvais russe que Djavatkhan dut le traduire. D'après le vieux, les blindés d'Arzo étaient arrivés au village la veille vers six heures du soir. Les soldats s'en étaient allés dans la montagne et, trois heures plus tard, sur la cime qu'on voyait à droite, là-bas (cime médiocrement boisée), les tirs avaient commencé. Au matin le vieil homme était monté avec son troupeau de brebis, pour y découvrir des cadavres qu'on était en train de filmer. Les soldats du commando, russes et tchétchènes, s'y trouvaient encore, qui avaient donné l'ordre au berger d'enterrer les morts. Il y était donc revenu deux heures plus tard avec des villageois, dont l'un, nommé Rasul, reconnut son neveu parmi les dépouilles, un étudiant de l'université de Torbi-Kala enlevé un mois plus tôt. Cris des villageois que les soldats avaient chassés en leur interdisant de revenir.

Pankov s'approchait des soldats quand il entendit un grondement qui venait du ciel. Un hélicoptère était en train de se poser, d'où descendit un homme en treillis qui courut vers les soldats à grandes foulées.

Il y fut avant la foule. A son commandement, les soldats se rassemblèrent et l'homme éructa de sa voix de basse :

— Debout tout le monde !

Ecartant Djavatkhan, Pankov s'avança. La mèche collée au front, la bouche ouverte comme une carpe, il se retourna : la foule qui le suivait se rompit pour envelopper le petit groupe de soldats d'un côté comme de l'autre.

— Qui es-tu, toi ? lança Pankov à l'homme qui ordonnait la formation.

— Major Streletski, groupe d'intervention spéciale Youg !

— Je suis Vladislav Pankov. Laisse passer ces gens.

La face tantôt blême, tantôt rouge, le major eut finalement un geste d'abandon et fonça à l'hélico : pour faire son rapport.

Le petit bois où s'était déroulé le combat ne donnait ni ombre ni fraîcheur. Des arbustes noueux s'élevaient sur une pente pierreuse, leur écorce envahie d'une mousse qui ressemblait à de l'urticaire. Les fédéraux n'avaient pas chômé : pas un cadavre en vue.

A l'écart du bosquet, une pierre blanche schisteuse faisait saillie à même la terre, surmontée d'un petit tertre de moellons. On voyait bien que ces pierres-là avaient été rapportées des éboulements voisins et, par ce temps humide et chaud, Pankov crut sentir de lourds relents qui lui soulevaient le cœur.

— Déterrez les morts.

Les hommes s'attaquèrent au monticule pendant que Pankov, assis sur un schiste saillant comme une tumeur de la montagne, regardait la vallée. On était si haut qu'on se croyait au niveau du soleil. Par-dessous la maigre ramure d'un arbuste qui jetait une ombre incertaine, il vit un troupeau de moutons sur une pente voisine délicieusement ombragée. Plus bas serpentait la route qui traversait le village et sur laquelle se traînaient deux blindés. On eût dit deux fourmis marchant sur du sucre mouillé.

Pankov montra les blindés à Djavatkhan qui fit oui de la tête. Vladislav avait très envie de faire venir quelqu'un d'autre – Khizri, Mahomedsalih ou Niyazbek lui-même – mais il voyait bien que c'était inutile. Personne n'avait de couverture mobile, l'antenne relais la plus proche se trouvant à une bonne cinquantaine de kilomètres. Il avait bien un téléphone satellitaire dans sa voiture, mais la voiture stationnait au fond de la vallée, coupée du satellite par la paroi rocheuse.

Il avait six gardes et Djavatkhan, trois. Plus une vingtaine d'hommes venus du village avec pétoires ou mitraillettes. Théoriquement, ça ne valait pas tripette contre deux blindés couverts par un hélico de combat, et Pankov tenta de refouler la peur irrationnelle qui le prenait. C'était idiot de penser que l'armée russe allait se battre contre le chef de l'état-major antiterroriste. "Tu as encore trop peur d'Arzo, pensa-t-il, mais il n'est plus séparatiste et tu n'es plus prisonnier dans sa cave."

Et pourtant l'ambassadeur du Kremlin en poste dans le Caucase éprouvait un étrange réconfort à l'idée que l'homme assis à ses côtés avait certes égorgé des soldats russes, mais uniquement par économie de cartouches.

Le premier cadavre fut extrait au bout de vingt minutes.

Djavatkhan lui fit un bref signe de tête, se leva et l'emmena.

L'homme en treillis gisait face à terre près d'une touffe de ronces. Détail curieux, il était pieds nus. Un des compagnons de Djavatkhan dit quelque chose à mi-voix.

— Quoi ? fit Pankov.

Djavatkhan s'accroupit et tendit le doigt :

— La nuque. Il a été tué d'une balle dans la nuque.

Puis il retourna le corps, dégrafa la tunique camo qu'il portait à même sa poitrine bronzée, dénoua la ceinture de son pantalon et fit apparaître un slip défraîchi sur une peau blanche.

Dents serrées, Pankov fit une aspiration brusque et vacilla.

L'homme avait été abattu d'une arme à feu, aucun doute là-dessus : entrée par la nuque, la balle avait tant mutilé le visage qu'on n'aurait su dire s'il s'agissait d'un jeune ou d'un vieux. Mais les balles n'étaient pas la cause de toutes ses meurtrissures, loin de là. Un corps efflanqué comme celui d'un déporté d'Auschwitz ou d'un prisonnier qui aurait subi le supplice de la faim, mais qui avait gardé le bronzage de l'été. Un slip alors que les wahhabites n'en portent jamais. L'épaule gauche marquée de brûlures grosses comme une belle pièce. Pankov comprit tout de suite que ce n'était pas la marque de cigarettes, trop petites, mais de cigares.

Djavatkhan lui remonta les bas de pantalon, trop lâches, et Pankov vit avec effroi qu'il avait les rotules en marmelade, brisées par balle ou autrement, mais c'était une meurtrissure ancienne qui ne datait pas de la veille ou de l'avant-veille, or quiconque a les rotules brisées est incapable de courir la montagne, à supposer que la douleur ne l'ait pas foudroyé d'entrée.

Un autre montagnard, aidé de Djavatkhan, se mit à ôter le pantalon du mort. C'en fut trop pour Sergueï Piskounov, le garde de Pankov, qui courut à l'écart et qui, penché sur un rocher, rendit tripes et boyaux.

Deux minutes plus tard, un deuxième cadavre était devant Pankov. Peu de gens pour le voir parce que les hommes de Djavatkhan bouclaient les abords de la clairière par égard pour les morts, mais la foule était bien visible, à trois mètres des pierres. Djavatkhan leva la main du deuxième défunt et la montra à Pankov.

— Il a les ongles arrachés.

— Je vois, dit Pankov ; sans doute avec des tenailles.

— C'est bien le problème. Crois-tu qu'on aille au combat avec une paire de tenailles ? Sache une chose, à toutes fins utiles : si tu captures quelqu'un au combat et que tu veux qu'il parle vite fait, le mieux est encore de lui mitrailler les doigts.

La chaleur et l'odeur de chair putrescente donnaient le vertige à Pankov. Il se croyait là-haut depuis une demi-journée au moins, et quelle ne fut pas sa surprise de voir à sa montre que seulement quarante minutes s'étaient écoulées. "Que va-t-il se passer si je perds connaissance ? se dit-il. Tous ces montagnards penseront que je suis une petite nature, alors que c'est simplement le poids de la chaleur."

Assis sur une pierre, il attendait silencieusement qu'on déterre les autres morts. Quand il leva les yeux, il vit que la foule se fendait à l'orée du bois au passage du général Chebolev, chef du FSB régional, et du colonel Khadjiev, commandant du Youg, groupe d'intervention spéciale du FSB.

Pankov se leva en jetant un œil en coin sur les cadavres. Il y en avait quatorze, certains avec les oreilles coupées. Il se rappela les images télédiffusées de la veille qui ne révélaient pas la moindre trace de torture. Le cadreur, pourtant, n'avait pas pu ne pas les voir. Chebolev non plus, qui semblait avoir choisi de couvrir Arzo jusqu'au bout, préférant lui décerner une médaille pour un combat jamais livré plutôt que de compromettre l'action de l'état-major antiterroriste.

— Faites venir ici les parents des personnes enlevées le mois dernier, ordonna Pankov à l'oreille de Djavatkhan, surtout par des ravisseurs en Niva blanche sans plaque d'immatriculation.

— Impossible, pas le temps. D'après la coutume, ils doivent être enterrés avant le coucher du soleil.

— Alors emportons-les à Torbi-Kala. Nous ferons le voyage dans une de tes voitures et les cadavres dans toutes les autres. Trouvera-t-on des sacs au village ?

Chebolev était déjà tout près et Pankov fit un pas énergique à sa rencontre. Le général avait la face couleur de betterave, la respiration bruyante, qui sifflait comme une bouilloire en ébullition, la chemise blanche en eau, sa cravate pendillant à son col comme un hareng crevé. Pankov éprouva une vague satisfaction à l'idée que l'autre en avait bavé plus que lui pour monter jusqu'ici.

Arzo Khadjiev se tenait immobile derrière le général, en tenue de camouflage et brodequins lourds. Il portait un gilet pare-balles sur son treillis, la manche gauche vide agrafée à la ceinture, un béret des troupes d'élite vissé de travers sur des cheveux poivre et sel. Et pas une goutte de sueur ne perlait sur son visage mat.

— On se permet bien des choses, Vladislav Avdeïevitch ! fit Chebolev. J'ai failli perdre la tête en apprenant que votre cortège n'était pas arrivé à l'aéroport ! J'ai pensé à un attentat terroriste ! A un enlèvement ! Et voilà que vous faites bande à part, maintenant...

— J'enquête sur des meurtres et des enlèvements.

— Ce sont des criminels ! Des wahhabites !

— J'en doute. De plus, Arzo Khadjiev n'est pas le plus à même de distinguer un wahhabite d'un non-wahhabite.

— Vous avez des *a priori* contre lui, dit Chebolev, des comptes personnels à régler avec lui, je le sais bien. Pour autant, votre aspiration à régler ces affaires personnelles ne doit pas vous conduire à saper l'autorité du pouvoir fédéral !

Vladislav attrapa le chef du FSB par le col :

— Oui, j'ai des comptes personnels à régler avec lui, tu as parfaitement raison. Un jour que je croupissais dans la cave d'Arzo, on m'a fait sortir pour m'obliger à jeter aux chiens des cadavres de soldats russes, en pitance. Et tu sais quoi ? Ces cadavres avaient le même aspect que ceux-ci. Il ne t'est jamais arrivé de faire manger des cadavres aux chiens ? Hein, Guennadi Vassiliévitch ?

Rouge comme un coquelicot, Chebolev faisait rouler ses yeux de Pankov à la foule et inversement.

— Fais gaffe, Slava, lança Arzo à mi-voix, tu ne seras pas le premier homme du Kremlin à disparaître dans les montagnes.

Hors de lui, Pankov lui fit face. Arzo ne bougeait pas, droit sur ses jambes, le treillis corseté d'un gilet pare-balles, le bras gauche remplacé par un tissu agrafé à la ceinture. Il posait sur lui des yeux noirs comme le cul d'une marmite avec la même indifférence que sur les cadavres, et les rides qui sillonnaient son visage semblaient pareilles à des tranchées creusées par le temps.

Neuf années durant, le visage du tueur avait hanté les cauchemars de Pankov. Neuf années durant, il avait eu peur de cet homme. Et voilà maintenant que, à peine cinq heures plus tôt, Vladislav Pankov le félicitait personnellement du succès de cette opération. Laquelle opération n'était autre qu'un déchargement de cadavres, comme on pouvait le voir maintenant au grand jour. Des cadavres d'hommes qu'on avait torturés durant plusieurs semaines et abattus d'une balle dans la nuque pour ajouter quelques sardines à de nouvelles médailles.

L'instant d'après, Pankov frappa Arzo. Il le frappa comme Niyazbek le lui avait montré, pas du poing ni non plus du revers, mais du plat de la main, en plein nez, de toutes ses forces comme pour l'amocher jusqu'aux yeux. Ou plutôt, il tenta de le faire. Car, de sa dextre puissante, le Tchétchène lui bloqua le bras et le retourna d'un coup déchirant. L'herbe et le ciel valsèrent, une force inouïe le tétanisa, qui le serrait comme une gigantesque menotte, et, dans la seconde, le brodequin d'Arzo l'éperonna au plexus.

L'homme du Kremlin s'écroula à quatre pattes comme un bichon, les lunettes égarées dans l'herbette. Pour parachever le tableau, il fut pris d'un violent, d'un atroce vomissement qui se fit devant tous.

Le général Chebolev hurla quelque chose, le chef de la garde saisit Pankov à l'encolure et le traîna à l'écart. Quand le premier commis fut sur ses jambes, suffoquant et rouge de honte, il vit ses gardes et Djavatkhan pointer leurs PM sur Arzo qui souriait, la main droite en l'air.

— Tu vois, Djavatkhan, c'est lui qui m'a frappé, dit Arzo. Je n'ai rien fait du tout.

— Partons de là, dit Serguéï, partons de là et vite.

Mais Pankov n'avait pas l'intention de partir. Il s'assit en silence auprès des cadavres, et Djavatkhan se posta à ses côtés. Certains corps étaient transportables mais d'autres se trouvaient dans un état tel qu'il fallait les envelopper à tout prix. Naturellement, il n'y avait pas de sacs appropriés au village, et l'on emballa les dépouilles avec ce qu'on avait sous la main : bâche, polyéthylène, draps blancs qui tournaient instantanément au rouge.

Assis par terre, Pankov se disait qu'il était tout autant responsable de ces cadavres qu'Arzo. Parce que si l'on charge un loup de garder un poulailler, on n'a pas le droit de se défausser sur le loup. Puis, écœuré par ses propres pensées, il se leva pour aider les villageois à envelopper les morts. Ses mains se couvrirent bientôt de sang et d'une espèce de souillure noire.

Ils entamèrent ensuite la descente avec les dernières dépouilles, et Pankov observa que Serguéï avait maintenant un pistolet-mitrailleur à double chargeur orange rayé de bleu.

Du haut de la montagne, le général Chebolev regardait en silence les hommes, petits comme des pions, charger les cadavres dans une Niva blanche, un Land Cruiser, une Mercedes.

— Il faut l'en empêcher ! s'écria-t-il. Il faut boucler la sortie du village !

Chebolev mit son talkie-walkie à sa bouche et tressaillit quand la dextre ferme d'Arzo prit son avant-bras en tenailles.

— Laisse-le partir, dit Arzo.

Le chef du FSB régional lui jeta un regard perplexe.

— Tu ne comprends pas, hurla le général, ils vont nous virer ! Ils vont tous nous envoyer paître ! Nous devons lui expliquer…

Le Tchétchène lui arracha le talkie-walkie de la main et le fracassa contre une pierre. Le plastique noir éclata en mille morceaux comme une petite grenade.

— Il n'y a pas d'explication qui tienne, dit Arzo. D'ailleurs, ça ne te concerne plus.

Ils roulaient en colonne à quatre voitures : deux Land Cruiser, une Niva blanche et, en tête, un Chevrolet Tahoe fort comme un bœuf à bord duquel s'entassaient Djavatkhan, Pankov et deux gardes – Pankov étant coincé entre Djavatkhan et le chef de la sécurité comme un steak haché dans un hamburger, avec un officier du FSB sur le siège avant. La Merco blindée avait été irrémédiablement semée au premier tournant.

La chaleur, la vue des cadavres, l'humiliation, tout cela faisait trembler Pankov. Il n'avait pas su frapper Arzo. Dans un monde où l'agilité physique passait pour la qualité première de l'homme, c'était un ratage impardonnable.

— Fils de chien, maugréa-t-il, je vais le réduire en purée. Et Chebolev aussi par la même occasion. Il le regrettera, d'avoir pris sa défense.

— Il ne pouvait pas faire autrement, dit Djavatkhan. Ces cadavres-là sont les siens.

— Que veux-tu dire par là ? fit le Moscovite d'une voix fatiguée.

— Que ce n'est pas Arzo qui les a enlevés. Mais les kagébistes. Les hommes de Chebolev. Ils les faisaient passer à l'interrogatoire et puis... Il fallait bien régulariser les cadavres. C'était la mission d'Arzo. Ça tombait bien : ces gens-là étaient fichés comme appartenant à des bandes, ils ont donc été liquidés en tant que bande.

— Et vous le saviez ?

— Niyazbek le savait. Je le savais. Khizri le savait. Tout le monde le savait.

Pankov mit ses mains sur ses yeux.

— Sais-tu ce qu'a dit la mère de Chakhbanov ? hurla-t-il. Elle a dit que je lui avais pris de l'argent contre la promesse de lui rendre son fils !

— Ça aussi, tout le monde le savait, dit Djavatkhan. Il allait de soi que tu étais au courant de l'enlèvement, et Chebolev aussi. Son ravisseur avait fait un deal avec Chebolev, Chebolev avec toi, et toi, sans doute, avec le président. C'est l'opinion générale ici. Qu'un subordonné ne fasse pas de deal avec son supérieur, on n'a jamais vu ça.

— Moi prendre de l'argent pour ça ?! se récria Pankov (mots piaulés plutôt que prononcés). Que je mette des gens en prison pour de l'argent ?! Que je les relâche pour de l'argent ?!

— Et pourtant tu as bien fait mettre Mahomedsalih en prison pour de l'argent, lâcha Djavatkhan d'un air philosophe.

— Quoi ?!

— Il ne t'avait rien fait de mal et tu le voyais pour la première fois. Ce n'était même pas à toi qu'il s'en prenait, mais à quelqu'un d'autre que tu ne connaissais pas non plus. Tu ne savais rien, ni qui il frappait, ni pourquoi. Donc tu as choisi d'en profiter pour te faire de l'argent, logique.

— Et combien d'après toi ?

— Deux cent mille tickets au minimum. Chebolev lui en a extorqué trois cent mille pour classer le dossier, lui disant qu'il enterrerait l'affaire gratis mais que, toi, il fallait te payer. A ce qu'on dit, tu as fait banquer les Ataïev. Pour la nomination.

— Et, toi, je ne t'ai rien fait payer ? s'enquit Pankov d'un ton cauteleux.

— A dire vrai, Chebolev m'a montré mon dossier : Pervomaïka, Hattab et compagnie. Il m'a demandé un million si je ne voulais pas disparaître comme Djanadov. Je le cite mot pour mot : Vladislav Avdeïevitch me prie de te dire que, après la mésaventure de l'Autrichien, exiger moins d'un million ne serait pas convenable.

Non sans peine, Pankov se rappela que Djanadov était le nom du chef adjoint du comité d'Etat à la Pêche enlevé deux semaines auparavant dans la fameuse Niva blanche.

— Et tu as cru que j'étais le demandeur ? gémit Pankov. Ça sent le bluff à plein nez…

— C'est pourtant toi qui as créé l'état-major antiterroriste.

— Arrête-toi, ordonna Vladislav.

Le chauffeur se gara docilement sur le bas-côté et l'homme du Kremlin se laissa tomber à genoux dans les ronces de bord de route. Comme il avait l'estomac vide depuis longtemps, il ne put vomir que des glaires marron-jaune. Ayant relevé la tête, il vit Djavatkhan qui lui tendait une bouteille d'eau. Il se rinça longtemps la bouche, puis l'autre le prit par l'encolure et le remit dans la voiture comme on soulève un chaton.

Il s'enferma dans un mutisme prostré. Il ne songeait même plus aux cadavres, trop hébété qu'il était à l'idée que pour l'entourage de Niyazbek le combat du nouvel homme du Kremlin contre le terrorisme et la corruption n'avait d'autre mobile que l'appât du gain. Plus ahurissant encore : si Djavatkhan croyait dur comme fer que l'état-major antiterroriste avait été créé exprès pour extorquer de l'argent aux Caucasiens, c'était parce que le résultat lui donnait raison.

— La vérité, dit le Lezghe, c'est que tu ne prenais pas d'argent. Tout le monde le saura maintenant.

— Merci, bredouilla le Moscovite.

Et dire qu'il s'étonnait du refus de Niyazbek de remplacer Arzo. Niyazbek l'avait-il vraiment tenu en mépris tout ce temps ? Ou seulement à partir de la création de l'état-major antiterroriste, c'est-à-dire à partir du moment où les disparitions s'étaient multipliées dans toute la région et qu'on avait commencé à exiger des rançons en son nom ?

A l'idée des cadavres qui étaient dans le coffre, Pankov fut pris de l'envie de hurler.

Passé un barrage hydroélectrique, on se retrouva sur la rive d'en face et le Moscovite ordonna à Sergueï de joindre le Kremlin par le réseau spécial. Mais la gorge, trop profonde, empêchait la connexion.

— Fils de chiens, balbutia encore Vladislav.

La route s'obscurcit brusquement. Elle courait maintenant au fond de la gorge et les rayons du soleil n'éclairaient plus que la ligne régulière de la crête, là-haut, où se nichait Dieu sait comment un village minuscule. L'endroit était si frais qu'il accueillait un petit bois, sans prétention certes, mais un bois quand même, avec des chênes difformes et des fourrés de verdure.

Les branches des arbres griffèrent le toit des voitures, la route tourna à droite et le Chevrolet ralentit parce que la chaussée était entamée par des coulées de boue de la saison passée et que le goudron le cédait maintenant aux graviers.

Un blindé les guettait au tournant.

Vladislav ne s'en inquiéta pas sur le coup : ce n'était pas le genre d'engin que devait redouter un haut fonctionnaire de rang fédéral sur les routes d'une république fidèle à la Russie. Puis le blindé s'ébranla et le canon de sa mitrailleuse oscilla de droite et de gauche comme la truffe d'un berger allemand reniflant sa proie.

Vladislav comprit ce qui allait arriver. Le Chevrolet de Djavatkhan était plutôt bien protégé. Il ne possédait pas de blindage d'usine (car alors il aurait perdu toute mobilité), mais le pare-brise faisait pare-balles et des gilets-cuirasses habillaient la carrosserie. Le véhicule aurait peut-être supporté un tir de Kalachnikov, mais pas de calibre antiblindage 14,5 mm à bout portant. Pas question non plus de sauter de la voiture en marche. Les compagnons de Djavatkhan n'avaient que des armes d'infanterie. Jamais ils n'auraient touché le blindé.

Encore quelques secondes et tout serait joué. Les hommes d'Arzo rapporteraient alors au commandement fédéral que des camarades des boïéviks abattus la veille s'étaient embusqués dans les bois et avaient attaqué le cortège de l'ambassadeur du président de la fédération de Russie. On dirait aussi qu'on était arrivé trop tard sur les lieux de l'accrochage, à trois minutes près ; et qu'on avait eu le temps d'exterminer les boïéviks, mais pas de sauver l'homme du président.

Comme dans une séquence tournée au ralenti, Vladislav vit la main de Djavatkhan l'attraper par la manche ; de l'autre main, le Lezghe ouvrait la portière. Apparemment, il criait quelque chose au chauffeur. L'ordre de serrer à gauche, semblait-il, vers l'affaissement raboté par les coulées de boue qui donnait droit sur le précipice. Ça leur laissait au moins une petite chance. C'était ça ou rien.

La portière du Chevrolet s'ouvrit, et Vladislav se sentit voler dans les airs.

La seconde d'après, le blindé explosa.

Vladislav le vit en se laissant rouler sur la pente encore douce de l'affaissement. Une flamme jaillit de l'arrière de l'engin masqué par une peinture de camouflage, puis une explosion éjecta le tireur par la trappe grande ouverte, après quoi les munitions détonèrent à l'intérieur.

A cet instant Djavatkhan le poussa derrière un pli du terrain et se laissa tomber par-dessus lui. Pankov atterrit le nez dans les ronces. Les explosions s'enchaînèrent l'une après l'autre comme les notes s'enchaînent en musique. Pour finir – balle ou éclat – il y eut un sifflement exécrable. Le Moscovite sentait l'horreur lui coller aux tripes.

Djavatkhan le souleva par l'encolure et le traîna droit devant.

Une Nissan noire stationnait tout là-bas, près de laquelle un homme appuyé sur un genou tenait à l'épaule un lance-grenade semblable à un énorme stylo plume : Niyazbek. Une rafale jaillit des bois. Niyazbek se retourna en un éclair et, dans la seconde qui suivit, une boule de feu roux-jaune fusa d'entre les arbres. La Nissan fit demi-tour et fonça en marche arrière vers le blindé en flammes.

— Vite ! cria le chef de la sécurité de Pankov.

Les balles arrachaient des geysers à une poussière grise de graviers. Une paire de bras – sans doute ceux de Dja-vatkhan – fit décoller Pankov, le traîna le long du blindé embrasé et le jeta dans le ventre frais de la Nissan.

— On se tire d'ici ! cria Serguéï en s'engouffrant dans la Nissan par l'autre portière.

— Pas question de les abandonner, lança Vladislav.

— Il y a assez de monde pour se battre, répondit le chauffeur.

Ce qu'ayant dit, il écrasa l'accélérateur.

Une foule de deux cents personnes attendait devant la villa de Pankov, et la foule savait tout. Personne ne savait rien, mais la foule savait. Dieu sait comment. Peut-être la Merco blindée du Moscovite avait-elle été aperçue par une voiture venant de Kharon-Yourte, ou peut-être avait-on téléphoné du village qui possédait une ligne fixe, toujours est-il que les femmes apprirent que Pankov s'était rendu sur les lieux du drame avant même qu'il ne revînt à la résidence.

Les voitures s'arrêtèrent devant la foule qui s'écarta puis les enveloppa comme une coulée de lave noire. Un cordon de miliciens se trouvait déjà sur place mais, ceux-ci venant du quartier et la foule n'étant composée que de femmes, tout se passait sans violence.

Le cortège était composé de trois véhicules : la Nissan Patrol de Niyazbek, le Land Cruiser et la Niva. La Nissan avait le capot percé de balles, le moteur toussotant perdait de l'huile en égrenant des gouttes qui ressemblaient à des taches de sang. Quant au Cruiser argenté, des marques de balles en émaillaient la carrosserie comme autant d'étoiles blanches.

Pankov descendit de voiture et comprit alors qu'il était blessé. Il avait la chemise trempée à l'épaule. Quand il s'appuya à la portière, il poussa un cri de douleur. Debout devant lui, les femmes semblaient espérer qu'il leur ramènerait leurs enfants vivants, et Pankov ne savait quoi leur dire. Aussi alla-t-il à l'essentiel :

— J'ai rapporté les corps, je... c'est tout ce que je peux dire pour le moment.

Les gardes surgirent du portail et le poussèrent à l'intérieur en le coupant de la foule. Un officier des transmissions l'attendait sur le perron :

— Vous avez le Kremlin en ligne. Une demi-heure qu'ils sont pendus au bout du fil.

Cinq secondes plus tard, Pankov essoufflé entrait dans son bureau et brandissait le combiné.

— Vladislav Avdeïevitch ? lança une voix froide et lointaine. Je suis au courant de votre virée d'aujourd'hui... dans les montagnes. Je dois vous dire que vous n'avez pas été envoyé dans le Caucase pour crapahuter là-haut. Laissez cela aux forces spéciales. Et ne vous mêlez pas de leurs affaires. Nous ne permettrons à personne, m'entendez-vous, à personne, de saper l'unité du pouvoir et du peuple ! Nous ne vous permettrons pas de régler des comptes personnels avec Arzo Khadjiev au détriment de l'intégrité de la Russie ! Nous ne permettrons pas à l'ambassadeur du président de prendre le parti des séparatistes et des perturbateurs.

— Apprenez, Ivan Vitaliévitch, que mon cortège a été mitraillé il y a quarante minutes. Sur ordre d'Arzo !

— Vous ne pouvez pas savoir qui est l'auteur de l'attaque, lui fut-il froidement répondu, et nous ne pouvons pas permettre à l'ambassadeur du président d'attribuer une exaction terroriste aux ennemis qu'il s'est faits parmi les fédéraux. M'avez-vous bien compris, Vladislav Avdeïevitch ?

— Je veux parler au président.

— Tenez ceci pour l'opinion du président.

Pankov jeta le combiné à l'officier des transmissions et partit d'un sanglot sourd et désespéré.

Niyazbek Malikov arriva au siège de l'ambassadeur du Kremlin vingt minutes plus tard avec à sa suite la Merco blindée de Pankov et quatre de ses gardes. Le corps du cinquième aussi avait été chargé dans la Mercedes. Blessé à l'entrejambe, l'un des hommes de Malikov venait d'être déposé à l'hôpital. Les autres en étaient quittes pour des égratignures.

Une chance pour Pankov que l'embuscade ait été préparée précipitamment avec un seul blindé en tout et pour tout. Une demi-douzaine d'hommes d'équipage s'étaient cachés dans les bois pour appuyer leurs camarades, et l'on eut toutes les peines du monde à les en déloger quand le branle-bas commença.

Au seuil de la résidence, Niyazbek ôta ses chaussures maculées de sang avant de passer dans le bureau du premier commis, suivi de Djavatkhan, Khizri et Mahomedsalih. Assis sur le divan, Pankov regardait le plafond sans le voir. Les cheveux roux englués de boue, il portait une chemise blanche comme neige signée Cerruti avec une auréole rouge vif qui séchait à l'épaule. Les yeux du fonctionnaire étaient couleur de cendre froide. Des bris de téléphone parsemaient le divan.

— Qu'est-ce que c'est que ça ? fit Niyazbek en shootant dans une moitié de combiné qui avait volé sur le tapis.

— J'ai essayé de joindre le Kremlin.

— Et alors ?

— Rien. Je n'ai pas été connecté.

— Excellente réaction, dit Mahomedsalih. Quand on a été canardé par quelqu'un à la mitrailleuse lourde, que reste-t-il à faire ? Téléphoner au président, bien sûr, il n'y a plus que ça. Sans un coup de fil au président, comment voulez-vous savoir ce qu'on doit faire ?

— Ah ! Momo, soupira Niyazbek, tu as toujours été un âne. Même sur le ring. Et surtout depuis que tu as été ministre.

L'ex-ministre des Travaux publics baissa la tête d'un air contrit. Il n'en voulait jamais à Niyazbek.

— Par contre, j'ai eu un appel d'Ivan Vitaliévitch, dit Vladislav. Il s'est posé en porte-parole de l'opinion présidentielle et m'a dit de ne pas faire de vagues et de ne pas régler mes comptes personnels avec des représentants des structures fédérales.

Mahomedsalih cracha par la fenêtre grande ouverte.

— Tu es blessé, dit Niyazbek à demi-voix.

Pankov glissa un œil en biais sur son épaule.

— C'est superficiel. Un médecin va venir.

— Il y a des gens devant le siège, s'immisça Khizri. Tout le monde est au courant. Tu es un héros pour eux. Va leur parler.

L'homme du Kremlin observa un silence.

— Tu... Y a-t-il des morts parmi tes hommes ? demanda-t-il à Niyazbek.

— Aucun. Chez toi, il y a un garde de tué.

Non sans peine, Pankov se rappela le garde assis à l'avant du Chevrolet. Au moment où la voiture avait quitté la route, l'autre s'était éjecté du côté où le blindé, une seconde plus tard, devait exploser.

Vladislav bougea, tendant la main vers le guéridon pour y attraper une bouteille d'eau. Sa main tremblait. Niyazbek prit la bouteille, versa de l'eau dans un verre et se mit à le faire boire comme un enfant.

Le pire, c'était que, à la moindre manipulation des faits, la vérité se retournait comme un gant. Contre qui s'étaient battus les hommes de Malikov ? Contre les séparatistes qui avaient tendu une embuscade à l'ambassadeur du Kremlin.

Et les hommes d'Arzo ? Contre les séparatistes eux aussi. Et où étaient passés les séparatistes ? Envolés.

Qu'avait-on trouvé aujourd'hui sur la montagne ? Des cadavres de boïéviks. Les boïéviks avaient subi un interrogatoire avant de mourir ? Et alors ? Le hasard faisait qu'on les avait capturés d'abord, interrogés ensuite. Un interrogatoire plutôt musclé aux entournures, ça d'accord. Qu'espériez-vous ? Arzo Khadjiev est un Vaïnakh, un montagnard. Pensiez-vous que, ayant égorgé des Russes comme chef de bande, il se mette à faire la guerre avec des gants de demoiselle après être passé du côté des Russes ? Les cadavres sont peut-être minés par la faim, mais ce sont des cadavres de boïéviks. Un boïévik, ça n'a rien à bouffer. Tenez, dans la bande à Bassaïev, la moitié est atteinte de la tuberculose…

Vladislav ne pouvait joindre le président au téléphone, mais il savait que son interlocuteur avait raison. Le président serait furieux de voir son ambassadeur faire tanguer la barque. Ambassadeur aujourd'hui, chômeur demain.

Etait-il prêt à devenir chômeur pour la seule raison qu'un salopard avait voulu lui loger une balle antiblindage entre les deux yeux et qu'au lieu de régler la question dans les plus hautes instances il avait joué les tribuns devant la foule ? Etait-il camelot ou fonctionnaire ? Etait-il disposé à laisser la région à quelqu'un qui ne le valait pas ? A quelqu'un qui prendrait vraiment des pots-de-vin pour libérer un homme de la salle de torture à la seule fin de le livrer froidement à la mort par les mains de bandits tchétchènes ayant passé l'uniforme russe ?

— Alors, vas-tu parler devant la foule ? redemanda Khizri.

— Je ne suis pas prêt à me faire limoger. La question, je la réglerai. Mais je la réglerai par la voie normale.

Silence total. Djavatkhan se moucha dans sa main qu'il essuya à un lourd rideau de velours.

— Vois-tu, dit Niyazbek, j'avais deux proches parmi les disparus. Je n'ai pas réussi à les racheter. C'est toi qui les as retrouvés et qui as rapporté leurs corps. Sans toi, ils auraient pourri comme des bêtes sauvages, sans sépulture ni personne pour lire devant eux les paroles du Coran. Tu as fait revenir des hommes de la mort. Tu as fait plus que n'importe quel fonctionnaire fédéral en dix ans. Ce n'est pas rien, tu peux me croire. Voir la tombe d'un parent et prier dessus, c'est plus important que de voir la tombe d'un ennemi.

— Peux-tu dire à ces gens, gémit le Moscovite, qu'ils ne fassent pas de… enfin…

— De provocation ?

— Oui.

— Je vais leur dire.

Niyazbek sortit accompagné de ses hommes. Le front dans les mains, Vladislav ferma les yeux. Quand la porte se referma, il pensa qu'il n'avait même pas dit merci à l'Avar de lui avoir sauvé la vie pour la deuxième fois.

Pendant que Niyazbek et Pankov se parlaient, la foule avait grossi devant la résidence. On en était bien à six cents personnes, et pas seulement des femmes ou des parents de victimes. Des voitures avaient investi la place. Outre la milice locale, l'OMON de Saratov avait été appelé en renfort.

Recouverts d'un plastique noir, les morts étaient exposés dans la cour de la résidence. Les hommes de Niyazbek eurent tôt fait d'organiser leur identification. On comptait vingt-deux cadavres au lieu de vingt-quatre. Les deux manquants se trouvaient dans le Chevrolet qui s'était abîmé au fond du précipice, et Niyazbek comprenait qu'on ne pourrait les en sortir avant le lendemain. On fit venir une vingtaine d'ambulances, les unes emportant les corps, et les autres, les proches évanouis.

Sortie on ne sait d'où, une caméra fit irruption dans la cour. Une journaliste maigrichonne à la mâchoire d'acier dirigeait le tournage à mi-voix. Surveillée de loin, mais sans plus. Envoyée par CNN, elle courait la république depuis une bonne semaine.

Quand Niyazbek s'avança vers la foule, il y eut un mouvement à sa rencontre, un murmure. Ainsi d'un courant électrique conduit par un fil. Quelqu'un demanda Pankov.

— Pankov est blessé, dit Niyazbek. Il a besoin de repos. Il est avec les médecins.

— Qui répondra des morts ? cria une voix dans le fond. C'est un coup des Tchétchènes et des Russes ! Nos frères croupissent encore dans les geôles du FSB ! Allons les libérer !

— Niyazbek ! Niyazbek ! lança la foule.

Niyazbek leva la main.

— Doucement ! Que voulez-vous ? Voulez-vous que ce Russe soit limogé ? Il vous a rendu les corps, voulez-vous qu'il soit remplacé par le général Chebolev ? Vous l'aurez bien cherché, par Allah ! Arrêtez de vous conduire comme des moutons !

Un grondement sourd roula dans la foule.

— Mes hommes sont ici, reprit Niyazbek. Ils resteront tout le temps qu'il faudra pour reconnaître les corps et les transporter chez eux. Si vous n'avez pas la possibilité de les transporter, venez me voir. Si vous n'avez pas d'argent pour l'enterrement, je vous en donnerai. Votre seul souci, à vous tous qui êtes là, c'est d'enterrer vos morts. Si vous n'êtes pas venus pour cela, que faites-vous à regarder le malheur des autres ? O vous tous, enterrez vos proches dignement, nous penserons au reste plus tard !

Parmi les gens entrés dans la cour de la résidence pour reconnaître les corps figurait un petit homme d'une cinquantaine d'années à la maigreur maladive. Tête blanche aigrettée, visage sombre creusé de tranchées et de crevasses comme un terrain vague en construction, épaules basses, il avait à la main droite un chapelet blanc de perles de bois semblables à des noyaux de cerise.

D'un pas mécanique, l'homme défilait devant les civières et, chaque fois qu'il arrêtait son regard sur le visage d'un mort, il poussait une perle.

A la cinquième perle, il s'arrêta et scruta longuement la face d'un cadavre avant de continuer sa marche. Il fit de même à la neuvième. Il marqua encore un arrêt à la dix-septième, puis à la vingt et unième, puis à la vingt-deuxième. Les deux derniers corps étaient ceux de femmes, les seules d'entre tous les cadavres de Kharon-Yourte, et Djavatkhan, qui avait observé la scène de l'autre côté de la cour, trouva étonnant qu'il s'arrêtât tantôt devant des femmes, tantôt devant des hommes.

— Eh quoi ! s'exclama Djavatkhan, tu ne sais pas qui tu as perdu ?

L'homme secoua la tête et se tourna pour partir quand Djavatkhan se rappela où il l'avait vu. On disait de lui, à l'époque, qu'il n'avait pas son pareil dans le maniement des explosifs.

— As-tu fait la guerre ? l'apostropha Djavatkhan.

— Oui, répondit l'autre doucement, mais c'était il y a longtemps.

Puis il passa le portail et disparut.

Le général Chebolev arriva sur les lieux du combat une demi-heure après Arzo. Ceci pour lui laisser le temps de tout remettre en ordre.

Il trouva le blindé éventré au détour de la gorge. Les hommes d'Arzo erraient autour comme des poules autour d'une mangeoire vide. En contrebas, dans les rochers, le Chevrolet Tahoe finissait de brûler.

— Que s'est-il passé ici, nom de nom ? demanda le général qui, flanqué de ses gardes, descendit de voiture.

— Des boïéviks, répondit Arzo, ont tendu une embuscade au cortège de l'ambassadeur du Kremlin. Nous sommes arrivés à temps. Pankov est parti, nous avons couvert sa retraite.

"La peste soit de cet Arzo, se dit le général, je n'ai pas signé pour ça. Dans quel merdier me fiches-tu ?"

A cet instant l'un de ses gardes le tira prudemment par la manche. Chebolev balaya les lieux d'un regard circonspect et constata que sa voiture stationnait au milieu d'une route défoncée par les coulées de pierre et cernée de Tchétchènes. Un silence assourdissant s'instaura, rompu par une phrase dite en tchétchène et des rires qui éclatèrent en réponse. Le rire des combattants du groupe Youg.

Chebolev comprit alors ce qui, dès le début, ne lui avait pas plu dans le plan d'Arzo.

Où pouvait se retirer un général du FSB après une tentative de meurtre du fonctionnaire russe le plus haut placé dans la région ?

Nulle part.

Où pouvait se retirer un ex-chef de bande ?

Dans les montagnes.

Chebolev se pétrifia comme un homme en fuite à la vue d'un chien prêt à l'attaquer. Il se prit un instant à penser qu'il regardait les yeux impénétrables d'Arzo en se murmurant à lui-même : "Mollo, Médor, mollo." Il fit un pas prudent en arrière et mit la main sur la portière de sa voiture.

— Bon, eh bien j'y vais, fit le général russe du FSB d'une voix molle et persuasive, entouré d'une vingtaine de Tchétchènes armés.

— Allons-y ensemble, ordonna Arzo.

— Où donc ? lâcha le général d'une voix qui le trahissait d'un frémissement.

— Chez moi, au village. Après on verra.

Quand Niyazbek eut parlé, la foule se calma quelque peu. Il put alors rejoindre ses hommes qui faisaient mêlée commune avec ceux de Pankov. En général, les gardes fédéraux n'avaient guère d'atomes crochus avec les forces locales, mais aujourd'hui tout ce monde s'était battu ensemble et chacun savait que, sans Niyazbek, on serait déjà mort.

De quinze hommes au moment de l'arrivée de Niyazbek, ils étaient maintenant près d'une centaine. Amis, parents, camarades d'entraînement au club de sport, tous étaient venus soutenir leur leader à la nouvelle du combat qu'on venait de disputer dans les montagnes. Plus nombreux que les flics au pied du siège de l'ambassadeur du Kremlin, ils avaient carrément pris possession de la rue du domicile de Niyazbek.

Tous étaient armés.

Serguéï Piskounov, le chef de la garde, s'était fait une entorse au bras en sautant du Chevrolet mais, pour l'heure, il ne quittait pas la cour. A la vue de Niyazbek, il s'en approcha.

— Combien d'hommes peux-tu laisser ici ? demanda Piskounov.

— Parce que vous en manquez ?

— Des hommes, on en a. Et beaucoup. Il y en a, par exemple, qui circulent en Niva blanche sans plaque d'immatriculation. (Puis, après un temps de réflexion :) Nous avons appelé le groupe Alpha de Moscou. Par nos propres réseaux. Mais il ne sera pas là avant deux heures.

— Je resterai ici jusqu'à la levée du dernier corps. Après, on verra.

Puis ils battirent le ralliement de leurs hommes. Piskounov remarqua que l'un de ses gars, un petit jeune nommé Choura, était blanc comme un linge. Assis sur les marches de la résidence, il tenait à peine son fusil. Touché par une balle au-dessous des côtes pendant le combat, il avait renoncé tout de go à son hospitalisation.

Niyazbek et Piskounov lui passèrent un bon savon, puis l'Avar appela l'un de ses parents nommé Mahomed-Rasul, lui demandant de conduire Choura à l'hôpital n° 1.

Mahomed-Rasul était le cousin germain de Niyazbek, autant dire son frère d'après les coutumes du Caucase. C'était un homme de cinquante ans, creux et vaniteux. Spécialiste du bâtiment, il avait beaucoup sollicité Niyazbek pour être placé dans la milice, mais l'autre n'en fit rien de peur de le voir déshonorer la famille, préférant le faire nommer à la tête d'un service de réparation où le bonhomme se trouva presque heureux. Mahomed-Rasul se fit fabriquer un sauf-conduit respectable frappé de l'aigle bicéphale et marqué des lettres GROu, initiales russes trompeuses associées au renseignement militaire mais qui se déchiffraient en l'occurrence comme "service général des réparations". Quiconque ouvrait le sauf-conduit pouvait y lire que son titulaire avait la qualité d'ingénieur en chef dudit service de la ville de Torbi-Kala, mais il était rare qu'on l'ouvrît parce que, à la vue de ces lettres d'or sur fond marron, les patrouilleurs rendaient les honneurs en blêmissant, et Mahomed-Rasul parcourait la république dans son quatre-quatre noir en treillis avec un PM sur le siège avant.

Si Niyazbek avait envoyé son cousin à l'hôpital, c'était surtout parce qu'il en avait marre de lui. Aux premiers coups de feu donnés à Kharon-Yourte, il s'était laissé tomber de sa voiture en roulant dessous comme un sac. Mais maintenant, devant la résidence de l'ambassadeur du Kremlin, il gesticulait comme jamais, galopait d'un coin à l'autre, agitait sa mitraillette sous le nez de la journaliste occidentale en lui montrant des impacts de balles sur son quatre-quatre, bref, il était à deux doigts de faire une grosse bêtise.

Une semaine déjà que le capitaine Stachevski, commandant de l'OMON de Novosibirsk, était en mission à Torbi-Kala. En fait d'OMON, la formation était constituée non de milices combattantes de l'Intérieur mais d'un service de patrouille ainsi baptisé au seul motif que la hiérarchie l'avait demandé pour une mission au Caucase. On devait annoncer aux supérieurs l'envoi de cinq mille combattants aguerris volant à la rescousse d'une république en détresse, mais où les prendre, tous ces hommes ?

Déjà qu'on en manquait pour soi... On avait donc envoyé des patrouilleurs.

Les cinq premiers jours, les hommes vécurent dans un gymnase à bouffer des saletés que les intendants du coin appelaient nourriture. A Novosibirsk, il y avait beau temps que le capitaine en aurait trouvé, des victuailles. Les routes en étaient pleines, de ces victuailles, à deux jambes ou à quatre roues. Le loup mange grâce à ses pattes, dit le proverbe ; et le flic, grâce à son uniforme.

Le hic, c'était qu'on ne les laissait pas travailler sur les routes. Peut-être que les chefs avaient d'autres chats à fouetter que de s'occuper des Sibériens, ou bien qu'on avait compris, à y regarder de plus près, quelle espèce d'OMON c'était. Donc : cinq jours de gymnase. Au sixième jour, on les embarqua dans un bus pour nettoyer un village de montagne. Mais ils n'allèrent pas jusque-là.

Parce que, aux abords du village, ils furent arrêtés par des gens du pays avec barbes et fusils. Ceux-ci bloquèrent le bus. Soit par amour des wahhabites, soit par détestation des flics. Les combattants de l'OMON de Novosibirsk se consultèrent et proposèrent un compromis aux villageois : laissez-nous aller jusqu'au village voisin et nous vous fichons la paix. "Impossible, répondirent les villageois, comment pourrons-nous regarder nos voisins dans les yeux ?"

Les combattants de l'OMON se consultèrent de nouveau et proposèrent un autre compromis : vous nous filez mille tickets US et nous fichons le camp. "Jamais de la vie", fut la réponse des villageois.

Nouveaux conciliabules des hommes de l'OMON qui demandèrent au moins un peu à manger parce qu'ils n'avaient pas de ration ni de solde non plus. Les villageois prirent alors les Russes en pitié et leur apportèrent des galettes, des khinkals et un long collier de saucisson sec.

Forts de quoi les gars de l'OMON repartirent pour rapporter à la hiérarchie que le village avait été inspecté. Pas l'ombre d'un boïévik.

Le soir même, les Sibériens furent affectés à un barrage aux abords de Torbi-Kala avec l'ordre d'arrêter toutes les voitures – surtout les Mercedes – et de les contrôler à la recherche d'explosifs et d'armes sans permis.

Les Mercedes, il en passait beaucoup. Toutes blindées et toutes avec des armes sans permis. Ces armes, on aurait pu les mettre à la pesée et les charger par tonnes dans des conteneurs ferroviaires. Outre les armes, les propriétaires de Mercedes possédaient aussi des téléphones cellulaires avec lesquels ils appelaient qui le président de la République, qui le ministre de l'Intérieur, qui un général du FSB, avant de passer le combiné au capitaine Stachevski.

Un chat devant un aquarium, tel était le capitaine Stachevski devant ces Mercedes. A chaque contrôle il se voyait déjà empocher mille *bucks* pour le passage d'une mitraillette, mais à chaque contrôle il devait ficher la paix à son client.

A cinq heures du soir, on eut vent de l'échauffourée survenue dans les montagnes. Un message d'alerte annonça que la foule se rassemblait devant la résidence du premier commis du Kremlin. Hystérique, l'émetteur-récepteur hurlait que les boïéviks pouvaient tenter de chercher refuge en ville. Là-dessus, le capitaine Stachevski vit un spectacle étonnant : un quatre-quatre noir dévalait l'avenue Chamil en direction du barrage.

Le capot criblé de balles. Un côté froissé, maculé de boue et de sang. Quand la voiture ralentit devant le barrage, le capitaine Stachevski aperçut par une vitre trouée de tirs la tête renversée d'un blessé et le profil d'un barbu armé d'un PM.

— Descends de là, ouste ! hurla le Sibérien.

La portière du conducteur s'ouvrit, par où surgit un homme en tenue de camouflage. On aurait dit un billot de bois mangé d'une barbe de trois jours.

— Fiche-nous la paix, dit le billot de bois, tu vois bien que je transporte un homme à l'hôpital. C'est un garde de l'ambassadeur du Kremlin.

L'hôpital n° 1 se trouvait à trois pâtés de maisons du barrage.

— Qui êtes-vous ? Et pourquoi ces PM ? Tous dehors ! Armes à terre !

— Ohé ! mais je suis dans les cadres dirigeants ! dit le billot de bois en sortant de son interminable pantalon baggy son livret de service aux lettres dorées : GROU.

"Des boïéviks", dit alors Stachevski horrifié qui tira avant même de comprendre quoi que ce soit.

Niyazbek parlait avec Khizri dans la cour de la résidence du premier commis du Kremlin quand le téléphone s'agita dans sa poche.

— Niyazbek ! Les gars de l'OMON ont abattu Mahomed-Rasul ! Au barrage de l'avenue Chamil !

Djavatkhan eut connaissance de la fusillade à sept heures zéro trois. Il se trouvait à ce moment dans la cour du domicile des Chakhbanov.

Il venait tout juste de ramener la mère du défunt avec la dépouille de son fils encore enveloppée d'un plastique noir dans le tacot qui servait d'ambulance. Patimat sanglotait sur l'épaule de son mari et ses cinq fils restants, mines sombres, étaient plantés au milieu de la cour.

Djavatkhan écouta ce qu'on lui disait, raccrocha le téléphone et conclut :

— Je dois y aller.

— Que s'est-il passé ? demanda l'un des frères de Chakhbanov, le cadet, d'environ seize ans, maigre et souple comme un fil de fer.

— Mahomed-Rasul a été abattu avenue Chamil. Apparemment, ils tuent tous ceux qui étaient à Kharon-Yourte aujourd'hui.

— Nous allons avec toi, dirent les frères.

Le barrage de l'avenue Chamil se trouvait à dix pâtés de maisons de la résidence du premier commis du Kremlin. Nul n'avait entendu les coups de feu, mais tout le monde vit la jeep de Niyazbek passer le portail de la villa à une vitesse folle et enfiler la descente en manquant d'écraser une volée de flics réduits à la débandade.

Puis Mahomedsalih apparut au portail, qui s'écria :

— Les fédéraux ont abattu le frère de Niyazbek !

La foule poussa un grondement sourd comme un ours qu'on aurait touché au lance-pierre.

Mains tremblantes, le capitaine Stachevski se tenait près du quatre-quatre amoché. Il n'y avait pas deux minutes que son fusil s'était tu. Deux corps gisaient à ses pieds sur l'asphalte, et le troisième homme, qui avait suivi les autres dans une voiture à part et sur lequel on n'avait pas tiré parce qu'il était russe, arrosait les gars de l'OMON d'une bordée d'injures encore inédites à leurs oreilles de Sibériens.

Le capitaine avait deux pièces d'identité à la main. L'une d'elles appartenait à Mahomed-Rasul Mahomedov, ingénieur en chef du service général des réparations de Torbi-Kala, et l'autre, à Alexandre Romanov, agent de la garde fédérale dont le cadavre était à terre.

Il y eut un hurlement de freins. Une Nissan noire décrivit une hyperbole qui lui fit contourner les miliciens de l'OMON avant de stopper devant le barrage. Ironie du destin, la Nissan présentait beaucoup plus de blessures que la jeep : aile gauche emportée, portière percée de balles et souillée de sang. Cette fois, Stachevski n'en avait que faire.

Quatre hommes bondirent hors de la Nissan, avec à leur tête un meneur, haut de taille, souple de corps, le cou balafré, des yeux sombres et cruels qui ne prêtèrent aucune attention aux miliciens. Il s'accroupit devant Mahomedov pour se relever aussitôt.

— Il est encore vivant ! Vite ! A l'hôpital !

Mahomedov fut relevé et traîné dans le quatre-quatre. Deux nouvelles voitures de marque étrangère apparurent soudainement au barrage, puis, l'instant d'après, une autre encore.

Le capitaine Stachevski prit peur pour de bon. Il s'était dit jusque-là que la pire bavure de la journée se résumait au meurtre du capitaine de la garde fédérale. Depuis maintenant deux minutes, il ne doutait pas que cela lui vaudrait d'être dépiauté avec ongles et dents et qu'il en prendrait pour au moins dix ans.

Mais quand arriva la dernière voiture, Stachevski comprit que dix ans de camp n'étaient pas la pire déveine qui puisse arriver. Il fut terrifié. Aussi terrifié que ce maigriot d'Ingouche qu'il avait surpris trois ans auparavant rasant le mur d'un passage souterrain à la vue de sa patrouille, et que Stachevski et ses camarades avaient réduit en marmelade avant de le laisser mourir sur place.

Niyazbek se tourna vers le capitaine qui n'eut même pas l'idée de lui demander ses papiers bien que l'autre eût à la main une Kalachnikov approvisionnée et chargée.

— Qui a donné l'ordre de tirer ? demanda Niyazbek.

— Je... ben... on...

Dans la seconde, Khizri surgit de derrière Niyazbek et tira dans la tempe du Russe.

L'un des gars de l'OMON, ahuri par la scène, tenta de mettre la main à son arme. Nouvelles détonations, et les trois patrouilleurs furent abattus en deux secondes.

Niyazbek se retourna vers Khizri.

— Tu as perdu la boule ou quoi ? hurla-t-il.

— Hé ! mais que veux-tu ? Qu'on se fasse tous descendre l'un après l'autre ? explosa Khizri. Ouvre les yeux, Niyazbek ! On n'a plus le choix ! C'est maintenant ou jamais !

Le regard de Niyazbek s'attarda quelques secondes sur Khizri, puis l'Avar baissa son arme.

— Tu as raison, dit-il.

Il était déjà huit heures du soir mais la Maison sur la Colline regorgeait de monde.

Le hasard avait fait qu'une importante réunion gouvernementale s'était tenue dans l'après-midi, consacrée au budget de l'année à venir. Un budget de deux milliards de dollars composé à quatre-vingt-dix-sept pour cent des subventions fédérales, tel était l'unique chapitre de revenu légal de la république car nul officiellement ne savait où passait l'argent du pétrole, de la pêche et de la vodka.

Certains postes budgétaires pouvaient éveiller l'attention : par exemple, soixante-dix millions de dollars étaient alloués à la création d'un musée de la culture des peuples du Caucase. Pourquoi tant d'égards prodigués à la culture ? Il n'était qu'à voir, pour projeter quelque clarté sur la réponse, la liste des parrains du musée, au premier rang desquels figurait à titre honorifique Rasul Aslanov, le frère du président en exercice.

Non moins étonnants paraissaient les soixante-dix millions de dollars affectés à la compagnie d'Etat Pétrogaz-Avarie. On avait quelque peine à imaginer par quel mystère un consortium extrayant du sol un hydrocarbure apparenté à de l'essence pure pût être déficitaire, et pourtant tel était bien le cas sur le papier.

Toutefois, le morceau le plus affriolant qui figurait de surcroît à la marge du budget et qui provenait directement du centre fédéral était le projet de création d'un parc de loisirs et de tourisme sur la base du vieux port maritime. Le programme prévoyait que le nouveau port accueillerait pas moins d'un million de touristes par an. Où les trouverait-on dans cette mer intérieure qu'est la Caspienne et que viendraient-ils faire dans une ville en proie à des attentats quotidiens à l'explosif, nul ne le savait. En revanche, il était de notoriété publique que le programme prévoyait un subventionnement global de trois cent soixante-dix millions de dollars pour les travaux d'approfondissement. L'approfondissement, c'est un truc aussi génial que la revalorisation de l'image du pays ou la bonification des sols. Où est le fond ? On l'a approfondi. Comment vérifier ? Plonge. Si tu y tiens vraiment, on peut même te prêter du matériel de plongée : une pierre au cou.

Bref, les ministres au grand complet et une légion de députés passèrent le plus clair de l'après-midi à se partager le budget. On y mit d'autant plus de temps que le nouveau ministre de l'Intérieur entama la séance par un long laïus sur les succès de la lutte contre le terrorisme, se disant ainsi fondé à réclamer une rallonge de trente millions. La rallonge rejetée, on adopta une déclaration commune à l'attention du premier commis du district fédéral du Caucase afin que le colonel Khadjiev se vît attribuer la médaille de Héros de la Russie pour la bataille de Kharon-Yourte.

Le député Gamzat Aslanov arriva en fin de séance, par suite de quoi un avenant fut ajouté au projet budgétaire portant sur l'octroi par le gouvernement de dix millions de dollars en vue du championnat de golf de la fédération de Russie.

Fin de séance à sept heures. On apprit à ce moment-là que Pankov était parti pour Kharon-Yourte. Du coup, la sollicitation d'une médaille de Héros de la Russie paraissait pour le moins prématurée. Quelqu'un émit l'hypothèse qu'il allait en découdre avec Khadjiev. Beaucoup s'en étonnèrent, n'ayant pas connaissance de l'histoire de Pankov. Vladislav et Niyazbek n'étaient pas bavards, et les autres acteurs de cette histoire préféraient ne pas s'en vanter.

Les choses s'éclaircirent quand Gamzat raconta que Pankov avait été aux fers dans une cave d'Arzo. "Arzo se préparait à l'abattre, mais j'ai pris sa défense, dit-il. En vérité, il nous doit tout à mon frère et à moi. Puis Arzo nous a livrés à Niyazbek qui voulait le tuer pour ne pas laisser de traces. Mon frère et moi avons eu toutes les peines du monde à le convaincre de relâcher le Russe."

Sur ce vint la nouvelle de l'échauffourée survenue au retour de Kharon-Yourte. Il était clair qu'on allait faire la peau à quelqu'un : soit Pankov aurait la peau d'Arzo et de Chebolev, soit Arzo et Chebolev auraient la peau de Pankov. Dans la mesure où l'ombre de Niyazbek se profilait derrière le premier commis du Kremlin, certains allèrent chez ce dernier : les uns pour faire allégeance, les autres pour espionner.

Toutefois, la plupart des fonctionnaires et députés restèrent dans la Maison sur la Colline. Certains approchèrent le speaker Abdulhamidov, le poussant à solliciter le président russe pour que Niyazbek, sauveteur de Pankov, soit récompensé de l'ordre du Mérite.

A huit heures cinq, Gamzat Aslanov eut un coup de fil lui annonçant que Niyazbek et ses hommes avaient fusillé une patrouille fédérale.

Cinq minutes plus tard commençait une réunion d'urgence dans le bureau du président. Lequel président se trouvait à Moscou depuis deux jours. Le haut fauteuil présidentiel, avec son dossier à rainure d'or, faisait donc un trône à Gamzat Aslanov, ce qui n'était pas du goût de toute l'assistance. On avait beau dire, mais Gamzat, à trente-cinq ans, était encore trop jeune.

Gazi-Mahomed siégeait à sa droite, tandis qu'à sa gauche avait pris place son cousin Nabi Nabiev, procureur de la République par intérim.

Aucun membre de l'état-major antiterroriste n'était présent. Le nouveau ministre de l'Intérieur et le chef des gardes-frontière Barskov avaient préféré se perdre en attendant de voir de quel bord serait le bon droit. Il y avait en revanche deux vice-ministres de l'Intérieur – des vieux de la vieille – et le procureur du quartier Rive droite, ennemi de sang de Mahomedsalih Salimkhanov.

— Je viens d'avoir un coup de fil, annonça Gamzat. Cette fois, Niyazbek Malikov a passé les bornes. Des patrouilleurs ont arrêté certains de ses hommes qui roulaient avec des armes sans permis. Arrivé sur place, Niyazbek a abattu les fédéraux.

— Mais c'est un attentat terroriste ! s'écria le procureur du quartier Rive droite.

— Il faut profiter de l'occasion, dit Gazi-Mahomed. C'est eux ou nous !

— D'accord, mais que peut-on faire ? s'inquiéta l'un des vice-ministres de l'Intérieur.

— Il est l'instigateur de tous les meurtres commis dans la république. Il a tenté de nous faire sauter, mon père et moi, j'en suis sûr ! Et voilà maintenant qu'il pousse l'insolence jusqu'à fusiller le cortège de l'ambassadeur du Kremlin !

— Pankov ne pourra jamais tolérer cela, crut bon de noter le procureur par intérim.

— Que si, renvoya Gamzat.

A quoi Gazi-Mahomed ajouta, mélancolique, après un temps de réflexion :

— J'ai vu Pankov jeter des cadavres de soldats russes en pâture à des chiens tchétchènes. Il cédera. Il pliera et cédera.

L'interphone poussa un cri strident. Irrité, Gamzat appuya sur le bouton :

— Quoi encore ?! J'avais dit : sous aucun prétexte...

— Gamzat Ahmednabievitch, là, dans l'antichambre... y a... Malikov.

— Comment ?!

La porte du bureau présidentiel s'ouvrit en grand. Niyazbek apparut sur le seuil, sans une arme, avec derrière son dos une tripotée de fonctionnaires et députés avertis de sa présence.

Le nommé Chapi, garde personnel de Gamzat dont il était aussi l'adjoint en charge de la sécurité présidentielle, passa comme une ombre derrière Niyazbek, se coula parmi l'assistance et souffla à l'oreille de son chef :

— Il est venu seul. Une chance incroyable. Nous le tenons, maintenant.

— Je suis venu pour te parler, dit Niyazbek.

Il ne s'était pas changé ni lavé depuis qu'il avait pris le chemin des montagnes, le matin même, et le poil noir qui mangeait ses joues était aussi dur et dru qu'une brosse à chaussures.

— Eh bien parle, dit Gamzat.

— Fais venir aussi une caméra de la télé pendant que tu y es, dit Niyazbek en balayant l'assemblée du regard. Vois-tu, il arrive parfois qu'on parle de trop devant les autres et qu'on se dise après coup : Comment ? Un tel a entendu ? Il faudrait le descendre.

Nabi Nabiev, procureur par intérim, se leva de son siège d'un air incertain :

— Je crois que je vais en griller une.

— Tout le monde dehors, ordonna Gamzat.

Tous prirent le chemin de la sortie. Une minute plus tard, ils n'étaient plus que quatre. Gamzat et Gazi-Mahomed siégeaient toujours devant le bureau cependant que Chapi, le garde du corps de Gamzat, s'était mis à l'écart pour laisser les gens sortir.

Gamzat se sentait très à l'aise. Chapi était moins son garde du corps que son bourreau, et la fantastique imprudence de Niyazbek apportait de l'eau au moulin de sa chance personnelle. "Il ne sortira pas vivant de ce bureau, pensa-t-il, il faut lui demander ce qu'il est venu faire, il faut le mettre en boîte, mais il ne sortira pas de là vivant. Nous dirons ensuite qu'il a trouvé le moyen d'introduire une arme et qu'il a tenté de me tuer. Ici, les murs n'ont pas d'oreilles."

Gamzat n'avait peur de rien en la présence de Chapi, mais il n'en ouvrit pas moins discrètement un tiroir pour y glisser la main : son père rangeait là un pistolet à ses initiales offert en son temps par l'ex-commandant en chef du Caucase.

Chapi referma la porte et donna deux tours de clé à la serrure. Le temps d'une seconde, il dut pour cela quitter des yeux Niyazbek planté devant lui.

Ce fut l'instant que choisit celui-ci pour lui planter deux doigts dans la gorge. L'autre poussa un râle et s'écroula. Il n'avait pas encore touché le sol que l'Avar lui arrachait déjà le Stetchkine qu'il portait à la ceinture.

— Pas un geste, dit Niyazbek à Gamzat. Personne ne bouge.

Gamzat resta de pierre, tout en cherchant le pistolet à tâtons dans le tiroir.

— Ta main, dit Niyazbek, lève doucement la main, ou je t'éclate la cervelle. Ici, les murs n'entendent rien.

Gamzat sortit doucement sa main. Sans quitter des yeux les fils du président, Niyazbek se pencha sur Chapi, le fouilla au corps et tira de sa cheville un Tokarev à la crosse garnie de bois. L'homme poussa un gémissement et Niyazbek lui ajusta un coup de pied à la charnière de la nuque et du dos. Les cervicales croustillèrent et l'autre ne bougea plus.

Couleur de fiente d'oie, telle était la face de Gazi-Mahomed, si pétrifié sur son siège qu'on eût dit un cadavre avant l'heure.

— Tu as perdu la tête, articula Gamzat, ça ne te sera jamais pardonné. Il y a vingt de mes gardes dans l'antichambre.

Niyazbek s'approcha et lui porta à la tempe un petit coup de crosse de Tokarev. Gamzat perdit connaissance et s'effondra.

Alors Gazi-Mahomed, déboussolé par la peur, fit une chose absurde. Il était devant un bureau de chêne lisse sans autre accessoire qu'un plateau portant des crayons bien taillés et une bouteille d'eau gazeuse entourée de verres comme une poule entourée de poussins.

Il attrapa le plateau, le jeta à la face de Niyazbek puis, poussant un cri aigu, se rua vers la fenêtre : blindée et inouvrable par définition.

En moins de temps qu'il n'en faut pour le dire, Niyazbek sauta par-dessus le bureau et lui ficha la pointe de son pied dans le coccyx sans se donner la peine de le frapper de la crosse du Tokarev. Gazi-Mahomed heurta la vitre blindée de la tête et, sans un cri, glissa au sol. Niyazbek le retourna, s'assura que le fils du président avait encore sa tête et qu'il clignait des yeux, puis fouilla ses poches pour en extraire un joli petit Nokia à clapet rouge.

Il tendit le Nokia à Gazi-Mahomed.

— Appelle la garde et donne l'ordre de laisser passer les voitures qui vont se présenter au barrage de contrôle. Tu diras que ce sont des hommes de Gamzat. Je te conseille d'être très persuasif.

La blessure reçue par Pankov se révéla bénigne, mais vilaine. Ce n'était pas une balle. Un éclat de RGD-5 s'était logé dans son épaule en fin de course, or cette grenade offensive possède une particularité désagréable : d'une portée et puissance inférieure à la F-1 (défensive), elle projette des fragments légers qui vrillent la chair comme un tire-bouchon et se laissent extraire beaucoup plus difficilement qu'une balle de Kalachnikov.

Il avait perdu plus de sang qu'il n'y paraissait. Les médecins lui firent des piqûres d'analgésiants, retirèrent l'éclat perdu, pansèrent la plaie et le mirent au lit après lui avoir administré une dose de cheval de somnifère. Pankov se laissa faire. C'était comme s'il avait construit une maison qui se serait écroulée sur lui. Dormir était ce qu'il voulait le plus au monde, dormir pour se réveiller le plus tard possible. Le somnifère lui en donnait la possibilité.

Il dormit jusqu'à deux heures du matin.

Dans le rêve qu'il fit, Niyazbek lui apporta un tapis avec Aminat enroulée dedans ; mais, une fois le tapis déroulé, un cadavre à demi décomposé s'en échappa. Il se réveilla parce qu'il se sentit secoué comme un prunier. Longtemps il ne put se rappeler qui il était ni où il était. Ayant enfin recouvré ses esprits, au bout d'une demi-minute, il comprit que son rêve n'avait été qu'un rêve. Les paupières plissées par la violente lumière des lampes, il se mit sur son séant et se frotta les yeux de sa main valide.

Il avait devant lui Sergueï Piskounov, le chef de sa garde.

— Qu'y a-t-il ?

— Une prise d'otages terroriste.

Pankov tenta de rassembler ses esprits. Or ses esprits, brouillés de somnifères, avaient du mal à s'y retrouver.

— Où ça ?

— Au siège du gouvernement.

— Qui a fait ça ?

— Niyazbek Malikov.

VI

LA RÉBELLION

Il était déjà trois heures du matin quand Pankov se rendit à la Maison sur la Colline. Pas la moindre tentative de bouclage de la place, mais une foule déjà importante se pressait là, d'environ quinze cents personnes. Les gens faisaient des feux, certains plantaient même des tentes. Pankov remarqua des hommes en armes qui déchargeaient des sacs de farine du côté de la rue Kokorev.

La milice était là, mais il s'agissait de la milice locale qui semblait approuver la situation. Du moins ne faisait-elle rien pour disperser le meeting.

Rue Lénine stationnait, tous rideaux tirés, un autobus avec des miliciens de l'OMON appelés de l'extérieur. Pankov crut discerner un œil espion derrière une vitre.

Quand on avait construit, dans les années 1970, le siège du Comité central du Parti communiste de la république en plein centre de Torbi-Kala, face à la mer, on était parti du principe que l'ensemble mer, siège et place devait constituer un tout : la mer en contrebas, un quai bordé de sable, un escalier de marbre, large et droit comme ceux des temples incas de naguère, et une place où s'érigeaient deux monuments à la gloire de Lénine – un bronze juché sur un socle en granit de deux mètres, et un autre de pierre et de verre dressé sur dix étages.

En regardant Lénine du bord de mer, on voyait s'étirer sur la droite un parc somptueux, et se profiler sur la gauche les contours d'un chien bâtard massif et gris gardant son maître : le siège du KGB, devant lequel était un petit monument, ou plutôt un buste, celui de Félix Dzerjinski.

Cela faisait maintenant trois ans qu'on avait séparé la Maison sur la Colline de sa place au moyen d'un mur de béton avec caméras de vidéosurveillance et barrière de contrôle.

La foule se pressait entre le mur et le monument, et les hommes armés qui tenaient le barrage n'étaient pas moins d'une dizaine. Combien y en avait-il à l'intérieur, le premier commis du Kremlin n'osait l'imaginer.

En revanche on voyait bien que les gens circulaient sans entrave de la place à l'enceinte et vice-versa.

Aux fenêtres ouvertes du siège du gouvernement pointaient çà et là des bouches de fusils. Par endroits pendillaient des drapeaux vert uni, ce qui déplut très fortement à l'homme du Kremlin. Tout cela faisait penser non pas tant à une prise d'otages par des terroristes qu'à une révolution. A en juger par la couleur des drapeaux, tout portait à croire que cette révolution, loin de virer à l'orange ou au jaune, resterait vert foncé comme une cornouille pas mûre.

Le cortège de Pankov traversa la place jusqu'à un vague cordon de sécurité qui séparait la foule du siège du FSB. Là, l'ambassadeur du Kremlin descendit de voiture. Dans le périmètre du cordon, c'était plutôt tendu : devant des hommes encagoulés qui avaient des PM aux poings, leur commandant sans cagoule – inconnu de Pankov – parlementait âprement avec deux combattants bardés d'armes. L'un d'eux était Djavatkhan.

— Comment va ton épaule ? lui demanda Djavatkhan qui le reconnut.

— Y a pire.

La main à la visière, l'inconnu se présenta :

— Colonel Migounov. Groupe Alpha.

Pankov se souvint d'avoir appelé l'Alpha en renfort cinq heures auparavant. Pour faire la chasse à Arzo. Après le sale coup qu'il venait de faire, le Tchétchène risquait fort de prendre le maquis dans la montagne ou de se retrancher dans son fief. Pour le déloger avec des patrouilleurs de Saratov, on pouvait toujours courir !

— Tu viens voir Niyazbek ? demanda Djavatkhan.

— Oui.

— Laissez passer les voitures de Pankov ! ordonna Djavatkhan à la foule en même temps qu'aux officiers de l'Alpha.

Ils se taillèrent un chemin à travers la foule jusqu'au barrage de contrôle. Devant le portail, Pankov avisa une caméra de CNN près de laquelle se tenait un bout de femme maigrichonne au menton ferme, un micro à la main.

Pankov descendit de voiture et d'un geste salua la foule. Celle-ci lui fit écho d'un cri amical, du moins n'y eut-il pas d'*"Allah akbar"*. Les gardes s'apprêtaient à le suivre, mais Vladislav les en empêcha :

— Piskounov et personne d'autre.

Djavatkhan, Piskounov et Pankov disparurent derrière le portail, et la femme au micro se plaça face à la caméra en disant :

— Nous venons de voir l'ambassadeur du président russe entrer dans le siège du gouvernement. Tout porte à penser que les autorités fédérales sont prêtes à parlementer et ne voient pas de défi au Kremlin dans la prise du siège gouvernemental par les insurgés.

Le rez-de-chaussée baignait dans l'obscurité. Un rai de lumière jaune s'échappait d'un couloir, des bris de verre crissaient sous les pieds, et une violente odeur sauta aux narines de Pankov. Jamais il n'avait remarqué de toilettes à ce niveau, mais il savait maintenant à coup sûr qu'elles se trouvaient là, à droite. Un long tapis enfilait un étroit corridor sur un sol dallé de marbre, par où coulait un véritable ruisseau qui traversait le hall et se déversait dans une fosse d'ascenseur.

Ça sentait le lisier. Il fallait voir à quelle vitesse le ruisseau s'était formé, Pankov en restait coi. Le matin même il avait présidé une réunion dans ces murs sans y remarquer le moindre filet d'eau. "Pourquoi, mais pourquoi toutes les révolutions du monde commencent-elles par des vécés qui fuient ?" pensa-t-il.

L'ascenseur non plus, curieusement, ne marchait pas, aussi dut-il monter à pied au dixième étage. A partir du troisième, le bâtiment était plus ou moins éclairé, et il découvrit sur les murs des impacts de balles.

Un combat sans acharnement particulier, mais auquel il fallait s'attendre. Au moment de l'assaut, le bâtiment était encore plein de monde. Un député ou fonctionnaire sur deux disposait de gardes du corps armés, et un sur trois portait sa propre pétoire. Quand les armes sont si nombreuses, elles finissent toujours par parler.

Sans doute les toilettes avaient-elles souffert des combats. "On a peut-être buté quelqu'un dans les chiottes", se dit Pankov.

Niyazbek l'attendait dans le bureau du président, son pistolet-mitrailleur posé sur le plateau verni de la table. Il portait toujours le même treillis mais avait trouvé le temps de se raser et de se laver.

Il y avait là sept ou huit personnes dans un décor rendu bizarre par la présence d'une montagne de billets de banque à même le sol, principalement des dollars irisés ici ou là de liasses de roubles.

Pankov, les yeux écarquillés :

— C'est quoi ?

— De l'argent, dit Niyazbek, partout nous avons trouvé de l'argent. Dans chaque bureau. Ils considéraient sans doute que c'était l'endroit le plus sûr.

— Et ça vient de partout ? fit Pankov en désignant le tas.

— Non. Seulement de ce bureau-ci. Là-bas, derrière la salle de repos, il y a un coffre que je te montrerai.

Vladislav battait des paupières. Le président de la République était certes un concussionnaire notoire. Les sommes volées se comptaient par centaines de millions et non par dizaines. Mais diable ! Il y en avait là pour une vingtaine de millions de dollars, foi de financier ! Et les comptes offshore ? Et les banques turques ? Si là n'était que la monnaie, que dire alors de la pièce ?

— Combien de morts pendant l'assaut ? demanda Pankov.

— Pas des masses. Qui voulait fuir a pu le faire, c'était pas sorcier.

— Où sont les fils du président ?

— Vivants.

— Et que veux-tu ?

Niyazbek lui tendit une feuille sur laquelle son pistolet-mitrailleur faisait presse-papier.

— C'est une déclaration du Conseil des ministres de la république. Ils revendiquent la démission du président Aslanov.

— Et combien de ministres l'ont-ils signée ?

— Tous ceux qui étaient présents dans le bâtiment quand j'ai donné l'assaut. Et tous ceux qui ont donné l'assaut avec moi.

— Est-ce là votre seule revendication ?

— Nous exigeons une enquête sur le massacre de Kharon-Yourte, sur toutes les disparitions inexpliquées, sur les meurtres les plus retentissants de hauts fonctionnaires et de parlementaires.

— Tu es toi-même coupable de la moitié de ces meurtres.

— Nous enquêterons sur l'autre moitié.

Pankov balaya les lieux du regard et remarqua un détail qui aurait dû lui sauter aux yeux sans ce tas de fric sur le tapis. Il n'y avait pas un drapeau dans le dos de Niyazbek. Or l'homme du Kremlin avait suffisamment rencontré le président pour ne pas oublier qu'il pavoisait toujours devant le drapeau russe tricolore à cordelières dorées, et celui de la république, tricolore lui aussi, où le vert remplaçait le bleu. Le président adorait se faire photographier devant les deux drapeaux aujourd'hui disparus, et Pankov songea non sans frémir aux morceaux d'étoffe verte qui pendaient aux fenêtres.

— Et c'est tout ?

— Cent vingt personnes ont disparu sans jugement le mois dernier dans la république. Vingt-quatre cadavres ont été trouvés à Kharon-Yourte. Les autres moisissent encore dans les caves du FSB et d'Arzo. Nous exigeons leur libération.

— Je veux parler aux otages, dit Pankov.

— Les seuls otages sont Gamzat et Gazi-Mahomed. Tous les autres se trouvent ici de leur plein gré.

Pankov leva les yeux au ciel. L'autre mentait sciemment. Certes, une partie des proches d'Aslanov – fonctionnaires ou députés – avait pu fuir à temps la Maison sur la Colline, d'autant qu'elle disposait d'une garde armée. Certes une autre partie avait fait le choix de rester : soit par sympathie pour Niyazbek, soit par conviction qu'il allait l'emporter.

Mais il n'était pas moins certain que d'autres parents ou confidents du clan des Aslanov – peut-être une douzaine ou peut-être deux – n'avaient pas eu le temps de prendre la fuite alors même qu'ils n'auraient jamais rallié le camp opposé. A l'évidence, Niyazbek les avait retenus : d'abord, quelle bêtise de relâcher des hommes qui, une fois dehors, auraient commencé par mobiliser les troupes adverses ; ensuite, pourquoi ne pas semer la pagaille dans les rangs de l'ennemi en lui faisant accroire que ses alliés étaient hors jeu, voire rangés à la cause des rebelles ? D'ailleurs, il n'était pas exclu que certains d'entre eux aient trahi leur maître.

Sans doute étaient-ils détenus quelque part pour être tués par Niyazbek en cas de défaite.

— Il y a des otages ici, dit Pankov ; et si tu veux obtenir la libération des prisonniers du FSB, tu devras les échanger.

Sans faire de commentaire, Niyazbek se leva et mit son PM en bandoulière.

— Allons-y.

Lui emboîtant le pas, Pankov manqua de trébucher sur les billets de banque.

— Pourquoi les avoir jetés par terre ? lança-t-il irrité.

— Pour abaisser ceux qui voudront les ramasser, répondit Niyazbek.

Conformément au dire de Niyazbek, les députés étaient bel et bien sains et saufs. D'ailleurs, ils se portaient à merveille. Réunis en salle des séances, ils faisaient comme d'habitude des discours de tribune. Il y avait quand même des hommes armés aux portes, et Pankov repéra trois ou quatre élus qui ne jouissaient pas de la même liberté de sortir que les autres.

Mais la plupart d'entre eux, à l'évidence, se trouvaient ici à titre volontaire, d'autant que trois caméras dont une étrangère faisaient face à la tribune. Un député de la république d'Avarie-Dargo-Nord avait-il souvent le loisir de s'exprimer en direct sur CNN ?

Dans la foulée, en la présence de Pankov, l'Assemblée adopta une résolution à l'unanimité pour demander la démission du président Aslanov et créer une commission d'enquête parlementaire sur les événements de Kharon-Yourte. Le speaker se leva de son fauteuil et prononça un discours. Le peuple, déclara-t-il, plaçait tous ses espoirs en Moscou et associait son avenir à la Russie. Quant aux citoyens députés, ils attendaient que le Kremlin prît les bonnes décisions en temps et en heure maintenant qu'on lui avait enfin décillé les yeux sur la situation de la république. "Nom de nom, songea Pankov, si ces gens ont attendu d'avoir un canon sur la tempe pour comprendre, est-il seulement pensable qu'ils soient fichus de prendre les bonnes décisions ?"

Mais il vit que la salle était encore pavoisée du drapeau russe, ce qui le réconforta.

Avant de quitter les lieux, il remonta voir Niyazbek au dixième étage et les deux hommes passèrent dans la salle de repos du président. Un petit couloir s'en échappait à la dérobée, qui donnait sur un rideau. Celui-ci tiré, Pankov vit une porte-coffre-fort armée d'une énorme serrure à crémaillère. Niyazbek composa un code et la porte, non sans mal, céda.

En fait de coffre, c'était plutôt une chambre forte : deux mètres sur deux, des murs d'acier, un plafond bas, une ampoule halogène. Il y faisait frais : sans doute était-elle ventilée. Deux hommes gisaient au sol, tous les deux menottés derrière le dos et fortement ligotés de scotch de la tête aux pieds. Gamzat et Gazi-Mahomed ressemblaient ainsi à des cocons gris emmaillotés par un insecte géant. Détail d'une absurde cruauté, on leur avait scotché la bouche.

Niyazbek se pencha pour arracher à Gamzat son bâillon adhésif.

— Tu as quelque chose à dire ? demanda Niyazbek.

Choqué, Pankov détourna le regard. Gamzat cracha au sol.

Niyazbek sortit, aussitôt rattrapé par Pankov.

— Et les toilettes ? demanda l'ambassadeur du Kremlin quand l'autre eut actionné la lourde crémaillère.

— Ils n'ont qu'à chier dans leur froc, renvoya Malikov indifférent. La république entière baigne déjà dans leur merde...

Niyazbek l'accompagna jusqu'à la barrière et, prenant congé de lui, demanda :

— As-tu besoin de ma garde ?

— De quoi aurais-je l'air ?

— Tu es le seul haut fonctionnaire russe rallié à notre camp. Que va-t-il se passer si tu te fais descendre ? Veux-tu que je te le dise ?

— De qui tiens-tu que je suis dans ton camp ?

Niyazbek marqua un silence.

— Fais savoir au président Aslanov que s'il ne démissionne pas, je tuerai ses fils de mes propres mains.

Quand Pankov passa le cordon de sécurité, Djavatkhan palabrait toujours avec le colonel de l'Alpha sous l'objectif zélé d'une caméra de CNN. Pankov fit arrêter sa voiture et descendit. La maigrichonne lui tendit le micro en disant :

— Le président Aslanov, qui se trouve à Moscou, a qualifié les événements de prise d'otages terroriste. Vos commentaires ?

— Où voyez-vous des terroristes ?

— Mais ces hommes sont armés, rétorqua la reporter.

— Avez-vous déjà vu des hommes sans armes par ici ?

— C'est donc que vous ne considérez pas l'occupation du siège gouvernemental comme une insurrection contre la Russie ?

— Je reviens de la salle des séances où j'ai vu les mêmes députés que d'habitude avec au mur le même drapeau fédéral qu'avant. Les gens ne veulent savoir qu'une chose : qui a tué leurs proches ? Je me suis rendu à Kharon-Yourte et j'affirme que ces personnes ne sont pas mortes en combattant. Et que nous punirons les coupables.

Après avoir raccompagné Pankov, Niyazbek s'en revint au bureau présidentiel. Sept personnes l'y attendaient à la table de réunion, sans compter le fauteuil vide du président dans lequel il prit place.

Le premier à sa droite était l'un des hommes les plus influents de la république en la personne du maire de Torbi-Kala, Charapudin Ataïev, qui avait acheté son poste à Gamzat Aslanov. Ces derniers temps, le torchon brûlait entre eux deux, comme souvent quand l'objet des transactions se révèle trop flou : Ataïev estimait avoir trop payé ; Gamzat estimait avoir trop peu gagné.

Il faut dire qu'Ataïev avait acheté son fauteuil deux années plus tôt lorsque le service de la sécurité présidentielle comptait cinquante hommes contre les cinq cents d'aujourd'hui : la garde grandissait en même temps que l'appétit de Gamzat qui se mit à faire main basse sur le business du maire et ses entreprises. Six mois auparavant, il avait soumis au racket toutes les pompes à essence de la ville ; en juin, il s'était taillé un terrain pour la construction d'un supermarché ; et, tout récemment, il avait carrément écarté Ataïev du projet de terminal portuaire en chantier sur la Caspienne.

Ataïev aurait bien pardonné à Gamzat mais il se disait que l'autre ne lui pardonnerait jamais. Il estimait que Gamzat estimerait toujours qu'Ataïev s'estimerait spolié.

Participait aussi à la réunion Muhtar Meïerkulov, vice-speaker du Parlement, un homme complètement étranger aux réalités économiques. Dans les années 1960, n'étant alors que doctorant à la chaire d'histoire de l'université de Moscou, il avait soutenu une thèse intitulée : *L'Imam Chamil, espion anglo-turc*. Un travail aussi bien-pensant lui avait ouvert les sous-sols de la Loubianka locale où il avait fini par dégoter, à la fin des années 1980, le manuscrit d'un ouvrage fondamental écrit par un officier de l'armée blanche de Denikine. Lui-même originaire du Caucase, ledit officier était rentré dans ses pénates au début des années 1920 pour se documenter trente années durant sur l'ère de l'imamat avant d'être fusillé en 1952 par manque de prévoyance. Son manuscrit avait donc atterri dans les archives du KGB régional où Muhtar l'avait volé pour le faire publier au début des années 1990, le sujet revenant en odeur de sainteté. Instantanément, il était devenu un expert incontesté de l'imamat, à la faveur de quoi on l'avait élu député. Un nouvel écrit historique, consacré cette fois à l'exploit héroïque du grand-oncle du président Aslanov pendant la Grande Guerre nationale, avait fait de lui un vice-speaker.

Malheureusement pour lui, Muhtar ne jouait là qu'un rôle de potiche. Il était si bête qu'on le savait infichu de faire du business et même d'extorquer des pots-de-vin. Vous conviendrez qu'une potiche n'est pas le genre d'homme à qui l'on s'empresse d'apporter de l'argent sans raison, surtout s'il n'en demande pas. Conséquence de cette honnêteté forcée, Muhtar était devenu petit à petit un pourfendeur invétéré des milieux au pouvoir dans la république, introduisant par ces mots chaque discours qu'il faisait à la tribune du Parlement : "L'imam Chamil en vingt-cinq ans n'a jamais eu d'argent dans les mains."

Le troisième participant s'appelait Daoud, député de l'Assemblée législative et triple champion olympique de lutte libre. Cet homme, parmi les plus vaillants que comptât la république, n'en avait pas moins le même défaut qu'Arzo Khadjiev : on ne pouvait pas l'intimider, mais on pouvait l'acheter.

Le quatrième participant – le speaker Hamid Abdulhamidov – était un homme profondément pieux. S'il occupait son poste, c'était pour la seule et bonne raison que les différents clans de la république, quand ils s'entretuaient, avaient besoin d'un médiateur. Abdulhamidov vivait dans un deux-pièces bien qu'il lui eût suffi d'une seule allusion pour que n'importe quel clan lui offrît une villa à quatre étages.

Quant aux trois autres, assis à la gauche de Niyazbek, c'étaient Khizri, Mahomedsalih et Djavatkhan.

— J'approuve de toutes mes forces la démission du président Aslanov, dit le maire de la ville. Son fils a passé toutes les bornes ! Le gouvernement fédéral débloque trois cent soixante-dix millions de dollars pour un terminal passagers situé sur le territoire de la ville, et voilà l'autre qui fait main basse sur le terrain !

— Le terrain sera restitué, dit Niyazbek.

— L'imam Chamil en vingt-cinq ans n'a jamais eu d'argent dans les mains, dit Muhtar. Pour lui, tout le mal venait de là. Et le président Aslanov a fait de la république une grosse cagnotte personnelle. Je lui ai remis une note écrite sur la création d'un centre d'études historiques du Caucase qui n'aurait coûté que trois millions de dollars. Eh bien, ma note, il me l'a renvoyée à la figure !

— Ce centre sera créé, dit Niyazbek.

C'est alors que Daoud poussa un rire sarcastique :

— Vois-tu, Niyazbek, j'ai de l'âge et peu d'instruction. L'histoire, les terrains de la ville, je suis loin de tout ça. Gazi-Mahomed est à la tête de PétrogazAvarie. Donne-moi l'entreprise et tu auras mes hommes en échange.

Niyazbek fit signe que non :

— Je ne peux pas te mettre à la tête de PétrogazAvarie parce que j'y placerai Mahomedsalih. Mais les Aslanov ont un consortium de vins et alcools. Prends-le si tu veux, parce que je ne permettrai jamais à mes hommes de travailler dans la vodka. Qu'en dis-tu ?

— Je marche.

Puis Niyazbek leva les yeux sur Hamid Abdulhamidov et lui demanda :

— Pourquoi ne dites-vous rien, Hamid Mahomedovitch ? S'il vous faut quelque chose, n'hésitez pas.

— J'aimerais savoir, répondit Abdulhamidov, qui sera président si le Kremlin destitue Aslanov.

Tout le monde se regarda. Personne ne s'était posé la question alors que les élections au poste de chef de l'exécutif régional avaient été supprimées par décret fédéral et que, si le Kremlin s'apprêtait à déposer le président, ce serait pour en nommer un nouveau sur-le-champ. Il était clair que l'avenir du terminal passagers ou de PétrogazAvarie dépendrait beaucoup plus du futur président que des arrangements conclus dans ce bureau.

— Bah ! dit le maire de Torbi-Kala, je pense que le président doit être un gestionnaire expérimenté. Pas un homme politique, non, mais un bon gestionnaire qui aurait consacré toutes ces années à faire son boulot, tout simplement, par exemple : à diriger une grande ville...

— Eh bien moi je pense que ce doit être un homme de science, coupa Muhtar, un philologue ou un historien, quelqu'un qui connaisse en profondeur la culture de notre pays.

Mahomedsalih tapa du poing sur la table :

— Sottises ! Le meilleur président, ce sera Niyazbek !

Nouveaux échanges de regards. "Holà ! je ne resterai pas longtemps maître du terminal passagers si Niyazbek devient président", songea le maire de Torbi-Kala. "Holà ! je ne resterai pas longtemps le patron du consortium de vins et alcools pour peu que Niyazbek fasse couper les mains aux ivrognes !" songea Daoud.

— Je crois, dit Abdulhamidov, qu'il n'y a qu'une seule solution si nous ne voulons ni narguer Moscou ni sombrer dans la zizanie. Le président de la République doit être quelqu'un qui ne représente aucun clan. Quelqu'un qui se soucie du peuple, pas de l'argent.

— Ne serait-ce pas à toi que tu penses ? lui lança Meïerkulov irrité.

— Non, le poste de président de la République doit revenir à Vladislav Pankov.

La réunion terminée, Niyazbek s'approcha de la fenêtre et regarda longuement les feux qui brûlaient sur la place. La foule ne cessait de grandir, pareille à une immense chenille noire à travers la vitre blindée.

— Jamais je n'aurais cru que nous serions soutenus par autant de fonctionnaires ! s'exclama Djavatkhan.

— Ils ne sont pas là pour nous soutenir, rétorqua Niyazbek. Ils sont là pour nous vendre au meilleur prix.

Après quoi Niyazbek convoqua son petit-neveu Nabi Abdulkerimov qu'il avait fait nommer directeur adjoint de l'aéroport de Torbi-Kala. Ayant reçu de son oncle des consignes claires, nettes et précises, Nabi regagna son poste de travail. Mêmes consignes données au directeur adjoint des Chemins de fer du Caucase-Nord.

Le troisième fonctionnaire en charge des transports convoqué par Niyazbek fut un certain Mahomed-Husein qui n'était pas de la famille. Les deux hommes s'étaient connus douze ans auparavant dans les circonstances que voici :

Au début des années 1990, Mahomed-Husein acheta deux pétroliers légers et monta un petit business. Ses tankers sillonnaient la mer et rachetaient aux capitaines de cargos leurs trop-pleins de carburant. Les capitaines de bateaux ordinaires leur vendaient le mazout de la flotte par simple transvasement de réservoir à citerne, et les transporteurs d'hydrocarbures leur cédaient un peu du fret qu'ils acheminaient en sous-traitance. Les militaires vendaient jusqu'au dixième de leur mazout en faisant passer les pertes sur le compte de leur consommation courante.

Par un beau matin de 1993, un tanker de Mahomed-Husein fut accueilli au port par des camions-citernes qu'avait amenés Niyazbek.

— A qui est ce mazout ? demanda Niyazbek.

— A moi, répondit Mahomed-Husein. Et tu n'y toucheras pas tant que tu ne l'auras pas payé.

— Arrête de dire des sottises et mets ton mazout où je te demande de le mettre. Sinon, ton pétrolier brûlera comme une torche.

A y regarder de plus près, Mahomed-Husein constata que les hommes de Niyazbek avaient deux lance-flammes, c'est-à-dire plus qu'il n'en fallait pour cramer un tanker.

— C'est d'accord, dit Mahomed-Husein.

Douze ans s'étaient écoulés depuis lors. Mahomed-Husein était devenu député à l'Assemblée législative, directeur du port maritime et l'un des bons amis de Niyazbek. Ils s'entretinrent une dizaine de minutes, se donnèrent l'accolade, et Mahomed-Husein repartit avec, il est vrai, un sac de dollars sur le dos.

Ceci fait, Niyazbek revint dans la chambre forte et se planta devant Gamzat. Il y resta un long moment, sans le frapper, sans dire un mot. Gamzat non plus n'ouvrit pas la bouche pour la bonne raison qu'elle était bâillonnée d'un scotch. Puis Niyazbek tourna les talons et sortit.

Les rumeurs les plus folles couraient sur les raisons de la rupture de Niyazbek avec le clan des Aslanov, mais seules cinq personnes connaissaient le fin mot de l'histoire : Niyazbek, Gamzat, son père, son garde du corps Chapi et le procureur de la République Makhriev.

Tout commença à cinq mois des élections présidentielles, quand Gamzat Aslanov s'engagea devant PétrogazAvarie à commercialiser cent mille tonnes de pétrole, les vendit mais garda l'argent pour lui. Le consortium pétrolier se trouvait à l'époque sous la coiffe d'un nommé Timour que l'affaire rendit furieux.

Gamzat courut demander de l'aide à son père.

— Et Niyazbek ? demanda ce dernier.

Ne voulant pas avouer à son père que Niyazbek avait interdit à son beau-frère de le solliciter dans quelque affaire que ce soit, il répondit :

— Niyazbek ? Ce bandit-là m'en a volé la moitié, justement ! Et il veut me faire porter le chapeau à présent !

A cette époque l'ancien président en exercice s'était disqualifié aux yeux du Kremlin et du peuple qui ne pouvaient plus le voir en peinture, et beaucoup disaient, nostalgiques, qu'on vivait mieux avant, du temps où Ahmednabi Aslanov était encore premier secrétaire du Parti dans la république. Ahmednabi décida donc de devenir président, sachant que plus personne alors n'oserait s'en prendre à ses fils.

Deux semaines après la validation des candidatures (on élisait encore les chefs de l'exécutif régional à cette époque),

Gamzat Aslanov tomba sur Niyazbek un jour d'enterrement. Il le prit à part et lui demanda de soutenir son père, lui promettant PétrogazAvarie en échange.

— Ce sont vos oignons, pas les miens, refusa Niyazbek.

— Vois-tu, Niyazbek, le directeur de PétrogazAvarie est en train de me traduire en justice alors tout que cet argent est passé en frais électoraux !

— Cet argent, tu l'as claqué bien avant la campagne électorale. Et je connais même le nom de cette chienne de Moscovite qui en a profité.

— Mais Timour est l'homme du président. Si nous perdons les élections, il nous réduira en bouillie et je suis sûr d'être tué.

— S'il te tue, je trouverai meilleur parti pour ma sœur, renvoya Niyazbek en s'éloignant.

Quinze jours de plus étaient passés quand Niyazbek, en rentrant chez lui, trouva Aïzanat en train de faire des confitures de cerises avec Farida. Ses enfants jouaient dans leurs jambes avec ceux de Gamzat. Niyazbek embrassa sa sœur et passa dans le salon où Aïzanat le rattrapa.

— Niyazbek, je ne t'ai jamais rien demandé mais aujourd'hui je t'adjure d'aider Gamzat au nom de nos parents et de tes neveux ! Voilà déjà plusieurs nuits qu'il ne dort pas. Hier, des hommes de Timour sont venus. Ils demandaient dix millions de dollars, une somme qui est passée depuis longtemps dans les frais de campagne !

— Je n'y crois guère.

— Timour le tuera !

— J'en doute.

Aïzanat le regarda.

— Je n'ai pas besoin d'un autre mari. J'aime Gamzat plus que moi-même. S'il vient à mourir, je mourrai avec lui.

Long silence de Niyazbek.

— D'accord, lâcha-t-il enfin. Tu peux dire à Gamzat de ne plus s'inquiéter ; et de ne plus jamais se servir de toi pour me parler.

Trois jours plus tard, Timour entama une tournée électorale à travers la région pour soutenir le président sortant dont il était très proche. Il se déplaçait avec une vingtaine de jeeps noires transportant armes et urnes, celles-ci pour une collecte préalable de bulletins. Ce préscrutin se faisait comme suit : les hommes de Timour débarquaient dans un village, rameutaient tout le monde sur la place et proposaient à tous de voter. Comment décliner pareille proposition quand chaque urne était flanquée de deux mitrailleurs ?

Non loin du village de Smelaya la bien-nommée (la Vaillante), une jeep se joignit au cortège, le suivit sur une vingtaine de kilomètres et s'arrêta aux portes de la bourgade avec l'ensemble du convoi. Une portière de la jeep s'ouvrit alors, par où sortit un homme armé d'un lance-roquette qui, s'avançant d'un pas martial, fit feu de son arme sur le quatre-quatre de Timour.

Tout crama d'un coup : le quatre-quatre, le stock d'armes, Timour et, bien sûr, les bulletins du préscrutin transportés par Timour. L'homme au lance-roquette sauta dans sa jeep, fit un tête-à-queue et s'enfuit dans la montagne jusqu'à un point de vue qui surplombait le village.

Là, le véhicule fut abandonné, brûlé, et ses passagers s'envolèrent en hélicoptère.

La prochaine virée électorale fut celle de Niyazbek et les choses tournèrent de telle sorte que quatre-vingts pour cent de la population de la république se prononça pour le président Aslanov par vote anticipé.

La victoire fut fêtée le lendemain soir à la datcha de Gamzat. Tout le monde était déjà paf quand la garde annonça l'arrivée du directeur général de PétrogazAvarie, celui-là même qui travaillait sous la coupe de Timour et qui avait traduit Gamzat en justice.

Ce directeur était un pétrolier russe d'une soixantaine d'années qui n'aurait jamais fait appel aux instances judiciaires si Timour ne lui avait collé un pistolet à la tempe. Maintenant que Timour n'était plus, le directeur avait très, très peur.

Au moment où il se présenta à la datcha, il n'y avait plus que cinq hommes à table : Ahmednabi Aslanov, le procureur de la République, Niyazbek, Gamzat et son garde du corps Chapi. Déjà bien aviné, le fils du président poussa un rire de rogomme et fit un pas chaloupé à sa rencontre :

— Tiens, voilà l'arroseur arrosé ! Ce salopard a tenté de fabriquer un procès contre moi. Qu'est-ce qu'on en fait maintenant ? Hein ?

— Je pense qu'il faut le renvoyer, dit Ahmednabi Aslanov, et le remplacer par Niyazbek.

— Eh bien moi je pense qu'il faut le mettre en prison, dit le procureur Makhriev.

Seul Niyazbek ne disait mot.

C'est alors que le directeur se mit à demander pardon en tendant à Gamzat l'attaché-case qu'il avait à la main. Gamzat jeta la valise qui s'ouvrit au sol en vomissant des paquets de dollars. Trop peu pour lui. Sous la menace de son flingue, il força l'homme à se mettre à genoux. L'autre s'exécuta et redemanda pardon à Gamzat qui lui fit embrasser sa chaussure et qui décida de l'effrayer pour de bon. Il ôta discrètement le chargeur de son arme puis, à la vue de tous, retira la sûreté, appuya le canon du pistolet sur le front de l'homme à genoux et pressa la détente.

Dans la seconde qui suivit, un coup de feu retentit.

Gamzat avait certes retiré le chargeur mais, dans l'ivresse, ne s'était pas préoccupé de vérifier l'absence de balle engagée dans le canon.

Le directeur s'écroula, la tête éclatée comme une pastèque sur le macadam. Sang et cervelle souillaient les liasses de billets échappés de l'attaché-case. D'un coup asséné à Gamzat, Niyazbek lui fit lâcher le pistolet. Le procureur et le président étaient fossilisés.

— Qu'as-tu fait, malheureux ?! hurla Ahmednabi Aslanov.

— Il voulait me frapper ! Légitime défense ! Pas vrai, Kamil Saïguidovitch ?

Le procureur de la République revint à lui :

— Légitime défense, mon cul ! As-tu envie de rayer d'un trait les résultats des élections ? Ce cadavre-là n'existe nulle part. Pas de cadavre, pas de crime.

— Très bonne idée, dit Gamzat. Entends-tu, Niyazbek ? Débarrasse le cadavre.

Niyazbek le fixa des yeux sans rien dire avec, dans la main, le pistolet qu'il venait de lui arracher. Tous crurent un temps qu'il allait tirer. Puis l'Avar prit une serviette sur la table, essuya minutieusement l'arme et la jeta par terre.

— Je ne vais pas te tuer, dit Niyazbek, mais à partir de cet instant je ne fais plus partie de votre équipe. Ta merde, tu la débarrasseras toi-même. Au moins une fois dans ta vie.

Il y eut un long silence jusqu'au moment où se fit entendre le bruit des véhicules quittant la cour. Gamzat glissa un œil à la fenêtre et constata avec horreur que la voiture du directeur stationnait toujours devant le portail avec son chauffeur tranquillement assis à l'intérieur. La musique mise à tue-tête dans l'habitacle avait sans doute assourdi la détonation.

— Confie-moi ce boulot, dit Chapi.

La voiture du directeur de PétrogazAvarie fut découverte carbonisée le lendemain soir. Elle était tombée dans un précipice à quarante kilomètres de la ville, et avait entièrement brûlé avec son propriétaire et son chauffeur.

Deux semaines plus tard, la voiture de Niyazbek sautait sur une bombe.

Quand il revint à lui après trois jours de coma, on lui annonça que sa sœur s'était suicidée.

Vladislav Pankov fut à sa résidence en un quart d'heure, escorté de ses gardes du corps et d'une poignée d'hommes du groupe Alpha conduits par le colonel Migounov. Le somnifère lui tenait le crâne aussi fort qu'un clou rouillé enfoncé dans une clôture.

Quand il eut mis en marche la ligne spéciale du Kremlin, hautement protégée, il demanda à parler au président mais il lui fut répondu que le président dormait. Pankov exigea qu'on le fît lever. On lui dit alors que personne ne réveillait le président pour des vétilles pareilles. Il dut faire observer que ces "vétilles" passaient en direct sur CNN sous la manchette "Rébellion dans le Caucase", à quoi on lui objecta que les services étrangers travaillaient depuis longtemps à tailler la Russie en pièces mais que le Kremlin ne se laisserait pas mener en laisse par les médias occidentaux calomniateurs.

Pankov ordonna qu'on le mît en contact avec le président Aslanov et alluma un téléviseur.

CNN retransmettait des images de sa résidence. Un bus stationnait place de la Trinité avec des miliciens de l'OMON de Krasnoïarsk. Il y avait là un petit rassemblement d'une centaine de personnes, à tout casser.

Les gens tenaient des cierges et des portraits de disparus. Fleurs et couronnes s'amoncelaient au pied de la grille extérieure. Un très vieil homme se détacha de la foule au-devant d'un reporter, une pétoire à la main, coiffé d'une haute toque en mouton blanc. Il dit que les gens exigeaient la démission du président Aslanov.

— Croyez-vous que le Kremlin acceptera ? Croyez-vous dans le Kremlin ? lui demanda la femme reporter.

— Je crois en Allah, répondit le vieillard.

Le tour vint des gardes du corps personnels des frères Aslanov d'être convoqués par Niyazbek. Ils étaient une vingtaine conduits par un certain Rouslan, le meneur depuis la mort de Chapi.

Sinistre réputation que celle de la garde de Gamzat... Mettre la main à son flingue en pleine conversation était une pratique très répandue dans la république, et généralement pardonnée aux hommes de sa sécurité. Ceux-ci pouvaient tabasser n'importe qui et même donner le coup de grâce quand il le fallait. Leur maître les appelait souvent pour redresser les torts de tel ou tel homme d'affaires.

Lorsqu'on fit entrer les gardes dans le bureau présidentiel, CNN rediffusait l'interview de Pankov pour la énième fois.

— Alors, on ne s'est pas battu pour son maître ? demanda Niyazbek.

Morne silence des gardes bientôt rompu par Rouslan qui cracha par terre en disant :

— Se battre d'accord, mais pour quelqu'un qui le vaille.

— De quand date votre dernière solde ?

Tous se taisaient, mais l'un d'entre eux finit par dire :

— On a touché celle du mois de mai.

Alors Niyazbek tira des billets du tas disposé par terre et distribua mille dollars à chacun hormis Rouslan.

— Mon conseil, dit-il : prenez vos cliques et vos claques et fichez le camp de la ville. Parce qu'à l'aube les gens auront déjà compris que Gamzat a plus de biens ailleurs qu'ici, et ses villas seront réduites en cendres fumantes.

Vingt minutes plus tard Vladislav Pankov arrivait au siège du FSB de la république, situé en dépit du bon sens, à l'opposé transversal de la Maison sur la Collline, de l'autre côté de la place. Un triple cordon de police (milice locale, troupes Alpha, OMON de Krasnoïarsk) le séparait d'une foule qui se multipliait aussi vite qu'un nuage de drosophiles.

Quinze personnes avaient répondu à la convocation de Pankov : quatre du groupe Alpha conduits par le colonel Migounov, les autres étant de l'OMON et de la section de lutte contre le crime organisé. Un seul adjoint de Chebolev représentait le FSB, le restant de la troupe ayant disparu de la circulation. Le président Aslanov avait débranché tous ses téléphones après avoir cochonné les dépêches de presse de son commentaire. Arzo et Chebolev s'étaient évaporés dans les montagnes. Le ministre de l'Intérieur, pauvre choute, fut signalé à l'hôpital avec un infarctus, et deux de ses adjoints téléphonèrent de la Maison sur la Colline pour faire libérer tous les prévenus de la région. Le procureur par intérim avait été vu pour la dernière fois au siège du gouvernement, d'où il se serait échappé, *dixit* la rumeur. En tout cas, pas un de ses téléphones ne répondait, et l'homme restait introuvable.

Voilà qui arrangeait parfaitement Pankov. Tous les cafards étaient planqués dans les coins, attendant de voir lequel des deux camps l'emporterait sur l'autre. Ce qui signifiait que, à part Niyazbek et lui-même, tout le monde ne pensait qu'à sa pomme et non à l'avenir de la république. Une réalité qu'il avait bien l'intention de tourner à son profit.

— Je me suis rendu à Kharon-Yourte hier après-midi, dit-il à l'assemblée, pour examiner personnellement les dépouilles des boïéviks qu'on prétendait morts au combat contre l'unité Youg du colonel Arzo Khadjiev. Pas le moindre boïévik. Rien que des corps de gens enlevés et torturés sans jugement. Khadjiev m'a menacé et... bref, il y a eu... euh... de la bagarre entre nous.

Disant cela, il rougit légèrement et rajusta ses lunettes. Difficile de qualifier de bagarre ce qui était arrivé, mais Pankov ne pouvait tout de même pas dire qu'Arzo avait frappé le premier. C'eût été trop malhonnête à l'égard du Tchétchène.

— Sur le chemin du retour, mon véhicule a été pris pour cible par un blindé du groupe Youg. Si mes gardes et moi en sommes sortis indemnes, c'est uniquement grâce à Niyazbek Malikov et à ses hommes qui ont occupé ensuite le siège du gouvernement. A l'heure où je vous parle, les occupants exigent la démission du président Aslanov, une enquête sur le massacre de Kharon-Yourte et la libération de tous ceux qui ont été enfermés sans enquête ni jugement. Pour la gouverne de ceux qui débarquent, il faut bien voir une chose : ce n'est pas une rébellion contre la Russie mais ça peut le devenir à la moindre provocation. Ce genre d'affaire se produit tous les mois. Cette fois, d'accord, il y a deux mille personnes dans la rue au lieu de cinq cents, et qui occupent le siège du gouvernement au lieu de barrer les routes. Notre mission à nous tous est de ne pas céder à la provocation. Encore une chose : combien y a-t-il de prévenus dans les cellules du FSB ?

— Soixante-deux, répondit le colonel Somov, chef adjoint du FSB.

— Qu'on les transfère en détention judiciaire. Ce bâtiment est trop proche de la Maison sur la Colline. Les parents des prévenus peuvent tenter de l'assaillir à tout moment.

Somov leva les yeux au plafond en signe de mécontentement, et les rabaissa sous le regard hostile et pesant de Pankov. Seul d'entre tous les présents, l'adjoint de Chebolev comprenait que le fond du problème n'était pas dans d'éventuelles provocations. Nul ne savait ce qui se passait dans les caves du FSB, pas même, apparemment, le représentant du Kremlin. Quant aux cellules de détention de la direction judiciaire de la région, c'étaient de véritables passoires : les prévenus se rendaient les uns chez les autres et passaient des heures accrochés à leurs téléphones portables. Il y avait même des spécimens particulièrement doués qui trouvaient le moyen d'aller tous les jours au travail. Transférer les prévenus des cellules du FSB à celles des services judiciaires, c'était la garantie que les familles sauraient tout au bout d'une heure et qu'on ne pourrait plus tuer personne sans procès ni jugement. Car alors nul ne prendrait le risque de s'exposer à une vengeance certaine. Mais le kagébiste n'osa pas contredire le premier commis du Kremlin.

— Où se trouve Khadjiev à l'heure actuelle ? se fit préciser le colonel Migounov.

— Dans les montagnes, maugréa le chef de l'OMON de Krasnoïarsk, et le plus malin qu'il puisse faire est encore d'y rester. (Une grimace, puis d'ajouter :) S'il avait la bonne idée de s'offrir du même coup la tête de Chebolev, nous lui devrions une fière chandelle.

A cinq heures du matin, le cortège de Vladislav Pankov s'arrêta devant une opulente villa du centre de Torbi-Kala. On ne dormait pas dans la maison. Un jeune gars faisait le planton devant un portail de fer de trois mètres de haut ; à la vue des immatriculations fédérales, il s'empressa d'ouvrir.

Une bâtisse en brique à quatre étages occupait le centre de la cour. A droite murmurait une fontaine éclairée près d'une gloriette qui abritait un barbecue et des tables de planches.

Le frère du maître de maison accueillit Pankov, le maître lui-même ne pouvant plus accueillir quiconque : on l'avait rapporté la veille de Kharon-Yourte dans le coffre du Land Cruiser. C'était le fameux directeur adjoint du comité d'Etat à la Pêche qui avait commandité le meurtre de son chef.

— Vladislav, se présenta Pankov en passant le bras à l'épaule de l'inconnu.

— Abdul-Kerim.

Ils entrèrent dans la maison où Pankov, d'un geste, arrêta les femmes qui s'apprêtaient à regarnir la table du salon.

— Je n'ai pas beaucoup de temps. Je voudrais savoir ce qui s'est passé avec votre frère. Suleïman, c'est bien ça ?

Décidément, il n'arrivait pas à retenir le nom de famille de cet homme.

— Il a été enlevé dans une Niva blanche sans plaque d'immatriculation. Tout le monde savait ce que ça voulait dire. Ensuite, on m'a fait savoir qu'il était détenu par le FSB qui enquêtait sur...

— ... sur le meurtre de son chef qu'il avait commandité, continua Pankov.

Abdul-Kerim se demanda un instant s'il devait ou non discuter, puis il opina du chef.

— Bref, ils exigeaient une rançon. J'ai demandé une preuve de vie. Ils m'ont conduit à sa geôle. Là, mon frère m'a dit de payer.

— Le montant de la rançon ?

— Deux millions pour commencer. Puis ils m'ont dit que Daoud (son chef) en donnait trois pour qu'on le tue. Mais nous n'avions pas une telle somme. Après tout, il n'était qu'adjoint, pas directeur. Ensuite, ils sont descendus à un million et demi, ce qui restait encore trop pour nous. Au bout d'un moment, j'ai rencontré Chebolev qui m'a dit ceci : Et si on tue Daoud, combien de temps vous faudra-t-il pour payer deux briques ? La solution a été envisagée pendant quelque temps jusqu'au jour où Chebolev m'a transmis ce message : Une brique, et on le relâche. Nous avons donc payé un million, mais Chebolev a fini par nous dire que l'affaire s'était trop éventée dans la ville. Il fallait rajouter un demi-million. Nous n'avions pas la somme, et résultat... (Abdul-Kerim se tassa, il eut un geste d'impuissance. Puis d'ajouter :) Je pense qu'on nous a fait marcher depuis le début. Parce que Daoud avait payé pour le faire liquider, et un chef a toujours plus d'argent que son adjoint, c'est bien connu.

— As-tu rencontré Chebolev personnellement ?

— Oui.

— Et ton frère aussi ?

— Je l'ai serré dans les bras que voici.

— Où était-il détenu ? Dans les taules du FSB ?

— Non. On m'a emmené dans les montagnes les yeux bandés, mais je pense qu'il était enfermé chez Arzo. Parce qu'il valait cher et qu'Arzo a l'habitude de détenir des prisonniers rançonnés. De plus, j'ai la certitude que notre argent est allé dans la poche d'Arzo. Il était justement en train de marier son fils. Une femme coûte cher pour un fils comme ça, et il lui a payé une fille vraiment magnifique.

— Se sont-ils servis de mon nom ? demanda Pankov.

— A vrai dire, oui. Mais la ficelle était un peu grosse. J'ai tout de suite pensé qu'un personnage de votre importance ne pouvait s'abaisser à pareilles vétilles. Vous venez de Moscou, en plus. Gamzat pourrait vous en donner en veux-tu en voilà, vous n'avez pas besoin de ces clopinettes. D'après moi, c'étaient Chebolev et Arzo.

— Fais-moi une déposition écrite, dit Pankov.

Abdul-Kerim secoua la tête.

— Fais-moi une déposition écrite. On a tué ton frère. Tu es chez toi, pas sur la Colline. Allez, écris, aboya l'homme du Kremlin.

Ce qu'il fit.

De retour à sa résidence, vers six heures du matin, Pankov trouva le général Chebolev assis comme si de rien n'était dans son coin préféré, enfoncé dans un lourd fauteuil de cuir près d'un guéridon vitré sous lequel il avait posé quelque chose à ses pieds. Pankov écarquilla ses yeux. Il croyait Chebolev enchaîné dans une cave d'Arzo. Comme l'avait dit justement le colonel de l'Alpha après avoir écouté le récit des règlements de compte de la veille : "Et voilà Chpigoun numéro deux !" – allusion au général des forces de l'Intérieur enlevé et supplicié par les Tchétchènes en 1999.

— Où étais-tu ? demanda Pankov.

— Dans les montagnes. Les boïéviks ont attaqué le village d'Arzo pour se venger de l'opération d'hier. Ils ont incendié sa maison.

— Est-ce qu'ils n'auraient pas brûlé aussi par hasard la cave où vous teniez les gens enfermés pour les vendre ? s'enquit l'ambassadeur du Kremlin du ton le plus posé qu'il pût prendre.

Alors le chef du FSB de la république se leva en silence et posa sur le guéridon une mallette bien pansue. Il la retourna aussitôt sous les yeux de Pankov, et des liasses de billets tombèrent en pluie sur la table.

— Il y a là cinq millions, dit Chebolev. Tu les prends et tu la boucles.

— De quoi ?! lança Pankov abasourdi.

— Je vois. Niyazbek a déjà donné plus, hein ? Ils ont des montagnes de fric qui traînent par terre, à ce qu'on dit…

Sans piper, Pankov s'approcha de son bureau et pressa le bouton de l'interphone. La porte s'ouvrit, par où s'introduisirent le colonel de l'Alpha et Serguéï Piskounov. Derrière eux se profilaient des têtes de hauts gradés convoqués pour une nouvelle réunion.

— Arrêtez cet homme, ordonna le chef de l'état-major antiterroriste.

— Quel motif ? se fit préciser le colonel de l'Alpha.

— Tentative de corruption active, pour commencer.

Les gardes relâchés par Niyazbek arrivèrent à la résidence de Gamzat à cinq heures du matin. Personne ne dormait. Les femmes s'affairaient en sanglotant. Les vigiles faisaient des messes basses devant la télévision.

La drôle de nouvelle qu'ils apportaient : on ne les payait plus depuis trois mois alors que la Maison sur la Colline regorgeait de fric. Même que Niyazbek s'était servi dedans pour leur donner mille dollars à chacun.

— Dommage qu'on n'y était pas ! déplorèrent leurs camarades restés dans la résidence, eux qui cinq minutes plus tôt se félicitaient encore de ne pas avoir été mitraillés dans le siège du gouvernement.

— Quoi dommage ? dirent les autres. Ici, à tous les coups, il n'y a pas moins d'argent !

Il y eut des échanges de regards. Peu d'entre eux tenaient Gamzat en estime et les paroles de Niyazbek étaient maintenant gravées dans toutes les têtes : il n'y avait pas moins d'argent ici que dans la Maison sur la Colline, et la foule aurait vite fait de venir la piller au petit matin. Pourquoi laisser à la foule ce qu'on pouvait prendre soi-même ?

Vladislav Pankov se trompait quand il se disait que, à part Niyazbek et lui-même, aucune force ni personne n'était capable de songer à l'avenir de la région plutôt qu'à sauver sa peau.

Une telle force existait bel et bien qui s'appelait Wahha Arsaïev.

A la vérité, ce grand démon de la république dont le seul nom épouvantait les engagés de tous poils, n'avait jamais voulu être terroriste.

Avant que de devenir terroriste, il avait été longtemps tricheur aux dés. Son gang de joueurs de dés sévissait à Moscou, Kiev, Riga et Odessa. On arrondissait les fins de mois grâce aux cambriolages. Un jour d'automne 1997, Wahha et ses hommes rentrèrent de Bakou avec un Perse de l'ethnie des Tats dans le coffre de leur voiture, lequel Tat devait de l'argent à quelqu'un. La deuxième voiture de Wahha avait le coffre bourré d'armes pour le cas où il aurait fallu se battre.

N'ayant pas trouvé le commanditaire de l'enlèvement à son adresse, Wahha rentra chez lui avec ses compagnons. On attacha le Tat à un radiateur avec une chaîne à chien, puis on se mit à table. La bonne cuite qu'on se prit alors !

Pendant que le Tat, au bout de sa chaîne, implorait qu'on le relâche, Tchétchènes, Karatchaïs et Lezghes (le gang de

Wahha était éminemment international, avec même un Ukrainien) évoquèrent un événement survenu dans la ville voisine de Minvody où des terroristes avaient pris un bus en otage, exigeant un avion, des stupéfiants et vingt millions de dollars.

— Et combien étaient-ils ? demanda Wahha.

— Ils devaient être cinq, répondit l'Ukrainien.

Il faut savoir qu'on leur avait promis dix mille dollars contre le Tat prénommé Ahmed. Aussi Wahha trouva-t-il très vexant que huit gaillards pleins de forces aient passé deux jours à courser un bougre dans la contrée voisine alors qu'il suffisait de faire cinq kilomètres jusqu'à l'aéroport pour empocher vingt millions – idée lumineuse dont il fit part à ses compagnons.

— Mais ils se sont fait pincer ! objecta l'un de ses amis qui s'appelait Chapi.

— Parce que ce sont des ânes ! se rengorgea Wahha. On ne se serait pas fait pincer, nous. On aurait décollé avec le pognon.

— Où partez-vous comme ça ?! s'époumona la femme de Chapi quand elle vit la joyeuse bande se mettre en route à deux voitures, des GAZ-09 sorties des usines de la Volga.

— Ta gueule, la femme ! coupa Chapi. On revient tout de suite, et avec vingt millions de dollars.

On jeta le Tat dans un coffre pour ne pas le laisser sans surveillance. La nuit tombait déjà quand ils arrivèrent à l'aéroport.

Le vigile de garde vit bien qu'ils étaient armés mais, étant le neveu de l'un des deux chauffeurs, il leur ouvrit le passage. De plus, tout le monde se faisait déposer en voiture au pied des avions avec des armes, et il eût été faux d'affirmer que Wahha en avait plus que les autres.

Ils s'engagèrent sur le tarmac et avisèrent un Yak-42 dont la passerelle sortait de l'arrière comme une langue de chien pendant par le cul. Un camion-citerne stationnait près de l'avion.

Wahha et ses hommes s'engouffrèrent dans l'appareil où ils ne trouvèrent personne d'autre que le commandant de bord en costume blanc.

— Où sont les autres otages ? demanda Wahha, si cuité qu'il crut voir deux commandants.

— Euh...

— Ils sont encore à l'aéroport, expliqua l'hôtesse de l'air.

— Je vois, dit Wahha qui tira sur l'un des deux commandants.

Par bonheur, il ne toucha que le commandant qu'il était seul à voir. Le vrai commandant, qui avait eu son content d'émotions, s'écroula entre deux fauteuils et perdit connaissance.

Wahha et ses hommes sortirent le Tat du coffre et partirent en quête des otages en emmenant l'hôtesse de l'air avec eux. Ils n'eurent pas à chercher longtemps : un bus ventru et jaune comme un canari se traînait justement vers l'avion. Wahha ouvrit la porte des toilettes, s'y introduisit en y poussant l'hôtesse qu'il menaça de son arme :

— Fais entrer nos chers voyageurs.

Au matin Wahha fut réveillé par un téléviseur qui lui vrillait les tympans. Il écarta les paupières et comprit que la télé faisait état d'une opération terroriste : des neuneus s'étaient emparés d'un avion sur le tarmac qui stationnait encerclé des forces spéciales et des troupes de l'Alpha. Le Tat de la veille se trouvait là, assis dans ses fers près du poste de télévision.

"En voilà des cons, songea Wahha, ils vont tous se faire flinguer avec leurs putains d'otages."

A cet instant, son portable sonna à son oreille. C'était le major du FSB Guennadi Chebolev, chef du service de sécurité de l'aéroport. Les deux hommes se connaissaient de loin : la femme de Chebolev avait de vagues liens de parenté avec un ami de Wahha.

— Ecoute-moi bien, Wahha, dit Chebolev, pour l'instant, nous n'avons collecté que dix millions de dollars. Mais nous ne les donnerons que si tu relâches les femmes et les enfants.

Alors Wahha se réveilla pour de bon et comprit que, le téléviseur, c'était ce qu'il voyait au-dehors par le pare-brise du cockpit.

Le major Chebolev s'approcha de l'avion encerclé à une heure et demie. Wahha et deux autres terroristes venaient enfin d'écarter leurs paupières tandis que les cinq autres, à l'inverse, s'étaient endormis. L'officier s'arrêta au pied de la passerelle et leva les mains en l'air pour montrer qu'il ne portait pas d'arme.

— Amène-toi, l'invita Wahha qui se tenait à l'ouverture, un PM à la main.

L'autre monta.

— Mais qu'est-ce qui t'a pris, Wahha ? demanda le major quand il fut dans le cockpit.

Connaissant un peu le bonhomme par des amis communs, il avait été très étonné d'apprendre cette histoire.

— Ça s'est trouvé comme ça.

— A vrai dire, nous n'avions pas l'intention d'attaquer un avion, avoua l'Ukrainien Nikolaï. On fait de ces trucs quand on est dans le cirage…

— Pour ça oui, acquiesça Chebolev, sur les huit que vous êtes, j'en vois au moins cinq qui sont en train de cuver leur vin. Et celui-là c'est qui ? ajouta-t-il le menton pointé sur le Tat.

— J'ai été enlevé, dit le Tat.

Nikolaï lui flanqua un coup de pied et le Tat ferma la bouche.

— Fichez le camp d'ici tous les huit puisque vous n'aviez pas l'intention de détourner un avion. Vous ferez six mois de taule, et bonjour la prochaine amnistie.

— Eh non, dit Wahha, ce qui est fait est fait. Il nous faut vingt millions et un couloir aérien jusqu'à Tel-Aviv.

Un appel à la prière retentit à la radio qui était allumée dans le poste de pilotage.

— Dis donc, Wahha, fit Chebolev, il est déjà une heure et demie et il y a des vieillards en cabine qui ont raté le *namaz*. Où veux-tu qu'ils prient ? Est-ce que tu fais la guerre aux vieillards ? Va, relâche-les si tu ne veux pas prendre sur toi le péché qu'ils commettront en ne priant pas.

Comme Wahha n'avait pas envie d'endosser la charge écrasante d'un tel péché, il ouvrit la porte du cockpit et, la tenant ouverte du bout de sa mitraillette, cria :

— Muslim ! Relâche les vieillards !

On relâcha les vieillards. Ceux-ci sortis, Wahha entendit le vagissement d'un bébé. Il braillait si fort qu'il empêchait le terroriste de penser.

— Dis donc, Wahha, fit Chebolev qui n'avait toujours pas quitté le cockpit, à quoi ça rime ? Vois le nombre de femmes que tu retiens dans l'avion. Tu fais la guerre aux femmes, ou quoi ? Va, relâche-les si tu es un homme.

Comme Wahha jugeait déshonorant de faire la guerre aux femmes, il ouvrit la porte du cockpit et, la tenant ouverte du bout de sa mitraillette, cria :

— Muslim ! Relâche les femmes !

Cinq minutes plus tard, il ne restait que des hommes à l'intérieur de l'avion : quarante-deux otages en comptant le Tat, huit terroristes et un major du FSB.

— Et maintenant écoute-moi, mon pote (comme nous l'avons déjà dit, il connaissait Chebolev et le tenait pour un type bien), j'ai rempli tes conditions, mais je te garde à leur place. Et tu resteras jusqu'à ce qu'on nous apporte le magot.

— Pas de problème, dit Chebolev.

Là-dessus, il sortit son flingue de sa ceinture et tira dans le ventre de Wahha. Simultanément, le groupe Alpha fit irruption dans la cabine de l'avion.

La libération des otages fut menée de main de maître par le major Chebolev. En s'appuyant sur ses liens personnels avec le leader des terroristes, sur la connaissance de son caractère et sur le contexte spécifique de la situation, l'officier avait su le convaincre de relâcher femmes, enfants et vieillards. Il savait que l'avion ne renfermait pas d'explosifs et que, sur les huit terroristes présumés, seuls deux veillaient dans le cockpit et un dans la cabine, les autres dormant ivres morts. Grâce à un capteur et à une mini-caméra sans fil, l'information avait été transmise aux assaillants.

Wahha revint à lui dans un hôpital pénitentiaire. Un miracle qu'il s'en soit tiré. Avaient aussi survécu un jeune gars nommé Chapi et le Tat ligoté à sa chaîne.

Commencèrent alors de noires journées. Le major du FSB Chebolev avait certes accompli un exploit, mais il n'avait pas manqué d'en tirer le maximum, voire plus. Une opération terroriste menée par ivresse, cela ne convenait ni à Chebolev ni à ses supérieurs. En l'ayant déjouée, on ne pouvait prétendre à la médaille de Héros de la Russie. Or Chebolev aspirait à la médaille de Héros de la Russie. A la rigueur, il n'aurait pas refusé l'ordre du Mérite.

De plus, Wahha était l'enfant d'une famille fortunée. Son père, directeur de la première faculté de médecine, était prêt à tout pour tirer son fils de là.

Wahha, Chapi et le Tat (assimilé pour son malheur aux terroristes) furent sauvagement battus. Le Tat avait beau tout avouer docilement, on le rouait quand même de coups. On exigeait de Wahha des aveux d'accointance avec Bassaïev, ainsi que le nom de ses complices. Wahha tenait bon.

On le ligotait à son lit avec un filet métallique auquel on envoyait un courant électrique. Wahha n'avouait rien.

On lui mettait un masque à gaz sur la tête en coupant l'arrivée d'air jusqu'à l'évanouissement. Wahha n'avouait rien.

Tout le temps que dura l'instruction, le major Chebolev rendit visite à la famille de Wahha pour lui extorquer de l'argent. Cent mille dollars, d'abord, pour qu'il ne soit pas torturé, et quand ses proches eurent vent de ce qu'on lui faisait, l'officier allégua que les kagébistes fédéraux l'avaient pris sous leur coupe. Alors il reçut cinq cent mille dollars pour arranger la chose avec les fédéraux, mais prétendit les avoir dépensés pour que la famille ne soit pas inquiétée. Huit cent mille dollars, enfin, pour organiser l'évasion de Wahha, après quoi les exécutants furent pris en flagrant délit.

Par suite de son évasion ratée, Wahha fut placé à l'isolement dans un cachot rempli à cinquante centimètres d'une étrange solution liquide. Quand on le tira de là au petit matin, il n'avait plus de peau jusqu'aux genoux et ses poumons étaient brûlés de l'intérieur. Alors Wahha demanda à voir Chebolev qui rappliqua avec deux nouvelles petites étoiles à ses épaulettes.

— Que fais-tu de moi, vieille chienne, dit Wahha, et dire que ta femme est une cousine de Chapi ! Toi et moi étions de la noce à manger des khinkals dans la même soupière !

— La noce continue, répondit Chebolev, à cette différence près que je suis là comme invité alors que, toi, tu es un khinkal dans la soupière.

Le Tchétchène Wahha Arsaïev, organisateur de la prise d'otages, écopa de vingt ans ; le Tat Ahmed et le Tabasaran Chapi, de dix-huit ans. "J'ai trente et un ans, dit Wahha après le jugement, j'en aurai cinquante et un à ma libération. Si Chebolev vit encore, je le tuerai. S'il est mort, je tuerai ses enfants."

Wahha n'eut pas à attendre vingt ans. Lors de son transfert au camp de détention, il s'évada. Guennadi Chebolev comprit l'allusion et se fit muter d'urgence à Novosibirsk.

Maintenant, après tout ce temps passé depuis la prise d'otages, Wahha Arsaïev n'était plus du tout le même homme. D'abord, il ne considérait plus cette action comme une bêtise d'ivrogne. Il considérait que telle avait été la volonté d'Allah désireux de le remettre sur le droit chemin.

Deuxièmement, il n'en voulait pas à ceux qui l'avaient torturé pour ajouter de nouvelles étoiles à leurs épaulettes. Il voyait là le châtiment de ses péchés d'avant : la boisson, le tabac, la luxure. Oui, Allah avait été bien clément de lui envoyer pareille punition de son vivant et non après sa mort.

Troisièmement, Wahha savait qu'il ne reculerait pas tant qu'un seul mécréant resterait en terre du Caucase, et peu lui importait de savoir qui était ce mécréant : homme, femme, enfant, scélérat, méritant.

Wahha ne distinguait en rien le général Chebolev de tous les autres Russes, parce que les sévices endurés huit ans plus tôt lui avaient été infligés non par Chebolev, mais par Allah. Le général n'était qu'un instrument aveugle entre les mains du Très-Haut qui avait voulu montrer à Wahha vivant ce qu'il advenait des impies après la mort.

Une conviction aussi ferme n'empêchait pas Wahha de louer les services de ses tueurs à tous les preneurs ni de maintenir le contact avec tous ses clients potentiels, y compris ceux du FSB. Tous ceux qu'il tuait étaient des suppôts de Satan condamnés au supplice par la volonté d'Allah. Car Allah avait jeté tellement de poudre aux yeux de ces gens-là que ceux-ci s'entretuaient et payaient même pour cela. De l'argent pour construire une route vers Allah, laquelle en vérité devait être construite sur les cadavres de ses ennemis.

Wahha aimait bien Niyazbek. D'abord, Niyazbek était un bon musulman. Jamais l'on n'avait entendu dire que Niyazbek ait manqué l'heure de la prière, et l'on savait qu'il payait chaque année un voyage à La Mecque à deux cents pèlerins.

Deuxièmement, Niyazbek était un brave, en quoi Wahha reconnaissait celui que lui-même avait été avant sa conversion. Troisièmement, Niyazbek était un ennemi des Aslanov, or Wahha tenait le président Aslanov pour un suppôt des Russes, un fils du diable et un sac d'immondices dont le pus abreuvait le pays entier.

Mais Wahha ne voyait que trop les défauts de Niyazbek. Celui-ci fréquentait les mécréants ; il obéissait au mufti officiel ; et, surtout, il enfreignait la parole du Prophète interdisant aux musulmans de vivre sous le pouvoir des impies.

En écoutant les nouvelles, Wahha n'en croyait pas ses oreilles : Niyazbek n'exigeait rien d'autre que la démission du président ! Le Parlement qui disait leurs quatre vérités à ces diables de Russes continuait de siéger sous le drapeau tricolore !

Vladislav Pankov n'avait guère apprécié les drapeaux verts pendus aux fenêtres de la Maison sur la Colline. Wahha Arsaïev non plus. Selon lui, ces drapeaux devaient être noirs.

Wahha ne tenait pas rigueur à Niyazbek de la fusillade de l'autre fois, avenue Lénine. Si Wahha n'avait pas dormi à ce moment-là, il n'y aurait pas eu de fusillade. Mais Wahha dormait parce que telle était la volonté d'Allah. S'il n'avait pas dormi ce soir-là, Niyazbek ne serait pas aujourd'hui dans la Maison sur la Colline. Maintenant, Niyazbek devait choisir : ou bien devenir un combattant d'Allah, ou bien mourir par la félonie des Russes en creusant davantage le fossé qui les séparait du peuple.

A sept heures du matin, les premiers hommes de Wahha s'infiltrèrent dans la Maison sur la Colline. Ils étaient peu nombreux par rapport à la foule ; peu nombreux aussi par rapport aux deux cents assaillants armés. Mais c'étaient des hommes qui vivaient depuis longtemps sur l'autre rive de la mort. Ce qui ne les empêchait pas à l'occasion de vendre leurs services de tueurs à gages.

Il était neuf heures du matin quand Pankov vit tomber un nouveau bulletin d'information sur son bureau. La foule avait grossi jusqu'à sept mille personnes devant le siège gouvernemental.

La route fédérale du Caucase avait été barrée par des hommes armés à la frontière de la république. Plus de liaison aérienne avec Torbi-Kala : un Antonov 24 bimoteur se trouvait coincé sur l'unique piste de l'aérodrome. Le directeur adjoint de l'aéroport aux prises avec cette fâcheuse panne d'Antonov avait des liens d'amitié et de parenté avec Niyazbek.

Même histoire ou presque du côté des Chemins de fer. Une bombe à fragmentation, selon une coutume bien établie, avait explosé à la frontière avec la Kabarda. Les cheminots faisaient tout leur possible pour réparer la voie, mais dans quel délai et pour quel résultat, le directeur adjoint des Chemins de fer, un certain Beïbulatov (cousin de Khizri Beïbulatov) ne pouvait le dire avec précision.

La république se trouvait coupée *de facto* du reste de la Russie. Sans doute n'était-il pas compliqué d'envoyer le groupe Alpha à l'aéroport pour débarrasser la piste du vieux coucou. Mais cela équivalait à une déclaration de guerre. Le plus simple était encore de fermer les yeux et de faire comme si de rien n'était. Va pour l'Antonov ! Au nom de quoi, gentilshommes, un Antonov n'aurait-il pas le droit de se planter sur la piste en pleine rébellion armée ?

Pankov avait enfin reçu la liste approximative des présents dans la Maison sur la Colline et des morts pendant l'assaut. Figurait parmi ces derniers le nom du procureur de l'arrondissement Rive droite, et Vladislav comprit que le dernier obstacle au mariage de Mahomedsalih avec Aminat venait de tomber : Niyazbek, qui le voulait pour gendre, n'aurait jamais donné sa sœur à un homme susceptible de la laisser veuve à tout moment.

Des geôles du FSB, les prisonniers furent transférés dans les cellules du centre judiciaire, lequel fut entouré d'un triple cordon de l'OMON et de blindés. Les détenus saluèrent leur transfert avec enthousiasme, et marquèrent plus d'enthousiasme encore à recevoir parmi eux un nouveau captif en la personne de Chebolev, aussi furieux que décontenancé. Celui-ci fut placé seul dans une cellule, évidemment, en dépit du surpeuplement carcéral.

Ce qui frappait le plus Pankov, dans cette histoire, c'était que Guennadi Chebolev utilisait le pouvoir en sa possession aux mêmes fins que ses prédécesseurs caucasiens : le lucre.

Maintenant Pankov avait la certitude que la terrible chasse livrée par Arzo à Khizri ne s'était pas soldée uniquement par un arrangement entre le Tchétchène et le patron d'Avarie-Transflotte. Jamais Arzo n'aurait osé monter un truc pareil sans l'aval de Chebolev, lequel n'aurait pas avalisé la chose s'il n'y avait trouvé sa part. Deux pétroliers promis à Arzo, cela voulait dire que Chebolev en aurait cinq.

Pankov s'était habitué à la manie qu'avaient les Caucasiens de lui fourrer des pots-de-vin. Il avait même appris à relativiser la pratique, sachant que proposer de l'argent dans le Caucase n'était pas forcément signe de scélératesse. C'était la coutume, tout simplement. Mais l'ambassadeur du Kremlin ne s'était jamais interrogé sur l'autre pendant de la question : d'où les Caucasiens tenaient-ils la certitude que le Russe accepterait cet argent ?

Depuis cette nuit, il avait la réponse.

Pankov croulait de fatigue. Il demanda à être mis en communication avec le Kremlin pour s'entendre dire une fois de plus que le président était occupé. L'homme qui lui parla lui laissa comprendre avec tact que toute la responsabilité du règlement de la crise reposait sur lui, Pankov, et qu'il serait autrement inspiré d'appeler le président une fois la crise dépassée. Avec de bonnes nouvelles.

De nouveau il fit chercher le président Aslanov pour s'entendre dire, cette fois, qu'il s'était envolé pour l'Iran. Drôle de réponse. L'Iran, quel Iran quand tes fils sont couchés par terre, ligotés de scotch, dans ton propre bureau ? Et pourquoi l'Iran ? Pourquoi pas le Burkina-Faso ?

La fatigue harassait Pankov qui avait passé la nuit sans dormir à vider une tasse de café par heure. Il s'en fit verser une autre par Sergueï, puis se vit soudainement accroupi devant un frigo de la salle de repos en train de dévorer goulûment un fromage pendant que l'officier des transmissions lui criait de l'autre pièce qu'il avait le Kremlin en ligne. Pankov laissa tomber son fromage comme le corbeau de la fable et courut au téléphone.

— Vladislav (c'était la voix du chef adjoint de l'Administration présidentielle), je t'ai vu sur CNN. Qu'est-ce que tu nous chantes là ?

Pankov serra les dents.

— Ivan Vitaliévitch, dit-il, ces gens ne veulent pas faire sécession d'avec la Russie. Pas pour le moment. Leurs revendications restent dans la limite du raisonnable. Nous n'avons

plus qu'une seule solution : démissionner le président Aslanov. Il acceptera forcément !

— Et pourquoi acceptera-t-il ?

— Parce que, s'il refuse, Niyazbek tuera ses fils.

— Niyazbek Malikov est un bandit, un terroriste, répliqua l'autre au bout du fil, il est en train de défier la Russie et,
s'il ne quitte pas le siège du gouvernement sur-le-champ,
force sera donnée à la loi.

— Le seul tort de Niyazbek Malikov est d'avoir un jour libéré les fils du président des mains de leur ravisseur tchétchène. Et comme ces deux-là s'étaient mis dans le pétrin
par cupidité et arrogance, ils ont décidé de supprimer leur
sauveur dès qu'Aslanov est devenu président. Au lieu de lui
dire merci.

— Le seul tort, dis-tu ? répartit l'homme qui avait fait nommer Pankov à son poste. Et combien d'hommes a-t-il tués,
d'après toi ? Combien de sang ses hommes ont-ils fait couler ? Et combien de fauteuils a-t-il achetés pour les caser ?

Pankov se tut, ne pouvant rien objecter. Certes, il aurait
pu rétorquer qu'il ne connaissait ici personne d'important
qui n'ait jamais tué, mais c'était une objection inopérante.

— Quant à savoir qui mérite ou non de gouverner le Caucase, reprit l'autre, il n'appartient à personne de le décider
à la place du président de la Russie. Quiconque cherche à im-
poser sa volonté à la Russie est un terroriste et un séparatiste.
On peut négocier avec des terroristes. On peut endormir leur
vigilance. Mais la Russie ne se laissera jamais manipuler par
un ramassis de bandits à la solde de l'Occident !

— Je veux parler au président.

— C'est là l'opinion du président. A la première tentative que tu feras de le joindre par-dessus moi, j'y verrai une
preuve de déloyauté de ta part.

Il était dix heures du matin quand Niyazbek Malikov sortit sur la place au-devant de la foule. En une heure, elle
s'était étendue à une dizaine de milliers de personnes. Elle
envahissait l'escalier, s'étirait de haut en bas jusqu'au bord
de la mer et, repoussant à franches coudées le cordon de
sécurité, s'approchait maintenant du triple encerclement du

siège du FSB. De l'autre côté, la foule s'emparait du parc, certains avaient même planté des tentes sous les arbres. Niyazbek était accompagné du maire de Torbi-Kala et du président du Parlement et, quand la foule les reconnut, elle se mit à crier et à tirer en l'air.

— Niyazbek ! Niyazbek !

N'importe quel journaliste de CNN filmant la foule pardessus l'épaule des gardes armés de Niyazbek l'aurait trouvée semblable à celle qui prit la Bastille en 1789 ou le palais d'Hiver en 1917. Et pourtant : la Bastille fut enlevée par des individus, là était toute la différence. Ils pouvaient être unis par une même idée, une même folie, entraînés par des amis ou même des parents mais, dans la vie courante, chacun des assaillants de la Bastille était savetier, bourrelier, ouvrier… et obéissait aux règles dictées par la loi, par le Très-Haut ou par soi-même.

Alors que, ici, l'unité de base n'était pas l'individu, mais la tribu, chacun agissant non en conscience, mais sous l'autorité des anciens. La foule se composait de parents ou de proches des occupants de la Maison sur la Colline. Niyazbek savait qu'il y avait peu d'âmes sensibles à l'idée de la liberté ou à la voix d'Allah dans le vaste cercle de ses partisans. Décider de ces choses-là était l'affaire de qui s'en était montré digne par ses actes, et Niyazbek voyait là un principe infiniment plus sage que les fadaises de la démocratie occidentale.

Comment Niyazbek eût-il pu se considérer comme l'égal d'un sergent de la milice routière (par exemple), sachant qu'il était de la tribu des Avars, lui Niyazbek, alors que l'autre était nogaï ? Comment pouvaient-ils être égaux si Niyazbek lui versait de l'argent que l'autre recevait avec force courbettes ? Comment pouvaient-ils être égaux alors que Niyazbek l'aurait tué sans hésiter après avoir essuyé un affront de sa part tandis que l'autre aurait ravalé cette offense avant de s'en retourner chez sa femme pour lui taper dessus ?

Non, décidément, Niyazbek et le sergent n'étaient égaux en rien sinon dans le droit imbécile de voter d'une même voix pour le même homme…

Les bus ne cessaient d'affluer sur le bord de mer. Niyazbek en vit un arriver de son village natal, et il savait que pas moins d'un tiers de la foule venait de la part du maire de Torbi-Kala.

Il n'aurait pu en être autrement. De l'argent, Niyazbek en avait. Mais plus on est brouillé avec le président, plus on se trouve écarté de la mangeoire du budget : aussi avait-il moins d'argent qu'Ataïev. Or toutes les sociétés, fussent-elles tribales, connaissent une loi étrange : plus tu as d'argent, plus grande est ta famille.

Niyazbek leva la main et la foule se mit à gronder comme si le leader des rebelles venait de soulever le couvercle d'une marmite où mijotait de la soupe d'homme.

Plus il dévala les marches et se tailla un chemin à travers la fourmilière. Nul ne comprit d'abord où il allait, mais il apparut bientôt qu'il se dirigeait vers la statue d'Ahmednabi Aslanov érigée en lieu et place du bronze de Vladimir Ilitch Lénine devant le siège du gouvernement. Moteur vrombissant, un blindé sortit du parc. On apprendrait par la suite que l'engin appartenait aux flics et qu'on le leur avait loué pour deux cents dollars.

D'un bond, Niyazbek escalada le socle de granit, se hissant tel un lynx à deux mètres de hauteur. Djavatkhan se montra hors du blindé et lui lança un câble d'acier. L'Avar s'apprêtait à le passer autour du bronze quand une idée lui vint subitement à l'esprit. Sur un ordre de lui, un vigile lui tendit une masse. Niyazbek en donna quelques coups entre les bottes et le socle. Puis, rejetant la masse, il se glissa derrière et l'enlaça par la taille.

La foule suspendit son souffle. Le cadreur de CNN qui filmait son reportage en direct leva même les yeux de son viseur pour s'assurer que sa caméra ne mentait pas.

A deux mètres de haut se joua une joute entre deux géants : un grand brun d'un mètre quatre-vingt-quinze en treillis et un bronze de deux mètres soixante. Durant quelques secondes, il sembla que rien ne se passerait. Les forces étaient trop inégales. Puis le socle craqua, Niyazbek vacilla, rajusta la prise et précipita son adversaire à terre. Le président s'écroula la tête la première, les bottes lancées en l'air, embarrassées de paquets de ciment.

La foule gronda. Niyazbek leva les bras au ciel, comme sur le ring, et quelqu'un lui jeta une Kalachnikov.

La photo de l'homme à la Kalache, juché sur un socle de granit au-dessus de son adversaire de bonze terrassé, le tout sur fond de drapeaux verts claquant aux fenêtres du siège du gouvernement – cette photo fit ce jour-là le tour des agences de presse du monde entier.

Il était deux heures de l'après-midi quand les voitures de Pankov arrivèrent aux abords de la Maison sur la Colline. La foule avait inondé les rues adjacentes. La statue déchue d'Aslanov était déjà réduite en miettes. Près du socle en granit dégarni, des vieux coiffés de toques en mouton pratiquaient le *dhikr*.

A ce moment Pankov vit des blindés surgir de derrière le siège du FSB. Il en compta huit. Ils roulaient étonnamment vite, semblables, de loin, à de petits marteaux sur roues. Quand les gens les aperçurent, ils se tournèrent et levèrent le poing. Bientôt la foule se mit à grogner comme un ours énorme.

— Qu'est-ce que c'est que ce foutoir ? tonna le premier commis du Kremlin. Qu'est-ce qu'il se permet, l'enfoiré ?!

Impossible de traverser la place en voiture. Pour accéder au siège du FSB, les véhicules du premier commis du Kremlin durent faire marche arrière et contourner l'ensemble par la rue d'Octobre. Enfin Pankov et les hommes de l'Alpha qui l'accompagnaient s'immobilisèrent devant la façade granitique de la bâtisse. Les blindés avaient déjà aligné leurs carapaces derrière l'OMON de Krasnoïarsk, les canons braqués sur la foule. Des silhouettes vert clair cagoulées s'en extirpaient et se déployaient en chaîne défensive.

D'un bond furieux, Pankov descendit de voiture.

Ce qui le jetait hors de ses gonds, ce n'était pas qu'Arzo Khadjiev ait osé se montrer moins de vingt-quatre heures après l'attentat qu'il avait raté contre lui ; ni même qu'il ait regagné ses quartiers personnels tout de suite après son échec, incendiant sa prison privée avec les détenus dedans.

Non, ce qui l'exaspérait le plus, c'était que la foule qui occupait la place en exigeant du sang pour venger Kharon-Yourte, la foule qui vouait au bataillon d'Arzo une haine encore plus féroce qu'à tous les Russes – cette foule était comme provoquée, narguée par l'entrée de ces blindés dont les roues portaient encore les entrailles de leurs victimes.

Cette fois, Pankov était sûr de lui. Il avait derrière lui sa garde et les troupes Alpha ; et plus loin, derrière le cordon de sécurité, grondait une foule de dix mille personnes toutes prêtes à dépecer Arzo.

— Fiche le camp d'ici, et vite ! hurla Pankov.

— Où ça ?

— Où tu voudras. En Tchétchénie, en Kabarda, où tu voudras ! Je ne veux pas voir ici le bout de ton nez ! Au premier coup de feu, c'est une boucherie assurée ! Qu'est-ce que tu viens foutre ici ?

— Un ordre de mon chef Chebolev, répondit Arzo.

— Chebolev est arrêté.

— Arrête-moi aussi, pendant que tu y es ! le défia Arzo en exhibant un insolent sourire.

Pankov en resta coi. D'un point de vue strictement formel, Arzo était subordonné à Chebolev. Pour autant, le chef de l'état-major antiterroriste comprenait parfaitement que, s'il pouvait faire arrêter le général russe, il n'était pas en état d'inquiéter le colonel tchétchène. Nul ne prendrait la défense de Chebolev. Même Ivan Vitaliévitch, qui avait mis les deux hommes en relation, ne lèverait pas le petit doigt pour récupérer un matériau non recyclable. On le jetterait comme on le fait d'un agent secret grillé ou d'une prostituée défraîchie. Mais s'il mettait Arzo aux arrêts, une boucherie commencerait ici et maintenant.

"Mais pourquoi ne s'est-il pas sauvé dans les montagnes ? songea Pankov dépité. Il pense peut-être avoir versé tellement de sang qu'il ne peut plus faire machine arrière ? Et il se dit que les Russes lui pardonneront plus facilement son attentat contre l'ambassadeur du Kremlin que les Tchétchènes ne lui pardonneront le massacre de ses frères ?"

— Faut qu'on parle, dit Arzo.

Pankov ne bougea pas d'un cheveu. Il se rappela soudain les paroles de Niyazbek : "Tu es le seul haut fonctionnaire fédéral qui soit de notre bord. S'ils te tuent..." Arzo aurait donné cher pour le tuer. D'ailleurs, à peine vingt-quatre heures plus tôt, il avait bel et bien tenté de le tuer. Arzo, c'était le genre d'homme qui n'avait pas besoin d'engager un cuisinier pour se faire cuire un œuf.

Arzo partit d'un gros rire :

— Tu as peur, ou quoi ?

Pankov rougit comme une écrevisse, jeta un regard en coulisse sur sa garde qui avait grandi en petite armée, et lâcha :

— Allons-y.

Ils gravirent des marches de granit gris et traversèrent un hall étonnamment désert. Pankov était flanqué de Sergueï et des hommes de l'Alpha, Arzo allait seul. Quand les hommes, bardés d'armes, passèrent le détecteur de métaux qui barrait l'entrée du FSB régional, le portique hurla de toutes ses sirènes mais nul n'y prêta la moindre attention.

On trouva un bureau ouvert au troisième étage. Un adjoint de Chebolev était là seul à se morfondre, qui décanilla vite fait. Sergueï et les gars de l'Alpha restèrent à la porte. Pankov se sentit l'aplomb d'un char : tous les bureaux de la bâtisse étaient sur écoute. Malheur à Arzo s'il avait l'audace de s'en prendre à lui.

Le Tchétchène promena le regard alentour comme un loup précipité dans une cage, puis il se faufila prestement derrière le bureau et s'installa dans le fauteuil de cuir du maître des lieux. A sa gauche, toute une batterie de téléphones blancs ; face à lui, la surface lisse de la table, plane et vierge comme l'exigeait le règlement, avec une pile soignée de papier et une écritoire en granit où était gravé : *Je sers la Russie !*

Derrière son dos pendaient une carte du Caucase ainsi que le drapeau tricolore de la Russie. Le visage mat du Tchétchène, creusé de rides comme une stèle fissurée de partout, paraissait encore plus noir dans la pénombre de la pièce.

— Dis-moi une chose, dit soudain Pankov, quand je suis venu chez toi au village, tu sais, après l'explosion de la bombe, et que je me suis approché de la cave où j'avais été enfermé, eh bien... y avait-il du monde dedans ? Ou pas encore ?

Arzo haussa les épaules, secoué d'un rire narquois.

— Je veux t'expliquer un truc, dit le Tchétchène. D'après toi, pourquoi t'a-t-on nommé ambassadeur du Kremlin ? Tu n'avais passé que trois jours de ta vie dans le Caucase. Et encore ! au fond d'une cave.

— Justement pour cette raison-là. Parce que je n'étais pas du sérail.

Arzo eut un sourire méprisant. Son front basané se plissa, ses prunelles noires de loup vrillèrent les pupilles de Pankov qui comprit alors, horrifié, combien il avait sous-estimé Arzo. Vladislav avait toujours su combien cet homme était cruel, combien cet homme était vaillant. Mais combien cet homme était intelligent, il n'y avait jamais songé.

— Un seul homme, dans cette république, était à même d'en devenir le président, dit Arzo. Un enfant du pays, pas un Russe. Il connaissait cinq langues européennes et trois caucasiennes. Il était capable de penser non pas au prix qu'il pouvait tirer des postes à responsabilités, mais à ce qu'on devait y faire. Il s'appelait Ibrahim Malikov et il était ton meilleur ami. Tous les autres font la paire avec Aslanov. En plus petit. C'est pour ça qu'on t'a nommé. Pour que tu nommes Malikov.

— Malikov pouvait être nommé sans moi. C'est toi-même qui le dis : il n'y avait pas d'autre candidature.

Le Tchétchène prit une feuille blanche sur le bureau. Encore un geste auquel Pankov ne s'attendait pas. Dans son esprit, Arzo ne savait pas écrire. On n'apprend pas aux loups à écrire, enfin quoi.

— Regarde bien, Vladislav Avdeïevitch. Voici le président Aslanov. Il contrôle toute l'économie de la république. Il reçoit deux milliards de dollars par an de subventions. Il en vole un milliard et laisse filer l'autre moitié entre ses doigts. Et combien rapporte-t-il au Kremlin ? Zéro. Parce que le président Aslanov tient la république d'une main ferme et qu'on ne lui connaît pas d'alternative. Or les gens du Kremlin veulent qu'il rapporte. Les gens du Kremlin n'ont pas besoin d'un Malikov qui ne leur rapportera jamais rien. Ce que veulent les gens du Kremlin, c'est qu'Aslanov les paie pour que Malikov ne soit pas nommé à sa place.

Assis devant Arzo, Pankov l'écoutait sans piper. Le silence qui régnait dans le bâtiment vide les isolait des cris de la foule et du fracas des blindés. Il y avait quelque chose d'envoûtant dans la logique du Tchétchène. Une logique des cavernes qui sentait la chèvre et les douilles de mitraillettes, mais c'était cette logique-là, Pankov le comprit, qui prévalait maintenant au Kremlin.

— Je n'ai rien à voir là-dedans, objecta Pankov. Ivan Vitaliévitch pouvait parfaitement nommer Malikov. Je veux dire : faire semblant de le nommer.

— Non. Tout le monde sait ici qu'Ivan Vitaliévitch se fait bakchicher pour chaque nomination. Et tout le monde sait que Malikov n'aurait rien donné. Conclusion : Ivan ne pouvait pas faire semblant de vouloir nommer Malikov. Personne ne s'y serait trompé. Bon, admettons qu'Aslanov lui apporte une enveloppe de cinq millions. A quoi bon prendre si peu ? Pour acheter des épingles de nourrice à sa femme ? Voilà pourquoi Ivan s'y est pris autrement. Il t'a nommé, toi, au prétexte que le Caucase à feu et à sang avait besoin d'un homme intègre. Et, là, tu as décidé de faire nommer Malikov. Du coup, Aslanov a pris peur pour de bon. Parce qu'on savait ici qu'Ibrahim était ton ami et que Niyazbek t'avait libéré de ma cave. D'après toi, qui a fait courir le bruit qu'Ibrahim allait devenir président ? Toi ? Aslanov ? Sa progéniture ? Tu n'y es pas ! La rumeur est partie du chef adjoint de l'Administration présidentielle fédérale.

Silence de Pankov.

— Mais Ivan Vitaliévitch s'est planté, continua Arzo. Ibrahim a été tué. Il s'est donc retrouvé sans son magot, mais avec toi pour premier commis du Kremlin. C'est alors qu'il a décidé de remettre le jeu sur le tapis. Avec Niyazbek, cette fois, dans le rôle de l'épouvantail. Evidemment, on avait peine à croire que tu nommerais Niyazbek président, il est trop...

— Trop montagnard, lança Pankov maussade.

— Si tu veux, oui, trop montagnard. Mais on pouvait pousser le bouchon assez loin pour qu'Aslanov se mette à y croire. Et il y a cru. Il a sauté dans un avion, direction le Kremlin. Pourquoi penses-tu qu'Ivan Vitaliévitch ne t'a pas appelé cette nuit ? Pourquoi a-t-il attendu ce matin pour t'appeler ? Parce qu'il a passé la nuit à mettre la pression sur Aslanov ! Tu imagines la somme qu'il a pu lui extorquer ? Deux milliards de dollars par an dont la moitié passait sur des comptes en Arabie Saoudite, et ce pendant les huit dernières années ! Ça fait combien d'argent en banque si des millions traînent par terre dans la Maison sur la Colline ? Hein ? On est bien au-dessus du millier de milliards de cash en roubles russes dans un wagon de chemin de fer, n'est-ce pas ?

Pankov tressaillit :

— Tu veux dire que...

— Oui ! Ce millier de milliards aussi était passé dans la poche d'Ivan.

La question suivante partit d'elle-même de la bouche de Pankov :

— Dis-moi, Arzo, pourquoi as-tu rallié notre camp ? Nous avons mutilé ton fils. Nous massacrons ton peuple.

Le Tchétchène était là, assis devant le Moscovite, droit, impeccable, cheveux grisonnants, et Vladislav se dit soudain qu'il connaissait la réponse et qu'il la tenait d'Arzo lui-même, Arzo qui mutilait toujours les soldats russes avant de les échanger. Non pour le plaisir, mais pour causer le maximum de nuisance à l'ennemi. La nuisance la plus terrible n'est pas un mort que tout le monde oubliera bientôt. La nuisance la plus terrible est un estropié qui ne peut pas travailler, vit de mendicité et sème la peur dans la société, la peur et la haine des mendiants. "Il nous aide à nous entre-mutiler, comprit soudain Pankov. Un estropié de la conscience installé au Kremlin, c'est mille fois plus terrible qu'un million de culs-de-jatte dans le métro. Aucun pays ne peut survivre à un tel estropié. Aucune économie."

Arzo dit en souriant :

— C'est du pareil au même. Ça paie mieux chez vous.

Pankov éprouvait la sensation d'avoir été retourné comme un gant, roulé en serpillière et traîné dans les chiottes publiques pour un lavage à grande eau.

— Va voir Niyazbek, dit le Tchétchène, et explique-lui qu'il doit vider les lieux. C'est foutu pour lui. Il sera déclaré séparatiste et l'assaut sera donné contre la Maison sur la Colline.

— ... en zigouillant dans la foulée la moitié du gouvernement ?

Arzo haussa les épaules.

— Les morts seront déclarés complices de Niyazbek ; et les survivants, otages libérés. Ce sera un assaut parfait, sans victimes innocentes. Tous les morts seront des terroristes, et tous les rescapés, leurs prisonniers.

Le premier commis du Kremlin se taisait.

— Il n'est pas dangereux, on le relâchera. Il a fait son boulot. Le fric est payé. Qu'il aille où il veut. (Large sourire d'Arzo, qui ajouta :) Sinon c'est moi qu'on enverra à l'assaut. Rigolo, non ? Arzo Khadjiev et les fédéraux sous ses ordres ont anéanti le terroriste Niyazbek Malikov. Aurais-tu rêvé d'une chose pareille du fond de ma cave ?

Quand Pankov et Arzo quittèrent le bureau, le Moscovite remarqua que le colonel de l'Alpha semblait bizarre et qu'il ne quittait pas le Tchétchène des yeux.

Ils sortirent de la bâtisse et, là, Pankov se rappela tout à coup où il avait vu le colonel Migounov. C'était le même officier de l'Alpha qui accompagnait Arzo dans les restaurants de Moscou en 1999.

Migounov jeta un regard détaché droit devant lui, vers Arzo qui donnait des ordres secs et méchants à ses hommes, et Pankov comprit que Migounov aussi l'avait reconnu.

— Je me trompe ou c'est bien là le Tchétchène dont nous avions la garde ? Il parlait de vous et de la cave où vous étiez aux fers.

— C'est bien lui.

— Vraiment ? Qui sont les terroristes, alors ?

— En fait, leur chef est l'homme qui m'a sorti de la cave, répondit l'ambassadeur du Kremlin.

Douze heures au moins s'étaient écoulées depuis la première visite de Pankov dans le bâtiment occupé, et le ruisseau qui jaillissait des chiottes n'avait fait que grossir. Quelqu'un avait arraché le tapis chemin qui faisait son lit et posé des briques à même le marbre, de sorte que le flot bruissait maintenant entre les briques dans sa course à la fosse d'ascenseur.

L'ascenseur marchait.

Niyazbek l'accueillit au même endroit que la veille, dans le bureau du président Aslanov. Il avait l'air calme dans sa tenue bien mise. Sous l'ample échancrure de son treillis, Pankov remarqua un maillot propre à la blancheur impeccable. Cheveux courts humides, fraîchement lavés, menton volontaire, rasé de près. Un tapis de prière plié en quatre reposait sur une chaise, et le Moscovite se dit, à la vue du tapis, qu'il ne s'était pas lavé depuis la veille.

Etaient aussi présents, outre les amis de Niyazbek, Daoud et le maire de Torbi-Kala. Ils visionnaient une vidéo en poussant des oh ! et des ah ! C'étaient des rushes filmés en caméra cachée, et Pankov comprit que les chambres fortes de la maison ne renfermaient pas que de l'argent. Les rebelles avaient mis la main sur une véritable mine de compromissions.

— Tu n'as pas l'air très réjoui, Slava, dit Niyazbek.

— Je veux te parler en tête à tête.

Niyazbek marqua un bref silence, hocha la tête et passa dans la salle de repos. Pankov le suivit. Khizri et Djavatkhan les imitèrent.

Pankov s'assit dans un large fauteuil de cuir tandis que Niyazbek resta planté à l'entrée. La crosse de son pistolet-mitrailleur, à son épaule, touchait presque le linteau de la porte. Khizri, tout sourire, se mit au comptoir du bar et scruta les bouteilles avec l'indifférence d'un végétarien devant un étal de viande.

— J'ai dit : en tête à tête.

— Considère que nous sommes seuls.

Pankov comprit que Niyazbek ne voulait pas qu'on l'accuse d'avoir traité avec un Russe seul à seul.

— Le président Aslanov ne démissionnera pas. Tu ferais mieux de vider les lieux avant que ça tourne à la boucherie. Je suis prêt à te promettre ce que tu voudras. Une enquête sur Kharon-Yourte. Le châtiment des coupables. J'ai fait arrêter Chebolev. Je limogerai Arzo. Tu seras un héros. Mais Aslanov restera.

Niyazbek se tut un temps.

— Pourquoi ?

— Parce que… au Kremlin, on considère qu'il est le seul capable de faire face à la situation.

— Parce qu'il a payé sa place, tu veux dire.

Pankov leva les yeux.

— Oui. Il a payé sa place. Quand tu t'es emparé de la Maison sur la Colline, si ça t'intéresse, il a dû doubler la mise. Mes supérieurs ont gagné beaucoup d'argent sur ton dos, Niyzabek.

Silence.

— Ecoute-moi, Niyazbek, il y a dix mille personnes sur la place. Et même plus, sans doute. Ils sont là parce que tu te bats contre les Aslanov. Ils sont là parce que leurs parents et leurs proches disparaissent sans laisser de trace. On va en finir avec ce problème. Tu seras un héros. Personne ne te touchera. Tu…

— Je serai même utile, dit Niyzabek. La prochaine fois qu'Aslanov rechignera à payer, on pourra me remonter contre lui encore une fois. Et si tu me donnais son téléphone, Slava ?

Que je le joigne directos en cas d'arriéré de paiement... Je pourrai prendre d'assaut quelque chose d'autre, au prochain coup. Le terrain de golf, par exemple. Ou la résidence de Gamzat. Dès qu'il l'aura reconstruite.

— Que veux-tu, Niyazbek ?

— La démission du président.

Pankov rajusta ses lunettes qui étaient embuées. D'un œil en coin, il vit une bande crasseuse au revers de son col de chemise.

— Si tu ne veux rien pour toi, pense au moins aux autres ! Vous pouvez tout exiger ! Khizri, ta nomination n'est pas encore confirmée à la tête d'Avarie-Transflotte ? Ce sera fait. Demain. Aujourd'hui. Dans une heure. Mahomedsalih, je t'ai retiré ton portefeuille de ministre ? Tu le retrouveras demain. Ou le veux-tu pour ton frère ? Veux-tu que l'on double le budget des Travaux publics ? Veux-tu qu'il te soit payé cash ?

Silence de Niyazbek.

— Les Aslanov sont des scélérats, reprit Pankov, mais les Aslanov n'ont pas tué ton frère. L'essentiel est là, non ?

Silence de Niyazbek.

— Réfléchis bien, Niyazbek ! Tout ce que tu voudras ! Des compensations pour les morts ! N'importe quel poste pour toi ! Je suis prêt à te donner tout ce qui est en mon pouvoir. Mais je ne destitue pas le président Aslanov. Le Kremlin a décidé que quiconque revendique la destitution d'Aslanov lance un défi à la Russie ! Qu'en dis-tu ?

— J'en dis que Wahha a raison, répondit tranquillement Niyazbek. Le problème, ce n'est pas le président Aslanov. Le problème est ailleurs : quand des mécréants gouvernent des musulmans, ça finit toujours dans la honte.

Vladislav, pantois :

— Quoi ?

— Va-t'en.

Pankov était muet.

— Va-t'en, articula Niyazbek, avant que je prenne une autre décision. Au nom de ce que tu as tenté pour nous, va-t'en, le Russe.

— Je reste.

— Alors tu restes comme otage.

— Soit. Je reste comme otage.

Ils sortirent du bureau à cinq : Pankov, Niyazbek, Khizri, Djavatkhan et Mahomedsalih. Deux caméras de télévision se campaient sur leur statif. Piskounov tournait en rond, un pistolet de service à la ceinture. A côté du lance-grenade sur pied qu'on avait placé à la fenêtre, canon braqué au-dehors, le pistolet avait l'air d'un bichon près d'un chien-loup.

Quelqu'un mit un micro sous le nez de Pankov.

— La situation est complexe, dit-il, les négociations conti-nuent. (Une hésitation, puis :) Afin d'éviter toute provoca-tion, j'ai décidé, en tant que chef de l'état-major antiterroriste, de rester au siège du gouvernement jusqu'à la fin des pour-parlers.

Piskounov le regarda avec les yeux d'un chien abandonné.

— Vas-y, Serguëi. C'est un ordre.

Pankov appela son adjoint, puis le colonel Migounov à qui il expliqua en quelques mots ce qu'il venait de déclarer à la presse. "Fais attention à Arzo et suis-le bien de près. A la moindre alerte, tords-lui le cou. Tant que je suis ici, c'est toi le chef."

Niyazbek regagna le bureau tandis que Khizri et Dja-vatkhan escortèrent Pankov au bout du couloir. Il y avait là l'antichambre de Gamzat Aslanov. Le temps d'un éclair, Vladislav fut pris d'une peur bestiale : il crut revoir la chambre forte du président, de deux mètres sur deux, et les prison-niers ligotés de scotch à même le sol. Mais on se contenta de l'enfermer dans une salle de repos. En sortant, Djavatkhan balaya les lieux du regard et, d'un geste nonchalant, sec-tionna au couteau un écheveau de fils téléphoniques : sur une table basse, près du téléviseur, il n'y avait pas moins de trois téléphones, y compris une ligne gouvernementale.

Tout le temps qu'ils avaient longé le couloir, ni Djavatkhan ni Khizri n'avaient échangé le moindre mot.

Tout beau, tout neuf, le divan de cuir couleur crème se tassa mollement sous le séant du premier commis du Krem-lin. Assis devant un guéridon, il laissa rouler sa tête dans ses mains. La moirure de la tablette, frappée aux coins des initiales dorées *GA*, lui renvoya l'image de sa face blême, pas rasée, barrée de la monture d'écaille de ses lunettes. Ses aisselles lâchèrent une brusque et rebutante odeur de sueur et Pankov songea que c'était une erreur, de s'être rendu aux pourparlers sans avoir pris soin de se changer. Il se dit aussi qu'il fallait allumer la télévision mais il n'en avait plus la force. Deux minutes plus tard, il se renversa sur le dossier du divan et bascula dans le puits noir du sommeil.

Il se réveilla au bout d'une heure et demie, dans le silence et l'obscurité. Quelqu'un était entré dans la pièce pendant son sommeil et avait baissé les stores occultants. Le double vitrage blindé faisait écran aux bruits de la place, et l'excellente isolation acoustique, à ceux de l'intérieur.

Il resta un temps allongé, les yeux posés sur l'unique rai de lumière qui, échappé par le haut du store, courait au plafond. Il alluma la télé et tomba pile sur les infos de la première chaîne. Il y eut un reportage sur la rencontre du président de la Russie avec le Premier ministre du Mozambique. On y fit même un peu de place au Caucase, avec un sujet sur une récolte exceptionnelle de céréales en Karatchaïevo-Tcherkessie où l'on montra d'heureux conducteurs de moissonneuses-batteuses préoccupés par le marché du grain.

Pankov coupa le son et comprit qu'il avait faim. Il découvrit un bar somptueux dans un coin de la pièce, mais rien dedans que de l'alcool. Il ne toucha pas à la vodka, bien qu'il en mourût d'envie. Ce n'était pas le moment de se bourrer à jeun.

Il aurait certes pu cogner à la porte et demander à manger, mais il n'avait pas envie de s'abaisser une fois de plus. Il claqua la porte du bar et constata que ses mains tremblaient. "Tu n'es pourtant pas dans la cave d'Arzo, ici", se rappela-t-il à lui-même.

Il joua du zappeur et tomba cette fois sur CNN, un reportage sur l'Avarie-Dargo-Nord. Il y vit Niyazbek étreindre le bronze et entendit sa propre voix en traduction synchronisée, annonçant qu'il restait à l'intérieur du siège gouvernemental. Pour finir, il y eut un plan sur la foule cernée de blindés. Apparemment, le sujet passait toutes les heures.

Pankov avait peur, très peur. Ces derniers mois, il s'était peu à peu habitué au Caucase. De ces gens étranges qui priaient Allah et saignaient les Russes dans la nuit, les montagnards étaient devenus ses amis, joyeux, joviaux, qui le régalaient de khinkals et de viande. Ils riaient ensemble des mêmes plaisanteries, partageaient les mêmes tables. Il s'avérait tout à coup que Khizri, ce tueur de sang-froid, savait préparer de succulentes brochettes ; que Djavatkhan, le ravisseur du businessman autrichien, était un garçon doux et bienveillant qui raffolait de sa femme russe et de ses trois enfants ; et que même le champion du monde de wushu Mahomedsalih, qui, sous les yeux de Pankov, avait tiré sur un homme à coups de Beretta, se montrait fort sympathique et plutôt doué aux échecs.

En un seul instant, tout avait basculé. Des vieilles connaissances qu'ils avaient été, ces hommes étaient redevenus des musulmans aux cheveux noirs, et Pankov savait que l'affable Djavatkhan comme le souriant Khizri lui couperaient la gorge avec la même légèreté que Wahha Arsaïev ou même, tant qu'à faire, Niyazbek en personne.

Ami, il avait cessé de l'être. Il était russe, et les Russes les avaient trahis.

Question : s'il frappait à la porte et demandait à partir, là, maintenant, le laisserait-on ? Ou le refoulerait-on à coups de crosse de pistolet-mitrailleur ?

La panique le gagnait. Il avait oublié, en s'engageant à rester dans le bâtiment, qu'il avait déjà été otage une fois dans sa vie. Les trois jours de captivité passés dans la cave d'Arzo s'étaient soldés par une névrose des plus sévères, un séjour en clinique psychiatrique, une addiction à la cocaïne. Les médecins l'avaient purgé de ses souvenirs comme un plombier l'aurait fait d'un siphon, et Pankov croyait avoir tout oublié. Mais maintenant les horreurs endurées neuf ans plus tôt refaisaient surface et lui noyaient la raison en s'insinuant dans les recoins les plus reculés de son cerveau.

Il fut pris de convulsions. Au bout d'un moment, il se retrouva affalé dans un coin, assis entre le bar et le divan, en train de sucer son pouce. Il se leva d'un bond et promena ses mains à tâtons sur les murs à la recherche d'un interrupteur. Rien. Seuls quelques pinceaux de lumière striaient le plafond, venant du poste de télé. Pankov se jeta sur la fenêtre. Le cadre était d'acier, et la vitre, blindée. Derrière la vitre, une baie de fenêtre large d'un mètre avec un store noir à l'intérieur qui le privait de la lumière du jour et de la foule amassée sur la place. "Il ne leur coûterait rien de prétendre qu'on m'a tué et de commencer l'assaut", songea-t-il en un éclair de panique auquel fit immédiatement écho une autre crainte : "Ceux-là aussi pourraient me tuer en un rien de temps."

Il s'agrippa au cadre de la fenêtre et le secoua comme pour crier : "Je suis là ! Je suis vivant !"

Clic, il y eut un bruit d'interrupteur et la lumière électrique inonda la pièce. Pankov se retourna. Debout dans l'encadrement de la porte, Khizri tenait un plateau de nourriture dans les mains.

— On a pensé que tu avais peut-être faim.

Pankov mit quelques secondes à se reprendre. Une goutte de sueur perla à ses cils et roula plus bas, vers le nez.

— Oui, dit Pankov, un bail que je n'ai pas mangé.

Khizri posa le plateau sur la table. Du pain, un fromage à pâte blanche et poreuse, des herbes aromatiques et de la viande. Pankov enroula le fromage dans un brick tiède à peine cuit et se mit à manger en s'efforçant de ne pas avaler de trop grosses bouchées. Khizri souleva du plateau une imposante théière de cuivre et lui versa un verre d'eau bouillante.

Pankov s'attendait à ce que l'autre parte, au lieu de quoi le boiteux prit un verre au bar et se servit à son tour. Puis il s'installa dans un fauteuil de cuir : Khizri adorait être bien assis.

— Que disais-tu tout à l'heure à propos d'Avarie-Transflotte ? demanda Khizri à brûle-pourpoint.

Surpris, Pankov manqua de s'étrangler. Puis il déglutit prudemment, mit un sachet de thé dans son verre et lapa l'eau qui menaçait de déborder.

— Je disais simplement que le Kremlin, à l'heure actuelle, dira oui à n'importe quelle demande de poste. Néanmoins, je ne suis pas sûr qu'il t'aurait confirmé à la tête d'Avarie-Transflotte. Le pétrole, sais-tu seulement ce que c'est ?

— Oui. C'est un truc qui coule d'un tuyau quand on y bricole un branchement.

— C'est bien ce que je disais. En temps normal, ça ne suffirait pas à faire de toi un directeur. Mais maintenant le Kremlin est prêt à tout vous donner. Mieux, le Kremlin veut voir les postes clés occupés non seulement par les amis du président, mais aussi par ses ennemis. Je te le garantis. Je peux régler la question en deux minutes. Même d'ici. Même tout de suite. Bien que ça n'ait plus aucun sens. Si vous avez décidé de proclamer l'indépendance de la république, ça n'a guère de sens que tu sois nommé à la tête d'Avarie-Transflotte ou pas.

Khizri, après un silence :

— Je ne trahirai pas Niyazbek, dit-il soudain.

— Je ne te demande pas de trahir Niyazbek. Mais vous faites une belle bêtise. Admettons que vous déclariez l'indépendance. Fort bien. De quoi vivrez-vous ? La république n'a pas d'industrie. Pas de potentiel scientifique. Votre pétrole, c'est un demi-milliard de dollars par an, plus deux milliards de subventions fédérales que vous partagez entre vous à coups de mitraillette. Admettons que vous ayez l'indépendance, mais pas les subventions. Qui vous donnera de l'argent ? L'Arabie Saoudite ? Cinq centimes par tête de pipe ?

— L'Arabie, oui, peut-être bien, fit Khizri sur le ton du défi.

— Très bien. Mais qui tiendra le pouvoir ? Crois-tu que Niyazbek restera au pouvoir quand vous aurez déclaré l'indépendance ? Crois-tu que toi-même resteras au pouvoir ? Moi je pense que c'est Wahha Arsaïev qui prendra le pouvoir. Voilà dix ans déjà qu'il se bat contre les Russes alors que Niyazbek leur fait des mamours. Si l'Arabie Saoudite donne de l'argent, ce sera à qui s'est battu contre les Russes.

Silence accablé de Khizri.

— Vois-tu, reprit Pankov, Niyazbek m'a dit de partir. J'aurais pu partir, rejoindre les miens et leur dire : Tirez sur ce tas de fumiers à coups de pièce de char. Au lieu de quoi je reste ici à me demander par qui je vais me faire descendre. Par vous ou par les autres ? J'ai fait ce choix parce que, s'il arrive ce que vous recherchez, ce sera un bain de sang. Vous allez vous entretuer, mais pas pour l'argent des Russes, pour rien. Niyazbek s'obstine. La tête d'une statue ne lui suffit pas. Dis-moi un peu : d'un côté, la tête des Aslanov, et, de l'autre, la moitié de la république que vous allez recevoir. La moitié, m'entends-tu ? Tu veux Avarie-Transflotte ? Prends-la ! Tu veux être député ? Vas-y. Même à la Douma fédérale, si ça te chante. Tu veux quel parti ? Russie unie ? Ou chez les communistes ? Ou peut-être que tu préfères le Sénat ? Sénateur de Krasnodar, ça te va ? Ou de Krasnoïarsk ?

Khizri fixait la table d'un air concentré. Pankov comprenait les tourments de son âme. Ce garçon de vingt-six ans, estropié natif de Chamkhalsk-la-Poussière, s'était hissé au sommet de la vie locale grâce à sa rage de tuer. Le sommet, c'était une place bien ancrée dans la suite du bandit le plus notoire de la république et le statut de député régional qu'il n'avait pas encore obtenu. Or voilà qu'on lui proposait d'être sénateur de Krasnodar et directeur d'une compagnie qui contrôlait les deux tiers du fret de la Caspienne.

Le jeune homme se leva si brusquement que son thé se répandit sur la moirure du guéridon.

— A propos, lança Pankov à mi-voix dans le dos de Khizri, ce serait bien qu'on me donne un téléphone. Ça fait le jeu de vos ennemis qu'on ne puisse pas me joindre.

La porte claqua derrière lui. Alors seulement Pankov découvrit l'interrupteur judicieusement niché entre la porte et le comptoir du bar, à côté de la commande du store.

Le téléphone arriva quarante minutes plus tard par les bons soins de Djavatkhan. Dans l'énorme patte du Lezghe, le petit Nokia en titane semblait perdu comme une balle sur un terrain de golf. C'était l'un des portables du Moscovite dont seuls les plus proches connaissaient le numéro. Ce qui ne l'empêchait pas de se trouver le plus clair du temps dans les mains de son adjoint : comme la plupart des hauts fonctionnaires de rang fédéral, Pankov n'avait presque jamais de mobile sur lui pour la bonne raison qu'un téléphone cellulaire, même débranché, pouvait servir de capteur d'écoute. Aussi les fédéraux préféraient-ils la ligne gouvernementale, elle aussi sur écoute (cherchez la logique), mais en revanche plus prestigieuse.

Djavatkhan lui tendit le Nokia et lui dit :

— Tiens. Ça fait trois fois qu'il sonne. Une vraie teigne.

Pankov prit le téléphone et reconnut la voix de son vieil ami oligarque. Celui-là même dont il avait raté l'anniversaire. C'était... Ah ! Seigneur. C'était hier.

— Slava, dit la voix joyeuse qui parlait de Moscou, jamais tu décroches quand on t'appelle ?

— Je dormais, répondit Pankov qui n'eut même pas à mentir. Deux jours de suite que je suis debout. J'ai plongé.

— Tu as plongé ? Et qui est ce loustic qui répond à ton téléphone ?

— Un ami. Un mec bien.

— Vraiment ? Ces mecs bien, ça fait deux jours qu'ils passent en boucle sur CNN. Tous plus pittoresques les uns que les autres. On les élève dans les montagnes avec les moutons, ou quoi ?

— Mollo la jactance.

— Holà ! (La voix du Moscovite se fit plus tendue :) Tu es vraiment là-dedans de ton plein gré ? Parce qu'il y a de ces rumeurs qui c...

Pankov comprit que tel était bien le motif du coup de fil de son ami moscovite. Un coup de fil sur commande.

— Ecoute-moi bien, dit Pankov. Première chose : je risque davantage de prendre un pruneau là-bas qu'ici. Il y a deux gus, en face, qui ont déjà tenté de me faire la peau. C'est d'ailleurs comme ça que tout a commencé. Deuxième chose : qu'on m'apporte la garantie qu'aucun taré ne s'amusera à nous tirer dessus avec le canon d'un char. Parce qu'il y a déjà dix mille manifestants sur la place. S'ils sont tous terroristes, c'est qu'on est mal barré. A supposer qu'il y ait vingt mille terroristes dans une république de la fédération de Russie, les Russes n'ont plus qu'à plier bagage.

— OK, dit le Moscovite, sans rancune. Macha fête son anniversaire en novembre. Tu peux venir avec ton copain. Est-ce qu'il sait se servir d'une fourchette, au moins ?

Pankov raccrocha. Djavatkhan avait l'ouïe fine et le Nokia parlait trop fort. Pankov craignait que le Lezghe n'ait suivi toute la conversation.

— Il me faut une ligne spéciale, dit Pankov, je dois parler à l'état-major.

Le Lezghe opina sans bouger de son fauteuil, ses longues et fortes jambes allongées devant lui dans leur pantalon camo.

— C'est vrai que tu as fait la guerre en Tchétchénie ?

Il fit oui de la tête.

— Tu as tué des Russes ?

Encore oui.

— Sur le front ? Ou c'étaient des prisonniers ?

Djavatkhan réfléchit longtemps.

— Là-bas, il n'y a pas de ligne de front. Pas de prisonniers non plus. Il n'y a que l'ennemi.

— Et pourquoi as-tu cessé de te battre ?

Il observa un silence, puis :

— Je pensais qu'une fois la guerre finie... tout serait différent. Je pensais que tout serait selon la volonté d'Allah. Et puis je suis rentré... Il y avait des barrages tous les kilomètres sur la route. Des bandits. Ils pillaient tout le monde en disant : Nous sommes des combattants d'Allah. Des combattants d'Allah, ça ? Je ne les avais jamais vus avant. Ni à Bamout, ni à Pervomaïka. J'avais la télé dans ma voiture. En couleurs, sur le tableau de bord. Nous approchions de Grozny, vers sept heures du soir. C'est là que j'ai vu, dans le poste, qu'on égorgeait un Russe. Qu'on puisse égorger un Russe, je comprends ça. Mais pourquoi à la télé ? Où est-il écrit dans le Coran qu'on doit couper les têtes à la télé ? Est-ce que j'ai déjà saigné quelqu'un sous les caméras, moi ? Si j'ai vraiment une gorge à couper, je fais ça dans mon coin. C'est comme aller aux chiottes, on ne s'affiche pas à la télé. Le soir même, nous étions invités chez quelqu'un. Un camarade à moi. Il s'est fait tuer depuis. Il nous a bien reçus. Des gamines dansaient sur les tables. Douze ans chacune, les gamines. Ils en ont pris une et l'ont posée sur mes genoux en me disant : Tiens, une vierge, qu'ils m'ont fait ; on l'a gardée pour toi, pour te faire plaisir. Alors je me suis levé et j'ai dit : Je ne savais pas qu'un musulman pouvait se conduire comme ça. L'autre m'a répondu : Imagine que nous sommes au paradis et que ce sont des houris. Moi, j'ai dit : Tu n'es pas au paradis pour l'instant, mais dans une porcherie. Bon, je suis resté un moment et j'ai repris la route.

Pankov marqua un silence.

— Donc, la charia, là-bas, ça n'a pas marché ?

— Non.

— Et, ici, ça marchera ?

Djavatkhan laissa la question sans réponse.

— Tu veux la même chose dans ton pays ? Des bandits sur les routes, des têtes coupées en *prime time* ? Des pères de famille affamés qui mangent des racines et leurs filles qui dansent sur les tables ? Pour les nouveaux maîtres de la charia.

— Jamais ça, coupa Djavatkhan.

— Personne ne vous demandera votre avis. Comment comptez-vous prospérer ? La république vit de ses subventions fédérales, deux milliards de dollars par an. Si vous plantez vos drapeaux verts sur ce bâtiment, les fonds seront coupés. De quoi vivrez-vous ?

— Nous avons du pétrole, ânonna Djavatkhan, les investisseurs suivront.

— Nous avons déjà eu la visite d'un investisseur... et ce n'est pas Gamzat qui l'a fait fuir. C'est toi ! Parfaitement ! Il n'y aura donc ni investissements, ni création d'emplois. La seule embauche, ce sera pour travailler de la Kalachnikov. Sauf que, au lieu de sortir les Kalaches pour vous disputer deux milliards de dollars, vous ne les sortirez plus que pour deux jerricanes d'essence. Vois-tu, Djavatkhan, ces choses-là ne dépendent pas de vous. Les bandits sur les routes, les têtes coupées à la télé et les filles sur les tables, ça ne dépend pas de vos décisions. Ça dépend de l'économie.

— C'est bizarre, tout de même, les autres pays arrivent bien à gagner leur vie, pourquoi pas nous ?

— Combien y a-t-il d'habitants dans la république, le sais-tu ?

— Deux millions et demi.

— Et combien sont partis ?

— Je n'en sais rien.

— Un demi-million. Un demi-million en quinze ans.

Vladislav tendit le bras et prit une feuille de papier. Une jolie feuille à filigrane marquée des initiales *GA*. Un joli stylo aussi, en or blanc couronné de nacre, qu'il tira d'un présentoir en daim gravé d'une dédicace.

— Regarde bien. Un demi-million de gens partis, qui voulaient travailler. Pas voler, pas tuer, travailler. Ibrahim Malikov voulait travailler, et il est parti. Imaginons que, dans le tas, seuls cent mille gagnent deux mille dollars par mois. Ce chiffre en vérité doit être bien supérieur parce que ceux qui partent sont les plus entreprenants, et deux mille dollars, pour quelqu'un d'entreprenant en Russie, ce n'est pas grand-chose. Mais imaginons qu'un cinquième seulement des émigrés gagne deux mille dollars par mois. Tu me suis ?

— Ben oui.

— Deux mille dollars par mois, c'est vingt-quatre mille dollars par an. Il existe un critère mondialement reconnu d'après lequel chacun ne gagne pas plus que le cinquième du revenu qu'il dégage. Allez, disons le quart. Celui qui gagne deux mille dollars par mois produit donc annuellement un minimum de cent mille dollars. Multiplie cent mille dollars par cent mille personnes, et tu découvres que les émigrés créent un produit brut de dix milliards de dollars. Contre les deux milliards que la république reçoit du budget fédéral.

Djavatkhan écoutait très attentivement, la mitraillette posée entre les genoux.

— Et maintenant dis-moi une chose, Djavatkhan. Pourquoi le président Aslanov et ses fils préfèrent-ils avoir deux milliards de dollars de subventions fédérales plutôt qu'un minimum de dix milliards qu'ils auraient dégagés s'ils n'avaient pas fichu tous ces gens à la porte ?

Djavatkhan ne répondit pas.

— Parce que, ces deux milliards, Aslanov est seul à en disposer. Il les distribue entre les siens. Alors que, les dix milliards, il ne peut pas les redistribuer entre les siens. Les gens les gagnent eux-mêmes. Le président trouve plus agréable d'avoir deux milliards et d'en disposer personnellement que d'être assis sur dix milliards qui lui échappent. Et maintenant dis-moi franchement : Niyazbek, Khizri ou toi, pensez-vous tolérer un jour l'apparition d'une source indépendante de business dans la république ? Es-tu jamais entré dans une raffinerie non pour en sortir de l'essence, mais pour y apporter des investissements ? Tu t'es rendu responsable du rapt d'un investisseur il y a deux mois avec l'espoir d'en tirer vingt milliards de dollars. Et tu comptes maintenant l'inviter à venir faire des forages ?

Djavatkhan fixait le sol d'un œil maussade, ses mains tripotant la bandoulière de son PM.

— Oh ! Slava, soupira enfin le montagnard, comme ce serait bien que tu te convertisses à l'islam et que tu sois notre Premier ministre.

Une fois Pankov enfermé, Niyazbek se garda bien de proclamer l'indépendance de la république, contrairement à la menace qu'il avait proférée. Au lieu de cela, il donna plusieurs coups de téléphone, dont l'un au chef du groupe Alpha et l'autre au directeur du centre de détention judiciaire, conversa avec quelques amis puis se retira en salle de repos.

Là, il déroula son tapis et se mit à prier.

Il pria longtemps. Son tapis replié, il enfila ses chaussettes et s'approcha de la fenêtre. La place était pleine. La foule avait noirci la place comme des lettres l'auraient fait d'une feuille de papier, elle se déversait par l'escalier et s'étalait plus bas le long du bord de mer. Elle paraissait si nombreuse qu'elle rendait minuscules les carcasses des blindés stationnés devant le siège du FSB. Au loin la mer faisait une anse où convergeaient de toutes parts ruelles et toits rouges, et le soleil gravitait sur les montagnes blanches comme une couronne ardente.

De là-haut, du dixième étage de ce bâtiment érigé au sommet de la colline, on voyait bien que pour les propriétaires de ce bureau les gens étaient comme des fourmis, mais que le ciel n'en devenait pas plus proche pour autant.

Si Niyazbek ne s'était pas pressé de proclamer l'indépendance, c'était aussi pour une raison toute simple. Il n'oubliait pas que le Parlement de la république, pour médiocre qu'il fût, siégeait ici dans ces murs, et le gouvernement aussi. Si lui, Niyazbek, se fichait comme d'une guigne des deux milliards de dollars invoqués par Pankov avec tant de conviction, d'autres, ô combien nombreux, ne pensaient qu'à se partager cet argent. Non qu'ils fussent pro-Russes ; mais parce qu'ils étaient pro-milliards.

En substance, leur rapport à la Russie tenait en ceci : les deux milliards, c'est le tribut du faible au fort, du boutiquier au rançonneur, de l'empire agonisant aux peuples arrogants des montagnes. Depuis quand le rançonneur refusait-il de tondre les marchands ? Deux milliards, c'était de l'argent ; cela permettait de corrompre l'élite de la république, même si le président en volait la moitié.

Deuxième raison. Niyazbek sentait que, encore un peu, et l'on aurait peur de lui plus encore que du président Aslanov. Le président Aslanov tuait des hommes, se faisait ériger des monuments et prenait des pots-de-vin. Mais le président Aslanov ne dirigeait pas la république, sauf à appeler "diriger" la possibilité de tuer ou d'arrêter n'importe qui sur son territoire. En matière de gouvernance, c'était le règne de la pagaille. Les deux tiers du pétrole de la compagnie dirigée par le fils du président s'envolaient par des trous percés dans les pipelines.

Tous ceux qui avaient grandi dans la pagaille jouiraient de voir le président privé de la moitié du pouvoir. Des deux tiers du pouvoir. Des neuf dixièmes. Mais si tout le pouvoir revenait à Niyazbek, on n'aurait plus qu'à se soumettre ou à mourir. Niyazbek Malikov n'était pas le genre d'homme à vendre des portefeuilles ministériels ou à laisser voler le pétrole par les trous.

Avant que le Parlement ne proclame l'indépendance – Niyazbek en était conscient – il devait y avoir beaucoup moins de partisans des deux camps : celui des milliards et celui de la pagaille.

Plus complexe était la troisième raison, elle aussi étrangère au manque de fermeté ou à l'économie.

Après s'être entretenu avec le premier commis russe, Niyazbek ne s'adressa pas au Parlement mais à Allah, et la conversation eut lieu seul à seul, sans reporters ni caméras de télévision.

En sortant de la salle de repos, Niyazbek se chaussa et prit son pistolet-mitrailleur. Dans le bureau, ses compagnons visionnaient une cassette tirée d'un coffre. Apparemment, une pièce compromettante à charge contre l'ancien procureur.

Niyazbek gagna l'antichambre où se trouvaient une vingtaine d'hommes, les uns assis sur des chaises, les autres accroupis ; d'autres encore se tenaient du côté du couloir. Un peu plus loin, il vit assis sur le rebord d'une fenêtre un petit gars qu'il avait entraîné autrefois, mais qui était maintenant sous mandat d'arrêt fédéral, et tenu pour un proche de Wahha Arsaïev.

Niyazbek s'approcha du gars et, tournant à peine la tête, lui lança :

— Dis à Wahha de venir lui-même. Où se planque-t-il, comme un lézard dans les rochers ?

— Et tu ne vas pas le tuer ?

— Soit je le tue, soit je ne le tue pas, répondit Niyazbek d'un air philosophe.

Premier coup de fil du président Aslanov au colonel Migounov à cinq heures moins le quart, par la ligne gouvernementale.

— Cessez toutes négociations et prenez-les d'assaut, déclara le président, combien de temps encore allez-vous supporter une honte pareille ? Votre premier commis est otage, mes fils sont otages ! Il faut les libérer sur-le-champ !

— Je n'en ai pas reçu l'ordre, répondit Migounov.

— Je vous le donne !

— Je n'ai d'ordre à recevoir que du président fédéral ou du chef d'état-major, répondit Migounov.

Il raccrocha et s'approcha de la fenêtre. La foule, coupée du siège du FSB par un triple cordon, continuait de grossir. Un nouveau meeting prenait forme près du port. On rapporta d'abord au colonel que c'étaient des partisans du président mais il s'avéra bientôt que le rassemblement était conduit par un gaillard qui ressemblait fortement à un centaure. En bas, un fauteuil roulant ; en haut, Schwarzenegger. Le type s'appelait Telaïev et, à en juger par ses biceps, ce n'était pas sous un tramway qu'il avait perdu ses jambes. Un vent d'ouest étirait une épaisse fumée noire : la résidence de Gamzat Aslanov achevait de brûler, mais les pillards en étaient restés là.

— Etais-tu à Grozny lors du premier assaut ?

Le colonel se retourna. C'était Arzo. Il se tenait à deux mètres de là, près d'une table de réunion bigornée, le visage creusé par le temps et les rides. La foule grondant au-dehors, Migounov n'avait pas entendu le Tchétchène entrer dans la pièce.

— L'assaut du Nouvel An ?

— Non. Celui de novembre. A l'arrivée de l'opposition.

Migounov secoua la tête.

Le Tchétchène se colla à la fenêtre, sa main unique posée sur le carreau. Il scrutait la foule.

— La ville était déserte, dit Arzo. Tous partis. Zéro soulèvement populaire. Deux cents pékins dans toute la cité. Trente chez Chamil, dix chez Guelaïev, et nous allions en voiture les uns chez les autres pour nous persuader que nous n'étions pas dix, pas sept, mais plus. Mais la ville était vide. Les uns se disaient : C'est un coup des Russes, comment peut-on vaincre les Russes ? Et les autres pensaient : On ne va tout de même pas se battre pour Djokhar ! C'est un règlement de compte ! Entre soi ! Une bonne moitié de ceux-ci avaient reçu du pétrole de Djokhar mais ne voulaient pas le rembourser.

Le colonel du groupe Alpha jetait sur le Tchétchène un regard en coulisse. Un visage moins expressif qu'une poêle à frire.

— Puis les chars sont entrés dans la ville et nous les avons brûlés. En un rien de temps. Va comprendre comment c'est possible. Mes gars ne savaient même pas tirer au lance-grenade, et voilà qu'ils brûlaient trois chars à la minute. Nous pensions que d'autres allaient venir qui nous taille-raient en pièces. Un gars de mon groupe a chié dans son froc. Tu vois un peu la scène : il a rempli son froc en tirant, et le char a cramé. Ensuite il s'est penché du toit et pan ! un deuxième char de mort.

Arzo marqua une pause.

— Et le lendemain, bonjour le soulèvement populaire. Les gens sont revenus dans la ville. Ils avaient vaincu les Russes. Et toutes ces choses qu'on se disait la veille encore, que c'était un règlement de compte entre soi, qu'on ne pour-rait pas se passer de la Russie…

— Sans la Russie vous n'aurez plus personne à piller… lâcha Migounov maussade.

Petit rire désabusé d'Arzo.

— En effet : qui va-t-on dépouiller quand nous n'aurons plus la Russie sous la main ? Eh bien, vois-tu, vient un mo-ment où ces choses-là, brusquement, ne veulent plus rien dire. Imagine-toi en train d'aller à la soupe. C'est vachement important, la soupe. Mais voilà qu'on te dit : Ton frère a été tué. Du coup, tu te fiches de la soupe.

— Où veux-tu en venir ?

— Ce que je veux dire, c'est qu'il n'y a que deux cents hommes prêts à se battre dans la Maison sur la Colline.

Un silence, puis :

— Ces gens, là, en bas, ils s'imaginent qu'ils sont venus demander des comptes. Quand l'eau est en train de bouillir, elle se prend pour de l'eau. Et pourtant elle est déjà de la vapeur. Niyazbek ne veut pas se dresser contre la Russie. Djokhar non plus ne le voulait pas. Sais-tu quelle est la dif-férence entre les Russes et nous ?

— Vous êtes musulmans, dit le colonel.

— Non. Quand on leur crache au visage, les Russes encaissent. Pas nous. Quand Gantamir fonçait sur Grozny, personne en Tchétchénie ne croyait à la guerre. Tout le monde croyait à une explication de texte.

— Et toi ? Tu savais que c'était la guerre ?

Arzo fit non de la tête. Un temps de réflexion, puis il ajouta :

— Mon frère le savait, lui. Mon frère aîné. Nous avions des jardins autour du village. Des jardins immenses, les jardins du kolkhoze. Une année, les récoltes ont été miraculeuses. Des pommes grosses comme des têtes d'enfant. Jaunes, presque diaphanes. Mais personne ne se donnait la peine de les ramasser. Elles pourrissaient par terre. Un jour qu'il regardait ces pommes, mon frère a dit : Les gens ne savent plus travailler. Bientôt la guerre.

— Où est ton frère à cette heure ?

La réponse tomba après un silence :

— Mort au premier assaut.

Il était cinq heures du soir quand Khizri conduisit Pankov de la salle de repos au bureau de Gamzat. Pankov passa plusieurs coups de fil et joignit Nabi Nabiev, procureur par intérim.

L'homme se trouvait dans le bâtiment, malgré tout. Il avait pondu toute une pile de circulaires pour ordonner des enquêtes sur le charnier de Kharon-Yourte, et Pankov fit allouer trente mille dollars à chaque famille de victime.

Une somme colossale pour le pays.

Une fois de plus, il ne put joindre le président de la fédération de Russie.

Quand il eut reposé le combiné avec un soupir de soulagement, il remarqua la présence dans le bureau du maire de Torbi-Kala.

— *Salam aleïkum*, dit Charapudin Ataïev.

— Bonjour, répondit Pankov, et les deux hommes se donnèrent l'accolade selon la coutume caucasienne.

L'accolade, dans le Caucase, est une façon de montrer à son ami qu'on ne porte pas d'arme dans le dos, or, quand Pankov étreignit Ataïev, il constata que le bonhomme avait non seulement une arme sous sa veste, mais aussi un gilet pare-balles.

— Il y a des bruits qui circulent, avança prudemment Ataïev, il paraît qu'Aslanov est au Kremlin...

— Ils ne vont pas virer Aslanov, coupa Pankov. (Une hésitation, puis il ajouta d'un air entendu :) Mais ils vont le plumer. Vous étiez en conflit avec lui, je crois, sur cette histoire de terminal passagers ?

Ataïev ouvrit la bouche, puis la referma. Rien que pour l'année à venir, la construction du port de tourisme de Torbi-Kala prévoyait, nous l'avons dit, l'octroi de trois cent soixante-dix millions de dollars pour des travaux de dragage. Gamzat Aslanov avait été désigné président du directoire de la société Terminal. On avait arraché le terrain à la ville, et Ataïev avait demandé sa part. Au lieu de quoi Gamzat s'était appliqué à lui démolir la mâchoire dans les murs de ce même bureau.

— Oui, dit Ataïev, il y a eu contentieux. Le terrain appartient à la ville. J'estime en l'occurrence que le maire de la ville devrait prendre la tête du directoire.

Pankov le dévisagea, prit une feuille de papier et écrivit : "Je soussigné nomme Charapudin Ibrahimovitch Ataïev, maire de la ville de Torbi-Kala, président du directoire de la société par actions Terminal, et recommande au Fonds fédéral des biens de transférer dans les meilleurs délais la part fédérale de la société au crédit des biens municipaux de Torbi-Kala. Signature : V. Pankov." Il data et signa, se disant à lui-même que ce papier transgressait au moins cinq articles de la législation russe.

— Je vous conseille de prendre ça, dit Pankov, et d'aller... (il marqua une hésitation parce qu'il n'y avait personne à qui présenter ce papier – pas au chef du groupe Alpha, tout de même...) d'aller à la mairie. Et de faire partir vos manifestants de la place.

— Ah bon ? fit Ataïev.

— Eh oui, répondit Pankov.

— Et le reste ? répartit l'autre du tac au tac.

— Le reste après, persifla l'ambassadeur du Kremlin.

Le prochain visiteur fut le vice-speaker Muhtar Meïerkulov. Celui-là s'était laissé acheter pour trois fois rien : sept millions de dollars du budget fédéral en vue de la construction du Centre d'études historiques du Caucase, projet immédiatement entériné par l'ambassadeur du Kremlin.

Pankov mit prudemment le nez dans le couloir en raccompagnant Meïerkulov, et fut aussitôt entouré de députés et de fonctionnaires. L'anxiété des parlementaires était palpable. La plupart se trouvaient là pour se partager les deux milliards de budget fédéral, comme nous l'avons dit, et s'inquiétaient fortement qu'il n'y ait plus rien à partager, d'ici peu.

Aussi sèchement que possible, Pankov répéta que Moscou était prête à discuter, voire à payer quatre milliards au lieu de deux, mais que le président Aslanov resterait en place.

Cette entrevue terminée, Pankov s'éclipsa dans les toilettes. En sortant de la cabine, il tomba sur un Koumyk grassouillet et petit de taille, celui-là même qu'il avait vu le jour de son entrée en fonction. L'homme commença par rappeler son nom :

— Arsène Isalmahomedov. Juste une petite minute, Vladislav Avdeïevitch. Il s'agit de la bonification des terres du district de Bechtoï…

Il s'avéra que la chose était du ressort du frère d'Isalmahomedov mais que, dans la mesure où le financement de la bonification relevait du contrôle exclusif du président Aslanov, Bechtoï se retrouvait sans rien, et pas bonifié. Pankov promit que le plan de subventionnement fédéral de l'année à venir comporterait une clause spéciale sur le district de Bechtoï. Alors le député l'étreignit de ses mains encore mouillées et s'en alla.

L'histoire l'étonna fort parce qu'il savait qu'Arsène avait fait la guerre en Tchétchénie et que l'autre nuit, en salle des séances du Parlement, c'était lui, Isalmahomedov, que Pankov avait entendu proposer "de mettre aux voix à main levée la question de l'indépendance de la république". Cela le rendit même plutôt triste que l'indépendance de la république soit mise sur le même pied que le problème de la bonification du district de Bechtoï.

Pankov se lava soigneusement les mains et se regarda dans la glace. Sa barbe de vingt-quatre heures le faisait ressembler à un wahhabite ou à l'oligarque Abramovitch, et ses yeux, bizarrement, s'étaient mis à papilloter. "Tu fais ce que le Kremlin t'ordonne de faire, se dit Pankov, nul n'a le droit de dicter sa volonté à la Russie."

Il sortit des toilettes, traversa le bureau du speaker et le hall qui donnait sur la porte grande ouverte de la salle des séances, porte surmontée d'un panneau de un mètre à l'effigie de l'aigle bicéphale. C'est alors qu'il fut pris d'un mauvais spasme au cœur. Il se retourna brusquement.

A trois mètres de lui, là d'où partait un escalier de marbre, un jeune efflanqué le visait avec un Stetchkine. Les yeux du type étaient d'un vide abyssal, et Pankov reconnut son visage au souvenir d'une photo d'archive de l'état-major antiterroriste. Ce gentil garçon s'était fait pincer après avoir tenté d'acculer sa fiancée à un attentat kamikaze. Les jeunes mariés devaient faire leur voyage de noces dans un camion bourré d'une demi-tonne de TNT. La fille l'avait balancé au FSB et l'autre, dans sa fuite, avait laissé deux cadavres.

Le garçon esquissa un sourire et arma son pistolet. Sans doute voulait-il régler ses comptes avec le chef de l'état-major pour venger la ruine de son bonheur nuptial. A cet instant surgirent Niyazbek et ses gardes. L'Avar posa la main sur l'épaule du gars et lui dit :

— Ce n'est pas à toi de décider.

Le type hésita, leva le canon de son arme et tira dans le panneau de marbre. Des miettes de l'aigle russe se dispersèrent aux pieds de Pankov qui se dit avec tristesse que, s'il n'avait pas été aux toilettes l'instant d'avant, il aurait fait dans sa culotte.

— Viens, dit Niyazbek.

Ces mots s'adressaient à Pankov. Les doigts de l'Avar se refermèrent sur son avant-bras comme des menottes.

Il s'attendait à ce que Niyazbek le ramène en salle de repos. Inconsciemment, il pensait aussi que l'Avar allait le frapper. Mais il comprit aussitôt que l'homme n'avait que faire du fonctionnaire russe : ses yeux fixaient un point donné et son regard semblait celui d'un possédé.

Niyazbek avala les marches plus qu'il ne les monta, et Pankov s'engouffra bientôt derrière lui dans le bureau présidentiel par la porte grande ouverte.

La pièce était pleine. Pankov remarqua Daoud, le maire de Torbi-Kala et le speaker du Parlement, Hamid Abdulhamidov.

Il y avait là, assis au beau milieu du bureau, un homme de petite taille d'une cinquantaine d'années, aux épaules tassées et aux cheveux précocement blancs. Il paraissait anormalement brisé, mais, à la vue du rouquin en veste, son visage s'enflamma d'une haine brutale qui, du reste, retomba aussi vite qu'elle était apparue, et l'homme dit alors :

— C'est bien lui qui a retrouvé les miens ?

— Les tiens ont péri à Kharon-Yourte ? demanda Pankov.

L'autre acquiesça.

— Ma mère, dit-il, et ma femme. Et mes fils. Et mon père. Tous des Ahmedov. Je m'appelle Roustam. Et mon père, Rezvan.

Silence de Pankov. Seuls deux des vingt-quatre corps étaient ceux de femmes et n'avaient pas encore été reconnus. Au total, on comptait six cadavres non identifiés ; il ressortait maintenant que, sur les six, cinq étaient d'une seule et même famille.

— Et pourquoi les a-t-on arrêtés ? demanda Pankov.

— Parce que c'est moi qui ai tué Ibrahim Malikov, répondit Roustam.

Niyazbek continuait de serrer le bras de Pankov qui, à ces mots, faillit hurler de douleur : il lui sembla que les phalanges de l'Avar venaient de lui broyer le membre.

— Continue, ordonna doucement Djavatkhan.

— Tu m'as reconnu hier, dit Roustam en se tournant vers Djavatkhan. Moi aussi j'ai fait la guerre. Comme tout le monde à l'époque. Les montagnes, c'était le chômage ; pour l'argent, il fallait faire la guerre. C'était craignos. J'étais dans les montagnes. Ensuite, j'ai rejoint Arsaïev. Et puis j'en ai eu marre. Trop de sang. Je suis rentré chez moi. J'ai dit à Wahha : Suffit, j'ai une femme, des enfants, cinq ans qu'on ne s'est pas vus ; je veux vivre comme vivaient les anciens. Et le quinze de ce mois, ils sont venus me chercher. J'ai eu le temps de me sauver. Planqué dans la montagne. Je dormais là-haut.

Au matin, une voisine est venue à mon repaire et m'a dit qu'on avait enlevé ma famille, que c'était un coup de Gamzat et que, si je n'allais pas le voir, il les tuerait tous. Je suis donc allé voir Gamzat. Il m'a dit que, si je voulais retrouver les miens, je devais tuer Ibrahim Malikov.

— Mais pourquoi une bombe ? demanda Pankov.

Roustam soupira.

— C'est que... je travaillais dans les Chemins de fer.

— Et alors ? Tu as trouvé la bombe dans les petites annonces du rail ? Ou peut-être que la régie faisait circuler une note disant qu'une FAB-250 était enfouie sous le passage à niveau ? Ou je n'ai pas tout pigé ?

— Je... j'ai été contacté par les hommes de Wahha. Ils m'ont demandé d'ordonner des travaux de remise en état pour un passage à niveau dans le cadre de mon service.

— Pour deux passages à niveau, rappela Pankov.

Roustam opina :

— Pour deux passages à niveau. J'ai compris qu'ils manigançaient quelque chose. Je ne leur ai rien dit, mais j'ai regardé. Et j'ai tout vu. Ce sont des gosses par rapport à moi. J'ai passé trois ans dans les montagnes. Eux, c'étaient des gamins de dix-huit ans. J'ai pensé que je ne trouverais pas mieux que cette bombe pour faire le boulot. Parce que, si Wahha se mettait à chercher qui l'avait trahi, il chercherait parmi les poseurs.

Roustam marqua un silence.

— Gamzat avait un type qui s'appelait Chapi, reprit-il. Il est venu avec moi au passage à niveau. Il a dit qu'il viendrait me couvrir, qu'il y aurait des hommes à lui avec des PM pour le cas où ça tournerait mal.

— Et il t'a couvert ?

Roustam secoua la tête.

— Je pense, dit-il, que Chapi avait ordre de me tuer. Il m'a promis de me couvrir, mais on n'a pas besoin de couverture après une explosion pareille. J'ai pensé que, si je montais dans leur voiture, ils me tueraient pour faire croire qu'Ibrahim avait été supprimé par des boïéviks ; et qu'ensuite ils tueraient ma famille pour empêcher la vérité d'éclater au grand jour. J'ai pensé que, si je prenais la fuite et que je m'en tirais sain et sauf, j'arriverais peut-être à trouver un arrangement pour ma famille. J'ai même repris du service chez Wahha pour remplacer ses hommes par des gens à moi. Mais ils ont quand même massacré ma famille.

— Gamzat savait comment Ibrahim serait tué ? demanda Niyazbek.

— Oui. Il savait tout.

— Amenez Gamzat, ordonna Niyazbek.

Si tant est que Pankov eût encore quelques doutes sur ce qu'il venait d'entendre, ils se dissipèrent dès qu'on fit entrer Gamzat. Celui-ci n'eut pas plus tôt aperçu Ahmedov au milieu de la pièce que son visage tourna au gris. L'horreur le mit en chiffe et il se serait étendu au sol s'il n'avait été tenu par les coudes. On le jeta sur une chaise en mettant Gazi-Mahomed près de lui. Ce dernier, qui semblait ne rien comprendre, regardait prudemment autour de lui.

— Parle, dit Niyazbek à son ex-beau-frère.

Il s'était installé dans le fauteuil présidentiel. Pankov s'assit près du maire sur le rebord de la fenêtre.

Mutisme de Gamzat.

— Gamzat, de quoi s'agit-il ? demanda Gazi-Mahomed.

Personne ne lui répondit.

Niyazbek se leva à demi en poussant devant Gamzat l'un des appareils qui trônaient sur le bureau. C'était un téléphone blanc rescapé de l'époque soviétique, avec un grand disque rond et beaucoup de boutons multicolores. Le premier secrétaire du parti Ahmednabi Aslanov, en son temps, avait dû s'en servir pour engueuler les directeurs de kolkhoze responsables de mauvaises récoltes.

— Tu n'as qu'une seule chance, dit Niyazbek. Appelle-le.

Gamzat composa un numéro, puis un autre. Coup de chance au troisième numéro. Il y eut un clic, un bruit de friture (toutes les communications partant de la Maison sur la Colline étaient sur écoute, pardi), après quoi l'on entendit la voix veloutée et pleine d'assurance d'Ahmednabi Aslanov.

— J'écoute, dit le président.

— Père, c'est moi. Tu dois venir et donner ta démission, je t'en prie. Sinon Niyazbek nous tuera, mon frère et moi.

— Il ne le fera pas au nom de ses neveux.

— Il sait que j'ai tué Ibrahim.

— Il ne le fera pas au nom de ses neveux, répéta le président.

Il avait la voix parfaitement assurée, comme si l'homme était assis là dans son bureau sous le drapeau tricolore, admonestant un ministre trop négligent ou donnant une interview sur les succès de la république.

Le visage de Gamzat se décomposa.

— Père, il va nous tuer ! hurla le fils du président.

Pankov quitta d'un bond le rebord de la fenêtre et se jeta sur le téléphone.

— Ahmednabi Ahmedovitch, vous perdez la tête, cria Pankov, vous tenez plus à votre fauteuil qu'à la vie de vos fils, ou quoi ?

Pas le moindre tressaillement dans la voix du président.

— N'exercez pas de pression sur moi, Vladislav Avdeïevitch ! Je sais que vous êtes du côté de Malikov. Vous briguez ma place. C'est un vilain coup tordu que de faire croire à Malikov que ma famille est impliquée dans le meurtre de son frère ! Vous ne l'emporterez pas au paradis ! Personne ne vous laissera impunément monter les peuples du Caucase les uns contre les autres ! Personne ne vous permettra de blanchir les extrémistes de leurs crimes sur le dos des fidèles compagnons du président de la Russie !

Là-dessus, il raccrocha.

Gamzat essaya de se lever, mais ses jambes ne le tenaient plus.

— De grâce, Niyazbek, non, marmonna-t-il. Au nom de ta sœur. Au nom de ses enfants. Il... tout simplement il...

Muettement, Niyazbek prit le pistolet-mitrailleur accroché au dossier du fauteuil, là où les gens normaux accrochent leur veste ou leur manteau.

— Non, Niyazbek, hurla Pankov. Pas de vengeance ! Aslanov, on finira par l'avoir !

Niyazbek se leva et arma son PM. L'instant d'après, d'un coup de pied bien ajusté, Djavatkhan lui arracha la mitraillette des mains, et l'autre sursauta sous le choc ; dans la même seconde, Mahomedsalih sauta droit sur lui pardessus le bureau.

C'était la première fois que Pankov voyait Niyazbek se battre contre deux adversaires à la fois, dont un double champion du monde de wushu et un favori toutes catégories de lutte libre. Du reste, le combat fut de courte durée. Quelques secondes plus tard, Mahomedsalih s'accroupissait, vacillant, avec un han ! de douleur, cependant que

Niyazbek se laissait asseoir sans résistance, le bras tordu dans le dos par Djavatkhan.

Des hommes armés s'engouffrèrent un à un dans le bureau. La main sur le ventre, Mahomedsalih se leva.

— Emmenez-les, dit-il en montrant les fils du président.

Gamzat et Gazi-Mahomed furent traînés au-dehors et Pankov les suivit, n'étant pas sûr qu'on ne les achèverait pas dans un coin. Mahomedsalih poussa les deux prisonniers dans la chambre forte, puis saisit Gamzat par le menton et lança entre les dents :

— Comment les Ahmedov se sont-ils retrouvés à Kharon-Yourte ? Vite ! Ou c'est à Niyazbek que tu répondras.

— Ben… ils étaient toute une famille… Il fallait s'en débarrasser. Je les ai passés à Chebolev. Ils ne savaient rien de ce qu'avait fait Roustam. Des boïéviks, un point c'est tout.

Mahomedsalih jeta un téléphone à Gamzat.

— Appelle ton père.

— Il a perdu la tête ! Par Allah, il ne voit rien d'autre que le pouvoir. Qui lui tendra la main dans la république s'il sacrifie ses fils au pouvoir ?

— Appelle, fils de pute !

Le réseau ne passait pas dans la chambre forte. On traîna Gamzat dans le couloir où on le jeta au sol, un téléphone à une oreille, un pistolet à l'autre.

Quand Pankov regagna le bureau du président, cinq minutes plus tard, le calme était revenu. La garde avait sorti Roustam. Daoud et le maire s'étaient envolés, sans doute pour répandre une nouvelle aussi renversante. Derrière la porte entrouverte, on entendait Khizri crier dans l'antichambre.

Assis sur une chaise, Niyazbek regardait muettement devant lui. Une belle ecchymose gonflait à sa pommette. Par la porte grande ouverte des sanitaires, Pankov aperçut Djavatkhan.

Penché sur le lavabo, l'autre crachait ses dents à grand bruit.

Pankov s'accroupit face à Niyazbek.

— Ce ne sont pas tes prisonniers personnels, lui dit-il, comprends-moi bien. C'est la dernière chance de ton peuple. Nous saurons convaincre Ahmednabi. Il finira par piger. Je te le promets.

La porte du bureau claqua si fort dans le dos de Pankov, rabattue par un puissant ressort d'acier, que Niyazbek leva les yeux malgré lui.

Puis, après avoir marqué une hésitation, il quitta son siège pour accueillir le visiteur. Pankov se retourna.

Et vit, debout devant la porte, Wahha Arsaïev.

L'autre fois, lors des obsèques, Pankov n'avait pu le voir de près, et les photos de police laissaient espérer mieux. Mais maintenant le chef de l'état-major et premier commis du Kremlin Vladislav Pankov avait l'opportunité sans précédent de dévisager en détail le premier terroriste de la république.

Wahha avait passé la quarantaine. Il avait le corps noueux et tressé de ligaments comme un câble à fils multiples, des cheveux noirs grisonnants et des yeux non pas bleus, comme Pankov avait cru les voir l'autre fois, mais plutôt violets. D'ailleurs, ce n'étaient pas des yeux. Si l'on avait enfermé la mort dans un coffre-fort en y perçant deux trous, alors ces deux trous-là seraient l'exacte copie des yeux d'Arsaïev.

Pankov avait espéré ne jamais le revoir vivant. Surtout dans ces conditions où l'autre était armé, et pas lui. On voyait bien pourtant qu'Arsaïev n'était pas aussi téméraire qu'on le disait. Son apparition tombait trop opportunément. Il avait dû se planquer dans un coin, de peur que Niyazbek ne lui fasse la peau. Mais dès qu'on lui avait rapporté l'histoire de Roustam Ahmedov, il était sorti d'un bond comme un diable de sa boîte.

Niyazbek s'approcha d'Arsaïev. Ils se donnèrent l'accolade. Puis les lèvres du terroriste s'allongèrent en un sourire inattendu. Il se tourna vers l'homme du Kremlin et lui dit :

— Je tiens à te remercier pour mon ami Chebolev. Merci de l'avoir mis en cabane.

— Et après ?

— On l'a tué. Tu veux voir comment ?

— C'est-à-dire ? fit bêtement Pankov.

Wahha fouilla dans sa poche pour en sortir un petit mobile.

— Il y a de tout dans les geôles de la préventive. Même des téléphones. C'est dingue ce que ça peut faire, vos derniers trucs. Ça enregistre le son et l'image. Ça peut même envoyer des enregistrements d'un portable à l'autre.

— Moi aussi je serai filmé en vidéo ? demanda froidement Pankov.

Pour toute réponse, Niyazbek tendit la main vers le bureau et lui donna à lire un papier qu'il sortit d'un tas.

"Gloire à Allah, Maître des Mondes", lut le premier commis du Kremlin en plissant l'œil. Suivaient trois ou quatre citations du Coran, puis ce texte : "Les Russes ont apporté le sang et la mort à notre terre. Leurs fonctionnaires potiches vendent leur peuple et tuent nos enfants. Nous répondrons au sang par le sang, et à la cruauté par la vengeance. Notre patience est à bout.

"Les occupants du Caucase nous ont déclaré une guerre à mort. Ils seront anéantis. Telle est la volonté d'Allah."

Le temps qu'il lise le texte, Daoud et le maire de Torbi-Kala entrèrent dans la pièce. Pankov s'assit au bureau, y chercha un stylo et se mit à corriger quelques fautes d'orthographe, dont une au mot potiche. Puis il rendit le texte à Niyazbek.

— Je vous recommande l'usage de l'ordinateur, dit Pankov. Il tient compte des lois de l'orthographe.

— Rien à foutre de vos lois, articula Wahha. Y compris de l'orthographe.

Niyazbek examina les corrections et donna le texte à Djavatkhan. Tout à coup, Pankov imagina ce papier aux archives. Super. Un appel séparatiste corrigé de la main de l'ambassadeur russe.

— Et qu'allez-vous manger ? demanda Pankov.

— De quoi ?

— Vous répondrez au sang par le sang, mais qu'est-ce que vous allez bouffer ? Vous allez vous manger les uns les autres ?

Niyazbek se tut, et Wahha répondit :

— J'ai déjà entendu cet argument. Sais-tu par où il pèche ? Il y a des familles où tout va bien, vois-tu. La femme abat de la besogne. Elle vaque à ses fourneaux. Elle élève les enfants. Mais l'homme, le jour où ça le prend, décide de divorcer.

Pankov, muet, écoutait.

— La Russie, c'est la femme, reprit Arsaïev. Et le Caucase, c'est l'homme. Si un homme ne veut plus vivre avec une femme, crois-tu qu'il restera rien que par intérêt ? Ou alors ce n'est pas un homme. Et toi qui prétends pouvoir m'entretenir, espèce de bonne femme…

Pankov fixait les yeux couleur bleuet du premier extrémiste de la république, et comprit soudain qu'il avait raison.

Tout ce qu'avait tenté Pankov ces quatre derniers mois, c'était justement de sauver un ménage en faillite. Il y avait longtemps que les deux parties se détestaient. Des milliers de choses les tenaient encore ensemble : les habitudes, les convenances, les enfants, les biens communs, le logement. Mais elles faisaient le compte de leurs rancunes réciproques.

Ce qui en rajoutait à la tristesse, c'était qu'on pouvait très bien vivre ensemble sans avoir à se ressembler. Les différences de coutumes, de goûts et de vues n'empêchaient pas qu'on s'aime quand même.

Il faut dire aussi qu'au moment où le ménage bat de l'aile – Pankov le savait très bien – un mot dit à temps produit cent fois plus d'effet. Qu'on le dise avant qu'il ne soit trop tard et le couple restera au nom des enfants, la discorde retombera, la blessure se cicatrisera et peut-être même que l'amour reviendra. Les années passeront et l'on ne comprendra plus qu'on ait voulu partager l'argenterie de la grandmère et la datcha du grand-père. Mais si ce mot vient trop tard, les deux époux divorcés deviendront les pires ennemis du monde au bout de cinq ans.

Pankov comprit qu'il n'avait plus qu'une chance. Prendre le téléphone et joindre directement le président de la Russie. Ou bien celui-ci limogerait Aslanov, ou bien les Russes seraient massacrés d'ici une heure.

Il s'approcha muettement du bureau et décrocha le téléphone à disque.

La ligne était morte.

Le petit rire de Wahha rompit le silence, qui sonna comme une queue de détente.

Pankov se retourna et promena le regard sur ceux qui étaient là. Wahha le dévisageait avec une haine froide et ostensible. Le prisonnier russe comprit que s'il était encore en vie, c'était aussi parce que le terroriste espérait le récupérer pour son propre compte. Sinon il l'aurait descendu à peine franchi le seuil de la porte.

Assis sur le rebord de la fenêtre, le maire de Torbi-Kala faisait grise mine. Même dans ses rêves les plus fous, il n'avait jamais vu plus loin que les trois cent soixante-dix millions de dollars du terminal passagers, et voilà maintenant qu'il découvrait que les terminaux passagers étaient une spécialité exclusive des gouvernements potiches. Khizri se tenait près du maire, le visage aussi inexpressif qu'un écran éteint d'ordinateur. Djavatkhan esquissait un vague sourire de compassion, et Pankov se souvint de lui avoir vu le même sourire sur une photo où ses camarades et lui égorgeaient un soldat russe.

Debout près de Wahha, Niyazbek posait sur Pankov un regard de mépris ostensible. Ce mépris ne s'adressait pas à Pankov, mais à l'autre bout du fil.

— Y a-t-il des caméras de télévision en salle des séances ? demanda Pankov.

— Pourquoi ça ? dit Niyazbek.

— J'ai une déclaration à faire. Devant les députés de l'Assemblée législative régionale et les médias internationaux.

— De quel contenu ?

— J'ai discuté de la situation avec le président de la Russie. Il m'a ordonné de punir sévèrement tous les auteurs du massacre de Kharon-Yourte. Il a limogé le président Aslanov et m'a nommé à sa place.

Niyazbek loucha sur le combiné de la ligne gouvernementale, qui gisait inerte sous un écheveau de fils bouclés.

— Et que vont-ils te faire pour une déclaration pareille ?

Pankov exhiba un sourire triomphal.

— Rien du tout, répondit-il, à condition que, en plus de ma déclaration, le Kremlin reçoive la tête de celui-ci.

Et de montrer Wahha.

Instinctivement, Arsaïev fit un pas en arrière. Sa main droite plongea dans sa poche, le temps d'un éclair, comme un cormoran plongeant après un poisson, et Pankov glacé se rappela que tous ces gens-là avaient une grenade sur eux comme d'autres portent un crucifix en sautoir. Les yeux de Wahha se firent noirs de haine, il se tourna vers Niyazbek et hurla :

— C'est ce que tu cherchais ? Tu t'es servi de moi, hein ? Comme un épouvantail ? Pour faire plier les Russes ?

"C'est qu'il a raison, se dit Pankov traversé d'une illumination. Diable d'Avar ! O mon Dieu ! Il ne m'aurait jamais laissé là s'il avait eu vraiment l'intention d'envoyer la Russie paître ! Il m'aurait abattu froidement. Aux côtés de Gamzat, et pan ! Sans le moindre battement de paupières !"

— Du calme ! dit Niyazbek. Je jure au nom d'Allah que tu sortiras d'ici sain et sauf, quoi qu'il arrive, Wahha.

Wahha avait toujours la main au fond de sa poche. Pankov recula prudemment d'un pas, puis d'un demi-pas. Il avait déjà vu de ces fameuses petites grenades artisanales "à la Hattab" rebricolées en projectiles de trente millimètres pour les canons à module monté. Ça logeait pile-poil dans un étui de téléphone mobile. Les éclats n'allaient pas bien loin, juste ce qu'il fallait pour se suicider. Allez savoir ce qu'il avait vraiment sur lui. Peut-être une grenade, peut-être une ceinture explosive.

— Wahha, répéta Niyazbek, je jure Allah que je ne tuerai jamais quelqu'un que j'ai invité à venir. Ce n'est pas toi qui as tué mon frère. Les fédéraux n'auront qu'à te faire la chasse.

— Non ! dit Pankov ; tu devras choisir, Niyazbek. Ou bien Wahha, ou bien ma conversation avec le président.

Niyazbek croisa les bras sur sa poitrine.

— C'est toi qui devras choisir, Vladislav. Ou bien ta conversation avec le président, ou bien...

Niyazbek reprit en main la proclamation écrite.

— Nous corrigerons l'orthographe, dit-il.

Pankov avala sa salive. Inutile de marchander. Maintenant qu'il avait proposé une issue, Niyazbek ne le lâcherait plus.

— Diable d'homme, dit Pankov, allons voir les députés.

Le maire de Torbi-Kala poussa un bruyant soupir. Djavatkhan ne se départait pas de son sourire trouble. Le visage de Niyazbek ne laissait rien paraître.

— Djavatkhan, ordonna Niyazbek, tes hommes et toi resterez ici. N'oublie pas que Wahha est mon invité. Si le moindre cheveu tombe de sa tête, ramasse-le et veille à ne pas le perdre.

Ils quittèrent le bureau à quatre : Niyazbek, Pankov, Ataïev et Khizri. Les gardes veillaient dans l'antichambre, les uns par terre, les autres sur des chaises.

— Niyazbek ! lança Wahha quand les hommes sortirent.

L'Avar marqua un arrêt.

— Les Russes te trahiront, dit Wahha. Ils te trahiront et te tueront. Qui fraternise avec le scorpion sera piqué par le scorpion.

Ils dévalèrent deux étages et entrèrent en salle des séances. Plus de la moitié des fauteuils se trouvaient occupés, mais tous les députés, naturellement, n'étaient pas présents. Il y avait beaucoup d'hommes en armes et en treillis, mais, là encore, tous n'étaient pas de simples combattants : pour moitié, c'étaient des députés.

Hamid Abdulhamidov, en proie à l'ennui, siégeait derrière le bureau de l'Assemblée. Un large écran plat occupait un coin de la salle, habituellement destiné à l'affichage des résultats mais qui retransmettait cette fois les images de la chaîne fédérale RTR. On passait un reportage sur une rencontre du président avec des représentants de la jeunesse.

L'ambiance de la salle était à la morosité. Les députés faisaient des messes basses. On avait posé un seau plein de raisin au pied du présidium. Odeur familière à Pankov, ça sentait l'air vicié des séances interminables, cet air cent fois respiré par d'autres poumons avec des relents de sandwiches et de café alourdi par une émanation de lubrifiants d'armes. Du drapeau fédéral, plus une trace.

Des amis de Niyazbek, seul Khizri était là. On avait laissé Djavatkhan avec Wahha et l'on ne voyait Mahomedsalih nulle part. On devait apprendre plus tard qu'il se trouvait auprès de Gamzat, occupé à le traîner sur le sol de son propre bureau pour le forcer, de temps à autre, à joindre son père. Tous les téléphones de celui-ci étant débranchés, on se remettait à frapper le fils pour qu'il appelle au moins les amis du père.

Pankov devait apprendre un peu plus tard qu'Ahmednabi avait dit à l'un de ses proches dans une datcha gouvernementale de Moscou : "Si je démissionne de mon poste de président, mes fils seront quand même fusillés. Ils seront fusillés dans un jour ou dans un an. Qu'il en soit selon la volonté d'Allah."

Au moment de passer la porte, Pankov stoppa Niyazbek d'un mouvement du menton. Ils eurent un aparté.

— File-moi Wahha, lui glissa Pankov à l'oreille.

— Non.

— Ils vont me bouffer au Kremlin...

— Va et parle.

Ils n'étaient pas plus tôt entrés que six ou sept caméras de télévision se braquèrent sur eux. Parmi les micros pointés sur la tribune, Pankov reconnut avec irritation les logos de deux grandes chaînes d'Etat. "Pourquoi diable filmer tout ça s'ils ne mettent rien à l'antenne ?" songea-t-il.

De la deuxième chaîne, l'écran plat perché à gauche de la tribune bascula sur CNN et Pankov aperçut la place noire de monde avec l'autre maigrichonne de reporter. CNN était retransmis par une chaîne locale, et quelqu'un avait eu l'idée de faire courir une traduction russe simultanée sur le texte anglais. "Apparemment, dit la reporter, quelque chose est en train de se passer dans le bâtiment. Nous changeons de caméra."

Pankov se dirigea vers la tribune et vit à l'écran sa propre image faire le même mouvement. La transmission se faisait par satellite et il marchait à l'écran avec un léger différé.

Ayant pris place devant les micros, il se tourna aussitôt vers Niyazbek. L'Avar était assis là, à trois mètres du présidium, flanqué de Khizri. Comme il faisait très chaud, il avait laissé au bureau la veste de son treillis et ne portait plus qu'un maillot de sport blanc à manches courtes d'où saillaient de puissants biceps. Sa Kalachnikov approvisionnée était devant lui, couchée sur la table, avec sa longue bandoulière grise. Il avait les cheveux noirs soignés, bien peignés, et le visage impassible aux traits épais et réguliers à peine altérés par un nez cassé depuis longtemps et une fraîche ecchymose sous la pommette.

Ses yeux marron foncé souriaient à Pankov avec un brin de tristesse et de mépris, comme s'il savait déjà tout. "Quelle est la première aspiration de tout un chacun ?" avait demandé Niyazbek à Pankov le jour des obsèques de son frère, à quoi Pankov avait répondu du tac au tac : "Garder sa place." L'autre était parti d'un grand éclat de rire, et Vladislav lui-même avait conscience d'avoir dit une bêtise. Une bêtise ? Non : c'était plutôt qu'il en avait trop dit. "Ce n'est pas de ma carrière qu'il s'agit là, songea Pankov. Ivan Vitaliévitch a raison. Nul n'a le droit de dicter sa volonté à la Russie."

Pankov se tourna vers la salle.

— Je me suis entretenu avec le président, dit Vladislav Pankov. Le président de la Russie est parfaitement au courant de la situation. Le président a ordonné la création d'une commission d'enquête indépendante sur le charnier de Kharon-Yourte. Les familles de toutes les victimes se verront octroyer une indemnité de trente mille dollars. L'état-major antiterroriste sera dissous. Toutes les personnes arrêtées par l'état-major comparaîtront dans les meilleurs délais devant des jurés populaires. Malheureusement, nous ne pourrons châtier tous les coupables. Le général Chebolev, arrêté cet après-midi et placé à l'isolement, s'est suicidé dans sa cellule.

La salle poussa un soupir à l'unisson. Apparemment, peu de gens avaient eu connaissance de la mort de Chebolev.

— Pour combattre la menace de terrorisme, continua Pankov, la force ne saurait être une menace suffisante. La seule méthode qui vaille consiste à garantir à la république sa prospérité économique. A cette fin, la Russie double le financement des programmes fédéraux existants, notamment celui du terminal passagers de la mer Caspienne. Pour une meilleure prise en compte de l'intérêt des peuples de l'Avarie-Dargo-Nord, je nomme Niyazbek Adievitch Malikov inspecteur fédéral de la République. Il sera le principal coordinateur des financements sur projet, mais aussi des nouveaux programmes d'investissement auxquels Moscou allouera huit cents millions de dollars supplémentaires.

Aux mots "terminal" et "doubler", le maire de Torbi-Kala tressaillit et souffla quelque chose à l'oreille de ses gardes.

— En ce qui concerne le président Aslanov, continua Pankov, il reste l'un des dirigeants les plus méritants de la région caucasienne, en dépit d'un certain nombre d'insuffisances à déplorer dans son travail. Toute rumeur de démission relève d'une manœuvre de désinformation visant à précipiter le Caucase dans l'abîme de la zizanie interethnique et religieuse.

Ce qui survint l'instant d'après fut transmis en direct par toutes les chaînes de télévision du monde entier, à l'exception, bien entendu, des chaînes russes.

Niyazbek Malikov se leva tranquillement.

— Je n'ai pas besoin de ton poste, dit-il, et mon peuple n'a pas besoin de tes pots-de-vin. Je viens de voir à quel point les Russes sont capables de tenir leur parole. Depuis dix ans, nous ne voyons rien des Russes que du mensonge et de l'argent. Le président que vous avez nommé a rongé la république jusqu'à la moelle. La terreur que vous semez tue nos enfants. Et la bêtise de Moscou n'a d'égale que son niveau de corruption. Vingt mille personnes exigent la démission d'Aslanov au pied de ce bâtiment. Tu leur craches au visage. Nous ne sommes pas des Russes pour nous cracher au visage. Nous…

Un coup de feu retentit. Niyazbek se tenait droit, le bout des doigts appuyé sur une table, et la balle jeta sa poitrine en avant. Il se redressa, l'air ahuri, et Pankov vit avec horreur une tache rouge grandir sur son maillot blanc. "Comment est-ce possible, pensa le Russe, je lui ai tout proposé ! J'ai fait de lui l'argentier de la république !"

Niyazbek amorça un mouvement rotatif et attrapa son pistolet-mitrailleur qui était sur la table lorsqu'un second coup de feu tonna. La balle, cette fois, lui entra dans la tempe, et de si près que les images, bientôt rediffusées au ralenti, feraient apparaître des fragments d'os et de peau jaillissant de sa tête. Le tir avait roussi ses cheveux coupés court. Niyazbek s'écroula pour ne plus se relever.

Khizri Beïbulatov était derrière lui, un Stetchkine à la main.

— Ne tirez pas, putain, ne tirez pas ! hurla le maire de Torbi-Kala quand les gardes et les proches de Niyazbek se mirent à dégainer.

Ce qui n'empêcha pas la fusillade d'éclater.

Après la fusillade commença l'assaut.

Les deux jours qui suivirent l'assaut, Pankov les passa à dormir. Quand il se réveillait, il posait un œil morne sur les murs de sa chambre d'hôpital et se rendormait de nouveau. Puis il alla au-devant des caméras de télévision avec le président Aslanov. Il n'avait plus guère la mémoire de ce qu'il faisait. Il avait dû décerner une médaille à Aslanov, croyait-il se souvenir.

Puis il se mit à boire. Il buvait du matin au soir, quelquefois avec Sergueï Piskounov, quelquefois avec les solliciteurs qui venaient chercher sa signature pour une nomination. Pour les nominations, il prenait de l'argent. D'abord par l'intermédiaire de Gamzat Aslanov, puis sans se cacher le moins du monde. Un beau jour, Pankov se réveilla non dans sa modeste chambre, mais dans une luxueuse villa avec tourelle vitrée et jacuzzi à la robinetterie plaquée or.

C'était, semble-t-il, la villa d'un rebelle tué pendant l'assaut. Gamzat avait choisi de l'offrir à l'ambassadeur du Kremlin.

Que Gamzat eût survécu à une telle boucherie relevait d'un hasard incroyable. Au moment où tout commença, Mahomedsalih avait cessé de le torturer et commencé de le tuer. Le fils cadet du président gisait au sol dans une mare de sang. De temps à autre, on le criblait de coups de pied. Quand la fusillade crépita, Mahomedsalih et ses hommes se précipitèrent. Ils pensaient que Gamzat serait achevé par les gens de faction près de la chambre forte ; mais quand ceux-ci firent irruption dans le couloir, ils crurent que l'autre avait déjà reçu le coup de grâce. Finalement, il fut récupéré par le groupe Alpha.

Si l'un des médecins ayant soigné Pankov neuf ans plus tôt avait pu l'examiner maintenant, il aurait conclu à une rechute de névrose. Tous les symptômes étaient là. Mais il n'y avait pas de médecins à son chevet. "Tu ne comprends pas, dit une fois Pankov à son ami oligarque – celui-là même qui fêtait son anniversaire le jour où tout avait commencé –, je m'en balance maintenant. Mais alors complètement."

Quelqu'un rapporta à Pankov que Mahomedsalih Salimkhanov, grièvement blessé lors de l'assaut, s'était encore échappé, cette fois de la salle de réanimation. Un avis de recherche fédéral avait été lancé contre lui, mais aussi contre Djavatkhan Askerov. Pankov était trop ivre pour s'y intéresser. Puis on lui rapporta que Mahomedsalih avait été abattu à Kehi, et là encore il n'y attacha aucune importance. Quand on lui dit qu'Aminat avait épousé Mahomedsalih, il ne dessoûla pas trois jours durant.

Deux mois après l'assaut, le premier commis du président de la fédération de Russie Vladislav Pankov se rendit à Chamkhalsk inaugurer une nouvelle école. Il en revint dans un cortège de trois voitures, son ami Khizri Beïbulatov partageant sa limousine. Deux Mercedes blindées roulaient devant (pas question qu'on sache laquelle des deux transportait le fonctionnaire fédéral), et un Land Cruiser fermait la marche.

Un énième poste de contrôle franchi, Pankov reconnut soudain la route par laquelle Niyazbek l'avait conduit neuf ans plus tôt. Elle serpentait vers une ville poussiéreuse située en contrebas le long d'une mer bleue moutonnant de vagues blanches, le tout sous un ciel vierge de nuage. Au loin scintillaient les cimes, comme nappées de sucre glace, et un chemin de métal en fusion brasillait sur les flots vers le soleil couchant. On allait contourner le Torbi-Taou et entrevoir au loin les marais salants et le plan vert du terrain de golf.

La route coupait un passage à niveau à l'abandon, battu par les roues d'innombrables camions. Le cortège ralentit légèrement à son approche.

L'instant d'après la Merco sauta en l'air. Pankov eut le temps de voir l'émail fondre sur la portière arrachée par l'explosion, puis le monde tournoya et s'éteignit.

La FAB-250 enfouie six mois plus tôt sous le passage à niveau explosa entre les deux Mercedes blindées parce que le terroriste ignorait dans laquelle des deux voyageait l'ambassadeur du Kremlin. La première voiture fut anéantie. La deuxième se froissa comme une boîte de conserve. Elle eut le capot arraché et fut projetée en arrière. Les passagers furent éjectés de leur siège comme des morceaux de viande propulsés par l'explosion d'une cocotte-minute.

Pankov se vit gisant au beau milieu d'une route à la blancheur éclatante. La route allait montant vers la boule d'ambre du soleil qui brillait aux portes du ciel. De lointaines montagnes la cernaient comme la clôture d'un jardin merveilleux, d'où s'échappaient de lourdes ramures aux fruits rubis sous des gazouillis d'oiseaux, et par cette route, droite comme un rayon de soleil ou la trajectoire d'une balle, un homme marchait vers Pankov. Il était très grand, plus grand que dans la vie, vêtu d'un blue-jean et d'une chemise blanche impeccable à manches longues, malgré la chaleur, avec une Kalachnikov à longue lanière grise, portée en bandoulière comme la sacoche d'un facteur. L'homme était rasé de près, les yeux aussi sombres que des cerises mûres, et n'avait pas plus de trente ans comme il sied à tout musulman reçu au paradis. Pankov sourit à la vue de cet homme et lui tendit la main pour qu'il l'aide à se lever.

— Niyazbek, dit Pankov, comme je suis heureux que tu m'aies pardonné. Tu es venu me secourir ?

— Non. Je ne peux plus rien pour toi maintenant.

— Parce que tu es musulman et pas moi ?

— Non. Pas pour ça.

Alors Pankov ouvrit les yeux et comprit que la route blanche n'existait pas. Il était étendu à la renverse avec, au-dessus de lui, très haut, un ciel bleu sans nuage. Çà et là s'étalaient les cailloux pointus du bas-côté de la chaussée. Plus loin, à trois mètres de là, les voitures étaient la proie des flammes. Le Russe ne ressentait aucune douleur mais se savait perdu, le dos baignant dans une espèce de flaque, et cette flaque, comme il ne tarda pas à le comprendre, était de son sang.

Il tourna la tête. Une Samara 09 blanche surgit de derrière les épaves en flammes, d'où sortirent trois hommes en treillis encagoulés de noir. Ils allèrent droit sur Pankov en ôtant leurs cagoules. Ils marchaient d'un pas confiant, sans pousser à la course, assurés qu'ils étaient de ne trouver là personne d'autre qu'eux-mêmes et le Russe à l'agonie.

Quand ils furent à visage découvert, Pankov reconnut Djavatkhan et Mahomedsalih, puis le troisième homme s'avança et le Russe vit les cheveux grisonnants et les prunelles violettes de Wahha Arsaïev. Ils approchèrent à un demi-mètre de l'homme qui baignait dans son sang, et Djavatkhan sortit un Stetchkine de sa ceinture. Pankov voulut le prier de le laisser mourir tout seul parce qu'il n'en avait plus pour longtemps, mais sa langue lui désobéit et le ciel s'assombrit comme avant l'orage.

Djavatkhan tendit le bras, et Pankov vit au-dessus de lui, au zénith, la bouche noire du canon où plus rien ne restait de la route étincelante qu'avait dévalée Niyazbek, ni du soleil d'ambre qui s'était répandu sur l'éden aux fruits rutilants. Les lèvres de Djavatkhan bougèrent et Pankov crut qu'il allait dire : "Pour Niyazbek."

— *Allah akbar*, dit Djavatkhan.

Et le monde s'éteignit.

TABLE